Lecture Notes in Computer Science 4560

Commenced Publication in 1973
Founding and Former Series Editors:
Gerhard Goos, Juris Hartmanis, and Jan van Leeuwen

Nuray Aykin (Ed.)

Usability and Internationalization

Global and Local User Interfaces

Second International Conference on
Usability and Internationalization, UI-HCII 2007
Held as Part of HCI International 2007
Beijing, China, July 22-27, 2007
Proceedings, Part II

 Springer

Volume Editor

Nuray Aykin
The New School
55 West 13th Street, New York, NY 10011, USA
E-mail: aykinn@newschool.edu

Library of Congress Control Number: 2007929581

CR Subject Classification (1998): H.5.2, H.5.3, H.3-5, C.2, K.4, D.2, K.6

LNCS Sublibrary: SL 3 – Information Systems and Application,
incl. Internet/Web and HCI

ISSN   0302-9743
ISBN-10   3-540-73288-8 Springer Berlin Heidelberg New York
ISBN-13   978-3-540-73288-4 Springer Berlin Heidelberg New York

Springer is a part of Springer Science+Business Media

springer.com

© Springer-Verlag Berlin Heidelberg 2007
Printed in Germany

Typesetting: Camera-ready by author, data conversion by Scientific Publishing Services, Chennai, India
Printed on acid-free paper   SPIN: 12082773   06/3180   5 4 3 2 1 0

Foreword

The 12th International Conference on Human-Computer Interaction, HCI International 2007, was held in Beijing, P.R. China, 22-27 July 2007, jointly with the Symposium on Human Interface (Japan) 2007, the 7th International Conference on Engineering Psychology and Cognitive Ergonomics, the 4th International Conference on Universal Access in Human-Computer Interaction, the 2nd International Conference on Virtual Reality, the 2nd International Conference on Usability and Internationalization, the 2nd International Conference on Online Communities and Social Computing, the 3rd International Conference on Augmented Cognition, and the 1st International Conference on Digital Human Modeling.

A total of 3403 individuals from academia, research institutes, industry and governmental agencies from 76 countries submitted contributions, and 1681 papers, judged to be of high scientific quality, were included in the program. These papers address the latest research and development efforts and highlight the human aspects of design and use of computing systems. The papers accepted for presentation thoroughly cover the entire field of Human-Computer Interaction, addressing major advances in knowledge and effective use of computers in a variety of application areas.

This volume, edited by Nuray Aykin, contains papers in the thematic area of Usability and Internationalization, addressing the following major topics:

- Designing Global and Local Products and Services
- Enhancing and Personalizing the User Experience

The remaining volumes of the HCI International 2007 proceedings are:

- Volume 1, LNCS 4550, Interaction Design and Usability, edited by Julie A. Jacko
- Volume 2, LNCS 4551, Interaction Platforms and Techniques, edited by Julie A. Jacko
- Volume 3, LNCS 4552, HCI Intelligent Multimodal Interaction Environments, edited by Julie A. Jacko
- Volume 4, LNCS 4553, HCI Applications and Services, edited by Julie A. Jacko
- Volume 5, LNCS 4554, Coping with Diversity in Universal Access, edited by Constantine Stephanidis
- Volume 6, LNCS 4555, Universal Access to Ambient Interaction, edited by Constantine Stephanidis
- Volume 7, LNCS 4556, Universal Access to Applications and Services, edited by Constantine Stephanidis
- Volume 8, LNCS 4557, Methods, Techniques and Tools in Information Design, edited by Michael J. Smith and Gavriel Salvendy
- Volume 9, LNCS 4558, Interacting in Information Environments, edited by Michael J. Smith and Gavriel Salvendy

- Volume 10, LNCS 4559, HCI and Culture, edited by Nuray Aykin
- Volume 12, LNCS 4561, Digital Human Modeling, edited by Vincent G. Duffy
- Volume 13, LNAI 4562, Engineering Psychology and Cognitive Ergonomics, edited by Don Harris
- Volume 14, LNCS 4563, Virtual Reality, edited by Randall Shumaker
- Volume 15, LNCS 4564, Online Communities and Social Computing, edited by Douglas Schuler
- Volume 16, LNAI 4565, Foundations of Augmented Cognition 3rd Edition, edited by Dylan D. Schmorrow and Leah M. Reeves
- Volume 17, LNCS 4566, Ergonomics and Health Aspects of Work with Computers, edited by Marvin J. Dainoff

I would like to thank the Program Chairs and the members of the Program Boards of all Thematic Areas, listed below, for their contribution to the highest scientific quality and the overall success of the HCI International 2007 Conference.

Ergonomics and Health Aspects of Work with Computers

Program Chair: Marvin J. Dainoff

Arne Aaras, Norway
Pascale Carayon, USA
Barbara G.F. Cohen, USA
Wolfgang Friesdorf, Germany
Martin Helander, Singapore
Ben-Tzion Karsh, USA
Waldemar Karwowski, USA
Peter Kern, Germany
Danuta Koradecka, Poland
Kari Lindstrom, Finland

Holger Luczak, Germany
Aura C. Matias, Philippines
Kyung (Ken) Park, Korea
Michelle Robertson, USA
Steven L. Sauter, USA
Dominique L. Scapin, France
Michael J. Smith, USA
Naomi Swanson, USA
Peter Vink, The Netherlands
John Wilson, UK

Human Interface and the Management of Information

Program Chair: Michael J. Smith

Lajos Balint, Hungary
Gunilla Bradley, Sweden
Hans-Jörg Bullinger, Germany
Alan H.S. Chan, Hong Kong
Klaus-Peter Fähnrich, Germany
Michitaka Hirose, Japan
Yoshinori Horie, Japan
Richard Koubek, USA
Yasufumi Kume, Japan
Mark Lehto, USA

Robert Proctor, USA
Youngho Rhee, Korea
Anxo Cereijo Roibás, UK
Francois Sainfort, USA
Katsunori Shimohara, Japan
Tsutomu Tabe, Japan
Alvaro Taveira, USA
Kim-Phuong L. Vu, USA
Tomio Watanabe, Japan
Sakae Yamamoto, Japan

Jiye Mao, P.R. China
Fiona Nah, USA
Shogo Nishida, Japan
Leszek Pacholski, Poland

Hidekazu Yoshikawa, Japan
Li Zheng, P.R. China
Bernhard Zimolong, Germany

Human-Computer Interaction

Program Chair: Julie A. Jacko

Sebastiano Bagnara, Italy
Jianming Dong, USA
John Eklund, Australia
Xiaowen Fang, USA
Sheue-Ling Hwang, Taiwan
Yong Gu Ji, Korea
Steven J. Landry, USA
Jonathan Lazar, USA

V. Kathlene Leonard, USA
Chang S. Nam, USA
Anthony F. Norcio, USA
Celestine A. Ntuen, USA
P.L. Patrick Rau, P.R. China
Andrew Sears, USA
Holly Vitense, USA
Wenli Zhu, P.R. China

Engineering Psychology and Cognitive Ergonomics

Program Chair: Don Harris

Kenneth R. Boff, USA
Guy Boy, France
Pietro Carlo Cacciabue, Italy
Judy Edworthy, UK
Erik Hollnagel, Sweden
Kenji Itoh, Japan
Peter G.A.M. Jorna, The Netherlands
Kenneth R. Laughery, USA

Nicolas Marmaras, Greece
David Morrison, Australia
Sundaram Narayanan, USA
Eduardo Salas, USA
Dirk Schaefer, France
Axel Schulte, Germany
Neville A. Stanton, UK
Andrew Thatcher, South Africa

Universal Access in Human-Computer Interaction

Program Chair: Constantine Stephanidis

Julio Abascal, Spain
Ray Adams, UK
Elizabeth Andre, Germany
Margherita Antona, Greece
Chieko Asakawa, Japan
Christian Bühler, Germany
Noelle Carbonell, France
Jerzy Charytonowicz, Poland
Pier Luigi Emiliani, Italy
Michael Fairhurst, UK

Zhengjie Liu, P.R. China
Klaus Miesenberger, Austria
John Mylopoulos, Canada
Michael Pieper, Germany
Angel Puerta, USA
Anthony Savidis, Greece
Andrew Sears, USA
Ben Shneiderman, USA
Christian Stary, Austria
Hirotada Ueda, Japan

Gerhard Fischer, USA
Jon Gunderson, USA
Andreas Holzinger, Austria
Arthur Karshmer, USA
Simeon Keates, USA
George Kouroupetroglou, Greece
Jonathan Lazar, USA
Seongil Lee, Korea

Jean Vanderdonckt, Belgium
Gregg Vanderheiden, USA
Gerhard Weber, Germany
Harald Weber, Germany
Toshiki Yamaoka, Japan
Mary Zajicek, UK
Panayiotis Zaphiris, UK

Virtual Reality

Program Chair: Randall Shumaker

Terry Allard, USA
Pat Banerjee, USA
Robert S. Kennedy, USA
Heidi Kroemker, Germany
Ben Lawson, USA
Ming Lin, USA
Bowen Loftin, USA
Holger Luczak, Germany
Annie Luciani, France
Gordon Mair, UK

Ulrich Neumann, USA
Albert "Skip" Rizzo, USA
Lawrence Rosenblum, USA
Dylan Schmorrow, USA
Kay Stanney, USA
Susumu Tachi, Japan
John Wilson, UK
Wei Zhang, P.R. China
Michael Zyda, USA

Usability and Internationalization

Program Chair: Nuray Aykin

Genevieve Bell, USA
Alan Chan, Hong Kong
Apala Lahiri Chavan, India
Jori Clarke, USA
Pierre-Henri Dejean, France
Susan Dray, USA
Paul Fu, USA
Emilie Gould, Canada
Sung H. Han, South Korea
Veikko Ikonen, Finland
Richard Ishida, UK
Esin Kiris, USA
Tobias Komischke, Germany
Masaaki Kurosu, Japan
James R. Lewis, USA

Rungtai Lin, Taiwan
Aaron Marcus, USA
Allen E. Milewski, USA
Patrick O'Sullivan, Ireland
Girish V. Prabhu, India
Kerstin Röse, Germany
Eunice Ratna Sari, Indonesia
Supriya Singh, Australia
Serengul Smith, UK
Denise Spacinsky, USA
Christian Sturm, Mexico
Adi B. Tedjasaputra, Singapore
Myung Hwan Yun, South Korea
Chen Zhao, P.R. China

Online Communities and Social Computing

Program Chair: Douglas Schuler

Chadia Abras, USA
Lecia Barker, USA
Amy Bruckman, USA
Peter van den Besselaar,
   The Netherlands
Peter Day, UK
Fiorella De Cindio, Italy
John Fung, P.R. China
Michael Gurstein, USA
Tom Horan, USA
Piet Kommers, The Netherlands
Jonathan Lazar, USA

Stefanie Lindstaedt, Austria
Diane Maloney-Krichmar, USA
Isaac Mao, P.R. China
Hideyuki Nakanishi, Japan
A. Ant Ozok, USA
Jennifer Preece, USA
Partha Pratim Sarker, Bangladesh
Gilson Schwartz, Brazil
Sergei Stafeev, Russia
F.F. Tusubira, Uganda
Cheng-Yen Wang, Taiwan

Augmented Cognition

Program Chair: Dylan D. Schmorrow

Kenneth Boff, USA
Joseph Cohn, USA
Blair Dickson, UK
Henry Girolamo, USA
Gerald Edelman, USA
Eric Horvitz, USA
Wilhelm Kincses, Germany
Amy Kruse, USA
Lee Kollmorgen, USA
Dennis McBride, USA

Jeffrey Morrison, USA
Denise Nicholson, USA
Dennis Proffitt, USA
Harry Shum, P.R. China
Kay Stanney, USA
Roy Stripling, USA
Michael Swetnam, USA
Robert Taylor, UK
John Wagner, USA

Digital Human Modeling

Program Chair: Vincent G. Duffy

Norm Badler, USA
Heiner Bubb, Germany
Don Chaffin, USA
Kathryn Cormican, Ireland
Andris Freivalds, USA
Ravindra Goonetilleke, Hong Kong
Anand Gramopadhye, USA
Sung H. Han, South Korea
Pheng Ann Heng, Hong Kong
Dewen Jin, P.R. China
Kang Li, USA

Zhizhong Li, P.R. China
Lizhuang Ma, P.R. China
Timo Maatta, Finland
J. Mark Porter, UK
Jim Potvin, Canada
Jean-Pierre Verriest, France
Zhaoqi Wang, P.R. China
Xiugan Yuan, P.R. China
Shao-Xiang Zhang, P.R. China
Xudong Zhang, USA

In addition to the members of the Program Boards above, I also wish to thank the following volunteer external reviewers: Kelly Hale, David Kobus, Amy Kruse, Cali Fidopiastis and Karl Van Orden from the USA, Mark Neerincx and Marc Grootjen from the Netherlands, Wilhelm Kincses from Germany, Ganesh Bhutkar and Mathura Prasad from India, Frederick Li from the UK, and Dimitris Grammenos, Angeliki Kastrinaki, Iosif Klironomos, Alexandros Mourouzis, and Stavroula Ntoa from Greece.

This conference could not have been possible without the continuous support and advise of the Conference Scientific Advisor, Prof. Gavriel Salvendy, as well as the dedicated work and outstanding efforts of the Communications Chair and Editor of HCI International News, Abbas Moallem, and of the members of the Organizational Board from P.R. China, Patrick Rau (Chair), Bo Chen, Xiaolan Fu, Zhibin Jiang, Congdong Li, Zhenjie Liu, Mowei Shen, Yuanchun Shi, Hui Su, Linyang Sun, Ming Po Tham, Ben Tsiang, Jian Wang, Guangyou Xu, Winnie Wanli Yang, Shuping Yi, Kan Zhang, and Wei Zho.

I would also like to thank for their contribution towards the organization of the HCI International 2007 Conference the members of the Human Computer Interaction Laboratory of ICS-FORTH, and in particular Margherita Antona, Maria Pitsoulaki, George Paparoulis, Maria Bouhli, Stavroula Ntoa and George Margetis.

Constantine Stephanidis
General Chair, HCI International 2007

HCI International 2009

The 13th International Conference on Human-Computer Interaction, HCI International 2009, will be held jointly with the affiliated Conferences in San Diego, California, USA, in the Town and Country Resort & Convention Center, 19-24 July 2009. It will cover a broad spectrum of themes related to Human Computer Interaction, including theoretical issues, methods, tools, processes and case studies in HCI design, as well as novel interaction techniques, interfaces and applications. The proceedings will be published by Springer. For more information, please visit the Conference website: http://www.hcii2009.org/

General Chair
Professor Constantine Stephanidis
ICS-FORTH and University of Crete
Heraklion, Crete, Greece
Email: program@hcii2009.org

Table of Contents

Part II: Enhancing and Personalizing the User Experience

Part I

Designing Global and Local Products and Services

Localization Issues: A Glimpse at the Korean User
(From the Western Perspective)

Björn-M. Braun and Kerstin Röse

Center for Human-Machine-Interaction, University of Kaiserslautern
P.O. Box 3049, 67653 Kaiserslautern, Germany
{bbraun,roese}@mv.uni-kl.de

Abstract. This paper shows how applying Chavan's Quick and Dirty User Profiling Technique proves to be an excellent first step for gaining first insights into users from a different cultural background, exemplified for the Korean market. On this hit products of the Korean market are reviewed, Korean design preferences are analysed, cultural context data is gathered and completed with findings of cultural dimensions.

Keywords: Cross-Cultural, Usability Engineering, User-Profile, South Korea.

1 Introduction

The user lies at the core of the user-centred design. Especially for the development of a localized product within a cross-cultural approach, in-depth understanding of the user and her culture is a prerequisite for success. "To grasp the native's point of view" [18] is the ultimate goal here. The scientific approach exploring an 'alien' culture is ethnography, which is rooted in the field of anthropology. One methodological approach thereby is to observe social conventions that guide attitudes and behaviours of a social system – the so called ethnomethodology [19; 5; 4]. The probably most famous method for gaining this understanding is applying etic dimensions and observing their occurrence in different cultures [6]. Triandis [29] points out that cultural characterization based on these etic constructs is far too simplistic and proposed these dimensions (collectivism and individualism in particular) to be conceptualized rather as polythetic constructs [28]. Hence further attributes are required to describe a researched culture.

As this research aims at the user-oriented, cross-cultural HMI-development the purpose of this paper is to broaden the developers understanding of the Korean culture to be enabled to implement culture-specific variables into the development-process. From this perspective innumerous attributes are thinkable for defining the target-culture. A method designed to arrive at a fast and frugal user-profile is the Quick and Dirty User Profiling Technique (QDUPT), as introduced by Chavan [1]. The QDUPT can be understood as a heuristic, based on three steps, to derive essential cultural variables from the vast amount of data and information available related to cross-cultural HMI-development.

N. Aykin (Ed.): Usability and Internationalization, Part II, HCII 2007, LNCS 4560, pp. 3–12, 2007.
© Springer-Verlag Berlin Heidelberg 2007

2 Step 1: Aspects of the Korean Culture's Lifestyle

In the first step diverse aspects of the target culture's lifestyle are analysed. This includes the examination of the hit products of the past five years to identify possible unique selling propositions and the scope of globalization or localization of products. Hence it is to determine if some kind of distinct local look, in terms of colours, layout, etc., can be identified. A review of book illustrations, advertisements or web unique selling proposition gives useful insights to answer these questions. Another interesting source to broaden the understanding of the target culture's recent lifestyle is to have a closer look at the past years top five films and music videos, as well as at the most successful local websites. [1]

2.1 Hit Product 2002: Colour Screen Mobile Phones [22]

Even though according to the Samsung Economic Research Institute (SERI) report the 2002 World Cup was the number one hit in 2002, colour screen mobile phones seem better suitable to generate a picture of the Korean user, as the World Cup as an international, single event might have its short-term impact, but doesn't necessarily enhance the understanding of the Korean user for our purpose here. The sales of mobile phones with colour screens sharply increased to 2.40 million and 5.71 million units in the first and second half of 2002 respectively; since its introduction in June 2001 (1.80 million units were sold in 2001). Out of all mobile phones sold in the latter half of 2002, around 72% had a colour screen; representing the fast adoption of new products and features by the Korean user. This also helped the rapid deployment of other advanced phone features such as high-definition pictures, various melody ring tones and built-in cameras rather than plain vanilla features like voice messages and short text messaging. In line with the rapid growth of the market for mobile phones with colour screens, the size of the mobile on-line content market has expanded to 258 billion won (ca. 230 Mio. EUR) in 2002 from 38 billion won (ca. 33 Mio. EUR) in 2001. Unique features of the mobile on-line content market include creating personal avatars or icons and messaging photos, what seems especially appealing to the younger Korean generation who increasingly wants to differentiate themselves.

2.2 Hit Product 2003: Digital Photos [23]

Monthly sales of mobile phones with built-in digital cameras surged from 300,000 units at the beginning of 2003 to 1 million units in October. The share of camera phones in the mobile phone market has thus skyrocketed from 24% to 72.7% during this period. In addition to the mobile phone market, up to 80,000 units of digital cameras were sold only in October 2003, dramatically higher than the monthly sales average of 20, 000 units recorded the prior year. Such rapid growth of the digital photo market is attributed to technological advances. The technology had reached a point where camera phones with more than 1 million pixels and digital cameras with around 8 million pixels already emerged in the market. The spread of digital photo equipment was accompanied by various services, such as internet photo shops, which provide free online storage space. It also created a culture with the younger generations to promote their self-image by uploading such photos to the web. This has even developed into a new type of 'beauty contest', where people would take self-portraits, upload them to the web, and the one who received the highest grade from netizens is called 'eol-jjang', meaning 'the best face'.

2.3 Hit Product 2004: www.cyworld.com [24]

The internet company Cyworld has drawn subscribers in excess of 10 Mio. as of 2004. For 2006 20 Mio. out of 33 Mio. internet-users are estimated cyworld-users; 96% of the 20 to 29 year-olds regularly use this site [3]. This website allows subscribers to choose background music, colour and avatars to decorate their own web-logs. Sales from these decoration items amounted to a staggering 150 Mio. Won (ca. 132,000 EUR) a day for 2004 (2006, 250 Mio. Won (ca. 210,000 EUR). Users have created new words like 'Cyzil' (to indicate uploading of articles and pictures on web-logs), Cyholic (referring to addiction to Cyworld activities) and 'Dotoeree' (=Acorn, to indicate electronic coins); these terms have gained a wide currency as a result of the website's popularity. Cyworld's explosive popularity indicates consumers' overwhelming desire to communicate with each other. On the website, users search other people's web-logs and form virtual families with close friends. They upload digital picture on their cy, download music and use their own homepage as some kind of juke-box. In addition, users can create and decorate their own web-logs with just a few clicks as the website provides simple and convenient tools. Stung by Cyworld's takeoff, rival portal sites have appeared, emulating its blog service. Daum Communications, Freechal and MSN have all launched their own blog services named Planet, SUM and HomeP, respectively. Now it's becoming a fad for business companies to create their own blog sites on Cyworld to boost corporate image and promote products.

2.4 Hit Product 2005: The Cheonggyecheon (청계천) Stream [25]

The Cheonggyecheon is a stream that flows right through the centre of Seoul meeting the Han River. For about 58 years the stream was covered by highways and concrete till in July 2003 the restoration-project was launched. Despite controversial discussion of the use of this project, it seems to have met Korea's ravages of time as the renewed stream was immediately after its opening in September 2005 voted for Korea's number one hit in goods and services. It seems like Koreans rediscover their love for nature, freedom and leisure-time what findings of the cultural context data also back.

2.5 2006: Apartments in Pangyo [26]

Appartments in Pangyo district in Seongnam-city, a satellite city south of Seoul, were the number one hit product in 2006, driven by competitive but steadily increasing housing prices as well as the fact that Pangyo is long-time considered as potential replacement for Gangnam-ku, which is popular for new (and expensive) apartments, IT and competitive schools. For the understanding of the Korean user particularly the effects of schools on housing decisions seem interesting. Education in Korea is highly competitive and considered as one of the most important factors throughout the society. Parents would spend their life-time savings to allow only the very best education for their children. They even chose their homes to close proximity to the best schools, if they can afford this as housing prices around first-class schools are considerably higher than elsewhere. Despite just ranked number two of the 2006 hit products, slim mobiles shall explicitly mentioned here as their success implies a change of user-preferences compared to previous years. While products in the past competed mainly with functions and technology users increasingly value design and hedonistic product features developers need to account for.

2.6 Korean Design Preferences

As the Korean culture itself, Korean design is strongly influenced by the Chinese as well as the Japanese culture. However, one would make a big mistake to assume that what makes successful design in Japan or China does it in Korea too, what studies like INTOPS show. INTOPS [21] and research conducted by Fuji Xerox (FX) [7] both proof that when it comes to colours, Koreans strongly favour bright and intense colours over pale ones. So chose 88% of subjects interviewed by FX bright green, blue and red over their pale counterparts and all of Koreans participating at INTOPS requested a colour-intensity of 100%. These observations are clearly confirmed when comparing 18 of Korea's most successful websites of different areas of interest. While the background of all pages is left simply white, buttons, navigation-bars and titles are embedded in a rather strong colour. Green and blue seem to be the most preferred ones when it comes to web-design, followed by orange. Despite the vast amount of textual content on most pages, they do not evoke the feeling of simple word-documents that are merely converted to HTML but rather seem quite sophisticated and well organized. One factor supporting this impression is the strong clustering of information on Korean websites. Information referring to the same or similar context is clearly, visually differentiated from other information. Findings of the FX research invigorate this idea, also. 76% of subjects asked preferred a strongly clustered page layout for a VCR manual with instructions and supplementary information in the left column and explanatory screens in the right column, or vice versa, over less clustered layouts, like supplementary information in the left and screen plus instructions in the right column, or the vertical arrangement of those. The differentiation between clusters is also improved through the widespread use of pictographs as cluster-titles. Also this preference is supported by findings of the FX research. So, do 96% of the survey's participants prefer rather icon-like pictographs over more word-like labels. Despite the abundance of animations, pictures and other icons on Korean homepages, these pictographs are rather kept simple and neat than fancy and pictorial. Yet other research proves, that when it comes to recognisability of icons and symbols Koreans perform significantly better when those are rather pictorial and less abstract [21, 17]. Hence, the right balance between pictorial and abstract is to be found to meet recognisability and aesthetic preferences.

3   Step 2: Cultural Context Data

In the second step of the QDUPT a closer look at existing cultural context data, as gathered by marketers or research institutes, gives further insights about the respective culture. Especially non-traditional data such as national character, self-expression, young/adult culture, individual- and/or group-perception, cultural bilingualism, etc., as opposed to traditional demographic data, can significantly improve the developers understanding of the culture in question. [1]

3.1 Demographic Data

As of July 2006 Korea has a total land area of 98,190 km² and a population of 48,846,823, of which 18,9% are under 15 years old, 71,9% are between 15 and 64, and 9,2% are 65 and older. Most Koreans (46%) are religiously not affiliated, 26% are Buddhists, the same ratio are Christians, 1% Confucians and 1% belong to another religion. The literacy rate is 97,9%. [2]. Over the past 40 years the new middle class – made up of specialists, technicians, and employed administrators/office workers – was the fastest growing class in Korean society [27]. With an average age of 38,2 years and about 14,1 years of education, this class is made up of comparatively young and highly educated people (50% of them graduated from four-year university or obtained higher degrees). This indicates how highly valued education is in the Korean society, as it is a mean for many to move up in their social status. The chance, however, to obtain good education strongly depends on the social background.

3.2 Cultural Context Data

Currently Korea is undergoing a massive social change fuelled by the impressive development of the Korean economy, globalization and the ever increasing internet abundance over the past decade. This has a significant impact on consumption patterns, life-style and the structure of society.

According to a survey on consumption features of Korean customers conducted by the Korean Chamber of Commerce and Industry (KCCI), the most significant factors influencing the buy-decision are quality (31.7%), followed by price (25.1%) and brand (17.2%) [15]. Especially high-income brackets, with an income over 3.85 Million won (ca. 3000 EUR), are very quality oriented, while the focus of lower income brackets, with an income less than 1.46 Million won (ca. 1200 EUR), is naturally more on price. When deciding for a purchase place, 62.4% of the consumers are mainly driven by price – one reason of the success of on-line shopping in Korea – and 17% by the shopping atmosphere. These preferences let more and more consumers purchase online [16]. Especially internet-based customer-to-customer (C2C) shopping significantly increased by 4% from 2004 to 2005 compared to other online businesses. 71.7% point out that they prefer C2C-shopping due to the very competitive prices. However, even when shopping online the product quality plays an important role for Koreans. In consequence poor product quality is the main reason of dissatisfaction in C2C-shopping, leaving online malls with a much higher customer satisfaction (56.3% compared to 49%) [8]. Quality preferences also let online-consumers spend in average 1.6 days comparing offers from at least 3 different online- or offline outlets before deciding what and where to buy, indicating how picky and conscious Korean customers are.

The steadily growing economy of Korea leaves more money in the country, and the peoples pockets (GDP per capita reached USD 24,200 in 2006 and South Korea joined the trillion dollar club of world economies already in 2004). Despite this 57.9% of Koreans reported a decrease in their disposal income in 2004 compared to 2003 [9] as prices, living-standards and other expenses are rising, too. As a result consumer confidence was in 2004 at an all time low ending in a sluggish consumer spending for this period [10]. 40.2% of questioned households reported that the fear for uncertainty of the economy is one of the main reasons for them to spend less, indication the high uncertainty avoidance of Koreans. These developments cause deep changes in the society. So reported 78.1% of the people asked that, as a result of decreased bargain-power, they stay at home more often, 77.3% increased their saving of energy [11] and 57.6% said to split bills, usually uncommon in Korea, became the norm at lunch or dinner with friends [13]. These developments can be added up to the three buzzwords of the domestic consumption in 2005: *Single*, *Security* and *Self-Satisfaction* [12].

Single refers to the recently spreading 'I-will-do-my-bit-and-you-mind-your-own-business'-thinking even among family members. While in the past Korean men and women lived with their families until they got married, the number of single house-holds is steadily increasing. People more and more are taking the right to live their own life, less constrained through their families. This will boost the sales of products which seem to be particularly relevant for singles, such as multi-functional monitors, large capacity MP3-devices, telematics and SNS (Social Network Services), such as Cyworld. The second buzzword, *Security*, relates to the increased number of crimes and suicides within the last decade. Thus the market of security related products, such as CCTVs or mobile devices with sophisticated internet-based accident surveillance systems, is expected to increase heavily. Recently, especially Koreans in their 20s, are increasingly consuming products for the sake of *Self-Satisfaction*. The success of mini homepages, as provided by cyworld, satisfying the consumers' desire for self-displaying, can be partially explained by this development, as people spend more time and money on doing things for their own satisfaction.

Amid these trends, an aging population leads to the emergence of new major *consumer groups* with different consumption patterns [14]. The first major group is characterised through *egocentric* and *sensible* consumption patterns. Those are the customers mainly aiming for subjective satisfaction, sensibility, beauty and first-hand experience. Among them those can be found who are only using first-rate brands, a rather small but old group, as well as lately emerging TONKs[1] and Metro-Sexuals. Increasing ecological problems, such as yellow dust or air pollution as well as the growing economical strength of Koreans lead to the second major consumption pattern that can be described as *nature-loving* and *simplistic*. Also the implementation of the 5-day workweek system in Korea in 2004 resulted in a growing amount of consumers higher valuing nature, family, health and leisure time. Finally there are those groups who fancy an *elite-style shopping*. Those are valuing planned consumption, are interested in efficiency, speed and self-development and spread steadily amid the trend for information and the emergence of internet generations. As the country becomes richer and information-technology more abundant people are getting more and more individualistic, family ties are becoming looser and people

---

[1] The acronym for 'two only no kids'.

start carrying more for their own quality of life. However, clearly the Korean mind is strongly influenced by its religious roots of Buddhism and Confucianism putting high weight on society and family in setting the boundaries between what is appropriate and what is inappropriate for individuals. In step 3 this impact can be observed.

4 Step 3: Cultural Dimensions

The third and last step of the QDUPT is to have a closer look at cultural dimensions, such as introduced by Hofstede, to compare the users' and developers' cultural background. The following table gives an overview of rankings and scores of Korea and Germany.

Table 1. Hofstede's Cultural Dimensions – South Korea vs. Germany (r = rank, s = score)

Country	PDI		IDV		MAS		UAI		LTO	
	r	s	r	s	r	s	r	s	r	s
Germany FR	42/44	35	15	67	9/10	66	29	65	14	31
South Korea	27/28	60	43	18	41	39	16/17	85	5	75

4.1 Power Distance (PDI)

Power distance refers to the extent to which less powerful members expect and accept unequal power distribution within a culture. As a country with a higher PDI, in Korean society inequality among people is rather accepted and welcome, parents teach their children obedience, the attitude towards authority is less dependent from education than in Western Countries, structures are in general strong hierarchical structures, a tendency towards centralization can be observed, privileges and status-symbols are expected and popular, employees expect orders, power is valued over right and is based on family, friends, status as well as the possibility to apply pressure. However, it shall be pointed, that this enumeration represents a simplistic generalization than cannot be applied on the individual lever.

4.2 Individualism vs. Collectivism (IDV)

Individualism in cultures implies loose ties; everyone is expected to look after one's self or immediate family but no one else. Collectivism implies that people are integrated from birth into strong, cohesive groups that protect them in exchange for unquestioning loyalty. As a rather collectivist country in Korean society identity is based on the social net a person belongs to, the credo is to avoid conflicts and keep harmony, the own opinion is determined by the group, collective interests have priority over individual interests, communication is highly context-dependant, degrees enable access to groups with higher status, the chief-employee-relation is based on moral measures (similar to family-relations), for hiring-/promotion-decisions the group is taken into account and relations are more important than the task to fulfil.

4.3 Masculinity vs. Femininity (MAS)

Masculinity and femininity refer to gender roles, not physical characteristics. Masculine roles refer to concepts of assertiveness, competition, and toughness, while feminine ones to orientation towards home and children, people, and tenderness.

In the rather masculine Korean society a decisive and authoritative performance-ideal is followed that supports the strong ones. On this the sympathy is with the strong; big and fast are beautiful, financial/material values are important, people live to work, while the working-life is focused on fairness, competition and performance and the resolution to conflicts is to carry them out (which, at the first sight, seems in contrast to the previously mentioned harmony ideal, but is non the less persuasive).

4.4 Uncertainty Avoidance (UAI)

People vary in the extent that they feel anxiety about uncertain or unknown matters, as opposed to the more universal feeling of fear caused by known or understood threats. Cultures vary in their avoidance of uncertainty, creating different rituals and having different values regarding formality, punctuality, legal-religious-social requirements, and tolerance for ambiguity. Due to the rather high UAI of Korea there is an emotional need for rules and laws, the country is rather conservative and intolerant to innovations (at least socially while technologically very open), values specialists and experts, people rather suppress aggressions and emotions as well as thought and behaviours which do not represent the norm. Despite uncertainty avoidance known risks and also unknown factors in the favour of speed are accepted resulting in the occasional referred to Korean 'pali-pali-syndrome' (pali = quick, fast).

4.5 Long-Term Orientation (LTO)

Long-Term Orientation seems to play an important role in Asian countries that had been influenced by Confucian philosophy over many thousands of years. Hofstede and Bond [7] found such countries shared the beliefs, that a stable society requires unequal relations, the family is the prototype of all social organizations; consequently, older people (parents) have more authority than younger people (and men more than women). Alike does virtuous behaviour to others means not treating them as one would not like to be treated, while virtuous behaviour in work means trying to acquire skills and education, working hard, and being frugal, patient, and persevering.

For the Korean society this implies a certain respect of social and status responsibilities within certain borders, a high social pressure of status-representation, a high saving-ratio and the importance of the protection of ones 'face' (status).

5 Conclusion

The QDUPT proves to be an excellent method to gain first, generic insights into a target-culture, particularly for the purpose of cross-cultural product development. So could be shown that even though the Korean culture is currently undergoing massive changes in its social-system, such as the desire for a single life and self-satisfaction particularly among the younger generation, the bonds within this social-system remain significantly strong, what the success of SNS and the desire to communicate backs. This could not have been shown by simply applying Hofstedes cultural dimension as these merely provide the rather rough frame, which can be considered as more past-oriented and simplistic, of the Korean culture.

This structural change is not at least fuelled by the huge success of technological innovations and the new media in Korea. The fast adoption of colour screen mobile phones, digital pictures and internet clearly show the openness and even the desire of Koreans for innovation. Amid this dynamic a stronger orientation towards life-quality, health and free-time which were certainly neglected in the Korean society can be observed.

More than just broadening the developers understanding of the target-culture, the QDUPT also provides useful insights in user-preferences. On this first insights are, that Koreans strongly favour intense colours, get along quite well with much information simultaneously presented (as long at it is clustered) and their cognitive models are best supported by applying rather pictorial icons (but be careful of too 'childish' designs). Also suggests the fact, that shopping-websites, which can be associated with free-time and 'playing', are making more extensive use of animations and picture, than rather sincere website (such as for banks and news), the context-orientation of Koreans. This finding is also backed by other research [20] as well as through own usability-tests with Korean systems. Based on this first, generic understanding of the target-culture further steps towards the cross-cultural product-development, such as the definition of cross-cultural variables to further scrutinize localization issues, can be build on.

References

1. Chavan, A.L.: A Quick and Dirty User Profiling Technique. In: Prabhu, G.V., delGaldo, E. M. (eds.): Designing for Global Markets 1, IWIPS 1999, First International Workshop on Internationalisation of Products and Systems, Rochester, New York, USA, May 20–22, 1999, pp. 79–93, Backhouse Press (1998)
2. CIA World Factbook: Korea, South, (January 16, 2007), (2007), URL: https://www.cia. gov/cia/publications/factbook/geos/ks.html
3. Ewers, J.: Cyworld: Bigger than YouTube? In: U.S. News & World Report, (November 9, 2006) (2006)
4. Garfinkel, G.: Studies in Ethnomethodology, Malden MA. Blackwell Publishing, Oxford (1984)
5. Geertz, C.: Dichte Beschreibung: Beiträge zum Verstehen kultureller Systeme. In: Frankfurt: Suhrkamp (1983)
6. Hofstede, G.: Cultures and Organizations: Software of the Mind. McGraw-Hill, New York, USA (1997)
7. Ichimura, M.: Intercultural Research in Page Design and Layout for Asian/Pacific Audience. Fuji Xerox Co., Ltd. Human Interface and Design Development, Planning Group for Manual Design, (July 26, 2006) (2001), URL http://www.stc.org/confproceed/ 2001/PDFs/STC48-000122.PDF
8. KCCI: Consumer Behavior at Internet Shopping Malls. Korean Chamber of Commerce and Industry (KCCI) (December 02, 2004) (2004)

12   B.-M. Braun and K. Röse

9. KCCI: KCCI's survey of consumers' recent purchasing pattern. Korean Chamber of Commerce and Industry (KCCI) (August 04, 2004) (2004a)
10. KCCI: Korean Consumer Confidence at all time low: Survey Results. Korean Chamber of Commerce and Industry (KCCI) (October 12, 2004) (2004b)
11. KCCI: A survey of changes in consumption pattern in the era of high oil prices. Korean Chamber of Commerce and Industry (KCCI) (September 20, 2005) (2005)
12. KCCI: Expected buzzwords in domestic consumption market in 2005. Korean Chamber of Commerce and Industry (KCCI) (January 19, 2005) (2005a)
13. KCCI: Survey of Recent Change in Consumption Behaviour. Korean Chamber of Commerce and Industry (KCCI) (January 28, 2005) (2005b)
14. KCCI: Emergence of senior citizens as a new consumer group and how business should cope with it. Korean Chamber of Commerce and Industry (KCCI) (August 08, 2005) (2005c)
15. KCCI: Consumers' online purchasing pattern in digital era. Korean Chamber of Commerce and Industry (KCCI) (August 29, 2005) (2005d)
16. KCCI: Consumption Features for Each Income Level and Suggestions. Korean Chamber of Commerce and Industry (KCCI) (September 29, 2005) (2005e)
17. Kim, J.H., Lee, K.P. (n.a.): Cultural Difference and Mobile Phone Interface Design: Icon Recognition According to Level of Abstraction. In: Deajeon, Korea Advanced Institute of Science and Technology (KAIST), Department of Industrial Design
18. Malinowski, B.: Argonauts of the Western Pacific. New York: E.P. Duttoon (1922 /1961)
19. Mark, G., Becker, B.: Designing believable interaction by applying social conventions. Applied Artificial Intelligence, (13), pp. 297–320 (1999)
20. Nisbett, R.: The geography of thought: how asians and westerners think differently and why. The Free Press, New York (2003)
21. Röse, K.: Methodik zur Gestaltung interkultureller Mensch-Maschine-Systeme in der Produktionstechnik. In: Kaiserslautern, University, Maschinenbau und Verfahrenstechnik, Dissertation (2002)
22. SERI: Korean Economic Trends. Samsung Economic Research Institute (SERI), vol. 6(49), Seoul (2002)
23. SERI: Korean Economic Trends. In: Samsung Economic Research Institute (SERI), vol. 7(45), Seoul (2003)
24. SERI: Korean Economic Trends. In: Samsung Economic Research Institute (SERI), vol. 8, No. n.a., Seoul (2004)
25. SERI: Annual Report. In: Samsung Economic Research Institute (SERI), vol. n.a., no. n.a., Seoul (2005)
26. SERI: Top Ten Hit Products of Korea in 2006. In: Samsung Economic Research Institute (SERI), Seoul (2006)
27. Shin, A.: The Growth of the Korean Middle Class and its Social Consciousness (July 26, 2006). The Developing Economies 41(2), 201–220 (2003), http://www.ide.go.jp/English/Publish/De/pdf/03_02_05.pdf
28. Triandis, H.C.: Individualism and Collectivism. Boulder: Westview Press (1995)
29. Triandis, H.C.: Cross-cultural psychology. In: Asian Journal of Social Psychology, (2), pp. 127–143 (1999)

Increasing the Usability of Text Entry in Mobile Devices for European Languages and Languages Used in Europe

Martin Böcker[1], Karl Ivar Larsson[2], and Bruno von Niman[3]

[1] BenQ Mobile, Germany
[2] LWP Consulting, Sweden
[3] vonniman Consulting, ETSI TC HF Vice Chairman and STF 300 Leader
bruno@vonniman.com

Abstract. Entering text through the 12-key keypad of mobile devices is one of the biggest usability challenges of mobile phone use. The user's problem is potentially increased if the text to be entered contains language-specific letters not included in the 26 letters of the Latin alphabet, as users cannot be sure which key of the 12-key keypad the letter they wish to enter is associated to. ETSI, the European Telecommunications Standards Institute, has published in 2003 a standard (ES 202 130) that specifies the assignment of characters on the 12-key telephone keypad for a range of European languages. That standard for letters, digits and special characters (such as the Euro symbol and punctuation marks) covered the official languages of the EU and EFTA members, Russia, as well as countries with applicant status for the EU at that time. This paper describes the further development of the standard to cover other major languages spoken in Europe including official languages, minority languages and immigrants' languages.

Keywords: Usability, user interfaces, standards, 12-key keypad, ICT.

1 Introduction

Telecommunications devices currently represent one of the largest global consumer product segments. As telecommunications devices and services converge with technologies such as information processing, broadcast services and the internet, while at the same time becoming mobile and ubiquitous, the usability of these devices and services becomes a critical factor in service uptake. One of the most challenging aspects of mobile-device usability is text entry using the standard 12-key telephone keypad.

At present, finding the characters necessary to enter a name in the terminal's phone book, searching for a name, writing an SMS (text) message or logging on to a mobile internet portal cannot always be performed easily, because manufacturers differ in terms of which European characters their devices support, how they are ordered in lists and how the specific characters are mapped onto the keys of the keypad. Character-set implementation varies sometimes even between devices and applications from one and the same manufacturer. Standardizing the way characters are mapped onto keypads gives users easier access to different communication devices and services, allowing simple, correct and efficient text input, search and retrieval. It also broadens

N. Aykin (Ed.): Usability and Internationalization, Part II, HCII 2007, LNCS 4560, pp. 13–21, 2007.

market opportunities for manufacturers and suppliers and reduces their development costs.

The original reason for assigning letters to the rotary dial pad and later to the numeric telephone keys was to provide alphabetic 'aliases' for digits, as mnemonics in dialling. The need to use a telephone keypad for entering text or data was not envisaged. Nobody in the pioneer days of telephony anticipated the concept of a 'phone books' stored inside the telephone, or a service like SMS, the very successful service for transmitting short text messages as an alternative to voice communication.

The only standards previously available (e.g. ETSI ETS 300 640 or ITU-T Recommendation E.161 (02/01)), addressing the assignment of characters to the 12-key telephone keypad, were limited to the assignment of the basic 26 Latin letters (a to z). Language-specific letters (e.g. ü, é, å, ä, ö) as well as other characters (e.g. '€' or '@') were not addressed. The lack of a standard on these issues has led to diverse and inconsistent solutions for European languages, obviously creating accessibility barriers to basic communication access in eEurope.

Europe has around 230 indigenous languages – worldwide there are close to 7000. The largest number of languages presently supported by a specific ICT device or service is approaching 50. Cultural and linguistic diversity is one of the key strengths of Europe. However, in ICT, it raises issues that need to be considered and solved in order not to limit access to services, their availability and usability, on the basic as well as more advanced levels.

The first version of ETSI ES 202 130 has been developed to solve the problem for some of the most important European languages by defining character repertoires, sorting orders and the assignment of letters to the 12-key telephony keypad for these languages. A new version of ETSI ES 202 130 will extend this work to cover other major languages spoken in Europe including official languages, minority languages and immigrants' languages. All of this work was aligned with the European Commission's initiative *eEurope*, a programme for accelerated uptake and inclusive deployment of new, important, consumer-oriented technologies (http://europa.eu.int/ information_society/eeurope).

2   Scope of ETSI ES 202 130 in Its Presently Published Form

The current version of ETSI ES 202 130 specifies the minimum repertoire and assignment of graphic (letter, digit and special) characters to standard 12-key telephone keypads on ICT devices with telephony functionality. It applies to public or private, fixed or mobile network terminals, without an alphanumeric keyboard but providing a 12-key keypad in hardware form (e.g. as push button keys) or software form (e.g. as soft keys on a visual display). It also applies to network-based services accessed through such terminal devices. It complements ETS 300 640 by additionally including European language-specific letters (Latin, Greek and Cyrillic scripts) and other common characters (e.g. '€' and punctuation marks). It specifies solutions for both language-independent and language-specific keypad assignments, mapped to the 12-key telephone keypad, also providing common and language-specific information on character repertoires and ordering.

The standard is fully applicable to the official languages of the European Union (EU) member countries as of 2005 and those of countries with candidate status (Romania, Bulgaria and Turkey) and, additionally, to the official languages of the EFTA (the European Free Trade Association) countries and Russian. The languages fully covered by the first version of ETSI ES 202 130 are therefore: Bulgarian, Czech, Danish, Dutch, English, Estonian, Finnish, French, German, Greek, Hungarian, Icelandic, Irish, Italian, Latvian, Lithuanian, Luxemburgish, Maltese, Norwegian, Polish, Portuguese, Romanian, Russian, Slovak, Slovenian, Spanish, Swedish, and Turkish. In anticipation of future expansions, the language-independent repertoires and keypad assignments specified also include letters needed in some of the remaining European official languages.

ETSI ES 202 130 does not cover any implementation related issues, e.g. specifics of predictive text input or user interface design.

3 User Requirements

Users of the standard are those implementing it, for example interaction designers and other developers of ICT devices and services, designing user interfaces deploying text input and output, applied to 12-key keypad arrays provided in hardware form (e.g. as push button keys) or software form (e.g. as soft keys on a visual display) and telecommunication-network based services accessed through such terminal devices.

End users addressed are the consumers (end users) of the ICT devices and services mentioned above, ranging from first time to experienced advanced users, who can produce tactile stimuli in the form of a key press and perceive written text. The end users' main goal is to efficiently use ICT devices and services under circumstances intended by these. The implementation of ES 202 130 enables users to reapply knowledge and previous experience between different ICT devices and services using a 12-key standard keypad array and a display. Control of common functions such as entering of characters and retrieval of text in a certain order will be simplified. Well-established services which rely on alpha mnemonics (e.g. '800 DOCTOR' rather than '800 362867' are not negatively influenced as the standard only complements ETS 300 640).

For certain end users with special needs, ES 202 130 is particularly helpful due to consistent implementations (same character always found in the same position, regardless of the terminal manufacturer). For certain disabilities, e.g. in the case of temporary or permanent difficulties caused by cognitive problems or the lack of necessary level of proficiency in the respective language and other communication impairments such as: visual impairments, the inability to produce distinctive tactile stimuli or difficulties in handling, distinguishing and understanding textual information, the standard is not expected to have any impact.

Uniformity in the basic interactive elements increases the transfer of learning between devices and services and improves the overall usability of the entire interactive environment. Such transference becomes even more important in a world of ubiquitous devices and services.

Guiding principles during the development of the ordering and assignments of the alphanumeric characters have been:

1. Consistent and harmonised across different devices and services
2. Easy to learn and remember
3. As natural as possible, matching previously acquired knowledge
4. Redundancy (multiple solutions possible to reach desired input)

4 Methodology

4.1 Initial Survey

As start of the work to developing the standard, an informal survey of the key assignments in a number of mobile phone models was carried out on several major
manufacturers' handsets. The survey was based mainly on specifications and user
manuals downloaded from the internet but also on 'hands-on' investigation.

4.2 Principles Applying to ES 202 130

In order to arrive at a consistent and easy-to-implement presentation of the requirements for character repertoires, ordering rules and character assignment to the 12-key
keypad, the principles listed in Table 1 were applied throughout the production of the
standard. Some of these are elaborated in the following.

4.3 Characters Needed

Approximately 240 Latin-repertoire letters are needed to cover the major European
languages. With Greek and Cyrillic letters added, the number increases to well over
350. This can be compared to the 75 Latin-repertoire letters (mix of capital and small)
supported by the present GSM 03.38 7-bit scheme generally implemented in today's
mobile phones and networks (85 letters all-in-all when the Greek capital letters of that
scheme are included). It was found necessary to include in the language-specific repertoires more letters than are contained in the "core" of those languages, called "Type
A" letters. This is because in all languages there is a user need to input also foreign-
origin words, some of them needing "foreign" letters. Further, in all countries there
exist user preferences in spelling of some names with "foreign" letters, and possibly
also a need to represent names – personal and/or geographical – correctly in recognised minority languages. The repertoire tables therefore also include "Type B" letters
(see Figure 1).

4.4 Character Ordering

Ordering of characters is a highly complex problem, and has been the subject of
very large amounts of work in several standardisation bodies, both national and international. Earlier ETSI and ISO/IEC standards specify principles based on a "multi-level"
approach for the ordering of strings of characters. However, it was found necessary to
adopt a simplified "single-level" method for this standard, considering the limited capabilities of telephone devices as compared to computer systems. As regards letters, the
two language-independent repertoire tables specify a deterministic ordering. For the

language-specific repertoire tables, however, some additional criteria were applied because of established practices in telecommunications, e.g. for printed telephone directories.

In all European languages, the letters A-Z are considered part of the alphabet even if, in many of them, some of the letters are not used in any indigenous-origin words. Also some languages have special-shape letters, like the Icelandic Þ and the German ß. Additionally, all languages use special variants of letters A-Z with diacritical marks, like the acute accent and the cedilla (e.g. É and Ç). For ordering, most languages consider such variants equivalent to the basic letter. In some languages, however, a few of them are considered letters of their own, and ordered differently. For instance, the letter Ö is ordered in Swedish as the last letter of the alphabet. As far as possible, national conventions

Table 1. Principles employed in character repertoires, sorting order and keypad assignment

Principle 1: Presentation of character repertoires and sorting orders
<ul><li>Combine repertoire and ordering information in one table</li><li>Provide language-independent tables per script (Latin, Cyrillic, Greek)</li><li>Cover in language-independent tables languages not covered in language-specific part by designing the language-independent tables to be "future-proof" (e.g. Ukrainian, Serbian and Croatian)</li></ul>
Principle 2: Character description
<ul><li>Describe letters in terms of standardized identifiers: (a) Letter: Representation of the letter, (b) GSM 03.38 7-bit coding, (c) ISO/IEC 6937 coding, (d) ISO/IEC 10646 (Unicode) identifier, and (e) ISO/IEC 10646 (Unicode) name</li><li>Order characters according to established standards, e.g. the Latin and Cyrillic language-independent repertoires are ordered according to ENV 13710</li></ul>
Principle 3: Language-independent repertoires
<ul><li>Latin: covers all Latin-based letters covered by the scope of the document</li><li>Cyrillic: Repertoire according to ISO/IEC 8859-5:1998</li><li>Greek-script repertoire is identical with the Greek language-specific repertoire</li><li>Provide minimum Latin subset ("A – Z") to be used with the Cyrillic and Greek repertoires</li></ul>
Principle 4: Language-specific repertoires
<ul><li>List essential alphabet of a particular language and letters typically used in that language (from various recognised sources). Usage type: A classification of each letter according to the following principles: (A) Letters essential to the language, and (B) Letters commonly used in writing the language, but not essential for it</li></ul>
Principles 5: Repertoire of digits and special characters
<ul><li>Only one (European) language-independent table of digits and special characters is provided</li><li>The need for language-specific tables is to be discussed</li><li>The digits and special characters are ordered (at present) according to ISO/IEC 14651 resp. CEN ENV 13710</li></ul>

Table 1. (*continued*)

Principle 6: Information contained in the keypad assignment tables
• Key: the key of the 12-key keypad the respective letters are assigned to, Letter: Representation of the letter, ISO/IEC 10646 (Unicode) identifier, and ISO/IEC 10646 (Unicode) name
Principle 7: Latin-script assignment principles
• If a character is assigned to a key of the 12-key keypad, it shall be assigned to the key specified in the respective table
• Letters with diacritical marks are assigned to the same key of the 12-key keypad as their respective basic letters (if existent), i.e. "ä" is assigned to key "2" because "a" is assigned to "2" according to ITU-T E.161
• A character may be additionally assigned to other keys
• Complete language-independent and language-specific tables may be implemented in any combination
Principle 8: Greek-language and Cyrillic-script assignment principles
• The Greek-language repertoire and the Cyrillic-script repertoire shall be assigned together with the minimum Latin-script repertoire
• Additional characters not covered by the present document may be assigned to a key
• Only tables for the assignment of small letters are specified, capital letters shall be assigned in the same way as the respective small letter
Principle 9: Assignment order for Latin-script letters
• Letters assigned to that particular key according to ITU-T E.161 (e.g. "abc" to key "2")
• The digit for the respective key according to ITU-T E.161
• Type A letters according to the tables in Section 6 (e.g. "ä" on key "2" for German)
• Type B letters according to the tables in Section 6 (e.g. "à" on key "2" for German) (e.g. the resulting assignment for key "2" for German is "abc2ää")
Principle 10: Language-independent Latin-script assignment
• Letters are assigned to the above-mentioned principles and ordered according to ISO/IEC 14651 resp. CEN ENV 13710
Principle 11: Assignment order for Greek-script and Cyrillic-script letters
• Letters assigned to that particular key in alphabetic order (e.g. "абвг" to key "2")
• The digit for the respective key according to ITU-T E.161
• Latin letters assigned to that particular key according to ITU-T E.161 (e.g. abc to key "2"). For example, the resulting assignment for key "2" for Russian is "абвг2abc")
Principle 12: Character ordering for Greek-language and the Cyrillic-script tables
• The characters of the Greek-language and the Cyrillic-script tables are ordered according to ISO/IEC 14651 resp. CEN ENV 13710

were followed for the language-specific repertoire tables. This may possibly cause "non-deterministic" ordering in specific cases. Although unsatisfactory in principle, it was concluded that this could be accepted for the relevant applications.

Letter	GSM 03.38 7-bit coding	ISO/IEC 6937 coding	ISO/IEC 10646 identifier	ISO/IEC 10646 name	Usage type	Notes
a	6/01	06/01	U+0061	LATIN SMALL LETTER A	A	•
A	4/01	04/01	U+0041	LATIN CAPITAL LETTER A	A	•
á	—	12/02 06/01	U+00E1	LATIN SMALL LETTER A WITH ACUTE	A	•
Á	—	12/02 04/01	U+00C1	LATIN CAPITAL LETTER A WITH ACUTE	A	•
ä	7/11	12/08 06/01	U+00E4	LATIN SMALL LETTER A WITH DIAERESIS	B	
Ä	5/11	12/08 04/01	U+00C4	LATIN CAPITAL LETTER A WITH DIAERESIS	B	
b	6/02	06/02	U+0062	LATIN SMALL LETTER B	A	
B	4/02	04/02	U+0042	LATIN CAPITAL LETTER B	A	
c	6/03	06/03	U+0063	LATIN SMALL LETTER C	A	‡
C	4/03	04/03	U+0043	LATIN CAPITAL LETTER C	A	‡
č	—	12/15 06/03	U+010D	LATIN SMALL LETTER C WITH CARON	A	
Č	—	12/15 04/03	U+010C	LATIN CAPITAL LETTER C WITH CARON	A	
d	6/04	06/04	U+0064	LATIN SMALL LETTER D	A	•
D	4/04	04/04	U+0044	LATIN CAPITAL LETTER D	A	•
ď	—	12/15 06/04	U+010F	LATIN SMALL LETTER D WITH CARON	A	•
Ď	—	12/15 04/04	U+010E	LATIN CAPITAL LETTER D WITH CARON	A	•
e	6/05	06/05	U+0065	LATIN SMALL LETTER E	A	•

Fig. 1. Extract of the table specifying character repertoire and sorting order for Czech

Key	Letter	ISO/IEC 10646 identifier	ISO/IEC 10646 name
2	a	U+0061	LATIN SMALL LETTER A
	b	U+0062	LATIN SMALL LETTER B
	c	U+0063	LATIN SMALL LETTER C
	2	U+0032	DIGIT TWO
	á	U+00E1	LATIN SMALL LETTER A WITH ACUTE
	č	U+010D	LATIN SMALL LETTER C WITH CARON
	ä	U+00E4	LATIN SMALL LETTER A WITH DIAERESIS
3	d	U+0064	LATIN SMALL LETTER D
	e	U+0065	LATIN SMALL LETTER E
	f	U+0066	LATIN SMALL LETTER F
	3	U+0033	DIGIT THREE
	ď	U+010F	LATIN SMALL LETTER D WITH CARON
	é	U+00E9	LATIN SMALL LETTER E WITH ACUTE
	ě	U+011B	LATIN SMALL LETTER E WITH CARON
4	g	U+0067	LATIN SMALL LETTER G
	h	U+0068	LATIN SMALL LETTER H
	i	U+0069	LATIN SMALL LETTER I
	4	U+0034	DIGIT FOUR
	í	U+00ED	LATIN SMALL LETTER I WITH ACUTE

Fig. 2. Extract of the table specifying character assignment to 12-key keypad for Czech

4.5 Keypad Input Sequences

In today's keypad-input implementations – foremost in mobile phones – the digits are generally placed as the last character in the key-press sequence, following not only the standardized letter assignments (ABC on key 2, DEF on key 3 etc.) but also all special letter variants assigned to the keys. The same principle was considered for ES 202 130. However, the special needs of visually-impaired users make the principle questionable. It was, therefore, decided to place, instead, the digits immediately following the presently standardized letter assignments; i.e. as the fourth key-press on all keys except 7 and 9 (PQRS and WXYZ) where it is the fifth (see Table 1 and Figure 2).

4.6 Digits and Special Characters

As the ordering and keypad assignment of digits and special characters turned out to be somewhat controversial, they were treated following a different set of rules. ES 202 130 defines a set of special characters that must be supported. In addition, other characters may also be supported. The order of appearance in the respective table is only a recommendation, valid for a language-independent implementation, and alternative orders of appearance of special characters are allowed. Furthermore, language-specific orders of appearance are also allowed. The full set of special characters must be accessible via one single entry point. It is recommended that this entry point is the "1" key. In addition, a device may use different other keys to access different sets of special characters and/or digits. In this case, Rule 1 and Rule 6 must still be followed. Thereby, the possibility to implement language-specific keypad assignments of special characters and digits is made possible.

5   Update/Extension of ES 202 130

ES 202 130 was met with positive responses from industry. An extension of its language coverage is therefore highly desirable, in particular in view of the strong emphasis on multilingualism by the European Union. In January 2006, ETSI decided to begin work on such an extension. This will take the form of either a revision of ES 202 130, or of a complementary standard. The Terms of Reference for the decided-on work specifies the extension as containing "major minority languages, some official European languages and ... non-European languages used by a considerable number of ICT users in Europe". The interpretation of this is not obvious, since different delimitations may be concluded from the wording.

Geographically, "Europe" is traditionally delimited in the south and the east by the Bosporus, the Caucasian mountain range, the Ural Mountains and the Ural River. The North Atlantic islands (but generally not Greenland) are also included, as well as those Mediterranean islands not in the proximity of the African continent. This definition is however unsatisfactory as a language basis for the Terms of Reference, since it contains only a small part of the nation of Turkey, also part of Kazakhstan, but not Cyprus, and further leaving the Trans-Caucasian states somewhat undefined. A more suitable definition of "Europe" should be the one of the Council of Europe (CoE), containing all "traditionally European" states, and also clarifying that Turkey and Cyprus are part of Europe, but that Kazakhstan is not. Also CoE concluded after a thorough investigation, considering historical and cultural as well as other factors, that the Trans-Caucasian states Georgia, Armenia and Azerbaijan shall be considered European, and therefore eligible for entry in the Council (and all three are nowadays members).

An adoption of this definition for the update/extension work does not necessarily imply that all of the CoE member states' official/majority languages will be covered in the decided-on extension/standard. In particular, the Armenian and Georgian unique script systems will have to be considered, and will be studied in the initial phases of the standard extension work. A complication of the CoE definition is that it includes all of the Russian state, which is obviously European as well as Asiatic. This, however, relates only to the selection of minority languages to be covered in the ETSI work, and not to the definition as such. Another complication is the overseas territories of some of the European states. This will need study, which will be performed in the initial stage of the work. As regards European-origin minority languages, special consideration will be taken of languages recognised in ratifications of the CoE charter ETS 148, "European Charter for Regional or Minority Languages". This charter has so far been ratified by about half of the CoE member states, and signed – although not yet ratified – by several more. The ES 202 130 update/complement could therefore cover the following categories of languages:

- official/majority languages of European countries not covered in the current version of the standard (e.g. Croatian);
- recognised European-country minority languages not already covered by the majority language (e.g. Sorbian in Germany)
- other important but (as yet) unrecognised minority languages (e.g. Friulian in Italy);
- large immigrant languages (e.g. Arabic);
- other important immigrant non-European languages (e.g. Vietnamese, which poses special character complications).

6 Summary

The implementation of ES 202 130 in its current version allows users to enter text into modern ICT devices in a number of major European languages, in a way that is logically consistent and that renders the learning of new keypad assignments superfluous when moving from the devices of one manufacturer to those of another. The usability of future ICT devices will be further increased by a revision/complement of ES 202 130 to expand the number of languages covered by the standard.

References

1. ETSI references are available free of charge at www.etsi.org.
2. CEN ENV 13710 (2000): European Ordering Rules - Ordering of characters from the Latin, Greek and Cyrillic scripts.
3. ETSI ES 202 130 Human Factors; User Interfaces; Character repertoires, ordering and assignment to the 12-key telephone keypad (European languages)
4. ETSI ETS 300 640 Human Factors (HF); Assignment of alphabetic letters to digits on standard telephone keypad arrays
5. ETSI TS 100 900 Digital cellular telecommunications system (Phase 2+); Alphabets and language-specific information (same as GSM 03.38 version 7.2.0, Release 1998)
6. ISO 8859-7: Information processing - 8-bit single-byte coded graphic character sets - Part 7: Latin/Greek alphabet.
7. ISO/IEC 10646-1 (2000): Information technology - Universal Multiple-Octet Coded Character Set (UCS); Part 1: Architecture and Basic Multilingual Plane.
8. ISO/IEC 6937 (2001): Information technology - Coded graphic character set for text communication - Latin alphabet.
9. ITU-T Recommendation E.161 (02/01) Arrangement of digits, letters and symbols on telephones and other devices that can be used for gaining access to a telephone network

User Centered Design Approach Applying CPV in Mobile Service Design

Chang K. Cho[1,2], Cheol Lee[2,*], and Myung Hwan Yun[2]

[1] CIRCLEONE Consulting Inc., Seoul, Korea
[2] Department of Industrial Engineering, Seoul National University
Seoul, 151-744 Korea
iehis@snu.ac.kr

Abstract. In this paper, applicability of CPV in mobile service design has been investigated in both phase of divergent and convergent thinking. During the scenario-based ideation, potential customer values can be used as ideation stimuli in the process of structured brainstorming. In divergent thinking, CPV can be applied as evaluation criteria in comparing new ideas with alternative services. For the efficient implementation, work templates for accelerated front-end UCD are developed in co-operation with mobile service staffs in Korean mobile operator.

Keywords: mobile service, user centered design, new service design, customer perceived value (CPV).

1 Introduction

From the view point of usability, phone-based mobile internet has very poor device and network capability in comparison with traditional PC-based internet. Additionally, high cost for internet access is also a major disadvantage of mobile internet. However, characteristics of mobile internet such as personalization, localization, instant accessibility and ubiquity can be utilized to enhance the value of mobile internet. Understanding of the trade-off between pros and cons of mobile internet and leveraging the advantageous characteristics of mobile internet is the key to the successful mobile internet service development. Several needs for user-centered approach for mobile service development can be identified in new business opportunity auditing in fuzzy front end, context-based idea generation during divergent thinking, CPV-based concept evaluation during convergent thinking, usability evaluation during service development, and post-launch management in service improvement. Especially application of CPV concepts can be strategically applied to design useful and usable mobile services that offer a high enough value to users to overcome the usability and performance constraints. In this paper, applicability of CPV in mobile service design has been investigated in either phase of divergent and convergent thinking.

---

* Corresponding author.

N. Aykin (Ed.): Usability and Internationalization, Part II, HCII 2007, LNCS 4560, pp. 22–29, 2007.
© Springer-Verlag Berlin Heidelberg 2007

2 Literature Survey

Customer perceived value has recently gained much attention from researchers and marketers because of its important role in predicting purchase behavior and achieving sustainable competitive advantage [1,2,3,4]. Customer value management has been used widely by market oriented firms to differentiate themselves from competitors [4,5,6]. The most common definition of value is the ratio or trade-off between quality and price, which is a value-for-money conceptualization [7,8,9]. Another definition of perceived value a consumer's overall assessment of the utility of a product or service based on perceptions of what is received and what is given [2]. CPV is the result of the customer's evaluation of all the benefits and all the costs of an offering as compared to that customer's perceived alternatives, which is the basis on which customers make decision to buy things [9]. According to their analogy every user has balance scale in mind, then weigh the benefit in one side and cost or sacrifice in the other side when he or she makes decision whether to buy or not.

Although quality and price have different and differential effects on perceived value for money, many other studies pointed out that viewing value as a trade-off between only quality and price is too simplistic and existing value constructs can be too narrow and that dimensions other than price and quality would increase the usefulness [3,8,10]. A more sophisticated measure is needed to understand how consumers value products and services and to apply it in developing and evaluating new product or service concept. Efforts on developing value measurement scale have been carried out based on utilitarian and hedonic value components [11,12]. Consumer choice is regarded as a function of multiple consumption value dimensions and these dimensions including social, emotional, functional, epistemic, and conditional value make varying contributions in different choice situations [13].

There are four characteristics of CPV. Firstly, customer value is market-perceived and customer's perception of value is most important. Secondly, customer value is complicated. Complex nature of CPV including identification of components of benefit and cost attribute, relative weight, value evaluation process, and aggregated value makes customer research more important. Thirdly, customer value is relative. It should be evaluated as compared to alternatives which also include do-nothing option as well as competitive offerings. Finally, customer value is dynamic. Customer perceptions of value keep changing and evolving due to the changes of circumstances [9]. During the new product development (NPD) process, CPV can help in identifying customer wants and needs early in the ideation or fuzzy front end, identifying factors or attributes that influence customer's judgment of a product value, determining the relative importance of value-related attributes, and determining how offerings are viewed on each of these attributes relative to the customer's alternative.

Although there are several variations considering sub-attributes and accompanying factors other than customer value, in general measurement of CPV can be classified into ratio model and additive model. In ratio model, attributes of benefit and sacrifice are compared relatively. It is intuitive and useful in visualizing the implications where CPV is represented as a slope in benefit-sacrifice space. As the slope of customer value is steeper, the service is considered as more acceptable and more satisfactory for customers. In comparison with competitive services also can be possible in the same space of benefit and sacrifice dimension. In additive model, benefit and sacrifice are considered as existing along to the same dimension [10]. Since in many cases benefit and sacrifice are interconnected, separate evaluation cannot be possible. Therefore weighted summation of CPV for each value dimension is the criteria for the evaluation. In either case, relative importance and relative performance of value attributes or value dimensions should be calculated by direct or indirect customer judgment. Surveys, choice modeling, or market experiments are used in determining relative importance and relative performance. Questionnaire, interview and conjoint analysis are frequently used in measurement of perceived value and analytic hierarchical process can be a potential alternative for determination of relative importance.

In summary, the concept of CPV is expected to be a potential answer for the current problems of mobile internet which has high penetration but low usage, low utility and high cost, limited and biased use of mobile internet services. By using the CPV, perceived quality of mobile service can be managed effectively. In combination with the principles of user centered design, CPV can be effectively applied in the stages of new mobile service design such as concept generation, concept evaluation, market survey, market performance estimation and launching plan.

3   Applying CPV in Mobile Service Design

3.1   Concept Generation

From the literature survey on customer value components, basic value components are selected in hierarchical structure including hedonic and utilitarian dichotomy [14], functional, emotional, social, and epistemic value components in PERVAL [8,13], and conditional or contextual value [10,13] as shown in table 1. From the successful mobile services in terms of high user acceptance in market which are supposed to deliver relatively high customer value, potential value components and sub-entities are derived by expert group discussion which is composed of five mobile service staffs in Korean mobile operator and three mobile service consultants. In order to reflect the market perception, results of internal and external market surveys are reviewed before and during the discussion. After mapping between generic set of value components and existing successful mobile services, potential mobile value components are grouped together and coupled with their representative example respectively for efficient association during idea generation. Seventeen potential mobile values are selected and their descriptions and examples are summarized in table 1. These potential mobile values can be used as ideation stimuli in the process of structured brainstorming techniques such as Osborn's checklist, Small's checklist and TRIZ [15].

For the perspectives on the relationship between potential mobile values and mobile characteristics, mobile characteristics are also considered based on the definition of mobility[16], which are subscription-based user characteristics, mobile phone oriented device characteristics, communication characteristics focused on phone calling as a main function of mobile phone, and personal characteristics. For example, mobile device has its own feature of battery, LCD display, key pads, memory storage, processing unit, and physical dimension of size. These can be thought as device characteristics of mobile service.

Table 1. Potential value components in mobile contexts

Potential value in mobile service		Descriptions in mobile context	Mobile service example
Cost	Economic	cost-saving	Membership discount
Quality	Available	urgent use, anytime, anywhere	Camera phone
	Effective	goal achievement, multi-purposed	CNID
	Efficient	time reduction, minimal efforts	SMS P2P
	Convenient	ease of use	SMS W2P
Social	Superior	superior to others	New phone
	Different	different from others, unique	Ring-tone
	Homogeneous	empathy, sympathy	Screensaver
	Isolated	private, with no interaction with others	Adults contents
	Etiquette	considering others	Ring-back-tone
Emotional	Fun	fun, exciting	Mobile Game
	Relief	peaceful, trustworthy, reliable	Kids phone
	Preferable	preference, taste, esthetic,	Ring-tone, Screensaver
Epistemic	Educational	knowledge, useful	Mobile news
	Curious	newness, curiosity	Mosquito repellant
Contextual	Magnifying	situation increasing value	CNID for salesperson
	Minifying	undesirable situation decreasing value	Stalking block

Characteristics of mobility and potential mobile values are compared and relationship analysis was carried out so as to find potential value drivers that enhance potential customer value from the characteristics of mobility. For example, by comparison between subscription-based user characteristics of mobile service and cost saving economic value, integrated billing capability was identified as a mobile value driver. Micro-payment services can be another typical service example incorporated with value driver of billing capability. Mobile operators already have their customers' billing address and account so that it makes possible for users to buy goods or services using micro-payment service with saved cost relative to credit card in terms of interest or commission. When it comes to device characteristics exemplified above, availability with no preparation can be a potential mobile driver to almost functional value. Features of mobile phone such as battery, display, key pad can be a source of new service opportunities that deliver functional value on availability such as portable power supply, portable display unit, and portable input device, respectively. Potential mobile value drivers derived from the characteristics of mobility used with potential mobile values during scenario-based ideation will be helpful to draw numerous promising new mobile service ideas by providing more perspectives on internal relationship among mobile characteristics, mobile potential values, and value drivers.

3.2 Concept Evaluation

Concept evaluation of mobile service design involves CPV and usability. For the application of CPV in concept evaluation, CPV measurement methods are investigated and proposed for mobile service development. During concept generation stage, lots of ideas are generated through new opportunity clues, target domain, related stakeholders, target users, related contextual attributes and most frequent and important scenario. Service ideas are clustered and ready for evaluation. Considering the relative nature of CPV, even for non-existing innovative service concepts, alternatives are selected for comparison in terms of perceived value. CPV measurement methods are classified into additive method and ratio method. During the conceptual evaluation, two ways of application of CPV are recommended. In the case that comparable competing service can be found, the sub entities of benefit and cost or sacrifice factors for each service should be broken down and the part worth or relative importance are calculated by use of conjoint analysis or analytic hierarchical process. In case that ratio method can be applicable, new service ideas are compared with competing services in terms of ratio of benefit over cost. When it is difficult to find comparable competing services, additive method can be useful. Value components are investigated and by summation of them magnitude of CPV can be evaluated whether it is positive or negative. In this context, CPV is considered as a representative measure of user acceptance. Market attractiveness can be evaluated by market volume in terms of potential customers and scenario frequency, which means that service ideas which are relevant in frequent situation and many potential users are considered as promising concept. By combining a series of considerations such as CPV, market volume, and scenario frequency, most promising concepts are selected and proceed forward to the next step of formal NPD.

Considering the compatibility with international standards on UCD, measures of usability defined in ISO 9241-11, which are effectiveness, efficiency, and satisfaction can be taken into consideration during the CPV evaluation since most benefit components involve effectiveness, efficiency, and satisfaction attributes. Effectiveness can be defined as the accuracy and completeness with which customers achieve specified goals. Efficiency is the accuracy and completeness of goals

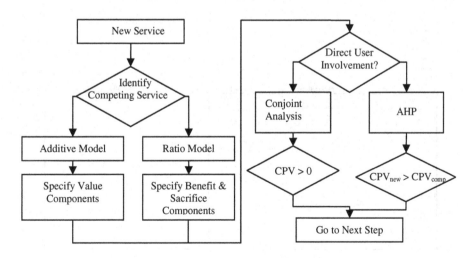

Fig. 1. Concept evaluation process using the concept of CPV

achieved in relation to resources. Satisfaction is the freedom from discomfort, and positive attitude towards the use of mobile service. Attributes of key performance indicators can be expressed in adjective such as useful, usable, unique, fun, efficient, attractive, simple, quick to learn etc. These attributes can be quantified by measurement of CPV. There are two main reasons for usability evaluation. One is to improve the service as part of development process by identifying and fixing usability problems (formative evaluation). The other is to find out whether people can use the service successfully (summative evaluation). In the front-end UCD, formative concept evaluations are focused, and precise summative evaluation would be implemented in later stage of formal NPD process as shown in figure 1.

4 Implementation

For the efficient implementation of CPV concept during front-end mobile service design, work templates are developed in co-operation with mobile service staffs in Korean mobile operator as shown in fig. 2 and 3. Template approaches are accepted as an efficient tool for process implementation and data management in new product or service process [17,18]. Templates include guidelines, checklists, work direction, and process data filled in by new service personnel. The proposed process was separated into separable activities and initial version of templates was provided. Pilot workshop was performed by five mobile service staffs. By forced relationship analysis with potential customer values in mobile context, new service ideas were generated. In convergent thinking during concept evaluation, customer perceived value is suggested as a critical criterion for the acceptance of end-user. Potential values in new service opportunity and competing service alternatives are identified and rated in terms of relative importance or part-worth by using analytic hierarchical process. Half day of pilot workshop was assigned to discussion on the problems of work templates. Based

Scenario Components		Scenario Description	by _____
Persona			
Others			
Artifacts			
Goal			
Activities			
Environment			

Customer Value		Description	Example	Related Idea
Economic		cost-saving	Membership discount	
Functional	Available	urgent use, any time, any where	Camera phone	
	Efficient	time reduction, minimal effort	SMS P2P	
	Effective	goal achievement, multi-purpose	CNID, manner call	
	Convenient	ease of use	SMS W2P	
Social	Superior	superior to others	New phone	
	Different	different from others, unique	Ring-tone	
	Homogeneous	empathy, sympathy	Screensaver	
	Isolated	private, with no interaction	Adults contents	
	Etiquette	considering others	Ring-back-tone	
Emotional	Fun	fun, exciting	Mobile Game	
	Relief	peaceful, trustworthy, reliable	Kids phone	
	Satisfaction	preference, taste, esthetic	Ring tone, Screensaver	
Epistemic	Educational	knowledge, useful	Mobile news	
	Curious	newness, curiosity	Mosquito repellent	
Contextual	Positive	situation increasing value	CNID for salesperson	
	Negative	undesirable situation, situation decreasing value	Stalking Block	

Fig. 2. Work template for scenario-based ideation with potential customer value

on the time measurement and discussion, total time required for the whole process is less than three hours. Considering individual differences and allowance time for break, it took about four hours which is equivalent to half day of working time to explore new service opportunity. During the discussion among participants in implementation workshop, concept of CPV, and the proposed work templates were referred to accelerate the iteration between divergent and convergent thinking.

Potential Value in ( )	Relative Importance (%)	Part-worth in NSO ( )	Part-worth in Competing Service ( )
	100 %	(A)	(B)

Monetary Cost

NSO (C)	Competing SVC (D)

CPV

NSO (E)	Competing SVC (F)
(A) / (C) =	(B) / (D) =

Relative Competitiveness

Competitiveness of NSO
(E) / (F) =

Fig. 3. Work template for concept evaluation with competing service

5 Conclusion

Pros and cons of mobile internet can be strategically applied to design useful and usable mobile services that offer a high enough value to users to overcome the usability and performance constraints by using the concept of CPV. During the implementation workshop, applicability of CPV in conceptual design stage in either way of divergent and convergent has been considered in mobile service design. Integrated conceptual design process from opportunity identification to concept evaluation incorporating scenario-based ideation and CPV-based concept evaluation were proposed and implemented in field so as to accelerate the iteration between divergent and convergent thinking. It is expected that the proposed framework can be used in managing mobile service development, identifying new mobile service opportunities, creating new service items, developing service scenarios, and evaluating user acceptance. CPV measurement research focused on direct and indirect user involvement can be the first suggestion for future research. Various CPV measurement methods by addition and ratio have been suggested by many researchers in various research area including marketing, service quality, cognitive science and so on. However, a majority of previous studies are focused on the constructs among CPV and related attributes such as loyalty, satisfaction and customer attitude are perceived value. Therefore, further research on direct or indirect CPV measurement is still required.

Acknowledgments. This work was supported in part by the Research Institute of Engineering Science at Seoul National University.

References

1. Parasuraman, A., Zeithaml, V.A., Berry, L.L.: A conceptual model of service quality and its implications for future research. J. of Marketing 49, 41–50 (1985)
2. Zeithaml, V.A.: Consumer perceptions of price, quality, and value: A means–end model and synthesis of evidence. J. of Marketing 52, 2–22 (1988)
3. Bolton, R.N., Drew, J.H.: A multistage model of consumers' assessments of service quality and value. J. of Consumer Research 17, 375–384 (1991)
4. Ulaga, W., Chacour, S.: Measuring Customer-Perceived Value in Business Markets. Industrial Marketing Management 30, 525–540 (2001)
5. Day, G.S., Fahey, L.: Valuing market strategies. J. of Marketing 52, 45–57 (1998)
6. Woodruff, R.B.: Customer value: The next source for competitive advantage. J. of the Academy of Marketing Science 25, 139–153 (1997)
7. Cravens, D.W., Holland, C.W., Lamb, C.W., Moncrieff, W.C.: Marketing's role in product and service quality. Industrial Marketing Management 17, 285–304 (1988)
8. Sweeney, J.C., Soutar, G.N.: Consumer perceived value: The development of a multiple item scale. J. of Retailing 77, 203–220 (2001)
9. Miller, C., Swaddling, D.C.: Focusing NPD research on customer perceived value. In: Belliveau, P., Griffin, A., Somermeyer, S.M. (eds.) PDMA toolbook for new product development, pp. 87–114. John Wiley & Sons, New York (2002)
10. Heinonen, K.: Reconceptualizing customer perceived value: the value of time and place. Managing Service Quality 14(3), 205–215 (2004)
11. Babin, B.J., Darden, W., Griffin, M.: Work and/or fun: measuring hedonic and utilitarian shoing value. J. of Consumer Research 20, 644–656 (1994)
12. Richins, M.: Valuing things: The public and private meanings of possessions. J. of Consumer Research 21, 504–521 (1994)
13. Sheth, J.N., Newman, B.I., Gross, B.L.: Why we buy what we buy: A theory of consumption values. J. of Business Research 22, 159–170 (1991)
14. Batra, R., Ahtola, O.T.: Measuring the hedonic and utilitarian sources of consumer attitude, Marketing Letters 2, 159–170 (1990)
15. Crawford, M., Benedetto, A.: New products management, Boston. McGraw-Hill, New York (2003)
16. Dix, A., Rodden, T., Davies, N., Trevor, J., Friday, A., Palfreyman, K.: Exploiting space and location as a design framework for interactive mobile. ACM Transactions on computer human interaction 7(3), 285–321 (2000)
17. Miller, C.W.: Hunting for hunting grounds: forecasting the fuzzy front end. In: Belliveau, P., Griffin, A., Somermeyer, S.M. (eds.) PDMA toolbook for new product development, pp. 37–62. John Wiley & Sons, New York (2002)
18. Travis, D.: E-commerce usability: tools and techniques to perfect the on-line experience. Talor and Francis. London (2003)

Design Guidelines to the Application of Extreme Design with Korean Anthropometry

Yongju Cho[1], Eui S. Jung[1,*], Sungjoon Park[2], Seong W. Jeong[1], and Woojin Park[3]

[1] Industrial Systems and Information Engineering, Korea University,
Anam, Seongbuk, Seoul, 136-701, Korea
[2] Industrial and Information System Engineering, Namseoul University,
21 Maeju-ri, Seonghwan-eup, Chonan, 330-707, Korea
[3] Department of Mechanical, Industrial, and Nuclear Engineering, University of Cincinnati,
University and Campus Drive-626 Rhodes Hall, Cincinnati, OH 45221-0072, USA
ejung@koea.ac.kr

Abstract. In this paper, we suggest guidelines related to the design limit or range by body dimensions based on 'SizeKorea 2004'. This paper describes three sequential tests. First, body dimensions' percentile curves were analyzed in order to find out their trends. Second, their appropriateness with respect to normality assumptions by gender and age was tested. Finally, the steepest slopes at both extremes of female and male percentile curves were checked and analyzed. By performing these sequential tests, five patterns of body dimensions were found. Findings from this research were two-fold. First of all, adult percentile curves, by and large, did not follow a normal distribution. The other finding was that the design limit for 33% of the male body dimensions must be from 5th to 97.5th percentiles and the limit for 85% of the female body dimensions must be from 2.5th to 97.5th percentiles, which shows their steepest slope at the extremes of the percentile curves. From this study, eight specific design guidelines for extreme design by patterns of body dimensions were found.

Keywords: Korean anthropometry, Extreme design, Percentile curves.

1 Introduction

Anthropometric data are widely used to accommodate mismatch between humans and their working environments. The three anthropometric design rules, design for the average, design for a specific population percentile, and design for extremes, are frequently used to design products and workspaces [1]. In particular, the design for extremes uses 5th and 95th percentiles which are normally the steepest slopes under the normality assumption that human body dimensions follow a normal distribution. It is for overcoming the limitation of space or cost as the second best design limits [2, 3, 4, 5]. However, it has continuously been criticized by the fact that it may be improper to apply a normal percentile value because of a gap between the normal percentile value and measured value. It is also shown to be influenced by body dimension [6, 7].

---

* Corresponding author.

N. Aykin (Ed.): Usability and Internationalization, Part II, HCII 2007, LNCS 4560, pp. 30–39, 2007.
© Springer-Verlag Berlin Heidelberg 2007

Moreover, anthropometric data show specific characteristics depending on race, gender, age and physical measurements of the human body [8, 9, 10, 11]. Therefore, Korean products and their workspaces should be designed with proper recognition of the Korean body dimension.

From this point of view, many Korean industries and researchers have faced ambiguity in applying a design guideline for Koreans. In order to overcome these problems, it is critical to answer these following three questions. Is it proper to apply body dimensions based on normal percentile values under the normality assumption? To what degree do gender, ages and body dimensions influence the design range? Is it appropriate to select 5th and 95th percentiles as a design limit although each body dimension has its own steepest slope at the extremes?

Research in this area in Korea has primarily focused on a practical use of basic data for applying Korean body dimension to products, a proposal for an optimal sizing system, and body type grouping based on factor analysis and cluster analysis [12, 13]. However, not much research has been made in finding proper design ranges regarding the body dimension for Koreans.

Therefore, in order to design products and workspaces for Koreans, it is necessary to suggest a modified design range as a type of design guidelines based on the results of "SizeKorea 2004" led by the Korean Agency for Technology and Standard. The goal of our present work, described in the paper, is to suggest guidelines related to the design range based on studying the body dimensions of 4,926 adults whose age ranged between 19 and 59, specifically for 27 selected body dimensions among 126 body dimensions based on SizeKorea [14].

2 Methods

2.1 Subjects

SizeKorea affiliated with the Korean government surveyed about 20,000 Koreans from 0 to 90 years of age for their body dimensions and shapes from 2003 to 2004. The male and female adults' body dimensions from 19 to 59 years of age in this study were gathered from 4,926 people. The details are shown in Table 1. Here, 20s' category includes 19 year-old people's data because no statistical difference was found between 19 and 20's and ordinary people usually start their job from 19 years old and older [15]. In the work of SizeKorea, the category of 20 years old, for example, includes people from 19.5 to 20.4 years old.

Table 1. Numbers of subjects depending on their age groups

Age	20s (19~29)	30s (30~39)	40s (40~49)	50s (50~59)
Male	958	712	408	736
Female	942	736	413	374

2.2 Selection of Body Dimensions

In order to choose necessary body dimensions for this study, 27 body dimensions were selected among 126 body dimensions based on SizeKorea. They were recommended more than three times by experts in industries (furniture, automobile, shoes, clothing, and human modeling) and researchers. The 27 body dimensions were height (9), breadth (7), depth (3), length (5) and circumference (3) variables.

2.3 Analysis

The selected 27 body dimensions were analyzed in three phases. First, the body dimension percentile curves were analyzed by correlation analysis in order to classify patterns and to figure out their trend. It was to provide foundations for the guideline by patterns and was analyzed by gender and age groups.

Second, the appropriateness to the normality assumptions of body dimensions by gender and ages was tested through results from Kolmogrov–Smirnov test, Skewness and Kurtosis. The application of a normal percentile value was analyzed based on the investigation on the gap between the normal percentile value and measured value.

Third, the steepest slopes at the extremes of the female and male percentile curves were analyzed in order to find a range for the most suitable design limits by body dimensions. The range was also analyzed by comparison between the percentile values of steepest slopes at the extremes and the 5th and 95th percentile values generally used.

Finally, design guidelines were suggested by patterns based on these results. For the first and second phases of analysis, SPSS 12.0.1 is used.

3 Results

3.1 Patterns of Percentile Curves of Body Dimensions

Five patterns of body dimensions resulted from the analysis of the percentile curves.

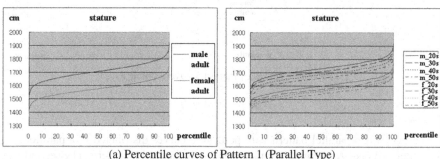

(a) Percentile curves of Pattern 1 (Parallel Type)

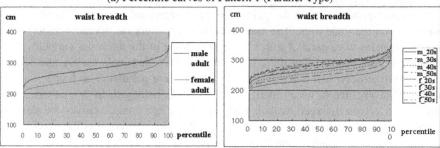

(b) Percentile curves of Pattern 2 (Convergent Type)

Fig. 1. Five patterns classified by types of adults and ages percentile curves

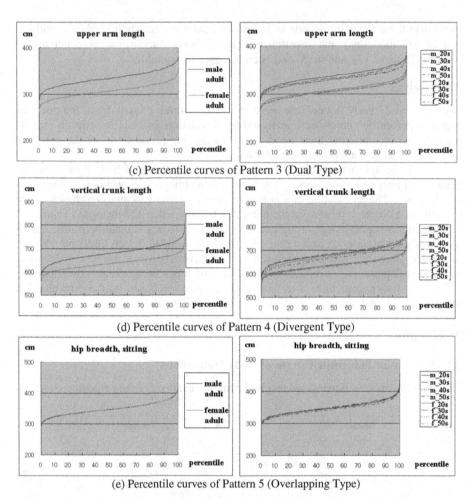

(c) Percentile curves of Pattern 3 (Dual Type)

(d) Percentile curves of Pattern 4 (Divergent Type)

(e) Percentile curves of Pattern 5 (Overlapping Type)

Fig. 1. (*continued*)

The first was a parallel pattern with percentile curves distributed in a parallel way by gender and age. All height variables were included in this pattern. The second was a convergent pattern that as the percentile value increased the female adult curves converged on the male ones. The male curves by age were distributed densely while those of females were parallel with a wider gap. Most of the thickness variables were included in this pattern. The third was a dual pattern that male curves and female curves were closely distributed while two curves were parallel. The fourth was the pattern of divergence to which many width variables belonged. In this pattern, male and female curves diverged at their ends and each age group's curves are densely distributed similar to those of the third pattern. The final pattern was the overlapping pattern. All curves for adults and ages in this pattern were overlapping. There were no discrepancies between male, female and age groups. Therefore they formed a massive group of curves. Hip variables belonged to this pattern. These five patterns of the selected 27 body dimensions are shown in Table 2.

In order to prove the validity of this classification by adult and ages percentile curves, a correlation analysis was performed as shown in Table 3. It showed that the correlations of body dimensions in the same pattern for both male and female were high which indicated the relevance of the classification of patterns.

Table 2. Five patterns classified by the types of percentile curves

Pattern (naming)	Body dimension	Number
Pattern 1 (parallel type)	stature, acromion height, waist height, hip height, knee height, sitting height, eye height, cervical height, crotch height	9
Pattern 2 (convergent type)	waist breadth, chest depth, chest circumference, hip depth, hand thickness	5
Pattern 3 (dual type)	upperarm length, palm length perpendicular, hand length, hand breadth, foot length, foot breadth(horizontal)	6
Pattern 4 (divergent type)	vertical trunk length, weight, biacromial breadth, chest breadth	4
Pattern 5 (overlapping type)	hip breadth(standing), hip breadth(sitting), hip circumference	3

Table 3. The results of correlation analysis of female adults' body dimensions

Pattern	Representative dimension	Results of correlation analysis (Coefficients of correlation above 0.7 are selected)
1	stature	acromion height(0.96), waist ht.(0.91), hip ht.(0.84), knee ht. (0.74), eye height(0.98), cervical height(0.98), crotch height(0.86)
2	waist breadth	chest depth(0.72), chest circumference(0.85), hip depth(0.74), chest breadth(0.70), weight(0.79)
3	hand length	palm length perpendicular(0.84)
4	chest breadth	weight(0.70), waist breadth(0.70), chest circumference(0.75)
5	hip breadth(std)	hip breadth(sitting)(0.79), hip circumference (0.80), weight(0.70)

* The underlined body dimensions represent the same pattern.

3.2 Test of the Normality Assumptions

Whether the body dimensions follow a normal distribution or not, was tested by the Kolmogrov-Smirnov test. According to the Kolmogrov-Smirnov test, when $\alpha \geq 0.05$, a body dimension is regarded as a normal distribution. The variable that satisfied this condition was tested afterwards with skewness and kurtosis.

There was no normally distributed curve in adults including both male and female. 7 dimensions including the vertical trunk length in the male and 3 dimensions in the female followed a normal distribution. They were usually height variables which belonged to Pattern 1. Other patterns, except for the vertical trunk length of Pattern 4, did not follow a normal distribution in adult.

Table 4. Body dimensions following a normal distribution

		Male	Female
Adult	adult (all)	none	
	adult	stature, acromion height, waist height, sitting height, eye height, cervical height, vertical trunk length	acromion height, waist height, eye height, crotch height
Age groups	over 2 age groups	stature, acromion height, hip height, waist height, knee height, sitting height, eye height, cervical height, crotch height, chest circumference, vertical trunk length, biacromial breadth, chest breadth, hip circumference	stature, acromion height, hip height, waist height, knee height, sitting height, eye height, crotch height, vertical trunk
	2 age groups	upperarm length, weight, hip breadth(standing)	cervical height, chest circumference, hip breadth (standing)
	under 2 age groups	waist breadth, chest depth, hip depth, hand thickness, hand length, palm length perpendicular, hand breadth, foot breadth (horizontal), foot length, hip breadth(sitting)	waist breadth, chest depth, hip depth, hand thickness, upperarm length, hand length, palm length perpendicular, hand breadth, foot breadth (horizontal), foot length, weight, biacromial breadth, chest breadth, hip breadth(sitting), hip circumference

More males followed a normal distribution than female by age groups. Body dimensions following a normal distribution in more than two age groups, were 14 in the male group (51%) and 9 in the female group (33%). They were mainly height variables in Pattern 1. Body dimensions following under two age groups were 10 in the male (37%) and 15 in the female (56%). This case belonged to Patterns 2 and 3 in the male and Patterns 2, 3, 4 and 5 in the female.

These analyses proved that many body dimensions did not follow a normal distribution by adult and age groups in spite of enough data sourcing from 374 to 958 people by age.

3.3 The Steepest Slopes of the Percentile Curves as Design Limits

In the adult body dimensions' percentile curves, the results of the analysis on the beginning and ending point of the steepest slopes are shown in Table 5.

In order to design for the extreme, the range for design generally used is the 5th and 95th percentiles regardless of body dimensions. The steepest slopes for the body dimensions in this research can be summarized in that the usual design limits which have a 90% range for design are not always suitable for all cases. For example, 9 male (33%) and 23 female body dimensions (85%) are the case in point. Although differences between male and female adults exist, usually Patterns 2 and 5 cover 90%, Patterns 3 and 4, 95%, and Pattern 1, male and female, 90% and 92.5%, for their design range.

Table 5. The results of analysis on the steepest slope of percentile curves

Body dimension	Pattern	The point of steepest slopes				FPC MB	MPC FE	Design range	
		male		female					
		begin	end	begin	end			male	female
Stature	1	5	95	2.5	97.5	69	36	90	95
Acromion height	1	5	95	5	97.5	69	40	90	92.5
Hip height	1	5	95	5	97.5	57	53	90	92.5
Waist height	1	5	95	5	97.5	50	58	90	92.5
Knee height	1	5	95	5	97.5	46	64	90	92.5
Sitting height	1	5	95	2.5	97.5	61	40	90	95
Eye height	1	5	95	5	97.5	70	42	90	92.5
Cervical height	1	5	95	5	97.5	70	41	90	92.5
Crotch height	1	5	95	5	97.5	52	50	90	92.5
Waist breadth	2	5	95	5	95	43	76	90	90
Chest depth	2	5	95	5	95	39	75	90	90
Chest circumference	2	5	95	2.5	97.5	57	54	90	95
Hip depth	2	5	95	5	95	33	70	90	90
Hand thickness	2	5	97.5	5	95	24	84	92.5	90
Upperarm length	3	5	95	2.5	97.5	56	49	90	95
Hand length	3	2.5	97.5	2.5	97.5	27	72	95	95
Palm length perpend.	3	2.5	97.5	2.5	97.5	20	82	95	95
Hand breadth	3	5	95	2.5	97.5	46	57	90	95
Foot breadth (hor.)	3	5	97.5	2.5	97.5	40	75	92.5	95
Foot length	3	2.5	97.5	2.5	97.5	40	53	95	95
Vertical trunk length	4	5	97.5	2.5	97.5	34	59	92.5	95
Weight	4	2.5	97.5	5	97.5	36	62	95	92.5
Biacromial breadth	4	5	97.5	2.5	97.5	44	42	92.5	95
Chest breadth	4	5	97.5	2.5	97.5	51	62	92.5	95
Hip breadth(sit)	5	5	95	5	95	5	95	90	90
Hip breadth (std)	5	5	95	5	95	8	92	90	90
Hip circumference	5	5	95	5	95	10	89	90	90

Female percentile values can be found to be a corresponding point that the male adults' steepest slope begins in the percentile curves (Female Percentile Corresponding Male's Beginning: FPCMB). Likewise, male percentile can be found as a corresponding female adults' ending points of the steepest slope (Male Percentile Corresponding Female's Ending: MPCFE) by body dimensions in Table 5. For example, the FPCMB of 69 means when a male's beginning point of the steepest slope is 5th percentile, a 5th percentile male is in accord with a 69th percentile female of 69 percentile for that specific body dimension. If the design limit for a male is selected as 5th percentile, 69 percent of female is not included in the design and MPCFE has an opposite meaning.

In the results of the counter percentile, as the value of the FPCMB is higher or the value of the MBCFE is lower, the gap between genders becomes greater. On this occasion, if design limit is determined by gender, many users of counter gender are out of range for the design. In the opposite case, the gap between genders has few differences. In the case of Pattern 5, although design limit is determined, there are few users of the counter gender beyond the design range because the value of the FPCMB is under 10 and MBCFE is over 90. It reconfirms the results of the classification percentile pattern analysis.

4 Discussion and Conclusion

The results of three analyses on 27 selected body dimensions are shown in Table 6. To summarize, the characteristics of the design range by patterns, Pattern 1 varies as ages in a parallel way from male 20s to female 50s. In the case that users are in a specific age group, it is prudent to use an adult or other age groups' data because male and female adults' data has a widely dispersed. Patterns 3 and 4 are densely distributed by ages, which mean that only gender has to be regarded without too much concern of age groups. In Pattern 5, both gender and age groups need not to be concerned because the percentile curves are all overlapping.

Table 6. The results of three analyses on body dimensions by percentile curves

Pattern	Characteristic of percentile curve		Varia-ble	Nor-mality	The point of steepest slopes		Counter point (average)		Design range	
	adult	ages			male	fe-male	male	fe-male	male	fe-male
1	parallel	parallel	height	N or non-N	5/95	2.5 or 5 /97.5	46~70 (60.4)	36~64 (47.1)	90	92.5 /95
2	con-vergent	massive in M, paral-lel in F	depth	non-N	5/95 or 97.5	2.5 or 5 /95 or 97.5	24~57 (39.2)	54~84 (71.8)	90 /92.5	90 /95
3	dual	massive in M and F	foot /hand	non-N	2.5 or 5 /95 or 97.5	2.5 /97.5	20~56 (38.2)	49~82 (64.7)	90 /92.5/95	95
4	diver-gent	massive in M and F	breadth	N or non-N	2.5 or 5 /97.5	2.5 or 5 /97.5	34~51 (41.3)	42~62 (56.3)	92.5 /95	92.5 /95
5	over-lapping	overlap-ping	hip	non-N	5/95	5/95	5~10 (7.7)	89~95 (92)	90	90

The results of Table 4 show that most of body dimensions except for the height variables do not follow a normal distribution not only for adults but also by age groups. There is a discrepancy between normal percentile values and measured values for body dimensions so caution is required when applying a normal percentile value [7]. In the female case, the discrepancy is illustrated in Table 7. To express the discrepancy of body dimensions, 'error in %' was used to normalize the difference. In the case of female adults, the discrepancy of Pattern 1 in which many dimensions follow a normal distribution was lower than 0.24% in average. Patterns 3 and 5, which do not follow a normal distribution, also have a low error in %. Although these patterns follow a non-normal distribution, their discrepancy between the normal percentile values and the measured values are small enough to neglect. Therefore, the application of normal percentile values of these patterns does not create any significant problem. In Patterns 2 and 4, which do not follow a normal distribution, the

Table 7. The discrepancy between the normal percentile value and the measured value for female adults (average error in %)

Percentile	Patten 1	Pattern 2	Pattern3	Pattern 4	Pattern 5
2.5	-0.24	-2.88	-0.83	-4.81	-0.93
5	-0.24	-2.03	-0.68	-3.94	-0.66
95	-0.10	-1.59	-0.45	-2.55	-0.42
97.5	-0.18	-1.88	-0.66	-2.94	-0.57

discrepancy becomes higher. For example, chest breadth shows 28.4% error at 5th percentile in the preceding research [7].

The result means whether or not a normal distribution makes the discrepancy of normal percentile values, but the discrepancy of some body dimensions becomes small although those do not follow a normal distribution. Therefore, the choice of design limit should be made based not only on which each body dimension follows a normal distribution, but also the pattern of body dimension.

Needless to say, reflection of user characteristics on the design becomes more important for industries and researchers in order to design sound products and workspaces. When considering Korean anthropometry, their gender, ages and body dimensions should be more specifically concerned. Through the results, the suitable design guidelines are founded by the patterns of body dimensions.

Table 8. Design guidelines to the design range according to body dimensions

Issue	Design guidelines	Body dimension
Use of normal percentile value	Height variables and hand/foot/hip variables are possible to use a normal percentile value	Patterns 1,3,5
	Breadth/depth/circumference variables must use a measured value	Patterns 2,4
Male or female	Gender must be separately applied	Patterns1,2,3,4
	Gender is not separately applied because of overlapping	Pattern 5
Ages group	Age groups are separately applied because of a difference of ages by gender	Patterns 1, 2 of female adult
	Age groups is not separately applied because of overlapping	Patterns 3,4,5
Range for design	The suitable design range is 95% coverage at 2.5 and 97.5 percentile	Except Pattern 1 of female adult
	The suitable design range is 92.5% coverage at 5 and 97.5 percentile	Pattern 1 of female adult

This guideline shows the design range for Koreans based on the analysis of male and female adults' percentile curves, a check of normal distribution by age groups, and the steepest slope point of curves.

Male and female adults' body dimensions are mainly analyzed in this study. If the age of target population is 20's, more detailed research is in need. In order to concretize the guideline for body dimensions, it is necessary to have an analysis of total body dimensions surveyed by SizeKorea and dimensions' trend by age groups.

The research provides industries and researchers with useful information by suggesting the guideline related to the design range focusing on Koreans.

References

1. Roebuck, J.A., Kroemer, K.H.E., Thomson, W.G.: Engineering Anthropometry Methods, p. 154. Wiley, New York (1975)
2. International Space Station Flight Crew.: Integration Standard NASA STD 3000T. SSP 50005 Rev. B. Aug. Johnson Space Center, Houston, TX. SSP (Space Station Program 1996)
3. Department of Defense.: Human engineering design criteria for military systems, equipment and facilities (MIL-STD-1472D). Philadelphia, PA: Navy Publishing and Printing Office (1989)
4. DOT/FAA/CT03/05.: Human Factors Design Standard (HFDS), U.S. Department of Transportation Federal Aviation Administration Technical Center Atlantic City International Airport, NJ 08405 (2003)
5. Peacock, B., Karwowski, W.: Automotive Ergonomics, Taylor and Francis London, Washington, DC (1993)
6. Panero, J., Zelnik, M.: Human dimension & interior space, Great Britain by the architectural press Ltd. (1979)
7. Vasu, M., Mital, A.: Evaluation of the validity of anthropometric design assumptions. Int. J. Industrial Ergonomics 26, 19–37 (2000)
8. Annis, J.F.: Aging effects on anthropometric dimensions important to workplace design. Int. J. Industrial Ergonomics 18, 381–388 (1996)
9. Tamburrino, N.: Apparel Sizing Issues, Part 2, Bobbin (1992)
10. Mokdad, M.: Anthropometric study of Algerian farmers. Int. J. Industrial Ergonomics 29, 331–341 (2002)
11. Barroso, M.P., Arezes, P.M., da Costa, L.G., Miguel, A.S.: Anthropometric study of portuguese workers. Int. J. Industrial Ergonomics 35, 401–410 (2005)
12. Kim, H.S.: Sizing System of Women's Ready-to-Wear. In: Journal of the Korean Society of Clothing Industry, 6(5), (2004)
13. Seong, D.H., Jung, E.S., Cho, Y.J.: A Methodology for Developing a Korean Apparel Sizing System by Body Types. Journal of the Ergonomics Society of Korea 24(4), 31–37 (2005)
14. Korean Agency for Technology and Standards, Ministry of Commerce, Industry and Energy.: Technical Standard Write Paper (2004)
15. Kang, Y.S., Seong, H.K., Choi, H.S., Yi, K.H.: Analysis of Men's Body Sizes for Garment Sizing System(Part I). Journal of the Korean Society of Clothing and Textiles 30(8), 1199–1209 (2006)

Developing Character Input Methods for Driver Information Systems

Youngseok Cho[1], Sung H. Han[1], Sang W. Hong[2], Yong S. Park[1], Wonkyu Park[1], and Sunghyun Kang[3]

[1] Dept. of Industrial and Management Eng., POSTECH, Pohang, Korea
[2] Technology Innovation Team 2, Technology Innovation Center, SK Telecom, South Korea
[3] Multimedia System Design Team, Hyundai-Kia R&D Centers, Hwasung, Korea
shan@postech.edu

Abstract. This study proposes a framework for developing an input method to enter characters into a driver information system (DIS). The framework consists of two phases. The first phase is a conceptual design phase that helps to create and design conceptual input methods and to conduct formative evaluation. The second phase is a detail design phase that helps to design detailed interfaces and interaction, and to select the most usable character input method. A case study is conducted to verify the effectiveness of the developed methodology and to find appropriate input methods for knob control. As a result, character input methods appropriate for knob control were developed, which were proved to work more effectively than an existing method.

Keywords: Character input method, DIS, Development framework, Usability.

1 Introduction

Cars have changed from pure transportation devices to mobile living space. As a result of the convergence of consumer electronic devices with a car, driver information systems (DISs) in cars provide services such as not only air condition control, but navigation assistance, wireless internet service, entertainment, office work, and so on. Drivers often need to input characters (i.e., alphabet, Korean characters, numerals, symbols, etc.) for using input services [1] [2]. Unlike other consumer electronic products, usability considering safety is one of the most important issues to design character input methods or devices for a DIS [3] [4] [5].

Numerous previous studies have been conducted to design efficient and safe input methods for navigation assistance, and almost all of them used a touch screen as an input device [2]. However, they have been focusing mainly on design guidelines for usable and safe input methods, and usability testing for comparing design alternatives. It is difficult to find a systematic framework for developing character input methods appropriate to the driver and input devices as well. In addition, there are only a few studies about the knob control that has been recently introduced as an input device in a car.

N. Aykin (Ed.): Usability and Internationalization, Part II, HCII 2007, LNCS 4560, pp. 40–47, 2007.
© Springer-Verlag Berlin Heidelberg 2007

The primary purpose of this study is to propose a framework for developing a character input method for a DIS. In addition, a character input method appropriate for knob control has been developed. Specific objectives of this study are as follows: (1) Constructing a framework for developing character input methods for a DIS; (2) Verifying the framework with a case study of developing character input methods using knob control; (3) Developing a usable character input method appropriate for the Korean characters through the case study

2 Framework for Developing Character Input Methods

The framework, proposed in this study, for developing character input methods for a DIS is composed of two phases. As shown in Fig. 1, the design steps of each phase were specified, and the design techniques needed at each step were provided.

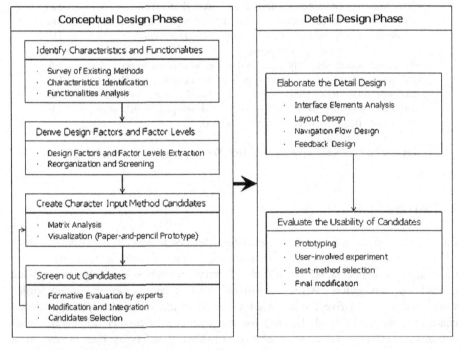

Fig. 1. Proposed Framework for Developing Character Input Methods for a DIS

2.1 Conceptual Design Phase

The first phase is conceptual design in which input methods are created and formative evaluation is conducted. The conceptual design phase consists of four steps.

The first step is to identify functionalities and characteristics of character input methods. Existing character input methods, used in PDAs, mobile phones, navigation assistance products, etc., are surveyed. The functionalities provided in various character input methods are investigated and classified according to the user's goals or tasks. Second, the characteristics of the character input methods are identified considering software/hardware aspects and usage context. Here, several constraints are applied to specify the characteristics such as display size, controller, target user, etc.

The second step is to derive design factors and factor levels. The meaning of the design factors and the factor levels are similar to those in the experimental design. Design factors are important features for designing character input methods and factor levels are values or specific conditions that a factor can have. For example, when a controller is a design factor, knob control, touch screen, and keypad can be the factor levels. Design factors are obtained from important characteristics identified in the previous step. For each design factor, design types of existing character input methods are listed and they become the levels of the factor.

The third step is to create design candidates of the character input methods. In this step, a design candidate can be created by taking one of the factor levels from each factor and combining them together. However, creating design candidates using all possible combinations is too costly and time-consuming. To reduce the number of combinations, it is necessary to reorganize and screen out design factors and factor levels by the importance level. Conceptual designs of each combination are then visualized. Paper-and-pencil prototypes are good methods for this purpose. Critical interface features and operating mechanisms are specified next.

The forth step is to screen out design candidates. The design candidates are presented to the experts and a pluralistic walkthrough is conducted. Each candidate is evaluated using the criteria such as compatibility, learnability, effectiveness, efficiency, and so on. In addition, pros and cons of each candidate are analyzed. When it is possible to create a more usable design by modifying or integrating the design candidates, visualization and evaluation are iterated from the third step. Finally, the number of candidates is reduced based on the evaluation results.

2.2 Detail Design Phase

The second phase is detail design in which interfaces and interaction are specified and the most usable character input method is selected (i.e., summative evaluation). The detail design phase consists of two steps.

The first step is to elaborate the detail design. The interface elements of each candidate are analyzed to determine the size, position, color, and shape. Next, a screen layout is designed by considering the design constraints.. Control functions to move cursors or select some interface element are allocated to each control mode (i.e. button push, rotating of the jog dial, etc.). Finally, navigation flows and feedback for a user input are designed.

The second step is to evaluate the usability of design candidates and to select the most usable method. Prototypes are implemented on the basis of interface/interaction designs of the previous step. A user-involved experiment is then conducted to evaluate the usability of the prototypes. Both quantitative measures and qualitative measure are collected together. Based on the experimental results, the most usable method is selected. Finally, the most usable method is modified by resolving any problems found in the evaluation experiment.

3 Case Study: Input Method for Knob Control and Korean Characters

A case study is conducted to verify the effectiveness of the developed framework and to design a usable character input method appropriate for knob control and the Korean characters. The pre-determined assumption about the knob control is that it has 7 degrees of freedom (i.e. 4-way joystick, 2-way rotary, and push).

To survey existing character input methods, 28 papers (i.e. journal, proceedings, and technical report), 67 patents, and 23 products were surveyed and 100 different types of character input methods were collected. The functionalities used in character input methods are presented in Table 1. There were three design constraints. The screen size was fixed at 800px*480px and a knob control was used as an input device.

Table 1. Functional requirements of character input methods

Function	Category (# of characters)	
Input	• Korean Alphabet –	Consonant: Single(14), Twin(5), Compound(9)
		Vowels: Single(10), Compound(11)
	• Alphabet – Big(26), Small(26)	
	• Figures – 0~9(10)	
	• Special Character	
	• Space	
Modification/ Delete	• Previous Phoneme • Previous Syllable • Between Words	
Finish/ Cancel	• Finish or Cancel of a Character Input	

Design factors for developing character input methods was made by considering interface, control, interaction, and Korean characters aspects. Eight design factors were extracted and the levels of each factor were listed by classifying design types of existing methods (see Table 2.).

However, creating design candidates using all possible combinations was too costly and time-consuming. Critical factors and factor levels were selected based on the importance, and a matrix analysis was conducted using the four factors that were expressed in bold in Table 2. Design candidates were created by taking one of the factor levels from each factor and combining them together. As a result of the matrix analysis, 100 conceptual designs were created. Fig. 2 shows some of the conceptual designs.

Table 2. Design factors and factor levels

Category	Design Factors	Factor levels
Interface (Display)	**Layout**	Keyboard type, **Matrix type, Circular type, Matrix + Circular**, None
	Mode change	**Yes** or No
Control	Controller	Touch screen/Pad, Numeric Keypad, 4 Arrow+ 'OK', Joystick+Push, Jog dial+Push, Glove, Mouse, Track point, Roller, **Joystick+Jog dial+Push**
Interaction	**Interaction method**	Two-step selection, Direct selection, Multi-press, Chording, Character recognition, Pattern recognition
	Support	Character unit, Word unit, None
Korean Alphabet	Layout of Cons. & Vowel	Left-Right, Top-Bottom, Main+Pop-up, Inner+Outer
	Consonant	**Type C1(Chun-ji-in), Type C2, Type C3, All**
	Vowel	**Type V1(Chun-ji-in), Type V2, All**

Bold: Critical factors and factor levels

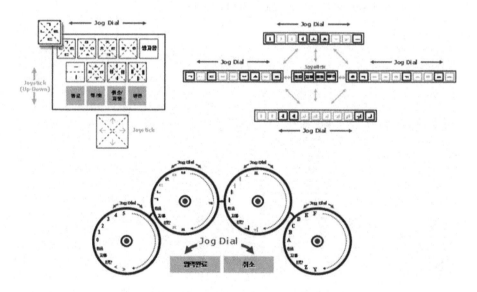

Fig. 2. Examples of Conceptual Design

Pluralistic walkthroughs were conducted by three usability experts. Efficiency, compatibility, simplicity, learnability, and memorability were used as the evaluation criteria and the weights of the criteria were estimated by using the analytic hierarchy process technique. As a result, three design candidates, i.e., single circle type, twin circle type, and two step type, were selected (See Fig. 3).

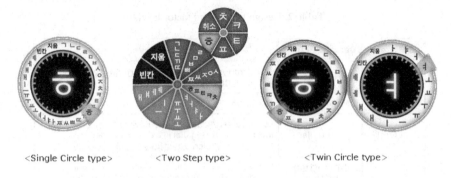

<Single Circle type>   <Two Step type>   <Twin Circle type>

Fig. 3. Selected Design Candidates

As a result of analyzing interface elements, 19 characters for consonants, 14 characters for vowels and soft buttons for changing the input mode (Korean, English, Numerals/Symbols) were included in the interface features to be implemented. In addition, spaces for a text entry box and an address list were allocated when designing the screen layout. As shown in Fig. 4, navigation flows and feedback for function selections were designed by paper-and-pencil drawing.

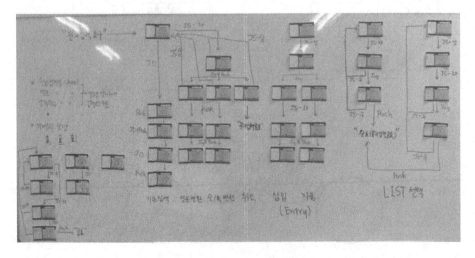

Fig. 4. Navigation Flows & Feedback Design

Each design candidate was prototyped using the MS visual studio .net and an HP multimedia keyboard. A traditional input type was also prototyped to compare with the new designs. Using the prototypes, a user-involved experiment was conducted. Ten subjects participated in the experiment. Their age ranged from 30's, 40's, and

50's because the target population for the DIS was restricted to these ages. The subjects performed text input tasks. They evaluated each design candidate based on six criteria (i.e. ease of use, ease of search, ease of learning, ease of adaptation, ease of recall, overall satisfaction) and the task completion time for each task was recorded. In addition, they were asked to provide ranking of the candidates, pros/cons, and improvement ideas, if any. As a result, the single circle type was found to be the most usable design in terms of both the objective (i.e., task completion time) and the subjective (i.e., usability score and overall satisfaction) measures. However, the best design was redesigned based on the suggestions made by the subjects during the experiment. Major suggestions were that characters and spaces were too small to find easily and it was difficult to distinguish the consonant part from the vowel part clearly. Thus, the single circle type was modified by combining the circles as shown in Fig. 5.

Fig. 5. Modified Design of the Single Circle Type

4   Conclusion

The framework proposed in this study helps to develop character input methods for a DIS easily and systematically. Most design work depends on the designer's creative ideas in the traditional development process. However, in this study, using a bottom-up approach for extracting design factors and a matrix approach for creating conceptual designs, a variety of design ideas could be created easily and systematically. Through a case study using the framework developed, this study designed a usable character input method appropriate for the knob control, which was proved to work more effectively than an existing method.

Design factors and factor levels extracted in this study are applicable to developing other input methods using different control devices in a DIS. It is also expected that the framework can be applied to developing character input methods for mobile phones, PDA, and so on.

References

1. Green, P.: Visual and Task Demands of Driver Information Systems. In: Technical Report UMTRI-98-16 (1999)
2. Tsimhoni, O., Smith, D., Green, P.: Destination Entry while Driving: Speech Recognition versus a Touch-Screen Keyboard. In: Technical Report UMTRI-2001-241 (2002)
3. Nowakowski, C., Utsui, Y., Green, P.: Navigation System Destination Entry: The Effects of Driver Workload and Input Devices, And Implications for SAE Recommended Practice. In: Technical Report UMTRI-2000-20 (2000)
4. Paelke, G., Green, P.: Entry of Destinations into Route Guidance Systems: A Human Factors Evaluation. In: Technical Report UMTRI-93-45 (1993)
5. Wright, P., Bartram, C., Rogers, N., Emslie, H., Evans, J., Wilson, B., Belt, S.: Text entry on handheld computers by older users. ERGONOMICS 43(6), 702–716 (2000)

Linguistic Analysis of Websites: A New Method of Analysing Language, the Poor Cousin of Usability

Sabrina Duda, Michael Schiessl, Gerald Wildgruber, Christian Rohrer, and Paul Fu

Eye square GmbH, Schlesische Str. 29-30, D-10997 Berlin, Germany
duda@eye-square.com, schiessl@eye-square.com
Humboldt Universität zu Berlin, Seminar für Ästhetik, Sophienstr. 22 a, D-10178
Berlin, Germany
gerald.wildgruber@rz.hu-berlin.de
eBay User Experience Research, 2145 Hamilton Avenue, 96125 San Jose, CA, USA
crohrer@ebay.com, pfu@ebay.com

Abstract. While text and concepts have always been acknowledged as key players in effecting the overall impact of a website, language - much like an attention-deprived stepchild - has always been allocated a little side role. The following work introduces a method for linguistic analysis which enables usability experts to examine language on a website at its various layers, and to carry out a user study about users´ perception of language. The method will be illustrated by an eBay case study in Germany and China and will be equipped with concrete examples. These examples indicate that this method is indeed easy to apply and that when used together with the classic usability test, enhances the study results and allows for a strategic optimization of the website.

Keywords: Linguistic Analysis, Usability, Web Usability, Usable Language, User Experience, User Test, Expert Analysis, Linguistics, Semiotics, Syntax, Semantics, Pragmatics.

1 Introduction

The increasingly user-centered development of websites have proven their impact: In terms of user-friendliness as well as in terms of graphic design and content, the quality of websites has in the last few years considerably gone up. And, in the web teams of big businesses these days, more and more psychologists are finding themselves working alongside linguists.

The unambiguous and intelligible designation of links and clear operation instructions are essential to the user-friendliness of a website. However, the naming of links and labelling of buttons deal with only one layer of language – that of meaning (semantic layer). An example of a semantic analysis is the study conducted in 2003 by Paivo Laine who analyzed the language of hyperlink and buttons.

All too often the diligence and care which should go into writing and shaping the text of websites are found to be lacking – supported of course by that well-known excuse that "online users do not read anyway". Indeed it is true that the manner with which people read the web differs greatly from the one with which they read books or

N. Aykin (Ed.): Usability and Internationalization, Part II, HCII 2007, LNCS 4560, pp. 48–56, 2007.

magazines. John Morkes and Jakob Nielsen (1997) found out in a study that 79 percent of the test users always scanned any new page they came across; only 16 percent read word-by-word. In our eye tracking studies however, we have found out that users actually read more and that women, in particular, read often more text than men (Duda, S., Schiessl, M., Thölke, A., Fischer, R., 2003).

A linguistic analysis of the language on a website would lend perspective and accuracy to the results of a usability test for language here is taken as a topic in its own right and subjected to close examination. The method of linguistic analysis offers several advantages. The first is that the results of a linguistic analysis allows for a quick yet concrete improvement. Furthermore, this improvement is considerably low in terms of expenses for it basically involves changing or rewriting of text rather than a redesigning of icons and graphics – which is a costly measure. Another plus point of the approach is the fact that an expert analysis will also deliver a model with guidelines and strategies for its further development.

Martín del Pozo (2005) points out that it is acknowledged by HCI experts from the beginning that linguistics as a discipline contributes to the field of HCI. Another important area of research regarding language and websites is the design of multilingual websites, localization and cultural particularities (Morgan, T., Luttrell, C., Liu, Y., 2001) (He, S., 2001). Nevertheless, research about the very issue of language on websites is rare. The online article "Linguistics and Web Usability" by María Angeles Martín del Pozo (2005) has identified this lack. She categorizes the research about language and usability in two fields: Reading materials which in the context of guidelines and checklists (e.g. Duda, S., 1998) briefly points to linguistic aspects, and articles on website writing and publishing.

In 2004, we were tasked by the internet auction company, eBay Germany to conduct a study of its selling pages. The following is a description of a linguistic analysis of those pages.

2 Theory

The method of the linguistic analysis was developed by eye square GmbH in cooperation with the linguist, Gerald Wildgruber from Humboldt Universität zu Berlin. According to the theory of signs by Ch. S. Peirce and C. W Morris (1868), it is possible to examine any kind of communication in terms of the syntactic arrangement and distribution of its signs, the semantic format of its contents and thirdly, the pragmatic embedment in a context of action.

The linguistic analysis method combines expert analysis with a user study. In the expert analysis, the language on the website is reviewed at the three levels (Syntax, Semantic and Pragmatic). In addition, the overarching themes of the website such as its metaphors and narration are also examined. Subsequently, the text on the website is put to a user test so that actual users get the chance to evaluate the language. Problems identified in the expert analysis are also reviewed in the user study. Results will then serve as both input in formulating concrete steps to improve of the text layout and as guideline for its future development.

2.1 Syntax: Text Is an Image

The subjects of analysis are the signs themselves – the way they are arranged and distributed on the page and their relationships and connections with one another. This has to do with the so-called iconic perception of the website, i.e. without taking into account the meaning of the words nor sentences (for this would make up the semantics); how the text is perceived, as a whole, as a picture.

2.2 Semantic: Meaning and Understanding

Semantic deals with the meaning of the signs. Here the question of whether the sign is understood in an effective manner takes centre stage. Are the concepts and instructions in use grasped intuitively by the user? The experience of having understood the system and the sense of security that accompanies that experience is an essential condition for a positive user experience.

2.3 Pragmatic: Meaning Is Use

Pragmatic here is used to denote the relationship between the sign and its user. The user is the one who acts. This aspect of language plays an important role when we consider the extent text can serve as an impetus or indeed as a commanding force for action. Language is never without a connection to action. The one who speaks does effect somebody else and wants to motivate for actions. Communication always has an aim.

2.4 Narrative

In order to provoke an (re)action from the user, mere comprehension (semantic level) and a simple call to action are often not enough. If the goal of the communication process is the action of the user we recommend for the generation of action impulse in the user the set up of a narrative. A narrative tells a story, a type of primordial story. It deals with primary conflicts and their solutions and addresses fundamental psychological needs. Finding such a tale would be enable one to address people at an emotional level that would directly appeal to them. A narrative can be seen as an extended and well-developed metaphor, a kind of meta metaphor ("Metaphora Continuata").

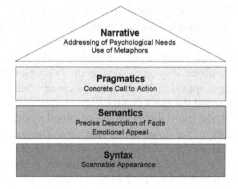

Fig. 1. Model of ideal language on a website

3 Method

3.1 Expert Analysis

Three experts - linguists and cognitive psychologists - analyzed independently from each other the language of the selling pages. The three levels of the text i.e. syntax, semantics and pragmatics were examined by each expert independently.

Syntax

- Is the amount of text appropriate?
- Is the text clearly laid out? Can the user quickly summarize the information in each block?
- Are the sentences clear and concise or clumsy and long-winded?

Semantics

- Cognitive effect: Is the wording comprehensible and informative? Is the wording consistent?
- Emotional effect: Is the style friendly and inviting? Is the user always addressed in the same way? Is the brand being conveyed?

Pragmatics

- Does the language call one to action?
- Is the point of the action being conveyed across?
- Does the user know which step to take next and how?

Narrative

- Which psychological needs could be addressed?
- Which narratives or metaphors could be used?

3.2 User Study

For the study we conducted in January 2004, a total of 10 participants were invited for single user sessions (90 minutes per person) in our media lab. These individuals had varying experience level - the group contained experts as well as novices. All participants used the same selected section of the website – the sales pages of eBay Germany. They went through the entire process of placing an item on the eBay pages. We used the thinking aloud method, and interviews. We focused our attention in having the following questions answered: What is the impression the users have of the language? Is the language appealing? Which terms cause confusion? Do users know what to do next? What would the users change?

After the website test, the user handed up the so-called association cards. These are cards on which the users wrote down terms that they associated with the language used on the pages. Subsequently, the participants evaluated the website using Semantic Differential, a procedure which measures connotative meanings of concepts: ratings on bipolar scales defined with contrasting adjectives at each end.

4 Results

4.1 Results of Expert Analysis

It becomes evident that in general, the user is offered too much text. The pages often come across as overloaded and have the effect of scaring off the user rather than inviting him to read them. A uniform layout for pages that belong together is also missing, for example, instead of having a specific position for the Help text throughout the pages, its placement changes. Often, the sentences were not only too long but also unnecessarily complicated in structure. The problem continues at the semantic level: Words were not always easily understood. The text was littered with technical terms for which definitions were not offered (e.g. "Verkaufsagent" and "Kaufabwicklung"). The mode used to address the user was inconsistent. In certain sections he is addressed politely with "Sie", in others he is the informal "Du". And yet in many parts, an appropriate tone of friendliness was found to be missing. Often, a direct call to action was missing. Sometimes the necessary steps were not clear or the processes were not described appropriately. It is also difficult for the user to have a complete picture of the selling process. He has to work through Step 1 to 5 without having any idea of what stage he is at and what is to come next.

The final task of the experts would be to find and formulate a suitable narrative that would take into account the results of the analysis. When looking for a suitable metaphor for the Selling procedure we found the shop metaphor: the eBay seller as a shop owner. For example:

- Putting articles in a shopping window (uploading items)
- Writing name tags for articles (item title) and price tags (auction starting price, or fixed price)

4.2 Results of User Testing

Examples of User Comments. The language is seen as factual and not very personal or motivating, but the latter aspects are not regarded as being important:

- Real estate agent, 55, newbie: "It's appropriate – it's like a manual!"
- Student, 35, user: "The language is appropriate for a form."

Though the informational aspect is regarded as the most important issue, some subjects thought it could nevertheless be more appealing:

- Consultant, 47, user: "A little bit too dry."
- Author, 31, user: "Could be more pleasing."

Interestingly, the very experienced as well as the inexperienced subjects thought the pages were not made for them. For the power-users there is too much additional text which they don't need and for the newbies there is not enough! Especially the compound nouns like 'Angebotsformat', 'Einstelloptionen' etc. are not comprehensible:

- Author, 31, user: "Two abstract terms combined, that creates a very special language!"

User Test Association Cards. The results of the free association together with the cards on which the users wrote down the adjectives produced a mixed picture of what they think of the selling pages. 44 overall associations (on average 4,4 per subject) were made; out of this 20 negative associations and 24 positive associations.

The positive adjectives were given by the two groups: usable language, positive user addressing. Several negative comments were found in the following three groups: complicated or incomprehensible language, too much text, factual style.

User Test Semantic Differential. The trend in the associations was further supported by the results of the Semantic Differential. The highest rated adjectives were: comprehensible, reliable, factual, and informative. The lowest ratings achieved: casual, motivating, and personal.

Here it is made clear that the eBay selling pages are perceived as fact-orientated and informative. They are however found to be unmotivating and impersonal – the emotional factor therefore is missing. To sum up: The pages worked well at the cognitive level but they were no fun to use.

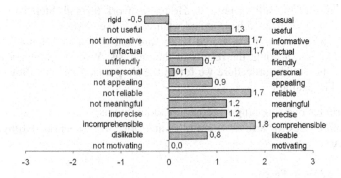

Fig. 2. Results user test semantic differential

5 Recommendations

The review of the syntax of the used language yielded the following recommendations:

- Use shorter sentences and reduce text.
- Take care about consistent positioning of text elements over different pages, according to content and function.
- Adapt user support to amount of user experience. Offer additional information and term definitions which are accessible through links.

Problems identified in the semantic and pragmatic analyses helped in making the following suggestions for improvement:

- Make the wording more friendly and motivating!
- Use clearer descriptions of objects and processes. Avoid complicated nouns.
- Use the friendly and polite addressing with "Sie" instead of "Du". Keep the addressing of the user consistent.

6   Case Study in China

eBay China site, in simplified Chinese, was launched at the end of 2004. Besides the unique features developed for eBay China, the content of the site was mainly translated from the English version. To analyze the site content the linguistic analysis method was adopted from eBay Germany. A combination of content-specific user studies and expert reviews were carried out in Shanghai. Again the user test consists of four sections: task-based website test, Semantic Differential, card association, and interviews.

In the expert analysis, two linguistic experts evaluated the buying and selling flows. The experts worked independently to evaluate the site by going through the typical buying and selling flows.

6.1   Results of Expert Analysis in China

From the linguistic analysis, forty seven buying-related and fifty selling-related issues were identified. In general participants thought that the site content needed improvements in the areas of precision, conciseness, call to action, informality, liveliness, and fun. Those ninety seven issues were then classified into six categories: content precision, content style, page design, business decision, legal content, and content bugs.

6.2   Selected Results of User Testing China

In China the study was conducted with the whole site. We want to present some general user comments and the results from the Association Cards and from the Semantic Differential from the selling pages user testing.

User Comments. Users felt the site is easy to use and intimate:

- "Although I've never been to eBay and not familiar with online purchase, I feel it easy to use the site when I use it for the first time today as if it was an old friend to me."
- "Its content is easy to understand and brings me sense of belonging."

Users put more emphasis on the fact that eBay is convenient; friendliness was less important:

- "Trustworthy, sincere, friendly and lively."
- "The reason I visit eBay simply is it brings convenience to my life."

User Test Association Cards. 26 overall associations (on average 3,3 per subject) were made; out of this 10 negative associations and 16 positive associations. The positive associations fell into three groups: Easiness, clearness, intimateness. The negative associations were: Missing conciseness/clearness, missing integration of both graphic and text.

It is very interesting that the results from Germany and China are rather similar. In both countries the positive associations were stronger; users found the selling pages comprehensible, concise, clear and easy. In both countries a considerable amount of users found that the pages are complicated, not concise. But in Germany more users than in China criticized the amount of text and the factual style.

User Test Semantic Differential. For the Chinese study the Semantic Differential was adapted to Chinese needs; therefore only some items can be compared directly. Nevertheless, the results point in a similar direction. In Germany rigid is the most negative item, followed by motiving, personal, likeable. In China formal is the most negative item, followed by boring and wordy.

Despite the different adjectives, one can see that in both countries there is a lack of nonchalance/ "lightness of being", and inspiring factors.

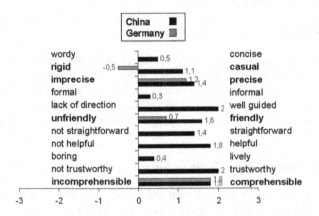

Fig. 3. Semantic Differential China-Germany

Comparing the adjectives that were identical (rigidness, preciseness, friendliness, comprehensibility) one sees that Chinese and German users rate the eBay selling pages equally comprehensible. As well preciseness is rated almost equally. Nevertheless, Chinese users experience the pages much more friendly! And regarding rigidness Chinese and German users have a different opinion: Germans think the pages are rather rigid, Chinese users not.

7 Recommendations China

High level recommendations from the study include:

- Cut back the content on each page. Simplify complex sentence structures. Make the content more scannable. Make sentence structure and presentation consistent.
- Update the content where it does not call out the benefits to the users and does not motivate users to action. Update the content where it uses eBay terms and is not expressed from the buyer's point of view.
- Minimize eBay technical terms. When technical terms are used ensure they are in the user glossary.

The eBay China use case illustrated the ease of adopting this linguistic research method, and the multitude and quality of the findings demonstrated its effectiveness. The China use case, combined with the German study, also provided evidence to the validity of the research method in the international context.

8 Conclusion

With our studies we wanted to throw light on the benefits of going beyond usability issues and paying more attention to the language on websites. We tried to show how looking at a website from a different perspective can help gain deepened insights how to improve overall user experience. We hope that these studies could demonstrate that language issues can easily be integrated in usability projects.

Research which systematically measures the effect of improved language on web pages on efficiency and user satisfaction is needed. What are the factors regarding language that influence users´ performance, and users´ emotional perception of the website? Especially the use of metaphors and narratives is a challenging and promising area of research that could involve linguists and HCI researchers.

We hope that research in linguistics and usability will continue to expand, and that both disciplines will work more closely together in the future.

Acknowledgments. We thank eBay Germany for giving the idea and the impulse for this project, and for realizing it with us; and we thank eBay China for adopting the method for their website.

References

1. Duda, S.: Design and Empirical Testing of a Checklist for the Evaluation of Multimedia Software for Children. In: Sutcliffe, A., Ziegler, J., Johnson, P. (eds.) Designing Effective and Usable Multimedia System, Kluwer Academic Publishers, Boston (1998)
2. He, S.: Interplay of language and culture in global E-commerce: a comparison of five companies' multilingual websites. In: Proceedings of the 19th annual international conference on Computer documentation (2001)
3. Laine, P.: Invited workshop on digital interaction: Explicitness and interactivity. In: Proceedings of the 1st international symposium on Information and communication technologies ISICT '03 (2003)
4. Martín del Pozo, M. A. Linguistics and Web Usability, http://www.nosolousabilidad.com/articulos/linguistics.htm
5. Morgan, T., Luttrell, C., Liu, Y.: Designing multilingual web sites: applied authoring techniques. In: Proceedings of the 19th annual international conference on Computer documentation (2001)
6. Morris Ch. W.: Foundations of the Theory of Signs. In: International Encyclopedia of Unified Science, Bd. 1, No. 2, Chicago, 1938, 9. ed (1957)
7. Peirce Ch. S.: On a New List of Categories. In: Proceedings of the American Academy of Arts. and Sciences 7, 287–298 (1868)
8. Schiessl, M., Duda, S., Thölke, A., Fischer, R.: Eyetracking and its application in usability and media research. In: Seifert, K., Rötting, M. (eds.) Sonderheft: Blickbewegung in MMI-interaktiv Journal - Online Zeitschrift zu Fragen der Mensch-Maschine-Interaktion, Ausgabe Nr. 6 (2003)

Human Communication Based on Icons in Crisis Environments*

Siska Fitrianie, Dragos Datcu, and Leon J.M. Rothkrantz

Man-Machine Interaction Group, Delft University of Technology
Mekelweg 4, 2628CD Delft, the Netherlands
{s.fitrianie,d.dactu,l.j.m.rothkrantz}@ewi.tudelft.nl

Abstract. In recent years, we have developed an icon-based communication interface to represent concepts and ideas. Users can create messages to communicate with others using a spatial arrangement of visual symbols. We deployed our icon-based interface in a serious game environment of a disaster and rescue simulator, which is capable of simulating real disaster situations using information from human user observers' reports. To support faster interaction, we designed a highly adaptive interface for optimizing the next icon look up. Inspired by the Fitaly keyboard, the system rearranges the icons menu's layout dynamically to minimize the searching time. Users are able to find their desired icons fast since the next icon selection is most likely to be one that is (on or) around the center. Our user tests showed that the developed icon-based interface could serve as a communication mediator. The experimental results also indicated that the Fitaly-based interface allowed for much faster and easier icon finding than the hierarchical menu.

1 Introduction

Nowadays, icons are used in almost every GUI-based computer software. Direct manipulation on the icons on a GUI allows us to have a fast interaction. Research showed that direct manipulation with a pointer has better time performance than form filling with Soft Input Panels or handwriting recognition [20]. As pictorial signs, icons can be recognized quickly and committed to human's memory persistently [12]. Therefore, icons can evoke a readiness to respond and quick ensuing actions [23].

Icons can form a language, where each sentence is created by a spatial arrangement of icons [4]. Each icon is understood as a representation of a concept, i.e. an object, an action, or a relation [27]. By virtue of resemblance between a given icon and the object or the movement it stands for, an icon functions as a mean of communication. Therefore, icons offer a potential across language barriers and a direct method for conversion to other modalities. Since icons are representations of models or concepts, with which humans are actually interacting, we expect this language is easy to learn.

Recent catastrophic events are stark reminders of the global implications of crisis management technology that can cope with nondeterministic environments. This is

---

* The research reported here is part of the Interactive Collaborative Information Systems (ICIS) project, supported by the Dutch Ministry of Economic Affairs, grant nr: BSIK03024.

N. Aykin (Ed.): Usability and Internationalization, Part II, HCII 2007, LNCS 4560, pp. 57–66, 2007.

because major incidents generally entail much informational and operational chaos [7]. Emergency response of such events involved collaborations of people from different backgrounds, roles and professions. The need of a standard representation to reduce the ambiguity and multitude of semantic interpretation of human observers' reports becomes more apparent. Moreover, due to potentially overloaded or destroyed wired-communication infrastructures, these observers may only rely on their mobile devices (e.g. PDAs) with wireless connection for communication. However, the user interaction options for a PDA are quite limited along with decreasing size of this device. Moreover, for adding speech recognition capabilities to a PDA, a close to mouth microphone is necessary. The environment in which the technology is used must be similar to the training environment of the system [3], whereas PDAs are often used in various environments under various conditions. The result is misrecognition of commands, which is frustrating to the user. This leads us to aim at a natural interaction style based on GUI using an icon-based interface for communication.

In earlier work, we have investigated icons in particular for a language-independent context application. We have developed an icon-based interface for communication in crisis situations on a PDA [11]. A user can report about crisis situations using spatial arrangements of icons. The use of icons to represent concepts or ideas makes user interactions on the interface particularly suitable across user diversity and differences between organizations and actors involved in the crisis management. However, a PDA represents a typical device, where a user has to carry out interaction tasks in a varying environment, with a small device and usually by using only one hand. The situation often requires multitasking, where the attention cannot be devoted fully on inputting. In demanding situations, e.g. crisis situations, usability and improvement in the input method performance are highly desired. Using our interface, users will likely interact with a large number of icons. To enhance the interface for usable and faster icon selections, we introduce an adaptive icon menu.

We have developed a method for adapting the icon menu layout adopted from the Fitaly keyboard [21]. The most relevant icons to a user's input context are placed on or around the center. Usability of the experimental implementation was examined with user tests. Verifiable measurement data and comments of test users were collected in order to guide further development.

This paper reports the basic idea of our adaptive icon-based interface. It is structured as follows. The following section starts with the related work. Then, the developed icon-based interface, which is deployed on a serious game environment, is presented. The next section presents our adaptive icon menu. We continue with describing our experiments. Finally, we report our conclusion.

2 Related Work

Semiotics approach provides theories and methods for designing and analyzing signs and symbols that can be understood universally. Recent attempts have been done in developing computer-based icon-based communication, for example: the Hotel Booking System [26], CD-Icon [2], Sanyog [1], and the Elephant's memory [15]. Most of these systems are too complex to learn or language-specific. A deep research has been done on designing such system that allows people to communicate with each other when they share no common language [22]. The system is based on the notion of simplified speech by reducing complexity and non-linear order. This is possible because as a visual language, sequencing and ordering may not be necessary.

In the field of crisis management, a comprehensive evaluation of existing symbols (or icons) for sharing information during crucial emergency situations has been performed by Dymon (2003) [7]. The US Government has promoted these symbols for emergency response applications on a national basis [13]. These symbols have been tested nationally with participations from private and public sectors. An icon-based interface for sharing and merging topological maps in damaged buildings has also been developed by Tatomir et al. (2006) [30]. The constructed map can be used for providing navigations or rescue action coordination.

Pen-based text entry on PDAs has been studied extensively [24]. Previous work in developing adapted keyboard layouts for PDAs and single-handed use has concentrated on alternative key configuration for improving entry speed, for example: Metropolis [33] and OPTI [25]. Fitaly keyboard (Fig. 1(a)) used an ad hoc optimization approach to minimize the distance between common character pairs [21]. The resulting keyboard contains two space bars and the letters are arranged so that common pairs of letters are often on neighboring keys. According to [24], this layout is one of the "fastest" for expert users.

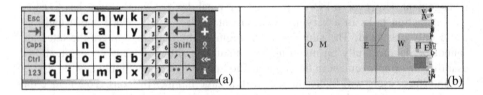

Fig. 1. (a) Fitaly keyboard [21] and (b) Dasher [33]

Some text input techniques have been developed with both movement minimizing and predictive features. T9 text entry works by comparing sequences of key presses to a stored database of possible words [31]. Dasher (Fig. 1(b)) employs continuous input by dynamically arranging characters in multiple columns positioning the next most likely character near the user's stylus [33]. The options are presented to the user in boxes sized according to their relative probabilities, to optimize the movement time. Our approach adopts these techniques for searching-minimizing and predicting input.

3 System Overview

3.1 Icon-Based Interface

We designed an icon-based interface for supporting people who must work collaboratively using knowledge from geospatial information and coordinate actions for resolving crisis. These people are professionals (rescue workers in the crisis field and crisis center room operators) and civilians (victims and witnesses). The interface provides icons, geometrical features, icon sentences, and text and photo selections for describing a crisis situation. A user can select and place them on a map where the crisis is occurring (see Fig. 2(a)). Sensed data, what the user sees, hears, smells, and even feels or experiences, can be transformed into icon representations. Geometrical features, e.g. arrow, ellipse, rectangle, can be used to indicate an area and highlight or emphasize an object, an event or a location on the map. Besides providing icons for representing observations, such as explosion, victim, ambulance, the interface also provides icons for reporting non-spatial information using text, photos, and 2D icon sentences. A pop-up window will appear when the user selects these types of icons.

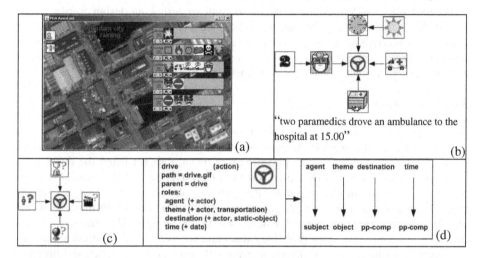

Fig. 2. The developed icon-based interface, (b) an example of two-dimensional icon sentences (15.00 is distinguished by the icon "noon" – represented by the image "sun"), (c) hints for the concept "drive", and (d) a schematic view of a case for the concept "drive"

Fig. 2(b) shows an example of 2D icon sentences. Inspired by Deikto [6], a user can construct an acyclic-graph of icons to represents a sentence. The graph connects icons using arrows, in which the former icon explains the latter. The sentence construction has no linear order. The user may start the string from anywhere she/he wants but if a verb is selected, the structure of the sentence will be determined.

We develop ontology by defining a case (i.e. a set of attributes) for each icon our ontology. For example: the icon "victim" contains number, location and status. For icons that represent verbs, we defined their case based on the theory of Fillmore [9] and VerbNet [19]. Each verb in ontology has a link with associated thematic roles (e.g. an agent, patient, and theme) and syntactic arguments (e.g. subject, object, and preposition) (Fig. 2(d)). Using this approach, the interface can give hints, which attributes can be filled in (Fig. 2(c)). As the icon is deselected, the hint will disappear. This hint can be selected and replaced by an icon to form a sentence. The approach gives a freedom to users to fill in the parts of a sentence, but at the same time the system can restrict the choices of icons which lead to a meaningful sentence.

The system uses Lexicalized Tree Adjoining Grammar (LTAG – [17]) to convert the icon sentence into text. Based on the case of every icon in a 2D string, a parser processes the 2D stream and maps each thematic role into the elementary trees of TAG families. The interface gives direct feedback on the user's selections. Therefore, although some icons are still unknown, the users can learn them on trials.

To help users find their way around a large number of icon vocabularies, we grouped related icons based on their semantic meaning. The icon vocabularies are displayed in a hierarchy tabular menu. The first version of the interface also provides an n-gram-based next icon prediction tool, which predicts and ranks most likely icons to follow a given segment of icon selections. The next version combined both approaches to be one icon menu layout (see section 4).

We took some guidelines and standards to guide us during our design process, such as: ISO/IEC [16], Horton's [14] and Schneiderman's [29]. Since the interpretation of icons is a subjective matter, in particular, we have tested each icon in the context of other icons based on Horton's [10]. To solve problems of linguistics and culturally bias, the test participants were selected to include different nationalities.

3.2 Serious Game Environment

We designed a simulation environment to facilitate the testing of the proposed interface. The simulation offers integration with real observations of a crisis situation. In this simulation, a human user plays the role of an observer using the developed icon-based interface on a PDA. Fig. 3(a) shows an overview of the simulator. In a *real world*, a crisis simulation plays out. In an *observer world*, the observers report their observations to a *crisis center* using their PDA. The data set of the real world and the observer world are geo-referenced overlay one another. The crisis center has an expert system to give most probable causes and advice about the current situation. For example: if the chances of fire are increased, the emergency is alerted and firemen are sent. The simulator receives the users' reports and updates the activities in the disaster simulator.

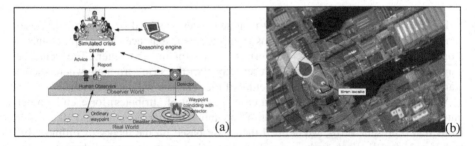

Fig. 3. (a) Overview of the simulation environment and (b) an example of a gas dispersion scenario shown by the simulator's interface

The geospatial knowledge of the real world is represented using grids and vectors that contain information about the environment. The simulator uses the vector values to model physical phenomena and its impact, such as spreading fire, gas dispersion, and spread of a hazardous material (Fig. 3(b)). The simulation is generated based on a scripted scenario. This scenario is a set of snapshots taken at every time unit on certain vector points. Each snapshot is advanced every minute. To enable real and mobile users to participate in a simulated reality, we provide knowledge of the virtual world. The current version of the implementation simulator is able to display an image of a situation relevant to the current scenario based on the location of an agent.

4 Fitaly-Based Icon Menu

Fig. 4(c) shows the Fitaly-based icon menu. The key ideas are the center placement of the most relevant icons to the current input context and different sizes of icons (the center menu has bigger icons than the outer). It has 28 icons and the double oversized icon "!" (to emphasis the message) and icon "?". In addition, two columns at the right side in the Fig. 4(c) are always and only available for constructing messages on a map. For constructing 2D icon sentences, they consist of numbers 0..9. The adaptive layout is formed in three sequence steps.

Firstly, the method uses an ontology-driven approach to bridge the heterogeneity of crisis domain context. As described above, we have represented domain knowledge of each icon in the system's ontology, which is stored as w3c-OWL [32]. The ontology represents context that binds verbal thought (to remember or recall) and icons together. The ontology provides a natural way to group icons based on their concepts. It also provides information about relations of a concept to other concepts.

We distinguish two algorithms in forming the menu layout based on user's task. For constructing icon-based messages on a map, the algorithm is based on the taxonomy of the concepts that indicates relevancy between concepts contextually. For example: the icon "fire" is closer contextually to "firemen" from the same super-concept "fire-event" than to "collision" from "accident-event". For creating icon sentences, the algorithm depends on the state of the sentence construction. In a new sentence construction, the algorithm uses the taxonomy information to display groups of icons. After the first icon is selected, it uses information about the relation between concepts. This information can be derived from the properties of the selected concept in the ontology. For the following sentence(s), this algorithm prioritizes icons that are closer contextually to the previous sentence based on the taxonomy information.

These algorithms ensure that the suggestion icons are contextually and conceptually relevant with the user's input so far. To measure the distance between concepts, based on [18], these algorithms calculate the smallest number of synonymy (synset) steps between the semantic representation of two direct linked concepts in the ontology (= MPL value) by employing WordNet [8]. Using this information, the distance (C_i) of an icon to the context of the one(s) that is currently selected by the user, is the summation of the MPL values of interlinked concepts.

In the second step, we use statistical models of a language and a predictive engine that increases icon throughput by guessing or suggesting what the user will select next. The probability of an icon sentence is estimated using Bayes rule:

$$P(s) = P(w_1, w_2, ..., w_n) . \frac{1}{C_i} = \prod_{i=1}^{n} P(w_i \mid w_1, ..., w_{i-1}) . \frac{1}{C_i} = \prod_{i=1}^{n} P(w_i \mid h_i) . \frac{1}{C_i} \qquad (1)$$

where h_i is the relevant history when predicting w_i and C_i is the distance of the concept of w_i to the concept of h_i. To predict the most likely icon in a given context, a global estimation of the icon sentence probability is computed by estimating conditional probabilities of n-grams type features. This approach needs a large amount of data to compute multi-grams model. The current implementation collects the data from user selections during interaction. For training, it uses the database of the previous version of the interface. Additionally, the system records whether the icon is really the intended one or the user points it by mistakes. This information can be derived from the corrections that the user makes before a message is sent.

Finally, the method arranges the most probable 28 icons following the order shown in Fig. 4(b) (starts from no. 1). The system constantly re-arranges the icons dynamically based on the prediction.

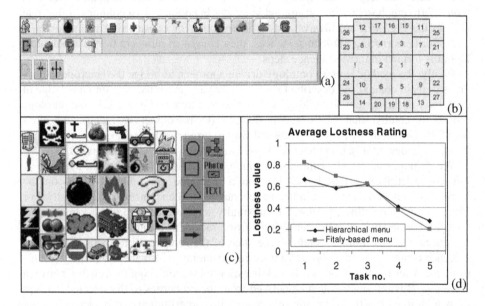

Fig. 4. (a) The hierarchical icon menu, (b) the ordering of icons, (c) the (adopted) Fitaly-based icon menu after a user selects "explosion", and (d) the average lostness rating

5   Evaluation

A set of experiments was performed to assess whether or not users were still able to create messages using provided icons from the Fitaly-based icon menu. It addressed the usability on interacting with the new interface. For this purpose, we compare the use of the hierarchical tabular icon menu (using the previous version - Fig. 4(a)) and the use of the Fitaly-based menu. Eight people took part in the test and one person as a pilot. They were selected in the range age of 25-50 years old. Four people used the hierarchical menu; the other used the Fitaly based menu. They were asked to walk around in certain locations. The tasks were created based on a crisis scenario that was fed into the simulator. The simulator used images of real crisis situations, which were sent to the participants based on their location in the world. The participants were asked to report what they saw or might sense using the icon-based interface on their

PDA. After the experiments, we interviewed their satisfaction. All interactions on the interface were logged and the interviews were recorded on a tape recorded, to be analyzed afterward. Fig. 5 shows an example of data for analysis.

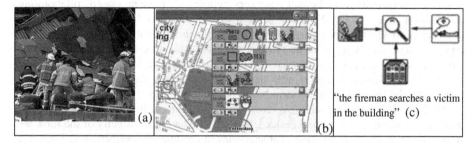

Fig. 5. Evaluation data: (a) an example of an image of a real crisis situation, (b) an example of icon-based message on a map and (c) an example of a 2D icon sentence created by a user

Smith's measurement of the sense of being lost in hypermedia [28] was adapted to measure disorientation (being lost) in an icon-based interface. As our icon space was made up by interlinked icons, we thought that an icon-based interface also might give cognitive overload and disorientation to its users. The problem referred to "after some trials, users cannot find what they are looking for". We compared the number of user selections whilst searching to the ideal path. For a perfect search, the lostness rating should have been equal to 0. From the results, it appeared that all users were able to express their concepts and ideas using icons. All participants could report crisis situations for the given images. The experimental results also indicate that our target users (using both interfaces) still had problems in finding their desired icons. This was indicated by the high number of the lostness rating of the first five sequence tasks (see Fig. 3(d)). One of the reasons was referring to problems in recognizing some icons. Another problem is caused of the limited icon vocabularies.

In the first few sessions, the lostness rating of the Fitaly-based menu was higher than the hierarchical menu's. The reason was that the proposed vocabulary was not the one that the users intended. It appeared that the test users tend to keep searching for the icon they intended. If they could not find their desired icon, time was needed to find more relevant concept to represent their message. The participants should have rethought other concepts that could fit with the current problem domain they faced. This usually occurred when our participants tried to familiarize with the interface.

All participants accomplished their tasks with relevant icon-based messages for given images. The result of the remaining tasks shows that the lostness rating of the Fitaly menu was lower than the hierarchical menu's. We viewed this decreasing lostness rating in terms of improvement of user performances. From the interview, it appeared that after few tasks, these users thought that the menu became smarter. The icon selection became faster and easier. We concluded that our test users only needed a small period of time to adapt to both interfaces.

6 Discussion and Conclusion

An experimental communication interface on a PDA has been developed, which is dedicated for reporting crisis situations. To reduce the ambiguity and the different semantic interpretations of human observers' reports, we have proposed collaborating information using icons. As icons offer a potential across language barriers, user interaction on the interface particularly is suitable in national and global aspects of crisis management. Users can describe a situation using icons, geometrical features, icon sentences, images and text on a map-based interface. It has been tested in a simulation environment that is able to capture and adapt the interactions between people and the interface in a scenario based on the users' reports.

We have developed an adaptive icon menu layout according to its usage and the user input context for faster and easier icon finding. Due to the novelty of the idea, we start with studying its qualitative characteristics to optimize its performance. From the experimental results, it appears that our target users are able to express concepts and ideas in their mind using a spatial arrangement of icons. However, the results also indicate that adaptation time is required, better icon designs and more icon vocabularies are necessary. In the first few tasks, users of the adaptive menu showed worse performance than the hierarchical menu. The reason is referring to the automatic result of the next selection prediction. The test users tended to keep searching instead of accepting the suggestions. In the following tasks, the users showed more familiar with the interface with better performance. The results indicated our test users had taken benefits provided by the menu layout and the prediction method.

The primary results show that the adaptive menu approach offers a usable tool to investigate. However, conforming MacKenzie et al. [24], it is potentially efficient and fast for expert users, but it may be difficult and slow for novice users due to the visual search requirement. Therefore, the interface should give the users both options of menu layouts to choose. Besides for more quantitative test results, future work should be done to gather data about how people might use the interface and how they experience in real crisis situations.

References

1. Basu, A., Sankar, S., Chakraborty, K., Bhattarcharya, S., Choudhury, M., Patel, R.: Vernacula Education and Communication Tool for the People with Multiple Disabilities. In: Development by Design Conference, Bangalore (2002)
2. Beardon, C.: CD-Icon, an Icon-based Language-Based on Conceptual Dependency. In: Intelligent Tutoring Media, 3(4), (1992)
3. Bousquet-Vernhettes, C., Privat, R., Vigouroux, N.: Error Handling in Spoken Dialogue Systems: Toward Corrective Dialogue. In: ISCA'03, USA (2003)
4. Chang, S.K., Polese, G., Orefice, S., Tucci, M.: A Methodology and Interactive Environment for Icon-based Language Design. Int. Journal of Human Computer Studies 41, 683–716 (1994)
5. Corballis, M.C.: Did language Evolve from Manual Gestures? In: 3rd Conf. of The Evolution of Language'00, France (2000)
6. Crawford, C.: Erasmatron. (2005), http://www.erasmatazz.com.s
7. Dymon, U.J.: An Analysis of Emergency Map Symbology. Int. Journal of Emergency Management 1(3), 227–237 (2003)

8. Fellbaum, C.: WordNet: An Electronic Lexical Database. The MIT Press, Cambridge (1998)
9. Fillmore, C.J.: The Case for Case, in Universals in Linguistic Theory. In: Emmon Bach and Robert Harms, Holt, Rinehart and Winston: New York (1968)
10. Fitrianie, S.: An Icon-Based Communication Tool on a PDA. In: Postgraduate Thesis, TU Eindhoven, the Netherlands (2004)
11. Fitrianie, S., Datcu, D., Rothkrantz, L.J.M.: Constructing Knowledge of the World in Crisis Situations using Visual Language. In: IEEE SMC'06, pp. 121–126 (2006)
12. Frutiger, A.: Sign and Symbols, Their Design and Meaning. Van Nostrand Reinholt: New York (1989)
13. Homeland Security Working Group. In: Symbology Reference. (2003), http://www. fgdc.gov/HSWG
14. Horton, W.: The Icon Book. John Wiley, New York (1994)
15. Housz, T.I.: The Elephant's Memory (1994-1996), http://www.khm.de/ timot
16. ISO/IEC. International Standard, Information Technology – User System Interfaces and Symbols – Icon Symbols and Functions, 1st edn, ISO/IEC 11581-1:2000(E) to ISO/IEC 11581-6:2000(E) (2000)
17. Joshi, A.K., Levy, L., Takahashi, M.: Tree Adjunct Grammars. Journal of the Computer and System Sciences 10, 136–163 (1975)
18. Kamps, J., Marx, M.: Words with Attitude. In: Global WordNet CIIL'02, India (2002)
19. Kipper-Schuler, K.: VerbNet: A Broad-Coverage, Comprehensive Verb Lexicon. In: PhD thesis proposal, University of Pennsylvania (2003)
20. Kjeldskov, J., Kolbe, N.: Interaction Design for Handheld Computers. In: APCHI'02, Science Press, China (2002)
21. Langendorf, D.J.: Textware Solution's Fitaly Keyboard V1.0 Easing the Burden of Keyboard Input. In: WinCELair Review (1988)
22. Leemans, N.E.M.P.: VIL, A Visual Inter Lingua. In: Doctoral Dissertation, Worcester Polytechnic Institute, USA (2001)
23. Littlejohn, S.W.: Theories of Human Communication. 5th edn. Wadsworth (1996)
24. MacKenzie, I.S., Soukoreff, R.W.: Text Entry for Mobile Computing: Models and Methods, Theory and Practice. Human-Computer Interaction 17, 147–198 (2002)
25. MacKenzie, I.S., Zhang, S.X.: The Design and Evaluation of a High-Performance Soft Keyboard. In: ACM CHI, pp. 25–31. ACM, New York (1999)
26. Mealing, S., Yazdabi, M.: Communicating Through Pictures. In: Department of Computer Science, University of Exeter, England (1992)
27. Perlovsky, L.I.: Emotions, Learning and Control. In: International Symposium: Intelligent Control, Intelligent Systems and Semiotic, pp. 131–137 (1999)
28. Smith, P.: Toward a Practical Measure of Hypertext Usability. Interacting with Computers, Elsevier Science Ltd B.V. 8(4), 365–381 (1996)
29. Schneiderman, B.: Designing the User Interface: Strategies for Effective Human-Computer Interaction, 2nd edn. Addison-Wesley Publishing, London (1992)
30. Tatomir, B., Rothkrantz, L.J.M.: Intelligent System for Exploring Dynamic Crisis Environments. In: Van de Walle, B., Turoff, M. (eds.) ISCRAM'06. NJ, SA (2006)
31. Tegic Communication, T9. (1998), http://www.t9.com/faq.html
32. W3C, OWL: Ontology Web Language, http://www.w3.org/TR/owlguide
33. Ward, D.A., Blackwell, A., MacKay, D.: Dasher – a Data Entry Interface Using Continuous Gesture and Language Models. In: UIST'00, pp. 129–136 (2000)
34. Zhai, S., Hunter, M., Smith, B.A.: The Metropolis Keyboard - An Exploration of Quantitative Techniques for Virtual Keyboard Design. In: ACM UIST, pp. 119–128. ACM, NY (2000)

ICT for Low-Literate Youth in Ethiopia: The Usability Challenge

Marije Geldof

Royal Holloway, University of London, Egham, Surrey TW20 0EX, UK

Abstract. How much can you do with a computer if you are not able to read or write like many people in Africa? This paper discusses the preliminary outcomes of a study into how Information and Communication Technology (ICT) can be made more usable for low-literate youth in Africa and help to empower their lives. It is based on fieldwork undertaken in Ethiopia in 2006 and 2007 and focuses especially on the challenges associated with designing and implementing such fieldwork, as well as some preliminary results.

1 Introduction

It is immensely challenging to enhance the basic education, literacy and livelihood of poor people. In January 2002, the United Nations General Assembly proclaimed 2003-2012 to be the United Nations Literacy Decade in which the commitment was made to achieve a 50% improvement in adult literacy by 2005, given that there are 860 million illiterate adults in the world.

But what does it mean to be literate in a world fundamentally transformed by technology? In the past the concept of literacy was primarily defined in terms of people's abilities to read and write, but with the emergence of new technologies it has come to encompass a broader range of human competencies needed to access and manage information, analyze and interpret this information, critically evaluate its relevance and credibility and use information to solve everyday problems [1].

More importantly, what impact does a lack of literacy skills, such as reading and writing, have on the use of ICTs? In order to be used, many ICTs require their users to have certain literacy skills. Poor and marginalized people in developing countries often lack these skills and are therefore not able to benefit fully from ICT, one of the reasons for the so-called "digital divide". The lack of literacy skills is often considered to be at the heart of this problem and therefore eradicating illiteracy is seen as the key remedy - in other words transforming people to fit the technology. However, another way to approach this problem is to determine how the technology can be made to fit this specific user group – in other words developing ICTs that can easily be used without literacy skills.

In order to fit technology to a specific user group and make a positive contribution to their lives, it is critically important to have a clear understanding of the abilities and needs of this group. It needs to be explored who the users are, what their daily lives look like, the kind of skills they already possess, the skills they would like to acquire, the knowledge they already have about ICT and how these could potentially

N. Aykin (Ed.): Usability and Internationalization, Part II, HCII 2007, LNCS 4560, pp. 67–76, 2007.

contribute to their lives. This paper is about shaping a methodology to obtain such an understanding, with the ultimate aim of identifying optimal ways in which ICT can contribute to empowering low-literate youth in Africa. It forms the first part of a comparative study between two countries, focusing in this instance on the design and implementation of the initial field survey in Ethiopia.

2   Interaction Design and Literacy Context

Both in designing computer-based interactive systems in the field of Human-Computer Interaction and in designing other interactive devices in the field of Interaction Design, there is a considerable concern regarding the usability of the final result; whether people can use them efficiently, effectively, safely and with satisfaction. Therefore prospective users should be carefully taken into consideration in the design process, such as who will be using the device and where it will be used. In addition to this it is vital to understand the kind of activities people are doing when interacting with the device.

Identifying user needs is not simply a matter of asking people "what do you need?" and then supplying it, because people do not necessarily know what is possible. Instead it is a matter of trying to translate who the users are, what they are doing and why they are doing it into possible innovation [2]. Moreover the design should be relevant and appropriate for the user cultures and languages [3]. Nonetheless up to now HCI research has mainly been Western dominated and limited to culturally homogeneous populations [4]. Knowledge about the usability of technologies for people in developing countries is still scarce. But technology development efforts in developing countries are likely to fail for the same reason products fail in markets anywhere: lack of awareness of what user needs really are, the failure to develop products that meet those needs and to continue relevant product support.

It is not only technological development which requires greater awareness of user needs, there are many examples of literacy campaigns that have failed because they were not functionally appropriate to the needs of the people [5]. As with HCI research, studies of literacy acquisition are heavily Western dominated and surprisingly little research has been undertaken in developing countries [6]. Many "literacy experts" and planners are often making assumptions about the needs and desires of future learners that may not be correct or appropriate. Local meanings and use of communicative and literacy practices may require alternative approaches in the design of literacy programs than those that may appear 'obvious' from outside. Therefore also in developing literacy programs, the first step should be talking and listening to people in order to find out what the needs are [7].

But what is literacy? For more than half a century the definition of literacy and how to measure it has been debated without much agreement being reached. Regardless of the definition used, in all cases literacy needs a social context from which to derive its existence and at the same time literacy itself has implications for its social context. In other words someone's level of illiteracy is the extent to which this person falls short of the demands for literacy current in his or her society [8].

At the same time the concept has not remained untouched by the quirks of new technologies. The use of ICT is currently transforming the literacy practices of people in many countries around the world and literacy and technology are more and more becoming interdependent [1]. With the new possibilities offered by ICT, a broader understanding of the concept of literacy that goes beyond the traditionally limited concept of functional reading and writing has become necessary [9]. Literacy in the digital age, among other things, means the ability to comprehend and critically analyze all that is read, viewed and listened to, engaging with the many forms of receptive and expressive symbol systems of the various multimedia sources, whereupon making rational decisions in the context of one's personal life [3]. Text, visual representations and sound are combined to give a new understanding to what it means to be literate.

When literacy and technology are becoming more and more interdependent, it is pertinent to ask what this means for all those lacking the traditional literacy skills such as reading and writing (in this research indicated as "low-literate"), something that is very common in developing countries. If they are not able to use ICT that has so far mainly been developed for industrialized countries, they might even get further behind. Therefore possibilities should be explored to design technologies that support people in their everyday and working lives, but do not require "traditional" literacy skills to use them. Progress in Artificial Intelligence is already making interaction with computers easier and more 'natural', which creates the potential opportunity for people with minimal reading and writing skills to some day be able to send and receive complex "written" communication via computers with only minimal input (possibly through voice commands) from their side [10].

3 Methodological Challenges

Worldwide Africa has the highest number of people lacking literacy skills, which was the most important reason why this continent was chosen as a research focus. Moreover because young people are the users of the future, the research particularly focuses on young people between the age of 10 and 20 years old. To obtain an understanding of the abilities and needs of this specific user group of low-literate youth in Africa, a three month field study was undertaken in two different parts of Ethiopia in late 2006 and early 2007. Young people participated in a combination of qualitative research methods, first in collaboration with Forum on Street Children Ethiopia (FSCE) in the urban setting of Nazret and then with the help of Action for Health, Education and Development (AHEAD) in the rural setting of Shakisso. Because research methods that require literacy skills, such as questionnaires, are not suitable for people without good literacy skills, a consideration had to be made what methods best to use. Three methods were eventually chosen: 153 semi-structured interviews and 18 focus groups with 6 participants each were held and 32 participants interacted with a digital camera. Five main challenges that are discussed in this paragraph were of particular significance in developing this study: sampling, answering behavior, visual representations, translation and the research setting.

3.1 Sampling

An initial challenge of this research was finding and selecting the proposed user group: low-literate youth in Africa. A first step in this direction was choosing Ethiopia as the country to undertake the field study. The EFA Global monitoring report 2006 [11] estimates a youth (15-24) illiteracy rate of 42.6% in Ethiopia. However the percentage of low-literacy is even higher than this, because these statistics still contain a number of people who are considered literate, but whose literacy skills are very limited. This means that by random selection in Ethiopia, the chances of selecting an individual with limited literacy skills are already quite high. Because subjecting participants to a reading and writing test before participation was ethically unfeasible, other strategies were used to ensure that low-literacy would likely be high among the selected participants. For example by working with street children who were less likely to have had good education and accessing participants in the lowest grades of schools, the chances were considerably increased.

Another challenge was selecting individuals in the targeted age range (10-20) of the research. Some individuals who were very eager to participate would adjust their age in the hope to be selected. Participants in rural areas often did not know their exact age and would just mention the guess from their parents or an age similar to their peers. Moreover particularly rural women were very reluctant to expose their real age (for reasons of preferable marriage age) and would preferably subtract a few years. In the rural setting this resulted in an accumulation of participants who stated to be around 15 and a low number stating to be over 16. This unreliability of the age range needs to be taken into account in any more quantitative analysis of the data.

A limitation of the selection methods used in this research was that it was somewhat biased towards certain subgroups and did not necessarily reflect the whole range of low-literate youth. In Nazret most participants were attached to Forum on Street Children Ethiopia that is running an ICT program. Because of that most of the participants were familiar with computers something that was not representative for most people of their age. In Shakisso, accessing participants via the primary school enabled the selection from lower grades, making low-literacy skills more likely, but on the other hand this approach excluded all those who were not enrolled in school and might have a very different profile. Therefore some street boys were also included in the research, but it was difficult to gain access to out-of-school girls who were usually involved in all of the household activities they have to fulfill.

3.2 Answering Behavior

One general observation was that, instead of trying to come up with something new, if they would get the chance most participants preferred to copy something already existing in their answers. Therefore it is not surprising that participants were struggling with questions that required creative thinking, such as inventing a new machine. For this reason, both in the interviews and focus groups, the researcher had to be very careful with clarifying questions with examples, because the participants were then likely to give the example or something related to it as their answer.

More importantly this behavior had a significant impact on the focus group dynamics. It was not uncommon that once the most talkative person from the group had answered, five identical answers would follow, even if the given answer did not make much sense. Therefore undertaking six individual interviews generally resulted in much more interesting and various data than if one focus group with the same six participants would have been undertaken. Although the focus groups nevertheless resulted in very interesting data, for example about gender inequality, in countries where there is a tendency to conformity focus groups require careful consideration and planning to prevent the group from conforming to the talkative group members.

3.3 Visual Representations

Singhal and Rattine-Flaherty [12] argue that pencil sketches and photos represent important tools for communication research and praxis, providing rich, descriptive insights into local worldviews and realities, as well as providing an alternative to 'textocentrism' – the privileging of text, writing and the lettered word as a mode of comprehension and expression. When working with people with low-literacy skills this truth may be of even greater consequence. Therefore in this field study an attempt was made to, apart from verbal interaction, include ways of visual representation.

First of all, in the interviews a set of cards depicting different ICTs was used to find out which of the technologies participants were familiar with and how they favored them. In practice the cards turned out to also be of great value throughout the remainder of the interview. Because participants had more difficulty answering questions in which they had to come up with something new than answering questions that addressed something concrete, referring to the pictures on the cards made it easier for the participant to imagine and greatly improved their responses.

Secondly, at the beginning of each focus group participants were asked to draw a visual representation in order to discuss the drawings in the group. Almost all participants, with the exception of those did not know how to hold a pencil, because they had never been to school, were able to express themselves in terms of drawings. Because coming up with something themselves was again a challenge, similar drawings produced in one focus group were not uncommon. Starting the focus groups with a drawing exercise turned out to be a good way for the participants to loosen up a bit before the real discussion started.

Finally some participants were invited to work with a digital camera and take pictures in the nearby environment. Participants were given a very short instruction about the functionality of the camera and would then be left to take pictures in the way they wanted. Usually participants easily grasped how to operate the camera and also stated afterwards that they did not experience any problems in using the camera. Not only did participants express their appreciation for being able to immediately watch the pictures on the screen, this functionality also gave them direct feedback about taking pictures, which accelerated the learning curve. Pictures, in which the head of someone was cut of, were usually immediately redone.

Ideally participants would be asked to capture things in terms of pictures instead of a verbal explanation to a question as also Singhal & Rattine-Flaherty [12] did, but in this field study this turned out to be difficult. Because a digital camera is a valuable object in a country like Ethiopia, particularly in the urban area there was a too high risk in letting participants just move around wherever they wanted. In the more rural areas the safety of the camera was less of an issue and participants could sometimes visit their nearby home environments and returned with very interesting collections of photographs. Despite precautions taken still an attempt was made to steal the camera in which a male participant was attacked by a group of boys. They failed in their attempt, but the camera got slightly damaged.

3.4 Translation

One of the challenges of undertaking the field study in Ethiopia is also of great importance in terms of usability, namely linguistics. In Ethiopia at least 70 different languages are spoken and Amharic, the official language, is only spoken by 30% of the people. In the urban Nazret, where Amharic is the dominant language, an Amharic translator was sufficient, but in the rural Shakisso the linguistic situation was more complicated. Although Oromic is the mother tongue of most people, Amharic is usually spoken in the streets and therefore there are many bilingual people in town. At the same time people only speaking Amharic or Oromic can be found and occasionally even people only speaking one of the other languages. Therefore a bilingual translator proficient in both Amharic and Oromic was required.

Getting a good translator turned out to be quite a challenge. In the urban area there were enough people speaking some English and interested in earning money, but in many cases their English was adequate for conversations but too poor for research purposes. An extra complication in the rural area was that apart from the need for a bilingual translator in Amharic and Oromic, the level of English in such areas is less advanced than in urban areas, limiting the choice for potential translators to well educated people who usually already have a fulltime job.

In addition to language proficiency, the translator's attempts to interpret what was said instead of providing a direct translation had a significant impact on both the interviews and focus groups. This was especially apparent when the translators made assumptions regarding participant's answers and asked questions on their own initiative. Particularly "interpreters" with limited knowledge about the possibilities of ICT can be very restrictive for the research and require an alert researcher.

Finally age and gender need to be taken in consideration in choosing a translator. In a culture where respect for older people is very important, the age of a translator may have significant influence on the responses of young participants. Apart from that, the gender of a translator can also impact the responsiveness of participants; as one female participant expressed how she felt uncomfortable about expressing herself freely in presence of the male translator.

3.5 Research Setting

In order for participants to express themselves freely the chosen research setting is very important. Even though the research was usually undertaken around a school environment, a quiet place in the surroundings would be sought and the interviews or focus groups were undertaken informally sitting on the ground. Getting and keeping this environment where participants could feel free was often a significant challenge. Willing school directors would ask whether they had to select the best students of the school to participate, instruct the participants not to fail in the research and bring comfortable chairs just for the researcher and translator, assuming that the participant could simply sit on the floor. More disturbing however, were all the curious and persistent people interested to observe and communicate with the white researcher. When they would get the chance they would approach the research setting or call from a distance, continuously disturbing the research in progress. Even when hidden somewhere in the bushes the research setting would always be found and then disturbed. Only when the presence of the white researcher became more normal after a while, the curiosity and the disturbance it provoked slowly faded.

4 Preliminary Results

Although the data from the field study still requires detailed analysis, there are already some clear patterns and observations that will be discussed in this paragraph.

1. There was a clear difference observable between the urban and the rural areas regarding familiarity with the technologies and use within the home. Even in the rural area there was a clearly observable difference between those living in the town and those living in nearby villages. ICT clearly does not have that much impact yet in rural environments as it has in the more urban area.
2. Currently the biggest contribution of ICT to people's lives is the ability to communicate with others over a distance and to provide information, for example about the country and the situation in the world. News broadcasts were often mentioned to provide information about disputes in the country, enabling people to move to safer places if necessary. Some participants explained how they preferred television over radio or tape, because television presents things audiovisually, whereas radio and tape can only be listened to.
3. Of all the ICTs the mobile phone was the device that was the most widespread and popular. Even in rural areas without electricity that are covered by a mobile network there are people who possess mobile phones, enabling them to contact people at a distance without traveling on foot. Interestingly, particularly in the rural areas many participants made reference to male relatives or other men when talking about mobile phones, which indicated that mobile phones are usually possessed and used by men rather than by women. In addition to enabling contact with relatives and friends, a very common answer was to use the mobile phone in emergency situations to call for help or to report the death of a relative.
4. Several participants who recognized the computer correctly ranked it quite high in their preference even though from their answers it was clear they had little knowledge about what it could actually be used for. They explained either that they had heard from others that a computer is something useful, that it can be used for educational purposes or that being able to use it can increase job prospects.
5. Technology was often perceived as something only to be used by educated people, because uneducated people are likely to damage it. Not only uneducated people, but also children seemed to be potential damagers of ICTs, a significant concern for parents, often resulting in children being forbidden to touch the devices. Thus even with exposure to technologies at home, many children have never operated any of them, or perhaps have only done so in secret without parental knowledge. As one of the participants remarked after he was given the digital camera "my heart started beating, because here people never give such things to children".

6. In addition to being educated, knowledge of English was often mentioned as a requirement for ICT use. Most technologies in one way or another require the ability to read in English, whether in reading the texts printed on the technology itself, being able to read the manual or the menus of, for example, the mobile phone or computer. So far there is little use of any of the Ethiopian languages with the technologies, not even the national language Amharic. Something explicitly mentioned by some of the participants as a point for improvement.

7. Several participants complained about the sustainability of ICTs. They explained how the technology market is saturated with fake versions of famous technology brands that usually break down very easily. Knowing that most of the technologies cost many people the equivalent of several months' salary their disappointment is quite understandable. The earlier discussed parental caution about children using the technologies might also be prompted by their financial circumstances rather than general unwillingness.

8. Reading and writing were among other things perceived as useful for education, for obtaining new knowledge, to write and read messages to relatives and friends and for better job opportunities. In addition it enables the possibility of secret written communication without requiring the help with reading and writing that would expose the secret to others.

9. Most participants had a tendency to copy what other people said and found it difficult to come up with new ideas. Because of this, questions about improvements to existing technologies and new inventions for the future were often too challenging. Also regarding ambitions for the future other than doctor, teacher or pilot, not many professions were aspired. As one participant responded "I actually never thought about this before". Particularly in the rural area the biggest talent of children was obeying their parents (as revealed in one focus group, disobedience is followed by physical punishment) and following their instructions. Children did not seem to be encouraged by their parents to make their own choices or to be asked for their ideas, but are taught to conform themselves to their parents will, perhaps a significant reason behind the children's limited ability to think in an innovative manner.

10. Particularly in rural areas people in daily life people are exposed less to impulses than in developed countries, which might be another reason for the limited ability to think in an innovative manner. The daily activities mentioned by participants in the rural areas are mainly focused around farming and household tasks, such as cleaning, cooking, fetching water, collecting firewood and looking after the cattle. The majority of new impulses these people are facing are actually coming from ICTs such as radio and television. Nowadays even in a small rural town in Ethiopia most people are familiar with Arsenal and Manchester United and there are people understanding Hindi who are translating Bollywood movies.

5 Usability Challenges Ahead

Data from this field study still need to be analyzed in more detail, but already five main preliminary recommendations can be made about developing usable technologies for low-literate youth in Ethiopia. Further work needs to be undertaken to see whether these are generalisable across Africa, and the second stage of this research will be to replicate the methodology in a different African context

Verbal communication and communication by means of visual representations did not cause any problems for the participants, regardless of their proficiency with literacy skills. Therefore designing ICT in such a way that they only use audiovisual representations is likely to improve usability for people with low-literacy skills.

In the Ethiopian education system there is not much attention for the individual learners, leaving particularly those with learning disabilities or other problems such as hearing or sight impairments behind. For example tall students with hearing impairments were found in the back of the classroom and students whose mother tongue is different from the teaching language already spent three years in school without understanding anything of what the teacher was saying. The rise of new technologies opens up many new opportunities for people with special needs. A well-designed educational system in the future will be one in which no two students follow the exact same route through the learning experience. In other words, there must be enough alternative routes so that learners will be able to find the support they need to master the content [3]. Therefore big gains can be made with educational technologies targeting those that remain unnoticed in the current education system.

Something that was often mentioned as a disadvantage in the rural context was the lack of electricity that is limiting the possibility of ICT use. Currently mainly things running on batteries like tape recorders, as well as mobile phones were being used in the countryside. Therefore developing technologies that run on alternative energies such as solar power could probably create a high demand in rural areas. Also in places with electricity people might favor these technologies, because they do not need to be plugged into a socket, decreasing the risk of electric shock that was a common complaint about ICT.

Further high prices of ICT were a common complaint which is not that surprising in a poor country like Ethiopia, where several technologies are more expensive than in Europe. At the same time because many of the technologies turn out to be not very sustainable, they can be a big burden for people who have invested several monthly salaries for the purchase. Designing technologies that are more break proof and have a higher life expectancy can therefore greatly improve the potential of ICT. Although it remains to be seen how people can distinguish them from the fake versions that will probably continue to exist.

Finally the linguistic diversity in a country like Ethiopia will inevitably ask for consideration in future designs. Currently most technologies are still dominated by English, disadvantaging those who do not master this language. Perhaps one day it will be possible for everyone in Ethiopia to operate their mobile phone in their mother tongue.

6   Conclusion

In order to get a good understanding of potential low-literate technology users in developing countries there is still a lot to be overcome and many challenges to be faced. As this research shows several issues such sampling strategy, visual representations, translation, answering behavior and research setting, need to be taken into account in designing and implementing the methodology. In addition to this, several cultural habits, the researcher might initially not be aware of, further influence the methodology.

ICT is already empowering the lives of low-literate youth in Ethiopia by providing information and means of communication for example through radio and telephone. It has the potential to do even more so in the future, for example through cheap, sustainable and audiovisual interactive devices. This will however require thoughtful design and consideration of how ICT can make a positive change in their lives.

Acknowledgements. This work was supported by Microsoft Research through its European PhD Scholarship Programme.

References

1. Wagner, D.A., Kozma, R.: New Technologies for Literacy and Adult Education: a global perspective. In: UNESCO, Paris (2005)
2. Preece, J., Rogers, Y., Sharp, H.: Interaction design – beyond human-computer interaction. In: Inc. John Wiley & Sons, New York (2002)
3. Withrow, F.B.: Literacy in the digital age: Reading, writing, viewing and computing, ScareCrow Press (2004)
4. Day, D.L.: Shared values and shared interfaces: The role of culture in the globalization of human-computer systems. Interacting with Computers 9(3), 269–274 (1998)
5. Downing, J.: Comparative perspectives on world literacy. In: Wagner, D. (ed.) The Future of Literacy in a Changing World, pp. 29–54. World Hampton Press (1999)
6. Wagner, D.A. (ed.): The Future of Literacy in a Changing, World Hampton Press (1999)
7. Street, B. (ed.): Literacy and development. In: Ethnographic perspectives, Routledge (2001)
8. Lewis, M.M.: The Importance of Illiteracy, George G. Harrap & Co, London (1953)
9. Wagner, D.: IT and Education for the Poorest of the Poor: Constraints, Possibilities and Principals. In: Technologia, pp. 48–50 (July/August 2001)
10. Raskin, V.: Naturalizing the Computer: English Online. In: Tuman, M.C. (ed.) Literacy online: The Promise (and Peril) of Reading and Writing with Computers, pp. 189–210. University of Pittsburgh Press (1992)
11. EFA Global monitoring report: Literacy for life. In: UNESCO, Paris (2005)
12. Singhal, A., Rattine-Flaherty, E.: Pencils and photos as tools of communicative research and praxis. International Communication Gazette 68(4), 313–330 (2006)

Design for Facilitating eBay Transactions Using Skype

Frank Y. Guo and Sulekha Nair

2145 Hamilton Ave, San Jose, CA 95129, USA
{fguo,sulnair}@ebay.com

Abstract. eBay has integrated Skype (a public voice over IP application) chat
and voice into hundreds of categories on eBay sites globally. By integrating
Skype in the marketplace, eBay sellers have the option of including Skype
functionality to their eBay listings. This fosters more consumer to consumer
(c2c) communication, in which eBay sellers can provide better customer care
and build trust with buyers by answering questions quickly. Buyers also feel
more confident to ask for details and get answers using chat or call, without
waiting for email responses. Challenges and design solutions regarding trust
and safety, building credibility, co-branding, and designing for global eBay
communities are discussed.

Keywords: VoIP, eCommerce, trust and safety, cross-cultural design, online
communication, user experience.

Disclaimer. The views expressed herein are those of the author and do not
necessarily reflect those of eBay Inc. or its subsidiaries, management, or
employees.

1 Introduction

Enabling efficient transaction and establishing integrated community are two
cornerstones underlying the success of consumer-to-consumer (c2c) ecommerce. The
lack of real-time communication, however, undermines the success with the two
aspects. Relative to brick-and-mortar stores, the lack of real-time communication is a
problem with ecommerce in general. Furthermore, it is a more prominent problem
with the c2c ecommerce model than with the business-to-consumer (b2c) ecommerce
model. This is primarily due to the trust and safety issue and the irregular inventory
issue that are inherent in c2c. Customer service has been shown by research to be an
important factor for online trust [1]. On eBay, buyers are sometimes concerned with
whether the seller is trustworthy and have questions about specifications of the item
that they are interested in (e.g., whether the item is brand new or used). Improving
seller customer service by incorporating real-teim communication will improve buyer
trust. Real-time communication is especially important for some categories that are
key contributors to eBay's business, such as the used cars category and the
collectibles category, where the trust and safety issue and the irregular inventory issue
are particularly pronounced. Currently, eBay buyers can use the "Ask Seller a
Question" feature to email sellers questions, but are unable to communicate with
sellers in a real-time manner. In addition, enabling real-time interaction allows for a

N. Aykin (Ed.): Usability and Internationalization, Part II, HCII 2007, LNCS 4560, pp. 77–83, 2007.
© Springer-Verlag Berlin Heidelberg 2007

greater sense of community, which leads to a consolidated customer base and is an important factor underlying eBay's success.

Globalization of ecommerce is another factor calling for the integration of real-time communication into ecommerce platforms. Some cultures (e.g., East Asian cultures) place great emphasis on substantial interpersonal interaction during transaction [2, 3, 4]. For example, the traditional Chinese way of transaction is characterized by "Tao Jia Huan Jia", which in Mandarin means bargaining. Whereas bargaining is no stranger to western consumers, it is one of the defining features of the Asian business culture. Trust and safety issues also underlie the need for real-time communication capability. In some developing countries, trust and safety issue, when coupled with the relatively immature ecommerce in those countries, becomes a more important problem relative to the United States. In addition, because many Asian cultures are not used to the "flea market" or "swap-n-meet" concepts that are familiar to Western consumers, nor are they familiar with auction, which has existed in the west for many centuries, buyers in those cultures need additional explanation and facilitation from sellers who sell used goods via online auction. Adding real-time capability to buyer-seller communication addresses these issues of global transaction.

On September 12, 2005, eBay purchased Skype, an EU-based company that developed popular VoIP software that enables people to make free voice calls over the Internet in real-time to other Skype users anywhere in the world. Skype also allows people to send instant text messages and make free video calls over the internet. Integrating Skype into eBay marketplace is a natural step for eBay in order to strengthen its c2c business model. The Skype project was developed with both eBay buyers and sellers in mind. For buyers, this helps facilitate a smooth and trustworthy transaction experience by efficiently communicating with sellers. For sellers, having the flexibility of real-time communication enhances their customer relationship management (CRM), which can in turn help reduce transaction friction. eBay also benefits from reduced friction on it's marketplaces via improved transaction velocity. The role of Skype is especially important for categories that involve a lot of interpersonal interaction, such as vehicles and other expensive items.

2   The Design

A coordinated effort of a group of eBay UI designers, product mangers, and creative designers was launched during the first half of 2006 to integrate Skype into eBay experience. The centerpiece of the project was implementing a series of buttons on eBay listings (i.e., items listed to sell), by which buyers can contact sellers using Skype. To realize this, the project involved UI changes on the buyer side as well as on the seller side. In this section, we will first describe the overall design, followed by specific design challenges and design solutions for these challenges.

2.1   Overall Design

The adoption of Skype starts with sellers. When sellers list their items, they will be prompted to specify whether they would like to offer Skype to buyers as a means to contact them. If a seller does not have Skype installed on the computer, he or she will be prompted to install Skype (see Figure 1). Once the seller has installed Skype and

Fig. 1. The page that prompts the seller to use Skype to facilitate transaction. This page appears after the item has been listed on eBay.

Fig. 2. The View Item page for an item listed by a seller who offers Skype as a means for communication – *before* the buyer installs Skype on computer

offered Skype as a means for buyers to contact him or her, the SkypeMe buttons will show up on the listings. On the buyer side, when the buyer visits the View Item page, the page where details of an item are presented, the buyer will be prompted to install Skype if the seller offers Skype for the listing (see Figure 2). Once Skype is installed, the buyer should go back to the listing to complete the transaction. The listing now

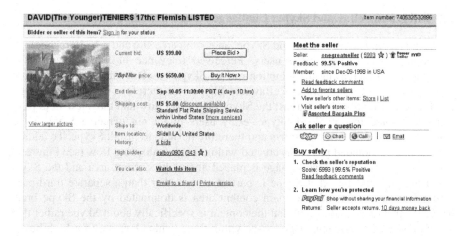

Fig. 3. The View Item page for an item listed by a seller who offers Skype as a means for communication – *after* the buyer has installed Skype on computer

has the SkypeMe buttons (see Figure 3), which allows the buyer to either call (using the Call button) or instant message (using the Chat button) the seller.

2.2 Preventing Frauds

Because Skype still exists as a separate service with its own registration, using the loophole created by the separation between the eBay and Skype registrations, there was concern that fraudulent acts could potentially be performed over Skype communication between buyers and sellers. For instance, a seller might use the eBay user name of a reputable seller during a Skype call with a buyer, and therefore is able to sell more items to buyers benefiting from the borrowed eBay identity. In order to prevent such frauds, we decided to require sellers to link their Skype names to their eBay accounts. When sellers first install Skype as part of a listing, they need to complete two actions, one is to install and register on Skype, the other is to link their Skype names to their eBay accounts. For this purpose, a message reminding sellers of the necessity of linking accounts is shown to sellers when they create the listing.

Fig. 4. This is the message reminding the seller to link his or her Skype name to eBay account

2.3 Integrating eBay and Skype: Challenge from a Branding Perspective

The relationship between eBay and Skype, an ecommerce site and a VoIP technology, is not apparent to most eBay users. Perceived relevance of the two entities is instrumental in increasing the adoption rate of Skype on eBay and creating coherent user experience. Co-branding of eBay and Skype was therefore implemented in the UI. This effort involved two areas: the Skype download flow and the View Item page. When prompted to download Skype, eBay users might not perceive Skype as an integrated part of the eBay platform and therefore hesitate to install Skype. To address this issue, a co-branded page was created within the downloading flow (see Figure 5). On this page, the eBay brand image is placed above the content area and the Skype brand image, indicating that Skype is part of eBay rather than a separate third-party entity. On the other hand, the main content area is dominated by the Skype brand image, so that users understand that the content is specifically about Skype rather than about eBay in general. This page exists within the downloading flow for both buyers and sellers.

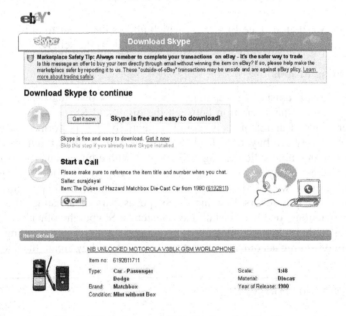

Fig. 5. This is A page within the downloading flow

The other area related to co-branding is the View Item page (see Figure 3). To create coherent visual representation, the Skype elements (i.e., the Skype button, the Chat button, and the Call button) were designed to have consistent look and feel as the rest of the page. For instance, blue is used as the color scheme for both the Skype and PayPal elements. The Skype icon is made of similar size of the PayPal icon, suggesting that the two are equally important subsidiaries of eBay.

2.4 Preventing Possible Loss of Business

Providing efficient communication tools to buyers and sellers might inadvertently create a loophole in transaction: the buyer and the seller reach an agreement to do transaction outside eBay, so that the seller does not need to pay eBay the obligatory seller fee. To discourage this behavior, when the buyer downloads and installs Skype, a message displayed on one of the downloading pages warns the buyer potential risks involved in off-eBay transaction (see Figure 5). In addition, because the installation of Skype on the buyer's computer is completed on the Skype site rather than the eBay site, buyers might accidentally forget to come back to eBay to finish the transaction. This message reduces the chance that the buyer forgets to complete the transaction and prevents possible loss of business due to the installation process.

2.5 Designing for the International eBay Community

With a global c2c model, eBay has international sites across the world, with UI customized to local contexts. The implementation of the SkypeMe buttons, as an integrated part of the local UI, is also localized. For instance, due to the unique look and feel of Chinese characters, the SkypeMe buttons on eBay Taiwan use different font and background color (compare Figure 6 with Figure 3) in order to enhance readability and visual appeal of the buttons. In addition, in the line below the SkypeMe buttons, number of questions and answers exchanged between the buyer and the seller is enclosed in the parentheses. By giving the buyer additional information regarding the communication, this potentially helps alleviate the relatively more severe trust and safety issue in Taiwan.

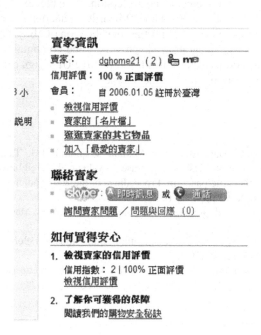

Fig. 6. The SkypeMe buttons on eBay Taiwan site

Many eBay users engage in cross-border trading. When users across two different time zones try to engage in real-time communication, both parties are not usually readily available due to misaligned schedules. Skype's off-line asynchronous communication capability addresses this issue. Skype can store the instant messages on a server, which can be read by the other party once he or she comes online.

3 Discussion

This project is among first attempts to solve the design challenge of integrating a VoIP tool and an eCommerce platform, two very distinct online platforms. The challenge came from both user experience and business considerations. In terms of user experience, we created consistent look and feel across eBay and Skype and integrated Skype downloading flows. In terms of business, we addressed numerous trust and safety issues and attempted to prevent users from accidentally dropping out of transaction after downloading Skype. Due to technical limitations, some issues have yet to be addressed in the design. For instance, the current platform is unable to pass item ID and description to the seller, so the seller does not know which item a Skype call is about. The buyer needs to specify which item he or she refers to during the Skype conversation with the seller. Future design effort should be made to address this issue.

Significance of this project can also be evaluated against the backdrop of the emerging trend of social networking. People increasingly look for a sense of community when engaging one another in the virtual space. This trend is impacting every aspect of online behavior, and eCommerce is no exception. Notable examples of this trend include MySpace, Craigslist, and YouTube. Primarily an auction site operating on a c2c model, community building is critical for the consolidation of eBay's customer base and expansion of business. By integrating Skype's real-time communication capacity into the eBay platform, this project showcases how effective UI design can help eCommerce benefit from a major emerging trend of the internet age.

References

1. Fogg, B.J., Soohoo, C., Danielson, D.R., Marable, L., Stanford, J., Tauber, E.R.: Focusing on user-to-product relationships: How do users evaluate the credibility of Web sites?: a study with over 2,500 participants. In: Proceedings of the 2003 conference on Designing for user experiences DUX '03 pp. 1–15 (2003)
2. Hofstede, G.: Cultures and Organizations: Software of the Mind. McGraw-Hill, New York (1997)
3. Marcus, A., Gould, E.M.: Crosscurrents: cultural dimensions and global Web user-interface design. Interactions 7, 32–46 (2000)
4. Nielsen, J. (ed.): Designing User Interfaces for International Use (Advances in Human Factors/Ergonomics, 13). Elsevier Science Ltd. New York

Localization in Korea of User Interface of the 3G Mobile Handset Built on Open OS

Sungmoo Hong

KTF, 7-18 Shinchondong, Songpagu, Seoul, Korea
sungmoo@ktf.com

Abstract. In order to minimize Korean users' conflict as they use global brand 3G handsets which are built on open OS, Symbian of Nokia and Windows Mobile of Microsoft, the research was operated by KTF, Korean mobile telecommunication company. To figure out the difference between ordinary mobile handsets and 3G open OS handsets, major European handsets and major Korean handsets were observed. According to the result of research the requirements for the handsets were established including key pad layout and key functions, information architecture of native menu, labels and input method of Korean language, and other user scenarios for main services like messaging.

Keywords: Localization, Mobile User Interface, Open OS Mobile Handset.

1 Background

1.1 Mobile Telecommunication Industry

Telecommunication industry is known as a local industry particularly in Korea where the world first CDMA service was commercialized. The Korean operators have been supplied mobile handsets for their customers by native handset venders. Besides several foreign manufacturers have been participated in Korean market, their market share is very low; handset business of Nokia had been withdrawn in 2003 after their 1.5 year-effort. After recent launch of WCDMA service by 2 major operators in Korea, SKT and KTF in August 2006, the condition of Korean mobile handset market is gradually changing, especially to the global handset venders which already had globally launched many UMTS - WCDMA devices who hope to sell their products to Korean operators.

1.2 Smartphone Industry

There have been little opportunities in Korea for manufacturers of PDA and smart phone because Korean users did not prefer these devices. As the difference among normal handsets, smart phones and PDA devices is being obscure and their size is getting smaller, customers pay attention to the featured phones. Additionally regarding the entrance of Koran operators into global industry by launching WCDMA

N. Aykin (Ed.): Usability and Internationalization, Part II, HCII 2007, LNCS 4560, pp. 84–90, 2007.
© Springer-Verlag Berlin Heidelberg 2007

service, both Korean operators and customers came to have global resources of mobile handsets.

1.3 User Interface

By communicating with customers for 20 years, Korean handset manufacturers set several tacit standards of user interface including key pad layout, access gate of wireless internet, etc. If KTF decided to commercialize global devices in Korea, it becomes necessary for KTF that make every effort to prevent the conflict between user experience from Korean tacit standards of UI and that from global devices.

2 Purposes and Process

The research was operated in order to minimize the Korean customers' confusion as they use the smart phones of foreign manufacturers: The specific purpose of research was to establish the requirements of KTF for the 3G handsets built on open OS, especially NOKIA Symbian handsets and Microsoft Windows Mobile handsets supporting WCDMA network regarding world wide market share.

2.1 Finding Out Facts Below

- What are the tacit standards of mobile handset UIs in Korea?
- Whose properties are those standards? Operating system companies, handset venders or operators?
- To whom KTF would require to implement these UIs?

2.2 Making Strategic Decision

- To maintain user experience in these tacit standards or to make users learn new interfaces
- If to maintain, what is the essential or mandatory requirements?
- If to make user learn, what is the essential or mandatory interfaces?

2.3 Making Documents of Requirement

- Requirement of UI for OEM venders and requirement of UI for OS companies
- Requirement of UI for the main applications: messaging, browser, WIPI internet platform
- GUI guidelines and image files

2.4 Process

- Researching the cases of mixed UIs of OEM's own UI and operator's UI on the handsets built on open OS: especially 3G handsets in Europe and Japan – handsets for O2, NTT Doccomo, T-mobile and Orange

Fig. 1. Handset models

- Researching the tacit standards of manufacturer's UI, Samsung, LG, Pentech & Curitel and KTFT
- Researching the user experience by monitoring consumer site of Korean handset users
- Interviewing UI designers in KTF
- Decision Making

3 Factors

In 2006 the standard UI guideline were released to Korean handset manufacturers by SKT, the largest Korean operator. Although it was the requirement made by SKT for the customers of SKT, there were several tacit Korean standards of user interfaces; key pad layout, key function, menu labels, navigation style and information architecture etc. Most initial differences between these tacit Korean standards and the user interface of global open OS handsets are as below.

3.1 Key Layout and Function

Table 1. Key Pad Layout and Key Function of Korean Handsets and Global Open OS Handsets

Key	Korean Handsets	Open OS Handsets
Power	• Front • Same as *End* key • No Profile	• Top or side • Separated from *End* key • Profile setting e.g. flight or normal mode etc.

Table 1. (*continued*)

Back	• Same as *Cancel* key	• Only as *Back* key; no function as *Cancel* key e.g. Windows Mobile • Only as *Cancel* key in a text input box; no function as *Back* key e.g. Symbian S60
Center	• Soft key as *confirm/select* • Same as *Wireless Internet* key	• *Confirm/select* function but not as soft key • No specific dedicated service
Left/Right Soft Key	• Left soft key as *Options* • Right soft key as *Back* key	• Left soft key as *Options* and right soft key as *Cancel/Back* – Symbian S60 • Left soft key as *Cancel* and right soft key as *Options/Menu*– Windows Mobile
Side Up/Down	• *Volume* key	• Rarely found except on music featured phone
* / Long Press	• Toggle to *Etiquette mode*	• Not assigned
# / Long Press	• *Lock* or *Unlock*	• Not assigned
0 / Long Press	• *Quick Dial* • *Search* exclusively by KTF	• *Wireless Internet* key
Direct Access Key	• Several *Direct Hot Keys* for special service e.g. VOD, telematics, banking	• Rarely found except *Message* key or *Internet* Key

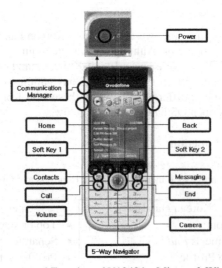

Fig. 2. Key Pad Layout and Function of V1240 by Microsoft Windows Mobile 5.0

Fig. 3. Key Pad Layout and Function of N70 by Symbian S60

3.2 Information Architecture

Table 2. Different Information Architecture of Korean Handsets and Global Open OS Handsets

Information Architecture	Korean Handsets	Open OS Handsets
Basic Architecture	• Tree structure	• Folder structure.
Menu Structure	• Service oriented	• Function oriented
Menu Layout	• Graphical, complexed and various	• Simple; list or grid
Navigation	• Arrow key to move to another menu in the same depth • C Key to go Back/Cancel/Exit	• Tab menu to another menu in the same depth • Soft key to go Back/Cancel/Exit

3.3 Application

Table 3. User Interface of Main Applications of Korean Handsets and Global Open OS Handsets

Application	Korean Handsets	Open OS Handsets
Call	• Start video call with *Video Call* button separated from voice call button	• Options in a call application; *Video* or *Voice call*

Table 3. (*continued*)

Messaging	• *SMS/MMS* application separated from *email* application; in general no *email* application	• One messaging application including *SMS, MMS* and *email*

4 Output

4.1 Consideration

The experience of Korean users, who would use both the open OS handset which has its own UI identity and also Korean normal device which is already familiar with, is seriously considered during the research. Preventing them from the errors and conflict between two different user interfaces, the cost and time which are demanded to manufacturers and OS developers by modification of user interfaces were also considered.

Table 4. Point of Consideration

User Interface	Business
• Intuitiveness to Korean users • Consistency in usability of the device and of other KTF services • Effectiveness: causing no error • Learnability for Korean users	• Importance of the feature • Supporting KTF identity

4.2 Mandatory Requirement

Table 5. Most Important Features from Mandatory Requirement

Feature	Mandatory Requirement
Power Key	• Front and same as *End Key*
Back Key	• Same as *Cancel Key*
Center Key	• Same as *Wireless Internet Key*
Side Up/Down Key	• *Volume* key
* Key / Long press	• Toggle to *Etiquette mode*
# Key / Long press	• *Lock or Unlock*
0 Key / Long press	• *Search* exclusively by KTF
Direct Access Key	• At least 2 *Direct Hot Keys* for KTF service
Menu Architecture	• Service oriented
Messaging	• *SMS/MMS* application to be separated from *email*

4.3 Output List

Final Delivered Documents

- KTF UI Requirement for Open OS 3G Handset – Nokia Symbian S60
- KTF UI Requirement for Open OS 3G Handset – Microsoft Windows Mobile 5.0

Content. Requirement of UI and GUI for OEM venders and OS companies including:

- Requirement of key pad layout and functions
- Requirement of information architecture of OEM menu
- Languages including labeling by Korean and input method of Korean language
- Scenario of main services; downloading and storing files, messaging etc.

Usability of Multilingual Communication Tools

Rieko Inaba

Language Grid Project, National Institute of Information and Communications Technology
(NICT), Kyoto 619-0289, Japan
`rieko.inaba@nict.go.jp`

Abstract. Multilingual communication tools are needed to support intercultural collaboration. I describe a tool that supports multilingual communication and propose a model of the tool in which usability subjects are extracted using empirically evaluated rules.

1 Introduction

The opportunity for intercultural communication is increasing as the Internet becomes more popular. Language barriers are one of the biggest problems remaining for intercultural communication using the Internet. Users of the Internet are an increasingly diverse population, and the percentage of people using the most common language, English, has fallen to about 35% [1]. Many people are actively working to increase opportunities for intercultural collaboration. In multilingual groups in which members' native languages differ, communication takes place in one language, requiring some members to communicate in a non-native language. Since members who must communicate in their non-native language frequently find communication difficult [2, 3], such collaboration tends to be ineffective [4, 5]. For these groups, machine translation is a promising tool because it would enable all members to read and write in their native language. Our project, the Language Grid Project [6], has been developing multilingual communication tools such as chat services and blackboards. The number of such communities and projects is expected to increase, and the number of multilingual communication tools that use machine translation is growing. However, the quality and usability of multilingual communication using machine translation is still quite problematic. This paper focuses on evaluating usability of tools that support multilingual communication.

2 Multilingual Communication Tools in the Language Grid Project

2.1 The Language Grid [6]

Previously, we proposed the Language Grid, which treats existing language services as atomic components and enables users to create new language services by combining appropriate components. The word grid is defined as a system for coordinating distributed resources with each other and uses an open standard protocol to create high quality services. The language grid has two main components: the horizontal and the vertical language grids. **The horizontal language grid** combines existing language services using Web service and workflow technologies, benefiting a wide range of users by providing standard language services for about 10 Asian languages and 20 other languages from around the world. **The vertical language grid**, on the other hand, layers community language services, such as medical parallel texts and pictogram dictionaries, to support intercultural activities.

We have two goals for the Language Grid: one is for everyone to be able to create community-oriented services and register them with the Language Grid and the other is for everyone to be able to use language services on the Language Grid easily.

2.2 Multilingual Communication Tools

The Language Grid project is developing several translation tools for multilingual collaboration support using the language services registered on the Language Grid. Users input texts in native languages to these tools, and the tools output texts in other languages as desired by users. Together, these tools can carry out multilingual translation by coordinating the workflows of several language services. In multilingual translation, users use back translation to check whether the translation of the input text is correct or not. The Language Grid also provides a tool to create community-oriented dictionaries. Users can add unknown words to the dictionary to make translation more accurate.

2.2.1 Multilingual Chat Tool – Langrid Chat [7]
Langrid Chat is a tool that uses multilingual translation developed on the Language Grid. When a user inputs a sentence in his or her native language, back translation texts are returned in the target languages set by the user as the user chats. The user can then decide whether the translation is reasonable.

2.2.2 Multilingual Sharing Blackboard –Langrid Blackboard
Langrid Blackboard is a multilingual blackboard tool that enables users to communicate using various types of graphics, such as labels, arrows, and pictures. It provides the user with two windows: a sharing window and an input window. In the sharing window, the user can use comment, image, and grouping labels. The user can also create labels to freely input his or her ideas in the input window. Such labels are shared among the participants and displayed in the same position on each participant's display. This tool enables users to converse in their native languages.

2.2.3 Repair Support for Multilingual Back Translation
The chat and blackboard tools provide a multilingual back translation function that can be used to check translation results in multiple languages. They also enable users to fix each translation individually. For example, a Korean back translation might be good while an English or Chinese one is not. It would be surprising if all the initial back translations from one input sentence were good given the homogeneity problem described above. As the number of target languages continues to increase, this will become even more of a problem.

3 Usability Evaluation Process

Groupware has been evaluated by researchers in the computer-supported cooperative work (CSCW) and groupware communities [8]. However, evaluation is still considered a difficult problem, and many researchers feel that the only way to get a true picture of a groupware system is to study it in an actual context with real users. Other studies have focused on the usability of multiple languages instant messaging [9]. This study focuses on translation quality by evaluating dialog with pre-defined subjects, casual dialog, and text translation.

We want to build a model usability evaluation process for multilingual communication tools. First, the elements of a multilingual communication tool are (1) groupware, and (2) a machine translation system. Therefore, we have to conduct two usability tests. Our preliminary study focuses on the evaluation of the system's communication usability. The second study focuses on translation quality using community words, that is, domain specific words. Multilingual communication tasks involve language translation processes. Both general usability and subject usability by way of a language translation process are described here.

We propose a usability evaluation process for multilingual communication tools, which is shown in Figure 1. The left side of the figure shows the general usability evaluation process. After the development team completed the prototype, we evaluated its usability. There are two approaches to evaluating usability. One is heuristics testing, which is an analytic technique, and the other is usability testing, which involves experiments. The result is feedback to the development process. The goal is multilingual communication. Therefore, in addition to a general usability evaluation, multilingual evaluation is also required. The evaluation items specific to multilingual communication are shown on the right side of Figure 1.

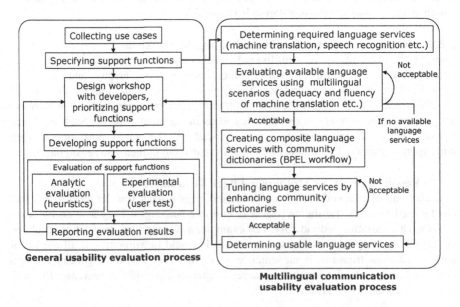

Fig. 1. Usability evaluation process for multilingual communication tools

3.1 Multilingual Communication Usability Evaluation Process

First, the user identifies a language pair. Then, the language service of Language Grid is checked to see whether it supports the language pair. If the pair is supported, translation accuracy is evaluated. An example of a translation accuracy evaluation of Japanese-German is shown below.

1. Create test data in Japanese and German.
2. Japanese test data is translated using Japanese -> English -> German. Similarly, German test data is translated using German -> English -> Japanese.
3. Native speakers evaluate the German and Japanese, which were obtained from machine translation, from the viewpoints of accuracy and fluency in comparison with the original test data.

When accuracy is judged by a language service that can understand semantic content, translation tuning using a community dictionary is evaluated. The optimal technique of a community word being replaced differs with kinds of machine translation. Therefore, it is necessary to identify the optimal cooperation technique and to provide it as a support language service. On the other hand, when accuracy is judged by a language service that cannot understand semantic contents in evaluation of language service, another interpretive language service is looked for. Again, the same semantic evaluation of a language pair is carried out. When there is no language service that can adequately evaluate the language pair, it is deemed to be unsupported. A support language is identified during the above-mentioned process. Moreover, while reporting the result to a development team.

The test data suitable for a community is created, and machine translation is carried out for a language pair. For example, machine translation may involve three hops (Korean-English-German). Furthermore, when the back translation of the communication tool is taken into account, six hops are involved. It turns out that translation accuracy deteriorates as the number of hops increases.

To deal with the synchronous and asynchronous characteristics of collaboration tools, the evaluation must be done in an Internet environment. Therefore, we prepared broadband and narrowband environments and clarified the relation between transmission speed and user satisfaction.

3.2 Usability Evaluation Issues

In this process, there are three usability evaluation issues.

3.2.1 Creation of a Multilingual Test Set

To evaluate the accuracy of multilingual translation, we need multilingual test sets. Test sets of a parallel corpus based on newspaper articles or similar material are currently available, but there are few language pairs. There is also a license problem. Researchers in the natural language processing area created several test sets to evaluate machine translations. However, they can only be used in a confined group. Moreover, communication on tools such as chatting tools is mainly done in a colloquial style. Furthermore, when we check cooperative machine translation systems with a community dictionary, we need a test set that includes domain words.

3.2.2 Evaluation of the Accuracy of a Translation System

Currently, machine translation is used as a language translation process. For some language pairs, two or more machine translation engines are sometimes used in a cooperative way. Our evaluation of the machine translation system must take this cooperation into account.

A subjective evaluation was conducted using the NIST (the National Institute of Standards and Technology) protocol[1]. Judges decide whether each translation of a sentence is adequate. Adequacy refers to the degree to which information present in the original is also communicated in the translation. Thus, for adequacy judgments, the reference translation serves as a proxy for the original source language text. Adequacy is judged on the following five-point scale:

	How much of the meaning expressed in the gold-standard translation is also expressed in the target translation?
5	All
4	Most
3	Much
2	Little
1	None

3.2.3 Evaluation of Optimal Tuning of a Community Dictionary

Recently, demand for higher quality machine translation systems has been increasing for a variety of reasons. Though carefully compiled community dictionaries are needed to do high quality translations, small machine translation dictionaries do not include vocabulary from various domains. The solution is community dictionaries that cover particular domains and that cooperate with existing machine translation systems. A system of evaluating the level of cooperation between the machine translation engine and the community dictionary is therefore necessary.

4 Lessons Learned

We tried to evaluate the communication tools developed by Language Grid Project in accordance with the proposing usability evaluation model. Two problems were revealed.

4.1 The Usability Evaluator's Problem

To evaluate the possibility of using a particular language, we must create test data that include community-oriented words and then evaluate the data's accuracy. For example, to determine whether the language pair of Japanese and Korean is supported, we need bilingual Japanese and Korean speakers. The evaluation is a two-step process that focuses on accuracy and specialized community words. In the first step of the evaluation, 'accuracy', it is not necessary to be a community expert.

---

[1] http://www.ldc.upenn.edu/Projects/TIDES/Translation/TransAssess02.pdf

However, in the second step it is important that the evaluator be able to understand the community words. Therefore, a community expert must do the evaluation.

We would like to focus attention on the difference in the evaluation of community-oriented words, rather than general words, when the evaluator is or is not a community expert.

4.2 Selection of General and Community Dictionaries

A community word often has two meanings: a community-oriented meaning and a general meaning. If we prioritize the community dictionary over the general dictionary, the system will select the community meaning. However, the user might actually want the general meaning. We found that a function is needed that can allow either the general meaning or the community-oriented meaning to be selected easily.

5 Conclusion

We proposed a process for evaluating the usability of multilingual communication tools.

To support intercultural collaboration, we need multilingual communication tools that can be tested for usability. By adding translation accuracy testing to general usability testing, we successfully specify a translation path that causes translation errors. In the process of usability testing, we also evaluate community dictionaries to improve translation results.

In this paper, we described a tool that supports multilingual communication and proposed a model of the tool in which usability subjects are extracted using empirically evaluated rules.

Acknowledgments. We are grateful for the assistance of the members of the Language Grid Project and the Language Grid Association. Translation services for this research were provided by Kodensha Co., Ltd. and Cross Language Inc. Morphological analysis services were provided by Kyoto University, Kookmin University, and Stuttgart University.

References

1. Andrews, T., Curbera, F., Dolakia, H., Goland, J., Klein, J., Leymann, F., Liu, K., Roller, D., Smith, D., Thatte, S., Trickovic, I., Weeravarana, S.: Business Process Execution Language for Web Services (2003)
2. Aiken, M., Hwang, C., Paolillo, J., Lu, L.A: group decision support system for the Asian Pacific rim. Journal of International Information Management 3, 1–13 (1994)
3. Takano, Y., Noda, A.: A temporary decline of thinking ability during foreign language processing. Journal of Cross-Cultural Psychology 24, 445–462 (1993)
4. Aiken, M. Multilingual Communication in Electronic Meetings. ACM SIGGROUP, Bulletin, 23(1), 2002.
5. Tung, L.L., Quaddus, M.A.: Cultural differences explaining the differences in results in GSS: implications for the next decade. Decision Support Systems 33(2), 177–199 (2002)

6. Toru Ishida. Language Grid: An Infrastructure for Intercultural Collaboration. In: IEEE/IPSJ Symposium on Applications and the Internet (SAINT-06), pp. 96–100, keynote address (2006)
7. Fujii, K., Shigenobu, T., Yoshino, T.: Application and Evaluation of Intercultural Communication Tool AnnoChat using Machine Translation. In: Proceedings of the Information Processing Society of Japan, GN-57-12, pp.67–72 (in Japanese) (2005)
8. Pinelle, D., Cutwin, C.: A Review of Groupware evaluations. In: Proceedings of WETICE, Workshops on Enabling Technologies: Infrastructure for Collaborative Enterprises, pp. 86–91. IEEE Computer Society (2000)
9. Ogden, B., Warner, J., Jin, W., Sorge, J.: Information Sharing Across Languages Using MITRE's TRiM Instant Messaging (2003)

The Universal Design Model of Set Top Box

Yen-Yu Kang and Han-yu Lin

Department of Industrial Design, National Kaohsiung Normal University,
Kaohsiung, 824, Taiwan
yenyu@nknucc.nknu.edu.tw, hanyu@nknu.edu.tw

Abstract. "E" life, a new trend to influence people's dairy-life since internet explored. No product or concept can be successful if it ignores the needs of its users and Digital Set Top Box (STB) is no exception. However, there has been a noticeable lack of real information about how STB are used. So, the objective of this study is established a series of surveys in an effort to help user in using STB. The study presents a process, based on user requirements, for users. Seven factors affecting E-books design are identified and discussed; these guidelines can be categorized into principles of universal design. Once the affected issues of universal design has been established, designers can get the relative understanding of developing ergonomic designed in STB development.

Keywords: STB, usability, universal design, human factors.

1 Introduction

The digitization of TV industry is a definite development policy of Taiwan in "Year 2002 to 2007 Country development key plan" published by Executive Yuan in 2002. The plan explains and defines clearly about TV digitization implementation strategy and process schedule. In the face of the transition and business opportunities brought by TV digitization, all kinds of media industries players devoted themselves into this big campaign. And the key factor of TV digitization is the application and promotion of DTV Set-Top-Box.

The Technology innovation goal for 21 century is digital live. Whatever are terrestrial communication, direct satellite, digital broadcasting TV, and wireless communication all enhance to digitalization. The digitalization trend is extended to every where around the world. The function of digital appliance is information sharing, easy using, and customization. Digital appliance includes information product appliance and appliance product information, personal communication, and entertainment.

There are three kind of application in digital appliance. The first application is that home display function device includes different display technology. For example, CRT TV,PDP TV, LCD TV, rear projector, and projector TV. The second application is home gateway for media and information processing device. For example, Set-Top box, Game console, DVD player, PVR (personal video recorder). The third application are mobile home entertainment device include DSC (Digital still camera), SHD (Smart Handheld Device), Mobile Game Console.

N. Aykin (Ed.): Usability and Internationalization, Part II, HCII 2007, LNCS 4560, pp. 98–102, 2007.
© Springer-Verlag Berlin Heidelberg 2007

Digital Set Top box is a main stream in home entertainment device market during five years. The shipment of this device is exceeded 10 million units and revenue is also exceeded 1 billion USD.

2 Objective

With the high development of information technology, consumers can be at a loss and uncertain in the face of "high-tech" products that overlooked "humanity." Therefore, an important issue that industrial designers work hard to deal with is how to use human factors engineering, or "user-centered" through industrial design to close the wide gulf between the user and the product. On the other hand, because technological advances have provoked a change in social structure, this has a caused a problem that needs to be resolved by the governments of many countries. The concept of "universal design" has derived from the multiplicity and differences among user groups, which has been catered to by product design. "Universal design," in accordance to the principle of human factors engineering, promotes the design concept that "a product should be capable of being used by a majority of people." For example, the design of chairs and tables for students must consider safe, effective, and comfortable usability by students with vastly different physical needs.

Norman [3] indicated a design principle that sets the user at the center, a philosophy that is based on the user's needs and interests that emphasize usability and understandability. In other words, only a principle that focuses on the user can grasp the whole issue involving "human / machine / environment" and "human / product / context." Therefore, a "user-centered" design principle needs to take into account elements such as the user's cognitive, psychological, and physical conditions. However, if there are individual considerations for users in a group, development of design necessarily becomes more difficult. As a result, this study attempts to develop a suitable human factors engineering and design assessment model. Its purpose is to extend the design principle of "user-centered" to the application of "universal design," according to human factors theory and differences in design practice. Then use the human factors analytical model, explore the human factors issues that relate to human-machine interface, as well as the functional issues related to engineering interface. Human factors analysis of operation interface and engineering exploration of engineering interface are used; these results are used as a basis for practice design, to ensure a human factors design that is user-centered.

3 Human Factor's Model

From the perspective of design practice, a product is not only merchandise of the manufacturer, but also a work of the designer and appliance of the user. In the process of communication transmission, a product passes from the contractor, designer, producer, to the user. Relative to different cognitive models of different entities, different meaning is infused in the product. In this way, the product is another symbol that transmits signals and expresses meaning. Thus, this study finally brings in the mental model of product semantics and cognition [3], combined with human factors engineering analysis to establish an assessment model that is centered around the "user," as shown in Figure 1 [1]. This is in attempt to lead designs to achieve the ideal of "universal design," and use this assessment model to elevate humanity-friendly design goals. Another goal of "universal design" is to response Donald Norman's concept that "a good design benefits the public." Also, the human factors assessment and analytical model proposed by this study can be used as a point of reference for the design of future products.

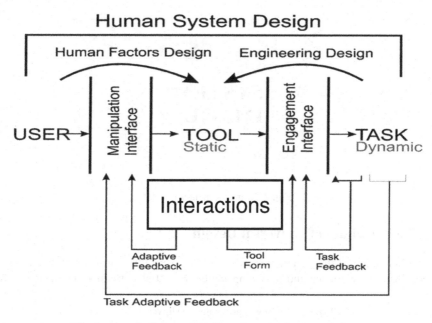

Fig. 1. A symbolic representation of user-tool system design

Norman [3] proposed a theory on the psychological model concept of users, dividing psychological models into three types: design model, user model, and system image. Design model is the designer's psychological concept of the product, user model is the user's idea of how to operate the product; the ideal situation is a coincidence between the design and user models. Thus, system image is exceptionally important, because the designer must ensure that all aspects of the product conform to an appropriate psychological model. Figure 2 shows the relationship of models.

This study uses this model as a basis to explore how human factors engineering can be applied in design practice. According to the psychological model of Don Norman, the relationship between human factors engineering and design practice establish their correspondence. A brief explanation is as follows:

1. With respect to the system (product), the product has an overall system image, including human factors engineering and functional design to convey the designer's creativity.
2. With respect to the designer, the designer uses the product image (form) to convey his creativity.
3. With respect to the user, through product image (form), assess creativity from the perspective of the user.

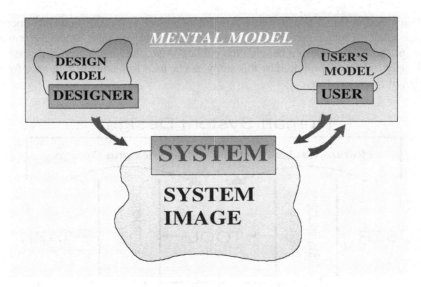

Fig. 2. Noman's mental models

4   The Principles of Universal Design

At the beginning of the 21st century, the world is very different from 100 years ago. People are living longer and surviving better. Potential consumers of designs who

Table 1. The seven principles of Universal Design

Principle	Subject matter
(1) Equitable Use	The design is useful and marketable to people with diverse abilities.
(2) Flexibility in Use	The design accommodates a wide range of individual preferences and abilities.
(3) Simple and Intuitive Use	Use of the design is easy to understand regardless of the user's experience, knowledge, language skills, or current concentration level.
(4) Perceptible Information	The design communicates necessary information effectively to the user regardless of ambient conditions or the user's sensory abilities.
(5) Tolerance for Error	The design minimizes hazards and the adverse consequences of accidental or unintended actions.
(6) Low Physical Effort	The design can be used efficiently and comfortably and with a minimum of fatigue.
(7) Size and Space for Approach and Use	Appropriate size and space is provided for approach, reach, manipulation, and use regardless of the user's body size, posture, or mobility.

may be limited in function by age or disability are increasing at a dramatic rate. Designers are trained to design for a mythical "average" group of people which in fact does not actually exist. Every individual is unique. The idea of Universal Design, proposed by Mace [2], began in demographic, legislative, economic, and social changes among older adults and people with disabilities [2] (The Center of Universal Design, 1998). Universal Design can be defined as the design of products and environments to be usable to the greatest extent possible by people of all ages and abilities. Ergonomic considerations are a part of "Universal Design". Therefore, it is very important to integrate ergonomic considerations into the principles of Universal Design as a major design strategy. The seven principles of this paradigm are shown in Table 1.

5 Discussion

Universal Design is an approach to creating everyday environments and products that are usable by all people to the greatest possible extent. By using Universal Design, companies can maximize their potential market. However, successful application of these principles requires an understanding of human diversity (ergonomic considerations). Design and manufacturing engineers seem well aware that the most efficient way of improving ergonomics in the manufacturing process is by becoming involved in the early phases of product development. This study presents an example of how to take ergonomic considerations into engineering design when applying Universal Design. This study is the first research project aimed at understanding issues related to evaluate of STB based on the concept of Universal Design.

Acknowledgments. This Study has sponsored by National Science Council in Taiwan. R.O.C. (NSC-94-2213-E-017-005-).

References

1. Lin, R.T., Kreifeldt, J.G.: Ergonomics in Wearable Computer Design. International Journal of Industrial Design 27, 259–269 (2001)
2. Mace, R.: The Center of Universal Design (1998). The Universal Design File –Designing for People of All Ages and Abilities. NC State University, pp. 6–84 (1970)
3. Norman, D.A.: The design of everyday things, New York, Doubleday (1990)
4. Wickens, C.D., Gordon, S., Liu, Y.: Introduction to Human Factors Engineering. Addison-Wesley-Longman, New York (1998)

"A Quick Dip at the Iceberg's Tip" - Rapid Immersion Approaches to Understanding Emerging Markets

Anjali Kelkar

Institute of Design, Illinois Institute of Technology, Chicago

Abstract. Remote research' enables the rapid gathering of activity-oriented data using structured data collection frameworks and disposable camera studies to gain a broad understanding of users and their contexts. This photographic data when used for Rapid Immersion workshops acts as a shared visual reference to enable multiple stakeholders with differing viewpoints to work together. Issues get addressed from multiple standpoints leading to rich concept generation, thus creating the potential for a win-win situation, for businesses and their customers.

Keywords: Emerging markets, BOP, India, user research, remote research, ethnography.

1 Introduction

"In less than 40 years, the BRICs' (Brazil, Russia, China and India) economies together could be larger than the G6 in US dollar terms. By 2025 they could account for over half the size of the G6 (USA, UK, Germany, France, Japan and Italy)." [1]

As the excerpt from the Goldman Sachs report 'Dreaming With BRICs: The Path to 2050' above suggests, if emerging markets continue to grow at their current rate, the buying power of consumers in these economies will be enormous and it is important therefore to begin considering them as a sizeable market. However this should not mean that this consumer is going to need and desire the same things that the developed market consumer does. The projected growth of the emerging markets is tantalizing to the marketer but the complexity of predicting what they might want can be confounding. For example in India, there are layers of economic classes between the standard stratification of the upper, middle and lower classes, and being able to discern between them requires being able to see them through a local lens. These three segments can easily be found in villages, towns, small and large cities and have varied modes of spending their earnings. In addition, general infrastructure and facilities such as education, safety, access to electricity and transport, proximity to the city, vary from region to region and state to state and affect what consumers spend as needs and luxuries. Layered upon these differences is the prevalence of age-old cultural and social systems, religion, local politics, corruption and gender bias which all play a role in purchasing behavior.

N. Aykin (Ed.): Usability and Internationalization, Part II, HCII 2007, LNCS 4560, pp. 103–108, 2007.
© Springer-Verlag Berlin Heidelberg 2007

1.1 Remote Research

Remote Research is particularly useful for researchers who are used to conducting research in a western context as well as executives who are considering investing in a new market. It acts as a quick and efficient initial design research step by enabling researchers a long-distance contextual understanding of the field, remotely. It would undoubtedly be most ideal if researchers had the time to engage in deep immersion, but this is not always possible from the perspective of business needs, nor advisable from the perspective of safety, access and unfamiliarity with the context. Ignoring these issues can potentially have a huge impact on design, understanding users and comprehending the context to make actionable design and these are be discussed in detail below.

1.2 Issues to Consider Before Conducting Contextual Research

1. Selecting researchers: Conducting ethnographic research in emerging markets is difficult largely because it is unfamiliar territory to western-centric methods, approaches and even environments. Everything is different and therefore bottlenecks in the research process should be expected. Selecting an appropriate research agency, budgeting for unexpected costs, trust in local research methods tends to be a fairly risky process.
2. Safety: Many locations in emerging markets, slums areas in Mumbai for instance or a rural area far from a city can be unsafe for researchers because they lack basic infrastructure that most researchers practicing in the western markets are used to. Sometimes these locations do not have proper roads, transport, healthcare facilities, communication systems, accommodation or support for personal safety.
3. Access: Most of the locations like those described above are difficult to reach, not just physically, but socially also. A researcher must be aware that users may not accept their presence in their communities because they do not naturally fit in as anything other than tourists and outsiders. As such, the information gathered might be 'made-up' or 'tailored to impress' rather than real.
4. Humility: Understanding the context is linked with issues of access as well as the ability of the researcher to be humble. From a cultural and social standpoint it is difficult to immerse oneself in a completely foreign environment and not find what we see as 'exotic'. It is important then to make every effort to remain objective.
5. Time: In unfamiliar environments the simplest things can take the longest time. This is partly due to our unfamiliarity with navigating a new environment as well as deep knowledge of the way the certain things work in that place.

Remote research addresses this cheaply and efficiently by hiring local unskilled researchers at local costs, giving them structured data collection formats to gather data, and in a timely way by couriering them research toolkits and having them courier back data. Using this data as Rapid Immersion helps gain an initial broad understanding of the day to day life of the user and can make a substantial difference in deciding what to research, who to design for and how to sustain the product or service in that market so it remains profitable.

2 'Quasi-Ethnographers': Addressing the Issues

Remote research using structured research frameworks and disposable cameras help address the above issues and enable data collection through a local lens. Researchers for such projects are typically untrained in ethnography or design research but since they are locals, are usually familiar with the context, cognitively understand issues of context and depending on their expertise can easily address issues of access. In past we have worked with graduate students from various academic fields including business, social work, design, and architecture.

2.1 Day in the Life Studies Using POEMS Frameworks

The POEMS framework books were first used in a hardcopy format for Remote Research when the Institute of Design, Illinois Institute of Technology (IIT), Chicago, started it's Design for the BOP (Base of the Pyramid) [2] research project in the summer of 2003 to study daily life in urban slums of India. Research toolkits comprising of disposable cameras and spiral bound POEMS framework books were couriered to our 'quasi-ethnographers' with the overall objective of getting a broad understanding of user's, their context and possible areas for business opportunity.

Our work at the Institute of Design, IIT, was inspired by C. K. Prahalad and Stuart Hart's article, Fortune at the Base of the pyramid [3]. They first coined the phrase 'The Bottom of the Pyramid' in 2002, to refer to approximately four billion people around the world who live on less than a $1-2 per day. In the book, The Fortune at the Bottom of the Pyramid, Prahalad argues that: "Despite the fact that these people subsist on annual per capita incomes of less than $1,500, this 'bottom of the pyramid' represents a multi-trillion-dollar market" [4]. It is believed that the bottom of the pyramid could grow to six billion people over the next 40 years. Taken together, nine developing nations -- China, India, Brazil, Mexico, Russia, Indonesia, Turkey, South Africa and Thailand -- have a combined GDP that is larger, in purchasing power parity, than the combined GDPs of Japan, Germany, France, the UK and Italy. The bottom of the pyramid, Prahalad writes, is "the biggest potential market opportunity in the history of commerce."

2.2 Speed and Efficacy Derived from Using Structured Frameworks

POEMS frameworks [5] are activity-oriented frameworks which are structured in a way that requires little or no training to gather data. POEMS stands for People, Objects, Environments, Messages and Services. Each framework page has fields for entering this information, as well as details and description of activity observed and human factors issues encountered. Each book consists of about 54 double spread pages, one side for pasting photographs from the disposable camera study and the other side for writing user data.

Observation is primarily conducted in two ways, either by researchers conducting direct observation of users or researchers helping facilitate participants (family members or individuals) document their own lives. In both cases research toolkits consisting of disposable cameras and POEMS workbooks are couriered to the researchers who facilitate the next steps. This helps save time and control quality as sourcing of cameras and printing of workbooks, and is done by us. Participants are typically given about 10 days to document their lives, and researchers another one week to 10 days to conduct interviews. Typically, it is a team of two researchers who do this, one who conducts the interview and the other who simultaneously notes down the data. Voice recorders, when available, are used to support interview data.

On completing the research, the workbooks filled with interview data and photos are couriered back to us. In situations where Rapid Immersion is necessary, due to tight deadlines, such as our BOP project, selected visuals from this data were used to conduct Rapid Immersion workshops. After this, data is put through a rigorous analysis and synthesis process by a research team in at the Institute of Design who enter the data in the User insights Tool [6]. This is a Microsoft Excel-based tool designed by Profs Vijay Kumar, and Patrick Whitney and is based on the POEMS framework. On an average we have about 15-20 workbooks. Each book typically takes about two hours to enter, this by default creates an immersion process for the researcher who by the end of the data entry process has a substantial understanding of the daily life of the users to derive insights and develop a direction for concept development.

In many other situations we have conducted Rapid Immersion workshops much after the research, this is often for new business clients who have a growing interest in emerging markets and find this approach to be quick, structured and compelling.

3 Rapid Immersion

3.1 Creating Shared Value Through Design Research

We first developed the Rapid Immersion process for a multi-stakeholder meeting about BOP that comprised of representatives from multinationals (MNCs), academia and non-profit organizations (NGOs). This being a BOP meeting, based on the work of C. K. Prahalad and Stuart Hart, everyone agreed that people who made $1-2 per day were consciously selecting where to spend whether it was for entertainment, purchasing daily needs or topping up their pre-paid cell phone card. We had noticed in past meetings though that despite this basic agreement, that there would be bitter arguments between the above-mentioned stakeholders regarding BOP. Each group had their own language and unique experience to describe needs, goals and issues at the BOP associated by the nature of their work. The disagreement lay in opinions they had of each other with no shared platform to work from. MNC's and NGO's often thought that academics were too removed from on the ground experience, NGOs considered MNCs were exploitative and MNCs considered NGOs to be against business. So the issue was, how could MNC's, academia and NGO's work together to develop products and services that the poor need and will buy, and in this way working out a win-win situation for all.

3.2 'Seeing Is Believing'

In this case, our general goal for the exercise was to bring these multiple stakeholders on the same page by creating a common platform to share their understanding using Institute Design's BOP research that were photo studies of daily life in the BOP.

We designed these workshops to be short immersion experiences not exceeding 2-3 hours with quick exercises that included a slide presentation of images from the field accompanied by verbal description, pattern identification and concept development. Each participant was asked to write down observations on post-its. Participants were then divided into teams that had roughly equal number of participants representing different interests and fields. Teams were then placed in different parts of the room, and teams members asked to share their observations with each other.

To their surprise most of them had similar observations- even though they were often worded differently. It was easy to agree with each other at this point because they had seen the same picture and identified the same issues such as lack of hygiene, long lines for water collection, lack of storage space in homes etc. The next exercise required them to analyze observations to write insights. These were then clustered together to identify patterns of use. These patterns helped identify opportunity for innovation and guide concept generation. Again the NGO's working alongside MNCs and academia and vice-versa experienced that they were comfortable working together and identifying similar user needs, such as: 'design products that are stackable so they are easily stored, design individual water treatment products, design reliable water deliver systems so children can attend school' etc. This process of viewing visual data simultaneously in multi-disciplinary teams ensured that when the context for discussion remained consistent, varying approaches to address BOP complemented concept generation. This visual approach acted as an information mediator, as images, not words were shared.

This process brought a discussion often had at 60,000 ft and largely through statistics, down to the ground realities gathered through design research which included photos of entrepreneurs in slum areas participating in day to day business, locations where they worked or socialized and the people they interacted with.

3.3 A Quick Dip

Rapid Immersion acts as a technique to rapidly introduce the context to a new audience or in other cases where the audience is familiar with the context, to encourage a proactive discussion using a shared context to reach a mutual understanding (if not a mutual agreement). It does not substitute for ethnography or other design research methods.

In other Rapid Immersion workshops conducted at conferences and with companies, students from the Institute of Design, IIT, have helped facilitate some of these sessions, helping teams brainstorm by drawing concepts as well as guiding them to make rapid prototypes. Again, taking the idea beyond words into tangible concepts that can be seen and experienced as informal models of a product or service. In addition, it also illustrated how some of the research methods used for design thinking can transform assumptions about a new market, often, leading to out-of-the-box approaches and outcomes for identifying new market opportunity.

4 Conclusion

This process is by no means complete in itself but it allows the researchers and clients to immerse in a completely unfamiliar environment in a short amount of time so a broad understanding of the ground reality can be gained. Our Base of the Pyramid (BOP) project at the Institute of Design [4] initially started with the goal of designing new housing for people living in poor urban areas. It is through Remote Research and Rapid Immersion that we quickly identified that ground realities were less about selling concepts about improved housing to the poor but more about developing pro-profit systems that enabled the poor to earn more money so in the longer term they could afford a better standard of living. This in-turn redefined our research scope so we could better understand the life cycle of economic activity in a slum dwellers life and helped us develop actionable design concepts which are now in the process of being prototyped and tested.

As the example above suggests, this process helps break or change assumptions about new and unfamiliar environments, encourages a participatory approach by multiple stakeholders and can be re-used in a more focused manner with higher budgets and trained design researchers once research direction has been identified.

References

1. Wilson, Dominic, Purushothaman, Roopa.: Dreaming With BRICs: The Path to 2050; Global Economics, Paper No: 99, Goldman Sachs p. 4 (October 1, 2003)
2. Whitney, Patrick, Kelkar, Anjali.: Designing for the Base of the Pyramid. In: Design Management Journal pp. 41–47 (Fall 2004)
3. Prahalad, C.K., Hart, S.L.: The Fortune at the Bottom of the Pyramid. In: Strategy+Business, Issue 26 (2002)
4. Prahalad, C.K.: The Fortune at the Bottom of the Pyramid: Eradicating Poverty Through Profits; Wharton School Publishing (2004)
5. Kumar, Vijay, Whitney, Patrick.: Faster, Cheaper, Deeper User Research. In: Design Management Journal, pp. 50–57 (Spring 2003)
6. Kumar, Vijay.: User Insights Tool: a sharable database for user research. In: Institute of Design White Paper, Illinois Institute of technology, Chicago (2004)

Adobe Approaches to Culturalization:
Two Case Studies

Hyolin Kim and Judy Shade

Adobe Systems Inc
International User Experience Team
345 Park Ave, San Jose CA 95110, USA

Abstract. Adobe uses diverse user research methods for our Asian geographies. Our approaches differ depending on the target market and the feature set under consideration. There is no cookie-cutter approach to software culturalization. The target user and software space is the starting point for determining research approaches and areas of focus for design. We will focus on two products from our Pro and Consumer product lines and provide case studies for how these approaches differ for two very different product lines that have been culturalized for the Japanese market.

Keywords: Adobe, Creative Professionals, Consumers, Creative Suite, Illustrator, InDesign, Elements, Photoshop Elements, Premiere Elements, Gaiji, Japan, Japanese, Culturalization.

1 Introduction

Adobe provides software solutions for creative professionals, enterprise users, and consumers worldwide. While Adobe localizes its products for many countries, those efforts are for the most part interface translations and basic support for international text handling needs. Adobe's culturalization efforts focus mainly on Japan, with small forays into the Chinese and Korean markets.

As experience designers in Adobe's iUx (international user experience) group, we play dual roles of both designer and researcher. Our team has been driving the culturalization of products for the Japan market. To date, we have succeeded in culturalizing all or parts of InDesign, Photoshop Elements, and Acrobat for the Japanese market, while ensuring that basic localization needs are met with the remaining range of our products.

2 Case Study One: Professional (Creative Suite)

Creative Suite's InDesign-J supports a Japanese print workflow with unique Japanese text handling features. Because Japanese print workflow has a long tradition, with a system that has been tried and tested over a long period of time, there are many challenges for traditional Japanese print houses to move from the old "Shashoku" print workflow system to a digitized DTP workflow such as that available with

N. Aykin (Ed.): Usability and Internationalization, Part II, HCII 2007, LNCS 4560, pp. 109–113, 2007.
© Springer-Verlag Berlin Heidelberg 2007

InDesign-J. Most Japanese book publishers and magazine companies now use a digital DTP system, but there are still many pain points in their workflow that have not been fully addressed in the software world.

2.1 Design Solutions for Gaiji

One of the previous biggest pain points for Adobe customers was the entry and management of "Gaiji" characters. Gaiji are non-standard characters that have no text encoding values. Before the advent of the Adobe Gaiji creation tool, there was no way for a user to enter Gaiji as text. Gaiji had to be laboriously created as bitmaps and then pasted into text. Users had to re-create bitmaps if there was any change to the font or style, and the bitmaps were hard, if not impossible, to reuse. The Adobe Type team recognized this problem and created a solution from the technology side. The International UE team got involved in the user research and interface design side of the solution.

The Gaiji Creation Tool. Gaiji are essentially tiny differences in certain glyphs. For example, "邊" is a variant of the character 辺, which are both read as "be." The former is considered to be a Gaiji character, while the latter is part of the standard Unicode text encoding character set. The first cannot be entered into a word processing document except as a bitmap, while the second can be entered and edited at will. In order to enter the variant example above into the application we used to write this paper, we had to paste it in as a bitmap.

A small mistake or mismatch in user expectations can have a huge impact on Gaiji creation usability. The Gaiji creation tool is an Illustrator palette that allows pro users to make Gaiji glyphlets in one step with minute levels of control; the palette contains more than 20 detailed controls.

The Gaiji Management Tool. Gaiji are technically not part of any character set, so there needs to be a Gaiji management tool which allows users to keep track of their Gaiji glyphlet creations. "Glyphlet" is the term coined at Adobe for a Gaiji creation. The Gaiji management tool (ASGM, or Adobe SING Glyphlet Manager) in Creative Suite is a stand-alone application that installs glyphlets created with the Gaiji creation tool into the user's system and allows the user to sort, search, add, or remove the glyphlets. The management tool is a mechanism which allows the glyphlets created in Illustrator to be used in other Creative Suite applications.

The Gaiji management tool allows users to view both basic and advanced sets of glyphlet attributes. Users can view five to six basic attributes for each glyhlet in the management tool, and can also go to a detailed view that displays over twenty more advanced attributes.

2.2 Japanese Pro Users

Japanese Pro users are very busy and don't want to spend time on even one additional click. As professionals, the users know the applications in and out. The relationship of Pro users to their bread-and-butter applications can be summed up as: "I want to be able to do everything with shortcuts." As designers, we need to see Creative Suite applications in the same way that our Pro users do, as work tools that allow for minute control without sacrificing quality.

2.3 Research Methodologies for the Gaiji Tool

Research for the Gaiji creation and management tools began by investigating the pain points of a Gaiji bitmap workflow. This initial investigation was followed up with validation and verification of the Gaiji glyphlet creation solution - through multiple design iterations - via a customer council and a pre-release testing program. These methodologies were chosen because it was necessary to confirm that the solution met pro users' needs in terms of time constraints (ease of use, limited number of clicks) combined with maximum control (allowing minute typographic adjustments to individual glyphlets).

Validation of Design Iterations. Adobe obtains user feedback in very early stages of the interface design process, sometimes even using paper mock-ups or drawings on a whiteboard. For this particular set of tools, we ran validation studies with more design iterations than usual and worked very closely with users because it was the first tool of its kind to be released in the market.

The Customer Council. The Customer Council consisted of a small number of professional users who we established a long-term relationship with. Unlike the users we normally recruit for lab-type studies, these users had the same level of passion in creating good tools for Adobe users. Their input was extremely valuable for quickly capturing a snapshot of a large number of professional opinions, without much turnaround time.

The Customer Council was also a mechanism whereby Adobe research could build a long-term relationship with council members. Long-term longitudinal study of pro users' professional tool use, including Gaiji creation, was an important criteria for choosing to funnel research via the customer council and pre-release program.

The Pre-release Program. In general, pre-release programs are a good way to get user feedback and statistical data. We were able to obtain a broader variety of feedback for the Gaiji tools through the pre-release program. We were seeking a larger variety of feedback from other customer segments – such as beginners –that did not exist in our Customer Council.

3 Case Study Two: Consumer (Elements)

The starting point for considering the needs of the Japanese consumer for both design and research is to examine the content requirements of the user. This is done via a broad survey of the culture-specific uses of technology – such as the advent and widespread use of QR Codes in Japan – as well as a deep dive into the yearly activities of our users – in understanding the significance of school "Sports Day," or seeing the subtle differences in how Valentine's Day is celebrated in Japan in comparison to America. This approach of examining broader cultural contexts in order to see the ramifications for Consumer-geared content design and content creation tools is radically different from the microscopic examination of Pro users' tool-use habits and workflows for Pro application features.

3.1 Design Solutions for Elements Creation

The Adobe Elements line, which is targeted toward consumer rather than professional image manipulators, comes packaged with a large amount of content; pre-created templates for users who are not creative design professionals. Content is extremely culture-sensitive, and Japan is a market where yearly events, holidays, and the childhood activities that consumers chronicle with their photo creations differ significantly from those of Western cultures. The New Year's Card and QR Code creation tools are two features in Photoshop Elements which are there to enhance and support the culturalized content experience of the Japanese user.

Content. A superficial comparison of calendar events in an American and Japanese calendar will only reveal the obvious differences, but will not reveal the hidden cultural differences with how these "same" holidays or traditions are observed. American and Japanese users of our products both celebrate events such as New Year's, Valentine's Day, Halloween, and Christmas. The oblivious designer based in America might create Christmas content for both users without realizing that the content is inappropriate and in some cases completely unusable for the Japanese user. In order to create culturally-specific and appropriate content, it is necessary to deeply examine the different traditions that are ascribed to even the same holidays. Field research and a collection of artefacts are both necessary components of sorting out and highlighting these subtle yet important differences.

Creation Tools. Photoshop Elements contains two creation tools - for New Year's Cards and QR Codes - that are designed specifically for the Japanese user. One additional tool, for Flipbooks (or stop motion animation) creation, was inspired by content creation influences from Japan, but is in all language versions of the application as stop motion animation is a global creation activity. The culturalized content in the Japanese versions of both Photoshop and Premiere Elements is intended to support and enhance all creations, but in Photoshop Elements is also tuned very specifically to creation needs for Japanese-style New Year's cards and QR Codes.

3.2 Japanese Consumer Users

Japanese consumers use image editing software for fun and enjoyment, rather than for work. Users want a large amount of content variety and the means to enhance their photos easily. Consumer tools are not used day-in and day-out like professional tools, so features and content must be easily accessible and not difficult to use; our consumers want to focus on quick, fun, easy creation rather than on the creation process itself. In addition, the Japanese consumer requires content and tools that are a natural extension of the Japanese cultural environment. For instance, a QR Code creation tool does not make sense in America, where mobile bar codes are not widespread or even viewable on American mobile devices, but the tool completely natural to the Japanese user, who sees and might even use QR Codes with their mobile on a daily basis - perusing a magazine, looking at a billboard, watching TV, or browsing online.

3.3 Research Methodologies for Elements Content and Creation Tools

The research focus is on how best to support the creation needs of the Japanese consumer. We have taken a two-pronged approach to research in our consumer segment.

Participant Interviews. A long-term strategic research project took a broad look at the means and meanings behind how users keep and archive their memories. Rather than researching a small number of people longitudinally, as was the case with the Pro Gaiji research, this particular Consumer-based research focused on interviewing a cross-swathe of the target user segment as to their image-taking and content creation habits. This type of research has provided invaluable information about the types of content and content creation tools our Japanese consumers desire and need.

Field Work. The second research approach was devoted to identifying and analyzing our users' content needs by closely examining yearly Japanese calendar events. This was done by going on field visits to a large variety of stores in Japan, with a particular focus on stores frequented by our consumers. We collected artefacts such as cards, books, magazines, and flyers from these stores. Our collected artefacts helped the content creator drill down in areas noted as particularly important by our interview participants and to identify the important events to create culturalized content for.

4 Conclusion

Our two case studies show the value of not only researching different geographies, but to also think about the target users' needs when identifying and running research studies that lead to the creation of satisfying culturalized design solutions. As we stated at the beginning, there is no cookie-cutter approach to software culturalization. The target user and software space needs to be examined for determining appropriate research activities as well as useful application features.

User-Centered Design: Component-Based Web Technology

Esin Kiris, Howard Abrams, and Roman Longoria

CA One CA Plaza
Islandia, NY 11749, USA
esin.kiris@ca.com, howard.abrams@ca.com, roman.longoria@ca.com

Abstract. In this age of rapid technological progression and heightened competition, designers of interactive systems, especially web applications, must be able to prepare for, cope with, and adopt to design processes that meet both customer needs and expectations and cutting edge-technology. This paper presents the authors' experience with designing and prototyping a web application using a new web user interface (UI) development technology. We describe how the technological progression forced significant changes in User-Centered Design (UCD) process and design tools. We then discuss the contributions of these changes to the design and development of an internationalized web application. We provide background information about an *Abstract UI* and the web implementation using JavaServer Faces (JSF)[1] technology. We describe how this new technology will be adopted into CA's UCD process and present a case study in which the new JSF technology solution is used for a prototype of an enterprise storage management application. We then discuss the pros and cons of using this technology at the design stage, providing some structure and guidance to designers who might be faced with similar situations. This paper suggests there may be a more appropriate alternative to the current design processes and tools used for designing web applications.

Keywords: UI technology, Java Server Faces (JSF), Prototyping, User-Centered Design, Internationalization, AJAX.

1 Introduction

In technologically-developed countries, people have become increasingly reliant on electronically-delivered information and services as information technology is embedded into more and more every day items. Users' expectations of the interactive performance of these items have also increased. Today's users expect to interact with electronic applications like they interact with the desktop applications – simply and intuitively.

To meet user expectations, web UI technology has been rapidly changing and web applications are providing more and more interactive UI functions and features similar to desktop applications. In other words, web application UIs are becoming "rich" interfaces. A rich interface reduces server round-trips, receives data from the

N. Aykin (Ed.): Usability and Internationalization, Part II, HCII 2007, LNCS 4560, pp. 114–122, 2007.

server without a full page refresh, and increases interactivity with desktop-like interaction. The new goal of web applications is to be as rich as possible. The web technologies used to create rich and universal web applications presented in this paper are JavaServer Faces (JSF) [1] and Asynchronous JavaScript and XML (AJAX).

This paper evaluates the JSF technology and new prototyping tool, Exadel Studio Pro[1] ™. In addition, a case study is presented on a pilot project which examined the implications for the web application design process and UCD methods.

2 Background

Several years ago, CA undertook the ambitious goal of creating a single UI look and feel across hundreds of products. One result of this effort is a large and continuously updated set of UI standards for the products.

Early in the standardization process it was realized that, without a set of reusable technologies, it would be extremely costly to implement any standard, let alone one as detailed as the company's. The technology standardization process started with typically web application artifacts: CSS stylesheets and Java Server Page (JSP) tags. But the limits of these relatively simple technologies became evident in the face of the evolving, complex UI standards. At the same time, there were non-web-based products that also needed a consistent look and feel.

To overcome these obstacles, CA has developed an Abstract UI. An Abstract UI is a defined, consistent set of declarative application programming interfaces (APIs), independent of the underlying technology and the UI's look and feel. This technique allows the technology and look of the UI to change with limited impact on the development team. It also allows UI designers to develop UIs that can quickly and easily be reused. The downside to this approach is the need to develop and maintain the API and a set of implementing technologies

3 UI Technology

The current Abstract UI implementation for web-based applications uses JSF as its underlying technology. While JSF is a relatively new J2EE standard for web-based UIs, it was chosen for three key concepts that it employs: components, renderers, and tool support. Instead of building a user interface with raw HTML, CSS, and JavaScript, JSF uses reusable components, like traditional desktop-based applications. Rendering is separated from the model of the component, allowing the rendering to change over time without affecting the developer's use of the component when programming. This separation can also mean the same UI could be rendered in two different styles without modifying the application. In Addition, this separation enables UI to be universal where UI can be localized into several languages [2]. Tool support was also an important consideration during the design of the JSF framework. Since tooling was standard, there were many tool venders to choose from. WYSIWYG design tools were important since they let UI designers, who are not trained as

---

[1] Trademark or registered trademark of Exadel, Inc.

programmers, build working UIs that development teams can then hook up to live data. This means the actual UI can be tested by users during UI design stage without having to build the application. This is a key feature in CA's overall UCD program.

To implement the Abstract UI and CA UI Standards, a comprehensive set of reusable JSF UI components were created. The rationale behind creating a set of CA-specific components rather than re-style a set of generic third party components was that CA's UI Standards are very specific and detailed, allowing the custom components to encapsulate knowledge of the standards beyond simple colors and fonts. The resulting reusable components encapsulate complex rules, for example data validation error message and icon display. By simply placing a label and a text field in the interface, the complex rules describing how, where, and when messages and icons should be used are automatically implemented for the developer or designer. Figure 1 shows an example from CA's UI Standards on message display.

Another example is that the CA UI Standards specify that the UI designer can place anchor links at the top of the page that allow the user to jump to specific sections within the page (see Figure 2). Under each section, a 'back to top' link is placed to return the user back to the top of the page. Rather than making the developer understand the UI Standard and place each anchor and 'back to top' link, the components allow the developer to specify an anchor bar and list each section it should contain. When the page renders, it not only renders the bar in the proper colors and fonts, but can automatically place the 'back to top' links under each section, set proper tooltips, etc.

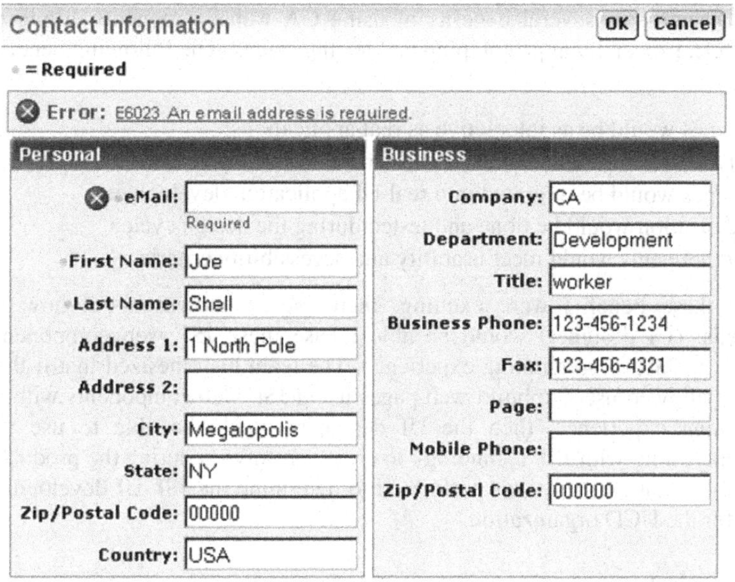

Fig. 1. An example of reusable components automatically implementing validation error message and icon display

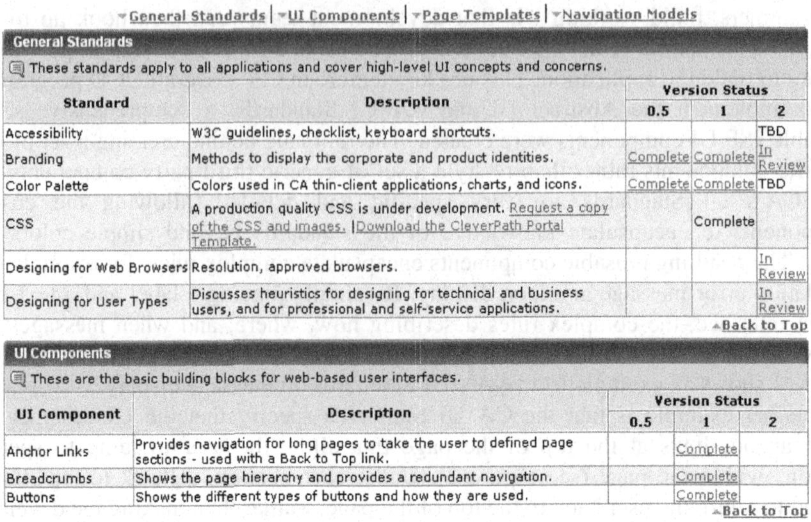

▼General Standards | ▼UI Components | ▼Page Templates | ▼Navigation Models

General Standards

🔲 These standards apply to all applications and cover high-level UI concepts and concerns.

Standard	Description	Version Status		
		0.5	1	2
Accessibility	W3C guidelines, checklist, keyboard shortcuts.			TBD
Branding	Methods to display the corporate and product identities.	Complete	Complete	In Review
Color Palette	Colors used in CA thin-client applications, charts, and icons.	Complete	Complete	TBD
CSS	A production quality CSS is under development. Request a copy of the CSS and images. |Download the CleverPath Portal Template.		Complete	
Designing for Web Browsers	Resolution, approved browsers.			In Review
Designing for User Types	Discusses heuristics for designing for technical and business users, and for professional and self-service applications.			In Review

▲Back to Top

UI Components

🔲 These are the basic building blocks for web-based user interfaces.

UI Component	Description	Version Status		
		0.5	1	2
Anchor Links	Provides navigation for long pages to take the user to defined page sections - used with a Back to Top link.		Complete	
Breadcrumbs	Shows the page hierarchy and provides a redundant navigation.		Complete	
Buttons	Shows the different types of buttons and how they are used.		Complete	

▲Back to Top

Fig. 2. An example of 'back to top' links being automatically place in the page based on the anchors links at the top

4 User-Centered Design Process and UI Technology

The UCD team saw several benefits of using CA web components during product design cycle, especially at prototyping and testing stages. The following benefits were identified:

- Prototypes would be as interactive as real applications;
- Prototype building time would be shortened;
- Prototypes would be migrated into real UI application development;
- UI localization would be done and tested during the design cycle;
- The components would meet usability and accessibility criteria.

While these benefits were exciting, there were concerns about how a UCD professional (UI designer) would be able to use these JSF web components with limited or no Java programming experience. The team hypothesized that if there was a tool that allowed users to build web pages using JSF web components without Java programming experience, then the UI designers would be able to use the web components along with JSF technology to create prototypes during the product design cycle. An evaluation study was performed to determine the JSF UI development tool suitable for the UCD organization.

4.1 Tool Selection

A UI designer and GUI developer conducted a tool evaluation study. The goal was to identify a tool that could easily be used by UI designers without Java programming experience. Since it is a new technology, tool availability was limited. Two candidate tools were identified and evaluated for ease of use from a designer's perspective. At the end of the evaluation, Exadel™ was chosen since it creates web project deployment automatically and had several features that eased UI prototyping such as a drag and drop feature for UI components, visual view mode, source code mode, outline features, and a graphical navigational model.

4.2   User-Centered Design Infrastructure Project

After Exadel™ was chosen, the UCD team planned an infrastructure project. The goal of this project was to create an infrastructure with a number of reusable template pages and applications for UI designers and change the UCD process from creating HTML prototypes to creating JSF prototypes. The initial step of this project was to engage a pilot design project and validate the selected tool and technology. An enterprise storage management web application project was selected as the pilot JSF project.

Pilot Project: An Enterprise Storage Management Web Application UI Design. The next release of enterprise storage management web application underwent a typical UCD process. This involved performing customer interviews to gather user interface requirements and determining user roles and features. After the process flow and architectural diagrams were complete, storyboards were created. A prototype of the user interface was then created using JSF technology and Exadel™. A remote usability evaluation was conducted to gather feedback on the prototype. A UI designer was assigned to this project.

JSF Prototype. Initially, the UI designer took an online training course to learn JSF technology and Exadel™. This was a week long course with a lot of hands-on lab exercises. At the end of the class, she became familiar with the tool, understood JSF technology, and was able to build a few simple JSF web applications. She spent few days on training herself on CA web components using the available documents and input from the component development team. At the end of two weeks, she became comfortable with JSF, Exadel™, and CA web components. However, she could not create Java source files for binding UI elements to the events, data, and navigational model. As a result, a Java developer joined the project to provide Java programming support. The UI designer built the presentation layer based on CA web components using Exadel™ and delivered them to the Java developer who added necessary Java source code behind the presentation layer. The result was an interactive UI prototype which could eventually be reused in application development. In addition, since the UI model was an Abstract UI where all locale-sensitive objects are separated from the core source [2], the user interface was also localized. This added value to the UCD process by potentially allowing the team to test a localized interface with users.

A remote usability evaluation was conducted to gather feedback on the JSF prototype. Since the JSF prototype was as interactive as the targeted application, the tasks that were designed to get user feedback were highly comprehensive. Some tasks included filtering, grouping, and deleting data. Participants were able to accomplish these tasks exactly as they could in the targeted application. This allowed the team to collect detailed and complete usability data on the proposed UI design.

Localization of JSF Prototype. Since localization of prototype results in cost and time savings in the development cycle, it is not common to localize prototypes at design cycle, due to the time consuming nature of this process. Most commonly, localization is left as a separate exercise at the end of development cycle during which problems resulting from word length or orientation often causes costly UI redesigns. Using JSF prototyping, it was easy to localize with no extra cost or time. This allowed the team to conduct expert design reviews and identify and solve potential localization design problems at early design stage. Although the team had a goal to conduct international usability tests, this was not accomplish due to difficulties in finding international participants as well as project time and cost limitations. However, the team did identify the most important localization issues on the user interface, such as tab and button labels and solved them before the development started.

JSF Template Pages. The pilot project results suggest that JSF Prototype has several potential benefits. However, the effort was not as minimal as it was thought at the beginning. To further streamline the process, it was decided to create reusable JSF template pages. The template pages were identified based on CA page layout standards. The identified template pages were: Dashboard (home page), Full Page with Tabs, Full Page with Tabs and Subtabs, Object Detail Page, Report Page, Wizard Drill-Down Page, and Wizard Multi-Tab Page. The UI designer reused the pilot JSF prototype and created the JSF template pages. Since no Java developer resource was available for this activity, these pages were not fully generalized in terms of Java source code. Currently, this part of the project is still in progress. However, the user interface design of template pages was completed as was the localization of the pages (see Figures 3 and 4).

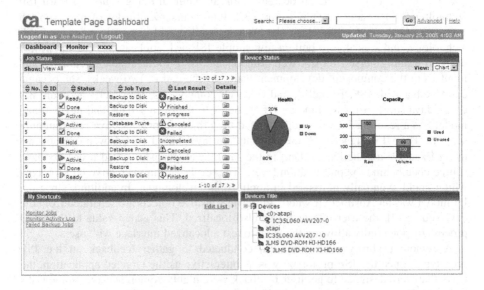

Fig. 3. An example JSF template page: Dashboard

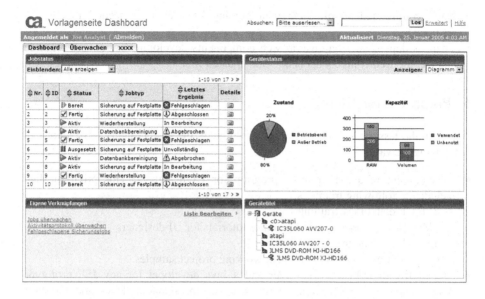

Fig. 4. An example JSF template page localized in German: Dashboard

5 Advantages and Disadvantages of JSF Prototyping

The pilot project study demonstrates that JSF prototyping has a number of advantages:

- The resulting prototype is as interactive as the targeted application.
- The prototype is the real front layer of the targeted application and is reusable in the development of application.
- Reusable CA web components are complete in terms of data validation, error messages, etc. The resulting prototype also becomes complete using these components.
- New technological updates on CA web components can automatically go into the prototypes built with them by updating the linked CA web component package.
- The UI designer directly contributes to the application development process. This eliminates the need for a detailed UI design quality test at the end of development cycle.
- The prototyping effort can be generalized using template pages. This results in savings in both cost and time in the product design and development cycles.
- The UI standards are converted into working JSF web components. This ensures the UI standards are implemented correctly and eliminates discrepancies that might be caused by different interpretations of the standards.

There are numerous challenges associated with JSF prototyping:

- Java programming experience is required to create fully interactive prototypes. This is not a typical experience owned by UI Designers.

- XML coding and simple Java data binding knowledge is needed for the UI designer.
- There is dependency on custom web components development. For any required change, the web components need to be updated first.

6 Preparing for Change

Based on the lessons learned from the pilot project, the requirements were identified for moving forward:

- Development of a JSF training program for UI designers. This program shall include the following trainings:
  - JSF UI technology training
  - CA web components training and/or tutorials for UI designers
  - Exadel tool training
- Development of CA web component working project samples.
- Availability of both a UI designer and a Java developer for any JSF prototype development. The UI designer will create the presentation layer and the Java developer will bind the presentation layer to the XML data file and navigational model.
- UI designers must understand the concept of XML and data binding.
- Simple, XML data models that allow the designer to add data to the prototype without a developer

While this change presents a challenge for UI designers, it brings significant potential benefits to the design and development process.

7 Future Direction

There is no a complete JSF prototyping tool for UI designers in the market. There is still plenty of work to be done in developing a tool that is easy to be used with no Java programming experience. As a next step, we will continue searching a complete tool suite to the UI designers' needs.

Template pages project is still in progress. The next step is to complete development of template pages and continuously enhance them in order to ease the task of creating JSF prototypes.

Another area that will continuously be renewed and maintained is CA web components. More AJAX technology will be applied to the components and they will be as "rich" as possible. In addition, bi-direction localization features will also be applied to the components

Acknowledgments. UI Web Component Development team, Rebecca Baker, and Kerry Harrison from UCD team at CA, Inc.

References

1. JavaServer Faces Technology, News and Information. Available as, http://java.sun.com/javaee/javaserverfaces
2. O'Conner, J.: Java Internationalization: Localization with ResourceBundles (1998), Available as http://java.sun.com/developer/technicalArticles/Intl/ResourceBundles

Color Your Website: Use of Colors on the Web

Irina Kondratova and Ilia Goldfarb

National Research Council Canada Institute for Information Technology
46 Dineen Drive, Fredericton, NB, Canada E3B 9W4
{Irina.Kondratova,Ilia.Goldfarb}@nrc-cnrc.gc.ca

Abstract. In spite of the wealth of information available on designing international user interfaces, it is not easy for web designers to acquire a deep understanding of culturally appropriate user interface design. There is a lack of tools that assist web developers in creating culturally appropriate user interfaces. In our paper we present an empirical study that identifies culture-specific web interface design elements for a number of countries using semi-automated approach, in order to incorporate the results into a cultural interface design advisor tool. The paper presents results of the pilot study on web design color preferences for a number of countries. Results show that along with ten colors that are used universally in website design for all countries studied, country-specific color palettes could be identified. Examples of these "preferred" palettes are presented in the paper along with suggestions on how designers can work with such palettes creating culturally appropriate websites.

Keywords: Color preferences, color theory, cultural user interface, usability.

1 Introduction

The need for culturally appropriate interface design for e-commerce applications is emphasized by many researchers [1], [2], [3]. Specifically, it is noted that the "culturability"[4], a combination of culture and usability in Web design, directly impacts on the user's perception of credibility and trustworthiness of websites [5], [6]. A culturally sensitive e-commerce framework [7] lists cultural appeal as one of the four important factors impacting on sustainability of e-commerce activity, along with economic appeal, usability and general attitude towards e-commerce; thus reflecting the importance of cultural factors in e-commerce applications.

Some theoretical models developed by researchers for managing the "subjective" aspects of cross-cultural interface design include cultural dimension (n-factor) models [8], [9], [10], [11], cultural markers model [12], and cultural attractor model [13]. Within their framework model, Barber and Badre [4] provide a detailed list of cultural markers corresponding to web design elements such as color, spatial organization, fonts, shapes, icons, metaphors, geography, language, flags, sounds, motion, preferences for text vs. graphics, directionality of how language is written (left vs. right), help features and navigation tools. Smith et al. [13] define cultural design elements as "cultural attractors", and list a smaller number of them: colors, color combinations, banner adverts, trust signs, use of metaphor, language cues and navigation controls. Sun [14], in

N. Aykin (Ed.): Usability and Internationalization, Part II, HCII 2007, LNCS 4560, pp. 123–132, 2007.
© Springer-Verlag Berlin Heidelberg 2007

turn, focuses on only four major categories of cultural markers: language, visuals, colors and page layout.

Empirical studies focused on evaluating the influence of cultural markers on user performance and acceptance of websites found some evidence of user preference for websites with cultural markers from their own cultures [15], improved performance for users on their local sites [16], or some cultural differences between websites for different countries [17], [14]. Based on these studies, it appears that it is easier to "map" the cultural markers directly into culturally appropriate design elements for a website [13]; therefore, in our cultural web user interface study we chose to use the cultural markers approach.

2 Cultural Web User Interface Study

The study investigates the usage of specific visual cultural markers for website design in a number of countries, in order to incorporate the results into a cultural interface design advisor tool. For the purpose of this study, cultural markers are defined as "interface design elements and features that are prevalent, and possibly preferred, within a particular cultural group"[18]. The visual cultural markers we are investigating are colors, font usage, number of images, and layout of the webpage.

This study is carried out via an automated "cultural audit" of a large number of websites from different countries. A Cultural Web Spider (Web crawler) tool, designed to extract information on culture specific Web page design elements (cultural markers) from the HTML and CSS code of websites for a particular country domain (eg: .ca for Canada, .fr for France, .jp for Japan, etc.) is used in the study [19]. The Cultural Web Spider application (CWS) utilizes Google SOAP APIs Web services [20] to search for particular cultural markers on web pages of top ranked websites for a country domain.

When using a Web Crawler to collect data for further analysis, it is important to make a proper choice of methodology for this survey, and , especially, of websites for data collection [21]. We are collecting data on the top ranked (popular) websites for a particular country domain in the Google index, thus we are capturing a representative sample of cultural design preferences for a particular country. In addition to this, Google API allows further restricting the search to country domain websites written in a particular language. In this way, we were able to limit the automated "cultural audit", of top ranked country specific domain websites, to sites written in the country's official language (e.g. Russian for Russia, French for France, Portuguese for Brazil, etc.) and assure reliability of our cultural study results. The Web crawler tool collects information on the color usage (e.g. page background colors, table background colors, font colors, etc.), font usage, and number of images on a website. This information is saved in a cultural database and is available for further statistical analysis and visualization.

To investigate the appropriateness of our approach, and the functionality and usefulness of the cultural analysis tools we are developing, we conducted a pilot study focused on Web design color preferences for 26 countries around the globe.

3   Color on the Web

Color plays an important role in different cultures throughout the history, and the choice of color plays a vital role in design, advertising and marketing [22, 23]. Some researchers suggest that certain colors have symbolic connotations in different countries, for example that green is preferred color in Islamic counties, red is preferred color in China and black is preferred in US, although has some unfavorable connotations in Asia, Latin America and Europe [24]. Others [25] connect colors with feelings, especially in advertising. Recent research study by Chattopadhyay et al. [24] suggests that most aspects of color (hue) preference are likely to be culturally universal, in fact, in their research they found that blue was the most preferred hue in every culture.

In our study on cultural preferences in website design for a number of countries we wanted to explore, in addition to other cultural markers, color preferences expressed by web designers in choosing colors for their websites, including colors chosen for webpage background, table background, graphics, text, imaging, etc. The underlying assumption is that the Internet, as a medium of communication, presents an opportunity for designers to truly express their color choices since the choice of colors for webpage is not constrained by cost or technical limitations that are frequently imposed when working with the print media.

3.1   Web Color Usage Pilot Study

The color usage pilot study investigates color use on the Web by studying a large number (from 900 to about 1000) of county-specific websites per each of 26 countries located in Africa, Asia, Europe, Latin America, North America, and Oceania. The list of the countries studied is presented in Table 1.

The first stage of the study involved web crawling with CWS tool and extraction of culture-specific information from HTML code by searching top-ranked (the most popular) pages in the Google index for a particular country and language. An analysis tool was developed to analyze all the information collected in the database and produce between countries comparisons for different cultural markers such as color usage, font usage, the number of images used on the page, usage of style sheets, etc. For the second stage of our study, the results collected by the CWS tool are statistically analyzed and visualized using a CWS visualization tool. This tool visualizes the results of analysis on a color usage in different countries and present most frequently used RGB colors for a particular country as color palettes [19].

3.2   Identification of Colors Specified in HTML and CSS Code

Designers have at their disposal a palette of about 16.7 million colors based on HTML RGB color code to create their interface designs. Therefore, the main inconvenience of using the CWS visualization tool is that the tool could not possibly show all the RGB design colors used in a convenient and user friendly format.

Table 1. List of countries for the pilot color study

Country	Language	Country	Language
Australia	English	Italy	Italian
Belgium	French	Japan	Japanese
Brazil	Portuguese	Korea	Korean
Canada	English, French	Mexico	Spanish
China	Chinese	New Zealand	English
Denmark	Danish	Norway	Norwegian
Egypt	Arabic	Poland	Polish
Finland	Finnish	Russia	Russian
France	French	Saudi Arabia	Arabic
Germany	German	Spain	Spanish
India	English	Sweden	Swedish
Indonesia	Indonesian	United Kingdom	English
Ireland	English	United States of America	English

To resolve this, we developed a color calibration tool that incorporates a proprietary color classification algorithm. This tool enables us to categorize all the colors discovered in our search into a manageable number of color categories corresponding to the user friendly "artistic" palette based on a well known "color wheel" palette of twelve hues [26]. The color calibration tool functionality allows us to manually adjust chosen color categories, if needed. Our "artistic" palette of 53 colors includes such intuitive and easy to understand color categories as white, black, three shades of gray (dark gray, gray and light gray), and four shades for each color hue such as dark blue, light blue, medium blue and shaded blue for blue; light yellow, medium yellow, dark yellow and shaded yellow for yellow, etc. (see Figure 1).

By using the color calibration tool for color clustering, we were able to analyze the color usage data harvested by the Cultural Web Spider more efficiently and visualize the results via an HTML Color Analyzer. The HTML Color Analyzer represents color information we collected as a pie chart color palette for a particular country and the results of this work are presented elsewhere [27].

In the process of further data analysis we have discovered limitations imposed by the nature of the automated Web "harvesting" process. For example, for any website that has images and graphics as most prominent design elements, image color information is lost in the automated cultural analysis using an HTML analyzer, since image color information is not contained in the HTML or CSS code.

Moreover, an HTML Color Analyzer counts instances of a particular color usage in the HTML code. The number of instances for a particular color does not necessarily gives a true indication of color preferences, since in this case the area of color coverage is not taken into account. For example, multiple usage of a color "dark blue" as a cell background color in the table will result in an overall higher count of "dark blue" color usage, than when the same "dark blue" color is used as a background color for the entire table (despite the fact that the resulting visual effect could be the same).

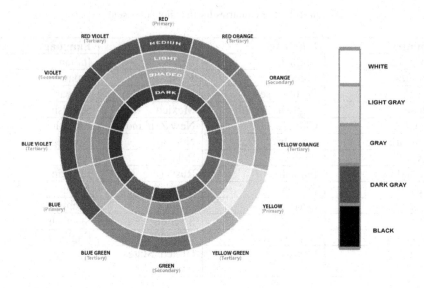

Fig. 1. "Artistic" color wheel

3.3 Finding Predominantly Used Colors Based on Webpage Snapshots

To overcome this apparent shortcoming of our data collection and analysis efforts, we developed another application for color analysis – the Image Color Analyzer. This application enables capturing a "snapshot" image of the webpage under review and analyzing color information in this image. This approach provides an opportunity to automatically analyze color usage on a large number of websites, and capture and

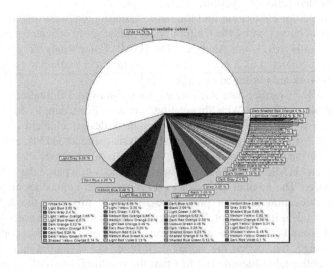

Fig. 2. Image Color Analyzer results: color palette for Japan

analyze a "visual appearance" of the webpage. This method provides us with an advantage in comparison with a labor consuming visual color analysis on the same number of websites (about 1000!) conducted manually by a researcher.

Image Color Analyzer tool permits us to precisely measure the relative coverage of different colors on the webpage of interest in percentage of the total webpage area. Color Analyzer also allows visualizing color usage and producing country-specific color usage pie charts, based on the color calibration scheme chosen via the color calibration tool. A color usage chart for Japanese websites produced by the Image Color Analyzer is presented in Figure 2. Similar color charts were produced for all countries previously studied using an HTML analyzer.

4 Study Results

We conducted our netnographic [28] color usage pilot study on a large number of website for a certain locale and harvested cultural markers usage data on the top ranked websites for a particular locale. We believe that the choice of colors, to a certain degree, reflects local users' preference for a particular color or color combinations on these "popular" local websites.

4.1 International Color Palette

In order to derive country-specific color palettes for fifteen out of 26 countries we studied, results obtained by utilizing both tools, the HTML Color Analyzer and the Image Color Analyzer, were examined using the following approach. We chose the sixteen most commonly used colors for a particular country, based on results obtained by the Image Color Analyzer. Thus, based on analysis of "snapshots" of web pages, we created country-specific color palettes. After this, we cross referenced these palettes with the results obtained by using the HTML analyzer. In this way we could eliminate colors that might be present in images on Web pages, but do not correspond to color preferences we identified though the HTML analyzer. This cross-referencing process helped us to choose a country palette of colors with both, a high coverage area and a high number of usage instances, verifying country-specific color preferences obtained by using each of the tools separately.

Results of our color usage analysis for the fifteen countries showed that some colors are commonly and preferentially used across all countries studied [29]. These colors include white, black, all shades of gray, all shades of blue and a light yellow color. We named this color palette the "international colors palette" (Figure 3).

4.2 Country-Specific Color Palettes

As a next step, we continued with further data analysis in order to single out country-specific color preference. As a result, we identified two to four additional "country-specific" colors by cross-referencing data obtained via HTML analysis and webpage snapshot analysis. The results for fifteen countries studied are presented elsewhere [29].

white	
light gray	
gray	
dark gray	
black	
shaded blue	
dark blue	
medium blue	
light blue	
light yellow	

Fig. 3. "International" color palette

In order to further expand the palette of country-specific colors for different countries, we chose to base our color usage recommendations on the range of preferred colors obtained through image analysis of webpage snapshots using the Color Image Analyzer. We believe that they represent the overall visual appearance of country-specific websites more precisely than the color information contained in HTML code. During the data analysis process, we removed the "international" colors from the color palettes obtained via Image color analysis of country-specific websites and obtained country-specific palettes presented with pie charts with relative percentage of the coverage area identified. An example of a country specific color palette for Japan is presented in Figure 4. Similar palettes are prepared for all 26 countries involved in the study.

As a next step in our investigation, we looked at the process of how these "country-specific" color palettes could be used to develop recommendations on country-specific color combinations for culturally appropriate interface design. Since our color palettes are based on the Johannes Itten's twelve-point color circle, we suggest that the process steps could follow the color theory approach to choosing colors from the color circle for determining complementary color pairs and harmonious color triads [26]. There are other relevant sources of information available for designers for choosing appropriate color combinations [30, 31], as well as some software resources such as ColorWheel software [32]. Design color decisions could be also supported by the tools that present information on "historical" meaning of particular colors [22, 23, 33, 34].

4.3 An Example: Color Combinations for Japan

As an example, we suggest how one can choose appropriate color combinations for Japan, based on the color palette in Figure 4 and utilizing a color theory. As seen from Figure 4, the following colors are prevalent in the country-specific palette for Japan: green (21.5% in total for dark, light and medium green), red orange (13.7% in total), orange (13.6% in total) and yellow orange (12.7% in total). In addition to these colors, yellow has significant presence in the palette of colors used in Japan (medium and dark yellow in total give 7.2 % and light yellow is popular as well as seen from Figure 2).

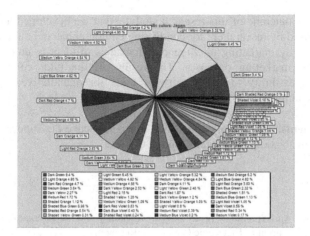

Fig. 4. "Country-specific" color palette for Japan

Based on the color theory, the designer will look for the appropriate color combinations (schemes) that could be used with these dominant colors. Such color schemes to chose from could be complementary, split complementary, analogous, etc. Complementary color pairs are any two colors which are diametrically opposite one another in the color wheel. Split complementary scheme could be achieved by substituting for one color of a complementary pair the two colors that lie on either side of the color wheel. For example, to harmonize green, the designer will choose a pair of colors such as red-orange and red-violet (or either one of them) to form the triple or pair harmony with the predominant green color. In the case of Japan, since red orange is predominantly used, it might be appropriate to use this color with green. To expand the analysis, based on the color wheel for Japan, an analogous color scheme that uses colors that are adjacent to each other on the color wheel would be yellow, yellow orange, orange and red orange.

It is important to notice that in our approach we do not restrict the choice of design colors, for example, a red orange color category contains a wide range of red orange hues to choose from. This is true for all other color categories.

5   Conclusion

The cultural interface design study investigates the usage of specific cultural markers for website design in a number of countries, in order to incorporate the results into a cultural interface design advisor tool. In particular, a pilot color study investigates usage of color for website design in different countries.

Results of the study show that, along with some colors (hues) used universally across the multitude of cultures, there are some preferred country-specific color palettes that could be used by web designers to create culturally appropriate web interfaces. The beneficial effect of utilising these palettes of colors for web design needs to be futher evaluated by conducting usability testing with end users for different locales.

An additional outcome of this research study is that we developed a suite of tools that could be used by researchers for conducting ethnographic and cultural studies on the Internet and by marketing intelligence companies to identify cultural trends for advertising and marketing purposes. The results of the pilot color usage study confirmed the feasibility of using software tools for quantitative and qualitative research on the cultural "look and feel" on the Internet.

Aknowledgements. The authors would like to acknowledge the support provided for the project by the National Research Council Canada.

References

1. Becker, S.A.: An Exploratory Study on Web Usability and the Internationalization of Us E-Businesses. Journal of Electronic Commerce Research 3(4), 265–278 (2002)
2. Hornby, G., Goulding, P., Poon, S.: Perceptions of Export Barriers and Cultural Issues: The Sme E-Commerce Experience. Journal of Electronic Commerce Research 3(4), 213–226 (2002)
3. Barron, A.E., Rickerman, C.: Going Global. Designing E-Learning for an International Audience. In: Proceedings ASTD TechKnowledge 2003 conference (2003), http://www1.astd.org/tk03/session_handouts
4. Barber, W., Badre, A.N.: Culturability: The Merging of Culture and Usability. In: Human Factors and the Web, Our Global Community, Basking Ridge, New Jersey, USA. AT&T Labs (1998), http://www.research.att.com/conf/hfweb/proceedings/barder/index.htm
5. Cyr, D., Bonanni, C., Ilsever, J.: Design and E-Loyalty across Cultures in Electronic Commerce. In: Proceedings of the 6th International Conference on Electronic Commerce Delft, The Netherlands, pp. 351–360 (2004)
6. Fogg, B.J.: Persuasive Technology. Morgan Kaufmann, San Francisco (2002)
7. Sudweeks, F., Simoff, S.: Culturally Commercial: A Cultural E-Commerce Framework. In: Proceedings OZCHI 2001 Fremantle Western Australia pp. 148–153 (2001)
8. Hall, E., Hall, M.R.: Understanding Cultural Differences. Intercultural Press, Yarmouth, Maine (1990)
9. Hofstede, G.: Cultures and Organizations: Software of the Mind. McGraw-Hill, New York (1991)
10. Trompenaars, F.: Riding the Waves of Culture: Understanding Cultural Diversity in Business. Nicholas Brealey, London (1993)
11. Khaslavsky, J.: Integrating Culture into Interface Design. In; Proceedings of CHI 98 on Human factors in computing systems Los Angeles, CA, pp. 365–366 (1998)
12. Barber, W., Badre, A.N.: The Merging of Culture and Usability. In: 4th Conference on Human Factors and the Web. Baskin Ridge, New Jersey (1998)
13. Smith, A., Dunckley, L., French, T., Minocha, S., Chang, Y.: A Process Model for Developing Usable Cross-Cultural Websites. Interacting With Computers 16(1), 69–91 (2004)
14. Sun, H.: Building a Culturally-Competent Corporate Web Site: An Exploratory Study of Cultural Markers in Multilingual Web Design. In: Proceedings 19th annual international conference on computer documentation, SIGDOC 01, Santa Fe, New Mexico, USA, pp. 95–102. ACM Press, New York (2001)
15. Barber, W., Badre, A.N.: Culturability: The Merging of Culture and Usability. In: 4th Conference on Human Factors and the Web New Jersey, USA. Basking Ridge (2001)

16. Sheppard, C., Scholtz, J.: The Effects of Cultural Markers on Website Use. In: Proc. 5th Conference on Human Factors and the Web Gaithersburg, Maryland (1999)
17. Juric, R., Kim, I., Kuljis, J.: Cross Cultural Web Design: An Experience of Developing Uk and Korean Cultural Markers. In: Proceedings of 25th International Conference on Information Technology Interfaces ITI 2003 Cavtat, Croatia pp. 309–313 (2003)
18. Badre, A.N.: The Effects of Cross Cultural Interface Design Orientation on World Wide Web User Performance. In: Georgia Instiutute of Technology, College of Computing, GVU Centre. Atlanta, GA (2001)
19. Kondratova, I., Goldfarb, I., Gervais, R., Fournier, L.: Culturally Appropriate Web Interface Design: Web Crawler Study. In: Proceedings the 8th International Conference on Computer and Advanced Technology in Education (CATE 2005) ACTA Press Anaheim/Calgary/Zurich pp. 359–364 (2005)
20. Google: Google Web Apis (2006), http://www.google.com/apis
21. Thelwall, M.: Methodologies for Crawler Based Web Surveys. Imternet Research:Electronic Networking Applications and Policy 12(2), 124–138 (2002)
22. Cage, J.: Color and Meaning: Art, Science, and Symbolism. In: University of California Press (2000)
23. Cage, J.: Color and Culture: Practice and Meaning from Antiquity to Abstraction. In: University of California Press (1999)
24. Chattopadhyay, A., Darke, P.R., Gorn, G.J.: Roses Are Red and Violets Are Blue - Everywhere? In: Cultural Differences and Universals in Color Preference and Choice among Consumers and Marketing Managers. Sauder School of Business (2002)
25. Gorn, G.J.C., Amitava, Yi, Tracey, Dahl, Darren, W.: Effects of Color as an Executional Cue in Advertising: They're in the Shade. Management Science 43(10), 1387–1400 (1997)
26. Itten, J.: The Art of Color: The Subjective Experience and Objective Rationale of Color. John Wiley and Sons, New York (1974)
27. Kondratova, I., Goldfarb, I.: Cultural Visual Interface Design. In: Proceedings EDMedia 2005 - World Conference on Educational Multimedia, Hypermedia and Telecommunications Montreal, Canada pp. 1255–1262 (2005)
28. Kozinets, R.V.: The Field Behind the Screen: Using Netnography for Marketing Research in Online Communities. Journal of Marketing Research 39, 61–72 (2002)
29. Kondratova, I., Goldfarb, I.: Cultural Interface Design: Global Colors Study. In: Meersman, R., Tari, Z. (eds.) On the Move to Meaningful Internet Systems 2006: CoopIS, DOA, GADA, and ODBASE. LNCS, vol. 4275, pp. 926–934. Springer, Heidelberg (2006)
30. Kobayashi, S.: Color Image Scale. Kodansha International (1991)
31. Mante, H.: Color Design in Photography (1972)
32. Colorwheelpro (2007), http://www.color-wheel-pro.com
33. Cabarga, L.: The Designer's Guide to Global Color Combinations. In: 750 Color Formulas in CMYK and RGB from around the Word. Cincinnati, Ohio (2001)
34. Vanka, S.: Colortool: The Cross Cultural Meanings of Color. In: IWIPS, pp. 33–43 (1999)

Cultural Environment for Social Learning and Adaptation in Different Countries - A Comparison of Minority Foreigners and Majority Foreigners

Masaaki Kurosu[1] and Masako Morishita[2]

[1] National Institute of Multimedia Education
masaakikurosu@spa.nifty.com
[2] Waseda University
ma-ko@msh.biglobe.ne.jp

Abstract. Before WWII, number of foreign people was not large in Japan. But after the war, it grew larger and now we have total of 2,011,555 foreigners (in 2005). There are some majority groups such as Koren (598,687), Chinese (519,561), Brazilian (302,080), and Filipinos (187,261). At the same time, there are minority groups such as Bangladeshi (9,707) and Iranian (5,769). Organizing local communities of such people and those of them with Japanese people plays important roles for their life in Japan. Information systems and communication devices such as the PC and the cell phone may play one of the key roles for maintaining such communities. Some people think that the use of such devices and systems may differ for majorities and minorities. Majorities can organize a local community far easily than minorities and will have more chances to meet friends face-to-face. They also have chances of getting information on their own country via the satellite TV, newspapers and magazines and other media. On the other hand, minorities may have only a small linkage with people from the same country. In such a case, the website on the internet or the cell phone may be important for them. Based on this hypothesis, we conducted interviews with and did research among Japanese Brazilians as the majority and Iranians as the minority to specify how the information system can serve a useful tool for their life and their social learning to adapt to the target society.

1 Introduction

Japanese people has been considering itself as a single ethnic group country despite the fact that there are Ainu-people, Koreans, Chinese and others who has the nationality of Japan. It was thus not easy for foreigners to adapt to Japanese society as its members. They tend to be regarded as foreigners almost always. This is quite different from such country as the U.S.

Authors are interested in how they are going to adapt to Japanese society, and how Japanese society is treating them, especially in terms of the social networking. And for organizing the social networking, authors are interested in the effective use of the ICT, i.e. the use of the cell phone and the internet.

N. Aykin (Ed.): Usability and Internationalization, Part II, HCII 2007, LNCS 4560, pp. 133–139, 2007.
© Springer-Verlag Berlin Heidelberg 2007

Table 1. Statistics on total number of foreigners based on their capacity (from Morris)

	2000	*2004*	*2005*
Total	1,686,444	1,973,747	2,011,555
University	6,744	8,153	8,406
Religion	4,976	4,699	4,588
Education	8,375	9,393	9,449
Technology		23,210	29,044
International business	34,739	47,682	55,276
Entertainment	53,847	64,742	36,376
Special skills		13,373	15,112
Short stay	68,045	72,446	68,747
Student	76,980	129,873	129,568
Temporary student	37,781	43,208	28,147
Short Student	36,199	54,317	54,107
Family Member	72,878	81,919	86,055
Specific Activity		63,310	87,324
Permanent Resident	145,336	312,964	349,804
Spouse to Japanese	279,625	257,292	259,656
Resident	237,607	250,734	265,639
Special Resident	512,269	465,619	451,909

Table 2. Statistics on foreigners staying in Japan based on their home country

Korea	598,687
China	519,561
Brazil	302,080
Philippines	187,261
Peru	57,728
USA	49,390
Thailand	36,347
Vietnam	26,018
Indonesia	23,890
UK	18,082

As shown in Table 1, there are 2,011,555 foreigners in Japan in 2005. It is 1.57% to the Table 1. Statistics on total number of foreigners based on their capacity (from Morris) total population of Japan of 127,756,815. There are various categories to some extent due to the historical reason.

The classification based on their home countries is shown in Tab. 2 and it can be seen that the majorities are Koreans, Chinese, Brazilian and Philippinos. People from such countries as Bangladesh, Iran, Nigeria, etc. can be categorized as minorities. Out approach is to survey the networking to and among majority / minority foreigners by taking Brazilians (Japanese Brazilians) as an example of the majority and Bangladeshi as an example of the minority.

2 Research and Its Results

Authors have been conducting the interview research for more than 5 years, Kurosu for Japanese Brazilian and Morishita for Bangladeshi, Iranian, etc. Based on those researches, results and findings are summarized in Tab. 3.

Table 3. Findings from interview researches for Japanese Brazilian and Bangladesh informants

		Majority	Minority
		Japanese Brazilian	Bangladeshi
Life	Stay in Japan	> Short stay (3-5 yrs.) > Goal is to earn money and send/bring back it to their homeland > Working in physical labor or simple work of which Japanese do not tend to work > Living in their own community (e.g. Hamamatsu, Ohta, etc.)	> Rather long stay (more than 10 yrs.) > Working as engineers, salespersons, actors, etc. > Do not have specific local community, hence living among Japanese community
	Motivation	> Less motivated to adapt to Japanese society because they can live in their own community	> They have motivations to adapt to Japanese society and have been making efforts to contribut to the local Japanese community
	Information Access	> Brazilian satellite TV and radio available > Portuguese magazines, newspapers, CDs, DVDs, Videos available > Can easily call to Brazil by the cellphone > Frequently communicate among them using cellphones > If PC is available, they can get information from Brazilian website quite easily > Many shops owned by Japanese Brazilian that have many kinds of products from their homeland	> Almost no information is available by their mother language > They are motivated to learn Japanese and English to communicate with them and get necessary information
	Japanese Language	> Less motivated to learn Japanese language and there are quite many who cannot talk/hear/read/write Japanese > For kids, there are Brazilian schools where Japanese is taught to them	> Less opportunity to learn Japanese in any formal organization > They are trying to get opportunities wherever and whenever it is possible by using the TV programs, by talking to Japanese colleagues, by attending the party, etc.

Table 3. (*continued*)

		Majority	Minority
		Japanese Brazilian	Bangladeshi
	Networking	> Though they form Brazilian local communities, the cohesive force among them seems not strong > But there are couples between Japanese Brazilian people, and sometimes they get married > Let their friends and family members come to Japan not just for pleasure but for providing them the job opportunity > Small sized networking among Japanese Brazilian is for certain extent necessary and it functions rather well as such > But large sized networking in the local community as a whole is not necessary be required and is not functioning enough	> Less frequent to form the local community of those who coming from Bangladesh > Trying to expand the network by making friends including Japanese and other foreign people > They are hosting the party, inviting friends to their home for the purpose of establishing the network > There are some who got married with Japanese > Many of them wish to live in Japan for a long time > Some of them have wishes to let their family members come to Japan, but actually it is rather diffcult
	Participation to Society	> They came to Japan with the support of family members or friends already living in Japan, got job positions by their introduction > After several years when they think they got enough money, most of them go back to Brazil	> After getting the job in Japan, they settle down in Japan > Many of them have experience of working in other foreign countries
Local Community	Local Government	> The policy is to support their life with satisfaction as much as possible by providing the website in Portuguese and publishing the newspaper in Portuguese > The language support is for Japanese, English and Portuguese	> Almost no service is provided in their native language > But such activity as to hold the foreigners society and to open the portal site for such foreigners has just begun
	Volunteer	> Supporting the Japanese language learning and the everyday issues	> Volunteers are not so much motivated to support foreign people but to enjoy the communication with foreigners
	Problems	> Sometimes the goal of activity is not clear whether they are intending to really support the life of Japanese Brazilian > Establishing a well disciplined and well organized symbiosis is still a goal that has not yet reached	> Opportunities for learning Japanese language are provided but just for primers and not for advanced level
Significance	Language	> Just a simple Japanese is needed in their workplace	> For the introductory level, most of them have already achieved their language skill

Table 3. (*continued*)

		Majority	Minority
		Japanese Brazilian	Bangladeshi
	Relationship	> Less motivated to establish a good relationship with Japanese people	> Motivated to support other foreigners based on their own experience
	Career Plan	> Short termed	> Motivated to live in Japan for a long time and is making efforts to establish a good relationship in their workplace and local community
	Problem	> Many conflicts exists based on the difference of living habits (e.g. how to separate trashes, how to entertain in the middle of night)	> Feels many kinds of barriers in the local community > Almost no opportunities for such foreigners to participate in the local community activity > Sometimes a good will based consideration is accepted as not treating them as a formal community member
Necessary Future Activity		> Understand more of their needs, necessity and expectation by using the depth interview, for example. > Consider a better solution for the networking among their community and between Japanese community > Find out the key person > Understand the individual differences	> Understand their situation and problems to adapt to Japanese society by tracing their human network > Mutual community activity is necessary than the one way support and Japanese people should consider more on how to establish such relationship with them

3 Discussion

In terms of the use of ICT to support the networking to and among foreigners, it could be summarized as follows.

3.1 For the Majority (Japanese Brazilian)

1. Communication using the cell phone is quite active among Japanese Brazilian. Most of the use is not by the calling but by the email in English. Although most of them are not fluent in English, they are using Japanese cell phone in English mode. Contents of emails among them are quite short and trivial, for example, "Hi what are you doing now?", "When are you coming here?", etc (of course, they are written in Portuguese). They exchange such emails during any time of the day even in working hours. In other words, their use of the cell phone is just like the everyday conversation. Based on such email communication, they are tightening their human relation.

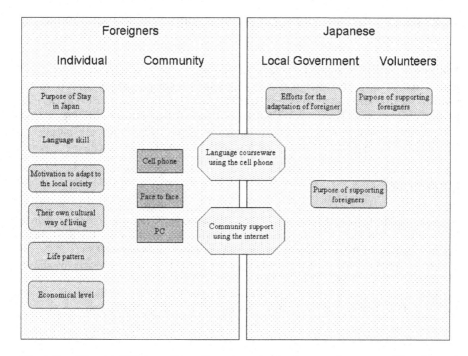

Fig. 1. Possible use of ICT to enhance the communication between Japanese and Foreigners

2. This tendency let them condense the relationship among them and put a distance from the Japanese community. This might be less problematic for Japanese Brazilian themselves at least at present. But considering the Japanese society as a whole, it might trigger some problems especially when something negative may happen. One of the worst case has happened during the big earthquake in Tokyo area in 1923 when there occurred a rumour that Koreans put some poison to the well and 233 (according to the government statistics) or 6000 (according to some private organization) Koreans were killed. The background for this incident is related to the fact that most of Koreans at that time could not speak Japanese language well and there was no good communication between Korean and Japanese.

3. Based on such fact, more effort to let Japanese Brazilian learn the Japanese language should be made, for example, by using the cell phone and the internet. Currently, the cell phone is regarded one of the effective tool for the e-learning. Besides almost all Japanese Brazilians own it.

3.2 For Minorities (Bangladeshi, for Example)

1. Because they are living in Japanese society and making efforts to establish a better communication among themselves each of which are living apart in Japan. Besides they have a motivation to be well-adapted to the Japanese society. Based on this fact, internet-based on-line community where Japanese and minority

foreigners can exchange information can be thought to be one of the good solutions to the situation.

Additional Notice. It should be noted that findings in our research can not simply be generalized to majority foreigners and minority foreigners. Many aspects in this research may be specific to Japanese Brazilian and Bangladeshi. For example, there are majorities such as Korean and Chinese who have a long history of living in Japan and generally have a good Japanese language skill. Hence, for the purpose of generalizing our hypothesis, more wide researches should be conducted.

References

1. Morishita, M., Kurosu, M.: The path of the participation to the Japanese society found in the narrative of foreigners – 1. In: Learning networking among minority foreigners, Annual Conference of Japanese Society of Qualitative Psychology (in Japanese 2006)
2. Kurosu, M., Morishita, M.: The path of the participation to the Japanese society found in the narrative of foreigners – 2. In: Learning networking among majority foreigners, Annual Conference of Japanese Society of Qualitative Psychology (in Japanese 2006)
3. Morris, J.F.: Foreigners in Japan.http://www.mgu.ac.jp/~jfmorris/Zainiti.htm

Transborder Data Protection and the Effects on Business and Government

Julian Ligertwood and Margaret Jackson*

School of Accounting and Law, RMIT University
239 Bourke St, Melbourne, VIC, Australia
{Julian.ligertwood,Margaret.jackson}@rmit.edu.au

Abstract. The expansion of the internet has brought with it a huge increase in the number of instances of personal information sent by businesses and governments from one jurisdiction to another. Concern arising out of Europe, in particular, over the adequacy of data protection measures in many jurisdictions around the world has resulted in increasing international pressure being applied to those countries not meeting adequacy requirements. This paper examines the nature and effect of this pressure particularly on Australian business and government.

Keywords: Australia, EU, India, data protection, law, business, government.

1 Introduction

This paper examines how Australian government and business is reacting to the data protection standards being set by the European Union (EU). It explains what legislative and other regulatory and contractual approaches are being taken in order to comply with the EU standards, examines the attitudes of business to the regulatory changes and the extent to which they are complying with the EU data protection standards.

The international data protection regulatory background is described, including the central role that Europe has had in setting the standard for trans-border data protection. The paper then discusses data protection regulation in Australia and how Australian government and businesses are reacting to the EU Data Directive in relation to personal data sent outside its national borders. Given growing international privacy concerns over its huge outsourcing industry, the response of India, which has little data protection regulation, to international pressure, is also briefly discussed. Whilst the aim of the paper is to explicate the legal developments in relation to transborder data protection, an examination of the social and cultural forces behind these developments is beyond the scope of this paper.

---

* The authors wish to acknowledge the support of the Smart Internet Technology Co-operative Research Centre in the development of this paper.

N. Aykin (Ed.): Usability and Internationalization, Part II, HCII 2007, LNCS 4560, pp. 140–149, 2007.
© Springer-Verlag Berlin Heidelberg 2007

2 International Data Protection Initiatives

Strong European data protection regulation is setting the international standard in transborder data protection. Indeed Europe has been the leader in protecting individual privacy throughout the digital age. This protection began in Europe in 1949 with the formation of the Council of Europe by ten European countries to strengthen democracy, human rights and the rule of law throughout the member states. In 1968, the Council of Europe concluded that national and international law was not adequately protecting privacy [17].

By 1974, the Council had adopted non-binding recommendations following the basic format of 'fair information principles': Information should be accurate, timely and relevant; confidentiality and security should be protected; individuals should have rights of access, notice, consent, and correction. The *Convention for the Protection of Individuals with Regard to Automatic Processing of Personal Data* (The Convention), adopted in 1980 was binding on the countries that signed it and required that national laws be consistent with it. The Convention set out basic data protection principles and provided a template for countries without data protection legislation. These principles required that automatic processed personal data be [24]:

1. obtained and processed fairly and lawfully;
2. stored for specific and legitimate purposes;
3. not used in a way that is incompatible with these purposes;
4. adequate, relevant and not excessive in relation to the purposes for which they are stored;
5. accurate, and where necessary, kept up to date;
6. preserved in a form that permits identification of data subjects for no longer than is required for the purpose for which the data are stored;
7. protected by appropriate security measures, and
8. accessible to individuals to enable checking the veracity of the information and enabling correction if necessary.

These principles have been one of the bases for subsequent privacy regulation in Europe, and between the EU and other jurisdictions. The other important influence has been the Organization of Economic Co-operation and Development (OECD) which adopted *Guidelines Governing the Protection of Personal Privacy and Trans-border Flows of Personal Data* adopted in 1980 [3]. This was the first trans-Atlantic agreement in relation to privacy protection. The guidelines were intended to harmonize national privacy legislation and to provide a framework to facilitate the international flow of data. They adopted data protection principles similar to those established by the European Convention, and based on the fair information principles developed in the US in 1972 by an advisory committee to the Secretary of Health, Education and Welfare. Although the OECD Guidelines are recognised by all member countries, they are not legally binding and are therefore implemented differently in different countries.

In 1995, the EU adopted the *Directive on the Protection of Individuals with Regard to the Processing of Personal Data and the Free Movement of Such Data*. (The Directive) [9] The Directive was not only intended to increase protection of privacy in the EU but also to promote free trade and ensure a single integrated market. It was based on the Council of Europe Convention. Under the Directive, data controllers are required to inform the data subject of the purpose of the processing and the recipients of the data. The data can be processed and used only for the purposes specified [10]. 'Sensitive' personal data cannot be collected and individuals must be informed before personal data is disclosed to third parties for direct marketing and must be offered the right to object to such uses. Individuals may challenge any decision significantly affecting them that is based on an automatic processing of data, including decisions involving credit worthiness or employment [11]. Individuals have the right to access and correct their personal data, to receive conformation of the purposes of processing the data, and to obtain the identities of third party recipients [12]. Member states are required to provide a judicial remedy for infringements of rights and an independent public authority must be designated to monitor the application of the Privacy Directive within each member state [13]. The Directive has been incorporated since 1998 into the laws of every EU member state.

Article 25 of the Directive requires EU member states to only allow transfers of personal data to third countries that have an *adequate* level of data protection, determined with reference to the nature of the data, the purpose of the data processing, the country of origin, the destination country, the law and professional rules and security measures in force in the third country. Articles 25 (4) and (6) enable the EU to determine whether a third country provides an adequate level of protection. The EU has declared that Canada, Argentina and the US Safe Harbor agreement provide adequate data protection [14].

Article 26 of the Directive allows transfers to third countries with *inadequate* levels of data protection on the condition that:

* the data subject consents to the transfer;
* the transfer is necessary for the performance of a contract with the data subject or for the data subject's benefit;
* the transfer is necessary or legally required on important public interest grounds or in exercise or defence of legal claims;
* the transfer is necessary to protect the vital interests of the data subject, or
* the transfer is made from a register which by law is intended to provide information to the public.

The member state's privacy authority may authorise transfers which do not comply with the above definition of adequacy, but which, in the authority's opinion, have adequate privacy safeguards. This discretion given to member state privacy authorities is aimed at allowing transfers made under appropriate contractual clauses. The European Commission may also approve standard contractual clauses for use when contracting with recipients that ensure adequate levels of data protection [15].

International privacy instruments such as the OECD Guidelines and the EU Data Directive provide frameworks through which consistent privacy standards can be implemented across national borders. In addition, recently additional international instruments have been drafted that have potential impact on improving and harmonizing data protection standards throughout the Asia Pacific region. Two examples are the APEC Privacy Framework and the Asia Pacific Privacy Charter.

The APEC Privacy Framework is the most significant international privacy instrument since the EU Directive. It attempts to promote privacy policy compatibility in a region that includes the US, Australia, China and Russia. It provides a relatively low set of privacy standards, at best equivalent to the OECD standards. One commentator believes it to be the weakest international privacy standard yet developed [18]. However, if it becomes a minimum standard to which Asia Pacific countries which are only starting to develop privacy laws can aspire to, it may be valuable.

The Asia Pacific Privacy Charter Council, a regional non governmental organisation formed by more than 30 privacy experts from APEC countries, has worked on providing higher independent privacy standards than the Privacy Framework provides for the Asia Pacific region. The Asia Pacific Privacy Charter is intended to be a 'high watermark' draft reflecting all the significant privacy principles from relevant international instruments [19].

In addition to international privacy standards, there are bilateral agreements on privacy. For instance, Australia and New Zealand have recently signed a new agreement creating formal guidelines for co-operation between privacy offices and for the sharing of resources. The agreement, based on the APEC Privacy Framework and OECD Guidelines, will govern the sharing of information in areas such as:

- surveys
- research projects;
- promotional campaigns;
- complaints information;
- education and training programs and initiatives; and
- investigative techniques relating to privacy violations and regulatory   strategies.

It is believed that the agreement will be used to set an example for other APEC and OECD nations to implement similar cross-border initiatives [26].

3   Australia

3.1 Data Transfers Out of Australia

In Australia, the federal public sector is covered by the Information Privacy Principles (IPPs) contained in the *Privacy Act 1988 (Cth)*. Private sector organisations with an annual turnover of more than three million dollars must comply with the legal obligations in relation to handling personal data set out in the National Privacy Principles (NPPs) in the Privacy Act. The IPPs and NPPs are substantially the same but there are differences, one of which is that the IPPs do not apply to the transfer of personal data out of Australia. Section B of the Privacy Act, on the other hand, does apply to acts done, or practices engaged in outside Australia by a private sector organisation. Its purpose is to prevent organisations avoiding their obligations under the Act by transferring the handling of personal information to countries with lower data protection standards [5]. NPP 9 dictates the circumstances in which an organisation can transfer personal data to a foreign country. NPP 9 is largely modelled on Articles 25 and 26 of the EU Directive which aims to ensure continued protection of personal data sent across national borders [27].

According to NPP 9, Australian private sector organisations, excluding small businesses, may only transfer personal data to a foreign country if [34]:

1. the organisation reasonably believes that the law in the country of the recipient of the information upholds principles of fair handling of the information that are substantially similar to the National Privacy Principles, or
2. the data subject consents to the transfer, or
3. the transfer is necessary for the performance or conclusion of a contract between the individual and the organisation, or for the implementation of pre contractual measures taken at the individual's request, or
4. the transfer is for the benefit of the individual, it is impractical to obtain the consent of the individual to that transfer, and it is likely that the consent would be forthcoming if it had been possible to obtain it, or
5. the organisation has taken reasonable steps to ensure that the information will be held, used or disclosed by the recipient of the information in accordance with the National Privacy Principles.

In relation to NPP 9(1), it is not easy for organisations to find out whether or not a country has privacy rules that are consistent with the Privacy Act. The Office of the Federal Privacy Commissioner does not maintain a list of countries with acceptable legislation and refers visitors to its website, to the EU website, to the websites of individual data protection regulators around the world, or suggests seeking legal advice [25]. Many businesses, have pointed out that they do not have the resources or expertise to determine whether data transferred out of Australia to other countries will be adequately protected, particularly where data is sent on to many jurisdictions [38]. The Privacy Commissioner has suggested that establishing which countries have privacy protections consistent with the Privacy Act is too complex a task even for it to carry out [29].

In relation to NPP 9(2), one way of obtaining the consent of the data subject is to use standard contractual clauses. The European Commission has suggested standard contractual clauses when transferring data to an entity outside the EU. The importer is required to comply with the nine standard privacy principles and the decisions of the European Commission concerning the standard of protection in the relevant third country [7]. The privacy principles form part of the terms. Standard contractual data protection clauses are rare in Australia, however, the Victorian Privacy Commissioner has recently taken the lead in providing model guidelines [39] similar to those that are available in the EU [16]. The Federal Office of the Privacy Commissioner, although not providing a standard clause contract, has indicated that it will release an information sheet outlining the issues that should be addressed as part of a contractual agreement concerning transborder data transfers, although it has not yet done so [28].

Australian organisations are generally fulfilling their NPP 9 obligations of ensuring that personal data is protected through contractual arrangements when it is sent to jurisdictions without privacy regimes through contractual arrangements [37] but, as noted above, there are concerns amongst business about the practical difficulties and costs associated with monitoring the compliance of their trading partners [30]. For instance, currently the Australian Federal Privacy Commissioner is investigating claims of certain financial institutions, including Australia's four largest banks, passing on financial information of their customers to the US without protecting that information as required under the Privacy Act. Eleven banks and 88 financial institutions in Australia use SWIFT (Society for Worldwide Financial Telecommunication), which has been in breach of EU data protection law [23]. These financial institutions may have been in breach of the Privacy Act in allowing personal data to be handed to US officials to track terrorist paper trails. This example illustrates that ensuring trading partners' compliance with Australian privacy law is not only a potentially difficult and costly task, it may be an impossible one in countries such as the US where privacy laws are weaker than in Australia and subordinate to national security interests.

3.2 Data Transfers into Australia

Article 25 of the EU Directive states:

> Member States shall provide that the transfer to a third country of personal data which are undergoing processing or are intended for processing may take place only if...the third country in question ensures an adequate level of protection.

Australia's Privacy Act has been assessed in its application to the private sector as providing inadequate protection of personal data transferred from EU countries to Australia [6]. A European Commission working party concluded that the Privacy Act provided inadequate data protection for various reasons, including the fact that small businesses were exempt from the Act and its associated NPPs.

Two solutions were proposed by the Working Party to address the inadequacy of Australia's data protection laws. The first was the use of industry self regulation, and the second was the use of contractual provisions. The objective of these provisions is to ensure that they result in the Australian data recipient having a legal obligation to apply the data protection principles of the EU Directive to the receipt, use, disclosure and storage of the transferred data [31]. The applicable law for the contract would be that of the EU member country from which the data was transferred to Australia.

The European Commission has adopted a number of standard contractual clauses that impose certain obligations on the data recipient [8]. The Council of Europe, the International Chamber of Commerce, and the Hong Kong Privacy Commissioner have also provided model contracts covering transfers of data to countries with inadequate data protection legislation [22]. Of course, non standard agreements are also possible, but they require approval from the relevant data subject's governing authority [20].

These self regulatory and contractual solutions to the inadequacy of Australia's data protection laws as determined by the EU appear to work, and business and trade with European organisations has not been impaired to any great extent [36]. Despite this, some industry groups including the Australian Banking Association are calling on the Privacy Commissioner to push for EU adequacy and the Privacy Commissioner has recognised that there may be long term benefits in achieving EU adequacy as well as implementing the APEC Privacy Framework [32].

4   International Pressure for Data Protection Regulation

India is currently the largest host of outsourced data processing in the world. Some estimates claim that India hosts 44 percent of the global market of outsourced software and 'back office' services [4]. Like many countries, India has been slow to enact comprehensive data protection legislation but it is facing increasing pressure internationally to do so. It had initially been proposed that legislation modelled on the EU Directive would be implemented; however, the Indian Government's position was revised in favour of a model more like the US Safe Harbor Agreement [1]. The Indian Government announced that data protection measures would be on the agenda for 2005, however, no legislation was drafted [2]. In October 2006, the Indian Government proposed amendments to the *Information Technology Act* (2000). Under the new amendments, fines may be imposed on businesses and individuals for failing to prevent data theft and leaking of personal information. They also aim to prevent phishing and identity theft. The amendments are expected to be passed in early 2007.

There has recently been a number of 'sting operations' exposing data theft in the Indian outsourcing industry. For example, the Information Commissioner in the United Kingdom is currently investigating claims of data leaks from outsourced call centres in India. A UK TV station ran footage of Indian call centre employees disclosing the financial data of 200 thousand UK citizens. Other Indian outsourcing frauds include Citibank accounts being stolen and a call centre employee in Bangalore selling credit card information to fraudsters who stole US$398 000 from British bank accounts [33].

Despite these examples of outsourcing fraud in India, one commentator has suggested that India has the lowest rates of data theft in the world and that there are more data security breaches in the UK and US than in India [35]. Another claims that many outsourcing businesses believe that data is safer in Indian hands than in the originating jurisdiction [21]. Whatever the real rates of data theft in India, confidence in Indian personal data security has been undermined due to the negative publicity mentioned above. As a result, the new legislation may be an attempt to improve the perception of data protection in India as much as it is an attempt to protect against privacy breaches.

5   Conclusion

International legal instruments such as the OECD Guidelines, the EU Data Directive and the APEC Privacy Framework have had an impact on national data protection regulation in countries such as the US and Australia, leading to some international consistency. The Privacy Act and associated NPPs in Australia, along with the Safe Harbor agreement and state privacy guidelines in the US are examples of this. International data protection initiatives have had less impact on India. But neither Australian nor US data protection laws are adequate when judged by the high EU standards so that, like India, standard and non standard form contracts must be agreed to when data is being sent between these jurisdictions and the EU.

In the US, many businesses believe contractual provisions required by the EU to be an unnecessary burden and there has been a relatively slow response to the Safe

Harbour initiative. In Australia, many businesses are beginning to accept that they have an interest in adopting a strong European style legislative approach to data protection with some industry groups pushing for stricter data protection laws that comply with the EU Directive and the APEC Framework. It appears that the Indian Government too realises the economic importance of taking steps to tighten data protection laws, although the response to date is unlikely to satisfy critics pushing for comprehensive data protection legislation.

References

1. Bender, D.: 'Data protection Law in India: A Change in Direction'. Privacy and Security Law Report (January 12, 2004)
2. Business Standard, Govt to introduce data protection laws, (November 3, 2004), http://www.business-standard.com/fulltextsearch/searchhome.php
3. Cooper, D.: 'Trans border data flow and the protection of privacy: The harmonization of data protection law', 8 Fletcher Forum 344; Patrick, P. 1981, 'Privacy restrictions on trans-national data flows: A comparison of the Council of Europe draft convention and OECD guidelines. Jurimetrics Journal 21(4), 405–420 (1984)
4. George, C., Gaut, R.: Offshore Outsourcing to India by EU and US Companies: Legal and Cross Cultural Issues that Affect Data Privacy Regulation in Business Process Outsourcing. 6 University of California Business Law Journal 13, 13 (2006)
5. Douglas-Stewart, J.: Annotated National Privacy Principles (2005)
6. EU Advisory Body on Data Protection and Privacy, Article 29, Data Protection Working Party, Opinion 3/2001 on the level of protection of the Australian Privacy Amendment (private Sector) Act 2000, pp. 15–17, (January 26, 2001) at 10/10/2006, http://ec.europa.eu/justice_home/fsj/privacy/docs/wpdocs/2001/wp40en.pdf
7. European Commission, 'Commission Decision of 15 June 2001 on standard contractual clauses for the transfer of personal data to third countries, under Directive 95/46/EC, at (10/10/2006),
http://www.privacy.vic.gov.au/dir100/priweb.nsf/download/8BCE83DBBB2B2996CA257 1870015C020/FILE/Model%20Terms%20Guidelines_June%202006.pdf
8. Ibid
9. European Commission, Council Directive 94/46EC, at 10/10/2006, article 10 (October 24, 1995),
http://europa.eu.int/smartapi/cgi/sga_doc?smartapi!celexapi!prod!CELEXnumdoc&lg=EN &numdoc=31995L0046&model=guichett
10. European Commission op cit, article 6
11. European Commission op cit, article 14 (b)
12. European Commission op cit, article 12
13. European Commission op cit, article 28
14. European Commission, 'Decisions on the adequacy of the protection of personal data in third countries', Note that a Safe Harbor Privacy Principles agreement has been negotiated between the US and the EU to provide for data transfers. Under Safe Harbor, an organisation 'self certifies' to the US Department of Commerce or another designated body its adherence to the seven privacy principles. See, at (10/10/2006), http:// ec.europa.eu/justice_home/fsj/privacy/thridcountries/index_en.htm at 31/1/2007, http://ec. europa.eu/justice_home/fsj/privacy/thridcountries/index_en.htm

15. European Commission, Model contracts for the transfer of personal data to third countries at (28/11/2006), http://europa.eu.int/comm/internal_market/privacy/modelcontracts_en. htm
16. Ibid
17. Evans, A.C.: Data protection in Europe. Journal of World Trade Law 15, 150–158 (1981)
18. Greenleaf, G.: 'APEC's Privacy Framework: A New Low Standard' 11 Privacy Law & Policy Reporter 1. In: Greenleaf, G. (ed.) 'APEC Privacy Framework Completed: No Threat to Privacy Standards' (2006) Privacy Law and Policy Reporter 5 (2005)
19. Greenleaf, G., Waters, N.: The Asia Pacific Privacy Charter, Working Draft1.0 Worldlii Privacy Law Resources, (2003) at (10/10/2006), http://www.worldlii.org/int/other/ PrivLRes/2003/1.html
20. Hill, G.: Harmony or Discord? Using Intra Group Contracts to address International Data Protection Standards 10. Privacy Law and Policy Reporter 31 (2003)
21. Holland, M.: 'NASSCOM 2007: India wants to be security leader. In: ITPRO website, (2007) at 13/2/2007, http://www.itpro.co.uk/internet/news/104067/nasscom-2007-india-wants-to-be-security-leader.html
22. Hong Kong Office of the Privacy Commissioner, Model Contract prepared jointly by the Council of Europe, the EU and the International Chamber of Commerce 1992, Fact sheet no 1, 'Transfer of Personal Information outside Hong Kong: Some Common Questions' (April 1997)
23. Lebihan, R.: Banks face privacy probe. Australian Financial Review (October 13, 2006)
24. OECD Recommendations of the Council Concerning Guidelines Governing the Protection of Privacy and Transborder Flow of Personal Data, (September 23, 1980) at 10/10/2006, http://www.oecd.org/document/18/0,2340,en_2649_34255_1815186_1_1_1_1,00.htm
25. Office of the Federal Privacy Commissioner. How do I know if the country I am sending personal information to ... at (10/10/2006), http://www.privacy.gov.au/faqs/bf/q6.html
26. Office of the Federal Privacy Commissioner media announcement. Cross Tasman initiative to promote privacy protection (September 19, 2006), http://www.privacy.gov.au/ news/06_20.html at 29/11/2006
27. Office of the Federal Privacy Commissioner. Guidelines to the National Privacy Principles, p. 58 (2001)
28. Office of the Privacy Commissioner. In: Getting in on the Act, The Review of the Private Sector Provisions of the Privacy Act 1988, Rec. 18 (March 2005)
29. Ibid, 79
30. Office of the Privacy Commissioner, Getting in on the Act, The Review of the Private Sector Provisions of the Privacy Act 1988, p. 78 (March 2005)
31. Ibid
32. Office of the Privacy Commissioner, Getting in on the Act, The Review of the Private Sector Provisions of the Privacy Act 1988, p. 76 (March 2005)
33. Out-Law News. In: Commissioner will probe call centre data leaks, (October 10, 2006) at 27/11/2006, http://www.out-law.com
34. Privacy Act 1988 (Cth), Sch 3, NPP 9. See also Privacy and personal Information Protection Act 1998, s 19(2) and Information Privacy Act (Vic), IPP 9
35. Raja, M.: India tightens data protection law. Asian Times, (October 20, 2006) at 28/11/2006, http://www.atimes.com/atimes/South_Asia.html
36. See Australian Direct Marketing Association submission to Office of the Privacy Commissioner. Getting in on the Act, The Review of the Private Sector Provisions of the Privacy Act 1988, p. 67 (March 2005)

37. See submissions of Coles Meyer, ADMA, Telstra and ABA to Office of the Privacy Commissioner. In: Getting in on the Act, The Review of the Private Sector Provisions of the Privacy Act 1988, fn 50, p. 78 (March 2005)
38. See submissions of Telstra and ANZ to Office of the Privacy Commissioner. In: Getting in on the Act, The Review of the Private Sector Provisions of the Privacy Act 1988, fn 49, p. 77 (March 2005)
39. Victorian Privacy Commissioner, Model Terms for Transborder Data Flows of Personal Information (June 2006)

Designing Globally Accepted Human Interfaces for Instant Messaging

Chiuhsiang Joe Lin[1], Dylan Sung[2], Ching-Chow Yang[1], Yung-Tsan Jou[1],
Chih-Wei Yang[1], and Lai-Yu Cheng[1]

[1] Department of Industrial Engineering, Chung-Yuan Christian University,
200, Chung Pei Rd., Chung- Li, Taiwan 32023, R.O.C.
[2] Department of Applied Linguistics and Language Studies, Chung Yuan Christian University,
200, Chung Pei Rd., Chung-Li, Taiwan 32023, R.O.C.
{Chiuhsiang Joe Lin,hsiang}@cycu.edu.tw

Abstract. This study investigated the perception differences of IM (instant messaging) icons between users of different cultural backgrounds. Two major parts were developed for this study. The first part investigated the frequent IM icons as a basis for improving the IM user-interface design. The second part tested the use of different graphical symbols using subjects from two different populations, Taiwan and the United States. From the result, there is significant difference between the two user groups on their recognition of those frequent icons. Confusion matrices further show that some icons were thought to be associated with same functions by the two groups while some others were linked with different functions. These similarities and differences could be due to the cultural differences between the two user groups. It is suggested that cultural differences should be effectively recognized by icon designers for globally accepted human computer interfaces in software products.

Keywords: Graphical User Interface, Globalization, Instant messaging, Icon.

1 Introduction

With the advent of the age of global information society, people's use of computers has become widespread throughout the world. The use of Internet in Taiwan is also becoming increasingly more extensive. According to a survey conducted by the Taiwan Network Information Center [15] the percentage of the Taiwanese population that use the Internet was 60.25% (13.8 million) at the end of December 2004, while about 53.78% (10.31 million) of residents in Taiwan age 12 and above have experience using broadband Internet. This number will rise as broadband Internet connections become even more prevalent in Taiwan.

Internet websites are often used internationally on a great variety of purposes. In a survey regarding top ten languages (i.e. English, Chinese, Japanese Spanish, German, French, Portuguese, Korean, Italian, and Russian) used in the web, Miniwats Group [12] pointed out that the number of recorded Internet users reached the staggering figure of 863,981,961 worldwide in 2006. With more than 37% of total Internet users, English is leading in absolute terms, while the other 541,381,124 users access the

N. Aykin (Ed.): Usability and Internationalization, Part II, HCII 2007, LNCS 4560, pp. 150–159, 2007.
© Springer-Verlag Berlin Heidelberg 2007

Internet in a different language. Internet users of non-English speaking were predominant in 2006. However, the greatest percentage of Internet users is English language users.

Because a considerable share of Internet users are from non English-speaking countries, using the global language for design of human-centered communication interfaces, such as product labels, traffic signs, and computer icons are of significant importance [9]. Still, icons and images are more universally recognizable than text [11]; [18]. As a result, research is needed to explore designs of globally-accepted, human-centered interfaces.

Most common presentation modes for icons are pictorial and verbal [4]. A graphical user interface (GUI) is a human-computer interface (i.e., a way for humans to interact with computers) that uses windows, icons and menus and which can be manipulated by a mouse [14]. It has also been indicated that icons are the most essential component of GUIs [7]. Horton [8] described icons as the small pictorial symbols used on the computer menus, windows, and screens. Icons alone are meaningless without a particular context.

In the realm of human-computer interaction (HCI), icons have dominated, especially since GUIs became increasingly common. Icons are extensively used because it can be easily remembered and recognized [16]. Additionally, icons offer the perception of affordance, which can facilitate human-computer interaction in terms of ecological perception [6], [11]. Goonetilleke et al. [7] suggested that there are three important aspects to consider when designing and developing icons: ambiguity, uniqueness, and dominance. Huang et al. [9] found that qualified computer icons should incorporate the following design criteria: styling, message quality, meaningfulness, locatability, and metaphor.

In the previous research on issues influencing icon design, this can be problematic in the designing of icons for international users. Bourges-Waldegg and Scrivener [1] conducted a study to understand culturally determined usability problems. It assessed the usability of the Netscape browser and "the Nemeton" website. Results of the study pointed out that the differences between cultures are basically representational differences; that is, although cultural factors such as religion, government, language, art, marriage, and sense of humor are universal, the way they are represented is specific. The results also further confirmed that if users do not understand a representation, it is harder for them to learn the functions of a technology. It was suggested that users will favor the system they understand better regardless of the fact whether it is in their native language or not. In an information display study, Nakajima [13] found that different populations play an important role in their cognitive processing of information. Americans prefer "easy-to-process" information displays rather than displays that require an extended cognitive commitment. At the reflective end of the continuum, the Japanese generally take greater time, and display a deeper processing commitment. Studies concentrating on the relationship between usability and culture can be considered very important.

Choong and Salvendy [4] investigated the cultural differences in cognitive abilities between American and Chinese populations by conducting a practical icon recognition experiment. The study assessed the participants' icon recognition, pointing out that Chinese participants performed more efficiently with pictorial rather than alphanumerical modes. They also seemed comfortable with high context information. A possible reason for this was thought to be their knowledge of the English language.

2 Globally Accepted IM Technology

The goal of globalizing IM applications is to create a core design for effective intercultural communication. The globalization process identifies the most common or shared features of the design of GUIs. The process thus identifies global functionality, interaction styles, communication patterns, and information that exceed cultural boundaries. The result of the globalization process is a product's core design. In computer user interfaces, functions such as open, close, save, and print are the most basic level functions. The above description becomes the global core. Thus, it would not seem sensible if the computer user interface designers ignore the global core.

Cultural differences exist in languages, orthography, symbols, number formats, and images. People from different cultures also vary in their appearance, perception, cognition, and style of thinking [4]. As progressively more cultural differences are found, increasingly more rules and guidelines have been developed, making the international design process more complicated at the same time. Additionally, such rules and guidelines make it hard to develop products that will fulfill the needs of many users. Consequently, international usage problems could arise if designers lack the motivation to gain understanding of the influence of cultural factors that may cause such problems.

Culture is a concept that is difficult to define and measure. The most striking cultural differences are noticed by us. However, it is difficult to talk about culture in a definitive way. Cultures change over time, so we often talk about traditional culture and contemporary culture. Particularly in the context of instant messaging, that is the phenomena of youth culture and other subcultures as formed by discussion and chat groups. Instant messaging, as a form of synchronously written communication, provides its users the ability to communicate with other people in real-time via the Internet [5]; [17].

International Data Corporation (IDC) predicted that corporate IM use was going to grow from 18.3 million in 2001 to 229 million users worldwide in 2005. Most IM users tend to be teenagers. IDC indicated that IM users would exceed 300 million users in 2005 [2]. Clearly, a growing number of people have used instant messaging, both for personal and business purposes. IM is also very popular with young people today. That is because IM is an easy way for them to keep in touch with friends. Besides, IM is much cheaper than the use of telephones. Youth can stay online to chat and not worry about the costs. As IM becomes widespread, further IM functions and icons are being extended and renewed. However, it is not yet fully established as to whether the existing functions and icons meet user's requirements, especially the design of the IM GUIs. It is, in actuality, imperative that GUIs are designed in a way that facilitates quick and accurate recognition by users, to ensure better usability for interfaces [4].

Although some of the aforementioned studies have shown that cultural diversity is important in HCI design, the issues have not been examined with respect to the use of IM software. Thus, this study will address the IM interface from a more global aspect.

In this study, the main emphasis falls on users' perception (recognition) on icons while using IM. Consequently, this paper attempts to evaluate possible differences between different cultural groups and to discern how those differences may affect user's perception on icon representations.

3 Method

The main purpose of this research was to investigate how cultural differences between different user groups may affect users' perception of icons when using IM. Based upon the previous discussion, three research questions were developed to guide the investigation.

RQ1: What are the most frequently used IM functions?

RQ2: Are there differences in the recognition of the functions referred to by the icons in IM software?

RQ3: What are the perception differences between users of different cultural backgrounds in their icon use with IM?

In order to resolve the above described research questions, two major parts were developed for this study. The first part investigated critical icons of IM user-interface design. The second part tested different graphical symbols using subjects from different populations from Taiwan and the United States.

3.1 Part 1: Frequent IM Function Investigation

This part was based on a survey of a large group of university students. The majority of them have some experience communicating using IM.

(1) Participants
A survey questionnaire was administrated to a random sample of students at a selected university in Taiwan. Data collection lasted a period of two weeks during April 15th to April 30th, 2006. Participation in this study was entirely voluntary. Five randomly selected classes of 163 Taiwanese students of a university participated in the study. The sample returned 148 usable and valid surveys (90.7%), with 129 undergraduate students (87.2%) and 19 graduate students (12.8%). The participants ranged in age form 20 to 29 years.

(2) Measures
This part sought to identify the frequent functions as a basis for part 2. The questionnaire consisted of two general sections: (1) IM function use frequency, (2) demographics and experience of IM use. A total of 29 items were developed and used in this survey. There were 20 questions representing 20 common functions in the first section. This section asked the frequency of use with each function in the IM activities. A five-point Likert scale was used, with "1"meaning "never use" and "5" meaning "frequent use". The second section asked the demographic characteristics which included 9 items concerning students' educational background, gender, and habits of using IM.

3.2 Part 2: Icon Perception

In this part, the study tested the difference in icon perception while using IM. The study examined the perception difference between two groups of participants from two countries.

(1) Participants
Participants selected from eastern and western cultural backgrounds are essential. The Taiwanese and American participants were considered to represent eastern and western cultures respectively. Eighteen Taiwanese and Eighteen American college students (total 36) participated in this experiment.

(2) Measures
The questionnaire was presented in the participant native language. The 11 functions (Table 2) as identified from the first part of the study (as will be explained in section 4.1) plus two additional functions, "to engage in voice chat" and "to use the webcam" were used in this part. These two functions, though not considered as frequent in use, were potentially of interest by the authors and were therefore added. For each function, three icons were selected from several common IM programs, resulting in a total of 39 icons as shown in Table 1. Icons were selected from IM software such as AOL Instant Messenger (AIM), ICQ, MSN Messenger (also known as Windows Messenger), Skype, and Yahoo! Messenger, which have attracted millions of daily users in recent years [3]. Each set of icons was based on selection from one major source in the above IM software. Each participant was asked to match each icon shown on a computer screen to a particular function from the 13 function lists.

Table 1. Icons utilized in the study [taken from AIM, ICQ, MSN, Skype, and Yahoo]

Num.	Item	Set 1	Set 2	Set 3
1	To engage in text messaging			
2	To change user handle			
3	To send files or photos			
4	To change user status (away)			
5	To change the display picture			
6	Add emoticons			
7	To multitalk with people			
8	To save the text messaging			
9	To send and receive email			
10	To change interface			
11	To change user status (invisible)			
12	To engage in voice chat			
13	To use the webcam			

4 Results

4.1 Frequent IM Functions

Statistical analyses were performed using SPSS 11.0. In terms of IM users' behaviors, the greatest percentage of respondents reported that they have been using IM more than four years (40.5%), followed by three to four years (25.7%), two to three years (25.0%), and one to two years (6.1 %). New users (less than one year experience) represented only 2.7%. Additionally, IM users believe MSN Messenger is the best IM software (89.2%) while most prefer MSN Messenger (98.6%). Most users spent an average of one to three hours chatting on a typical day (54.1%). They used IM at least once a day (62.8%). Most of them used IM between 10 pm to 12 am (57.4%). Additionally, 60.8% of respondents log onto IM from home. Based on the study of part 1, the functions with mean ratings of frequency of use over 3.0 were selected as the critical functions, shown as the 11 functions in Table 2.

Table 2. Frequent functions utilized in IM

Order	Function	Mean	Std.
1	To engage in text messaging	4.18	0.81
2	To change user handle	3.95	0.91
3	To send files or photos	3.92	0.77
4	To change user status (away)	3.83	0.93
5	To change the display picture	3.80	0.92
6	Add emoticons	3.72	1.05
7	To multi-talk with people	3.19	0.79
8	To save the text messaging	3.18	1.22
9	To send and receive email	3.11	1.19
10	To change interface	3.04	0.98
11	To change user status (invisible)	3.01	1.02

4.2 Icon Perception Differences

In order to address research questions two and three, there are several statistical analyses shown in this section, including descriptive statistics analysis, ANOVA test, and confusion matrices analysis.

There were 36 participants joined in the questionnaire survey which included 18 Taiwanese and 18 Americans. There were totally nine males (50%) and nine females (50%) in Taiwanese participants. In American participants, there were three males (16.7%) and fifteen females (83.3%) joined this survey. From descriptive statistics, 66.7% of Taiwanese used IM software over four years. However, there were only 38.9% of American participants used IM software over four years. Results also show that 94% of Taiwanese participants and 72% of American participants used MSN Messenger.

To assess the perception difference between the two groups of participants in their IM icon recognition, ANOVA was performed for the correct recognition rate against the participant group (Taiwan/U.S.), icon set (3 sets), and function (13 key functions).

The result indicated that there was significant difference between Taiwan and U.S. participants ($F_{1, 24}$=6.69, P<0.05). The icon set was significant ($F_{2, 24}$=86.65, P<0.001). The function was also significant ($F_{12, 24}$=45.48, P<0.001). The interaction between icon set and function was significant ($F_{24, 24}$=9.93, P<0.001). The interaction between icon set and participant group was significant ($F_{2, 24}$=9.14, P<0.001). Finally, the interaction between function and participant group was also significant ($F_{12, 24}$=3.99, P<0.01).

Table 3 shows the correct recognition rate of the Taiwan and U.S. participants with the three icon sets and the 13 functions. The ISO (International Standards Organization) 3864 [10] suggests a minimum correct recognition rate of 66.7% for icons. Based on this standard, 40 icons (51.3%) in the questionnaire survey were found lower than 66.7% and were thus difficult to recognize. To the Taiwanese participants, 18 (48.7%) icons had the low recognition rate. However, 22 (56.4%) icons were difficult to recognize for the American participants.

Table 3. Correct recognition (CR) rate for Taiwanese and U.S. participants

N.	Item	CR rate (Set 1) (%)		CR rate (Set 2) (%)		CR rate (Set 3) (%)	
		Taiwan	US	Taiwan	US	Taiwan	US
1	To multitalk with people	61	56	89	100	33	44
2	To send and receive email	100	100	100	94	94	94
3	To change user status to *away*	100	83	67	39	44	39
4	To engage in text messaging	44	61	61	39	11	28
5	To change user handle	94	39	61	11	17	17
6	To engage in voice chat	100	83	100	78	89	72
7	To send files or photos	67	61	61	50	61	72
8	Add emoticons	94	94	100	94	78	83
9	To use the webcam	78	78	67	61	78	100
10	To change interface	78	61	39	33	6	17
11	To save the text messaging	33	39	56	56	6	6
12	To change user status to *invisible*	83	83	50	67	17	33
13	To change the display picture	94	83	39	22	39	44
	Average	78.9	70.8	68.5	57.2	44.1	49.9

In order to determine the relationship between culture differences with each icon design, this study also performed a confusion matrix analysis. As shown in Table 4, there are six matrices (3 sets×2 countries). Each matrix has 13 rows and 13 columns. Each row demonstrated a specific icon. The corresponding 13 functions were displayed as the 13 columns. In the questionnaire survey, the participant choose the most suitable function they regarded to match each icon. The number of correct matches (persons) was recorded on the diagonal. The incorrect choice was recorded off the diagonal.

From Table 4, one can observe that, for example, in set 1, Taiwanese participants tend to have more problems with the fourth icon "To engage in text messaging", mismatching it with the eleventh function "To save the text messaging". As a result, some of the notable confusion results were shown in Table 5.

Table 4. Confusion matrices

		Taiwan													American												
Set	Icon\Item	1	2	3	4	5	6	7	8	9	10	11	12	13	1	2	3	4	5	6	7	8	9	10	11	12	13
1		11			1			2			1	3			10			1	1		1	1	1	2		1	
			18												18												
				18											1		15					2					
		3			8					7					4		11	1				1	1			
						17					1				3		2	3	7			1	1	1			
							18								1			1	15		1					
		4					12				2				2	1			11				4			
								17				1						1	17							
							1	14	1			2			1			2	1	14						
				1		1		1	14			1							2		11	2		3		
					8		3		1	6					2	7		1		1	7					
				1				2			15			1						2	15					
								1				17		1						2			15			15
2		16			2										18												
			18												1	17											
				12	1			2				3			1		7	1	1		3		1	1		2	1
				2	11		1		2	1	1				1		2	7	1	2		1	2	2			
		1			4	11			1	1					3	8	2		1			1	1	1	2	
							18								1	1		1	14				1			
				2			11	1	1	2	1				2	1		2	9		3			1		
								18							1					17						
					2		12	1		2	1						1	2	1	11	1	1	1			
					4		2	7			5			1		1	1		1		2	6	1		5	
				1		1		3	10	1	1						1		1	2	4		10			
		1		2				1	3	9	2	2	2									2	12			
					6			4		1	7					9	1				4			4		4
3		6			1	1		1	2		3		3	1	8		2	5						1	2	
			17								1				17					1						
				8		2			3	1	3	1		1		7		1		2		2	1	4		
		1			2	1		1	1	5	1	3	3		3		5	2	2			3	3			
				1	6	3	1		2	2	2	1		2		4	3			6	1	2			
		1		1		16								2		3	13									
				2	1		11		4					1				13			4					
		1			1		14		1	1									15			3				
				1		1	14	2												18						
			1		2	2	4		1	8		2			3			5			3	5				
		1	9	1	1			1	2	3	1	11			1				1	1	1	2			
		5		2	3		1	2		3	2	3	1	1	1				2		6	4				
		3		2	3			2	1		7		4		5				1			8				

Table 5. The most confused icons by the two groups of participants

Set	Function	Icon	Confusions	
			Taiwan	US
1	To engage in text messaging		To send files or photos (7)	0
	To save the text messaging		To engage in text messaging (8)	To change user handle (7)
	To change user handle		0	To engage in text messaging (8)
2	To change the display picture		To change user handle (6)	To change user handle (9)
	To change user handle		To engage in text messaging (6)	To save the text messaging (6)
3	To change interface		To save the text messaging (8)	0
	To save the text messaging		To change user status to away (9)	To change user status to away (11)

*. Confusions shown were the ones with over 6 mis-matches (total is 18), so that the correction rate is lower than 0.67, as suggested by ISO [10].

5 Discussion and Conclusions

It is important for HCI designers to consider international user backgrounds in their cultures, as the IM software is being marketed globally. International and intercultural usability research will offer valuable information for future efforts to develop products for the international market. This study contributes to IM designers by discovering users' perception of the IM icons with different cultural backgrounds.

The results of this research could have important implications for the globally accepted IM design of additional user-friendly icons.

There are three major results gathered from this study. First, 11 most frequently used functions in IM software were identified. These functions deserve more attention by IM interface designers to improve these key icons so that the IM software can be more user-friendly.

Second, the recognition rates between different participant groups of different cultures (the Taiwan and the U.S., in this study) in their IM icon use was discovered, despite the fact that many of the icons were selected from some of the most popular IM software. The result seemed to suggest that cultural background is of significant importance on how users think the icons may be. People from different cultures indeed vary in their appearance, perception, cognition, and style of thinking [4]. Shneiderman and Plaisant [14] also concluded that the graphical icon design may be strongly influenced by the designer's own experiences. If the designer does not consider the culture differences carefully, the usability of icons may be decreased due to the users from different cultural backgrounds. HCI designers should always bear the cultural background in mind when designing global products. More importantly, cultures can change over time. It would also be interesting to know whether the recognition eventually converges between different populations, as affected by product marketing, training, and globalization.

Finally, the icon perception similarities and differences between Taiwanese and American users can be observed from the confusion matrices analysis. The results suggest that among IM users in both countries, there were still many icons that could easily be confused by the users. From the confusion matrices and the results in Table 5, two icons turned out to be mis-matched into the same but wrong functions by both groups. This is interesting because the graphical representations behind these icons appear to be common between the two populations. There are differences too. Two icons each was matched into two different functions by each group. This indicates there are different thinking about the graphical representation of the icons between the two populations. Piamonte, Abeysekera, and Ohisson (2001) found that icon confusions are very important in design considerations and early stages of use. The confused symbols should be changed or redesigned if possible, or training should be offered and emphasized during the early stage of using the symbols. The confusion results presented in this study offer a possibility to further understand the cultural differences behind the graphical and symbol design of these IM icons for their future redesign.

References

1. Bourges-Waldegg, P., Scrivener, S.A.R.: Meaning, the central issue in cross-cultural HCI design. Interacting with Computers 9, 287–309 (1998)
2. Cameron, A.F., Webster, J.: Unintended consequences of emerging communication technologies: Instant messaging in the workplace. Computers in Human Behavior 21(1), 85–103 (2005)
3. Chatterjee, S., Abhichandani, T., Haiqing, L., Tulu, B., Jongbok, B.: Instant messaging and presence technologies for college campuses. IEEE Network 19(3), 4–13 (2005)

4. Choong, Y.-Y., Salvendy, G.: Design of icons for use by Chinese in mainland China. Interacting with Computers 9, 417–430 (1998)
5. Cunningham, P.J.: IM: Invaluable new business tool or records management nightmare? Information Management Journal 37(6), 27–33 (2003)
6. Gaver, W.W.: Technology affordances. In: Conference on Human Factors in Computer Systems, New Orleans, pp. 79–84. Addison-Wesley, London (1991)
7. Goonetilleke, R.S., Shih, H.M., On, H.K., Fritsch, J.: Effects of training and representational characteristics in icon design, International. Journal of Human-Computer Studies 55, 741–760 (2001)
8. Horton, W.: The icon book: Visual symbols for computer systems and documentation. John Wiley & Sons, New York (1994)
9. Huang, S.M., Shieh, K.K., Chi, C.-F.: Factors affecting the design of computer icons. International Journal of Industrial Ergonomics 29, 211–218 (2002)
10. International Standards Organization (ISO). In: International standard for safety colours and safety signs: ISO 3864. Geneva, Switzerland (1984)
11. Lodding, K.: Iconic interfacing. IEEE Computer Graphics and Applications 4(12), 13–23 (1983)
12. Miniwatts Marketing Group, Internet world users by language. (September 20, 2006) Retrieved (January 1, 2007, from http://www.internetworldstats.com/stats7.htm
13. Nakajima, Y.: Why are Figures Made All-Inclusive in a Computer Manual: The Elimination of Cultural Preference. In: Proceedings of the Society for Technical Communication. Arlington, VA (1993)
14. Shneiderman, B., Plaisant, C.: Designing the user interface: strategies for effective human-computer interface. Addison Wisley, New York (2005)
15. Taiwan Network Information Center. Internet Broadband Usage in Taiwan: A Summary Report of the January Survey of (2005), http://www.twnic.net.tw
16. Weidenbeck, S.: The use of icons and labels in an end user application program: an empirical study of learning and retention. Behavior & Information Technology 18(2), 68–82 (1999)
17. Weller, M., Pegler, C., Mason, R.: Use of innovative technologies on an e-learning course. Internet and Higher Education 8, 61–71 (2005)
18. Wickens, C.D., Hollands, J.G.: Engineering psychology and human performance, 3rd edn. Prentice Hall, Englewood Cliffs (1992)

User Validation of Cultural Dimensions
of a Website Design

Aaron Marcus and Chava Alexander

Aaron Marcus and Associates, Inc.,
1196 Euclid Avenue, Suite 1F, Berkeley, CA, 94708 USA
{Aaron.Marcus,Chava.Alexander}@AMandA.com
www.AMandA.com

Abstract. The majority of Websites are constructed with a single homogenous user in mind, or a limited number of user profiles, usually from one country or culture. In order to accommodate the international growth of the Internet, this mono-cultural bias of Website design must change. If crucial steps of user-centered user-interface (UI) development for Websites are omitted, which happens when people unconsciously apply their own rules to interactive communication intended for others, effective communication of the Website will be less successful, or may even be dysfunctional.

People from different countries/cultures have certain expectations of a particular site that may differ significantly from other countries/cultures. For example, many middle-class Germans may typically prefer a design that is more subdued and easy to navigate, while many middle-class Mexicans may prefer a more colorful screen and tolerate more ambiguity.

The present study is derived from the previous efforts of Marcus and Baumgartner [4, 5]. Using five cultural dimensions (from Hofstede, as a useful, well-known set) and the schema of five UI design components, Marcus and Baumgartner created a five-by-five matrix that allowed for twenty-five fields of interest. The authors analyzed 12 corporate business-to-business and business-to-consumer interactive Websites and found patterns in divergence from corporate design standards. Baumgartner, with Marcus' assistance, also analyzed a set of 29 culture dimensions abstracted from nine models and presented to a group of 57 experts. The two authors analyzed the experts' evaluations of the importance of each dimension [2]. They reviewed this list to derive which items comprised the top five in levels of importance. "Best of breed" culture dimensions are context, technology, uncertainty avoidance, time perception, and authority conception, in that order.

Context is described as the amount and specificity of information in a given communication. The cultural dimension of technology is comprised of the experience of technology and technological development. As a cultural dimension, technology has to do with the development and attitude of the members of a certain society towards technological development. The cultural dimension of uncertainty avoidance takes into account the behavior of the user regarding uncertain or unknown situations. Time perception concerns whether one has a long- or short-term orientation to achieving objectives and whether one is oriented to the past, present, or future. This cultural dimension can be related to the perceived amount of time that it takes to comprehend and utilize a

N. Aykin (Ed.): Usability and Internationalization, Part II, HCII 2007, LNCS 4560, pp. 160–167, 2007.
© Springer-Verlag Berlin Heidelberg 2007

Website. Authority conception concerns how people think of authority and the way their behavior is influenced when reacting to a Web UI design as official and authoritative, or not [4, 5].

Hofstede's five cultural indexes include power distance, individualism vs. collectivism, gender roles, uncertainty avoidance, and long-term time orientation. Power distance is defined as the extent to which the less powerful members of organizations and institutions (like the family) accept and expect that power is distributed unequally. This index measures whether or not there is a strong representation of inequality of a society. Individualism is the opposite of collectivism. This index demonstrates how loose or tight the ties are between individuals and their society at large. Masculinity is generally understood to be the opposite of femininity. This index refers to the roles people play according to their genders. Uncertainty avoidance concerns a society's tolerance for uncertainty and ambiguity. This index includes to what extent a culture programs its members to feel either comfortable or uncomfortable in unstructured situations. Long-term time orientation is generally the opposite of short-term time orientation. Long-term time orientation values thrift, education, and perseverance, while short-term time-orientation is concerned more with the achieving short-term goals, fulfilling obligations, and protecting one's self under changing conditions [3]'.

This study concerns an analysis of certain (undisclosable) public-facing pages of a financial-related Website by individuals from different countries and cultures. Based on the previously cited studies and after Website design interviews with twenty-four individuals from eleven different countries, the authors of this paper intend to shed light on these two questions: which dimensions seem to have the strongest impact or effect on a particular ethnic group? What considerations about culture should developers take into account when designing Websites for specific cultures/countries?

The authors used a working Website and carried out user-preferences tests. Preferences were extracted from a questionnaire of seven distinct questions that were based on the usability of and user opinions of the Website. The questionnaire consisted of three parts. The first part inquired about demographic variables. The second part contained questions based on the navigation of the Website. The third part measured the user experience and preferences. The goal of the user tests was to examine whether users with culturally different backgrounds experience and evaluate Websites in a way that is consistent with their culture-specific attributes.

The participants selected for this experiment ranged from students to professionals, with an age range of 20-50, all living in the San Francisco Bay area of California. The participants had been living in the United States for less than five years and came directly from their respective countries, which included Argentina, Canada, France, Germany, Italy, Mexico, the Netherlands, Poland, Russia, Slovakia, and the United Kingdom.

When comparing the final results with Hofstede's cultural dimensions, the following results became clear: cultural dimensions must be considered in order for a Website to be effective. For example, cultures like Russia and Slovakia, with a high level of power distance find Websites most useful when they have concise language and demonstrate a high level of professionalism. Countries such as Germany, the Netherlands, Poland, Great Britain and Canada, which have a shorter-term time orientation, desire a Website that is quick to navigate and does not require a lot of time and effort through which to browse. Participants from countries with a high index score for uncertainty avoidance, such as Argentina, France and Mexico, are not trusting of Website content, want Websites that look highly official and professional, want them in their own languages. Countries that ranked relatively higher in individualism, such as Italy, need to have a Website design that is particular to their culture and country.

Keywords: culture, design, dimensions, interface, user, Web.

1 Introduction

At its origin, the World-Wide Web claimed only a selective group of users: primarily male researchers and military project-managers located in a small area of the USA. Only a decade ago, the Web community was a male-dominated, Western-oriented society, with the design of Websites reflecting the homogenous audience. Now, a wide variety of users, from all demographics, are participating in Internet activities. According to Marcus [4], the Web implies the availability of and easy access to knowledge-based products among all peoples in all countries worldwide. Moreover, according to Cook and Finlayson [1], in 2005, roughly 75% of the Internet population is estimated to be non-English speaking.

Assessing the rapid international expansion of the Internet, it is widely understood that the current homogenous Website design should change. Currently, many Web pages have a form designed to appeal to North Americans. According to Simon [7], the World-Wide Web is a creation of technology developed primarily in the USA and Europe that exemplifies the values and norms of these advanced industrial countries. The value systems of these countries favor rationality, technology, speed, time saving, profit, individuality, and a democratic, egalitarian political model. English is the dominant language on the Internet and is present on most sites, including multi-language sites.

According to Cook and Finlayson [1], merely recognizing differences such as language, geographic location, and religious orientation is inadequate. Although these differences play a role, differences in attitudes, expectations, and the nature of social structures and relationships prove even a greater concern.

These cross-cultural differences indicate that there is a need to change the user-interface design depending on the culture/country of the user. This study uses Marcus and Baumgartner' five cultural dimensions [4, 5] and Hofstede's Cultural Index scale [3] to determine which cultural dimensions have the strongest impact on user-interface (UI) or human-computer-interaction (HCI) design. The current study examines the differences in preferences for Website design of participants from eleven different countries.

As Hoft [2] has described cultural dimensions, they can be divided into two categories: objective and subjective. Objective categories are "easy-to-research cultural differences like political and economic contexts, text directions in writing systems, and differences in the way that you format the time of day, dates, and numbers. Subjective categories cover information like value systems, behavior systems, and intellectual systems." This paper will focus on subjective categories based on the responses of the participants.

2   Research Approach and Research Questions

Available evidence about user preferences for localized or globalized Websites is limited at present. This study intends to fill this gap by presenting empirical evidence that enables user-interface designers to develop more culturally appropriate Web designs. In addition, the study aims at identifying the expectations and preferences of members of various cultures concerning Website design.

The authors examined a working international Website (oriented to financial-related content) and carried out a usability study of preferences. The test was comprised of three main sections. The first section examined the participants' backgrounds and their overall beliefs regarding what they thought would be contained in the Website. The second portion directed the participants to use the Website in order to find items in different locations and categories. The third portion asked the participants about their personal opinions about the Website. The final portion was used to assess the participant's opinions about the overall imagery of the site.

Research questions for the user tests included the following:

- How would you describe the imagery of the site in your personal opinion?
- Would this Website appeal to people in your country?
- What content is missing?
- What features would you like to see included?
- What would be two changes you would make to the site?
- Is there anything in the Website that you feel is inappropriate?

3   Evaluation Study

The goal of the user tests was to examine whether users with culturally different backgrounds experience and evaluate Websites in a way that is consistent with their cultural-specific attributes as described and predicted by a culture model.

3.1 Method

Based on results of research previously conducted by Marcus and Baumgartner [4, 5], the authors developed a questionnaire composed of questions related to the usability and aesthetics of the Website. The questionnaire consisted of three parts. The first part inquired about demographic variables. The second part contained questions about the navigation of the Website. The third part measured the user experience and preferences. The test as a whole focused on the usability issues as well as the cultural dimensions of the Website.

The participants selected for this experiment ranged from students to professionals, with an age range of 20-50, all living in the San Francisco Bay area of California. The participants had been living in the United States for less than five years and came directly from their respective countries, which included Argentina, Canada, France, Germany, Italy, Mexico, the Netherlands, Poland, Russia, Slovakia, and the United Kingdom.

3.2 Results and Conclusions

In total, 25 participants returned questionnaires to the author's firm.

Examinations of the findings for the user preferences regarding the test Website showed that the majority of participants agreed the visual image shown (a golfer or a baseball player) was not culturally acceptable and could even be insulting to their cultures. As a subsequent recommendation, the authors believe that when designing a Website for a country outside of the USA, an internationally admired sport such as soccer should be used, or a sport suitable for a specific country, such as ice-fishing for Canada, when appropriate and feasible.

Participants' comments indicated a feeling that golf was a "rich American sport" that would deter the participant from looking through the site. In addition, when initially seeing a baseball player, individuals from other cultures would assume that the Website was specifically for an American audience. This emotional reaction seems especially important when considering cultures that have a high score on Hofstede's individualism index [3, p. 53], which represents the fact that people from these countries have a strong desire to have a personal representation of their own country in the imagery they see. In addition, this strong emotional response also seems important for countries that have a high score on Hofstede's uncertainty-avoidance index [3, p. 113], which implies that people from these countries would avoid what they feel is not meaningful and/or familiar to them.

According to research conducted by Marcus and Baumgartner [4, 5], when designing Websites, it is necessary to consider the context of the Website. This would include items such as images, color, user audience, *etc.* A factor under consideration is the difference in peoples' visual or aesthetic preferences. Participants from Argentina, France, Mexico, Russia, Slovakia, and the United Kingdom preferred less white space in the visual layouts and screens. These participants expressed the desire to view a Website that contained fewer words and more imagery and color. In addition, the imagery of the test Website tended to be repetitive and was not relevant to the information at hand. On the other hand, participants from Canada, Germany, Italy, the Netherlands, and Poland did, in fact, like the fact that there was a lot of white space on the screen. They did not mind that there was a relatively small use of colors or of large images on the Website.

Although these differences suggest some design guidelines, further research must be conducted in order to have a clear understanding of the precise relationships linking the amount of white space, color, layout and imagery to cultural dimensions for specific countries when designing Websites. Based on the above study, it seems practical and feasible to gain these data for better Website design.

When choosing images, several participants suggested that there should be a direct, explicit relationship between the actual image and the purpose of the Website. According to Hofstede's data, this is especially important when designing Websites for countries with a high level of uncertainty avoidance [3, p. 113]. Marcus and Baumgartner [4, 5] also have mentioned the importance of considering uncertainty avoidance when designing Websites. This cultural attribute implies that it is important to make the purpose of the Website clear, so that users feel comfortable and capable of working with the site. In addition, countries with a high uncertainty avoidance index score will avoid a Website through which they feel they do not understand how to navigate or of which they do not understand the purpose. Marcus and Baumgartner [4, 5] have also noted the importance of considering time perception, including the length of time it requires to navigate through a site. The images and colors must strongly effect and make the users feel more comfortable with the site. For example, a participant from the United Kingdom mentioned that she did not feel the test Website was secure because the official company logo colors were different than the ones that she was used to in the United Kingdom (the corporate logo was undergoing gradual change worldwide). Also, there should be a clear image denoting the purpose of the Website in order to enable the user to feel more comfortable with the site.

Marcus and Baumgartner [4, 5] have discussed at length the importance of environment and technology. Participants from countries such as Mexico, Russia, and Slovakia who are used to a very basic Website took longer to locate the information for which they were searching. On the other hand, participants from countries that are more technologically advanced were disappointed and felt that the Website could have been designed with a higher level of technological development. This was especially true for the German participants.

In addition, countries with a low score on Hofstede's long-term time-orientation index [3, p. 261] seemed to need to have a quick and concise idea of the purpose of the Website. The Website needed to be attention-grabbing and eye-catching. These participants had little desire to spend much time searching for what they were looking for. They were impatient and preferred to have a picture of what they were interested in purchasing. For example, "shorter-term" German participants stated that they only wanted to see images with which they were working with directly. These images must be useful and functional. External images are not viewed unless they have a correlation with the materials for which they are looking. A direct contrast would be "longer-term" Chinese individuals who enjoy images in lieu of text.

The size of the images is also an important technological factor to consider when designing Websites. According to Marcus and Baumgartner [4], the technological abilities of the audience must be considered. Even though a large majority of the participants stated that they preferred to see the actual images larger, participants from countries with a lower economic status, such as Russia and Slovakia, mentioned that they would be concerned that it would take longer to navigate through the site because the graphics were too large and would cause some delays in downloading them. In addition, the total amount of imagery is also an important factor when designing a Website. This comparison is strongest between Germany and Mexico. The German participants stated that too many graphics would clutter up the site, versus the Mexican participants, who mentioned that they desired a larger number of graphics.

According to Marcus and Baumgartner [4], the context in which the Website is presented varies across cultures. A clear comparison of the importance of the nature of Website design would be between statements from four different groups of participants. The participants from Canada and Germany liked the fact that there was no use of Flash and that the user could click on the featured offers without leaving the Home page. On the other hand, participants from Mexico and the United Kingdom would have preferred a Website that contained more use of Flash and allowed them to navigate thoroughly through the Website. The second group of participants felt that if there were added Flash components, the designers would make the Website appear to be more legitimate.

As stated earlier in the introduction, when designing a Website, it is crucial to have a precise understanding of the audience. Several of the participants thought that the Website was not designed for them because there were no images displayed with which they could identify. This lack of identification was particularly clear when participants mentioned the desire to view images of athletes playing their national sport, such as ice fishing or soccer, and was especially strong with participants who had a low score on Hofstede's power-distance index [3]. These participants seemed to want to feel they were on equal levels with the sponsors of the Website and that the sponsors of the Website appreciated their visiting.

When designing the search functionality of a Website, it is also important to have a clear understanding of how people from different countries and cultures navigate through information. Acceptable design can be done with appropriate visual cues and images. One participant from France and two from Mexico did not understand how to navigate at all through the Website, and the majority of the other participants did not successfully find that for which they had been looking. The improper understanding of Website navigation and losing one's way through the navigation can contribute to a negative experience for the overall usability of the Website.

4 Conclusion

There is a clear and identified need to understand the role that images, layout, color, and navigation play when designing Websites from a cross-cultural prospective. As expected from the literature of culture analysis, the findings of this limited study demonstrate that there are clear patterns of difference among user preferences and experiences of Websites for people from different cultures. Some of these preferences have been described in previous research; others need to be researched further to be understood completely.

As the Web becomes more application-based versus catalogue- or document-based, different culture-related design considerations may need to be considered and implemented. For example, for some groups, in only a few more years people may not have the need to carry around laptops, and the primary use of the Internet will be for service.

After thorough review of the literature at present, the authors recommend that that customized sites should be designed for different cultures not just for language translation or country localization. In addition, designers in those regions should organize an appropriate design strategy as well as perform user testing in those regions to study the relations of culture to user-interface design more thoroughly.

The experience gained from these user tests led to important insights, confirmed previous notions, and helped bring about changes in the client's approach to Web design. This example may inspire others to undertake similar analysis and design efforts. Further analysis of culture and other dimension and more detailed measurement may yield further insight and more specific design recommendations in the future.

References

1. Cook, J., Finlayson, M.: The Impact of Cultural Diversity on Website Design. Advanced Management Journal, Summer 70(3), 15–23 (2005)
2. Hoft, N.L: Developing a Cultural Model. In: Galdo, D., Elisa, M., Nielsen, Jakob (eds.) International User-Interfaces, pp. 41–73. John Wiley and Sons, New York (1996)
3. Hoftstede, Geert.: Cultures and Organizations. McGraw-Hill, New York (1997)
4. Marcus, Aaron, Baumgartner, Valentina-Johanna.: User-Interface Design vs. Culture. In: Proceedings, International Conference on Internationalization of Products and Services (IWIPS 2003), July 2003, Berlin, Germany, pp, 67–78 (2003)
5. Marcus, Aaron, Baumgartner, Valentina-Johanna.: A Practical Set of Culture Dimensions for Global User-Interface Development. In: Masoodian, M., Jones, S., Rogers, B. (eds.) APCHI 2004. LNCS, vol. 3101, pp. 252–261. Springer, Heidelberg (2004)
6. Marcus, Aaron, Gould, E.W.: Crosscurrents: Cultural Dimensions and Global Web User-Interface Design. Interactions, ACM Publisher 7(4), 32–46 (2000), www.acm.org
7. Simon, S.: The Impact of Culture and Gender on Websites: An Empirical Study. Database for Advances in Information Systems, Winter 2001 32(1), 18–37 (2001)

Usability Challenges in Designing Foreign Language Keypads for Handheld Devices

Parul Nanda and Kem-Laurin Kramer

Research In Motion Ltd., 415 Phillip St. Waterloo, Ontario N2L 3X2
{pnanda,kkramer}@rim.com

Abstract. This paper discusses the importance of language and culture in the effective design and widespread acceptance of handheld devices in foreign markets. To this end, key challenges that usability experts and interaction designers face while designing foreign language keypads for handheld devices are discussed and analyzed. The discussion presupposes English as the point of reference for design decisions but focuses on the challenges faced when considering foreign language devices. For the context of this paper, Arabic is cited as the 'foreign' language in the design of BlackBerry devices.

Keywords: Handhelds, keypads, Arabic, language, culture, usability, design.

1 Introduction

Handheld devices allow users to communicate while they are on the move, creating a world where "anywhere, anytime, and anyhow access is allowed for anybody" [6]. However, the potential of personal and ubiquitous computing promised by handheld devices has not been fully realized, especially for users in foreign markets [10]. This is due to the dominance of research and technology taking root in the Anglo-American world. Consequently, many handhelds continue to be designed using Anglo-American conventions and standards [19], [21]. The devices, therefore, designed for non-English markets are often removed from the culture in which they will be used, ignoring one of the fundamental aspects of product usability – context of use [9]. Further, users' language preferences and social context of use of the device are ignored while designing the devices. Reusing the context of use of one culture and expecting that it works for another is termed as the "deficit-driven" approach [11], [21].

This paper suggests that following a "languacultural" approach, defined as the interdependence of language and culture, when designing handhelds can improve foreign users' experience with the devices [1]. The paper proposes that displaying the character set of the users' native language on the keypad, instead of providing only software support for the native language, not only pays homage to the users' culture but also motivates users to use the device (see [20]). However, there are several usability challenges in designing handhelds [23] and they tend to increase when designing for an international audience, which goes beyond a process of merely translating a product from one culture to another [13], [16]. In order to mitigate some of these challenges and to ensure that the languacultural approach is followed, cross-cultural

N. Aykin (Ed.): Usability and Internationalization, Part II, HCII 2007, LNCS 4560, pp. 168–177, 2007.
© Springer-Verlag Berlin Heidelberg 2007

usability guidelines have to be developed. One step towards framing these guidelines is to identify the usability challenges in designing keypads that can support languages other than English. This paper specifically explores the need for the languacultural approach in designing Arabic keypads for BlackBerry devices, a leading wireless handheld device solution [2]. The paper further proposes a design solution that addresses the usability challenges identified in this paper.

2   Arabic Language and Culture: Background Research

Focus of the paper is on the design of Arabic keypads due to the following three reasons:

- There is a growing market for handheld devices in countries where Arabic is spoken. According to Madar Research, mobile phone market in the Arab world will comprise 109 million subscribers by end of 2008, reaching a penetration rate of about 32 percent [12].
- There is a large part of the world's population speaking Arabic. Arabic is the 6th most commonly spoken language in the world, with approximately 206 million native speakers [5].
- There are a number of other languages that are similar or share the same script with Arabic; these include languages such as Persian, Urdu, Kurdish, Hebrew that are similar to Arabic, with respect to the direction of text, right-to-left (RTL). However, it is not necessary that all design rules applicable to Arabic keypads will apply to these languages; rather, standards and guidelines used in the design on Arabic keypads may help in generating guidelines for these other languages.

The paper also draws upon Hofstede's research on cultural dimensions to understand the Arab culture and how this understanding can be applied in designing effective handheld interfaces for this market [7], [14], [15]. Two of Hofstede's cultural dimensions, Uncertainty Avoidance Index (UAI) and Individualism (IDV), bear relevance for this study and will be used to support the position of this paper.

- *UAI* deals with a society's tolerance for uncertainty and ambiguity. The Arab world has a high UAI index, which indicates a low tolerance to accepting change and taking risks. This is in sharp contrast with the Western countries, which are tolerant of uncertainty and readily accept change [7]. Also, a high UAI index creates a rule-oriented society for the Arab world, which places more importance on tradition than Western societies.
- *IDV* versus its polar opposite, collectivism is the degree to which individuals are integrated into groups. Middle East has a low value for IDV, i.e., the society is collectivist, which is "manifested in a close long-term commitment to the member 'group', that being a family, extended family, or extended relationships" [7]. On the other hand, Western society is individualistic, which is manifested in "individualistic attitude and loose relationships" [7].

These distinctions in culture justify following the languacultural approach rather than a deficit-driven approach in order to penetrate and sustain the Arab handheld market. One consequence of the cultural distinction between the Western World and the Arab

World is the distinct perspective of the role of language in the two societies [24]. Arabic is not only a tool for transferring information, as English is in the Western World, but is also a social instrument used to affect people's feelings through three socio-historic forces – art, religion, and nationalism [8], [25]. Since handheld technology is increasingly changing the landscape of communication, we propose that by displaying the Arabic characters on the handheld, the Arab users can have a more positive emotional experience with the device. Such an interface will emphasize Arab users' beliefs of placing value in language, culture, and tradition [24], [25]. It, therefore, becomes important to involve users who are proficient in Arabic in the design of Arabic keypads.

3 Usability Evaluation: Methodology

Multiple iterations of usability evaluation were conducted to get user feedback on the preliminary design of Arabic keypads. Recent Arabic immigrants to Canada were selected to participate, as these users were the closest and most accessible representative users of a wider market for which the devices are destined.

3.1 First Iteration: Methodology

In an effort to fully embrace the culturally sensitive approach to usability evaluation [3], the method followed in the first iteration of the study was tailored to meet the collectivist nature of Arabic society, as indicated by a low IDV value in Hofstede's research [7]. A co-discovery learning method was used to simulate the collectivist nature of the Arabic culture and better foster the solicitation of input from users [4]. This was in contrast to the traditional one-on-one interview sessions. A total of 6 Arabic-speaking users were divided into 3 groups of 2 members each and were asked questions related to the Arabic language. They were also asked to provide their feedback on the challenges an Anglo culture would face in designing an Arabic keypad for a handheld. In addition to allowing users to think in conjunction with each other, users were also provided with cultural tools and implements such as the full Arabic character set. By allowing users to interact with individuals and other cultural tools, emphasis was placed on users' environment, which helped in distributing and redesigning users' social aspects of cognition [18], [22]. This also allowed users to benefit from the advantages of recognition over recall so that they could focus on other cognitive tasks rather than remembering the Arabic characters [17].Users were also given the opportunity to co-design and modify existing designs. The session resulted in generation of previously unforeseen usability challenges, which were not obvious while following an ethnocentric approach to design.

3.2 Second Iteration: Methodology

The goal of this iteration was to address the usability challenges related to font and layout that were encountered in the first iteration. Mini-focus groups were conducted to gather user feedback. A total of 11 users, 3 groups of 3 users each and 1 group of 2 users, participated in this iteration. The users were shown four variations of fonts and three different layouts of the Arabic keypad and were asked to select the keypad which they thought was the most representative of the Arabic keypad. The iteration resulted in selection of font for the Arabic keypad.

3.3 Third Iteration: Methodology

The goal of the third iteration was to evaluate the proposed design, which addressed most of the usability challenges discovered in the first iteration. A traditional usability test was conducted to evaluate both the software and the hardware of the handheld. In total, 9 users individually completed several typing tasks. At the end of the session, one-on-one interviews were conducted to gather user feedback.

4 Usability Evaluation: Results

4.1 First Iteration: Results

In the usability study, the participants were shown the following initial design of the Arabic keypad (See Fig 1).

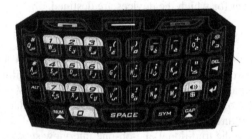

Fig. 1. Initial Arabic Keypad design (not to scale)

The issues encountered during evaluation have been presented as usability challenges faced while designing Arabic keypads.

1. *Arabic character set:* Majority of the participants mentioned that basic Arabic alphabets were missing from the initial design. This is because English character set has 26 alphabets whereas the Arabic character set has 28 alphabets (see Fig. 2). *Usability Challenge 1 (UC 1): How to accommodate the two extra alphabets on the keypad that was initially designed to accommodate 26 alphabets?*
2. *Layout of Arabic characters:* The participants commented that they were confused with the layout of the Arabic characters with respect to the English characters. The QWERTY layout is a tested method for inputting the English language on a computer. However, there is no research indicating whether the QWERTY layout fully supports the Arabic language. It should be noted that the AZERTY and QWERTZ layout were designed to accommodate French and German languages respectively.

   UC2: Is there an equivalent of QWERTY for the Arabic language, which is standardized and universal?

   UC3: Provided that there is a QWERTY equivalent for Arabic, does Arabic lend itself to a QWERTY style layout, as it is more a sound-based language?

IPA	Latin	Name		Final	Medial	Initial	Isolated	IPA	Latin	Name		Final	Medial	Initial	Isolated
[tˤ]	ṭ	ṭāʾ	طاء	ـط	ـطـ	طـ	ط	[ʔ]	ʾ(a)	ʾalif	ألف	ـا	—	—	ا
[ðˤ]	ẓ	ẓāʾ	ظاء	ـظ	ـظـ	ظـ	ظ	[b]	b	bāʾ	باء	ـب	ـبـ	بـ	ب
[ʕ]	ʿ	ʿayn	عين	ـع	ـعـ	عـ	ع	[t]	t	tāʾ	تاء	ـت	ـتـ	تـ	ت
[ɣ]	ġ	ġayn	غين	ـغ	ـغـ	غـ	غ	[θ]	ṯ	ṯāʾ	ثاء	ـث	ـثـ	ثـ	ث
[f]	f	fāʾ	فاء	ـف	ـفـ	فـ	ف	[dʒ]	ǧ	ǧīm	جيم	ـج	ـجـ	جـ	ج
[q]	q	qāf	قاف	ـق	ـقـ	قـ	ق	[ħ]	ḥ	ḥāʾ	حاء	ـح	ـحـ	حـ	ح
[k]	k	kāf	كاف	ـك	ـكـ	كـ	ك	[x]	ḫ	ḫāʾ	خاء	ـخ	ـخـ	خـ	خ
[l]	l	lām	لام	ـل	ـلـ	لـ	ل	[d]	d	dāl	دال	ـد	—	—	د
[m]	m	mīm	ميم	ـم	ـمـ	مـ	م	[ð]	ḏ	ḏāl	ذال	ـذ	—	—	ذ
[n]	n	nūn	نون	ـن	ـنـ	نـ	ن	[r]	r	rāʾ	راء	ـر	—	—	ر
[h]	h	hāʾ	هاء	ـه	ـهـ	هـ	ه	[z]	z	zāy	زاي	ـز	—	—	ز
[w]	w	wāw	واو	ـو	—	—	و	[s]	s	sīn	سين	ـس	ـسـ	سـ	س
[j]	y	yāʾ	ياء	ـي	ـيـ	يـ	ي	[ʃ]	š	šīn	شين	ـش	ـشـ	شـ	ش
		hamza	همزة	ء	—	—	—	[sˤ]	ṣ	ṣād	صاد	ـص	ـصـ	صـ	ص
								[dˤ]	ḍ	ḍād	ضاد	ـض	ـضـ	ضـ	ض

Fig. 2. Arabic consonants

3. *Typography:* The participants were dissatisfied with the fonts used to represent Arabic characters and called it a "pointy slanted" font, which is not representative of the cursive Arabic writing that the users are accustomed to. For instance, the participants pointed out the difference in how the Arabic characters خ, ح, ج were actually written and the way they were represented on the keypad on the U, I, O keys respectively (see Fig. 1). Users also mentioned that the same font color for English and Arabic characters added to the difficulty in recognition and recall of Arabic characters. Further, Arabic has many characters, which to the untrained eye, could look very similar. The choice of fonts used and whether these fonts are italicized in the design of the keypad could be critical. For example, there could be a confusion between the Arabic characters L (lām) and R (rā'), because lām should be straight, like ل and R should be slanted, like ر but with an unnecessary 7-degree slant created by italicizing the two as in the initial keypad design, the confusion becomes apparent. Also, the size for the character, ر , is smaller than the character, ل because it depends if it is written below the line or above the line. Moreover, unlike the English language, Arabic does not have any capital alphabets

   UC4: Which fonts would best enhance recognition and recall of characters on a smaller handheld keypad, preserving the integrity of the language in terms of design, script, and typography while respecting the handwritten conventions that mark the written form of a language?
4. *Variation in the alphabet depending upon its location in the word:* Each Arabic alphabet can have four variations depending on where it appears in the word: isolated, initial, middle, or final. Majority of the participants noticed that the initial keypad design did not consistently display all the alphabets based on where the alphabet is located in a word. For example, users commented that some alphabets were displayed in the initial form while others were displayed in the isolated form.

   UC5: Which form of the Arabic alphabet should be displayed on the keypad?
5. *Combination of characters:* The Arabic keyboard provides users with some combination characters, which are conjunction of two Arabic alphabets, to improve typing efficiency. Participants really liked that the combination character lām-alif, was available on the keypad, displayed on the "C" key (see Fig. 1). However, they also mentioned that these characters should not be made available at the expense of the basic alphabet.

   UC6: Should combination characters be displayed on the keypad?

6. *Special characters and vowel diacritics:* Arabic language supports various vowel diacritics, which, if used, can change the meaning of the word. Participants mentioned that some of the key symbols like hamza were missing on the keypad (see Fig. 2). They also recommended that it was not necessary to display all the vowel diacritics on the keypad, as they are rarely used (see Fig. 3a).

UC7: How to support the important diacritical mark?

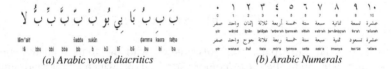

    (a) *Arabic vowel diacritics*   (b) *Arabic Numerals*

Fig. 3. Arabic language symbols and numerals

7. *Punctuation symbols:* The punctuation symbols in Arabic are written differently than in English. For example, a comma in English (,) is written differently in Arabic (،). Participants mentioned that they did not expect Arabic punctuation symbols be displayed on the keypad.

UC8: What is the ideal way to support Arabic punctuation symbols on the Arabic device?

8. *Hindu-Arabic numerals:* The Arabic numerals are different from the English numerals (See Fig. 3b). Participants were divided in their opinion about displaying Hindu-Arabic numerals on the keypad.

UC9: Arabic mobile phones display English numerals. Should Arabic numerals be displayed on handhelds? Changing the numerals to Arabic on BlackBerry may not match users' mental models

9. *Icons and Symbols:* Besides addressing textual components of the keypad, the issue of icons and symbols needs to be addressed. For example, the use of the (◄Del), meaning delete, on the BlackBerry is understood by most users of the QWERTY keypad, but it may not be understood by a native Arabic speaker. Participants also mentioned that the key, CAP is useless when in the Arabic mode. The "$" key does not have much significance in the Arab world. Other such keys are NUM, SPACE, and SYM.

UC10: What should be the rules surrounding the use of icons and symbols on handheld devices?

4.2 Second Iteration: Results

The first usability challenge addressed in this iteration was related to fonts (UC4). The following four font choices were given to users (see Fig. 4). All the participants in each group unanimously selected font choice 2 because it was representative of the cursive Arabic characters and writing.

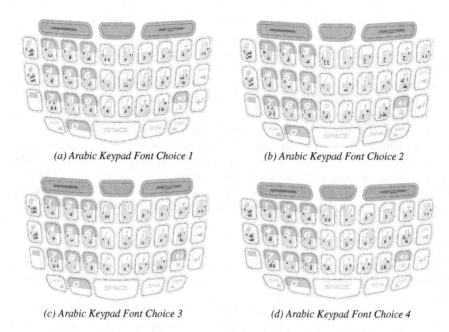

(a) Arabic Keypad Font Choice 1   *(b) Arabic Keypad Font Choice 2*

(c) Arabic Keypad Font Choice 3   *(d) Arabic Keypad Font Choice 4*

Fig. 4. Arabic keypad font choices secondary designs (not to scale)

The next usability challenge addressed in this iteration was related to layout (UC2 and UC 3). The users were shown the following three layouts for the Arabic keypad and were asked to choose one (see Fig.5).

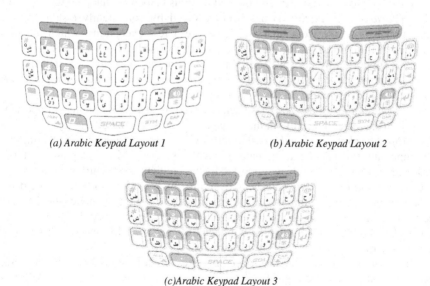

(a) Arabic Keypad Layout 1   *(b) Arabic Keypad Layout 2*

(c)Arabic Keypad Layout 3

Fig. 5. Arabic keypad layouts: secondary designs (not to scale)

Users were divided in their opinion about the choice of the layout. Two groups of three users each (6 users in total) preferred layout 3 because each Arabic character was mapped to one English character and the font size for Arabic characters was bigger as compared to the other layouts. Some users of these 2 groups later realized that some characters were missing from layout 3 but did not change their choice. One group of 3 members preferred layout 2 over layout 1 because it displayed Arabic numerals. The last group comprising of 2 users preferred layout 1 because it displayed English numerals. Although, more users preferred (6 versus 5 users) one-to-one character mapping for Arabic and English alphabets, this data was not considered reliable due to three reasons. First, the influence of the collective decision over the individual in the focus groups compromised the results. Second, the inherent drawback of focus groups is that the data gathered is unreliable for quantitative analysis. Third, real user experience was lacking due to absence of tasks being performed with the device.

4.3 Third Iteration: Results

Based on the usability evaluation of the keypads, an Arabic keypad layout has been proposed (see Fig. 6). The proposed design attempts to overcome some of the challenges outlined in the previous section.

UC 1 (Arabic Character Set) has been resolved by mapping two Arabic alphabets to one English alphabet in some cases. The current design supports predictive text entry, i.e., when user presses the Arabic key with two alphabets, the software effectively disambiguates between the two. In the usability test, all the users commented that the software support provided a satisfying typing experience.

UC4 (Typography) was mostly resolved in the second iteration. However, proposed design has been further improved by using bright orange-yellow colour to display the Arabic characters. Users commented that this helped in character recognition.

UC5 (Variation in alphabets) has been resolved by consistently displaying the Arabic alphabets in the isolated form. There are a few exceptions, which are displayed, in the initial form as they are more commonly used. Also, the variation in the alphabet is supported by the software. Majority of the users commented that the device was extremely good at providing a calligraphic experience while typing and adhered well to the rules of the written language.

UC6 (Combination characters) has been resolved by displaying the most important combination character, lām-alif, on the keypad to increase typing efficiency.

UC7 (Special characters and vowel diacritics) has been resolved by displaying the most important special character, hamza, on the keypad. Also, integration of the hamza with the basic alphabets is supported by the predictive text entry software.

UC 8 (Punctuation symbols) has been overcome by providing software support for the Arabic punctuation symbols, i.e., when in Arabic language mode, the English punctuation symbols are automatically converted to the respective Arabic form.

UC 9 (Hindu-Arabic numerals) has not been fully resolved. More research needs to be conducted to find user preferences for numerals.

UC10 (Icons and symbols) has not been fully resolved. Designs for more universal icons and symbols will be considered for future research. However, the $ key has been removed to accommodate additional Arabic characters.

(a)Arabic keypad design for BlackBerry 8700   *(b) Arabic keypad design for BlackBerry 8800*

Fig. 6. Proposed Arabic Keypad Designs for BlackBerry 8700 & 8800

UC2 and UC3 (QWERTY layout of the Arabic keypad) have been partly resolved. The QWERTY layout has been proposed as users were very receptive to the design. Until research yields a more appropriate fully-localized layout for the Arabic language, similar to the German layout (QWERTZ) and France layout (AZERTY), which respects the character differences, designers and users found the designs satisfactory. Continuous research that embraces a fully languaculture approach to design will yield better design solutions in the future.

5 Conclusion and Future Work

User-interface design for foreign language keypads of handheld devices requires design experts to follow a languaculture approach rather than a deficit driven approach. This allows for wider acceptance and higher pervasiveness of the device and technology within its intended market. We assert that the display of native language alphabets on the device keypad is the first step in this direction but it must be driven by a fuller understanding of other language, culture, and social aspects. However, there are considerable usability challenges in displaying the foreign language character set on a handheld device. It is, thus, essential to work towards language and cultural related guidelines, respecting both the device-centric elements and the user–centric aspects for wider acceptance of handheld devices across cultures.

References

1. Agar, M.: Language Shock. Morrow, New York, 1994 (1994)
2. BlackBerry, (2007), Online http://www.blackberry.com
3. Chavan, A.L: Another culture, another method. In: Proceedings of HCII 2005 [CD Rom], Lawrence Erlbaum, Mahwah (2005)

4. Dumas, J.S., Redish, J.C.: A Practical Guide to Usability Testing, Ablex Publishing (1999)
5. Raymond Jr, G. (ed.): Ethnologue: Languages of the World, 15th edn. In: Dallas, Tex.: SIL International. (2005), Online http://www.ethnologue.com
6. Gorlenko, L., Merrick, R.: No wires attached: Usability challenges in the connected mobile world. IBM Systems Journal 42(4), 639–651 (2003)
7. Hofstede, G.: Cultures and Organizations: Software of the minds: Intercultural cooperation and its importance for survival. Mc-Graw Hill, New York (2004)
8. Hourani, A.: Arabic thought in the liberal age 1789-1939. Cambridge University Press, Cambridge (1983)
9. International Organization for Standardization (1998). In: Ergonomic requirements for office work with visual display terminals (VDTs) – Part 11: Guidance on usability. Geneva, Switzerland (1998)
10. Käpyaho, J.: Internationalization in operating systems for handheld devices. In: University of Tampere, Department of Computer and Information Sciences, Master's Thesis (2001)
11. Katre, D.S.: A position paper on cross-cultural usability issues of bilingual (Hindi and English) mobile phones. In: Proceedings of Indo-Danish research Symposium (2006)
12. Madar Research, Knowledge Economy Research on the Middle East. Online: http://www.madarresearch.com/archive/archive_edit.aspx?id=19
13. Marcus, A.: International and Intercultural User Interfaces. In: Stephanidis, C. (ed.) User Interfaces for All, pp. 47–63. Lawrence Erlbaum Associates, New York (2001)
14. Marcus, A., Gould, E.W.: Crosscurrents: cultural dimensions and global Web user-interface design. Interactions 7(4), 32–46 (2000)
15. Röse, K.: Models of culture and their applicability for designing user interfaces. In: Luczak, H., Cakir, A. (eds.) WWDU, Work With Display Units, World Wide Work. In: Proceedings of the 6th International Scientific Conference on Work with Display Units, Berchtesgaden, May 22-25, 2002, pp. 319–321 (2002)
16. Nielsen, J.: Designing user interfaces for international use, Elsevier Science Publishers Ltd. Essex (1990), (1990)
17. Nielsen, J.: Heuristic evaluation. In: Nielsen, J., Mack, R.L. (eds.) Usability Inspection Methods, John Wiley & Sons, New York (1994)
18. Perry, M.: Distributed Cognition. In: Carroll, J.M. (ed.) HCI Models, Theories, and Frameworks: Toward an Interdisciplinary Science, pp. 193–223. Morgan Kaufmann, San Francisco (2003)
19. Russo, P., Bloor, S.: How fluent is your interface design? Designing for international users. In: Ashlund, S., Mullet, K., Henderson, A., Hallengel, E., White, T. (eds.) Proceedings of INTERCHI 2003, pp. 342–347. ACM Press, New York (2003)
20. Ruuska, S.: Mobile communication devices for international use – exploring cultural diversity through contextual inquiry. In: Proceedings of the first International Workshop on Internationalization of Products and Systems, pp. 217–226 (1999)
21. Sacher, H., Tng, T., Loudon, G.: Beyond Translation: Approaches to interactive products for Chinese customers. International Journal of Human Computer Interaction 13(1), 41–51 (2001)
22. Salomon, G.: Distributed cognitions: Psychological and educational considerations. Cambridge University Press, Cambridge (1993)
23. Weiss, S.: Handheld Usability. John Wiley & Sons, NewYork (2002)
24. Zaharna, R.S.: Understanding cultural preferences of Arab communication patterns. Public Relations Review 21(3), 241–255 (1995)
25. Zaharna, R.S.: Rhetorical Ethnocentricism. In: Speech Communication Association, New Orleans, November 1994 (1994)

Comparing User and Software Information Structures for Compatibility

Thomas Plocher[1] and Torkil Clemmensen[2]

[1] Honeywell Laboratories
3660 Technology Drive,
Minneapolis, Minnesota 55418, USA
tom.plocher@honeywell.com
[2] Department of Informatics,
Copenhagen Business School,
Howitzvej 60, 2.10
DK - 2000 Frederiksberg C
tc.inf@cbs.dk

Abstract. Eastern and Western cultures differ quite systematically in how they group objects, functions and concepts into categories [1,2,3]. This has implications for how navigation features, such as menus, links, directories, should be designed in software applications. This is particularly of interest when the application is developed in one culture for use in a second culture. This paper presents this problem and discusses some approaches to comparing user and software information architectures both visually and quantitatively.

Keywords: culture, cognition, information architecture, usability, visualization.

1 Introduction

Eastern and Western cultures differ quite systematically in how they group objects, functions and concepts into categories [1,2] and [3]. Earlier, Choong [4] also found some evidence for these cultural differences in category formation when people used an online shopping system. Eastern cultures tend to place objects together that share relationships. Western cultures group objects together based on similar object attributes. As a simple example, assume that we show Eastern and Western people three pictures: a cow, a dog, and a patch of grass, and ask them to group the pictures. Western people will tend to place the cow and dog in the same category because from their physical attributes, they are both animals. Eastern people will tend to group the cow and the grass together because of the relationship, "cows eat grass".

So what does this mean for user interfaces? Categories form the basis for the information architectures underlying user interfaces to software systems. The content and organization of menus in Windows[TM] interfaces, links in websites, and file directories in most software applications are based on categories. But who's categories? Most likely those of the software designer, and reflecting the particular biases in category formation associated with her culture or personal cognitive style.

N. Aykin (Ed.): Usability and Internationalization, Part II, HCII 2007, LNCS 4560, pp. 178–182, 2007.
© Springer-Verlag Berlin Heidelberg 2007

What happens when a user from one culture, say, the United States, attempts to use a software application that is based on categories, e.g. an information architecture, developed in another culture, such as India? The result can be poor usability, as the user attempts to locate functions in menus or information organized in an unfamiliar way by an original designer or engineer thinking in a different style.

2 Visualizing and Comparing User and Software Information Structures

A first step in understanding how the user interface is affected by these cultural differences in category formation is to have some useful methods to make these comparisons and describe the similarities and differences. Initially, it would be of great value to the designer and researcher to have tools for visualizing graphically the information structures of user and software and comparing them in a qualitative manner. Eventually, more quantitative methods of comparison can be developed. The current paper reviews some techniques for visualizing information hierarchies and how these might be applied to the problem of comparing user and software information architectures. We also discuss some ideas for metrics that would allow the usability expert to describe those differences more quantitatively. Such metrics can be used to evaluate usability and re-design an information architecture for a software application. They also can be used to design information architectures for cross-cultural research that deliberately and quantifiably vary from some cultural preference. This is how these metrics will be used on the CULTUSAB project [5]. In the future, one can envision how such metrics could also be integral to software applications that can adapt their information architecture and resulting menus, links, etc., automatically, to better match the preferences and cognitive style of the user.

2.1 Desired Functions

In this context, what does it mean to "compare" two information architectures, the user's versus the application's? First of all, we assume that the information architecture underlying a software application and user interface can be described as a branching hierarchy of main categories and subcategories, X levels deep. Assume also that the hierarchy can be derived by analysis for a given software application from its menus, links, or directory structure. A user's preferred hierarchy can be derived by having him perform a "card sort" exercise (6). Each object or function is written on a card and the user's task is to organize them into categories. Once the hierarchies are documented, tools can be applied to compare them.

At a minimum we would like to have a tool that allows us to:

1. Compare the gross or overall form of one structure to another. It would be useful to display two structures, side by side, and look at them from a bird's eye view. Then rotate them in X, Y, Z to identify gross similarities and differences in number of nodes at each level of the hierarchy (width) and number of levels (depth). From this bird's-eye view we could identify branches of a hierarchy that stand out by being being extremely simple or extremely complex. Further, it would be useful to

be able to zoom in on the dissimilar portions of the structures and then make more detailed comparisons, looking at the content or meaning of individual nodes.
2. Systematically compare the nodes and branches of one structure to another. The designer would like to compare mother nodes at each level of the hierarchy and look in detail at the children of each specific mother node. The ability to zoom in on a single node and read its description would be valuable.
3. Cross reference between structures. It would be useful to select a node in one structure and instantly be connected to its location in the other structure by means of a line connecting the two or highlighting the two nodes.
4. Estimate the degree of difference between the two structures. Ideally a tool for comparing two information structures would compute some quantitative measure of similarity or difference between the two.

2.2 Available Visualization Tools

Andrews [7] provides a survey of tools for visualizing information hierarchies. One of the classical approaches to this problem is that of Cone Trees [8] and their more recent and enhanced derivatives, Reconfigurable Disc Trees [9]. Cone Trees provide a three-dimensional representation of an information hierarchy. Each node in the hierarchy is represented as the apex of a cone. The "children" or nodes underneath the apical node are arranged in a three-dimensional circle. The height of each cone is scaled so that the entire hierarchy fits on the screen. Each cone is slightly shaded to make it distinct but without occluding other cones in the tree. The tree can be rotated by the user to explore its structure. Also, clicking on a node causes it and all the nodes in its path to rotate to the front and center of the tree in animation. The text describing each node is also displayed when the node has been rotated to the front. Cone Trees are searchable, with the nodes identified by the search highlighted in color.

Unlike textual two-dimensional depictions of information hierarchies, the three-dimensional Cone Tree allows a rather large hierarchy to be displayed and viewed on a screen without scrolling. Cone Trees can accomodate up to 1,000 nodes on a single screen but, beyond that, begin to suffer from visual clutter. To solve this problem and accomodate larger hierarchies, Jeong and Pang [9] developed Reconfigurable Disc Trees (RDTs). An RDT uses discs rather than cones to represent node and children relationships. The children are arrayed around a circle rather than a cone. This improves the ease of visual projection on the screen, reducing occusion between elements of the tree and increasing the number of nodes that can be displayed on a single screen. Figures 1 and 2 show examples of Cone Trees and RDTs.

Cone Trees and RDTs provide useful tools that can be used in their current form for analyzing user and software information architectures. However, these tools were intended to support analysis of a single information hierarchy, not the systematic comparison of two hierarchies. To support the latter task, these tools need to be modified in several ways. First, the two hierarchies being compared should be displayed side-by-side, on the same screen. Second, it would be highly desireable if Cone Trees and RDTs provided the ability to map a node in one structure to the node with the same content in the second structure. This is analogous to the problem of mapping one database schema or ontology to another. A number of tools are available for that, most notably Microsoft's BizTalk Schema Mapper and its recent

Fig. 1. Cone Trees for simple and complex (516 nodes) information hierarchies. From Jeong and Pang [9].

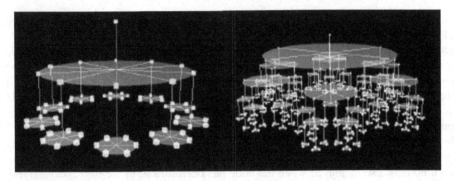

Fig. 2. Reconfigurable Disc Trees for simple and complex (516 nodes) information hierarchies. From Jeong and Pang [9].

enhancements described by Robertson, Czerwinski and Churchill [10]. While the latter clearly map one schema hierarchy to another, node by node, the representation is still two-dimensional and largely textual. The 3D graphical visualization that makes Cone Trees and RDTs so useful for our purposes and so efficient in the use of screen real estate, are missing. These capabilities need to be combined.

3 What Could We Measure?

The visualization tools reviewed by Andrews were intended for viewing a single information hierarchy, not for comparing two such structures. So it is not surprising that none of these hierarchy visualization tools is currently capable of computing measures of dissimilarity between two structures. The ability to do so is critical to this line of research on the CULTUSAB project so that we can systematically manipulate similarity of information structures as an independent variable in our experiments. We are contemplating various ways of measuring similarity.

1. We can simply count the number of nodes at each level of each structure and compute the difference in number of nodes at each level.
2. We can evaluate the cross-reference maps of nodes in one structure to the same nodes in the second structure and compute the differences in where the same nodes are placed within each hierarchy. We could measure differences in depth of placement down through the levels of the hierarchies. For example an item placed at Level 1 in one hierarchy and Level 3 in the second hierarchy would have a difference score of 2. These placement difference scores could be summed or combined in some way to produce a depth of placement score for the entire structure. Structures can also differ in where nodes are placed laterally. That is, nodes can be placed under different high level mother nodes and could be scored accordingly. Dissimilarity of placement of a node could be comprised of both the depth difference score and the lateral difference score.

Of course, such measures are subject to validation with experimental data. A validation experiment is currently in progress.

References

1. Nisbett, R.E., Peng, K., Choi, I., Norenzayan, A.: Culture and systems of thought: Holistic vs. analytic cognition. Psychological Review 108, 291–310 (2001)
2. Nisbett, R.E.: The Geography of Thought: Why We Think the Way We Do. The Free Press, NewYork (2003)
3. Choi, I., Nisbett, R.E.: Culture, categorization, and inductive reasoning. Cognition 65, 15–32 (1997)
4. Choong, Y-Y.: Design of computer interfaces for the Chinese population. In: PhD Dissertation. Purdue University (1996)
5. Clemmensen, T., Plocher, T.: The Cultural Usability Project (CULTUSAB): Studies of Cultural Models in Psychological Usability Evaluation Methods. In: HCI International Conference, Beijing, China (2007)
6. Dong, J., Martin, S., Waldo, P.A: user input and analysis tool for information architecture. In: CHI '01 Conference on Human Factors in Computing Systems, pp. 22–24 (2001)
7. Andrews, K.: Information Visualization. In: Tutorial Notes, IICM, Graz University of Technology, pp. 10-21 (2002), http://www.iicm.edu/ivis
8. Robertson, G.G., Mackinlay, J.D., Card, S.K.: Cone trees: Animated 3D visualizations of hierarchical information. In: Proceedings of the ACM SIGSCHI conference on Human Factors in Computing Systems, pp. 194–1890. ACM Press, New York (1991)
9. Jeong, C., Pang, A.: Reconfigurable Disc Trees for visualizing large hierarchical information spaces. In: Proceedings of Information Visualization '98, pp. 19–25 (1998)
10. Robertson, G.G., Czerwinski, M.P., Churchill, J.E.: Visualization of mappings between schemas. In: Proceedings of CHI 2005, Portland Oregon pp. 431–439 (2005)

Regulating India's Digital Public Cultures:
A Grey or Differently Regulated Area

Nimmi Rangaswamy

Microsoft Research India Labs
ninnin@microsoft.com

Abstract. The paper draws on ethnographic studies of urban, peri-urban cyber cafes in Western India, to understand public norms governing digital security and privacy in a context brimming with inconsistent and arbitrary state telecom regulation and a widespread culture of software piracy. We focus on issues emerging from three interrelated contexts crucial to cyber regulation in India: the grass-root, the state and the non-formal economy. While café managers dismiss their responsibility to police on-line security, state level initiatives show contradictions in their stated enthusiasm for an IT enabled society and sporadic regulatory behaviour directing public usage of the internet. There is a lack of will and genuine bemusement in the state apparatus to handle cyber regulation in non-formal and para- legal economies.

1 Introduction

The paper reports on an ethnographic study of urban, peri-urban cyber cafes in suburban Mumbai, Alibaug town and the city of Surat, all in Western India. Our research probes concern on-line security and privacy in public and shared computing experiences, in this case, the cyber café. We focus on issues emerging from three interrelated contexts crucial to cyber regulation in India: the grass-root, the state and the non-formal economy. Our earlier work on rural PC kiosks [19] and on going research among urban/peri-urban internet cafés are showing evidence of a weak culture of internet and on-line privacy and inconsistent demands for robust web security. We also noted broader socio-economic processes supporting a non-formal/informal culture holding sway over the sustainability of cyber cafes[1].

Designing for or even promoting secure and private cyberspaces require careful and deep understanding of larger contexts: of ad hoc state regulation, the shadow economy, human-mediated services, and unconventional usages of cyber cafes and spaces for leisure and friendly pursuits.

At the grass-root level, articulations about cyber security take place in an atmosphere of arbitrary norms and regulatory practices and an everyday tolerance of pirated software transactions. From initial investigations[2]and interviews with café

---

[1] Haseloff (2005) [9] is probably the only comprehensive study of cyber café presence in India to date.

[2] We have covered, thus far, 20 urban, peri-urban cafes, spending several days in each café doing qualitative interviews, participatory observation, maintaining field journals, recording and transcribing interviews.

N. Aykin (Ed.): Usability and Internationalization, Part II, HCII 2007, LNCS 4560, pp. 183–192, 2007.
© Springer-Verlag Berlin Heidelberg 2007

managers and participant observation in cafe premises, we found café owners and managerial staff viewing security as a non-issue and regulation as more business and ethics oriented.

Cyber security in India is limited to concerns of protecting its knowledge out source industry with increasing amounts of personal data from other countries flowing into India's backend processing units[3].

State level initiatives show contradictions in stated enthusiasm for an IT enabled society[4] and sporadic regulatory behaviour in directing its reach and impact in the public sphere. There are sudden surprise moves to monitor cyber cafés and equally startling cool-offs [22, 23]. They reveal a certain lack of will and genuine bemusement in the state apparatus, quite typical of a developing economy, to handle cyber regulation amidst non-formal and para legal economies. No special licenses are needed to run cyber cafés. We note most cyber cafés are run in an environment that may not strictly belong to the domain of formal economies despite business licenses and registrations. There are inconsistencies in billing, evidence of pirated software and multiple businesses running under a single business title. In an environment rife with non-formal business relations, cyber security fails to be a primary concern or priority among providers of public internet access.

2 Foregrounding Debates

The Indian state introduced the Information Act of India [21] in 2000, granting legal validity to digital data, signatures, communications and to retain data in digital formats. The Act was popularly viewed, as inadequate to tackle legal complexities arising out of cyber regulatory practice to suit and meet demands of a global IT driven economy in a developing nation[5]. Privacy is not just a matter bracketed by cyberspaces. It is embedded in a society's cultural prescriptions to which its members conform. These in turn affect and touch social transactions, in private and public, in the realms of the social and economic, and define frameworks of privacy that feed

---

[3] India's $23.4 billion outsourcing industry accounts for most of the country's software and services industry, which makes up nearly 5% of gross domestic product. The industry employs 1.2 million workers, has sparked a consumer revolution in India, and is accelerating at more than 30% a year.[10]

[4] 1994 was a major turning point for India's engagement with ICT's. The 1994 National Telecom Policy (NTP) laid the foundation of allowing private sector to operate Basic Services. This policy document attempted to clearly enunciate the goals of the liberalization process. In 1997, establishment of Telecom Regulatory Authority of India (TRAI) was a major gain leading to 1998 Internet Policy, Around the time, the Indian software and services industry grew from $12.8 billion in 2003 to $17.2 billion in 2005 -- a 34% increase (DIT, 1996-97,   2005)[4]. The IT industry was given a 'bureaucracy free environment' for prospective investors in the late 1990's after India's economic reforms took off the ground. This marked a shift from the era of state planning in industries and businesses to a new ideology of more local ownership and private initiatives [16]. Following the development of India's national strategies for ICT, the government made a concerted effort to bring low-cost connectivity and ICT enabled services to the 'rural masses' [18].

[5] Duggal (2004) [6, 7]. Telecom regulation gets to be debated mostly by dot.com owners on internet forums.

into its functioning. Definitions of domains of privacy in India, public or private, on-line or off-line, are not built alone by legal prescriptions but by how people relate to, communicate and share each other's professional, familial and personal information[6]. A brand new BPO industry with stringent norms of privacy and security is unlikely to quickly transform existing norms of privacy in the interplay of private and public realms in India.

Cyber cafes in India belong to the business environment of the unorganized and non-formal sector (Satyam Infoway and Reliance Infocomm are the only two cyber café franchises backed by large business houses) [25], [26]. Eighty six per cent of India's businesses are in the non-formal sector but account for 92 per cent of the Indian labour forces [15] and contribute 60 per cent of its GDP [12]. The informal economy and its employees operate outside the state's jurisdiction. Nevertheless they are promoted by the government, as these businesses are cheaper, more flexible, and more conducive to competitive global markets than formal labor [14], [20], [3]. In particular, Mumbai is a city where

> ...service economies involving law, leisure, finance, and banking, and virtual economies involving global finance capital and local stock markets live in an uneasy mix... Shifting from economies of manufacture and industry to economies of trade, tourism, and finance, they usually attract more poor people than they can handle and more capital than they can absorb. ....But they often contain shadow economies that are difficult to measure in traditional terms' [2: 627].

Into this economy fits the cyber café, bound by norms that govern and drive small and non-formal businesses. In our study, we find cyber cafés operating within the socio-economic ambit of small and informal business in Mumbai and nearby towns with varying degrees of formality, permanence and flows of business[7].

Public internet cultures and services in India have yet to include vital services, especially in areas of health, transportation, commerce or real estate. Most services are human mediated and still follow conventional processes. Many people experience computers mainly through shared access outlets (home PC penetration remains as low as 5%) in the form of audio/video channels, chat rooms, photo share and e- mails rather than serious information search and e-banking activities. Cyber café become places that are sought for reasons of leisure and individual pursuits[8]. Urban areas report plenty of unregulated leisure pursuits, with income coming from the sale of internet time by the hour. Rural PC kiosks have different barriers to make security and privacy a serious matter in shared access scenarios. There is little internet time with

---

[6] With regard to cultural prescriptions and privacy, Kumaraguru and Cranor (2005) [13] refer to the lack of an explicit privacy concern be it amongst family members running family business or in the work place where exists a certain amount of naiveté about data bases of personal information traded and sold between trading companies. They mention that even the constitution of India permits only the use of personal liberty rather than privacy in outlining its constitutional guarantees to the individual.

[7] For a case-study of small business environment in Bangalore, see [5].

[8] Nisbett(2005) [17] , in his study of cyber café in Bangalore, the IT capitol of India, notes the transformation of café space to a hang out joint for middle class youth in the absence of affordable spaces for such pre-occupations.

huge power crunches, hardware breakdowns and a small clientele who see value in net scapes and surfing [11]. In places that had the wherewithal to run a connected kiosk the same (non) regulatory practices governed internet activity. Rural kiosks reported pornographic web activities among clients, and considerable portions of para legality governing business ethics. The issue was simple. There was no felt need for cyber security when the larger public culture did not need or demand it.

3 Can Hutch Be Sued for a Bomb Scare Issued Through a Mobile Phone?

3.1 The Small Business of Internet Cafes

Sustaining the café business takes precedence over security issues. Cyber cafes in the city and suburbs of Mumbai, Surat, Alibaug, cities/towns close to Mumbai, are embedded in informal business environments. There are definite differences with regard to café owner profiles, client driven popular services and allied business alongside the café. Rather than being rooted in clearly defined formal and legal/ institutional relationships, cafes increasingly seek out and manage a diversity of services running under one business title. Several cafes assemble PCs for a local market, and operate through socio-economic networks to procure and assemble hardware components. Some also provided software solutions to local offices. Many had pirated software. Here is a small compilation of businesses that were tied to cyber cafes: A lending library of popular fiction and education guides, a fast-food catering service, a photo studio, a restaurant, mobile repair and maintenance service provider and the more popular Xerox/scanning/printing centers. More interestingly, several cyber cafes in Mumbai made most of their income from offline rather then internet based services. All of them were registered business with licenses but showed irregularity in billing, accounting profits and in maintaining records of business dealings. Many of them hosted their café in premises showing unclear legality in their ownership.

A café in South Mumbai, around 3 Kms from the stock Mumbai stock exchange in Dalal Street, ran a stock trading centre till 4 Pm. The idle PCs were offered for public use in the evenings. Pankaj, the café manager says:

> This is a market place. In this locality you won't find any cyber café. So it is a major source of income, right now, for it's just a month old café. It's not completely rooted. And also it is not just the cyber café that we operate here. Our prime business is trading, National stock exchange and the Bombay stock exchange. And the cyber café is actually part time business. We first started the trading business then the cyber café. We are on trial basis. So it is not necessary that we run this cyber café business for long. If it is beneficial to us then we will continue other wise we will wind-up. And the 4-5 PCs that are idle after four, because the market is open for trading up to four, so to utilize the PCs we started the cyber café.

Similarly, most cafés become gaming centers, raking profits based on the kind of network, quality of PCs, upgrades and variety of software support. Some made money only through gaming services. In Sunderbaug, a slum area in an eastern Mumbai suburb, the café transformed from a coin operated video parlour to a gaming centre. The owner makes additional money from a phone booth and a Xerox centre. Radhe, the manager/owner started the café having learnt computer programming and hardware but realized his neighbourhood had little value for the internet. A snippet from a conversation with Radhe (all the names are pseudonyms):

> Interviewer: So your major income is from gaming
> Radhe: Yes
> Interviewer: What made you think that gaming would earn you money and that so many kids will come to play games on your computers?
> Radhe: Earlier, kids would play games on those gaming boxes (machines).
> Interviewer: Okay those ones where you have to put a coin and play'.
> Radhe: Yes. A lot of kids rushed to play games on them so I thought after those machines have been shut down kids would turn to computers to play games.
> Interviewer: So has your communication business been affected by the cyber café?
> Radhe: No it has not affected my communications business. The two work together.

His clients are children between the ages of eight and 16, some school going and others daily wage laborers, mostly construction workers. He even had flexi rates, as low as Rs10 per hour for these children.

Ganesh runs a cyber café attached to his book lending library. He used to sell greeting cards, and found business was decreasing during the last five years due to the growth of on-line greeting exchanges. "I used to do a lot of business with cards, especially Valentines Day that has caught on in India. But people switched to e-cards and business dipped... I thought of opening a café to get the same market that brought cards... "

Café owners sited the unviability of a stand alone café, especially in urban areas with high real estate rates, maintenance costs for computers, and competition from other aspiring café businesses. Cafés break even because of profits from allied businesses. Hitendra, café owner in Alibaug town, makes money from the mobile retail shop tied to the café. He said,

> I started out as a computer hardware engineer and mobile repairer and used to operate from my house, as I didn't have an office... people don't buy computers everyday. Mobile repairing is a good business and the Cyber cafe brings me hard cash everyday... rather than monthly profits...

Vinod, 36, owns a café in outer suburban Mumbai. He said,

> I began the café in 1998, when an internet café was an exciting option... I began with data entry work and moved to selling internet time. I charged Rs80 an hour.... I always start with the most expensive and the best service provider and my rates are always high... It was the beginning of the software boom. The same boom has now pushed home PC penetration and low browsing rates, broadband and all. I charge Rs 30 per hour, which is still high... A café in my neighbourhood charges Rs 10 though the going rate is Rs20 per hour... I have moved to assembling PCs and providing hardware solutions. I cannot sustain a stand alone café relying on internet...

3.2 Voices from the Café

> Ok. So there is no software which is safe?
> There is no solution to this problem and if someone has, then he'd be richer
> than Bill Gates[9].

The Internet cafés we observed were mostly managed by independent entrepreneurs, who were hardware literate to some extent. This was an important skill for maintaining multi-PC cafés or kiosks. Hence, they are individuals with a know-how of computer cultures and business. They understood issues of cyber security and its unclear public status in digitally emerging public cultures. Amidst considerable computer literacy, notions of privacy and security were conceptually construed to mean several things.

Hitendra, 32, owns and manages a café in the tourist and coastal town of Alibaug, 100 Kms form Mumbai. A self taught computer engineer, he is ambitious to begin his own trading site for on-line trading. He said,

> ...being in the IT industry I know the importance of security. We have all the
> necessary anti viruses and firewalls installed. We update our software
> regularly. People do all kinds of banking transactions from our café...
> ... We don't allow two persons on one pc. Personally, I feel nobody must be
> able to see what you are typing or which site you are surfing. Before
> registering anybody we tell them to take a look at the rules... we do this to
> avoid any unlawful deed. We make the customers realize about their
> responsibility.... We don't allow anybody to download any software...We
> won't allow him directly to use a CD or floppy. We will transfer the file for
> that person. We don't allow pen drives or flash drives.

Anup, 22, who helps Prem, the owner, in managing the café on the other hand said: "You know, if I pull this wooden board here and here, bring them close, there is privacy..."

We noted in smaller cities and towns there was a shift in monitoring privacy and an element of everyday trust creeps in. Security meant a decent clientele who do not indulge in suspicious on-line practices. Jagadeesh manages his café in the city of Surat, in a busy commercial district. He has no dearth of clients and is upbeat about computing technologies. He said,

> In a city of business like Surat, computers are a boon. There are new
> products for new markets cropping up all the time.... My café is always full
> of people and (they) use internet for practically everything... mailing,
> information, chatting, surfing...I have no problems with security... I know
> everybody who visits my cafe...

Bhavesh, 29, is a Software engineer, providing client solutions and runs the café in his office. He said, "We do have clients who trade, use credit cards etc....provide security? What can we do about it? We are just service providers. Like the ICICI web site has tight security... What is the need for us to provide anything?" He adds in a

---

[9] Quote from a café owner about securing cafes and sites from tampering and fraud.

serious vein, "If offences take place are we to blame? ...Can Hutch be sued for a bomb scare issued through a mobile phone...?"

Echoing Bhavesh, Prem, another café owner and hardware engineer who offers maintenance services and assembles PCs for a small suburban market, "Well, what could we do about security? It's not our problem. We have enough problems running services and a business ..."

These statements are expressive of the broader issue of the responsibility for internet security. Café owners believe the on-line bankers and the vendors stand to gain and lose the most in matters of security and privacy. The cyber café wallah is probably the last in this chain of web access providers with the least control over the provision and securing of web sites. It is reasonable to assume concerns for security and privacy extending to protect only their businesses and clientele. Installing firewalls and site blocks, in part, to protect PCs from viruses and dubious internet content, were more to appease state machinery and moral policing rather than protect consumers' identities. Most café managers suggested a non-role for themselves with the onus squarely on companies encouraging e-services. The issue of a café as a secure space to conduct electronic transactions never seem to arise.

3.3 The State and the Café

"It might just be a general business like a vada pav business"[10]

The Indian state's first Information Technology (IT) Act was formulated in May 2000 [8] and it became law in November 2000. India's first cyber law makes 'punishable cyber crimes like hacking, damage to computer source code, publishing of information which is obscene in the electronic form, breach of confidentiality and privacy, and publication of digital signature certificate false in certain particulars'[7] . It provides the legal infrastructure for electronic commerce "which involve(s) the use of alternatives to paper-based methods of communication and storage of information and to facilitate electronic filing of documents with the government agencies" with little mention of directly regulating cyber spaces in the form of commercial public access outlets like cyber cafés. However, amendments to this are supposedly in queue before the Parliament [1].

There are generic government regulations to run cyber outlets. Cafés need to register, seek necessary permission from local governing bodies, and inform local police machinery that a certain café is opening in their jurisdiction. Insights gained from the 'field', point to a serious lack of regulation or governing body overseeing the functioning of cyber cafés, with regard to on-line content/services, client activity or securing café transactions through commercial and penal laws.

There is much 'ad hocism' in monitoring cyber cafés. A case in point is the aftermath of the bomb blasts that shook Mumbai suburban Metro railway killing 209 citizens and leaving hundreds wounded[24]. The blasts triggered huge debates on national security and serious suspicion about neighboring states playing a major role in instigating these blasts. Cyber policing was stepped up and café premises were treated as potential sites triggering terrorist action. Cafés were asked to put up posters

---

[10] Quote from café owner in Mumbai. *Vada Pav* is a typical low cost fast food readily available in street corner restaurants and carts.

against cyber crime with a reference to bomb blasts. The state police demanded formal registration of clients, frisking for IDs and cross checking with mobile phone numbers. Café owners, maintaining registers since the blasts, again showed irregularity. Cyber policing was a matter of tracking crime, in this case, combating terrorism rather than securing on-line transactions and monitoring internet practices

A conversation with Prem 32, who runs a café next to central Mumbai suburban station;

> Prem...You see this poster... This happened after the metro rail bomb blasts... We have this register here, where each person who steps in had to register with his name and mobile number. We give him an ID and check by calling his mobile number. There is some surety that he has a photo ID at the time of purchasing his mobile.
> Interviewer: You think this is fool proof?
> Prem... yes it is. What more do you need.....
> Interviewer: Did clients object to all this... I mean, were they uncomfortable?
> Prem: Initially clientele dropped. But once we insisted, it has become normal. Every one has an ID of some sort... We follow these rules. I do not know if others are doing it. I do it...

Vinod, 36, a café owner in Suburban Mumbai, was quick to note the irregularity in framing and implementing laws governing cyber spaces. He said,

Before the bomb blasts took place, we were asked to install a sort of security software issued by the state police, less than two years ago, due to a sudden ad-hoc government regulation for the cyber café operators. We were advised not (to) allow anybody to access sites containing offensive material... We can't block all sites (with) this security software... It was provided to us on monthly trial... It was sadly inadequate and blocked good sites more than (the) offensive (ones)! Basically it has to do with our legal system. Nobody bothers whether you implement it or not as long as their hands are free. It's a grey area...The business of running a cyber café is pretty much like any other business.

Hitendra, who strictly monitors client activities, aspires to begin his own web shop. He has a view that shifts the onus of security from the state to the site provider. He says,

> I have my own e-commerce site but I am not confident about using it. I still find it unsafe for trading. I am still not convinced about the protection this method of transaction provides... I think the culprits feel that they now have another method or way of cheating the masses and earning easy money. I have seen commercial sites like eBay but there (are) plenty of loopholes in it... I am a little worried. My website is completely ready. I have installed security software and everything else. I can accept payment. It has all (the) shopping cards.... Somehow in India the mentality is not ready for it. .

He admits like most others, to clients using negligible internet time for payments and purchase.

Pankaj's café being a share trading site is not a cause for worry. His files are secured by passwords and robust software provided by the Stock Exchange. He or a supervisor keeps strict vigilance while trading is going on. Like most others, even

Pankaj has 'full faith' (or ignorance) in security provided by online e-banking and other buying facilities where credit cards or other personal information are shared. He says, "They maintain the (online) security. So I don't need to install any software for extra security." For Pankaj, 'safe' stock trading is vital to his business and he ensures it. But regulating on-line activities is a matter that did not bother him with little pressure coming from customers or the government to provide secure and private internet activity.

4 Concluding Remarks

Privacy and security are not priority issues for cyber café owners. For the café owners, sustaining business, servicing a steady clientele, maintaining and upgrading computers are crucial every day issues. With leisure pursuits defining café usages, clients are satisfied if they get connected preferably fast, to the internet. Security is then the owners' responsibility, so that he or she can ensure the PCs are virus free and firewalled. He does not necessarily do it because the state law imposes it.

The research presented framed the cyber café as embedded in broader economic and business contexts. These, in various capacities, constrained provisions for privacy and security in public access to internet in these spaces. The State inconsistently regulates cyber spaces and its customers. The attention is focused on the outsourcing sector, so that there is only occasional concern about monitoring public Internet cultures. The café is thus left alone to stay afloat, make the most of available ICT technology and services, and ensure enough security to keep internet services on-going.

References

1. Amendments to Information Technology Act -2000 (Last accessed on February 20, 2007), http://www.naavi.org/naavi_comments_itaa/index.htm
2. Appadurai, A.: Spectral housing and urban cleansing: notes on millennial Mumbai. Public Culture 12(3), 627–651 (2000)
3. Agarwala, R.: From Work to Welfare: The State and Informal Workers' Organizations in India, Center for migration and development, working paper series, Princeton University (2005) (Last accessed, February 1, 2007), http://cmd.princeton.edu/papers/wp0407.pdf
4. DIT, Annual Report, Department of Information Technology, India (2005)
5. Donner, J.: Internet use (and non-use) among urban micro enterprises in the developing world: An update from India. In: Paper presented at Conference of the Association of Internet Researchers (AoIR) Brisbane, Australia (2006)
6. Duggal, P: License to shoot. Yahoo! India News. December 24, 2004. (Last accessed, February 1, 2007) http://in.news.yahoo.com/041224/48/2in9n.html
7. Duggal, P.: India's Information (Act 2000), http://72.14.235.104/search?q=cache: Rs7VRQlwxRAJ:unpan1.un.org/intradoc/groups/public/documents/apcity/unpan002090.p df+India%27s+first+information+technology+act&hl=en&ct=clnk&cd=2&gl
8. Extract from The Gazette of India Extraordinary, (Last accessed on February 20, 2007), http://www.naavi.org/importantlaws/itbill2000/preamble.htm

9. Haseloff, A M: Cybercafés and their Potential as Community Development Tools in India. The Journal of Community Informatics 1(3), 53–64 (2005)
10. India's outsourcing industry employs 1.2 mln people, contributes $23.4 bln to GDP, (Last accessed on February 20, 2007), http://www.itfacts.biz/index.php?id=P5840
11. Kiri, K., Menon, D.: For Profit Rural Kiosks in India: Achievements and Challenges (Last accessed, January 29 2007) (2006), http://www.i4donline.net/articles/current-article.asp?articleid=700&typ=,Features
12. Kulshreshtha, A.C. Singh, G.: Gross Domestic Product and Employment in the Informal Sector of the Indian Economy. Indian Journal of Labour Economics 42 (1999)
13. Kumaraguru, Cranor.: Privacy in India: Attitudes and awareness. In: Privacy enhancing Technologies, Lecture notes in computer science. Book Chapter 243-259, Berlin, pp. 243–259. Springer, Heidelberg (2006)
14. Kundu, A., Sharma, A N: Informal Sector in India. New Delhi: Institute for Human Development and Institute of Applied Manpower Research (2001)
15. National Sample Survey Organisation. In: Employment and Unemployment Situation in India. 1999-2000. New Delhi (2001)
16. Nayar, B.R.: Political Structure and India's Economic Reforms of the 1990s. Pacific Affairs 71(3), 337–360 (1998)
17. Nisbett, N.: Growing up Connected: The role of Cybercafés in widening ICT access in Bangalore and South India. In: Paper presented to the Information, Technology and Development Panel, Development Studies Association Annual Conference, Milton Keynes (2006)
18. Pohjola, M.: The New Economy in growth and development. Oxford Review of Economic Policy 18, 380–396 (2002)
19. Rangaswamy, N.: Social Entrepreneurship as Critical Agency: A study of Rural Internet kiosks. In: Social Proceedings of the International Conference on ICT and Development. pp. 143–152. Berkeley (2006)
20. Report of the 2nd National Commission on Labour (NCL). Ministry of Labour, Government of India. New Delhi (2002)
21. Right to information act, India 2005, (Last accessed on February 20, 2007), http://persmin.nic.in/RTI/WelcomeRTI.htm
22. Saboo, A.: Cyber safety week workshop for cyber cafes concludes successfully, 2005 (Last accessed February 20, 2007), http://apiap.blogspot.com/2005/11/cyber-safety-week-workshop-for-cyber.html,
23. Saboo, A.: Fake police raids, 2004, (Last accessed on February 20, 2007), http://apiap.blogspot.com/2004/08/fake-police-raids.html
24. Scores dead in Mumbai train bombs (Last accessed on February 20, 2007) July 11, 2006, http://news.bbc.co.uk/2/hi/south_asia/5169332.stm
25. What a wonderful world. Reliance Communications. (Last accessed on February 20, 2007),
http://www.reliancecommunications.co.in/Communications/Aboutus/aboutus_business_web world.html
26. What our franchisees have to say. Sifi iway. (Last accessed on February 20, 2007), http://www.iway.com/beourbizpartner_main.php

Entrepreneurial Digital Photography - A Case Study for Design Research Method in the Emerging Indian Market

Naznin Rao

Human Factors International
310/6 H.R. Complex, 5th block, Koramangala,
Bangalore, Karnataka-560 030. India
Tel.: +91 80 2504 2204
naznin@humanfactors.com

Abstract. This paper describes a research method termed "Contextual Invention" used by Hewlett Packard Research Labs for design research in emerging markets like India. The core value of this method lies in its multi-disciplinary approach towards design research. The process takes inputs from design, business and technology in order to reach a comprehensive solution. It involves a deep understanding of user needs and cultural context [1] to drive design ideas, business modeling and technological investigations. It aims to inspire and generate new technology inventions with high social and business value. The method has been developed and tested through a project, namely, "Entrepreneurial Digital Photography in India". This process describes how needs and opportunity spaces were identified in the domain of digital photography within the Indian context. It goes on to delineate steps that led to the mapping of those user needs onto opportunity spaces and culminates into implementable guidelines and research findings.

Keywords: design research, multi-disciplinary, contextual invention, iterative process, user research, digital photography.

1 Introduction

The project started as an offshoot of a Media study [2] conducted by HP Labs in 2003. The media study was taken up to:

- Create a framework for a robust methodology to do multi-disciplinary research to develop solutions for emerging markets.
- Develop business opportunity spaces drawn from the fieldwork and at the intersection of user needs, design, business models and technology feasibility (Fig. 1)

Various combinations of these disciplines have been used together in the past, both inside HP Labs and in the wider industry. However, all four disciplines are rarely harnessed together in the pursuit of innovation and new business opportunities [2].

N. Aykin (Ed.): Usability and Internationalization, Part II, HCII 2007, LNCS 4560, pp. 193–200, 2007.
© Springer-Verlag Berlin Heidelberg 2007

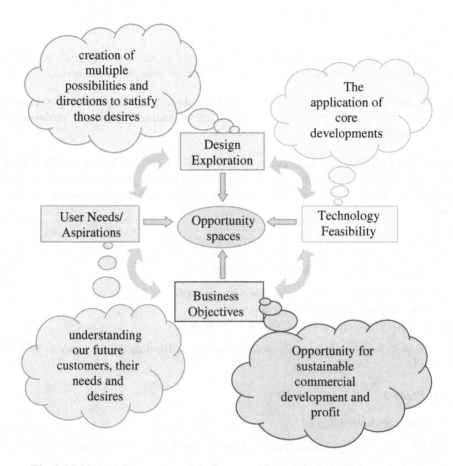

Fig. 1. Multi-disciplinary approach in Contextual Invention model. Source: Author.

1.1 Background

Business research at HP Labs suggested that Photography has an extremely strong growth potential in India. The Media Study carried out at HP Labs identified a very strong need in the burgeoning middle class of India which has extremely limited access to cameras [3]. The existing products of HP did not meet the requirements of this emerging Indian market as is also the case with other similar companies [4]. Hence it was anticipated that there might be a need for new products specifically designed [5] to penetrate this identified segment [4].

2 Methodology

The methodology was broadly divided into 3 phases

2.1 Phase 1

Identifying end-user needs and the associated initial concepts drawn from the Media Study. At the end of Phase I, two distinct categories of entrepreneurs emerged.

Photo Active segment. Entrepreneurs who are directly in the photography related business. These include photo lab owners, photo studio owners and professional photographers.

Non Photo Active segment. Entrepreneurs who, at present, are not in the photo retailing business but might enter as they have access to the end customer. These include STD/PCO booth owners, cyber cafes and entertainment centers like cinema halls.

2.2 Phase 2

This phase involved qualitative understanding of

- Digital photography in India and the various barriers to it
- Evaluating the challenges to photography
- Evaluating concepts for the Photo Active segment

It also included validating the concepts identified from the media study as well as Phase I

2.3 Phase 3

Qualitative understanding of

- Business challenges and the criteria defining new business opportunities among the Non Photo Active segment [3]
- Evaluating scenarios and hypotheses developed for this segment
- Validation of the concepts (new and from phase 2)
- Prioritization of concepts

2.4 Phase 4

- Consolidation of findings from each phase
- Concepts for prototyping and final testing
- Roadmap of future potential research

3 Iterative Design Process

The research process was of iterative nature (Fig. 2). Each phase used concepts and analysis of user study from the previous phase and validated the same, while deriving new concepts and recommendations from the present analysis. In this way, end of the final phase led to prominent concepts and potential findings from each phase that could be taken ahead for future research and/or testing. Being a multi-disciplinary approach, each phase had inputs from user, design and market research.

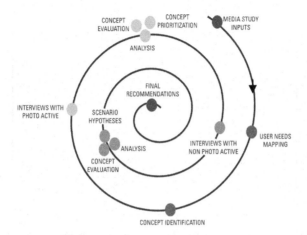

Fig. 2. Design Process diagram showing the iterative nature of the process. Source: Author.

4   Tools and Techniques

Some specific tools and techniques were used to progress from field data to insights to concepts. They have been listed below:

1. Domain Brainstorming to derive user needs (Fig. 3)

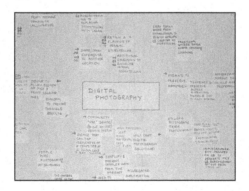

Fig. 3. Brainstorming to identify user needs. Source: Author.

2. Relationship mapping associating user needs from other categories to the digital photography category (Fig. 4)

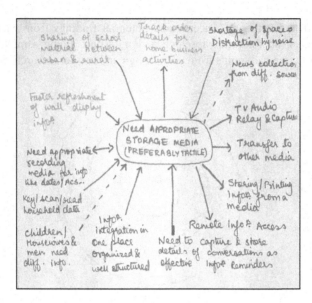

Fig. 4. Mapping relationship of user needs to digital photography domain. Source: Author.

3. User Needs Matrix mapping needs onto broad categories within the digital photography realm vs. different types of users from whom these needs were derived (Fig. 5)

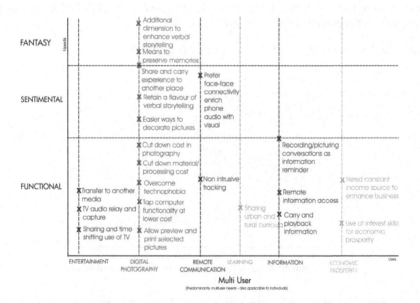

Fig. 5. User needs matrix. Source: Author.

4. Fishbone Analysis to highlight cause-effect relationship of each pain point (Fig. 6)

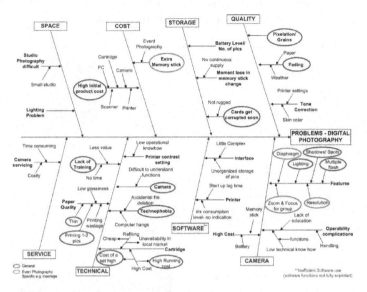

Fig. 6. Fishbone structure of digital photography problems in Indian context. Source: Author.

5. Concept Rating Scale- Preference of concepts (along with specific characteristics) qualitatively rated by end users (Fig. 7)

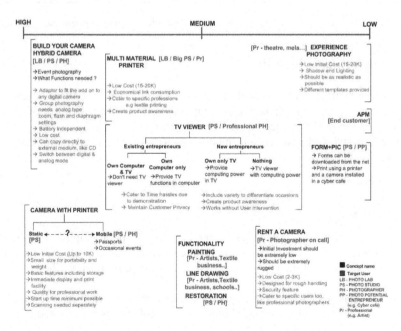

Fig. 7. Qualitative rating of concepts. Source: Author.

6. Summary sheet of findings– A single sheet covering demographic information of the user, main findings from the interview, important comments and images from the interview; very useful in getting information at a glance (Fig. 8)

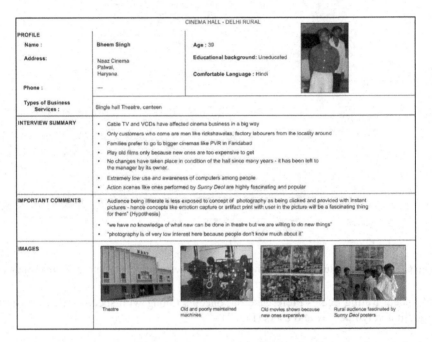

Fig. 8. Summary sheet of a user interview from the non-photo active segment. Source: Author.

5   Discussion and Results

The outcome from each phase acted as a platform for the next one. Every cycle of in-depth interviews culminated into insightful findings, further validation of previous concepts and some new concepts.

The end of Phase I resulted into main categories of user needs related to digital photography. These were

– Functional needs
– Sentimental needs
– User fantasies

The needs from other categories (other than digital photography) were mapped onto these three broad categories. This resulted into a matrix of all user needs. The matrix also represented the type of users (individual or group) from whom the needs arose.

Based on this matrix in-depth interviews were conducted in Phases 2 and 3. The interviews helped in understanding photography as well as business related challenges concerning the entrepreneurs. The questionnaire from Phase 2 was tailored to suit the user segment in Phase 3. A set of hypotheses from Phase 2 was also taken forward for validation in Phase 3.

The findings were presented such that one could understand, at a deeper level, what led to an identified problem (cause and effect relationship). End of the project resulted into

- Concepts that could be further taken up for prototyping.
- Findings that proved useful for similar work in the photography domain.
- Scope for future research in *Experiential photography.*

6 Conclusion

The case study of Entrepreneurial Digital Photography was an experiment towards evaluating the effectiveness of *Contextual Invention* as a design methodology for emerging markets like India.

The outcome of this approach was highly dependant on the iterative nature of the process and the cultural context. The project was successful in creating business opportunities and design concepts that were at the intersection of user needs, design, business models and technology feasibility. We hope the methodology and results prove useful for similar work in other emerging markets too.

Acknowledgments. Special thanks to Dr. Girish Prabhu whose expertise in this area was one of the main driving forces for the project. Also, thanks to Mr. Vivek Singh, friend and colleague for his valuable inputs during the project.

References

1. Frohlich, D.M., Greving, W.: Contextual invention: An approach, workshop and study outline for HP Labs India. In: HP Working paper (October 2002)
2. Prabhu, G., Frohlich, D.M., Greving, W.: Contextual Invention: A multi-disciplinary approach to develop business opportunities and design solutions. FutureGround 2004, Melbourne, Australia. Hewlett-Packard Development Company, L.P (2005)
3. Kim, S., Chung, A., Ok, J., Myung, I., Joo Kang, H., Woo, J.K., Kim, M.J.: Communication enhancer—appliances for better communication in a family. In: Pers Ubiquit Comput. Springer-Verlag London Limited, pp. 221–226 (2004)
4. Greving, W., Ramani, S., Gopal, G.: A strategy for contextual design applied to emerging markets. In: Internal HP Labs Working paper (2002)
5. Balanovic, M., Chu, L.L., Wolff, G.J.: Storytelling with digital photos. In: Proceedings of CHI (The Hague, April 2000), pp. 564–571. ACM Press, (2000)

Culturally Adaptive Software: Moving Beyond Internationalization

Katharina Reinecke and Abraham Bernstein

Department of Informatics, University of Zurich,
Binzmühlestrasse 14, CH-8050 Zurich, Switzerland
{reinecke,bernstein}@ifi.unizh.ch

Abstract. So far, culture has played a minor role in the design of software. Our experience with *imbuto*, a program designed for Rwandan agricultural advisors, has shown that cultural adaptation increased efficiency, but was extremely time-consuming and, thus, prohibitively expensive. In order to bridge the gap between cost-savings on one hand, and international usability on the other, this paper promotes the idea of *culturally adaptive software*. In contrast to manual localization, adaptive software is able to acquire details about an individual's cultural identity during use. Combining insights from the related fields *international usability*, *user modeling* and *user interface adaptation*, we show how research findings can be exploited for an integrated approach to automatically adapt software to the user's cultural frame.

1 Introduction

One of the largest impediments for the efficient use of software in different cultural contexts is the gap between the software designs - typically following western cultural cues - and the users, who handle it within their cultural frame. The problem has become even more relevant, as today the majority of revenue in the software industry comes from outside market dominating countries such as the USA.

Research conducted on the effect and usability of culturally adapted web sites and interfaces has already shown enormous improvements in working efficiency [1-4]. These results were further emphasized in our experience with *imbuto* [5], a program designed for Rwandan agricultural advisers (see Fig. 1). The conceptualization of *imbuto*'s learning platform, which holds information about newly-developed methods for increases in agrarian productivity, was accomplished on-site in Rwanda. In particular, this allowed for a circular development: To begin with, we thoroughly investigated the cultural particularities of the target group with the help of interviews and questionnaires. The result was a first version of *imbuto*. As a next step, the software was alternately enhanced and tested with Rwandan subjects. Since the provisional test system was designed and implemented by a member of western culture, evaluations soon revealed that Rwandans could not optimally use the software in terms of information perception and handling. We observed that difficulties emerged from too much freedom in the choice of functionalities: Rwandans, who learn to strictly follow instructions from a young age, seemed to be

N. Aykin (Ed.): Usability and Internationalization, Part II, HCII 2007, LNCS 4560, pp. 201–210, 2007.

overwhelmed by the range of functionalities available in the software. A playful arrangement of constituents, allowing for explorative behaviour, and a colorful user interface with a realistic appearance, were further adaptations that were needed for reconciling the software with the target culture.

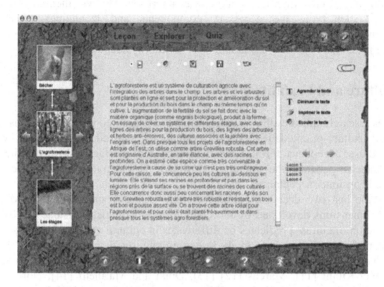

Fig. 1. Learning Platform for Agricultural Advisors in Rwanda

After these extensive circular adaptations to the cultural frame of Rwandans during a time span of approximately five months, evaluations finally fulfilled the expectations of improved usability and a reduction in time required for familiarization with the software. However, extending the target group to other cultures would necessitate even greater time.

Hence, cultural adaptation of software reveals two major problems:

1. The development cycle is extremely time-consuming, making it prohibitively expensive.
2. The elusive nature of cultural background makes it hard to recognize one's own preferences and thus, where the system should be adapted [6].

For economic reasons, software manufacturers therefore often neglect cultural adaptation that goes any further than a mere localization of the interfaces, such as the adaptation of language and date format.

One answer to general adaptation problems proposed by Maier [7] is the use of adaptive or personalization systems that "represent the most promising solution to the contradiction between striving to achieve cost-savings on the one hand, and high-quality training and customer satisfaction on the other". Extending this to the problem of cultural adaptation, we propose to approach the issue by developing *culturally adaptive software*.

Essentially, the idea of culturally adaptive software spans inter-disciplinary research fields that underlie the premises of successful Human-Computer Interaction.

In order to reveal the culture-dependent components of software, it is necessary to build a user model based on cultural particularities before the adaptation can be accomplished. In the following, we start with a literature review on international usability and culture. This review is the basis for an introduction on the current state of the art in user modeling and adaptive user interfaces. We will then combine these fields by identifying the necessary components and techniques of artificial intelligence (AI) required for automated software culturalization. The paper closes with the presentation of our research plan for culturally adaptive software.

2   Culture and Usability

Previous research indicates that usability can be only assured if future systems will be designed culture-oriented [8]. These evaluations showed improvement and an increased user acceptance through manually localized interfaces. However, they were not yet able to persuade the software industry of the positive economic effect of an increased consumer acceptance.

Over the last two decades, cultural usability research primarily focused on the cultural dimensions developed by the cultural anthropologist Hofstede [9, 10]. His classification of culture predicates on differences in cultural values. He points out that particular responses are "more likely in certain cultures than in other ones" [10]. In recent years, evaluations applying his cultural dimensions include studies by Voehringer-Kuhnt [11], Marcus [12] [13], Dunn and Marinetti [14], Dormann and Chisalita [15], Ford and Gelderblom [3], Hodemacher et al. [4] and Kamentz [16].

Hofstede's dimensions also built the basis for studies conducted in the area of *culturability*, a brigading term invented by Barber and Bardre [2] for "the merging of culture and usability". They also defined the so-called "cultural markers": elements of an interface that are preferred by a specific culture. Analyzing many hundreds of web sites, they found that cultural markers strongly influence the usability of software interfaces.

Hofstede's dimensions were enhanced by many researchers including Trompenaar who coined the metaphor that culture is like an onion consisting of many cultural layers [17]. Dunn and Marinetti [14] used Trompenaar's additional cultural dimensions to point out that one must peel this onion "to get to the core values, the things that really matter" in order to plan for cultural adaptation. Later, Marcus [18] developed a set of cultural dimensions by ranking a given list of these dimensions with the help of 57 participants from 21 different countries around the world. Doing so, he was one of the first researchers to attempt to build a bridge from evaluations on culturability to their application. The outcome was a practical set that can be used as a preliminary user model.

Nevertheless, research conducted in the interdisciplinary field of culturally adaptive user interfaces cannot presume that generic models of culture can be simply applied to the area of user interfaces. After measuring Hofstede's dimensions in an evaluation, Smith and Chang [10] are apprehensive that "in the case of China the four Hofstede dimensions have greatly differing significance". Some researchers also criticize the employment of cultural models as too generalizing and stereotypical [19]. Regarding the rigid one-to-one mapping of a single culture to a whole nation, as exemplified by Hofstede, the adaptation to culture in its redefined meaning for our globalized world is indeed questionable. However, concerning an initial user classification, we suggest using this simplistic view as a starting point from where adaptivity algorithms will refine it stepwise to cross-cultural particularities. These would then be assignable to people who belong to a single culture, as well as to culturally ambiguous users.

3 User Modeling

While it is increasingly encouraged to consider culture in interface design [1, 12, 20-23], various branches of research have concentrated on ascertaining "cultural fingerprints" in an interface [10]. Nevertheless, little progress can be found on combining these with an actual strategy about making predictions about the cultural background of users. Recently, Kamentz [16] looked into this new direction by investigating components needed for cultural user modeling. She states that cultural adaptation must be considered in the context of the user's background, while knowledge, aims and plans, preferences and individual user properties form important attributes that are to be modeled, but do not as such involve the cultural component. Apart from learner specific adaptivity, she also investigated layout, interaction and navigation and its cultural particularities in her studies.

However, to date it is still a moot point of how culture can be comprised in the construction of a user model. Moreover, it is unknown which methods to use in order to automatically acquire culturally related facts about individual users. Kobsa, who has been one of the key researchers in the area of automated user modeling, states that useful methods for user modeling strongly depend on the application domain of a system and are often combined [24]. Consequently, it can be assumed that current methods are widely applicable to cultural user modeling. We will therefore discuss the most common methods for the acquisition of user models in the following section, before returning to a discussion of our "cultural problem".

3.1 Acquisition of User Models

A key concern when ascertaining user modeling information, is whether data should be gained through an integrated acquisition process in the background, or through separate acquisition that is discrete to the normal interaction between the user and the system [25]. So far, almost all organizations of user groups into common characteristics with *stereotypes*, or into common interests with *communities*, as suggested by Paliouras et al. [25], have been carried out manually. This is not only difficult because it "involves the classification of users by an expert and/or the analysis of data relating to the interests of individual users" [25]; for cultural user modeling, manual acquisition is also questionable due to the intangible perception of cultural values and is therefore only feasible for an initial classification.

Such challenges in the manual construction can be abated by making use of *user modeling shell systems* that are similar to expert systems in Intelligent Tutoring Software. Shell systems offer a number of integrated mechanisms for user modeling. They still require the provision of primary assumptions about users [26], and thus involve separated acquisition. However, they take on all essential functions of a user modeling component of a system, "including user model representation, inference on the basis of the user model, consistency maintenance, and automatic user classification" [24] by shifting the mostly heuristic acquisition rules onto the shell.

Further endeavors towards automated acquisition have been made by the use of *machine learning techniques* for the automatic acquisition of data for the user model [25, 27, 28]. Given their wide use in personalization (see, e.g., [29]), machine learning algorithms are able to manage user models, supporting the automatic acquisition and constant updating of data [30]. Hence, they are useful for automated cultural adaptation.

An alternative strategy for user modeling is the *interaction history method* that is suitable if a continuative analysis of users is not applicable [24]. By monitoring the user, the system collects data about the interaction behavior before using clustering techniques to group this information. Clusters will then be classified and linked with a user group or an interaction, thereby generalizing the information to "interaction patterns" [31].

Focusing on our problem of *cultural user modeling*, we propose the use of stereotypes and communities that are highly beneficial for an initial (though very rough) user classification. By incorporating existing cultural models from other disciplines, this approach helps to outperform costly manual internationalization. The user's country of origin and his language, for instance, already provide first hints of their cultural cues and can activate an assigned interface layout. However, the acquired profile at this stage is unlikely to correlate with all facets of the user's culture. As a consequence, their interaction with the system has to be continuously monitored and evaluated in order to refine the assumptions about the user's cultural scope. Such further acquisition and step-wise refinement of stereotypes and communities has been proven to be successful with the help of established machine learning methods [25]. As described above, tasks such as those involving the maintenance of the user model are suited to be taken over by a shell system.

After these considerations of user modeling techniques, it can be assumed that cultural user modeling can take advantage of existing approaches to user modeling that base on AI techniques. However, such a combination of methods and in particular linking them to software adaptations, has yet to be studied in practice. To that end, the next section will introduce the work on user interface adaptation (i.e., methods for the dynamic re-arrangement of user interface elements), which will pave the way for integrated culturally adapted approaches.

4 Adapting the User Interface

Although the theoretical concept of adaptive computer systems has been an important subject for the research community, most approaches have been applied to adaptive hypermedia (or web) systems and only involve "the level of the content of the provided information (as opposed to the level of information presentation at the interface)" [24]. One reason for this might be that the advantages and disadvantages of providing generically filtered information are relatively easy to evaluate. Besides, it can be assumed that the objections to adaptivity at the user interface level also led to a stagnation of research in this area. In reference to this, Shneiderman [32] points out that „machine initiated changes to user interface features seem to be troubling to users".

Nonetheless, much research supports the thesis of user performance improvement with the help of adaptive interfaces (see, e.g., [33], [34] or [35]). If doubts persist, it is because none of these results can to date be readily generalized. Thus, many objections stem from "a fear that intelligence at the interface will violate usability principles" [36]. An important issue in this regard is the choice between automatic or computer-supported adaptation, the latter leaving more control to the user. Kobsa [26] points out that computer-supported adaptation is the better alternative if adaptations only seldomly occur but are nevertheless more important. This is fundamental for changes of the user interface since the users attention might have to be drawn to the new possibilities [26].

Regarding culturally adaptive interfaces, we have to keep in mind that most users are not used to an adaptation to their cultural frame, but have become acquainted with software embedding western cultural values. Thus, computer-supported adaptation risks a rejection of cultural adaptation measures before the user might experience its advantages.

We suggest to *automatically* adapt the software after initially having acquired the user's cultural background. In order to allow users to retract changes at any time, we plan to include an easy-to-access history log of recent adaptations. Further changes to the software should later underlie computer-supported adaptation and allow for the user's intervention if proposed changes are not desired. Here, too, are thorough evaluations essential in order to ensure that users can easily cope with adaptations and the way they are executed.

To clarify the concept of adaptive user interfaces, we will explain the idea behind it in the following section by referring to some developments in the past.

4.1 Recent Developments

Recent approaches to adaptive arrangements of interface components include the AVANTI system for disabled users that uses "a single unified user interface" but offers alternative interaction components to suit the user's need [37]. With the help of a rule-based adaptivity mechanism that communicates with the unit responsible for the user modeling, the interface can be adaptively enhanced at run-time.

Menkhaus and Pree [38] developed a new approach to dynamic user interface adaptation by remodeling "the widgets of a window into a new composition of 'small' windows", basing it on a "linking strategy" of two graph hierarchies. This method was originally developed to provide adaptation possibilities for a range of displays, input devices and mobile computing gadgets. Likewise, it has proven to be applicable for the flexible rearrangement of user interface components on the basis of a hierarchical structure of windows.

While the techniques mentioned above can be classified as the restructuring of components with the basic interface remaining the same, several approaches have proposed to offer different interfaces. Shneiderman's idea of a multi-layer design for complex systems, for example, associates the user's experience with a certain interface layer. It thereby offers the user a lower level with less functionalities or a higher level with an augmented number of interaction possibilities [32].

Regarding the adaptivity strategy, many researchers have proposed to increase consistency between applications. Lennard and Parkes [39], for instance, suggest to re-use the user's model of the interface in all applications. This is a big step towards a holistic usability that is not limited to single applications but instead supports different interfaces in providing a consistent look and feel for the user.

5 Heading Towards Culturally Adaptive User Interfaces

After reviewing the current state of the art in the three disciplines of culture & usability, user modeling, and interface adaptations, we find that the distinct research areas have yet to be combined and results have yet to be aligned with one another.

For instance, existing techniques for the initialization and maintenance of a user model can almost certainly be adopted for cultural user modeling. However, we do not know how the transfer of these techniques to culture can be carried out. "Is the user's culture tangible enough to establish a user model?", "How can we distinguish between cross-cultural and interpersonal differences?" as well as "Is it possible to assign one culture to a particular person in our globalized and multicultural world?", are questions that we will only be able to answer after hands-on experience with cultural user modeling and thoroughly investigating the measurability of culture in regard to adaptive user interfaces.

In addition, we have to map certain cultural behavior to an interface layout. It is therefore necessary to identify cultural markers that are universally valid for user interfaces. Again, existing research in this direction, such as the investigations of cultural markers in web site design (see [2, 40, 41]), can be used as a starting point for redefining these elements to suit user interface constituents.

The highly diverse adaptation of the interface can presumably be best modeled by systems that support a modular composition of the interface. Here too, the different possibilities regarding the user interface layout have to be investigated with special attention to established usability guidelines. Factoring in cultural markers, we will have to define the necessary level of flexibility required by individual elements and their composition as a whole. Thereafter, one can deliberate regarding the use and benefit of existing strategies for the adaptation of user interfaces, such as the graph hierarchies developed by Menkhaus and Pree [38]. The approach needs to be flexible enough to support all conceivable culturally adapted interface layouts, but still simple enough in order to avoid unnecessary overhead in adaptation complexity.

If we manage to merge research on culturability with guidelines on the usability of adaptive user interfaces (see [36, 42]), we will be able to develop culturally adaptive user interfaces that follow established culturability rules.

6 Conclusions and Future Research

In this paper we have proposed to overcome the problem of missing "culturability" with culturally adaptive user interfaces that enable people to use software within their cultural frame. Our opinion is that culturally adaptive software is the only possibility to overcome the two main problems of manual localization, which are, firstly, the extremely laborious and costly development process and, secondly, the elusive nature of cultural background.

Introducing artificial intelligence to the internationalisation of user intefaces makes it possible to provide a highly flexible interface adaptation that avoids to stereotypically assign a static layout to all users. Automizing the process of internationalisation throughout the use of the software will therefore allow for a less laborious and costly development.

We have presented a research summary of the core issues surrounding culture & usability, user modeling, and the adaptation of interfaces, and identified possibilities for combining these areas to achieve a concerted effort towards the topic. There are still many open questions and challenges facing the merging of different research disciplines. Consequently, our future research will firstly involve an analysis of cultural markers for software adaptation in order to establish a procedure for the software engineering and design process. With this, we will also outline how the software's architecture has to be designed to allow for an adaptation to different cultures. Furthermore, it is essential to find suitable knowledge representation techniques for the user model, as well as adaptivity strategies.

We intend to develop a prototype system in a participatory design process to test the most promising adaptivity algorithms over a longer time frame with members of different cultures. These evaluations will ensure an overall high quality of culturally adaptive software without significant investments of software-engineering resources.

References

1. Yeo, A.: World-Wide CHI: Cultural User Interfaces, A Silver Lining in Cultural Diversity. SIGCHI Bulletin 28, 4–7 (1996)
2. Barber, W., Badre, A.: Culturability: The Merging of Culture and Usability (1998)
3. Ford, G., Gelderblom, H.: The Effects of Culture on Performance Achieved through the use of Human Computer Interaction (2003)
4. Hodemacher, D., Jarman, F., Mandl, T.: Kultur und Web-Design: Ein empirischer Vergleich zwischen Grossbritannien und Deutschland (2005)
5. Reinecke, K.: Conceptual Design and Development of an XML-based Ergonomic Multimedia Information and Learning Platform for the Education of Agricultural Advisers in Rwanda (2005)
6. Kobsa, A.: User modeling: Recent work, prospects and hazards. In: Adaptive user interfaces: Principles and practice. North-Holland, pp. 111–128 (1993)
7. Maier, E.: Activity Theory as a Framework for Accommodating Cultural Factors in HCI Studies. In: Workshop-Proceedings der 5. fachübergreifenden Konferenz Mensch und Computer. A. Auinger, Wien: Österreichische Computer Gesellschaft (2005)
8. Röse, K.: Kultur als Variable des UI Design, Berücksichtigung kultureller Unterschiede bei der Mensch-Maschine-Interaktion als zeitgemässe Gestaltungsaufgabe der nutzerorientierten und ergonomischen Gestaltung von Mensch-Maschine-Systemen. In: Mensch und Computer: Fachübergreifende Konferenz. B.G. Teubner, Stuttgart, pp. 153–162 (2001)

9. Hofstede, G.: Culture's Consequences: Comparing values, behaviours and organisations across nations. Sage Publications Inc, Thousand Oaks (2003)
10. Smith, A., Chang, Y.: Quantifying Hofstede and Developing Cultural Fingerprints for Website Acceptability. In: Designing for Global Markets 5: Proc. Fifth International Workshop on Internationalization of Products and Systems (IWIPS 2003) Berlin, Germany pp. 89–102 (2003)
11. Voehringer-Kuhnt, T.: Kulturelle Einflüsse auf die Gestaltung von Mensch-Maschine Systemen (2001)
12. Marcus, A.: Cross-Cultural User-Interface Design. In: Human-Computer Interface Internat (HCII) Conf. New Orleans, LA, USA, vol. 2, pp. 502–505. Lawrence Erlbaum Associatest, Mahwah (2001)
13. Marcus, A.: Cultural Dimensions and Global Web Design: What? So What? Now What? (2001)
14. Dunn, P., Marinetti, A.: Cultural Adaptation: Necessity for Global eLearning (2002)
15. Dormann, C., Chisalita, C.: Cultural Values in Web Site Design (2002)
16. Kamentz, E.: Adaptivität von hypermedialen Lernsystemen - Ein Vorgehensmodell für die Konzeption einer Benutzermodellierungskomponente unter Berücksichtigung kulturbedingter Benutzereigenschaften. Universität Hildesheim (2006)
17. Trompenaars, F., Hampden-Turner, C.: Riding the Waves of Culture: Understanding Cultural Diversity in Business. Nicholas Brealey Publishing Ltd (1997)
18. Marcus, A.: A Practical Set of Culture Dimensions for Global User-Interface Development (2004)
19. Bourgges-Waldegg, P., Scrivener, A.: Meaning: the Central Issue in Cross-Cultural HCI Design. Interact Comput. 9, 287–309 (1998)
20. Marcus, A., Armitage, J., Frank, V., Guttman, E.: Globalization of User-Interface Design for the Web (1999)
21. Hall, P., Lawson, C., Minocha, S.: Design Patterns as a Guide to the Cultural Localisation of Software. In: Designing for Global Markets 5: Proc. Fifth International Workshop on Internationalization of Products and Systems (IWIPS 2003) Berlin, Germany pp. 79–88 (2003)
22. Thissen, F., Wingert, B.: Interkulturelles Interface Design und Interkulturelle Kommunikation (2004)
23. Heimgärtner, R.: Messen von kulturellen Unterschieden in der Mensch-Computer-Interaktion (MCI). Linz, Austria (2005)
24. Kobsa, A.: Supporting User Interfaces for All Through User Modeling. In: Proceedings of HCI International, Yokohama, Japan, pp. 155–157 (1995)
25. Paliouras, G., Karkaletsis, V., Papatheodorou, C., Spyropoulos, C.: Exploiting Learning Techniques for the Acquisition of User Stereotypes and Communities. In: Proceedings of the International Conference on User Modelling (UM '99) (1999)
26. Kobsa, A.: Adaptivität und Benutzermodellierung in interaktiven Softwaresystemen. In: Schütt, D. (ed.) Grundlagen und Anwendungen der künstlichen Intelligenz (17. Fachtagung), pp. 152–166. Springer, Heidelberg (1993)
27. Pohl, W.: Learning about the user - user modeling and machine learning. In: Proc. ICML'96 Workshop, Machine Learning meets Human-Computer Interaction, pp. 29–40 (1996)
28. Langley, P.: Machine Learning for Adaptive User Interfaces. In: KI - Kunstliche Intelligenz, pp. 53–62. Springer, Heidelberg (1997)
29. Adomavicius, G., Tuzhilin, A.: Expert-Driven Validation of Rule-Based User Models in Personalization Applications. In: Data Mining and Knowledge Discovery Journal 5 (2001)

30. Semeraro, G., Costabile, M.F., Esposito, F., Fanizzi, N., Ferilli, S.: Machine Learning Techniques for Adaptive User Interfaces in a Corporate Digital Library Service. Machine Learning and Applications. In: Proceedings of the ACAI-99 Workshop on Machine Learning in User Modeling, Chania, Crete, Greece, pp. 21–29 (1999)

31. Pitschke, K.: User Modeling for Domains without Explicit Design Theories. In: Proceedings of the Fourth International Conference on User Modeling, Hyannis, MA, USA, pp. 191–195 (1994)

32. Shneiderman, B.: Promoting Universal Usability with Multi-Layer Interface Design. In: Proceedings of the 2003 Conference on Universal Usability, Vancouver, Canada, pp. 1–8. ACM Press, New York (2003)

33. Greenberg, S., Witten, I.: Adaptive personalized interfaces - A question of viability. Behaviour and Information Technology 4, 31–45 (1985)

34. Sears, A., Shneiderman, B.: Split menus: Effectively using selection frequency to organize menus. ACM Transactions on Computer Human Interaction 1, 27–51 (1994)

35. Höök, K.: Evaluating the Utility and Usability of an Adaptive Hypermedia System. In: Proceedings of 1997 International Conference on Intelligent User Interfaces, Orlando, Florida, USA (1997)

36. Höök, K.: Steps to take before Intelligent User Interfaces become real. Interacting With Computers 12, 409–426 (2000)

37. Stephanidis, C.: Designing User Interfaces for All. In: Proceedings of the 13th Annual Conference Technology and Persons with Disabilities, Los Angeles, USA (1998)

38. Menkhaus, G., Pree, W.: A Hybrid Approach to Adaptive User Interface Generation (2002)

39. Lennard, A., Parkes, A.: An Architecture For Adaptive Interfaces (1995)

40. Badre, A.: The Effects of Cross Cultural Interface Design Orientation on World Wide Web User Performance. In: Georgia Institute of Technology (2001)

41. Sun, H.: Building a culturally-competent corporate web site: an exploratory study of cultural markers in multilingual web design. In: SIGDOC '01: Proceedings of the 19th annual international conference on Computer documentation, Sante Fe, New Mexico, USA, pp. 95–102. ACM Press, NewYork (2001)

42. Benyon, D.: Adaptive Systems: a solution to usability problems (1993)

Local Websites as the New Existence of Traditional Local Cultures in the Virtual Space: An Overview on the Local Websites of Turkey*

Kerem Rızvanoğlu and Özgürol Öztürk

Galatasaray University, Faculty of Communication, Ciragan Cad. 36,
34357 İstanbul, Turkey
{krizvanoglu,ozozturk}@gsu.edu.tr

Abstract. With its original traditions and values dating back to hundreds of years in seven different regions, Turkey distinguishes by its own cosmopolite culture from the others. The local sites of the regions also differ by their aspects reflecting the old culture at both the content and the design level with original tools like "virtual graveyard visit, condolence function etc." Benefiting from the Internet technologies creatively and pragmatically, the sites actually enable the citizens (townsman) who live geographically apart to share the traditions and values of their culture. In other words, by providing the familiar cultural experience on the web, the sites enable a kind of virtual access to hometown. Being a former step of a larger study, this study aims to investigate qualitatively this new existence of the local cultures on the Internet by focusing on the content and design aspects of the sites involved.

Keywords: Local, Culture, Web Site, Cultural Experience, Content, Design.

1 Introduction

In recent decades, the continual expansion of computer technologies -particularly the Internet- in the society is widely acknowledged. Even in developing countries, the use of Internet for different purposes has grown far beyond the expectations.

Considering the widespread use of Internet by different cultures, culture and identity appear to be the foremost subjects when speaking about the Internet and its social aspects. But as Zurawski (1998) [1] stated "there seem to be only two views when it comes to the relation between technology, society and culture at large: The Internet then is either bad or good for society and its culture in general". Though at one side of the coin, through a deterministic view of technology it is claimed that the Internet creates a worldwide monolithic culture by erasing local cultural boundaries, we adopt the view that the cultural identity lines stay the same in the virtual space. As mentioned by Hongladarom (2002) [2], "the Internet reduplicates the existing cultural

---

* This study has been realized under the coordination of Assist. Prof. Şule Tankut with the support of Galatasaray University Scientific Research Fund.

N. Aykin (Ed.): Usability and Internationalization, Part II, HCII 2007, LNCS 4560, pp. 211–218, 2007.
© Springer-Verlag Berlin Heidelberg 2007

boundaries. What the Internet does, is to create an umbrella cosmopolitan culture which is necessary for communication among people from disparate cultures".

At this point, the cultural identity mostly appears to be represented by the local e-content. Though the powers that 'push' global or just non-local content are often much stronger than those 'pushing' local content and though most formal content and communication 'channels' in developing countries help only to push 'external' content into local communities, especially in developing countries (Ballantyne, 2002) [3] counter efforts to push local content on to global stages can be observed recently.

Mostly designed by amateur initiatives, many local cultures represent themselves on Internet by separate websites based on culture-specific local content. Designed by the motives to create a communication and information platform for the people who come from the same cultural origin but live apart, these sites seemed to offer much more. Benefiting from the Internet technologies creatively and pragmatically, these sites enable the reconstruction of the cultural experience on the Internet for the users living worldwide. Reflecting the traditional local culture at all aspects, these sites imitate the real life experience that those people had once lived through and in a way enable a kind of virtual access to hometown.

In this context, it is thought that these original cultural web sites -which can be called also as the cultural artifacts- offer a lot for the HCI researchers and professionals at both the design and content level. Besides the efforts for designing for an international audience by means of ethnographic field studies, cross-cultural usability tests, internationalization, localization and relevant procedures, it is claimed that an in-depth analysis towards these sites can present new metaphors and design hints for the designers, content developers and researchers. Therefore, being a former step of a larger study, this study aims to investigate qualitatively this existence of the local cultures on the Internet through the reconstruction of real life cultural experience by focusing on the content and design aspects of the sites involved.

Culture is defined by several dimensions which also serve as the axis of analysis for the study. The analysis will consist of Turkish local sites which distinguish by original web site tools adapted or developed for providing the real life cultural experience for the users on the Internet. Seven web sites of different villages were chosen to represent the seven different geographical regions of Turkey.

2 Theoretical Background

As Williams (1983) [4] points out, "culture is one of the two or three most complicated words in the English language". There are various definitions for the term 'culture' in the field of cultural studies and cultural anthropology. Focusing mainly on experience and interaction with surroundings, Evers' (1999) [5] definition presents an optimal view of culture for our study: "Culture shapes the way people behave, view the world, express themselves and think. It is formed by historical experiences and values, traditions and surroundings". The interaction with daily surroundings results in common cultural experiences which constitute the traditions and values in other words the culture at all.

In addition to that, with an accent on the production of cultural artifacts, Kroeber's and Parsons' and also Triandis' definitions of culture seem to overlap with our theoretical approach. Kroeber and Parsons (1958) [6] claimed that culture is transmitted and created content and patterns of values, ideas and other symbolic meaningful systems as factors in the shaping of human behavior and the artifacts produced. In other words, it supports the notion that production of artifacts, such as websites may be determined by culture (Evers, 1999) [5]. Triandis (1972) [7] also states that a cultural group's characteristic way of perceiving the environment is expressed in objective artifacts. In this definition he suggests that the way people view the world around them is expressed in cultural products such as paintings, books, folklore and clothing.

Arising from those approaches, it is claimed that local sites can be considered as the embodiment of those local cultures in cyberspace. Therefore, it is assumed that analyzing a website of a local culture should lead us to the elements composing the culture itself and visa versa.

2 Research Methodology

Briefly in this study, it is aimed to investigate the adaptation of cultural experience into local e-content at both content and design levels by the analysis of local village web sites of Turkey. Firstly the term culture is decomposed into several dimensions which acted as axes for the analysis succeeding. Involving different dimensions of culture, the above definition of Evers provides the axes for the analysis of the sites referred in the study. Considering this definition, three main axes revealing the cultural experience are proposed: Daily Life Experience, Traditional Values and Nationalistic view.

When defining these dimensions, it is considered that they reflected the common real life experiences of a typical villager in Turkey. Also in discussing through these variables, it is benefited from one of the researcher's past experiences within village surroundings and day life.

Daily Life Experience. Besides the work routine, this dimension includes the activities in the typical daily life of a villager in Turkey. One of the main activities is meeting with the others in the "village public room" which include other varying activities. In the village room, the villagers chat and play games with each other. They watch the performances of local musicians playing traditional instruments like "saz", singing local songs called "turku" and reading poems which are part of the cultural heritage. Also "village room" is a place of humor where funny anecdotes are told, traditional games are played together. The other daily activities can be stated as worshiping in the mosque and visiting the neighbors. Also as a part of daily routine, all the events are announced by the loudspeakers.

Traditional Values. These values include the Bairam greetings which is an important ceremony at the religious Bairam days of Muslims and also include the regular graveyard visits. With pre and post stages, the wedding ceremony is also a complicated procedure that takes place between families. Besides, the dialects spoken and the food served in different regions of Turkey have also culture-specific qualities. As a part of dominant feudal and masculine tradition, the family origins of the inhabitants are still important. The legal authorities of the government in the villages: the reeves –called Muhtar in Turkish- are also accepted as the public leaders.

Nationalistic view. Having a history made of imperial and independence wars, the Turkish culture still has a rough nationalistic view which idealizes the warrior profile ready for any threat towards the country. This results with an insistent accent on the symbols like Turkish flag and anthem as well as the military service. In most of the parts of Turkey, the departure of someone for military service is still a great ceremony.

In the study, it was aimed to find out the design and content elements matching these dimensions by employing a qualitative method of analysis. The study consisted of seven local village web sites[2] each representing a region in Turkey. Though there are hundreds of similar village web sites on the Internet, considering their varying content, these seven sites were chosen as representatives for the qualitative analysis employed. Although there are cultural differences between these geographical regions, these seemed to diminish on the Internet and a focus on similar axes is observed to be common. The names of the villages and their geographical locations are stated in Table 1.

Table 1. The Names Of The Villages And Their Geographical Locations

Region	City	Village
East	Erzincan	Kozlupınar
Central	Çankırı	Bucura Yenice
Southeast	Adıyaman	Karaburun
Marmara	Sakarya	Dikmen
Mediterranean	Mersin	Dalak Deresi
Aegean	Kütahya	Karamanlar
Blacksea	Trabzon	Sugeldi

3 Results

The results of the analysis show that the local sites have elements that match directly with the activities and values provided by the cultural dimensions proposed. Either existing web tools or their creative adaptations are used to reconstruct the common familiar experience.

Daily Life Experience. Considering this dimension, it was seen that the tradition of "village public room" is reconstructed by new options in the websites. The village room concept is again considered as a meeting place with guestbook, chat, forum and game links. The preference of the name "village room" for the chat link in a web site supports this statement. The folkloric performances are carried on to pictures and videos whereas humor and poetry links also take attention as cultural elements in the navigation bar. Being a focus in the daily life, the mosque still has a priority in the hierarchical design of the site. Besides the photos showing the exterior structure, some sites also give access to the interior parts of the mosques by photos and videos. Relationships with the neighbors still have an important role at the content and design level. The daily announcements are transferred into news panels found at the homepages. Photos and links to the sites of the neighbor villages are also presented in most of the sites. The elements of village web sites that match the dimension of "Daily Life Experience" were stated in Table 2.

---

[2] The web addresses of the sites referred in the study is given in the Appendix.

Table 2. The web site elements matching the "Daily Life Experience"

Village	Daily Life Experience							
	Links to Neighbors	Mosque	Guestbook / Forum	Photos	Video	Humor	Poetry	News
Kozlupınar			*	*			*	*
Bucura Yenice	*	*	*	*	*			*
Karaburun	*		*	*	*			*
Dikmen	*	*	*	*	*		*	*
Dalak Deresi	*		*	*			*	*
Karamanlar	*		*	*	*	*		*
Sugeldi	*		*	*	*	*		*

Traditional Values. The most exact matches were detected by this dimension. A web option is assigned for nearly every traditional value mentioned within this topic. The feudal panorama of the villages is also embodied in the web sites. There is focus on the profiles of the families and inhabitants by photo links. "Family tree" link which is used to trail the old generations is seen to be frequently used. Legal authorities like reeves are still considered as social leaders, since separate clear links for these profiles are presented in the navigation bars. Cultural heritage is highly valued by the detailed informative links about the local accent and food. Another notion to support this idea was found in the surveys proposed by the sites. Most subscription surveys demand local knowledge from its users. Table 3 shows some of the links proposed by the sites which match the "traditional values" dimension.

Table 3. The web site elements matching the "Traditional Values"

Village	Traditional Values					
	Reeve (Muhtar)	Inhabitants	Family Tree	Local Food	Survey	Local Accent
Kozlupınar					*	*
Bucura Yenice	*					*
Karaburun		*		*	*	*
Dikmen	*		*	*	*	*
Dalak Deresi	*	*	*	*	*	*
Karamanlar	*					
Sugeldi	*	*	*		*	*

Although existing web tools are employed in the sites, it was surprising to find out that new tools are also adapted or developed in order to experience the tradition remotely. The "virtual graveyard visit" interface is a perfect example for this statement. As mentioned before, graveyard visit is an old cultural tradition which is adopted by most of the Turkish people. Most people living far away from their hometown complain on this issue, since they can't find the opportunity to visit the graveyard, but the "virtual graveyard visit" interface seems to solve this problem, as it pragmatically gives direct access to the photo of every gravestone found in the graveyard of the village. This option was found to be used in some other sites even with a "condolence button". The "virtual graveyard visit" interface of the web site of Bucura Yenice village is showed in Fig. 1.

Fig. 1. The "Virtual Graveyard Visit" interface

In the context of this dimension, wedding ceremonies, local music and dance links were also employed as the main links in the navigation bars. Most of the stages of the wedding ceremony and even Bairam greetings that took place in the villages are provided online for the ones that have missed those experiences. Direct access is enabled to the interpretations of the local songs by the local singers. Descriptive videos of the folkloric dance of the regions are also important parts of the content proposed. Table 4 shows the other links proposed by the sites which match the "traditional values" dimension.

Table 4. The other web site elements matching the "Traditional Values"

	Traditional Values			
Village	Bayram Greetings	Graveyard Visit	Wedding Ceremony	Local Music and Dance
Kozlupınar			*	*
Bucura Yenice		*		
Karaburun	*		*	*
Dikmen			*	*
Dalak Deresi	*		*	*
Karamanlar			*	*
Sugeldi		*	*	*

Nationalistic View. The elements mentioned under this topic as part of the Turkish local culture are found to be reflected to the content and design of the websites involved. All the nationalistic symbols are placed at visual focus corners in the layouts. Most of the sites have banners with animated Turkish flags at the home page. Some of the sites provide access to the lyrics of the national anthem whereas some offer even the audio recording of it. Links praising the boys at the military service and even the list of martyrs accompanied by their photos is also frequently used. The web site elements matching the "nationalistic view" dimension are shown in Table 5.

Table 5. The web site elements matching the "Nationalistic View"

Village	Turkish Flag	National Anthem	Military Service	Martyr
	Nationalistic View			
Kozlupınar	*			*
Bucura Yenice	*	*	*	*
Karaburun	*			
Dikmen	*		*	*
Dalak Deresi				
Karamanlar	*		*	
Sugeldi				

5 Conclusion

In this study, the local web sites of seven villages from different regions of Turkey are analyzed by the cultural dimensions proposed. Culture is taken as the sum of common cultural experiences based on the interaction with daily surroundings. Designed by amateur initiatives from the same culture, these local websites are considered as cultural artifacts just like the folkloric products that carry all the qualities and the fingerprint of the culture. The dimensions used in the analysis are derived from the decomposition of the definition above. It is observed that besides functioning as a communication platform, by benefiting from the possibilities of web technologies, these sites were successful enough to provide the common familiar cultural experience for the users living geographically apart. Therefore, it was assumed that an analysis towards these amateur local sites would lead us to an insider view of that culture.

Having analyzed the sites through the cultural dimensions proposed, the findings showed that these local sites represent every notion of that culture by the use of pragmatically created or adapted web tools. By the words of Hongladarom (2000) [2], "cyberspace mirrors real space". All the elements of Turkish rural culture are found as options or tools in these local web sites. Maybe the motives for creating and pushing such an e-content are just enabling the users to share the traditions and values of their own culture even if they live geographically apart, but on the other hand the findings of the study showed that, through their amateur but culture-specific content and design, local web sites could offer an important potential for the experts in HCI who work on the cross-cultural user interfaces. It is thought that before heading to extensive field studies for designing cross-cultural interfaces, the local sites of the target cultures can present the necessary metaphors and creative design elements as in the case of this study. Besides, it should be certainly noted that the creation and push of local e-content by local initiatives should be valued and motivated.

As mentioned before, this study is the first step of a larger study on local sites in Turkey and provides a brief overview. Further research will include a user centered ethnographic study with the target audience of these sites in order to gain better insight.

References

1. Zurawski, N.: Culture, Identity, and the Internet. In: Proceedings of INET 98. 1 (1998), http://www.isoc.org/inet98/proceedings/7x/index.htm
2. Hongladarom, S.: Global Culture, Local Cultures and the Internet: the Thai example (Special issue on culture and technology). AI & Society 13(4), 404 (2000)
3. Ballantyne, P.: Collecting and Propagating Local Content Development. In: Report of a project carried out by IICD in association with the Tanzania Commission for Science and Technology (2002)
4. Williams, R.: Keywords: A Vocabulary of Culture and Society. Glasgow: William Collins & Sons (1983)
5. Evers, V.: Cross-Cultural Aspects Of The Human Computer Interface. Doctoral Thesis. United Kingdom: Open University. 21 (1999) http://staff.science.uva.nl/~evers/pubs/Final%20thesis%20and.pdf
6. Kroeber, A.L., Parsons, T.: The concepts of culture and of social systems. American Sociological Review 23, 582 (1958)
7. Triandis, H.C. (ed.): The Analysis of Subjective Culture. Wiley, New York (1972)

Appendix: List of the Web Addresses of the Local Sites Referred in the Study

Village	Web Site Adresss
Kozlupınar	http://members.lycos.co.uk/kozlupinar/index.php??=& ____ord____=1171634099?&____ord____=1171634102
Bucura	http://www.byenice.gen.tr/AnaSayfa.aspx
Yenice	
Karaburun	http://www.karacoluk.com/
Dikmen	http://www.hendekdikmenkoyu.com/
Dalak Deresi	http://www.dalakderesi.net/
Karamanlar	http://karamanlarkoyu.com/
Sugeldi	http://www.sugeldi.com/

Word Processing in Spanish Using an English Keyboard: A Study of Spelling Errors

Nestor J. Rodriguez and Maria I. Diaz

Institute for Computing and Informatics Studies
University of Puerto Rico at Mayagüez
nestor@ece.uprm.edu, mdiazfigueroa@gmail.com

Abstract. This article describes a study of spelling errors made by writers while typing in Spanish using an English keyboard. The most important contribution of this study is the identification of a profile of errors made by writers using a word processor and an English keyboard to write in Spanish. The study revealed that a large number of the errors are related with words that have a character such as á, é, í, ó, ú or ñ. Another important finding of the study was that a substantial number of errors (approximately one third) are not corrected and that backspace was used to correct approximately two thirds of all the words corrected. The study supports the conclusion that the lack of straightforward support for characters such as á, é, í, ó, ú or ñ in the Spanish language can cause a significant number of errors.

Keywords: spelling errors detection, spelling errors correction, spell checking, word processing, Spanish writing.

1 Introduction

Grammatical correctness in writing is emphasized since a person starts learning to write because it is essential for clear transmission of thoughts, ideas, concepts or facts. Since we are unable to recall the correct spelling of every word of a particular language we usually seek help in order to achieve grammatical correctness in writing. The best resource for helping writers produce grammatically correct texts has been the dictionary. This resource is often used when the writer does not know the correct spelling of a word. However, the writer must has an idea of the spelling of the word to be able to search it through the dictionary. The effectiveness of the dictionary depends on the ability of the writers to detect words with incorrect spelling. Thus, there is a need for tools that can help them become aware of misspelled words an appropriately correct them. This type of help has been made available to writers through computer technology in the form of word processors with spell checking tools. Word processors with spell checkers are able to detect any pattern of letters that does not match a word in its dictionary. They can also suggest words for correcting the misspelled ones and automatically correct some of them.

There is no doubt that word processors with spell checking software have been tremendously effective in helping writers detect and correct misspelled words. However, this technology is not always 100% effective. A word processor could

N. Aykin (Ed.): Usability and Internationalization, Part II, HCII 2007, LNCS 4560, pp. 219–227, 2007.
© Springer-Verlag Berlin Heidelberg 2007

indicate a correctly spelled word as being incorrect and a misspelled word as being correct. This problem is treated in a study conducted by D. Galletta et al. [1]. The study identified three outcomes that can result from using spell checkers: correctly identified errors, false positives errors and false negatives errors. A "correctly identified error" occurs when the spell checker detects and actual misspelled word. A "false positive error" occurs when spell checkers indicates that a correctly spelled word is misspelled. A "false negative error" occurs when the spell checker does not detect a word that is misspelled. The study revealed that when the spell checkers correctly identified errors, it helps low verbal people (people with less experience in a given language) to write almost as high verbal people. On the contrary, high verbal people that rely on spell checkers end up making more errors than when they don't rely on them. This is mainly due to false negative and false positive errors.

Spelling errors are generated for a variety of reasons. In a study by Huang and Powers [2] six types of common errors were identified: typographical, homophone, grammatical, frequency disparity, learners, and idiosyncratic. Typographical errors typically manifest when a writer types a letter that is adjacent in the keyboard instead of the correct letter. Homophone errors are words that sound similar but they have a different meaning (i.e. piece and peace). Grammatical errors occur when a word with similar meaning is written instead of the intended word (i.e. "among" instead of "between"). Frequency disparity errors result when a writer tries to type the abbreviation of a word but types a similar unintended word instead ("their" instead of "they're"). Learner errors are those made by writers that are learning to write in a language that is not their first language. Idiosyncratic errors are those made for an unknown reason [3].

Spelling errors detection and correction has made its way through the World Wide Web as evidenced by two research studies. In the first study [4] the World Wide Web was used as a database to correct grammar and spelling errors. A client/server system was implemented in which the client sends a string or a phrase to the server and the server makes a search using a search engine on the web. The system counts the occurrence of that word or phrase in the web and lets the writer know the number of hits of the incidence of that word or phrase. It assumes that words with high frequency are very likely to be correct. In the second study Bolshavok and Gelbukh [5] proposed a solution for malapropism, writing words with similar sound but different meaning. For example, in the phrase "the boy is eating a peace of pizza" the word "peace" was used instead of "piece". Collocations and a search engine were used to correct this kind of error. Collocations are phrases composed of words that co–occur for lexical rather than for semantic reasons. If a specific combination of words does not exist in the collocation database, a search engine searches that combination. It is assumed that if a combination of words occurs several times in the web, it is correct. The problem with these two studies is that they assume that text on web pages is grammatically correct.

Spelling errors detection and correction has not been well documented for the Spanish language. The Spanish language has some characters that are not used in languages such as English. These characters are not well supported by English keyboards. This lack of support may cause writers to make spelling errors. These issues with the Spanish language motivated the study presented in this document. The goal of this work was to study the spelling errors made by writers while writing in Spanish using an English keyboard and how these errors are corrected.

2 Methodology

As a first step in this research, a study was conducted in which twenty people were asked to write for an hour using MS Word. The participants were college students and recent college graduates. They were asked to write in Spanish something related with their lives. They were asked to type as they normally do. All the participants used Microsoft ® Office Word 2003.

The participants' interaction with the computer was recorded using the TechSmith Morae software. This software records and synchronizes user and system data for usability analysis. The software consists of three components: Morae Recorder, Morae Remote Viewer, and Morae Manager. Morae Recorder is the component of the software that captures the interaction of the user while he/she is using the computer. This part of the software was installed in the users' computers. This component can be configured to capture important activity from the screen, keyboard, and the mouse to be used in the analysis of the interaction. The Morae Remote Viewer allows experimenters to watch the interaction of a user remotely through Internet. For this study, this component was not used because it was not necessary to monitor the participants while interacting since the recording of the interaction provided the necessary data for the study. Finally, Morae Manager was used to analyze the recorded interaction of every participant. Morae Manager allows the researcher to place markers on the recording, so he/she can easily move to that point of the recording while reviewing it.

The Morae Recorder software was configured to record the keystrokes (input from the keyboard), screen text, and mouse clicks (highlight mouse cursor, left and right mouse clicks). It was set to record the writer activity for a period of one hour. The recording was done once for each participant.

The collected data was analyzed to identify the type of errors made by writers while typing. The behavior of the spell checker was also studied to identify words automatically corrected. In addition the strategies used by the participants to correct misspelled words were also studied. Pilot tests helped identify the types of errors commonly made by people while typing. Eleven errors categories were identified. Some of these errors such as typographical, homophone, transposition, extra letter, wrong letter and missing letter have been previously identified in the literature for the English language [3, 6]. Three of the error categories identified (Accent, Ñ Error and Special Accent) are non-existent in the English Language but very common in the Spanish language. The description of these errors follows.

- Extra Letter - The writer types an extra letter in a word (i.e. "estuudio" instead of estudio).
- Missing Letter – The writer does not type a letter in a word (i.e. "esudio" instead of "estudio").
- Homophone - Words that sound similar but they have a different meaning (i.e. "ciervo" and "siervo").
- Typographical – The writer types an adjacent letter in the keyboard instead of the correct one (i.e. "sin" instead of "son").
- Transposition & Disorder – Disorder corresponds to the case where the writer types a word with all its letters but in an incorrect order (i.e. Aoccdrnig instead of

According), while transposition is a special case of disorder in which two adjacent letters in a word are exchanged (i.e. "etsudio" instead of "estudio").

- Wrong Letter – The writer types a wrong letter in a word (i.e. "estgdio" instead of "estudio").
- Grammatical – The writer types a word with similar meaning instead of the intended word (i.e. "among" instead of "between").
- Caps Lock – The writer is typing the first letter of a word in a sentence and turns on the Caps Lock and continues typing in capital letters.
- Ñ – The word has a ñ or Ñ but the writer does not type it and usually types a n instead.
- Accent – The writer types a word that must has a vowel with an accent and writes the vowel without the accent.
- Special Accent – The writer does not place an accent on a word that should has an accent or the writer places an accent on a word that should not has an accent (i.e. cambie, cambié). In both cases, both words are correct words of the dictionary but only one of them is correct in the context of a sentence.

3   Results

In order to make a fair analysis of the results the number of errors made by each of the participants was normalized by dividing the number of errors by the total number of

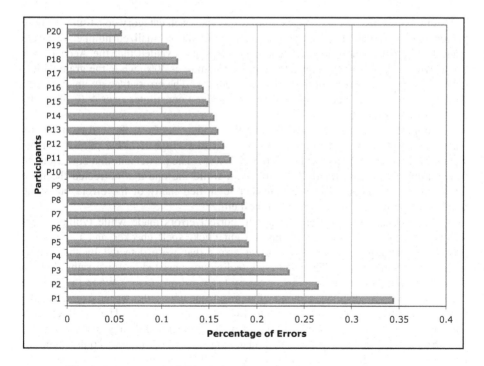

Fig. 1. Percentage of All Words that Were Errors Made by Each Participant

words written. Figure 1 shows the variability in the percentage of errors made by the participants. Results indicate that of all the words written by the participants an average of 17.31% were erroneous with a standard deviation of 6.16%. The maximum percentage of errors made by a participant was 34.29% and the minimum 5.78%.

Table 1 shows the mean, standard deviation, minimum and maximum values of the normalized number of errors made by the participants in each error category.

Table 1. Errors Made by the Participants Normalized by Total Number of Words Written

	Mean %	Standard Dev. %	Minimum %	Maximum %
Transposition & Disorder	0.91	0.61	0.07	2.22
Extra Letter	2.16	1.11	0.89	5.00
Wrong Letter	1.80	0.98	0.59	4.33
Missing Letter	2.29	1.15	0.91	5.47
Typographical	1.51	1.18	0.47	5.39
Homophones	0.48	0.50	0.00	1.72
Grammatical	0.02	0.05	0.00	0.19
Caps Locks	0.16	0.19	0.00	0.72
Accent	5.29	2.14	0.15	7.83
Special Accent	2.12	1.28	0.07	4.73
Ñ	0.57	0.44	0.00	1.49

Figure 2 presents the percentages of all errors that each category constitutes. These percentages were calculated using the averages of the normalized number of errors made by the participants for each category. Results revealed that the Accent error category is the one with the highest occurrence with over 30%, while the grammatical error category is the one with the lowest occurrence. The errors that are unique when writing in Spanish (Accents, Special Accents and Ñ) constitutes over 46% of all the errors made by participants.

An important action observed during the study was how the errors made by participants were corrected. Results indicate that an average of 73.0% of all the errors were corrected with a Standard Deviation of 19.0%. The participant that corrected the fewer number of errors fixed 29.6% of them while the one that corrected the most fixed 100.0% of them. The spell checker identified many of the errors but some writers did not review the document to fix them.

The participants used different ways to correct errors made while typing. Four techniques were identified: backspace, right click, spell checker and undo. The backspace technique was used to correct errors that were detected by the writers immediately while typing. The right click technique consisted in doing right click on the mouse on a word marked as incorrect by the word processor. When this is done the word processor displays a menu of words from which the writer can select the correct one if available and substitute the erroneous word. The spell checker technique is the case when the writer types in all the text and then go back to correct the erroneous words using the spell checking command in the Tools menu of Microsoft Word. The undo technique consists of hitting the undo button after the word processor automatically corrects a word that was typed correctly.

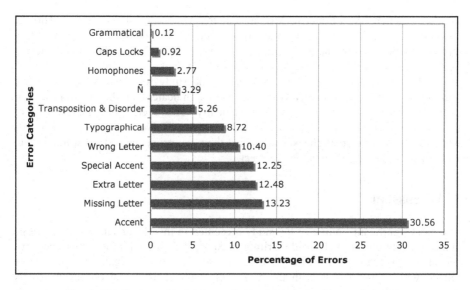

Fig. 2. Distribution of Errors Made by the Participants by Error Category

The percentage of errors made with each technique is presented on Figure 3. The results reveal that most of the errors were fixed with the backspace technique. Thus, most of the errors were fixed right at the moment they occurred.

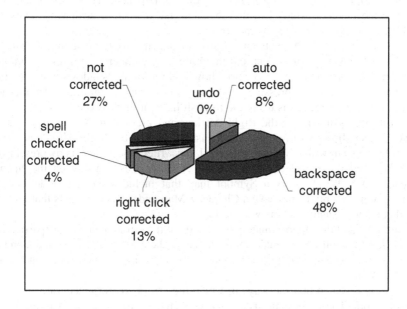

Fig. 3. Percentage of Errors Corrected with Each Error-Correction Technique

The study revealed that the percentage of errors corrected varies with the type of error. Error types that are easily identified by the writers or the word processor such as Wrong Letter, Extra Letter or Missing Letter, Typographical and Transposition & Disorder errors exhibit high percentage of correction. On the other hand, error types that are not detected by the word processor or easily identified by the writers such as Special Accent and Ñ errors exhibit a lower percentage of correction.

Another interesting aspect observed during the study was how many words the spell checker fixed automatically. The results indicate that the word processor attempted to fix 7.57% of the errors automatically. However, approximately 13% of the words automatically corrected resulted in false positive errors [1]. The words were correct but the spell checker identified them as erroneous and substituted them with a words that ended up being incorrect.

4 Discussion

The most significant finding of the study presented in this document was that a large number of the errors made while writing in Spanish is related with words that have accented vowels (á, é, í, ó, ú) or a "ñ" character. The study revealed that the errors related with typing words with these characters (Accents, Special Accents and Ñ errors) constitute over 46% of all the errors made by the participants. For obvious reasons these types of errors do not happen when writing in English. The errors that are common in the English language are the other eight error types identified with this study. In our study, if the errors related with the special characters are removed, the combination of Transposition, Wrong Letter, Extra Letter or Missing Letter errors constitutes 77% of all the errors made by the participants. These results are very similar to the Damerau study [7], that revealed that these four error types constitute over 80% of all the error made by the writers.

The Accents, Special Accents and Ñ errors occur mostly because the methods for typing the vowels with the accent and the ñ are very cumbersome in most computer systems and the writers do not remember how to do it. In the Windows platform these characters can be typed by pressing the Alt key and a sequence of digits. Another way of entering these characters is using the English International Keyboard Setting. With this setting the writer holds the Right Alt key and presses the vowel they want to accent. It also allows writing the ñ letter just by holding the Right Alt key and the n letter. On a system with a Spanish keyboard, the writer places accents by pressing the accent key and the vowel to be accented. Also there is a ñ key on the Spanish keyboard. MS Word offers a Symbol map that includes the accent letters. In addition, Windows platforms have a Character Map under System Tools that includes special characters such as letters with accent.

Result revealed that approximately two thirds of the errors made by the participants were corrected. In the large majority of the cases the errors were corrected using the backspace key. The remaining words were corrected using the spell checking features of the MS Word.

The study revealed that the ways in which the errors are corrected varies with the types of errors. The large majority of Wrong Letter, Extra Letter or Missing Letter, Typographical, Transposition & Disorder errors are corrected by the writers using backspace. This is because these types of errors are easy to identify by the writers and they corrected most of them on the spot. All the Caps Lock Errors were corrected either by the writers or the word processor. This is due to the fact that words in capital letters are easy to spot and writers can identified them easily. On the contrast, none of the Grammatical Errors were corrected. This is because Grammatical Errors are errors in which another word is written instead of the intended word. Since the word written is a correct word the word processor does not detect the error and it passes unnoticed by the writers.

About half of the Accent errors were corrected by the writers, most of them with the speller features of the word processor (spell checker, right click and autocorrect). The large majority of the Special Accent errors were not corrected. This is because the MS Word spell checker does not detect the large majority of this type of errors and in most of the cases the writer is unaware of the problem. Most of these errors were corrected with the speller features of the word processor. In the case of the Ñ errors about half of them were corrected by the writers and almost another half were left uncorrected. Some of these errors can be easily detected because of the presence of a tilde character (~) on the word. However, other cases are difficult to detect by the word processor and the writers because the word is written with an "n" instead of the "ñ" and that word is a correct word of the dictionary.

5 Conclusion

The most important contribution of this study is the identification of a profile of errors made by people using a word processor to write in Spanish. Eleven error categories were identified. The most significant finding was that a large number of the errors made are related with words that have a character such as á, é, í, ó, ú or ñ. These characters are very common in the Spanish language but non-existent in the English language. The errors caused when typing words with these characters were classified as Accents, Special Accents and Ñ errors. Most of these errors were made because the methods for typing the á, é, í, ó, ú and ñ characters were very cumbersome and the writer usually did not recall them. Thus, we conclude that the lack of straight-forward support for special character of languages such as Spanish can cause a significant number of errors.

Our study produced results consistent with the Damerau [7] study. If the Accents, Special Accents and Ñ errors are not considered, the percentage of the combination of transposition, wrong letter, extra letter and missing letter errors found in our study is very similar to the percentage reported in [7]. Thus, the Accents, Special Accents and Ñ errors are additional errors that are associated with the Spanish language. These findings supports the conclusion that writers can make a significant number of additional errors when writing in Spanish using Microsoft Word and a standard English keyboard than when they do it in English.

Another important finding of the study was that a substantial number of errors (approximately one third) are not corrected. Most of these errors pass undetected because the word processor does not detect them and thus does not provide a warning to the writers. From the study we identified that writers used basically three techniques to correct errors while writing in Spanish language: backspace, right click and spell checker. The backspace technique was used by the writers to correct approximately two thirds of all the words corrected. The writers used this technique to correct most of the errors that they detected at the moment they made them. Thus, we conclude that writers correct most of the errors on the spot by recalling the correct spelling of the word.

The study revealed that the percentage of errors corrected varies with the type of error. Error types that are easily identified by the writers or the word processor such as Wrong Letter, Extra Letter or Missing Letter, Typographical and Transposition & Disorder exhibit a high percentage of correction. On the other hand, error types that are not detected by the word processor or easily identified by the writers such as Special Accent and Ñ exhibit a lower percentage of correction.

As it is documented in [8], with simple algorithms most of the Accent, Special Accent and Ñ errors can be detected. In addition the writer can be provided with alternatives to correct the error. The adoption of such algorithms by commercial word processor can improve error correction for Spanish writers.

Acknowledgments. This study was made possible in part by NSF grant EIA 99-77071.

References

1. Galletta, D., Ducikova, A., Everard, A., Jones, B.: Does Spell-checking Software Need a Warning Label? Communications of the ACM, 48(7), (July 2005)
2. Huang, J.H., Powers, D.: Large Scale Experiments on Correction of Confused Words. In: Computer Science Conference, Proceedings 24th. Australasian, pp. 77–82 (2001)
3. Powers, D.W.: Learning and Application of Differential Grammars. In: CoNLL97: Computational Natural Language Learning, ACL Association for Computational Linguistics, pp. 88–96 (1997)
4. Fallman, D.: The Penguin: Using the Web as a Database for Descriptive and Dynamic Grammar and Spell Checking. In: CHI'02 Extended Abstracts on Human Factors in Computing Systems (2002)
5. Boshakov, I.A., Gelbukh, A.: On Detection of Malapropisms by Multistage Collocation Testing. In: 8th International Conference on Applications of Natural Language to Information Systems (2003)
6. Durham, I., Lamb, D., Saxe, J.: Spelling Corrections in User Interfaces. Communications of the ACM. 26(10), (October 1983)
7. Damerau, F.J.: A Technique for Computer Detection and Correction of Spelling Errors. Communications of the ACM. 7(3), (March 1964)
8. Diaz, M.I.: A Study of Spelling Errors in Word Processing: Detection and Correction. M.S. Thesis, University of Puerto Rico-Mayaguez, Mayaguez, Puerto Rico (2006)

Introducing New Methodologies for Identifying Design Patterns for Internationalization and Localization

Nicole Schadewitz and Timothy Jachna

School of Design, The Hong Kong Polytechnic University,
Hung Hom, Kowloon, Hong Kong, China
sd.nic@polyu.edu.hk, sdtim@polyu.edu.hk

Abstract. This paper describes a new methodology for deriving interaction design patterns from an analysis of ethnographic data. It suggests using inductive and deductive analysis processes to identify and articulate patterns that address the needs of culturally diverse users of interactive, collaborative systems. This might inform the internationalization and localization process of computer supported collaboration systems.

1 Introduction

A growing number of design and usability researchers and practitioners are beginning to take an interest in design patterns as a method to capture and communicate effective design solutions. The practical format of patterns enables designers to reuse and share design knowledge among various stakeholders in the design process. The concept of design patterns has received less attention in the field of internationalization and localization of products and systems than in other related areas of research. This might be due to the uncertainty as to whether or not patterns are an appropriate method to capture and communicate appropriate design solutions to support the use of interactive systems by culturally diverse users. Generally, the process of enabling localization of systems for different cultures starts with the development of a core interactive system, which is considered international. The core system is designed to receive local specific data, when it is localized. This paper introduces a methodology for studying and analyzing designs in culturally varying contexts in order to represent the findings in the format of design patterns that support the localization of collaborative systems.

2 Background

Since Alexander (1979) introduced the design patterns format into the field of architecture and Gamma et al. (1995) developed patterns to communicate reusable parts of computer engineering knowledge, a discussion among interaction design researchers has evolved regarding which role design patterns could take in the usability and interaction design process (Borchers 2001), (McInerney 2002) (Tidwell 2005) (Erickson 2000). Two teams of researchers are currently investigating the

N. Aykin (Ed.): Usability and Internationalization, Part II, HCII 2007, LNCS 4560, pp. 228–237, 2007.

possibility of patterns-supported cross-cultural usability in the field of internationalization and localization (Alostath and Wright 2004), (Mahemoff and Johnston 2001). Mahemoff and Johnston (2001) suggest design patterns that are closely related to usability standards for internationalization and localization. These researchers' patterns offer support for the design process of internationalization of computer systems but do not give consistent advice as to which cultural differences and models need to be considered and communicated in different design and development contexts. Some patterns reference cultural dimensions (i.e. Hofstede 1997) to describe culturally varying forces that determine the usability problem. However, this information is not provided consistently throughout all patterns.

Researchers have discussed the importance of context descriptions and appropriate naming of design patterns (Alexander 1979), (Borchers 2001), (Hall 2003), (Tidwell 2005). Based on their research in the area of internationalization and localization of products, Hall et. al. (2003) suggest that the same problem can have a different solution depending on the culturally varying context of use. A design pattern is a description of a solution to a problem in a certain context (Alexander 1979). The depiction of conditions that lead to a successful design solution in this context is very important in order to communicate the purpose and scope of an interaction design pattern. Suitable choices of terminology, writing style and graphical representations of design patterns contribute to the understanding and correct of use of a pattern. In this view, the author believes that the way patterns are articulated is greatly influenced by the methodology by which patterns are identified. In the past, pattern researcher accepted that pattern identification is based on the long term work and research experience of the composer. Although, literature provides information how to construct a pattern language (Meszaros and Doble 1999) or how to improve patterns in a shepherding process, researchers criticize that there are few concrete descriptions of methodologies to identify design patterns (Baggetun et al. 2007). Therefore, this paper introduces a qualitative methodology for identifying design patterns in ethnographic data of cross-cultural computer-supported collaborative interactions.

3 Methods

In the context of a long-term ethnographic study over a period of three years, inductive and deductive qualitative analysis methods were explored and developed for supporting the identification and articulation of interaction design patterns. In the inductive approach to data analysis all findings are grounded in the data. The deductive approach to ethnographic data analysis uses scientific theories to structure, code and report the data to test or extend an existing theory or hypothesis. (Tesch 1990)

From September 2003 to December 2005, I observed an undergraduate university design studio subject entitled "Only Connect - international collaboration project". This was a 6-7-week course organized by the School of Design at the Hong Kong Polytechnic University and taught in collaboration with partner universities and design schools in Korea, Austria and Taiwan. Each year, teams of 2-4 second year Hong Kong students from product, visual communication and environmental design were paired up with partner teams of 1-3 students from a similar design discipline and

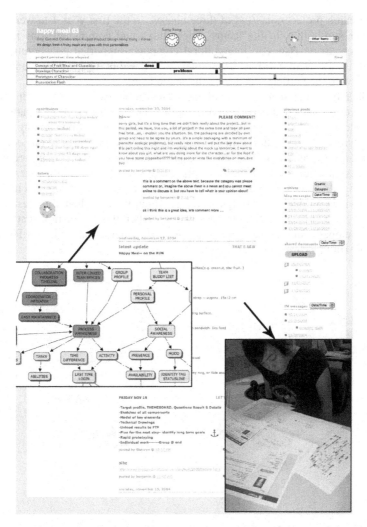

Fig. 1. Development Cycle of Interaction Design Patterns: from Deductive Mapping to Prototyping and Testing of the Prototype

from another country. Each time, there were approximately 110 Hong Kong participants and 50 international partners. Each discipline had 2-3 tutors from Hong Kong and from the respective partner university. Though distributed geographically, students collaborated using various communication technologies. Teams utilized synchronous communication tools like MSN or ICQ chat systems or Video-chat. In addition teams used asynchronous communication media like email, shared documents and different community and group websites like weblogs or Yahoo! Groups. Data about the collaborative interactions between distributed international design teams were collected using naturalistic observation, in-depth and informal interviews, as well as online conversation protocols.

The research project consisted of three phases. In the first year data were gathered to discover similarities in the teams' interactions and communications in order to identify reoccurring issues in intercultural computer-supported collaboration. Those identified issues were used as guidelines to carry out observations and conduct interviews with the participants during the second year.

The data from the second year of the observations were analyzed in cycles of inductive coding and deductive mind mapping. The emerging design patterns were mapped into a hierarchical graph to discover possible connections among individual design patterns. While patterns in the upper hierarchy informed about concepts of cross-cultural differences in interaction design, patterns lower in the hierarchy related possible design solutions to those concepts. A few emerging solutions were tested in design scenarios and paper prototypes. A cycle of the process is displayed in Figure 1. These activities produced 14 design patterns, which were evaluated in design pattern workshops with novice and expert designers. After this evaluation, patterns were further developed using a deductive analysis of the interactions between Hong Kong and remote (in this case Korean) participants.

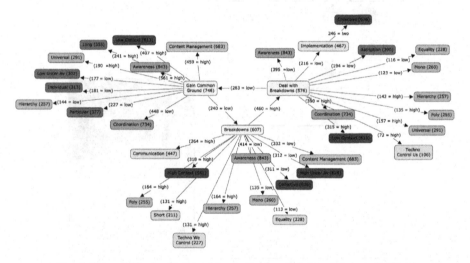

Fig. 2. Network Design Patterns Map to Explore Relations between the Data

For this development, a coding scheme informed by theories from intercultural and cross-cultural communication, and collaborative learning and design was utilized in the third stage of the study (Hofstede 1997), (Gunawardena, et. al. 1997), (Preece 2002). The computer-assisted analysis software package TAMSAnalyzer[TM] and GraphViz were used to view, sort, code and analyze the data. In this deductive analysis code frequencies and co-coding frequencies were used to compare the data, find patterns and explore relations among the patterns. The deductive analysis process was more rigorous than the previously-used, inductive analysis process. Due to the differences in the values of coding frequencies, dominant patterns in the data could be captured without difficulty. Moreover, patterns of stronger and weaker relations were acquired comparing the co-coding frequencies with other codes. This could be mapped and explored visually. The exploration of relations was accomplished mainly through mind mapping activities as shown in Figure 2. In comparison to the previous analysis technique, the emerging patterns were not structured in a predetermined hierarchical map; instead a network map evolved through inherent relations in the data. As a result, 18 design patterns for cross-cultural computer-supported collaborative design learning were written.

Having compared the methodologies for writing design patterns, I will now turn my attention to presenting findings from each stage of the study to demonstrate the evolution of the process of identification and articulation of patterns.

4 Findings

In this long-term ethnographic study, knowledge about intercultural collaborative activities and how they could possibly be supported by the development of interactive systems in the internationalization and localization process evolved gradually. The results of the first stage of the research project produced guidelines for the further study. Measures such as the coordinated use of synchronous and asynchronous communication tools, collocated intensive workshops, online tutorials, and indicators supporting the presence and background information of other participants emerged among others as central topics in intercultural collaborative design learning. Building on these findings, the second stage of this research generated 14 fully articulated patterns and an abundance of pattern beginnings. It is beyond the scope of this paper to present all fully articulated patterns. Nevertheless some design pattern thumbnails are detailed below:

- Blended Collaboration: This pattern suggests blending local and remote teamwork activities seamlessly into one collaboration process.
- Community Workshop: This pattern builds on the previous pattern, recommending running a collocated community workshop to start the project and establish trust through a mix of social and task-related communication.
- Community Portal: The design solution in this pattern advises setting up a virtual community portal to strengthen the relation of the members in the newly established virtual team and the entire learning community.
- Personal Profile: This pattern details the use of a personal page to represent information on each member in the team and community.
- Awareness Indicator: This pattern suggests conveying information about past activities, present states and possible future events of the artifacts used and members represented in the project.

In 2005, the author conducted an evaluative pattern workshop to investigate how the identified interaction design patterns were perceived and used in the design process. A set of interaction design patterns from the first analysis was handed to groups of experienced and novice designers for comment. Some workshop discussion results suggested that while design patterns were instructional, the writing style was slightly too prescriptive. For more experienced practitioners the patterns' contents were perceived as being "too close to the data" and not descriptive, inspiring or revealing enough. Also, the relation of cross-cultural concepts and internationalization and localization of systems was judged to be too weak. To address this problem, the first group of workshop participants suggested the grouping of patterns into domain-specific clusters such as cross-cultural dimensions or technological concepts, whereas the second group proposed less generic pattern names to increase curiosity while browsing the patterns map. After the first workshop I concluded that giving usable problem-solution description was difficult without explaining concepts of cross-cultural and intercultural communication as contextual information. Hence, for the further development of the patterns I decided to use intercultural and cross-cultural communication concepts throughout my patterns to achieve a less, prescriptive more descriptive and informative writing style.

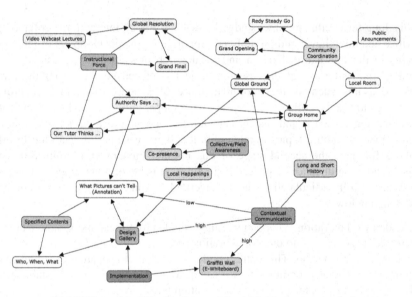

Fig. 3. Hierarchical Design Pattern Map of the Inductive Analysis

Some patterns were followed-up in the second deductive analysis. While a few patterns proved not to be as good as initially thought and were hence disregarded after the second analysis, other findings seemed to propose entirely new patterns that were not identified in the first, inductive analysis. Patterns were grouped around concepts of "Instructional Force", "Community Coordination", "Collective Awareness", "Contextual Communication", "Specified Context" and "Implementation" as presented in Figure 3.

The formerly identified pattern ""Personal Profile" could not be confirmed as a successful solution to represent an individual in collaborating collective cultures and was not further developed. Patterns that evolved from previous ideas were "Grand Opening", which takes up the idea of the previously identified solution of "Community Workshop" and contextualizes the solution within the need for a public display of a strong community in collective cultures. A further development of the "Awareness Indicator" pattern produced the design solution "Co-presence", which builds on the idea of a local team sharing one online chat account, even though the actual individuals who are chatting might change. This addresses strong collective community orientation and suggests the development of co-presence indicators of locally nearby collaborators for one chat account. The following is example of an entirely new pattern that derived from deductive analysis:

PATTERN: "GLOBAL RESOLUTION" ***

Thumbnail: Visually and textually supported synchronous tutorials help in gaining common ground among culturally diverse distributed learning teams and their tutors.

Breakdown: After a local, face-to-face tutorial, students discuss remotely the options for the development of the designs but cannot gain common ground about the direction they want to follow. This might be due to differences in the local and remote tutors' advice or because some students do not want to adopt the tutor opinion without discussing the feasibility. However, since local teams are assessed locally, the local tutors' opinion has a high significance for students. A breakdown between the local and remote teams occurs because the possibly contradictory instructions of the tutors cannot be resolved in the global team. Hence, instructing distributed design-learning teams exclusively in local face-to-face tutorials causes breakdowns in the coordination and decision-making process of the global virtual team.

Forces: Collective and hierarchically oriented cultures have a tendency to follow the tutor's advice without question. Maintaining harmony in the global virtual team is also important. However, if tutors give different advice in separate local tutorials, the harmony in the global virtual team is disturbed and can only be restored if both tutors' views are balanced and a decision is ether imposed from above or negotiated between all participants.

Solution: Establish several synchronous communication sessions over the project period involving local and remote instructors and students of the global team in computer-supported peer tutorials. To schedule at least three sessions, one at the beginning of the project, one interim and a final presentation, is a minimum requirement for establishing common ground within the design learning community. Synchronous peer tutorials involving local and remote tutors and teams are major project milestones and offer full awareness of the team's progress and of the opinions and suggestions of both tutors. Design decisions can be made instantly. Possible conflicts in advice can be discussed on the spot. In textual synchronous communication tutors can refer to representations of the designs stored in the DESIGN GALLERY as references for the discussion. However, video-supported presentations of the teams' designs are especially successful. In the discussion and comparison of local implementations, students and tutors can communicate in reference to shared physical design artifacts. Since sound quality is sometimes a problem, textual synchronous communication can be used to support the visual demonstration of the design artifacts.

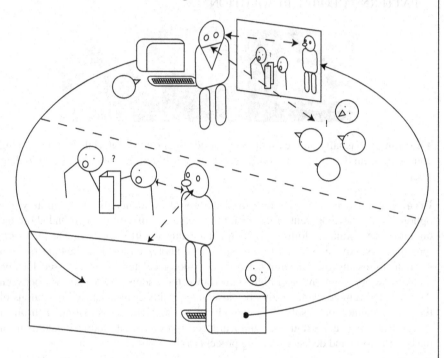

Why: In visual and textual supported synchronous discussion and tutorial sessions, students explain their design implementations in detail by means of sketches and prototypes. The discussants can immediately check and clarify misunderstandings in the design process. Both teams share and explain the design process from their local point of view, which fosters equality among the teams. All attending students and tutors gain awareness and common ground through high contextual communication. Having gained an understanding of the entire picture of the global team's process and progress, tutors can discuss the proposal among themselves and communicate their decisions and instructional advice immediately and in unity to the global team. High contextual and multi modal information about the designs enables tutors to give low contextual, clear and direct advice. Due to the strong hierarchical orientation of the students the advice is taken without objection. This resolves possible uncertainties among the students and restores harmony in collective oriented cultures. While the conclusion of the discussion satisfies achievement-oriented cultures, the involvement of the entire community reassured ascription-oriented cultures that they are aligned with the projects values and goals, too. Therefore, global resolutions given by the tutors may address universal goals and directions, but tutors should refrain from giving concrete tasks for the teams. Even if the teams' abilities and skills do not match the assignment or task, students from collective-oriented cultures would not object to the tutors' instruction, not wanting the tutor to lose face. Afterwards, while discussing the new design direction, teams can clarify new tasks and roles that emerged from the tutorial.

The identification of this and similar patterns was strongly influenced by the deductive coding scheme used in the second analysis. Since it was informed by ideas from collaborative learning and design, collaboration support and intercultural and cross-cultural communication theories, the terminology used to describe the phenomena and scope of the patterns were more consistent. The format of the developed patterns is descriptive and informative rather than prescriptive. The descriptions of breakdowns that cause a design problem and the forces that can resolve this problem suggest efficient design solutions that are embedded in the context of cross-cultural computer-supported design learning. Designers, educators and system developers who use such patterns are not only informed about possible solutions but also about the socio-cultural principles that underlie the solutions.

5 Conclusions

This paper has presented a qualitative methodology for identifying and articulating cross-cultural computer supported design-learning patterns in ethnographic data. It suggests a combination of inductive and deductive data analysis to articulate design patterns that take a cross-cultural context into consideration and aim at informing designers and developers in the process of internationalization and localization of products and systems. In addition to several pattern thumbnails, one fully articulated pattern called "Global Resolution" was presented in this paper. Based on these examples, I suggest that an inductive analysis of ethnographic data to establish pattern categories followed by a deductive analysis of this data to compose patterns with consistent style is an suitable process to identifying and articulating interaction design patterns for cross-cultural computer-supported collaborative design learning.

References

Alexander, C.S.: The timeless way of building. Oxford University Press, New York (1979)
Alostath, J.M., Wright, P.: Pattern Languages towards a tool for cross-cultural user interface design development. In: Proc. of 7th International Conference on Work With Computing Systems (2004)
Baggetun, R., Rusman, E., Poggi, C.: Design Patterns For Collaborative Learning: From Practice To Theory And Back. (Last accessed February 2007), http://dspace.ou.nl/bitstream/1820/302/2/Design+patterns+for+collaborative+learning_edMedia.pdf
Borchers, J., Buschmann, F.: A Pattern Approach to Interaction Design. John Wiley & Sons Inc. New York (2001)

Erickson, T.: Lingua Francas for Design: Sacred Places and Pattern Languages. In: Proc of Designing Interactive Systems DIS 2000, ACM Press, NewYork (2000)

Gamma, E., Helm, R., Johnson, R., Vlissides, J.: Design Patterns - Elements of Reusable Object-Oriented Software. Addison-Wesley, Reading, Mass (1995)

Gunawardena, C.N., Lowe, C.A., Anderson, T.: Analysis of a global online debate and the development of an interaction analysis model for examining social construction of knowledge in computer conferencing. Journal of Educational Computing Research 17(4), 397–431 (1997)

Hofstede, G.: Cultures and Organizations: Software of the Mind. McGraw-Hill, New York (1997)

Mahemoff, M.J., Johnston, L.J.: The Planet Pattern Language for Software Internationalisation. In: the Proc. of Pattern Languages of Program Design (PLOP) (1999)

Mahemoff, M.J., Johnston, L.J., Mahemoff, M.J., Johnston, L. J.: In Proc of Human-Computer Interaction: Interact '01 (2001)

McInerney, P.: UI Patterns: A Workshop for Designers a CHI 2002 Workshop (Last accessed February 2007) (2002), http://www.welie.com/patterns/chi2002-workshop

Meszaros, G., Doble, J.: A Pattern Language for Pattern Writing (Last accessed February 2007), http://webclass.cqu.edu.au/Patterns/Resources/writers/language

Preece, J., Rogers, Y., Sharp, H.: Interaction Design: beyond human computer interaction. John Wiley and Sons, NewYork (2002)

Tidwell, J.: Designing Interfaces: Patterns for Effective Interaction Design. O'Reilly (2005)

Tesch, R.: Qualitative research: analysis types and software tools. Falmer Press, New York (1990)

The Globalization of User Research:
Emerging Trends and Complexities

Robert M. Schumacher and Yiner Ya

User Experience, LLC, Suite 1802, Tower 16, JianwaiSOHO, 39 East Third Ring Zhong Lu,
Chaoyang District, Beijing, China 100022
rschumacher@usercentric.com, yya@usability.cn

Abstract. With the ubiquitous reach of the Internet, products and services that
were once mostly limited to local audiences now have global reach. To support
this shift, user researchers have developed new tactics and refined old methods.
As usability practitioners who frequently perform global usability tests for our
clients, we focus on maintaining the integrity of the research objectives
irrespective of location and culture. From this perspective, we have faced many
challenges in testing both in country and remotely.

Keywords: Global User Research, Multi-Country Testing.

1 Role of Global User Research

The mission of the user research community is to diagnose, understand, analyze,
recommend, convince and guide. To ensure a product will be engaging, useful, and
usable, we serve as the advocate for the users and a trusted adviser to the owners of a
product or service. As products and services gain global audiences, we have raised
our awareness of:

- The need for precision and sensitivity in how we frame research questions when
  conducting user research in different regional markets,
- Potential differences in the user's mental model among regional populations,
- Regional variations in enduser expectations of the product (based on prior
  technology use, integration of technology with daily life, basic consumer and
  business expectations),
- Assumptions we make about user reactions and willingness to share feedback with
  user researchers, and
- Applying insights from regional studies to global products.

Based on our experiences testing for multinational organizations in different
regional markets, we have created a starting list of global user research approaches
that work well when testing in different countries.

2 Developing Strategies for Multi-country Testing

Testing at home in your own lab is easy. Testing in a nearby city is not too difficult.
Testing in four countries 10,000 kilometers from home can be very challenging. Not

N. Aykin (Ed.): Usability and Internationalization, Part II, HCII 2007, LNCS 4560, pp. 238–248, 2007.
© Springer-Verlag Berlin Heidelberg 2007

surprisingly, we have found that building consistency into the user research/ testing procedures and final deliverables is essential.

Our experience is that preparation for global projects requires an additional time investment of 25 - 50% over same-Country user research projects. Aside from obvious challenges like language, other issues include recruiting, facilities and technology, testing protocols, translation, cultural differences, geopolitical issues, time zones, and travel.

- *Recruiting* – Practices differ widely within and across countries. Demographic classifications in one country simply do not align in another country: e.g., job titles, job functions, Internet usage, etc.
- *Facilities and technology* – Facilities below standard in one country might be exceptional in another. Sufficient Internet bandwidth may not always be available. Sometimes the most innocent things can trip you up, like not having the right power converters.
- *Testing script* (a.k.a. Moderator's guide or protocol) – Processes and procedures for development and construction can make unifying test scripts across multiple languages complex.
- *Translators and Interpreters* – Translations can be the source of many problems. However, there are specific things to look out for and many techniques you can implement, such as double translation.
- *Cultural differences in user testing* – User experience research techniques vary from practitioner to practitioner, firm to firm, and country to country.
- *Geopolitical issues* – There are countries where high-End participants would not be comfortable with going to an unfamiliar place (such as a market research facility) because of concerns with the possibility of violence or kidnapping. While this may seem unlikely to us, it is an unfortunate reality for people in areas like Brazil and Mexico, and one that needs to be accounted for.
- *Travel* – Travel must be planned in advance to allow for the coordination of visas and other details, including differences in time zone.

2.1 Elements of a Successful User Research Project

Let's assume that you are a usability practitioner and have a sponsor that is excited because they just received funding for a benchmark study that tests the usability of three mobile devices in four countries: China, Germany, US, and Brazil. The study objective is to determine which device is best overall and develop recommendations for improving the sponsor's product.

But there are a couple more things to consider:

- Mobile phone users must be between 18-29
- Observers will be in three locations (China, US and Germany)
- Desired data should include user preference, user performance and qualitative feedback
- Test analysis and recommendations are needed in six weeks
- Your test findings will drive future product strategy
- Some of the product team's jobs are on the line if one of the devices doesn't "win"

- One more wrinkle: because the design team cannot go to all these places, can you set it up so they can observe remotely?

This may seem like an especially complex research study but international user research projects are almost always, by definition, complicated. With so many issues to consider for global testing, one might easily feel overwhelmed. However, approaching the effort from the perspective of a more general project can help significantly.

Each user research effort has four elements of success:

- Preparation
- Fieldwork
- Analysis & reporting
- Project management

This paper will explore each of these elements in depth.

Preparation. Detailed preparation for international user research is essential; the importance of dedicating adequate time to this part of your project cannot be overemphasized. When testing in multiple countries, often your first step is to seek out experienced, professional usability practitioners who live in the test country and are fluent in the native language. There is no substitute for local knowledge. Not surprisingly, finding experienced usability practitioners is a particular challenge in emerging markets. As we have found, sometimes these practitioners, for a variety of reasons, no longer live in the country and will have to come from other parts as well.

There are two approaches to completing the work: "hands on" and "hands off". The "hands on" approach involves networking, interviewing, seeking and checking references. In short, you need to perform due diligence to ensure that you support your customer's business objectives by engaging the highest quality local firm.

Another approach is more "hands off": simply "farm the work out." Find good partners in each country and trust these partners to do the testing and send the analysis and recommendations to you. While this may work if you know and trust the in-Country partners well, our advice is to resist this temptation. High quality results demand quality control. Quality control means that you should plan on observers from the sponsor and from your own organization to attend sessions in each location. Without these in-Person observers, the quality of moderation may suffer. Budget savings are often not worth poor results.

Once you have retained an experienced, local consulting firm, there are several additional steps to consider:

- Understand the research objectives
- Create a test plan
- Complete the discovery process
- Develop a recruitment screener; recruitment and incentives
- Develop a moderator's guide (script, protocol); run pilot sessions

Understand the research objectives. Take the time to assess sponsor objectives. This is integral to the success of any engagement; you should not conduct user research unless the purpose of the study is clear.

More is at stake with international projects because budgets can become higher, expectations are higher, and goals a bit broader. You must make sure you invest time up-Front to thoroughly understand what the sponsor expects to achieve from testing in order to call the project a success. For example, does the sponsor need more qualitative or quantitative data ("hard numbers"). What will they do with the results? You may also wish to pay special attention to whether or not the study involves a new product or a poorly received product.

Overall, you must investigate why testing is important to the sponsor and how the sponsor intends to use the test findings. It is essential that your research methods be properly aligned with these sponsor objectives.

Create a test plan. A test plan identifies all of the points of the testing, including:

- Test objectives
- Research design
- Participant screener(s)
- Detailed description of the moderation procedures, including prompts for follow-up questions when participants succeed or do not succeed during each usability task or activity (if relevant)
- Data collection methods
- Recording details
- Expected means of presenting/reporting results and analysis.

Test plans are the key to successful planning and preparation. They confirm that you and the sponsor are properly aligned and also help ensure that outcomes will be met.

Complete the discovery process. 'Discovery' is a generic term for learning as much background information as you can about the project, stakeholders, technology and budget. Specifically, you should explore the sponsor's motivation for this user research project, identify and understand any product manuals or marketing materials, and determine which sponsor group(s) may be involved and their exact role is in the study. To give some perspective, we have a list of over 100 questions that we might ask during the scoping and discovery process for any given project.

Discovery also applies to learning about the device, application or site. You may need to ask questions such as, "When will prototypes be ready?" "What are our contingency plans if the prototype is are not ready in time for the study?" "Will a prototype be available offline?" (for Web-based user interfaces.) "How do you accomplish tasks in multiple languages?"

Develop a recruitment screener; recruitment and incentives. You will need to recruit participants for your study and pay some form of incentive for participation in the project. Depending on the nature of the study, this can be a complicated process; recruitment practices can often differ widely from country to country.

Some of the issues and examples you should explore include: "What is the 'show rate' in each country?" "Is the sponsor firm on the quota? If so, what do you do when you're short on recruits?" "Should 'extras' or 'floaters' be scheduled? If so, how many?"

Recruiting is usually completed by a third party and thus out of the direct control of the local practitioner – this is why the recruiting process has to be monitored very closely; two degrees of separation does not allow one to sleep well at night. Requirements should be obtained as soon as possible so that recruitment can be launched early during a study's timeline. Details, such as job titles, descriptions and tasks (often provided by the sponsor) don't always match the real-World conditions in the particular market that you intend to test in. This is why it is essential to allow extra time for recruitment.

And if another language is involved, you must make preparations to ensure the screener is well translated. Be sure to take the time to closely review recruiting lists to check that they are as accurate as possible. It is also a good practice is to arrange for the translated screener to be reverse-Translated to verify its accuracy to the original screener.

Even if you feel that you are prepared for every possibility, you should still make sure the sponsor understands all risks. Unexpected circumstances often arise in unfamiliar settings. In a supplier position, the first time we worked for one Asian client we were surprised that they expected to have a list of "applicants" (recruits) from which they could choose which participants we should solicit. This was a serious disconnect in assumptions and cultural practices – from which we all recovered, but not without some last-Minute scrambling.

The nature and value of incentives can differ widely from country to country. Carefully determine the proper incentive for a given location and user group. In some countries such as Sweden and France, paying cash over a certain amount is very difficult due to tax regulations. Also, to certain high-End user groups, cash would be considered insulting – they have all they need. Thus, offering a nice bottle of wine or an iPod may be a more intriguing alternative.

The best approach when completing recruitment is to know exactly where you can be flexible, yet remain true to the research objectives. It is also crucial that you know the incidence rate (estimated percentage of your target participant in the general population) before you provide a quote to the sponsor. For example, low-Incidence participants are harder to find and require more effort to recruit, so recruitment costs would most likely be higher. Not having yet learned this lesson, we quoted a price to the sponsor based on our best guess as to the incidence rate (because we were familiar with the high incidence rate of usage of this product in our country). We soon discovered that the incidence rate in this Asian city was 16 – not 16%, but 16 people! We paid a very large sum of money to obtain one recruit.

Develop a moderator's guide; run pilot sessions. The moderator's guide ties the business objectives to the operational elements (the tasks). It must be carefully worded and meticulously translated because the moderator will be preparing for the user research sessions and is likely to be reading directly from the guide. To ensure an accurate translation, use simple, high-Frequency words when writing the original script. Additionally, consider that reviewing the guide is typically the only way an interpreter can prepare in advance. The interpreter may want to read the guide in both the test language and the source language.[1]

---

[1] We use "translator" as one who transcribes the written word from one language to another. An "interpreter" is one who hears the native language spoken during a session and produces the target language verbally.

It is very important to localize the moderator's guide for language and cultural issues. If another language is used, be sure to hire an experienced, native translator and use reverse translation (i.e. translate the translated script back to the native language).

Once the screener is launched and the guide is prepared, schedule and run at least one or two pilot sessions. These sessions, which take place in advance of the "official" sessions, will uncover any "residual" issues and help confirm timings and recording details. It is a precaution that is well worth the additional investment in time and effort.

Fieldwork. 'Fieldwork' refers to the actual testing. Steps that may seem fairly straightforward under normal user research parameters need to be cautiously reviewed for an international effort. The elements of fieldwork include:

- Moderation
- Moderation and cultural differences
- Locations, Facilities and Technology
- Interpreters
- Data Collection
- Remote Observation
- Remote Testing

Moderation. There are many questions surrounding the cultural and language skills of user testing moderators. Therefore, you must consider such questions as who should moderate – native speakers only? Or are fluent, non-native speakers acceptable? How do you best address not only issues of language, but culture as well? If the goal is to make the participant as comfortable as possible (so that they will be more forthcoming with their comments) qualities of the moderator make a difference. There are certain word choices and language usage patterns that can introduce subtle artifacts into testing. Thus, we favor using moderators who are as culturally similar as possible to the participants. This is a point of professional discussion, however; for example, we have seen instances where nationality issues argue against Americans moderating even as close to home as Canada.

There are other logistical details to consider when planning the moderation. For instance, are one- or two-person test teams more beneficial? How many sessions can the moderator reasonably complete per day (without "burning out")? What should the schedule look like for each day (to ensure sufficient spacing between each session)?

Once these details are in place, there are some additional steps you can take to make sure the sessions run smoothly.

- Mention the task objective (the study-Related goal of each task) next to each task/question in the script to guide the moderator
- List the data that needs to captured/written down by the moderator and the format it should be written in
- If the data is limited to yes/no or other constrained data (ratings on a scale from 1 to 7, for example), simply list these data with the instructions "Circle One"
- Provide the moderator with the test plan and moderator's guide, but also provide detailed one-on-one training.

- Finally, as mentioned above, schedule one or two pilot sessions to train local moderators before the actual test. Also allow time to debrief after the initial sessions at the end of each day, and upon completion of the fieldwork.

Moderation and cultural differences. When you prepare for multi-Country testing, one of the most important steps is to acknowledge differences in how testing is conducted across borders. As mentioned previously, user experience research techniques vary from practitioner to practitioner, firm to firm and country to country. Some moderators closely follow the script, while other moderators are more flexible and adapt the order of the tasks and questions to the flow of each particular session.

Techniques used in another country may be quite different from what your team considers to be standard procedures. It is important to maintain the integrity of your objectives while remaining appreciative of cultural standards. It may also be valuable to consult the sponsor about their own perspective on how to address these issues.

Plan for at least one full day ahead of time to meet and brief the local staff and set up technology; plan two days ahead if you require an interpreter.

Location, Facilities and Technology. One of the biggest sources of potential discomfort when organizing a global project is that the facilities are often unfamiliar to the practitioner. Even with pictures, you usually cannot get a true sense of the facility's quality unless you (or a trusted colleague) have tested there before.

Some important considerations include: What are the sponsor expectations (for location, distance from hotels, etc)? What properties does the facility need to have? (Does it need to have a one-Way mirror, for example? Wifi?)

Your local practitioner should recommend a high-Quality research facility. If this is not possible, sources like the Human-Computer Interaction Resource Network (HCIRN), Quirk's or the Society for Technical Communication (STC) may be able to provide information.

You will also need to know how many participants and sponsors or observers will be arriving and whether or not they will require access to public transportation. It will also be necessary know how early or late the sessions will be taking place. (Beyond the local "business hours," there may be extra fees for opening the facility or leaving late.) If any of the observers or guests has dietary restrictions, you will need to mention this to the facility (especially important when arranging for catering).

When booking a facility, it is also best to ask for floor plans, a list of available technology, and pictures in advance. It is also advisable to obtain a list of nearby business-Grade hotels.

Technical requirements. Sponsors usually expect a flawless recording of the sessions with dual-Channel audio (native + translated). These requirements are not always easy to meet. You will need to determine how the facility records sessions, what recording software is used (Morae, VNC or a special request from the sponsor) and whether the recording should be in analog or digital format. It is also important to consider the video format – PAL, SECAM or NTSC. Also, you will need to determine in advance whether the facility has the technology you need; otherwise you will need to provide the equipment, which requires logistical planning all its own.

There are additional miscellaneous details to consider such as Internet connection and power setup. Will you need the Internet for testing, sponsor access to email and live streaming of the sessions for remote observers (see below)? If so, what kind of bandwidth does the facility have?

Power requirements can also differ from country to country. You will need to find out if the local power is 110 volts or 220 volts. Depending on the answer, you may need to take a transformer to make sure your equipment works. But this is not always easy – really researching power requirements is important. We learned right before a trip to test in a South American city that part of the city is supplied with 110v, while other parts have 220v. Which did our facility have? We had to ask. In places like India, where power blackouts are still sometimes common, it makes sense to check if the facility has a backup power generator. (Some of the facilities on corporate campuses may have access to more than one generator.) Plug adapters are also very different from location to location.

Once you have determined what equipment you will need to provide yourself and ship to the test location, you will need to check on the customs regulations for that destination. We routinely use high-Quality wireless audio microphones during testing. While planning testing in Beijing, we discovered that it is expressly prohibited to bring these into the country; we had to move to "Plan B". Being deprived of property like this at the border can have devastating impacts. To give a more extreme example, one client of ours recently had their lab held up in US customs *for months*.

Interpreters and Translators. Proper data collection for user research requires the users to think out loud. This means that it is impossible to accurately collect good data if the session is "lost in translation". Therefore, the highest quality translation is required. Do not try to save money by hiring inexpensive interpreters. Professional simultaneous interpreters, like those used in market research, technical conferences, or high-Level business negotiations are an absolute requirement.

In addition to the interpreter's quality, time and logistics of translation are also factors. When arranging the translation, be sure to send the moderator's guide in advance of the study and take the time to explain the general goal of user testing and the specific goals of each usability task to the interpreter.

Interpreters should to be positioned so that they can see the participant's face in order to note gestures and expressions. The length of the language is also important to consider in advance. For example, translating from English into German will require more time than translating from German to English. Also, how many observers will there be listening live to each language? Will they need to be physically separated? Paying attention to practical matters such as these is essential for the translations – and the data for that location– to have value to the sponsor.

Data Collection. The process of data collection is as important as any other part of the user research process. Every effort should be made to ensure that data collection/notation is as easy as possible for all notetakers and moderators. When possible, provide tools like checklists and pre-populated forms to enhance accuracy and efficiency. These items can then be turned into a data collection worksheet (e.g. in Excel) and the data notetakers can be trained to record and look for the required data. Check that the data are recorded properly both at the beginning of the study and after each session. If necessary, debrief the moderators between sessions and remind them to consistently take notes by following the moderator's guide.

Remote Observation. It is now possible to routinely stream usability testing sessions from anywhere in the world to remote observers. About half of the project work we do now requires streaming of sessions. Remote observation is practical because it reduces costs and the need for travel. Remote observers are often connected in real-Time to the test site via tools like instant messenger and can have an effective real-Time hand in test execution. Team members can then join for one or all remote sessions, as their schedules allow. (However, the majority of sponsors justifiably continue to send at least one in-Person observer.)

The tools and knowledge necessary for streaming have in the past been formidable, but they are becoming increasingly approachable. Streaming occasionally requires knowledge of network infrastructure. It must to be planned in advance because high bandwidth network administrators may not allow it, observers must have updated technology, and it can often be difficult to stream from a remote site.

A simple solution for streaming is Windows Media™ Encoder v9 – it has the capability to stream the observing laptop's screen live over the network or even across the Internet. Products like LiveMeeting, WebEx, GoToMeeting, etc. are also available to connect the test (or observation) computer to the Internet. VoIP options like Skype can then be used to inexpensively carry the audio. There are many resources available to assist you on the Internet.

Although testing the solution in advance with the sponsor will help identify obstacles, remote observation should only be offered to sponsors on a "best efforts" basis because you will not have control beyond the local facility.

Analysis and Reporting. During analysis and reporting, you will need to focus on the style of the report and the nature of the session videos. Reporting is based on the results and analysis of the fieldwork's findings. It is intended to "tell a story" and speak directly to the sponsor's objectives.

During "Discovery", you should have determined the number of reports needed, the level of detail required ("top-Line"/key findings versus a full report), the key questions of interest to stakeholders, and the target audience for the report (marketing, engineers, senior executives). When identifying the audience, do not forget to consider if the report will need to be in multiple languages.

Ideally, the report should not be too formal; it should be approachable by all readers and be "actionable". Clients should have a clear idea of what to do when they are finished reviewing it. However, you do not want to overwhelm the reader with too many recommendations or details – it is important to balance how much can actually be consumed or applied. To address this concern, try assigning priorities to the issues raised. And remember not to just be a critic – be sure to mention what worked well.

Because you have gone to the trouble of recording the sessions, you need to consider how the sponsor will make best use of the video. Will the sponsor require highlight videos or just a complete video of the sessions? (Highlight videos are more expensive because they must be edited.) What language(s) should the video include? Should there be subtitles or dubbing? Finally, you will need to consider how the video should be delivered – online (via file delivery services or an FTP server), via

CD/DVD or via iPod? The answers to these questions will determine which tools you use to assist you in the video production.

One final note: we have experienced mixed results in reporting when local staff members are asked to write test reports. There are obvious issues of language, but local staff members simply do not have the knowledge of the nuances of the sponsor, test plan, or politics. For this reason, we almost always send staff to observe in-Country testing to ensure consistency and first-Hand knowledge. While this practice is more expensive, it is a trade-off that is almost always worth the cost. We also have regular debrief sessions with local partners to ensure we completely understand the issues at hand; but ultimately, we are accountable for the research. Aside from the data interpretation issues, this also sidesteps the need to piece together multiple sources of data to create the report.

Project Management and Budgeting. Effective project management requires determining partners and/or vendors, staffing, and finalizing schedules and budgets. It is impossible to over-Prepare for multi-Country testing, so allocate as much time as you can to this step. You can eliminate up to 90% of your logistics-Related frustrations through careful planning.

Partners and Vendors. You will need to identify partners, vendors and staff well in advance of the study's formal start. The skills of the people you engage should support the business objectives of the project.

Finding vendors is sometimes challenging and sometimes easy. If you need assistance, there are several sources you can turn to including colleagues, sponsors and resource networks. Resources such as the Usability Professionals Association (UPA), UPA China, HCIRN, STC, the Human Factors and Ergonomics Society (HFES), and search engines can all be quite beneficial.

Make sure the vendor you hire is a business-Grade provider with a known professional history. This can be challenging to determine from a distance, but there are a few steps you can take to assess quality. First, you should check references and ask for names and CVs for the vendor's staff. Next, ask about experience with recent sponsors, specifically with foreign sponsors.

Staffing. Your sponsors will want a project leader who understands usability (preferably one who is a practitioner outright) and who has experience with project management supervising the study; often, many people have to be involved in large studies. To reassure the sponsor, be sure to choose a project leader who can easily travel and who has some experience with international efforts – preferably one who is familiar with some of the languages involved.

There is also a fair amount of coordination that is necessary for this stage of the process. For example, you will need to decide whether one person will go to all the sites or if different people will go to different sites. If you select different people to go, then you will need to make certain that the entire local team is trained to ensure consistency and team coherence.

Scheduling. Creating and maintaining an organized schedule will help avoid challenges and mistakes. This will also help you manage sponsor expectations.

Projects should primarily be scheduled based on the availability of fieldwork and facilities. However, you may also need to schedule them based on:

- Sponsor due date
- Prototype availability
- Resource availability

When scheduling multi-Country tests, it is also important to find out from the local usability vendor whether testing is encouraged or discouraged on the weekends and evenings. Also keep an eye on national holidays, which can extend for more than a couple of days depending on the location.

Finally, plan accordingly for jet lag and allow extra time on both ends of travel.

Budgeting. Budgeting is not all about money. It is also about allocating human and physical resources. Be warned that other countries may approach budgeting differently. For example, in some countries it is standard practice to provide an initial (non-fixed) estimate and later provide a final bill once work has been completed (this can create unwelcome surprises). It is also common for different payment terms to be in place.

The best practice is to over-Budget for test-Related resources during a multi-Country test. Because there are always hidden costs (such as visas), it is better to be on the generous side. Currency fluctuations can also have measurable budget impacts. In the end, be aware that agreements are largely built around trust between companies, and are therefore legally difficult to enforce. Working with vendors you trust (or can learn to trust) is certainly preferred.

3 Conclusion

Global organizations are increasingly aware that their products must be both usable and appealing to international audiences to be successful. Recent experiences indicate that global user research poses certain challenges with regard to both logistics and the actual process of user research. To address these challenges, it is imperative you allocate sufficient time to plan not only for your own team members, but also for arranging local usability vendors, facilities, and translators. If you have a goal with your first multi-Country study, it should be to over-Plan.

When testing in different countries, you must ensure that after having been adapted to other cultures and languages, your study is still:

- Asking the same questions,
- Getting at the same type of data, and
- True to the sponsor's objectives.

As the amount of international user research grows, we look forward to a growing collective wisdom on global usability testing, where we share resources, strategies and approaches for adapting to changing regional environments and sponsor needs.

Chinese Web Browser Design Utilising Cultural Icons

Siu-Tsen Shen[1], Stephen D. Prior[2], Kuen-Meau Chen[3], and Man-Lai You[4]

[1] Department of Multimedia Design, National Formosa University,
64 Wen-Hua Rd, Hu-Wei 63208, Taiwan
stshen@nfu.edu.tw
[2] Department of Product Design and Engineering, Middlesex University,
Trent Park Campus, London N14 4YZ, United Kingdom
[3] Visualization & Interactive Multimedia Lab, Natl. Centre for High Speed Computing,
Hsin-chu Science Park, Taiwan
[4] Department of Industrial Design, National Yunlin University of Science & Technology,
Dou-liu City, Yunlin, Taiwan

Abstract. This study investigates the appropriateness and effectiveness of the design of icons for a Chinese web browser. Web browser developments are outlined, together with the future potential growth of Chinese internet users. The findings of the study show that the subjects shown icons and text, had higher recognition rates, and had higher satisfaction ratings. Furthermore, some evidence points to a gender bias in favour of males in terms of recognition and females in terms of satisfaction. Future work is suggested in terms of refining the web browser icons and exploring the usability of colour and 3D effects.

Keywords: Web browser, Icon design, Chinese users, Metaphor, GUI.

1 Introduction

With the advent of information technology and global networking, graphical user interfaces (GUIs), which include interactive images and animation, have opened a new dimension for visual language and transformed our whole symbolic system into a much more complex one.

A repertoire of computer-generated graphical symbols is not restricted to the desktop of computers but extensively applied to the interface of IT appliances, e.g. The interface of mobile phones display small iconic buttons, which offer complex function directories such as a personal phone book, settings, text and voice messages [1].

On the one hand, that brings a great convenience to individual and global communication; on the other hand, it reflects great cultural and linguistic differences in the degree of comprehensibility of an interface. To avoid iconic ambiguity and misinterpretation it seems that standardisation is the solution; however, this will require learning and adaptation. That is to say, numerous cultural-oriented graphical symbols have to be traded for universal standardisation. Therefore, this has inevitability led to a loss of cultural and individual identity.

N. Aykin (Ed.): Usability and Internationalization, Part II, HCII 2007, LNCS 4560, pp. 249–258, 2007.
© Springer-Verlag Berlin Heidelberg 2007

1.1 Iconisation Trends

Icons have increasingly been used for the communication of information or instructions on labels, packaging, in manuals and interfaces. Many such icons have become standardised and carry a silent authority that is rarely questioned [2]. The International Standards Organisation is responsible for the standardisation of icons and signs that are applied to product interfaces [3].

Certain disadvantages of the sole use of icons may include usability problems, metaphor breakdown, direct manipulation, and user difficulties in maintaining a suitable directory system. The major arguments are that standardisation may not be the only permanent solution, and the inconsistent design of visual representations across different media has complicated interface interaction and navigation. On the other hand, the advantages of using icons in interface design over text, is enormous.

1.2 Advantages of Visual Representations

Research exists to show that icons and symbols are more efficient and effective in communications. For example, Walker et al. [4] stated that symbols and signs are more easily interpreted and learned, because of their greater perceptual simplicity. Rogers and Osborne [5] found that people tend to crystallise abstract concepts in terms of concrete symbols that can be visually represented. Therefore graphic symbols are often considered as a potential universal means of communication, which can convey certain types of information more directly and immediately than words [6].

1.3 Disadvantages of Visual Representations

Hutchins, Hollan and Norman [7] proposed the term "articulatory directness", that is the relationship between the meanings of expressions and their physical form. If the visual representation is more close to the intended meaning, then the articulatory distance becomes shorter.

Choong and Salvendy [8] examined the impacts of cultural differences in cognitive abilities between American and Chinese users in terms of their performance time and errors with three different icon displays, i.e. pictorial icons only, verbal icons only and combined modes of both pictorial and verbal elements. Their results indicated that it is better to design a combined presentation mode for facilitating better initial performance. Furthermore, American subjects had better verbal ability with alphanumeric icon displays, whereas Chinese subjects had better visual distinction ability with pictorial icon displays, if both of subjects are not provided with combined modes.

Shneiderman [9] pointed out some problems within direct manipulation. Direct manipulation usually requires graphical representations, which are not suitable for all tasks. Limited screen space leaves valuable information off screen and needs scrolling and multiple actions. Users have to learn the meaning of visual representation (icons) and require more learning time than with a word.

User Directory Problems. A hierarchical management organisation of icons is supposed to help users manage their daily files and easily trace them. Horton [10] stated that users prefer a hierarchical to a linear organisation of menus. They make fewer errors in a hierarchical structure because it creates a clearer mental map. In fact, people deal with massive information daily and it requires a good arrangement of their personal files in their system.

2 The Development of Web Browsers

Web browsers, such as Netscape Navigator, Mozilla, Konqueror, Microsoft Internet Explorer and Apple's Safari, are software applications which enhance the user's experience of interacting with computers.

The first web browser was the generic WWW (later named Nexus) introduced in December 1990 by Tim Berners-Lee [11]. Since its inception, there have been at least 29 different web browser packages available, most of which have been free. The most popular of these have been Netscape Navigator (c.1994) and Internet Explorer (85% market share worldwide) (c.1995) for the PC, and Safari (c.2003) for the Mac.

The graphical user interface, including the toolbars, menu bars and scrollbars with which the user is familiar, is applied to all Web browsers. By double-clicking on the iconic buttons on the web desktop, users can surf through web pages, which connect to the URL, HTTP supports the transmission between the web server and web browser, and HTML/XML that displays hypertext or hypermedia links. In terms of the Web metaphor there are aesthetic similarities between all web browsers, which indicate certain functions on the toolbar such as the Back, Forward, Stop, Refresh and Home icons (see Fig. 1).

Fig. 1. Internet Explorer web browser interface for the Macintosh Version 5.2

From the latest Macintosh OS X and Windows XP there appears to be a trend of integrating software and operating system in the evolution of the interface. The *Leopard* interface of the Apple Macintosh operating system and *Vista* interface of the Microsoft Windows XP operating system have some similarities, i.e. the 3D icons which are smooth, translucent, colourful and big, a range of customisation for desktop management and multimedia internet tools. In particular, the display of the desktop has developed into a browser like-window.

2.1 The Maxthon Web Browser

Frustrated by censorship in search engines, web surfers in China have been turning to a little known company, Maxthon, based in Beijing. So far 60 million people have downloaded the browser since its launch in 2003. It has been stated that 14% of Chinese users have used the browser and 17% employs it for web searching through

Baidu (the largest search engine in China) [12]. The reasons for its success are its customizable and innovative features, fast speed and the fact that it is built on top of the IE engine.

The recently published 18th statistical survey report – 'Internet Development in China' (July 2006), states that there are approximately 54.50 million computer hosts and 123 million Internet users in China. This only amounts to a penetration rate of 9.4% of the population [13]. Even with this low rate, China is second only to the USA (205 million) in terms of the number of Internet users. The number of internet users in China has grown by 400% during the period (2000-2005) [14], and If as predicted, China continues to grow at a conservative estimate of 10% per annum, it will overtake the USA in 2010 and approach saturation (≈66% penetration) by 2018. At this point China will have 900 million internet users.

According to the July 2006 report from the Taiwanese Network Information Centre there was approximately 15 million Internet users (68% penetration) in Taiwan. 81% of the population uses ADSL to access the Internet and the most frequent use was for Web browsing (71%) [15].

However, most of the existing web browsers have been developed in Europe and the USA, and not all of them could support Chinese text (Simplified and Traditional) [11]. Brandon [16] has suggested that a majority of internet users primarily speak languages other than English, Sun [17] has suggested that this could be as high as 70%. It has also been reported that 75% of users in China and Korea prefer content in their own languages [18].

3   What Makes a Good Web Browser Icon?

Over the years there have been many suggestions and design guidelines for what constitutes good usability, however few have focussed on the subject of what would make a good web icon [19, 20].

Howell and Fuchs [21] were one of the first to put forward the criteria for correct recognition of symbols. These being grouped into categories: *identifiable* (60-100%), *medium* (30-60%) and *vague* (0-30%). According to the International Standards Organisation (ISO) icon recognition rates should be at least 67% to achieve acceptability [22].

Lindberg and Nasanen [23] state that processing of visual information involves locating the correct piece of information, recognising the physical object and understanding what it means in the current context of use. According to Barr et al [24], who used the semiotic approach to compare two sets of icons for the same functions within the Mozilla and IE web browsers:

"...most of the icons utilised by the two browsers are symbolic signs. This is likely because there is no dominant metaphor for the internet, and thus no real-world phenomenon to create iconic and indexical icon forms."

Other researchers [25] have investigated the role of aging in icon recognition stating that search performance deteriorates with age and the size of icons. Sung and Hu [26] state that the recall-precision measure was almost perfect for 'plant' icons in a test of effectiveness.

The growth and importance of worldwide e-commerce is further driving the need for cross-cultural research into iconic interfaces [27-29].

4 Method

The test website consisted of the design of a Chinese Operating System (COS) environment, developed to act as an alternative to the desktop metaphor, involving the 'Garden' as an overarching metaphor. The COS was designed to be culturally rich, and have both visual and aural stimuli.

The study investigated the recognition and acceptance of intuitive icons for the web browser element of the Garden COS. The testing involved online evaluation, screen recording and user feedback.

4.1 Participants

The study was conducted in Taiwan during June 2006 and involved 20 participants (60% male, 40% female) who were recruited from 1st and 2nd year BA Multimedia Design students studying at the National Formosa University. The ages ranged from 18-31 yrs, the mean age being 20 yrs. Participants were not paid or given extra credit for joining this experiment.

4.2 Tasks

The testing was conducted in two phases. Phase I involved a pre-experiment (online) questionnaire to determine the participant's recognition of a series of eight Chinese localised web browser icons in monochrome (see Fig. 2).

Fig. 2. Chinese web browser icons

The choice of monochrome relates to the work of Horton [10] who suggests that icons should first be made in B&W, and that colour be added to make them work better.

Phase II consisted of dividing the participants into two groups A and B. Group A consisted of 7 males and 3 females (not by design), whereas group B consisted of 5 males and 5 females. Group A were given the task of experiencing the Garden COS (including browser) icons without any text labels, for 3-5 min. Group B were given the task of experiencing the Garden COS (including browser) icons with text labels, for 3-5 min. Both groups were then asked to perform various tasks within the COS and browser Favourites environment, which included creating new folders and files.

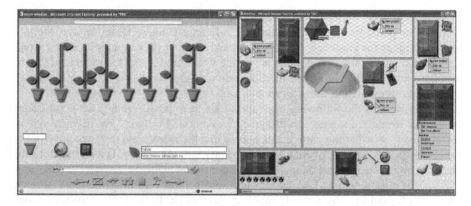

Fig. 3. Views of the File Manager and Chinese Operating System Windows

4.3 Experiment Rationale and Hypotheses

The rationale behind the experimental tasks listed in 4.2, were derived from various research hypotheses and findings [8, 20, 30, 31].

In brief, the evaluation sought to test out four hypotheses:

H1 - The web browser icons are easily recognisable (intuitive) without text.
H2 - There will be a difference in user recognition and satisfaction between groups shown icons and those shown icons with text – the latter group will perform better.
H3 - There will be no difference between the genders in each of the groups.
H4 - Chinese users will appreciate the culturally rich web content.

5 Results and Discussion

With reference to the results and analysis of the pre-experiment questionnaire it can be stated that four of the web browser icons were easily recognised and associated with their correct functions, as per Howell's criteria. The Home icon had the highest success rate (93%), followed closely by the Forward icon with 91%, the Back icon with 88% and the Stop icon with 76% (identifiable).

Two icons were partially recognised (medium); these were the Search icon with 31%, and the Go/Visit icon with 29%. The last two icons were not well recognised at all (vague), these being the Refresh icon with 19% and finally the Favourite icon with only 12%.

In general terms, Group B (icons and text) performed better than Group A (icons only) by 8% points, thus confirming hypothesis H2. It was also interesting to note that in both groups the male participants outperformed the female participants by 2% points, this is too small a margin to confirm hypothesis H3, but it is an interesting result none the less. In summary, hypothesis H1 was not confirmed, with only 50% of the icons being clearly identified by Group A (icons only).

With reference to the main questionnaire, the first two questions referred to whether the participants were familiar with a famous Chinese fable about a frog in a well (metaphor for knowledge acquisition), and whether they thought that this visual representation was appropriate for starting the web browser. All the participants were familiar with the fable, however, there was mixed agreement as to whether the use of this visual representation was appropriate.

The answers to the following eight questions were based on the five point Likert Scale (1 = strongly disagree, 2 = disagree, 3 = neutral, 4 = agree, 5 = strongly agree), and related to whether the participants agreed that the icons were representative of the functions. In this context, overall the participants agreed (mean ≈ 4) with the icons for Back, Forward, Home and Stop. This was consistent with the answers for the pre-experiment questionnaire. The participants were neutral regarding the Go/Visit icon (mean 3.14), and broadly neutral regarding the Search, Refresh and Favourite icons (mean 2.69). It is also interesting to note that overall the male participants from Groups A and B (SD=0.84) had much higher mean standard deviations than the female participants from Groups A and B (SD=0.50), thus indicating their greater levels of disagreement between participants. The answers to questions 6 & 8 produced the highest mean standard deviations (0.85 & 0.81), however, it is noted that these are less than unity, and therefore acceptable.

Overall, both groups could be classified as having a preference between neutral and agree, with the females (mean 3.55) slightly higher than the males (mean 3.37).

Questions 11 and 12 (multiple parts) related to tasks within the browser favourites section. With regards to Question 11, both groups were able to complete the tasks successfully within a 71-95% range. The result of Question 12 to 12.2 indicated that both groups would prefer to interact with icons and text (89%), followed by icons-only (45%), and then text-only (17%). This supports hypothesis H2, and is in agreement with the results of Choong and Salvendy [8] and Horton [20].

The overall satisfaction of the participants was broadly neutral to agree (mean 3.32).

Question 13 and 14 enabled the participants to give written feedback on the overall advantages and disadvantages of the Chinese web browser interface design in terms of usability. The written feedback for Question 13 was entirely positive with the use of words such as creative and meaningful from Group A and words such as interesting, innovative and fresh from Group B, which supports hypothesis H4. They also commented on the fact that they liked the 'computer game' feel of the interface design. The written feedback from Question 14 highlighted the weakness of visual representation using icons-only.

6   Conclusions

At the rate that China's Internet community is expanding, it will overtake the USA to become the largest Internet user base in the world by 2010. By 2018, there is estimated to have over 900 million Internet users. Of the currently available web browsers, very few have found favour amongst Chinese users. The leader amongst these is Maxthon browser.

The success of a Chinese web browser will depend on iconic appropriateness, effectiveness and cultural richness. The GUI should be both intuitive and easy to navigate. With the rapid growth of the use of the Internet, designers need to be culturally-sensitive to the potential of culturally-specific users [32].

The results of this study support three general conclusions. Firstly, four of the icons were clearly identified by both groups. However, there is a lack of satisfaction with the other four icons, especially the Favourite and Refresh. Therefore, it is essential to re-think these icons and reinforce their visual look, perhaps by using colour, shade, outline, etc. Secondly, most participants ignored the icons of the web browser in the bottom of the screen, when trying to complete their tasks. This indicated that there is a need to improve the layout of the screen for tracking users' eye attention. Thirdly, within the Favourites function, most participants spent time on distinguishing the difference between the Fire icon (Delete) and the Compost Heap icon (Temporary Save) during the testing. This showed that there is a need to rethink these icons.

Furthermore, most participants tend to click the mouse once, rather than twice, in order to evoke the actions of the icons. This suggested that we need to strengthen the icon's functionality. Moreover, the results indicated that the participants had a preference between neutral and agree (3.32).

In addition, under the pressure of the limited time (3-5 minutes) for users to complete the task, it might have affected their performance to some extent and created unexpected errors. The use of young subjects also has implications, in terms of their experience of computing and good eyesight.

In their study, Cheng and Patterson [33] found that many commercial icons used on e-business websites had extremely low recognition rates. Although selected from actual websites, certain icons did not appear to make any sense at all to the subjects of their study. Interestingly, it was found that some icons were used for different functions on different websites.

The results of this small-scale study provide a solid foundation for future development of a Chinese web browser, based on the methodology of Culture-Centred Design. More experimental settings are currently being developed, such as further questionnaires of icon recognition, consistency of 2D or 3D visual icons, user performance and preference, and 3D navigation orientation (see below).

Fig. 4. Developmental Images of the 3D Chinese Web Browser

References

1. Ben, C.: Notes from China: Handset design, in Interactions, pp. 38–39 (2006)
2. Evamy, M.: World without words, London: Laurence King (2003)
3. ISO Draft International Standard (DIS) 9241-11: Ergonomic Requirements for office work with visual display terminals, Part II: Guidance on Usability, International Standards Organisation: Geneva, Switzerland (1997)
4. Walker, R.E., Nicolay, R.C., Stearns, C.R.: Comparative accuracy of recognising American and international road signs. Journal of Applied Psychology 49, 322–325 (1965)
5. Rogers, Y., Osborne, D.J.: Pictorial communication of abstract verbs in relation to human-computer interaction. British Journal of Psychology 78, 99–112 (1987)
6. Tzeng, C.S., Trung, N.T., Rieber, R.W.: Cross-cultural comparisons on psychosemantics of icons and graphics. International Journal of Psychology 25(1), 77–97 (1990)
7. Hutchins, E.L., Hollan, J.D., Norman, D.A.: Direct Manipulation Interfaces, in User centered system design: new perspectives on human-computer interaction, D.A.D. In: Norman, S.W. (ed.) Hollan, J, Hillsdale, N.J. London, pp. 87–124. Lawrence Erlbaum Associates, Mahwah (1986)
8. Choong, Y.Y., Salvendy, G.: Design of Icons for use by Chinese in Mainland China. Interacting with Computers, Elsevier Science B.V., 9(4), 417–430 (1998)
9. Shneiderman, B.: Designing the user interface: strategies for effective human–computer interaction [4] of plates, 2nd edn. p. 573. Addison-Wesley, Reading (1992)
10. Horton, W.K.: Designing and writing online documentation: help files to hypertext, vol. xii, p. 371. Wiley, New York (1990)
11. Wikipedia, Comparison of Web broswers, Wikipedia (2006)
12. Olsen, S.: Mexthon: China's hip browser. In: CNET News.com (2006)
13. CNNIC, Statistical Survey Report on the Internet Development of China, China Internet Network Information Centre (2006)
14. Miniwatts, Internet World Stats, Miniwatts International Inc (2006)
15. TWNIC, The report of the use of broadband networting in Tainwan July 2006, TWNIC (2006)
16. Brandon, D.: Localization of web content. Journal of Computing in Small Colleges 17(2), 345–358 (2001)
17. Sun, H.: Building a culturally-competent corporate web site: An exploratory study of cultural markers in multilingual web design. In: SIGDOC 2001, Santa Fe, New Mexico, USA, ACM, NewYork (2001)
18. Ferranti, M.: From Global to Local. In: Infoworld (1999)
19. Fernandes, T.: Global Interface Design, London, p. 191. Academic Press, San Diego (1995)
20. Horton, W.K.: The icon book: visual symbols for computer systems and documentation, p. 417. J. Wiley, New York (1994)
21. Howell, W.C., Fuchs, A.H.: Population stereotypy in code design. Organizational Behavior and Human Performance 3(3), 310–339 (1968)
22. Thatcher, A., Mahlangu, S., Zimmerman, C.: Accessibility of ATMS for the functionally illiterate through icon-based interfacers. Behaviour & Information Technology 25(1), 65–81 (2006)
23. Lindberg, T., Nasanen, R.: The effect of icon spacing and size on the speed of icon processing in the human visual system. Displays 24(3), 111–120 (2003)
24. Barr, P., Noble, J., Biddle, R.: Icons R Icons. In: Fourth Australasian user interface conference, Adelaide, Australia: Australian computer society (2002)

25. Lindberg, T., Nasanen, R., Muller, K.: How age affects the speed of perception of computer icons. In: Displays. (in Press, Corrected Proof) (2006)
26. Sung, S.Y., Hu, T.: Iconic pictorial retrieval using multiple attributes and spatial relationships. In: Knowledge-Based Systems. (in Press, Uncorrected Proof) (2006)
27. De Angeli, A., Kyriakoullis, L.: Globalization vs. localization in e-commerce: Cultural-aware interaction design. In: De Angeli, A. (ed.) in AVI 2006, Venezia, Italy, ACM, NewYork (2006)
28. Li, K.F., Yu, L., Liao, W.: A study of Chinese Web characteristics and their implications on Web search. In: Li, K.F. (ed.) First International Multi-Symposiums on Computer and Computational Sciences, IEEE Computer Society Press, Los Alamitos (2006)
29. Fang, X., Rau, P.: Cultural differences in design of portal sites. Ergonomics 46(1-3), 242–254 (2003)
30. Hackos, J.T., Redish, J.: User and task analysis for interface design. Wiley, Chichester (1998)
31. Goonetilleke, R.S., Shih, H.M., On, H.K., Fritsch, J.: Effects of training representational characteristics in icon design. International Journal of Human-Computer Studies 55, 741–760 (2001)
32. Bourges-Waldegg, P., Scrivener, S.: Meaning, the Central Issue in Cross-Cultural HCI Design. The role of culture in the globalisation of human-computer systems. Interacting with Computers. Elsevier Science B.V. 9(3), 287–309 (1998)
33. Cheng, H.-I., Patterson, P.E.: Iconic hyperlinks on e-commerce websites. Applied Ergonomics 38(1), 65–69 (2007)

Evaluation and Usability of Back Translation for Intercultural Communication

Tomohiro Shigenobu

Language Grid Project, National Institute of Information and Communications
Technology, 3-5 Hikaridai, Seika-cho, Soraku-gun, Kyoto, 619-0289, Japan
shigenobu@nict.go.jp

Abstract. When users communicate with each other via machine translation, it
is important to improve the quality of the translations. The "Back Translation"
technique can improve the translation accuracy. A back translation, first,
translates the input language into the target language (outward), and then
translates the target language into the input language (homeward). This allows
the users to confirm the accuracy of the machine translation by themselves. If
the user finds that his input sentence is unsuitable for machine translator, he can
rewrite the input sentence. For effective multilingual communication, it is
important that the back translation offer good accuracy and good usability. This
paper focuses on these two points; we evaluated the accuracy of back
translation, and developed a user interface that improves the usability of
back translation. The outward and homeward translations show a correlation.
Back translation can improve the accuracy of outward translation for users.

Keywords: Machine translation, Back translation, Intercultural communication,
Usability.

1 Introduction

Several communities are now communicating via machine translation[1], and such
communities are expected to increase [1]. While machine translation is useful, it
comes with some risk. As users depend on the accuracy of the translation, the lack of
any necessary information could lead to misunderstanding and confusion [2]. This
problem was elucidated in the Intercultural Collaboration Experiments in 2002
(ICE2002[2]) with Chinese, Korean and Malaysian colleagues [3]. More than forty
students and faculty members from five universities joined this experiment. The goal
was to develop open source software using the participants' first language: Japanese
participants use Japanese; Chinese participants use Chinese, and so on. The
experiment used the multilingual communication tool TransBBS (bulletin board
systems) to translate the message of one user into the other languages. We found that
the accuracy of current machine translators was inadequate for intercultural
communications. Even if the message was written as usual, other users did not

---

[1] Enjoy Korea: http://www.enjoykorea.jp/
[2] Intercultural Collaboration Experiment: http://www.ai.soc.i.kyoto-u.ac.jp/ice/

N. Aykin (Ed.): Usability and Internationalization, Part II, HCII 2007, LNCS 4560, pp. 259–265, 2007.
© Springer-Verlag Berlin Heidelberg 2007

understand its translation. We took a new approach to remove this problem. Participants check the result of translation and rewrite their message before posting. Most participants could understand English to some extent. They translated their messages into English and confirmed the English translation. If the translation appeared to be incorrect, they altered the original message and retranslated it. When the English version was adequate, or no further improvement could be discerned, the message was posted. We found that this incremental improvement did raise the quality of the message significantly. However, most people who doesn't understand the reference language cannot execute this method. One method for solving this problem is "Back translation."

Users need to know what information is being sent to their partners. Back translation allows a user to write a sentence that is machine-translatable using only the user's mother language. Back translation is therefore an important technique as it provides confirmation of translation accuracy and highlights significant problem areas. Back translation is defined as the original language obtained by translating input into a target language and then retranslating the resulting text back into the original language. The effectiveness of back translation is based on the assumption that when back translation (homeward) is correct, the target language translation (outward) must also be correct. This method enables the translation accuracy to be confirmed in the input language. When the outward and homeward translations differ greatly from each other estimating the accuracy of the target language translation is difficult. Correcting text using back translation makes no sense without reliability of accuracy. We need to evaluate the accuracy of outward and homeward translations.

Many communication tools have been developed to date, but most of them only display the translated text [4]. Furthermore, existing back translation tools only show the translation results, and a user must decide whether the input text needs to be corrected [5]. Therefore, by examining the experiences from past applications, the following problems became apparent. 1) Users require a long time to complete the cycle of correcting input and back translated text because users usually prepare an entire message and then translate it. 2) As users do not know what part of the input should be corrected, they have to repeat the process of correcting the input and executing back translation many times. 3) The accuracy of translated sentences does not improve even if users correct the input sentence due to operating in a multilingual environment. These problems have reduced a user's willingness to initiate corrections. From a practical viewpoint, merely using back translation will not provide effective support. Developing a more effective user interface for back translation is necessary.

This paper describes our evaluations of the relation between the outward and homeward translations offered for Japanese-English machine translation as an example. Furthermore, the development of a user interface that makes back translation more effective is described.

2 Accuracy of Back Translation

When both quality of an outward translation result and that of back translation result are far from each other in quality, it is difficult to estimate the quality of target language. Therefore, outward and homeward quality evaluations of back translation are necessary. This section describes evaluations of the relation between the quality of outward and homeward translation using Japanese-English machine translation as an example.

2.1 Method of Evaluation

Hereafter, target language translation is referred to as "outward translation" while back translation is called "homeward translation." The instructions given in the subjective human evaluations followed those used for TIDE [6]. 5-step evaluations were performed. The evaluation method compares translated sentences and reference sentences to judge how much information was transferred correctly. Evaluation criteria were "How much of the meaning expressed in the gold-standard translation was also expressed in the target translation?" the evaluation scores were "5: All, 4: Most, 3: Much, 2: Little and 1: None". We used J-Server by KODENSHA[3] as the machine translation system. As the evaluation texts, we used 186 sentences extracted at random from material provided by NTT[4]. The material examined consisted of a set of original Japanese sentences and paired original English sentences. The evaluation contents are described below:

- Evaluation A: We compared outward translations (English) to the reference sentences (original English). This represents the outward evaluation.
- Evaluation B: We compared the homeward translations (Japanese) to the input Japanese sentences (original Japanese). This represents the homeward (back translation) evaluation.

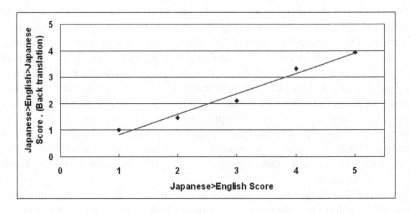

Fig. 1. Correlation between outward and homeward

2.2 Results

Figure 1 shows the relation of evaluation values between outward (Evaluation A) and homeward (Evaluation B). We found that the two translation directions were

---

[3] KODENSHA: http://www.kodensha.jp/
[4] NTT Natural Language Research Group: http://www.kecl.ntt.co.jp/mtg/resources/index-j.php

correlated. The homeward evaluation value was about 20% less than the outward evaluation value. Figure 2 shows the relation of evaluation values between outward and homeward translations based on the number of words. The point size represents the number of samples. As an inevitable consequence, values of both evaluations tend to fall as the sentences become long. Additionally, the homeward evaluation becomes lower as the outward evaluation become low. The average value of outward translation was 3.1 and that of homeward translation was 2.4. Given that the quality of evaluation value 5 is 100% and that of evaluation value 1 is 0%, the quality of outward decreases to 77% of its original value and that of homeward quality decreases to 60%. However, given that evaluation value 3 is the "threshold limit value for understanding contents", understandable outward translated sentences consist of about 8 words on average and homeward translated sentences consist of about 5 words on average. The evaluation texts is used for testing of machine translator, the evaluation value is low as there are several sentences that the machine translator finds difficult to translate. We consider that the evaluation value will improve as users tend to write suitable sentences for machine translation. The evaluation value decreased if the machine translation result was used as the input sentence since these sentences were generally incomplete; however, there is a high possibility that when back translation (homeward) is correct, the target language translation (outward) also is correct.

The quality of back translation in which outward translation is used as input sentence decreases significantly as sentence becomes long. However, the quality between outward and homeward translated sentences has correlation; thus, it is highly possible that if quality of back translation is high, quality of target translation becomes high. Therefore, users may be able to estimate the quality of outward translation by confirming homeward translation sentences.

We will evaluate various viewpoints, and increase the number of subjects and translators to be evaluated.

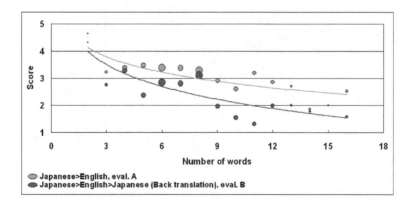

Fig. 2. Relation of outward and homeward translation quality

3 Usability

Our case studies showed that back translation suffers from several problems. Back translation needs some support functions if it is to become truly practical. Simply showing the result of back translation to the user is not good enough. This section describes a user interfaces to improve the usability of back translation.

3.1 Real-Time Back Translation

When users used the back translation provided by our first tool, they had to push the back translation button by themselves. The back translation result was shown only after they input their entire message. Since the system took several seconds to display the back translation result, the user quite often gave up on using the result. Our solution is real-time incremental back translation. It shortens the response time and improves usability so that users can obtain the back translation results while inputting their message. An incomplete sentence is likely to yield errors in the back translation. However, users can find their typographic and grammatical errors. We abut the input area and the back translation area to grab the user's attention. Figure 3 shows the display position of the back translation result.

3.2 Highlighting Translation Unsuitable Parts

Users who tried to correct sentences made many unsuccessful attempts because they did not know what part of the input caused problems for the machine translator. To help the user in locating problem areas in the input sentence, we have developed a

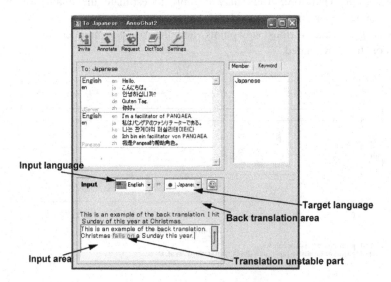

Fig. 3. Display of back translation result

function that highlights the translation unsuitable parts. This function is based on natural language processing technologies. Based on morphological analysis and syntactic parsing, it uses the degree of similarity as employed for the automatic evaluation of translation accuracy. This method can calculate the degree of similarity between an input message and the back translation result automatically [7]. When the degree of similarity is low, the method simplifies the original text gradually. The processes of simplification yield several texts. The method can estimate unsuitable parts by the differences of these texts [8]. The user is shown which parts of the message are unsuitable for translation. This method has been shown to improve message quality for machine translation [9]. Figure 3 shows the user interface with modification candidate words highlighted.

3.3 Multilingual Environment

Corrections performed by Japanese users when referring to the back translations based on English were very effective in improving the accuracy of the English translations. However, the corrections were not so effective for Chinese and Korean translations [10]. When a user corrects input using back translation, the accuracy of the translations is not improved for all languages simultaneously. Therefore, we extended the back translation function described above to suit multilingual environments. Figure 4 shows the user interface of this extended function. Users can write a suitable message for each language. When they decide that the translation quality is suitable (via back translation), they select the "fixed" check box to fix the translation or that language.

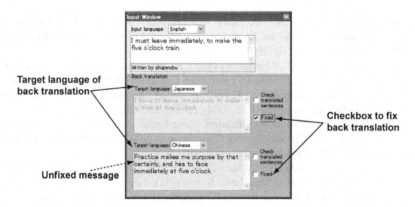

Fig. 4. Fixing function for back translation in multilingual environment

4   Conclusion

Current machine translation systems have insufficient quality to support intercultural communication. Therefore, repairing input messages by back translation is essential to improve translation quality. We verified the effectiveness of back translation by evaluating the relation between outward and homeward translations, and developed am effective user interface for back translation.

The quality of back translation in which outward translation is used as input sentence decreases significantly as sentence becomes long. However, the quality between outward and homeward translated sentences has correlation. Therefore, users may be able to estimate the quality of outward translation by back translation. Moreover, to improve the usability of back translation, we developed a user interface that offers real-time back translation, back translation proceeds automatically as the message is being input. We arranged the input area close to the back translation result area so that the user can notice typographic and grammatical errors immediately. The interface also highlights message passages that unsuitable for translation. For multilingual environments we developed an interface in which users can repair and write messages for each language.

References

1. Climent, S., More, J., Oliver, A., Salvatierra, M., Sanchez, I., Taule, M., Vallmanya, L.: Bilingual Newsgroups in Catalonia: A Challenge for Machine Translation. In: Journal of Computer Mediated Communication, 9(1), (2003)
2. Yamashita, N., Ishida, T.: Automatic Prediction of Misconceptions in Multilingual Computer-Mediated Communication. In: International Conference on Intelligent User Interfaces (IUI-06), pp.62–69 (2006)
3. Nomura, S., Ishida, T., Yamashita, N., Yasuoka, M., Funakoshi, K.: Open Source Software Development with Your Mother Language: Intercultural Collaboration Experiment 2002. In: International Conference on Human-Computer Interaction (HCI-03) vol. 4, pp. 1163–1167 (2003)
4. Raymond, S.F., Chris, C.B.: Secondary Benefits of Feedback and User Interaction in Machine Translation Tools. In: Workshop paper for "MT2010: Towards a Roadmap for MT" of the MT Summit VIII (2001)
5. Yoshino, T., Shigenobu, T., Maruno, S., Ozaki, H., Ohno, S., Munemori, J.: Development and Application of an Intercultural Synchronous Collaboration System. In: Proceedings of Eighth International Conference on Knowledge-Based Intelligent Information Engineering Systems & Allied Technologies (KES 2004), pp.869–882 (2004)
6. Linguistic Data Annotation Specification: Assessment of Fluency and Adequacy in Arabic-English and Chinese-English Translations. (2002), http://www.ldc.upenn.edu/Projects/TIDES/Transl ation/TransAssess02.pdf
7. Uchimoto, K., Hayashida, N., Ishida, T., Isahara, H.: Automatic Rating of Machine Translatability, 10th Machine Translation Summit (MT Summit X), pp. 235–242 (2005)
8. Uchimoto, K., Hayashida, N., Ishida, T., Isahara, H.: Automatic Detection and Semi-Automatic Revision of Non-Machine-Translatable Parts of a Sentence. In: International Conference on Language Resources and Evaluation (LREC-06) (2006)
9. Hayashida, N., Ishida, T.: Performance Prediction of Supporting Self-Initiated Repair by Translation Agents, IEICE, vol. J88-D-I(9), pp, 1459–1466, (Japanese 2005)
10. Ogura, K., Hayashi, Y., Nomura, S., Ishida, T.: User Adaptation in MT-mediated Communication. In: Su, K.-Y., Tsujii, J., Lee, J.-H., Kwong, O.Y. (eds.) IJCNLP 2004. LNCS (LNAI), vol. 3248, pp. 596–601. Springer, Heidelberg (2005)

Contextual User Research for International Software Design

David A. Siegel and Susan M. Dray

Dray & Associates, Inc.
2007 Kenwood Parkway
Minneapolis, MN 55405
US

Abstract. This paper, which is based on our many years of experience conducting research in more than 20 countries, examines both the importance and pitfalls of doing contextual field research when developing software, websites, or interactive products for the international market. We examine the ways in which field research gives crucial information that complements what can be obtained from other methods such as usability testing. We identify a number of core challenges in doing international fieldwork and recommend ways to address them. We conclude with at least one case study.

1 Introduction

User centered design involves the use of a range of methodologies to ensure that a user focus is introduced into the process of planning and designing products and software. Increasingly, companies have begun to recognize that without a disciplined user-centered design effort, their products have too high a risk of failing in the market because product planning and design decisions will be too heavily influenced by their enthusiasm for their own ideas.

Globalization requires an intensified focus on user-centered design. The need for systematic efforts to understand the user becomes even greater when products are being designed for users in another country and culture than your own. Beyond the usual difficulties we have imagining how other people differ from ourselves, people working in one country or culture can have difficulty imagining the enormous number of ways in which people can differ internationally. As a result, not only does the risk of design error increase, but, in particular there is a greater deep level at the conceptual level of product planning, such as a basic mismatch between the concept of the product and the usage context. The size of the investment at stake when doing business internationally can also contribute to making failure exceptionally costly.

Fortunately, many companies are realizing the need for international user-centered design (UCD) work. However, this probably most often takes the form of usability testing, which by itself is insufficient. Usability testing does not directly address the issue of contextual fit. Even designing a good usability test requires knowledge about patterns of usage and typical user goals which may differ radically from country to country.

N. Aykin (Ed.): Usability and Internationalization, Part II, HCII 2007, LNCS 4560, pp. 266–273, 2007.
© Springer-Verlag Berlin Heidelberg 2007

For example, without knowledge of local usage patterns, user expectations, and goals, you can not design task scenarios that will be meaningful to people. Two problems can result from this. You may design task scenarios that assess whether people can accomplish the tasks you ask them to do but which may have little to do with how users will ultimately value the experience the product provides for them. In more extreme cases, users may not even understand what the task is asking them to do. Fortunately, you may be able to derive indirect useful information from this, because it can be a clue pointing to an area of fundamental mismatch between the product team's assumptions and the local reality.

2 A Case Example

In order to take root, technology innovations require a good fit with existing behavioral patterns, social and economic conditions, and technology infrastructure. The overall dynamic created among these factors can differ from one country to another in ways that powerfully affect the adoption of technology. One good example that many people are well aware of is related to the gap between the adoption of mobile phones and in particular SMS functionality between the US and other countries. Although this gap is decreasing, it still exists. Many visitors to the US have been surprised by this, and have tended to wonder how people in such a tech-nologically advanced country could be so "behind" in adoption of a functionality which seems to be the wave of the future elsewhere. One can not address such questions without understanding all of the contextual factors that determine the appeal of and need for a technology in contrast to the available alternatives, the fit with people's lifestyles, and the obstacles to adoption including economics and technical infrastructure.

A similar question has arisen in regard to adoption of smart card technology. There have been many failed attempts to introduce smart cards (containing a computer chip as opposed to simply a magnetic strip) in the US. In the early 1990's, one of us assisted in a study commissioned by the US Office of Technology Assessment (a government agency whose mission was to assess potential policy implications of new technologies in order to inform relevant legislation) regarding the adoption of smart cards in the French health care system, to evaluate their potential for the US. At the time, there were a number of seemingly promising initiatives underway in France. Some projects focused on using the cards to store health insurance benefit and utilization information. Another project focused on using them for tracking dialysis information for kidney patients. The applicability of models like these to the US was in question.

Many of these factors that seemed to contribute to the fit of these approaches in France have probably changed significantly due to the evolution of the Web since that time. However, what is relevant for our purposes is that comparing the potential attractiveness of these approaches between France and the US required understanding the entire context. Following are some of the specific factors that seemed to create a fit in France that were not the case in the US.

The French government perceived this technology as promising and as an area where France had a lead internationally. It therefore provided a great deal of support and subsidy for these initiatives. France is a more centralized country than the US, and so it was likely national government policy would have a more direct effect on this. For example, to pursue larger policy goals the national telephone company could simply mandate the use of these cards as stored valued cards to replace coins in public phones.

The fact that use of smart cards as stored value cards was already well-established was likely to facilitate public acceptance of their use in other domains. For example, in addition to being used for phone cards, they were also used in credit cards to handle authentication and management of daily limits, without requiring authorization from a central data center. However, there were factors that made these uses appealing in France and that did not apply in the US. In France, higher telecommunications costs were an obstacle to the kind of credit authorization process used in the US, where merchants used terminals that communicate over telephone lines to get credit card authorization. Rates of credit card fraud were significantly higher in France than in the US, which made it economically worthwhile to create the infrastructure for more powerful security on credit cards, which could be supported by chips as compared to magnetic strips.

The structure of the health care system and of the mechanisms for health care financing differed radically between France and the US. In France, there were economies of scale that did not apply in the US. For example, France had a national single-payer health insurance system applying to most of the population, and the majority of clinics participated in it as health care providers. This made it reasonable to consider installing a single system of card readers in clinics nationwide, and to use a single format for information records and benefit information that would apply across the vast majority of patients and providers. In contrast, in the US, the system was much more fragmented. There were (and still are) a large number of different insurers providing health coverage. Some were national and some regional. Different clinics even in the same area participated with different subsets of the plans. Each plan requires its participating providers to go through different administrative procedures. Although medicare is a nationwide, federally-funded program for retires in which most clinics are participating providers, medicare enrollees could represent widely differing percentages of the case load for different providers.

3 Challenges and Solutions

Carrying out research internationally to understand the constellation of local factors likely to affect adoption of a technology presents a number of basic challenges. Some of these are particular to international research, while some are like the challenges of any contextual research, only rendered more difficult by the international setting of the research. In this section, we review a number of these and offer recommendations about how to address them.

3.1 Defining the Focus

Field research typically adopts a broader focus than usability evaluation, because it has to be open to a wide range of things that may influence the design. This is true regardless of whether you are trying to provide input early in the design process or are evaluating the "fit" of the product in the users' real life circumstances. The challenge is that how you plan the study will still influence what you see. This includes how you define both the people and contexts you are going to study. This requires proactive planning based on the research focus.

Some people believe that being overly specific about your focus is a mistake. Their argument is that this narrows your focus of attention excessively, based on your preconceptions, and blinds you to things that you would not have known to look for. We disagree with this. If you do not have a planned focus, your attention is more likely to be too diffused, so that you only capture vague impressionistic information. Planning the focus in detail will allow you to plan all aspects of the methodology in a targeted way, so that you have the opportunity to drill more deeply into interesting observations. One risk of failing to do this is that you are actually more prone to being influenced by stereotypes without realizing that this is happening. Another advantage of having an explicit focus is that it can give you a baseline against which unexpected observations will actually stand out more dramatically.

There are two main approaches we take to developing a useful focus. They are logically connected to each other. The first is to do an intensive brainstorming exercise, including the product team as much as possible, to identify as many of the contextual factors that may influence how people are likely to respond to the product, and could potentially affect its adoption and usage, and to plan what type of things you might look for as clues to these things. The goal of this is not to make sure you think of every possible factor that might matter. No matter how thoroughly you do this exercise, you will almost always discover relevant cultural and contextual factors that you did not anticipate. This is an example of where the conscious development of the focus helps increase the contrast between what you were looking for and what you find. This helps to more clearly reveal where the gaps in your initial mental model were.

The second method for developing a focus is to identify the team's implicit assumptions. It is almost inevitable that you will find the team making assumptions about user populations and their local context. No matter how early in the development process the team is, and no matter vague their product plan or how open they are to new information, it is extremely unusual for them not to have some mental image of their future product possibilities. This image includes assumptions about the people they are trying to appeal to, the potential benefits of the product in the lives of those people. Whether they are right or wrong, these assumptions should influence the focus of the research. Since the goal of the research is to advance the team's understanding of their users and their contexts, these assumptions should be made as explicit as possible, so that they can be treated as hypotheses to validate or invalidate.

3.2 Defining Who and What to Study

Developing a screener for international research is very challenging, because the criteria that you operationalize in the screener reflect your working assumptions about how to define your target audience. Assessing those assumptions themselves may be among the most important things you need to focus on in the research.

When doing field research in one's own country, one can be guided by a great deal of implicit knowledge about local conditions that helps one make more accurate initial guesses about what will be relevant, and where to look for that information. Although it is still challenging, one has an easier targeting the research to provide an opportunity to observe those things. When working internationally, we typically know less in advance about the factors that will turn out to be most relevant, and we therefore have to adopt a broader focus, with higher level questions. In local studies, we often can focus on understanding how certain groups of people do certain types of tasks. When we do international work, especially when we work in a culture different from our own, we often have to wrestle with whether the basic working definition of the groups and their contexts is even relevant.

Screener items tend to be simplistic efforts to capture much richer concepts using easily administered and easily scored items. For example, one may use an income level criterion in an attempt to target middle-class participants. However, the concept of "middle class" is much richer and more complex than can be captured in a simple numerical criterion. The author of the screener may imagine the product appealing to someone who fits an image of a middle class lifestyle, personal history, and experiences associated with a certain income level in his or her own country. However, this constellation of factors is itself culturally dependent.

Adjusting the income criterion to the fit the income range of the target country is not sufficient, because the entire structure of income distribution may be different in the target country from what it is in the product team's country. For example, in one case, we observed that people who fit the local definition of "middle class" often had personal servants, which would not have been true in the US. As another example, if we recruit people who have owned a personal computer for a certain length of time from an economically developed country and from a developing country, the latter person is more likely to be exceptional in a variety of ways in relation to their own context, such as having characteristics of an earlier adopter or having a special motivation to buy the computer that the criterion would not imply for someone in the developed world.

Researchers often try to deal with this by using multiple criteria to better target the people they have in mind. However, this can produce difficulties as well, because the relationship among the criteria can be different from what you expect. For example, in one project that we worked on several years ago, our client wanted to target people in a lower income range who had dial up connections on their home computers. It turned out that this definition of a category of people was filled with contradictions for that local context. People with home computers, who had telephone lines to their homes, and who were willing to use them for an internet connection despite that fact that time charges made this expensive, tended to be affluent. This does not mean that one could not find less affluent people who fit this description, but it does mean that those people were likely to be unusual in other ways.

When doing international research, we often encourage our clients to keep the recruiting criteria simple, rather than specifying them very precisely. This is because the more you specify, the more likely you are to be building your definition on mistaken assumptions about how to define what you are interested in given the local context, and to end up with a sample that is exceptional in some way that you are not aware of. It may be possible to find people who meet your tight criteria, but you will have little idea of how exceptional those people are. Simpler criteria have the advantage of allowing you more opportunity to learn how much heterogeneity there is within a particular group of interest, and what constellations of factors tend to go together meaningfully.

3.3 Balancing Depth with Breadth

Contextual field research is often described as emphasizing depth over breadth, in the sense that it uses small samples, and that you spend a significant amount of time with each informant. However, going "deep" with a participant means that your methodology allows you the possibility of understanding the processes broadly in the sense that you have the opportunity to look at the very wide range of factors that influence the user experience dynamics in the domain of interest, rather than simply focusing on practices most related to the behaviors you hope to support with your technology. For example, if you are considering delivering a service over the Web, it is not enough to focus only on how people interact with and utilize websites similar to yours. In fact, there may be no analogous web tools in their environment. Therefore, you may need to look broadly at factors that influence how they currently fulfill the life functions relevant to that website, because these things will influence whether and how people will adopt a tool like yours.

For example, we did a study related to potential use of electronic tools for coordinating family activities in a developing country. We had to go beyond trying to learning how families attempted to coordinate with each other and how they accomplish this now. We also had to try to understand the vast range of factors in the local context of social norms, rules, infrastructure, etc. that supported the existing practices. How much variability is there in people's activities across days and weeks? What introduces variability? How far in advance are different activities planned? What are the activities that families need to synchronize with each other? When do families expect to come together and what influences how they accommodate each other's schedules? What are the logistical challenges they face in coordinating? What roles do different family members assume in regard to all of the above?

3.4 Dealing with Pressures to Overload the Study

Companies' understandable desire to get the most value from their investment in international research can create pressure to broaden the scope of the study beyond what the resources of time and sample size can really support. Another factor that contributes to this is that international studies often have large numbers of stakeholders within the company, all of whom wants to be sure that their particular agenda is addressed. As explained above, while contextual field research can provide both breadth of understanding in the sense of examining the broad context of a process, it is unrealistic to think that it can show you every major variation in the ways that process plays out in an entire country. Attempting to cover too much can spread your efforts too thin and ensure that you only bring back superficial information, which will be misleading if it is over-generalized. It is more appropriate and effective to allow each study to have a clear focus, and to assume that you will need to gain information over time from an accumulation of research. Instead of trying to answer every imaginable question within one research study, plan your studies to make sure that you get a view of conditions in the country or of the process you are interested in from contrasting vantage points with each study. This means recruiting samples that will contrast with or complement each other, or planning the study to observe different parts of the process. Planning a series of complementary studies in this way is more likely to deepen your understanding.

For example, one series of studies attempted to understand the reasons that a particular innovative product being introduced into the developing world was not selling well. Some initial studies looked at people who were recruited through store intercepts while shopping for in the general category of that technology product. These studies revealed negative reactions to the product. This raised doubts about the fundamental desirability of the product, which was disappointing because it had been planned specifically in an effort to have a particular appeal to a particular hypothetical segment in the developing world. However, we pointed out that there might have been a built-in bias in the recruiting method. The shoppers found in the stores may not actually have been representative of the target group, unless those particular stores attracted a representative sample of the target group. We did a subsequent study in which we used conventional recruiting methods to find people who were in the target group according to screener criteria and were verifiably in the category of product we were interested in. We then did an accompanied shopping study with them, in which we let them choose the venue for shopping, but also arranged to exposed them to the product of interest. We discovered that these people tended to gravitate to very different types of retail settings than those where the product was being marketed. Also, when they were exposed to the product they had a much more positive response, often choosing it over the competition. This suggested that the problem may not have been in the product concept itself, but in its marketing strategy, which was systematically failing to reach the intended audience.

3.5 Using a Multicultural Team

We strongly believe that international research requires a combination of perspectives, including those of the design team and its culture, along with the local perspective. Different types of information will be visible to people with different backgrounds. For example, a local research team member may be well aware of local conditions that help explain an observation but that might not have been discovered by an outsider during the study. The local person is probably also more likely to know whether a participant's circumstances or behavior are atypical in the local context (although it can be a serious mistake to assume that people have objective and unbiased knowledge of their own local contexts.) Conversely, astute outsiders brings a wealth of contrasting experiences (especially if they have extensive international experience already) they can raise questions the local would not think to ask, or perceive the significance of things that the local person does not even notice simply because they are so common they are taken for granted.

However, simply sending design team members and engineers to work with local researchers does not guarantee a synergy between these perspectives. Someone on the team needs to be expert in cross-cultural research, interpretation of ethnographic data, and cross cultural communication to bridge between these perspectives and to extract the significance of observations. Whether it is a local researcher or a foreigner, what is important is important for this person to combine skills in understanding the team's mindset and identifying their underlying assumptions, which are often only implicit, and in making sense of local conditions, so that they can identify the discrepancies between these.

Language Issues in Cross Cultural Usability Testing: A Pilot Study in China

Xianghong Sun[1] and Qingxin Shi[1, 2]

[1] State Key Laboratory of Brain and Cognitive Science, Inst. of Psychology, Chinese Academy of Science, Beijing 100101, China
sunxh@psych.ac.cn
[2] Department of Informatics, Copenhagen Business School, Denmark
qs.inf@cbs.dk

Abstract. Language effect (Chinese vs. English), and power distance between evaluator and user in usability test were investigated. 12 participants from China, Swede, and Denmark formed 7 evaluator-test user pairs. Test users were asked to use a software. Evaluators were asked to conduct the usability test, and try to find usability problems. Participants' conversation, behaviour, and screen operation were recorded by behaviour observation system. Results showed that Speaking Chinese made evaluator giving more help in detail, and encouraging users more frequently; Speaking English asked evaluator and user look at each other more often to make themselves understood, and evaluators paid more attention to check task list. Power distance also had effect on evaluators and users. When evaluator's title were higher than users, evaluator would pay more attention to users' doing, not like to give user detailed instruction, usually loose communication with user, and spent less for task management. In contrast, talking to evaluators with higher rank, users tend to use more gesture to express themselves.

Keywords: Language, think aloud, cultural usability, field study.

1 Introduction

With the progress of economic globalisation, more and more international enterprises start to do usability test in different cultures during the last decade. In China only two, or three years ago, usability was quite a new word for most of people. Right now the situation has been changed dramatically. Many domestic enterprises have reckoned the importance of usability test for their products, especially for IT business. Many western researchers were interested in Chinese users' preference, behaviour, and mental models [3,4,5,8]. Since China is not an English speaking country, like India, and Singapore, and most users in China can't speak English at all. It brings the biggest communication problems when conducting usability test by international moderators.

There are several choices to avoid this problem. The first is using bilingual moderators to test user. The second is finding users who can speak English. But both professional moderators and English speakers are very rare in China, and they all are

N. Aykin (Ed.): Usability and Internationalization, Part II, HCII 2007, LNCS 4560, pp. 274–284, 2007.
© Springer-Verlag Berlin Heidelberg 2007

youth and probably with western education background, it means that there is no way to get the real feedback from all kinds of users in China. So the third and the most regular way they do is that, they use both remote and local moderators working together with Chinese users to ensure they really get the feedback from the right users and understand it.

Local moderators here mean someone who got training in Human Factors, or had working experience on usability test for at least one year in China. They usually can't speak English very well. Remote moderators mean someone who got training in Human Factors and had experience on usability test for at least one year in foreign countries. They usually can speak English and their hometown language very well.

Previous studies on cross cultural usability evaluation show us that culture broadly affects the usability evaluation processes [9]. Vatrapu R, and Pérez-Quiñones M.A (2006)[10] investigated the evaluator effect, and found that participants found more usability problems and made more suggestions to an interviewer who was a member of the same (Indian) culture than to the foreign (Anglo -American) interviewer. The results of the study empirically establish that culture significantly affects the efficacy of structured interviews during international user testing.

In this study, the primary questions are how to avoid cultural bias in requirements elicitation and usability data collection, and what user based evaluation methods address cultural diversity in both the moderator and user? Before we can answer them completely, First thing we need to do is to find what kinds of cultural factors could affect usability test. In this paper we investigated specifically two factors: one was language, and the other was power distance.

The reason why we picked language as a factor to be investigated is that, language is a kind of representation of culture. And language situation among India, European countries, and China is totally different. Although English is not hometown language for Indian and Danish either, most people in these two countries can speak English very well. But in China few people can do it well. Therefore, if conducting usability test in China, First thing you have to do is to change the testing interface into Chinese. We usually say if someone is speaking English, he/she must be thinking in English. So, by which language test user and evaluator choose during the usability test, they probably think in the way of that language. It means that speaking different language could affect the process of usability test even if all the participants are Chinese.

Since China is a kind of society with very clear and strict hierarchy. Different kind of relationship between evaluator and test user could cause different results. So, power distance is considered as another factor.

2 Method

The following section will describe the methodology, results, and conclusion of the pilot study and discusses the findings on language issue.

2.1 Materials

The pilot study was based on the 'usability test of cultural clipart' paradigm (Clemmensen, 2005)[1]. Here cultural clipart was a collection of culturally specific images and icons and several text documents with preformatted invitation text. The application was aimed at supporting a test user in the design of invitations. In this study, test users were asked to make a wedding invitation for themselves.

Totally 150 images and icons with wedding symbols were selected and saved in a subfolder with the name "Chinese clipart" in My Collections, in which 20 image and icons with Korean and Japanese symbols and another 10 with western style were mixed with others as interference (see table 1) to increase the chances of measuring culturally specific interaction between test user and evaluator.

Test user could access the images in "Chinese clipart" folder with Microsoft's clipart organizer.

Table 1. Potential usability errors in Chinese Cultural Cliparts

Culturally wrong symbols	Label errors	Invitation text errors
A Korea flag in the collection		Wrong time
An image of cherry flower (Japanese national flower)		Wrong place for wedding banquet
		Wrong name and title
Image of bride in traditional Korean wedding dress		
Japanese rope node		Wrong telephone number

2.2 Procedure

The pilot study in China had the same three phases like the other two experiments did in Denmark and India: phase one was Questionnaire phase which gave us the information about the experience of the user and evaluator; phase two was Usability testing of the Cultural Clipart application with Microsoft word. This phase included two parts, first was the testing, and second was interviewing the test user by evaluator. The third phase was the interview phase: the researchers interviewed the evaluator and test user on the basis of their observations during phase two.

The whole experiment was conducted at a standard usability lab in Institute of Psychology, which included one test room with several video camcorders installed in different viewpoints, and one observation room with one-way mirror between the two rooms. All the conversation between evaluator and test user, their behaviour, and the screen events were recorded by four-channel behaviour recording system.

2.3 Participants

Table 2 showed the basic information of all the seven evaluator-user pairs. Here all the test users were chosen from China. They are young staff, or graduate students studying in the Institute of Psychology, which ensure them all familiar with think aloud technology, and speak good English. The evaluators were chosen from Europe and China. Only one evaluator who was from Swede had not any knowledge about usability. But he got half an hour of training before he conducted the usability test. Since there is few people in China now could be treated as professional usability test leader, one of the evaluator was used three times with different test users.

Table 2. Description of participants

ID	Role	Age	Gender	National culture	Language used in the test	Expertise in usability test
E1	Evaluator	34	F	China	2 in English 1 in Chinese	Professional
U1	Test User	31	F	China	English	
E2	Evaluator	37	F	China	English	Professional
U2	Test User	25	F	China	Chinese	
E3	Evaluator	45	M	Danish	English	Professional
U3	Test User	27	M	China	English	
U4	Test User	29	F	China	English	
U5	Test User	27	M	China	English	
E4	Evaluator	25	F	China	Chinese	Non-professional
U6	Test User	24	F	China	Chinese	
E5	Evaluator	27	M	Sweden	Chinese	Non-professional
U7	Test User	23	M	China	Chinese	

Table 3. Different combinations of evaluator-user relationship

Cultural Pairing	Status	Age Relation	Language	Gender
Chinese Chinese	Prof. – Prof.	Young-Young	English – English	F- F
Chinese Chinese	Prof. – PhD student	Young-Young	Chinese – Chinese	F- F
Chinese Chinese	Prof. – PhD student	Young- Young	English – English	F- M
European Chinese	Prof. – Prof.	Older–younger	English – English	M - F
Chinese Chinese	Prof. – PhD student	Young - Young	English – English	F - M
Chinese Chinese	PhD student – PhD stud	Young- Young	Chinese – Chinese	F - F
European Chinese	Bachelor – PhD stu.	Young- Young	Chinese – Chinese	M- M

3 Results

Coding system. Watching evaluator and test-users' conversation and behaviour, it's found that, even for a single event, for example, silence, the duration of the event last were varied from several seconds to several minutes. But in the original coding system used in India and Denmark experiments, no matter how long the event lasted it was count as once. It brought us two problems. First, how long the event last could be treated as one event? Secondly, when we found the number of silence for one evaluator-user pair was higher than that of another pair, did it mean the former pair had more silence than the latter? It's probably not true. If the former pair fallen into silence 10 times during the test, and it last around 30 seconds each time, the total time in silence is 300 seconds. If the latter pair in silence twice, and 5 minutes each, the total time was 10 minutes. So the real situation could be opposite.

In order to eliminate the system error we encode, a chronological coding system was developed, by which we encoded the behaviour data by time period instead of by event. Each time period last 10 seconds. For example, if the usability test lasted 20 minutes, there would be 120 time points were coded. Therefore, times that an event happened during the test must be equivalent to how long that user or evaluator spent on that event.

Since the focus of our study was the process of usability test, especially the interaction between user and evaluator, in the chronological coding system, evaluator's conversation, evaluator's behaviour, test user's conversation, test user's behaviour, and screen operation were all coded. (See Appendix. Coding system)

Language Effect. The first row in Table 4 showed how many time points for each evaluator-user pair were coded. The third row illustrated which pair spoke Chinese (C), and which spoke English (E). Here the focused issue was whether for Chinese people speaking English, not native language – Chinese, would make the test process different. Since there was one European participant in the pair No.2, and pair No.3, we only do analysis with the other 5 Chinese-Chinese pairs.

Table 4. Classification of participant pairs and the test duration for each test pair

E-U pairs No.	1	2	3	4	5	6	7
Number of time points for coding	345	131	181	134	189	295	199
Test session duration (mins)	88	20	30	20	31	49	33
Language they used (Chin, Eng)	C	C	E	E	E	C	E
Status (at same level, or not)	Same	Same	Same	No	Same	No	No

Table 5 showed different content of evaluators conversation. From the data, we found most of time evaluators were keep silent. But in speaking Chinese condition, silence kept longer than speaking English. Numbers of reminder kept the same between the two conditions. Numbers of affirmative express, and answering user's questions didn't show any clear trend. But under Chinese condition, evaluators tend to give more help, tell more introductions in detail, and encourage users more frequently.

Table 5. Classification of evaluators' conversation

Language	Chinese		English		
	1	6	4	5	7
1 Affirmative express	12	8	52	1	16
2 Remind user keep thinking aloud	3	1	1	0	1
3 Tell user what is next step	**25**	**12**	2	7	17
4 Interrogative express	5	15	5	2	8
5 Answer user's question	33	4	3	1	18
6 Help out	**15**	**15**	1	9	0
7 Encourage user	**6**	**9**	2	0	0
8 silence	243	225	68	169	138

Table 6 showed different kinds of behaviour of evaluators during the test. It's found watching PC screen was the most behaviour. The second most behaviour was checking task list to find what was the next step, or to ensure everything was done. Chinese evaluators seldom expressed their thought with gesture. They didn't turn their face only to look each other with user either. But when watching PC screen they did have a look of the user. Comparing the two language conditions, evaluator when speaking Chinese didn't do so much on task management as they did when speaking English. And English condition asked evaluator and user look at each other more times to make them understood. In addition, under English condition, evaluators paid more attention to check task list.

Table 6. Classification of evaluators' behaviour

Language	Chinese		English		
	1	6	4	5	7
1 Turn face to user	0	0	0	1	2
2 Express himself with gesture	0	0	0	2	0
3 Watch PC screen	295	111	125	208	162
4 Task management	14	20	61	33	15
5 1+3	28	3	3	34	6
6 2+3	1	0	0	9	10
7 1+2	2	0	0	0	1
8 1+2+3	5	0	0	8	2

Combining the above two results we found speaking different language affected evaluators' behaviour. Speaking Chinese made evaluators easier to give help and more detailed instruction. And speaking English made evaluator and user have to look at each other more frequently to ensure there was no misunderstanding between them.

Table 7. Classification of test-users' conversation

Language	Chinese		English		
	1	6	4	5	7
1 evaluation	21	21	16	36	24
2 suggestion	0	0	0	3	0
3 explanation	0	1	0	1	0
4 question	20	3	7	9	25
5 description	115	72	87	116	57
6 confirmation	29	2	5	24	16
7 silence	159	15	73	99	73

Table 7 and Table 8 showed user's conversation and behaviour. From Table 8 it's found that, user didn't use gesture either, and seldom look back to evaluator. Different from Table 6, user never spent time on task management. That meant they didn't check what task should do next. They gave the responsibility totally to evaluator.

Conversation of user was classified into 7 types. From Table 7, we found that users didn't have so much silence as evaluators had, which was what users were supposed to do. Only one user made suggestion to the clipart organizer. Chinese users didn't explain how did he/she think, and why he/she picked this picture, not that one. What he/she spoke out mostly were what he/she was doing. So they just described their screen operations to evaluator.

Table 8. Classification of test-users' behavior

Language	Chinese		English		
	1	6	4	5	7
1 Turn face to evaluator	0	0	1	2	0
2 Express him/herself with gesture	0	0	0	0	0
3 Watch PC screen	338	86	188	271	156
4 Task management	0	0	0	0	0
5 1+3	7	1	0	15	0
6 2+3	0	38	0	2	33
7 1+2	0	3	0	2	2
8 1+2+3	0	6	0	1	6

Comparing the two language conditions, there seemed no difference exist on the amount of evaluations to Chinese clipart, amount of questions, descriptions, and confirmation. So for users, whatever language they spoke, it didn't affect their conversation content and behaviour.

Power distance. Reviewing all the participant pairs, we found two of them were student-student pair, another two of them were professor-professor pair, and the other three were professor-student pairs (See the last row in Table 4 and Table 3). The first four pairs were treated as at the same status level. In each pair there was not power distance exist. The last three pairs were treated as at different level of status. Professor as evaluator in think aloud session was at least one layer higher than student.

Table 9 and Table 10 showed the evaluators' behaviour at different groups. From the data in the two tables, we found if evaluator's title were higher than users, the evaluator would more like to ask user what was he/she thinking at that time, would not like to give user more detailed instruction, and didn't remind user so much on keep thinking aloud as evaluator at the same level with user did. In addition, from the Table 10, evaluator with higher rank would loose more communication with user, and spent less time for task management.

So, evaluator's status had affected the interaction between user and himself.

Table 9. Effect of relationship between evaluator and user in evaluator's conversation

Status	Same level				Different level		
	1	2	3	5	4	6	7
1 Affirmative express	12	5	49	1	52	8	16
2 Remind user keep thinking aloud	3	7	1	0	1	1	1
3 Tell user what is next step	25	10	22	7	2	12	17
4 Interrogative express	5	9	2	2	5	15	8
5 Answer user's question	33	1	10	1	3	4	18
6 Help out	15	2	3	9	1	15	0
7 Encourage user	6	0	3	0	2	9	0
8 silence	243	93	89	169	68	225	138

Table 10. Effect of relationship between evaluator and user in evaluator's behavior

Status	Same level				Different level		
	1	2	3	5	4	6	7
1 Turn face to user	0	6	4	0	0	1	2
2 Express himself with gesture	0	0	0	0	0	2	0
3 Watch PC screen	295	81	69	125	111	208	162
4 Task management	14	11	65	61	20	33	15
5 1+3	28	17	23	3	3	34	6
6 2+3	1	2	13	0	0	9	10
7 1+2	2	7	2	0	0	0	1
8 1+2+3	5	3	3	0	0	8	2

Table 11 and 12 showed the difference of users' behaviour between participants at same level group and at different level group. It illustrated that users in No.2 and No.3 gave more explanation to their evaluators, paid more attention to task management, and had more face-to-face communication with evaluators. But it didn't mean that user with the same title would give more communication and explanation than user with lower title would do. Since the evaluators in participants pair No 2 and 3 were from European countries, probably it's because they were foreigners, users in this two pairs had to explain more, and had more face-to-face communication.

But in the Table 12, there was a power distance effect showed in row 6: watching PC +communicate with gesture. When evaluator's rank was higher, users tend to use more gesture during the test session. What could be the reason? When we went back to review the videotapes, we found evaluators with higher rank would sit a little farther with user than they did in another situation, and users felt a little nervous when they talk to evaluator with higher rank. It could be the reason.

Combining the data from user and evaluator, we can say power distance affected not only e valuators' behaviour, but also the users. But in this study, there was another factor involved with the power distance factor.

Table 11. Effect of relationship between evaluator and user in user's conversation

Status	Same level				Different level		
	1	2	3	5	4	6	7
1 evaluation	21	7	28	16	21	36	24
2 suggestion	0	0	1	0	0	3	0
3 explanation	**0**	**3**	**5**	**0**	1	1	0
4 question	20	8	15	7	3	9	25
5 description	115	55	107	87	72	116	57
6 confirmation	29	8	16	5	2	24	16
7 silence	159	39	9	73	15	99	73

Table 12. Effect of relationship between evaluator and user on user's behaviour

Status	Same level				Different level		
	1	2	3	5	4	6	7
1 Turn face to evaluator	0	5	0	1	0	2	0
2 Express himself with gesture	0	1	0	0	0	0	0
3 Watch PC screen	338	98	143	188	86	271	156
4 Task management	0	**13**	**14**	0	0	0	0
5 1+3	**7**	**12**	**10**	0	1	15	0
6 2+3	0	1	10	0	**38**	**2**	**33**
7 1+2	0	0	1	0	3	2	2
8 1+2+3	0	0	3	0	6	1	6

4 Discussion and Conclusion

Comparing with the results in pilot studies in India and Denmark, we didn't find much data related to comments, especially to culture. Only when evaluator was from another country, not from China, users would explain more about his/her choices of pictures and icons (see Table 11). It implied that when evaluator and user came from same culture background, although the test session could go through very quick and smoothly, they could probably miss some cultural usability problems. Another reason could be that, users were not get used to the way of think aloud, especially in process of design. Five of seven users mentioned in the follow up session that they were not satisfied their wedding invitation design because of the time pressure. For this point, we need rethink the experiment design including the wedding invitation task, and the think aloud method.

Although there were three phases for each participant pair, we didn't analyse the amount of usability issues that evaluator found. That because in this study, one evaluator was used three times, the number of usability problems she found was cumulated test by test. So there was no way to compare them between different conditions.

Another reason for that, when we go back to the original videotapes, we found not any user found the invitation text error. Many user did noticed some culturally wrong symbols in images and icons, but they didn't mentioned them until evaluator asked them pick them up. So, after the think aloud session, when researcher asked users the reason why they couldn't find the culturally wrong things, they told us they were so concentrated to fulfil the whole task so that they missed out all the details. And sometime although they noticed the wrong picture, but what they were asked to do was find an appropriate one as a decoration, so they thought it's not necessary to point it out.

From the data shown in Table 7 and 8, there was not much behaviour difference whatever users spoke Chinese, or English. It probably didn't mean that there was no influence of language on users. As mentioned before, it might because of the task requirement asking users doing what they did not do usually. The effect of task difficulty might have impact on the effect of language.

So, let's look back to the users' think aloud behaviour (Table 7), and calculate the percentage of each kind of conversation content. We found Chinese user spent about 30% of time on silence, another 30% of time on description, the other 30% on other contents, such as asking question, and evaluate the interface. Ramey doubted the think-aloud method in usability test [6]. In this study, there seemed having the same question: do we think keep talking about 60% of test time mean a real think aloud? Do we think half of talking time were spent on describing what he/she is doing is really a think aloud? Is it true that what a person's doing is what the person's thinking? Do we need to give more training before we start the usability test session? All the questions need to be answered in further study.

Briefly we can make conclusions here that, speaking different language and power distance affected the process of usability test. Speaking Chinese made evaluator giving more help, telling more about introductions, and like encouraging users more frequently; Speaking English made evaluator and user look at each other more often to make themselves understood, and evaluators paid more attention to check task list. When evaluator's title were higher than users, the evaluator would pay more attention to users' doing, would not like to give user more detailed instruction, usually loose more communication with user, and spent less time for task management. In contrast, talking to evaluators with higher rank, users tend to use more gesture to express themselves.

Acknowledgments. This study was co-funded by the Danish Council for Independent Research (DCIR) through its support of the Cultural Usability project. Thanks to the people who gave us access and helped us in this study.

References

1. Clemmensen, T.: Community Knowledge in an Emerging Online Professional Community: The Case of Sigchi.dk. Knowledge and Process Management 11(2), 1–10 (2005)

2. Hornbæk, K.: Current practice in measuring usability: Challenges to usability studies and research. International Journal of Human-Computer Studies 64, 79–102 (2006)
3. Marcus, A.: International and intercultural user interfaces. In: Stephanidis, C. (ed.) User Interfaces for All: Concepts, Methods, and Tools, pp. 47–63. Lawrence Erlbaum, Mahwah (2001)
4. Marcus, A.: Fast Forward: User-Interface Design and China: A Great Leap Forward. ACM, New York (2003)
5. Marcus, A.: Cross-cultural, global, and mobile user-interface design. In: HCI International: 11th International Conference on Human–Computer Interaction, Las Vegas, USA (2005)
6. Ramey, J., Boren, T. et al.: Does Think Aloud Work? How Do We Know? In: CHI, proceedings (2006)
7. Rau, P.-L.P., Choong, Y.-Y., Salvendy, G.: A cross cultural study on knowledge representation and structure in human computer interfaces. International Journal of Industrial Ergonomics 34(2), 117 (2004)
8. Shen, S., Woolley, M., Prior, S.: Towards culture-centred design. Interacting with Computers 16, 1–33 (2006)
9. Smith, A., Yetim, F.: Global human – computer systems: cultural determinants of usability. Interacting with Computers 16, 1–5 (2004)
10. Vatrapu, R., Pérez-Quiñones, M.A.: Culture and Usability Evaluation: The Effects of Culture in Structured Interviews. Journal of Usability Studies 1(4), 156–170 (2006)

Extending the User Experience to Localized Products

Yanxia Yang

Trend Micro Incorporated
10101 N. De Anza Blvd., Cupertino, CA 95014, USA

Abstract. One of the research and development goals for Trend Micro, Inc. is to improve the user experience and process for product localization. To achieve this goal, we need to understand the localization process. *Localization* is the process of modifying an application or product to support the requirements of a particular locale. The paper was based on the discussions between the user experience group and localization teams. It involved studying the existing localization process, identifying the common pain points, and then proposing solutions for them. Because localization is the last link in the product development chain and focuses on content rather than function, there are obvious dependencies on product development, user interface design, and documentation. We found that to improve the user experience and process for localization, different functional groups must collaborate from the start of the project and design their deliverables with localization in mind. The proposed solutions to localization teams from the user experience group (including User Interface Design and Documentation) were aligned with the software development processes and helped to improve localized products.

Keywords: User Experience, User Interface Design, Information Presentation, Usability, Documentation, Localization, International Use, Software Product Development.

1 Introduction

The Internet connects computers, and languages connect people. If you want your products to be easily accessed and used among all peoples in countries all over the world, or your Web applications to be easily applied to different regions, then you need to have a good localization process and user experience.

What is localization?

Localization is the process of modifying or adapting an application or product to support the requirements of a particular locale [1], [2], while at the same time keeping the localized version in synch with the original. Successful localization generates a high-quality language translation and maintains the functionality of applications or products. Localization, however, is much more than just translation. Localization should consider providing a better user experience which means we should not only consider the common localization requests, but also consider cultural difference for

N. Aykin (Ed.): Usability and Internationalization, Part II, HCII 2007, LNCS 4560, pp. 285–292, 2007.

different locale. Some studies on globalization and localization provide some general guidelines for localization [3], [4], [5], [6].

A successful localization project is expensive. It involves manual work of highly-paid professionals, it requires a set of reviews to improve the quality of translations comparing the previous software release, and it also needs testing for the functional and user interface after the software localization. A tried and proven localization process will save localization cost in the end.

This paper discusses the industry practice of collaboration between user experience group and localization teams, and how to improve user experience on localized products.

2 Method

The study was conducted through the discussion and communication between User Experience Group and Localization Teams. We discussed with localization managers and identified their pain points and provided suggestions from user experience perspective. So the first part of the study is to identify the pain points, and the second part of the study is to provide improvement recommendations to support localization team and try to achieve the best user experience align with the their localization goals.

3 Localization Process

To better extend the user experience in localization process, there must be an understanding of the localization process and the user interface design and document-tation processes must be adjusted for localization issues. The general localization process can be illustrated as follows:

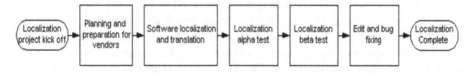

Fig. 1. Localization Process

When product development team freezes of the English UI completely - which means no additional UI windows or major elements will be introduced, localization project is at this point is launched. The localization team then plans and prepares the localization kit for vendors to localize the product. At this time, changes from the product development team can be incorporated. After software has been localized and translated, localization QA will do alpha and beta test. Based on the certain criteria, localization team will find issues and bugs. The issues and bugs will be fixed before the localized product is released.

4   User Interface Design and Documentation Processes

User experience group delivers user interface design and documentation that are closely related to the localized products. Improvement on user interface design and documentation processes will support localization process. To ensure the timely deliverables and quality of user-centered design and documentation, the different roles inside the user experience group, such as user researcher, UI designer, visual designer, technical writer, and usability engineer closely communicate and collaborate during the design and development process. Detailed information about different roles, their responsibilities and ownerships at different design and development stages can be referred in [7].

The following diagram will help to understand the general user interface design process:

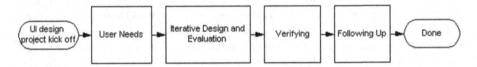

Fig. 2. User Interface Design Process

The user experience group starts the UI design project by gathering user needs. They receive and understand the detailed project content and raw requirements from in-house domain experts. Based on the requirement and user analysis, determine what design should do in order to cover the needs and goals of different user types. Then generate detailed UI design prototype. This is an iterative process. It needs quite a bit of communication among UI designer, product manager, and user researcher to come up the design, and the UI designer and product development team need to assess technical capabilities. The UI prototype needs a UI review and validation from technical writers to check wording, from visual designers to check the style guide and standards, and from usability engineers to test product usability. During product construction stage, user experience team should verify R&D's product build to ensure the product usability and installation. The final user interface will then be localized by localization team.

One of the major efforts of localization is translation, which is highly depends on the documentation from English version. The general documentation process can be illustrated as follows:

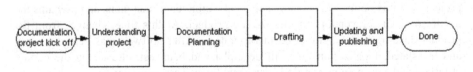

Fig. 3. Documentation Process

Technical writers are responsible for product information, or documentation, which appear in many forms – online, on-screen, and in print. After the documentation project kicks off, writers will study the product related materials and work on their documentation plan. The writers help UI designers for the on-screen content during the design phase, and work closely with product development team to draft online help, user manual, and readme during development and release stages. The document-tation is thoroughly reviewed to ensure the functionality accuracy and writing quality. Then the delivered documentation will be translated at different locales during localization process.

5   Issues Found During Localization

The user experience group is responsible for deliverables facing customers, such as the user interface, documentation and product packaging, which all related to future localized products. So the user experience group extends its interest to work with localization teams. The user experience group had discussions and interviews with localization managers including the regions of EMEA, Japan, and APAC. After discussion, we identified some pain points that related to localization and user experience. The details are found below.

5.1   Issues Related to User Interface Design

Since localized products are based on their original English version, if products that are not designed from the beginning for multinational or multilingual use, they often can not be deployed globally with ease. In this case, there would be some issues in localized products, such as: (1) UI is not fully resizable. Due to the difference in the size of an English string of text and a localized string, more space is needed in the localized languages. (2) Sometimes it is difficult to translate text correctly when the UI/control box is placed into a sentence, since the grammar is different from one language to another one. (3) Sometimes the data format is hard-coded. Since the specific locale has its own data format, it should not be hard-coded. (4) If there is text embedded in the graphics, it costs more to localize this text.

Other issues found by user experience groups are the following: (1) Sometimes the graphic being used in our localized products are inconsistent with its English version, and sometimes they look unprofessional and this reflects poorly on our brand. (2) Sometimes the layout of some controls changes (e.g., buttons being stretched out and distorted) due to the language translation, which influences the aesthetics.

5.2   Issues Related to Documentation

The languages connect people in different regions that are using Trend products. It is even more important to write sentences and present information in English version with localization in mind, so it can be easily translated into different languages in Europe, Asia and other regions. Through discussion with localization team, we found some issues related to documentation: (1) There are too much duplicated and unnecessary bits of information and screenshots in the documentation. (2) The new terms and glossary in English are either too late or insufficient for the localization team. (3) The tool we use to generate online help (RoboHelp) has some compatibility issues in the FireFox browser, which causes some problems at information presentation.

5.3 Issues Related to Development Process

Due to the lack of communication and collaboration between different functional teams, some development process related issues raised by localization teams are the following: (1) There are many necessary localization UI changes during the localization testing phase, due to late UI changes. This cost a lot of time, money and effort. (2) The localization teams should be involved earlier in the development process. The localization team should do source code and design reviews, repeatedly, after each design and major source code change, particularly when globalization or localization specific changes have been made. (3) The documentation should be finalized as early as possible. Technical writer should provide detailed information in what changes of a file have been made, not only what file has changed after the documentation sent to localization team.

6 Improvement Recommendations

The proposed solutions from user experience group to address the above issues can be classified as recommendations for processes and for guidelines and practices.

6.1 Improvement for Processes

Because localization is the last link of the product development chain, there will be ultimate impacts to localized products from user interface design and documentation processes. See the diagram below for the software development processes, which includes the product development process, user interface design process, document-tation process and localization process. Using product development process (R&D team) as the base timeline, we can see the other three processes corresponding timelines.

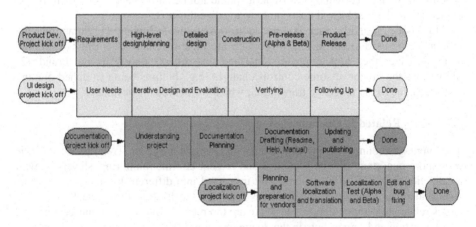

Fig. 4. Software Development Process

In the industry, the products delivered to customers are always under the limitation of time. "Time to Market" is an important factor to any product development. "What can be done in the short amount of time we have" is always challenging user experience group members. User experience group proactively collaborates with R&D and localization teams, and then try to address the issues raised by localization team. We do not want to increase development effort for R&D, and we do not want to increase costs for localization. Furthermore, we want our customers have best user experiences with our non-English products as well as English version.

From the above figure, we can see the timelines for user interface design and documentation processes, compared with the localization process. User interface design and documentation are involved in the early stage of product development. Therefore, to address the localization team's concern: "The localization teams should be involved earlier in the development process," user interface designers send the close-to-final UI prototype to localization team, and writers post their documentation plan to localization managers. This way, localization team can have a concrete idea for their project planning.

From localization's point of view, they would like the UI to be developed as early as possible, with no change after the final UI prototype. They also want the documentation to be finalized as early as possible. Thereby allowing the localization teams to work on the translation and testing earlier. This will save money, as the text would not have to be retranslated. However, in reality, user interface design and documentation have a lot of dependency on marketing product requirement and R&D engineering constraints, UI and documentation changes cannot be avoided. To address this concern, we build up the review mechanism. Localization teams will review UI prototypes and documentation (at certain milestones). The review feedback from localization team can be incorporated into the final UI design and document-tation, which will ultimately help the localized products. Effective communi-cation and collaboration between user experience group and localization team are the key to ensure the best user experience in localized products.

User experience group sometimes even goes further to help out localized products when there is an urgent need. For example, when the buttons in the localized products got stretched out due to translation, the user experience group did not want our customers using our non-English products to have an unprofessional UI compared the English version. So we made an extra effort to create English buttons and buttons that would accommodate every language version for which we localize. This way the product could be released on time, while RD saved time in creating a new button control that allows precise placement of text on image buttons, L10N saved their cost to use vendors for creating the localized images, which may not acceptable from user experience perspectives (branding and aesthetics).

Another recommendation is to have usability testing for localization products. Though the user interaction for tasks has been tested through the English version products, it is still necessary from the information visualization perspective due to the language and layout changes during the localization process.

6.2 Guidelines and Best Practices

To support localized products, the user experience group includes some guidelines and best practices related to localization address issues related to the UI and documentation. Therefore the software may be translated or adapted for other language and cultures easily. Some guidelines and best practices are listed below.

The development of Web-based UI and documentation are intend for users in many different countries with different cultures and languages, so it is very important to understand the needs of users from many different regions, demographics, experience, education, roles in organizations, and their daily tasks. Therefore, more thorough user research will benefit product localization and globalization.

Avoid embedding text within bitmaps and graphics to minimize the need for different versions to account for varying scripts.

Try to externalize any style and layout information from the HTML files into the style sheet, because the cost is quite high to match due to the large amount of tags within the HTML files.

Avoid embedding data fields and/or controls into sentences because the language changes significantly and therefore alters sentence format. For example, German sentences often have verbs at the ends of sentences, while English and French place them in the middle.

Use simple sentence structures when possible, because a shorter sentence is easy to translate.

Ensure consistency within one document and throughout the doc set, which means all references to the same item should use the same term. If there is a new term introduced, inform to localization teams.

The out-of-date file name should be removed from the project site. The maximum length of file name should be 64 characters (includes file extension) no matter the file is compressed in the build package. Do not use the special characters such as "\:;,*?<>" in the file name.

Allow for roughly 30% text expansion when English is localized into some target European languages. Based on the feedback from Trend Micro's localization managers, different languages need different enlarge space for the text string. For example, German: it is safe to allow 25% of increase; Spanish, French and Italian: it is safe to allow 75% of increase; Portuguese: it is safe to allow 35% of increase.

The adjustment of the appearance and orientation to account for national or cultural difference may distort the look and feel of user interface or online help. When localization team has some questions regarding the user interface and information presentation because of locale needs, user experience group will work with localization team to come up the best solution.

7 Conclusions

The industry practices used by Trend Micro improve the user experience for localized products, lower cost and prevent product delays. Different functional teams collaborate from the early stage of the project with localization in mind. The proposed solutions to the localization team from user experience group (including user interface design and documentation) are aligned with the UI design process, documentation process and localization process. A better understanding of the needs of different users in different cultures helps to develop successful products and increases the acceptance of localized products. As more emerging technology for information becomes available (such as AJAX and Web 2.0, and computer-based communication media becomes more popular), the challenge for more internationally compatible UI designs and information designs increases. More research needs to be done to provide a better user experience for localized products.

Acknowledgments. The full support of Trend Micro Incorporated helped to make this article possible. I would like to express my gratitude to my manager and colleagues in Trend Micro's Human Interface Engineering department, and to localization managers. I appreciate their support and involvement with this study.

References

1. http://www.localizationinstitute.com/switchboard.cfm?page=terminology
2. http://www.w3.org/International/questions/qa-i18n
3. Marcus, A.: Globalization of User Interface Design for the Web. In: the Proceedings of the 5th Human Factors and the Web conference in Gaithersburg, MD (1999)
4. Nielsen, J. (ed.): Designing User Interfaces for International Use, vol. 13 in the series Advances in Human Factors/Ergonomics. Elsevier publisher, Amsterdam (1990)
5. Fernades, T.: Global Interface Design: A Guide to Designing International User Interfaces, AP Professional, Boston (1995)
6. Del Galdo, E.M., Nielsen, J. (eds.): International User Interfaces. Wiley Computer Publishing, New York (1996)
7. Ektare, M. et al.: User Experience and Design Team: Efficient Handshake between Different Roles. In: Proceeding of Asia Pacific Computer Human Interaction 2006, Taipei, TW (2006)

Part II

Enhancing and Personalizing
the User Experience

The Technologist and
Internet Security and Privacy Practices

Greg Adamson

IEEE Society on Social Implications of Technology, Australia
18 Fourth St, Parkdale, Victoria, Australia

Abstract. The Internet's underlying architecture poorly supports many users' current security and privacy needs. This architecture reflects decades-old design decisions by technologists involved in creating the Internet. It can be viewed as an example of the separation between the interests and understanding of technologists and those of the subsequent technology end users. Alternatively, it can be considered the outcome of the needs of a particular set of users, technologists. This view, of the technologist as part of a technology culture among many cultural groupings using the Internet, goes further in explaining the security and privacy characteristics of the Internet today than an alternative critique of technology and usage, that there is an inevitable divide between technologists and non-technologist users.

Keywords: Internet, technology usage, engineering and society.

1 Introduction

Existing limitations in the implementation of security and privacy within the Internet are well documented. This paper examines some of these limitations and the assumptions of technologists who developed this technology. Most examinations of the role of technologists in the development of technology focus on the separation between technology tradition and practice and broader society (a separation variously seen as positive, neutral, or negative). I propose that Internet technologists can be seen as one (or more) particular cultural group. This moves the discussion from a choice between a technical view or a culturally informed view, to one in which technical players can be understood as part of the cultural landscape.

In this research I drew on a historical perspective of the Internet's development. The research examines the changing requirement for security, from the development of packet switching in the US military research environment in the early 1960s to the 1989 design of what would become the World Wide Web in a European science-research environment.

A second basis of this research is the philosophy of technology. I examined Winner's concept of 'autonomous technology'. The concept states that technology itself, rather than societal or usage factors, determine the development of technology.

This research also looked at usage theory, including the technologist as a user. The network technologist as user can be observed at least since the late 19th century. At

N. Aykin (Ed.): Usability and Internationalization, Part II, HCII 2007, LNCS 4560, pp. 295–304, 2007.

that time the number of people employed in the electric, telegraph and telephone industries had grown from a handful to hundreds of thousands in less than two decades. However, rather than seeing themselves as users, technologists have typically presented themselves as problem solvers standing outside the social context, providing the necessary solutions.

This paper examines the period of the Internet's technical development, an unusual period for the technologists involved. Technologists had broad opportunity to influence the Internet's architecture, free from commercial constraints, prior to the Internet's commercialisation around 1995. This makes the Internet atypical of technology uptake, but provides an opportunity to examine the direction in which technologists themselves may take a technology.

In this paper I am not considering the issue of unexpected implications of technology, in order to focus attention on the technologist as user. This is not to suggest that any new technology has exactly and only the effect that its developer or promoter expects. However, for simplicity, issues related to this have been removed from this discussion.

I have not considered whether an alternate set of design decisions, for example the construction of a secure network such as proposed by Baran [1], would have affected the Internet's subsequent success (for example due to increased cost or limits on accessibility). This research has been limited to the field of Internet technology. While important, the development path, structures and current state of Internet technology are not typical of technology in general. Further investigation could examine whether the 'technologist as user' has influenced the development of other technology fields.

2   How the Internet Got Its Security and Privacy Characteristics

The Internet has significant limitations in providing security and privacy. By default, the Internet's set of technical rules, or 'protocols', takes no responsibility for these. Specifically the Internet provides very little inherent support for the three requirements of secure and private communication: confidentiality, integrity and authentication.

- Confidentiality involves keeping information hidden from parties other than the intended recipient. As the Internet transmits clear (unencoded) text, confidentiality is not provided by default.
- Integrity of a message is whether it has been deliberately or accidentally altered. Has the figure or name on an order or cheque been changed? Have words been added to or deleted from a document? The Internet technology is based on 'packet switching', breaking messages into small discrete packets that are then sent across the network. Packets traversing the Internet infrastructure, which is owned by thousands of separate companies and organisations, will travel by an unspecified path that could include almost any country in the world, even when communicating between two users in the same city. By default all data is sent in a form that can be read and modified.
- Authentication is ensuring that each party in an exchange of information is who they claim to be. The Internet by design is an anonymous network. The Internet's

protocol suite TCP/IP provides no mechanism to certify parties to a communication. Co-inventor Cerf [2] identifies this as one of the key weaknesses of the protocol.

This lack of inbuilt security and support for privacy may appear surprising, given the origin of the Internet's technology in the US military environment. Its absence reflects the 'accidental' origins of the Internet. In his seminal work on packet switching Baran [1] included a chapter on security. This involved a complex two-level security approach built into the network providing encryption both between network devices and end-to-end across the network:

> One key difference between a civilian and a military communications system is the provision made in the latter for the preservation of secrecy and for immunity from destructive tampering. These considerations are most effectively integrated into a network as an integral part of the switching mechanism, rather than in the form of 'black boxes' tacked on as an afterthought... It is acknowledged that the approach represents a departure from conventional practices, which have traditionally maintained a separation between the design of the communications network itself (which is most often a slight modification of a system originally designed for civilian use) and the design and implication of cryptographic safeguards. (section IX, p. v)

Baran's comments on integrating security into initial design, rather than adding it on later, are now accepted standard practice within the IT security field. Baran's proposed network was never build. However, his work came to the attention of the US Department of Defence group working on Arpanet, which would later become the core of the Internet. Project manager Larry Roberts described his response on reading Baran's work: 'Suddenly I learned how to route packets' [3]. (p. 37) While the first network devices were steel-encased military-grade computers, and funded by the Department of Defence, Baran's security approach was not included. Two histories of the Internet [4, 5] make no reference to security considerations in describing the development of Arpanet ('security' does not even appear in their index). The first Internet standard to mention security problems is dated December 1973 [6]. Eighteen years later, a further standard echoes the same security concerns [7]:

> Because the Internet itself is neither centrally managed nor operated, responsibility for security rests with the owners and operators of the subscriber components of the Internet. Moreover, even if there were a central authority for this infrastructure, security necessarily is the responsibility of the owners and operators of the systems which are the primary data and processing resources of the Internet. There are tradeoffs between stringent security measures at a site and ease of use of systems (e.g., stringent security measures may complicate user access to the Internet).

The Internet developed in the 1970s and the 1980s. For much of this period technologists were the primary end users, as well as the Internet's developers. Technologists found that the services which the Internet provided, primarily e-mail and file transfer, were useful and valuable. In the absence of more pressing military applications, this provided technologists with the opportunity to develop a network to do what they wanted and needed. Technologists developed a technology that was well designed for their user needs.

By the early 1990s the Internet had grown into a widely dispersed network used by millions of people. The rapid uptake of the World Wide Web from 1993 created the Internet that users recognise today. This was based on work at the CERN European physics research centre. In his original proposal for what became the Web, Berners-Lee [8] addressed the issue of security as follows:

> Non requirements: Discussions on Hypertext have sometimes tackled the problem of copyright enforcement and data security. These are of secondary importance at CERN, where information exchange is still more important than secrecy. Authorisation and accounting systems for hypertext could conceivably be designed which are very sophisticated, but they are not proposed here. In cases where reference must be made to data which is in fact protected, existing file protection systems should be sufficient. (p. 12)

3 The Internet and Technology Tradition

These brief historical points on the origin of the approach to security during the Internet's development emphasise the central role of the technologists who developed the Internet's standards. There is a large body of literature examining the role of technologists in such decision making. Winner [9] summarises this debate including the work of Galbraith [10] on technocracy. At times the influence of technologists on decision making reaches into the political field. Winner quotes US President Dwight D. Eisenhower, who identified a 'danger that public policy could itself become the captive of a scientific technological elite.' (p. 148)

While the literature on technocracy points to controlling and centralising tendencies, the Internet's development history has been very different from that of other major technologies [11]. The single over-riding design requirement for Baran [1] in inventing packet switching was to build a network capable of continuing to wage war after a nuclear bombardment of the United States. He begins his introduction: 'Let us consider the synthesis of a communication network which will allow several hundred major communications stations to talk with one another after an enemy attack.' (section I, p. 1) This was achieved using packet-switching over a distributed network, in contrast to the centralised structure of the US telephone system of the 1960s. This explains the apparent contradiction of a hierarchical US military environment producing a distributed and difficult to control Internet technology.

The culture of the Internet was similarly non-hierarchical, as shown by its standards development process. The Request For Comment (RFC) standards are semi-formal documents available without charge and freely contributed by a community of thousands of technologists. This was possible because until the mid-1990s, from an infrastructure or business point of view, the Internet just wasn't very important. Handley [12] describes the last major change to the Internet's architecture in the 1980s:

> No-one likes changing such a key part of an operational network – such changes are driven by necessity. However, as the Internet was not a key

> infrastructure in the 1980s, the pain caused during transitions was comparatively low. Besides, many people regarded the Internet as an interim solution that would eventually be replaced by the [International Organisation for Standards'] OSI protocols, and therefore, with the glare of political attention diverted elsewhere, the engineers of the Internet were allowed to do good engineering. They learned from their mistakes by trying things out for real and fixed problems as they became pressing. (p. 120)

Despite its 'humble' origins, by the turn of the century the Internet had become critical infrastructure for the global economy. While the relative importance of large centralised information technology systems such as the mainframe, and the predominant mainframe communication protocol, a hierarchical technology from IBM called SNA, were in decline, the importance of the technologist was not diminishing. The introduction of CIOs (Chief Information Officers) to leading roles in corporations during the 1990s showed this strong and continuing importance of the technologist.

The rapid and unexpected growth of the Internet from 1995 created a demand for experts who 'understood' the Internet. While a new communications medium had been anticipated for the previous decade, and promised as an 'information superhighway', the actual Internet was far less predictable or controllable than previous technologies such as television or the telephone. In this sense the technology was 'out of control'. While the traditional technocrat was seen to have power through holding arcane technical knowledge, the Internet-era technologist in addition is expected to anticipate the direction and impact of complex technology. Stefik [13] provides a technologist's perspective on understanding the Internet. He presents four metaphors for what the Internet does, based on personality characteristics: the keeper of knowledge or conservator, the communicator, the trader, and the adventurer. He presents these four views as collectively exhaustive, missing the technologist (creator, planner of the Internet), and thereby providing no reflective examination of the Internet itself. This validates Winner [9], 'Technological society ... has never shown any great commitment to self-reflection, self-criticism, or the study of its own history.' (p. 128) In this view, the technologist sits above or outside of the world of problems to be solved. If technology is out of control (in either a negative or positive sense), who better than a technologist to intercede on an organisation's behalf?

Despite technologists' ability to do things with technology, and the clear role provided by technologists in the design of the Internet, there is no evidence that technologists in general have a greater ability to predict or control the direction and effect of technology than other professional groups. Technologists may be less prepared for unexpected results of technology. For example, uncritical enthusiasm for technology's promise can be found among technologists working for technology vendors. The experience of technology-led network vendor Cisco after the 2000 dot.com financial crash shows this. In 2000, one description of Cisco's production process [14] glowingly describes Cisco's inventory system:

> Because real-time information on sales requests and inventory levels is constantly online and available to Cisco and its manufacturers, Cisco can maintain lower inventory levels without increasing the risk of part shortages. Direct delivery from the factory cuts lead times at least in half—from four or

five weeks to two. As a result of the inventory online connection, Cisco has reduced its own inventory by 45 percent, saving $5.6 million. (p. 150)

Cisco shareholders were surprised in early 2001 when Cisco wrote off $US2.5 billion of $US4.1 billion inventories on its books. Looking back on this period some years later:

> CIO Brad Boston found that Cisco had nine order status tools. Each of them used data from different sources, which used different definitions for key terms. As a result, the systems couldn't give the company a clear picture of its orders. There were similar problems in the sales organization' [15]. (p. 146)

In retrospect the issue becomes clear, while at the time confidence in the technology left no room for doubt.

4   A Technologist Culture

The self-confidence of the technological profession is examined by Winner [9] in terms that go beyond the technical, to the basis of technology knowledge:

> A typical response of engineers ... is to announce that they are merely problem solvers. 'Tell us the problem,' they demand. 'We will find a solution. That's our job. But you may not presume to question the nature of our solution. You are not a member of a technical profession and, therefore, know nothing of relevance. If you insist on raising questions about the appropriateness of the means we devise, we can only conclude that you are antitechnology.' ... It soon becomes clear that in this enlightened age there is almost no middle ground of rational discourse, no available common language with which persons of differing backgrounds can discuss matters of technology in thoughtful, critical terms... Indeed, anyone seriously critical of conditions in the technological society soon meets up with the demand from technically trained persons that in order to speak at all, one must first 'learn technology.' A version of the mode of legitimisation through expert knowledge, this advice is, in my experience, usually less a plea for understanding than an urging to compliance. (p. 11)

Marvin [16] describes the creation of the electrical engineering profession within the United States. Electrical engineering first emerged as a profession in the 1870s. The American Institute for Electrical Engineers (AIEE) was founded in 1884. *Electrical World* estimated in 1890 that at the time 250,000 people depended on the electrical industry (including telegraph and telephone) for their livelihood. While investment in electrical technology created the engineering workforce, the creation of an engineering profession was not an inevitable consequence. Marvin describes this as a process of 'inventing the expert', and summarises the experts' goals as:

> ...to harness public adulation to improve their own social and professional standing while keeping public admirers at arm's length... The proper naming of persons, gadgets, and concepts in their electrical contexts and relations

was among the most important performative indicators of technological literacy. (pp. 15-16)

In recent decades there has been evidence of a more reflective attitude among technologists, partly responding to commentary from professionals outside the technology field. Schneier, author of *Applied Cryptography*, a seminal work on information technology security [17], for example reflectively examines the issue of technology security practices:

A colleague once told me that the world was full of bad security systems designed by people who read *Applied Cryptography*. Since writing the book, I have made a living as a cryptography consultant: designing and analyzing security systems. To my initial surprise, I found that the weak points had nothing to do with the mathematics. They were in the hardware, the software, the networks, and the people. Beautiful pieces of mathematics were made irrelevant through bad programming, a lousy operating system, or someone's bad password choice [18] (p. xi).

Schneier summarises this: 'If you think technology can solve your security problems, then you don't understand the problems and you don't understand the technology.' (p. 385)

The discussion of whether there is a technological or other basis for discussion of technology approaches goes beyond the field of technology. I suggest that we can think of technologists as one or more groups, with their own culture. The discussion of technologist as expert then becomes a discussion of the way in which various cultures approach technology, with the technologist's culture as one or more particular instance. (On cursory examination the approach of technologists across different countries and the existence of technical standards established by international organisations such as the International Telecommunication Union and International Organisation for Standards suggest a shared global technologists' culture.)

The tradition of technology described by Winner above has both strengths and weaknesses. A strength is that a great deal of valuable technology has been introduced into the world. A weakness is that technologists often believe that technologically satisfactory solutions are generally satisfactory for users. A recent and widely discussed debate between technologists and a non-technologist (business) audience occurred following the publication in *Harvard Business Review* of an article, 'IT doesn't matter' [19]. This took up the well established business concept of 'competitive advantage', a term coined and defined by Michael Porter [20]. Competitive advantage describes a situation in which a company has some ongoing advantage in relation to its rivals. For example, this could be lower cost production techniques, favored access to raw materials or markets, a more desirable product, key patents, or turnover of skilled staff at a rate substantially lower than an industry average. It doesn't mean high productivity, advanced technology or fast time to market if all its competitors also have these or can quickly get them. Competitive advantage is easy for a company to understand, but is outside the realm of practical experience for a technologist, who will generally promote the wide uptake of technology.

Carr suggested that information technology has become a commodity item, and does not provide competitive advantage in itself. In the following press debate, Carr [21] examines the technologist's view, provided by *Fortune* technology writer David Kirkpatrick.

> The most telling quote comes from the CEO of a software company that, Kirkpatrick tells us, 'builds sophisticated software for collaboration.' Says this CEO: 'We just closed several deals with leading Fortune 100 companies using our software to differentiate their ability to get vast international sales and marketing ecosystems working together to respond faster and more correctly to customers. "This is not a 'me too!"' But if he's already sold the same system to 'several' Fortune 100 companies, one has to wonder how differentiating the technology really is. It's difficult to purchase competitive advantage from an outside supplier who's peddling the same 'advantage' to your peers.

While it is easy to point to areas where technologists have a narrow technically defined view of a problem, there are many examples of technologists showing an awareness of the limitations of this approach. The Institute of Electrical and Electronic Engineers (IEEE) is a mainstay of the global technology community. Writing in the journal *IEEE Internet Computing*, Gong and Sandhu [22] describe a significant difficulty with security resulting from a disconnection between technology potential and uptake:

> The focus on deployment reflects the frustration, shared by the majority of the computer security research community, over the glaring gap between state-of-the-art security research and state-of-the-art security practice. Although a tremendous amount of new research is published each year ... the commercial adoption rate of this research is miserably low compared with adoption rates for other technologies, such as high-speed networking. In fact, you can count on one hand the number of innovative and effective security technologies that have been widely deployed in the past three decades... Why such a gap exists is a mystery, and to attempt an analysis is beyond the scope of this article. Our emphasis on deployment for this special issue is a small effort toward narrowing this gap. In the end, we failed to attract articles that explain why certain security technologies are adopted while others are not— Any historians out there reading this? (pp. 38-39)

The Xerox PARC laboratory in the US has a reputation for taking a non-technical view of technology challenges. Brown [23] describes his experience there:

> ...innovation is not about technology alone but also about the work practices in which technologies are used. In fact, we have anthropologists, psychologists, and sociologists on our research staff to help us find better techniques for linking to the world, listening in different ways for latent needs and tacit knowledge, and learning from actual work practices... Instead of merely hurling inventions over the transom into the hands of business developers, technologists share in the responsibility for making inventions into innovations. (pp. xii-xiv)

Brown calls this alternative approach among technologists 'seeing differently'. This complements the self-awareness of security researchers mentioned above. Such an approach increases the relevance of developed technology by linking technologists to the broader society for which they are developing and implementing technology.

5 Conclusion

This research has described the role of a technological perspective in the state of security and privacy functionality within the architecture of the Internet. The technological perspective has established a global data network which despite being used by hundreds of millions of people poorly supports security and privacy in its fundamental design. This could be cited as an example of the limitation of having a technological focus during technology design. I am proposing a different approach. This is to consider the Internet's architecture as representing the intentions of technologists in the 1970s and 1980s designing a network for the technologist user. Once incorporated into the Internet's architecture in the 1970s and 1980, these characteristics have been difficult to change.

In this view, technologists represent one or more groups of technology users with their own particular culture. From this perspective technologists can be considered as one voice among many in decision-making with regard to technology, rather than as the exclusive holders (or withholders) of expertise necessary to understand and manage technology.

References

1. Baran, P.: On Distributed Communications. In: United States Air Force Project RAND, RAND Corporation, viewed 25 January 2007 (1964), http://www.rand.org/about/history/-baran.list.html
2. Cerf, V.: Vint Cerf Talks About Internet, Slashdot, viewed 17 October 2002 (2002), http://interviews.slashdot.org/
3. Abbate, J.: Inventing the Internet. MIT Press, Cambridge, MA (1999)
4. Hafner, K., Lyon, M.: Where Wizards Stay Up Late: The Origins of the Internet, Touchstone, New York (1998)
5. Naughton, J A: Brief History of the Future: The Origins of the Internet, Phoenix, London (2000)
6. Metcalfe, R.M.: The Stockings Were Hung By the Chimney with Care, RFC 602, viewed 1 February 2007 (1973), ftp://ftp.rfc-editor.org/in-notes/rfc602.txt
7. Pethia, R., Crocker, S., Fraser, B.: Guidelines for the Secure Operation of the Internet, RFC 1281, viewed 1 February 2007 (1991), ftp://ftp.rfc-editor.org/in-notes/rfc1281.txt
8. Berners-Lee, T.: Information Management: A Proposal, internal CERN document, viewed 21 August 2006 (1989), http://www.w3.org/History/1989/proposal.html
9. Galbraith, J.K.: The New Industrial State, New American Library, New York (1968)
10. Winner, L.: Autonomous Technology: Technics-Out-of-Control as a Theme in Political Thought. MIT Press, Cambridge, MA (1978)
11. Adamson, G.: The Mixed Experience of Achieving Business Benefit from the Internet: A Multi-disciplinary Study, RMIT University, Melbourne, Viewed 31 July 2006 (2004), http://adt.lib.rmit.edu.au/adt/public/adt-VIT20041105.112155

12. Handley, M.: Why the Internet Only Just Works. BT Technology Journal 24(3), 119–129 (2006)
13. Stefik, M.: Internet Dreams: Archetypes, Myths, and Metaphors. MIT Press, Cambridge, MA (1996)
14. Bunnell, D., Brate, A.: Making the Cisco Connection: The Story Behind the Real Internet Superpower. John Wiley & Sons, New York (2000)
15. McAfee, A.: Mastering the Three Worlds of Information Technology, Harvard Business Review, pp. 141–149 (November 2006)
16. Marvin, C.: When Old Technologies Were New: Thinking About Electric Communication in the Late Nineteenth Century. Oxford University Press, New York (1988)
17. Schneier, B.: Applied Cryptography: Protocols, Algorithms, and Source Code in C, 2nd edn. John Wiley & Sons, New York (1996)
18. Schneier, B.: Secrets and Lies: Digital Security in a Networked World. Wiley Computer Publishing, New York (2000)
19. Carr, N.G.: IT Doesn't Matter. Harvard Business Review 81(5), 41–49 (2003)
20. Porter, M.E.: Competitive Advantage: Creating and Sustaining Superior Performance. Free Press, New York (1985)
21. Carr, N.I.: Doesn't Matter: Responses, viewed 16 February 2007 (2003), http://www.nicholasgcarr.com/articles/matter.html
22. Gong, L., Sandhu, R.: What Makes Security Technologies Relevant? IEEE Internet Computing 4(6), 38–41 (2000)
23. Brown, J.S.: Seeing Differently: Insights on Innovation, Harvard Business School Press, Boston (1997)

A Statistical Model of Relationship Between Affective Responses and Product Design Attributes for Capturing User Needs

Sangwoo Bahn[1], Cheol Lee[1,*], Joo Hwan Lee[1,2], and Myung Hwan Yun[1]

[1] Department of Industrial Engineering, Seoul National University
Seoul, 151-744, Korea
[2] POSDATA Co.Ltd., Seoul, Korea
iehis@snu.ac.kr

Abstract. Customer's satisfaction is a critical factor to a product's success and identifying key affective response factors which customers mainly perceive is critical to satisfy customers. This study aims to identify the key affective response factor of satisfaction for passenger car interior material using statistical approach. Related variables of satisfaction consisting of 10 affective response variables associated with look-and-feel and touch feel of a surface material was systematically identified through literature survey, customer reviews, and expert opinions. Thirty participants evaluated 41 different crash pad samples using a questionnaire survey with 9-point semantic differential scale and 100-point scale. Based on the survey results, softness was identified as the key affective response factor of satisfaction for car crash pad. Then the relationship between softness and related engineering variables was identified. It is expected that the results could suggest the optimal combination and provide specific design guidelines quantitatively.

Keywords: Affective response, Satisfaction, Crash pad, Quantification Theory Type I, Softness.

1 Introduction

Understanding what buyers value within a given offering, creating value for them, and then managing it over time have long been recognized as essential elements of every market-oriented firm's core business strategy [1,2,3,4]. In the last decade, understanding how customers perceive products and how to reflect their subjective feelings or preferences in product design is becoming more important [5,6,7]. In addition, topics such as 'hedonic quality' [8], 'image/impression quality' [9,10], and 'total ambience quality' [11] are being increasingly recognized in the product design.

In most industry, customers' concerns with the aesthetic aspects of design have recently increased as the functional characteristics have reached to a satisfactory level [12]. Especially, design considerations such as sophisticated finish, harmony of

---

* Corresponding author.

N. Aykin (Ed.): Usability and Internationalization, Part II, HCII 2007, LNCS 4560, pp. 305–313, 2007.

colors, and luxurious material have been emphasized to enhance customer satisfaction as well as competitiveness in the market [13]. With this trend, a number of studies which handled affective responses of design characteristics using questionnaire survey and statistical method have been conducted [11,12,13,14]. These studies shows that analyzing user's affective responses which expressed in verbal is an effective way of analyzing user's affective response and enhancing user's satisfaction. However, previous studies considered limited visual characteristics of engineering variables such as interior shapes, colors and materials partially. In addition, these results give only abstract results, which cannot provide practical guidelines. Hence, to improve customer's satisfaction, more detailed study that can give more specific guidelines of the optimal level of engineering variables is still needed. Therefore, this study aims to identify critical affective response factor of satisfaction and relationship between critical factor and each level of engineering variables with a case study of car crash pad.

2   Method

The overall procedure of this study is as follows. First, related affective response variables of car crash pad are collected through literature survey and FGI (Focus Group Interview) of customers and designers. Second, in order to identify the relationship between satisfaction and affective response variables of crash pad, evaluation experiments were conducted using a questionnaire survey. Third, based on the survey results, key factor of satisfaction was identified and the relationship between key factor and engineering variables of car crash pad was identified quantitatively by using quantification theory type I method.

2.1   Crash Pad

This study focused on the passenger car crash pad placed in front of driver seat. The crash pad has strong influence on customer feeling on overall interior quality of automobile (see Fig. 1).

Fig. 1. Example of a car crash pad

2.2   Related Affective Response Variables of Satisfaction for Car Crash Pad

Through extensive literature survey, FGI of designers, salespersons, and customers, and expert opinions about crash pad, initial 20 affective response variables of crash pad were collected. After selecting and integrating, 10 variables were selected from the initial variables based on the expert opinions. As a result, hierarchical structure of essential affective response variables of satisfaction was developed as shown in Table 1.

Table 1. The hierarchical structure of selected variables

Hierarchy			Definition
Satisfaction	Touch feel	Feel of a material	Degree of softness
			Degree of smoothness
		Feel of elasticity	Degree of solidness
			Degree of elasticity
	Look-and-feel	Feel of harmony	Degree of tactile oneness
		Feel of shape	Degree of hard-looking
			Degree of delicate
		Feel of color	Degree of warmness of color
			Degree of brightness of color
			Degree of gloss

2.3 Evaluation Experiment on Satisfaction

Table 2 presents the quantity and characteristics of crash pad samples used in the experiment. Based on their design specifications, crash pads were characterized by their material type, embossing type, and color.

Questionnaire used in evaluation experiment was formulated based on the hierarchical structure of affective response variables and 9-point likert scales and 100-point scales were used (see Fig. 2). Thirty participants who have more than 1 year driving experience employed in the evaluation experiment.

Table 2. The quantity and characteristics of crash pad samples

Design specifications		Quantity
Material type	Hard IP	10
	PU Spray	7
	TPO	4
	PVC PSM	11
	PVC ABS	4
	TPU PSM	5
Embossing type	Cell type	14
	Wave type	16
	Technical type	6
	Geometric type	5
Color	Black	12
	Dark Brown	7
	Brown	7
	Dark Blue	9
	Grey	6

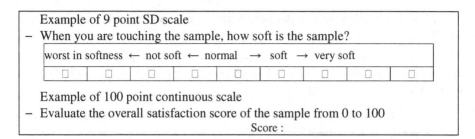

Fig. 2. Example of questionnaire used in evaluation experiment

2.4 Analysis and Modeling Method

Quantification Theory Type I method were utilized to analysis the relationships between satisfaction and related variables. Rating scores of 100-point scale were normalized in order to avoid the effect of individual variation in subjective evaluation. For the statistical analysis, SPSS (ver. 12.0) and SAS (ver. 9.1) S/W packages were utilized.

3   Results

3.1   The Results of Quantification Theory Type I Analysis

In order to identify the relationships between affective response variables and satisfaction, Quantification Theory Type I analysis was conducted. The results are presented in Table 3, and this shows the ranges of partial regression coefficients of each variables and the relative importance of each variable. According to the Table 3, satisfaction is mainly influenced by 'softness'.

Table 3. Relative importance of each variable ($R^2 = 0.53$, p-value<0.001)

Variable		Range	Relative importance (%)
Tactile variables	Softness	55.02	27.88
	Smoothness	17.98	9.11
	Solidness	10.56	5.35
	Elasticity	16.91	8.56
	Tactile oneness	19.53	9.90
Visual variables	Delicateness	15.69	7.95
	Hard-looking	13.41	6.80
	Warmness	17.44	8.84
	Brightness	6.53	3.31
	Gloss	24.27	12.30

3.3 Identifying Relationships Between Softness and Engineering Variables of Car Crash Pad

With respect to the key factor of satisfaction of car crash pad (softness), related engineering variables were collected based on the expert's opinion. Table 4 shows collected engineering variables.

Table 4. Collected variables Related with softness of car crash pad

Engineering variables	Dimension	Type of variable
The type of embossment	1. Geometric	Categorical
	2. Cell	
	3. Wave	
	4. Technical	
The hardness of surface	HS	Continuous
The length of embossment	mm	Continuous
The height of embossment	mm	Continuous
The size of embossment	mm^2	Continuous
The depth of embossment	μm	Continuous
The coefficient of static friction	Dimensionless	Continuous
The coefficient of dynamic friction	Dimensionless	Continuous

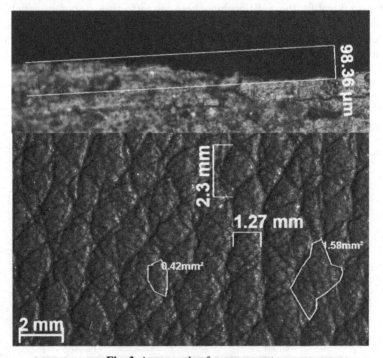

Fig. 3. An example of measurement

As the same way, the relative importance of each variables and the effect of each levels were identified using Quantification Theory Type I analysis. Before the analysis, continuous variables were categorized into 10 to 17 levels with respect to the values of softness (shown in Figure 4).

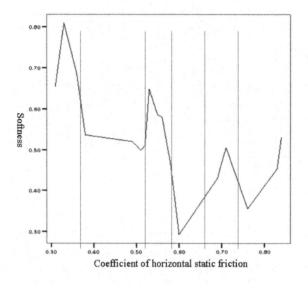

Fig. 4. An example of categorizing continuous variable

With the categorized data, we conducted Quantification Theory Type I analysis. The results of analysis are shown in Table 5~6. According to Table 5, softness of surface was mainly affected by the coefficient of friction. And Table 6 shows the effects of each level of variables and with these results. We can see the effects of each level of variables to softness and identify optimal combination of engineering variables according to the results of Table 6.

Table 5. Result of Quantification Theory Type I analysis ($R^2 = 0.49$)

Variable	Range	Relative importance (%)
The type of material	14.8	11.28
The type of embossment	10.3	7.85
The hardness of surface	22.2	16.92
The length of embossment	8.1	6.17
The height of embossment	7.4	5.64
The size of embossment	8.6	6.55
The depth of embossment	5.8	4.42
The coefficient of static friction	27.8	21.19
The coefficient of dynamic friction	26.2	19.97

Table 6. The partial regression coefficient of each level of engineering variables

Variables	Levels & their partial regression coefficients																	
The unit width of embossment (mm)	~0.8	0.8 ~1.1	1.1 ~1.3	1.3 ~1.63	1.63 ~1.7	1.7 ~1.75	1.75 ~1.8	1.8 ~1.955	1.955 ~2	2 ~2.015	2.015 ~2.1	2.1 ~2.26	2.26 ~2.4	2.4 ~2.46	2.46 ~2.7	2.7 ~2.9	2.9~	
Coefficient	-9.8	-20.4	-2.6	-4.5	-0.4	1.2	2.2	3.0	8.8	14.2	2.3	9.7	3.0	2.6	1.09	20.5	8.99	
The unit height of embossment (mm)	~0.65	0.65 ~2	2 ~2.29	2.29 ~2.46	2.46 ~2.55	2.55 ~2.9	2.9 ~3	3 ~3.55	3.55 ~4	4 ~4.4	4.4 ~4.55	4.55 ~5.2	5.2 ~5.8	5.8 ~6.4	6.4 ~8	8 ~9.2	9.2~	
Coefficient	-0.4	-4.1	-10.1	-1.9	-10.4	-1.8	-12.2	0.3	6.1	20.6	7.5	-0.2	20.5	9.0	0.9	11.9	2.9	
The unit size of embossment (mm2)	~0.5	0.5 ~0.85	0.85 ~1.2	1.2 ~1.5	1.5 ~1.813	1.813 ~1.83	1.83 ~1.88	1.88 ~2.1	2.1 ~2.3	2.3 ~2.4	2.4 ~3.69	3.69 ~4	4 ~5	5~ 5.85	5.85 ~6.4	6.4 ~16	16~	
Coefficient	-2.3	-10.4	-5.5	5.1	7.3	-3.6	6.1	-6.0	9.6	-5.5	7.2	1.7	16.6	8.1	-20.6	2.3	8.6	
The depth of embossment (μm)	~48	48 ~55	55 ~70	70 ~80	80 ~85	85 ~90	90 ~97	97 ~102	102 ~106	106 ~111	111 ~120	120 ~124	124 ~130	130 ~140	140 ~150	150 ~175	175 ~215	215~
Coefficient	3.6	21.0	1.0	8.7	8.1	-6.1	16.1	3.6	-6.5	4.6	-9.3	4.3	-12.6	10.5	-10.6	0.2	-5.2	3.9
The coefficient of static friction	~0.75	0.75 ~0.9	0.9 ~0.97	0.97 ~1.15	1.15 ~1.2	1.2 ~1.26	1.26 ~1.4	1.4 ~1.425	1.425 ~1.5	1.5 ~1.7	1.7 ~1.9	1.9 ~2.0	2.0~					
Coefficient	-3.8	-9.8	-1.9	9.8	22.4	5.7	10.0	-9.8	8.4	-7.2	7.8	-17.6	-5.0					
The coefficient of dynamic friction	~0.2	0.2 ~0.23	0.23 ~0.25	0.25 ~0.3	0.3 ~0.35	0.35 ~0.38	0.38 ~0.4	0.4 ~0.41	0.41 ~0.42	0.42 ~0.427	0.427 ~0.45	0.45 ~0.47	0.47 ~0.5	0.5 ~0.55	0.55~			
Coefficient	-3.8	-9.8	-1.9	9.8	-9.9	10.0	-9.8	8.4	-7.2	7.8	17.6	5.0	12.7	7.8	-9.9			
The hardness of surface(HS)	65 ~67.5	67.5 ~70.5	70.5 ~74	74 ~76.5	76.5 ~79	79 ~80.5	80.5 ~81.5	81.5 ~85	85 ~90	90 ~100								
Coefficient	1.7	5.9	2.0	1.2	9.4	4.7	14.6	-6.6	-13.3	-14.2								
The type of material	Hard IP	PU spray	TPO	PVC PSM	PVC ABS	TPU PSM												
Coefficient	-13.6	6.8	3.6	14.2	-8.4	6.2												
The type of embossment	Geo	Cell	Wave	Tech														
Coefficient	-19.3	6.9	5.7	-3.7														

4 Conclusion

This study identified the key affective response factor of satisfaction for car crash pad and its optimal levels of related engineering variables using statistical approach. Regarding with collected affective response variables of crash pad, evaluation experiment using a questionnaire was conducted to identify key affective response factor of satisfaction. Through the Quantification Theory Type I analysis, relationship between key affective response factor of crash pad and engineering variables of crash pad and desirable combination of engineering variables were identified. According to the results of this study, satisfaction of softness of surface was identified as the key affective response factor of satisfaction and to elaborate the satisfaction of softness, friction of surface should be controlled first.

The previous studies which analyzed affective responses were about relationships between limited part of the engineering variables and satisfaction, which can provide abstract implications. However this study analyzed more detailed and specific variables, so it can provide more specific and quantifiable design guidelines. Using the methodology used in this study, the key affective response factors of other products could be identified.

References

1. Drucker, P.F.: Innovation and Entrepreneurship, Harper and Row: New York (1985)
2. Porter, M.: Competitive Advantage. Free Press, New York (1985)
3. Porter, M.: Competitive Advantage: Creating and Sustaining Superior Performance. Free Press, NewYork (1998)
4. Slater, S.F., Narve, J.C.: Customer-led and marketoriented: let's not confuse the two. Strategic Management Journal 19, 1001–1006 (1998)
5. Hsu, S.H., Chuang, M.C., Chang, C.C.A: A semantic differential study of designers' and users' product form perception. International Journal of Industrial Ergonomics 25, 375–391 (2000)
6. Lai, H., Lin, Y., Yeh, C., Wei, C.: User-oriented design for the optimal combination on product design. International Journal of Production Economics 100, 253–267 (2006)
7. Lin, R., Lin, C.Y., Wong, J.: An application of multidimensional scaling in product sementics. International Journal of Industrial Ergonomics 18, 193–204 (1996)
8. Helander, M.G., Zhang, L.: Forget about ergonomics in chair design? Focus on esthetics and comport! In: Helander, M.G., Khalid, H.M., Than, M.P. (eds.) Proceedings of the International Conference on Affective Human Factors Design, pp. 256–261 (2003)
9. Yun, M.H., Han, S.H., Ryu, T., Yoo, K.: Determination of critical design variables based on the characteristics of product image/impression: case study of office chair design. In: Proceedings of the Human Factors and Ergonomics Society 45th Annual Meeting, pp. 712–716 (2001)
10. Yun, M.H., Han, S.H., Hong, S.W, Kim, J.: Incorporating user satisfaction into the look-and-eel of mobile phone design. Ergonomics 46, 1423–1440 (2003)
11. Jindo, T., Hirasago, K.: Application studies to car interior of Kansei Engineering. International Journal of Industrial Ergonomics 19, 105–114 (1997)

12. You, H.C., Ryu, T.B., Oh, K.H., Yun, M.Y., Kim, K.J.: Development of satisfaction models for passenger car interior materials considering statistical, technical and practical aspects of design variables. The Korean Journal of IE Interfaces 17, 482–489 (2004)
13. Nakada, K.: Kansei engineering research on the design of construction machinery. International Journal of Industrial Ergonomics 19, 129–146 (1997)
14. Tanoue, C., Ishizaka, K., Nagamachi, M.: Kansei Engineering: A study on perception of vehicle interior image. International Journal of Industrial Ergonomics 19, 115–118 (1997)

Guidelines to Develop Emotional Awareness Devices from a Cultural-Perspective: A Latin American Example

Cesar A. Collazos[1,2], María Paula González[1,3], Andrés Neyem[4],
and Christian Sturm[5]

[1] Group GRIHO – University of Lleida – Jaume II 69, 25001 – Lleida, Spain
mpg@diei.udl.es, mpg@cs.uns.edu.ar
[2] Department of Systems, Universidad del Cauca – FIET-Sector Tulcan, Popayán, Colombia
ccollazo@unicauca.edu.co
[3] VyGLab Laboratory – Computer Science Department – Universidad Nacional del Sur
Av. Alerm 1253, 8000- Bahia Blanca, Argentina
[4] Department of Computer Science, Universidad de Chile
Av. Blanco Encalada 2120 – Santiago, Chile
aneyem@dcc.uchile.cl
[5] Instituto de Electrónica y Computación - Universidad Tecnológica de la Mixteca
Huajuapan de León, 69000 - Oaxaca, México
csturm@mixteco.utm.mx

Abstract. Interpersonal communication involves more than just words; it involves emotional issues that can be roughly seen as complex organized internal states. Awareness of those states allows human beings to evaluate social information and develop strategic social intelligence. In this setting, developing emotional awareness devices can be successfully achieved under a Cultural Centred Design perspective, as social and cultural features are crucial to ensure an adequate level of emotional awareness. However, cultural-oriented recommendations are not always included to lead the promoting of an adequate emotional awareness in digital and physical devices. To cope with this problem, this paper presents a minimal set of cultural guidelines that should be taken into account to develop emotional awareness devices under Cultural Centred Design. To illustrate the proposal, the development of an extended virtual portrait is discussed by highlighting a cultural viewpoint form a Latin-American perspective.

1 Introduction

In the last decades, the importance of social and cultural aspects in the HCI field increased significantly. Applying Cultural Centred Design (CCD) [11], Ethnographic Observation [17], ethnographically-informed systems design [2] and localization methods that go beyond simple language translation shifted the focus from the individual human-computer interaction to contextual and social-cultural issues. This enhance the importance of systems supporting interpersonal interactions where non-verbal clues are closely connected to the emotional state of a person (like body

N. Aykin (Ed.): Usability and Internationalization, Part II, HCII 2007, LNCS 4560, pp. 314–323, 2007.

language and gestures). However, part of these non-verbal information seem to be missing when communication is mediated by technology. While the new developments in information technology lead to new ways of interpersonal computer-mediated communication, facilitating international and intercultural communication, the human basics of how trust and sociability is developed haven't changed [5].

In the above scenario, alternative ways have been proposed ranging from basic features such as the "emoticons" up to more sophisticated tools such as specialized emotional awareness devices based on Phidgets [9]. Note that in general the communication of emotional states has to be brought from an unconscious to a conscious level for both the sender and the receiver of the message, leading to evolve a common ground of emotional context in which the message can be interpreted correctly. Consequently, the support of emotional awareness is identified as one central issue that need to be developed further within the field of interpersonal computer-mediated communication [13, 16]. To address this problem, this paper discuss a minimal set of cultural guidelines that should be taken into account to develop emotional awareness devices under CCD. Taking as stared point the building of an emotional awareness device called *Emoti-Picture Frame*, the existing guidelines of User-Centered Design (UCD) associated with the production of social-oriented interactive systems are extended to include emotional awareness as a core function.

This paper is structured as follows. First, Section 2 discussed the most relevant characteristics of emotional awareness devices. Next, Section 3 describes the proposed guidelines. Section 4 presents the device *Emoti-Picture Frame* as an example wich illustrated the use of the settled guidelines within a Latinoamerican context. Finally, Section 5 concludes and depicts some further work.

2 Emotional Awareness Devices

Human emotions are valuable sources of information wich help us make decisions and communicate with others [4]. They play a major role in human interaction [4]. In particular, facial expressions can convey a wide range of emotions (as hapinness, nervousness or fear). Therefore, recently many areas of HCI research have been converging on the important implications of emotions and emotional awareness in software development, where emotional awareness is measured in terms of levels of awareness. As a consequence, novel types of software-based devices are emerging, including physical user interfaces augmented by computing power [9]. These new gadgets are called emotional awareness devices (EADs).

EADs enables new types of communication (e.g. tangible interfaces) and novel ways of emotional interactions, as the one-bit communication artefact described on [19]. Further on, existing products are often enriched by adding new communication functions to promote emotional awareness. Researchers have also addressed the "glancing" metaphor with the exploration of MediaSpaces, Portals, and awareness devices [6]. Various physical interfaces have enabled remote individuals to arm wrestle,[1] blow kisses,[2] exchange simple touching [3], and send gestures [7]. Similarly, there has been a tremendous amount of sociological studies of mobile phone usage.

In this setting, and according with UCD and CCD, cultural-based issues and restrictions comming from the final user's context of use should be strongly taken into account during all the development process of EADs. However, even some researches have investigated how to represent emotional characteristics using colors [16], most EADs are designed without considering the cultural characteristics of the people who use them as crucial requirements to achieve. In our opinion, a set of multicultural elements as those proposed in the next section needed to be more strongly considered for achieving an appropriate level of emotional awareness in a final EAD product.

3   Cultural-Based Guidelines for Emotional Awareness Devices Development Our Proposal

In this section a set of guidelines to better support a cultural-based development of EADs devices are presented. The proposal is based on the premise that final user's emotions are strongly related to their cultural context. Even we are aware of the great amount of discussions dealing with inborn universals and cultural induced characteristics of man, these issues are not addressed here. A review of cross-cultural differences in emotions can be found in [1]. The definition of culture proposed by [8] (culture is "a system of meanings", a direct connection between both cultural context and emotions can be drawn) is assumed as a theoretical underlying framework. Also the four-factor theory described by [12] are taken into account. In fact, while [12] defines the appraisal of external stimuli or situations as a starting point for an emotional experience (where facial expressions, action tendencies and body reactions are involved), [8] pointed out that stimulus can be seen as a central aspects of culture.

Based on [8] and [12], the author of [18] defined four levels that need to be taken into account when developing and adapting systems for different user groups: *technology*, *language*, *culture* and *cognition*. The first level deals with all the technical aspects of a system and is shaped by norms and given characteristics (e.g. the power supply). The second level deals with the translation of the words used in the user interface. The cultural level includes basically the context in which the technical system will be used and which assigns a meaning to it as well as meanings of user interface elements (such as icons, colours, music and metaphors). The fourth level describes the concrete human-interaction and the cognitive processes involved. According to this approach, the model described in this paper is related to both the cultural and the cognitive level because user interface elements as well as the overall cultural context are addressed.

---

[1] See Telephonic Arm Wrestling Report (1986) at http://www.bmts.com/~normill/artpage.html
[2] See more information at http://www.we-make-money-not-art.com/archives/007274.php

Putting into practice all the above ideas while developing EADs is neither a clear nor easily achieved task. Consequently, our goal is to propose a set of cultural-oriented guidelines which should be taken into account to ensure an appropriate emotional awareness level in a final EAD product. In what follows we will assume the existence of a current EAD E that is being constructed for the context of use C by means of a prototyping-based development process under a CCD perspective. This development process involves a number of intermediate stages that are performed cyclically on the basis of active user participation.[3]

First, according to CCD participants belonging to the context of use C should be included in the development team of E. This way, cultural behavior of end-user can be perceived more clearly when analyzing controversial information (e.g. when processing unclear information comming from ethnographic studies, or when taking design decisions influenced by cultural issues). Respecting to the Requirement Analysis Stage, a cultural-based elicitation procedure is recommended in order to achieve a satisfactory set of minimal requisites for E. End-user studies guided by Ethnography or other similar methodology should highlight the next issues when analyzing the context of use C under consideration:

- significance of colors and their relation with emotions [16]
- cultural premises associated with the use of technology and gender [14]
- grade of face expressiveness and spontaneity to transmit emotions [20]
- significance of emotional feedback and expected frequency [10]
- basic rules in C for relationships [15]

When performing the Design Stage for E, Participatory Design [17] is highly recommended. Besides, the development team needs to be focused on the elements which enhance final user's communication, since emotional awareness is directly related with messages transmission. Cultural variables of C related to communication as style, grade of contextualization and implicit communication rules in C (individualism, competitiveness, etc) should be reflected in the design of E. With respect to the Implementation Stage, it is desirable to make the functionality core of E independent from cultural-based features and to follow a localization procedure to promote the scalability of E. Finally, when considering the Evaluation Stage, adopting a cross-cultural usability viewpoint will ensure an appropriate evaluation of E.

4 The Emoti-Picture Frame: A Latinoamerican Example

This section describes the application of the cultural guidelines proposed on Section 3 when developing an EAD portrait called "Emoti-Picture Frame" (EPF).

---

[3] We are aware that in actual software development projects some parts of the above stages might overlap, as system lifecycle is not always characterized in a uniform and linear manner within the existing models in HCI.

C.A. Collazos et al.

4.1 Brief Description of the "Emoti-Picture Frame"

The EPF is an emotional awareness device constructed for the Latinoamerican context of use. It allows anyone with Internet access to transmit their feelings by displaying them on a TUI or a GUI interface (see Figure 1, left). By means of this kind of device, a user can send (sending-user) and receive (receiving-user) emotional awareness. The EPF interface is composed by two main parts (Figure 1, left): a picture area storing a picture of the sending-user, and a feeling area which allows the perception of the sending-user current emotional state. The feeling area is composed by different features as colored emotional buttons, a Heart-Emotional Indicator and a set of history-emotional buttons.

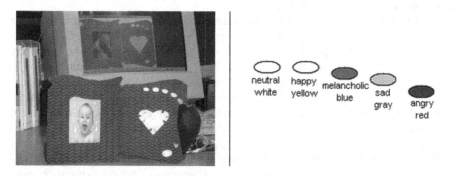

Fig. 1. Physical prototype of the Emoti-Picture Frame Device. Left: TUI and GUI versions. Right: colors associated with emotions.

Table 1. The emotional that users can communicate

Emotion			Emotional Buttons Pressed	Touch the picture
I am thinking about you			*None*	*Yes*
I am neuter			*white color*	*No*
I am happy			*yellow color*	*No*
I am melancholic			*blue color*	*No*
I am sad			*gray color*	*No*
I am angry			*red color*	*No*
I am neuter with you			*white color*	*Yes*
I am angry with you			*red color*	*Yes*
	happy	*Because*	*yellow color*	*Yes*
I am	*melancholic*	*I am thinking*	*blue color*	*Yes*
	sad	*about*	*gray color*	*Yes*

As shown in Figure 1 (right), each emotional button is linked to some emotional state of the sending-user: white color represents a neutral emotional state, yellow color represents a happy emotional state, blue color represents a melancholic emotional state, gray color represents a sad emotional state, and red color represents an angry emotional state. Moreover, each possible emotional state is intended to transmit a particular user feeling according to the correspondence summarized in Table 1.

When a sending-user wants to transmit a particular emotional state form the available range in Figure 1 (right), he/she has to press the correspondent emotional button in order to set a particular value in the EPF interface of the receiving-user. Then, this setting is captured by the EPF system which stored it in an historical database in order to allow the receiving-user to replay it later on by pressing the heart-like shape button in the set of history-emotional buttons. Indeed, pressing the heart-like shape button lead to the automatically painting of the Heart-Emotional Indicator with the color corresponding to the last emotional state sent by the sending-user. Besides, any time a novel emotional state arrives to the EPF interface of the receiving-user, some leds located around the Heart-Emotional Indicator blink, indicating that a new emotion sent by the sending-user has been received.

The EPF device also provides mechanism to send a special message to indicate the receiving-user that the sending-user is currently remembering him/her. To perform this action, the sending-user has to touch the picture of the receiving-user currently stored in the emotional picture zone of his/her EPF interface. When this action is carried out, some green leds blink on the Heart-Emotional Indicator of the receiving-user device. To stop this blinking the receiving-user has to touch the surface of the Heart-Emotional Indicator. Additionally, the receiving-user can block the reception of emotions by closing the portal of the Heart-Emotional Indicator. It must be stressed that this action is never informed to the sending-user, as the emotional state sending by him/her after the receiving-user blockage is received by the end EPF device and stored in the history database for a later optional recovery. If the receiving-user wants to erase the lasts recorded sending-user emotional states (which are stored in the historical database), he/she has to press the ellipse-like shape button in the historic-emotional buttons area.

4.2 Applying the Proposed Model to Develop the "Emoti-Picture Frame"

As suggested in the proposal of this paper, the EPF development team included people belonging to the context of use under consideration. In fact, the development team was formed by two Computer Engineers (both PhD students in HCI and Computer Supported Collaborative Work), and one specialist in HCI. One of the PhD students was Chilean, the other PhD student was Argentinean and the HCI specialist was Colombian. Besides, the development team was

Following the guidelines of Section 3, the Requirement Analysis for EPF was focused on understanding portrait manipulation in the Latinoamerican context of use. Indeed, a questionnaire including the items shown in Table 2 was performed in two different Latinoamerican scenarios (Chilean and Colombian scenarios) with the participation of a group of 15 Latoniamerican people. The analysis of the answers in Table 2 and the personal experiences of the EPF development team suggested that photos are an important part of many people's life in Latinoamerica, as they are symbols of a personal bond and provide a constant reminder of the feelings and emotions associated to that particular time frame or circumstance. However, this type of casual but personal communication can be very difficult at a distance, because it imposes restrictions on physical access to the personal space and artifacts of others.

Table 2. Questionnaire for the Requirement Analisys of the Emoti-Picture Frame

Question	Answer (Portrait)
When is a portrait used?	When I want to see a picture. / When I want to show a picture to other people. /When I want to remember "loved beings" or "unforgettable moments".
When do you need to put attention on the portrait?	Only when I want to see the picture.
How do you handle a portrait?	Putting the photograph in the portrait. / Locating the portrait on a visible place facing towards me.
How do you know it is working well?	Putting the photograph in the portrait. /Locating the portrait on a visible place facing towards me.
How do you know it is working well?	Because the photograph fits to the portrait and I can see the picture
What is the direct consequence of using a portrait?	It remains in the last place I put it on. /It shows the last picture placed there.
What do you do with a portrait?	Hold the portrait. /Put pictures on it
Who can use the portrait?	Anyone who faces the portrait or can grab it when it is on a visible place.
What is the cost of a portrait?	The economical cost is cheap. / The time spend in setting up is short.
Can you notice it was used?	Yes, when the picture or location has changed.
What is the user intention when have a portrait?	Providing a constant reminder of the feelings and emotions associated with this person or moment.
What do you do with a portrait?	Watch the picture hold by the portrait. Get close to the picture and grab it
How do you know if a portrait was used?	When the picture or location has changed. When my emotions distort the picture.
What is the relevance with a portrait?	Emotional. It maintains bonds with people, animals, places, etc.
What kind of value has a portrait for me?	Emotional, personal.
Who can use the portrait?	Close people (friends and family).
Who can watch you when you are using a portrait?	Sometimes it should be private, sometimes it could be public.
How many times you need to put attention on the portrait?	When I am thinking about someone. / When I am melancholic because I am distanced of people pictured on the portrait. / When I am happy and I need to bond with someone. / When I need emotional support.

The analysis of the answers in Table 2 and the personal experiences of the EPF development team were compiled in the information shown in Table 2. This analysis suggested that photos are an important part of many people's life in Latinoamerica as relevant symbols of personal bond, providing a constant reminder of the feelings and emotions associated to that particular time frame or circumstance. However, this type of casual but personal communication can be very difficult at a distance, because it imposes restrictions on physical access to the personal space and artifacts of others. In addition, the development team also studied different media and devices for remote affective communication. On the basis of these activities, the EPF development team decided to create a physical augmented portrait keeping some Latinoamerican cultural features. In consequence, and to cope with the proposal of this paper, during the Design Stage of EPF the development team focused on elements which enhance final Latinoamerican user's communication, such as:

- Represent emotional state of only one person per portrait using the guidelines depicted in Table 1
- Communicate the feelings and emotions of the sender-user depicting his/her photo in the portrait in order to reinforce the information received by the receiving-user
- Communicate several tokens of affection in a semi-transparent way
- Provide an interpersonal communication though an emotional awareness device.

Then, a first physical prototype of EPF was constructed, as one shown in Figure 1. Following the suggestions of Section 3, the technical core of the EPF was completely independized from the more high-level code corresponding the implementation of the information in Table 1. This way, the localization for the EPF for the Latinoamerican context was encapsulated in the interface level, thus promoting a simple future adecuating of EPF to others contexts of use.

Finally, the Evaluation Stage of EPF was carried out by applying the recommendations given in Section 3. The evaluation team was stated with the participation of the three EPF developers plus three teams of final-user comming from the Latinoamerican context. Whith the active participation of the six final user, the evaluation team pursed three case studies in order to cope with the usability evaluation of EPF stressing cultural associated issues: Case 1: Mother (GUI) and son (GUI and TUI), Case 2: Brother (GUI and TUI) and sister (GUI), Case 3: Boyfriends (GUI and TUI). The first two cases involved people living in distant cities which do not visit eachother frequently. In these cases the EPF was tested in the final users' homes during free time. The third case involucred a couple of boyfriends who were separated for work reason. In this case the EPF was tested at the final users' workplace during working time. More relevant results of the performed evaluation highlighted:

- No problems were detected associated with the chosen values for the cultural-biased elements of the EPF interface (those based on the information shown in Table 1). All users reported that the EPF system presented a useful and enjoyable way of transmitting emotions. They described EPF as a simple physical device that remains common everyday object often associated to emotional attachment such as a portrait. Users emphasized the EPF functionality which allows them to control which pictures are the appropriate to convey a particular emotion.
- Users declared that in their opinion, EPF stimulated other types of communication among people (as phone calls or e-mails interchange) due to the strengthening of people bonds through the increase of affective communication In addition, users reported that the increase in these communications does not affected the normal flow of their working day or free time.
- At the beginning, the EPF was perceived as a disrupting element for the activities in the workplace, since a lot of attention was given to the emotional interaction.

Later on, the EPF was assimilated and incorporated in a natural way. This evaluation result provided evidence of a usability problem. Therefore, it will be necessary to improve EPF GUI in order to make it less intrusive (for instance, instead of being a physical window, next version of EPF prototype could be embedded as a notification icon in the operative system task bar). Similarly, the TUI interface could be replaced by a touch screen, flattening the device so that it can resemble more closely to a regular portrait.

– Several problems were presented regarding the configuration and synchronization of the remote connection within the physical device EPF. As the evaluation of EPF was carried out in the real final users' environment (in opposition to a controlled laboratory circumstances) no conclusion about accessibility problems related to EPF could be established. However, the evaluation demonstrated that in a naturalistic environment everyday restrictions and heterogeneity make difficult to set up the device. Consequently, a transparent way for configuring EPF needed to be developed for next prototype version.

In addition to the case studies described above, the EPF evaluation team also experiented the use of alternative media and devices for remote affective communication as part of the EPF usability evaluation. Even some EPF features needed to be improved, note that the Evaluation Stage of the current EPF version concluded satisfactorily.

5 Conclusions and Further Work

As communication technologies increase their presence in the whole World, cultural issues and CCD are becoming important in HCI. Many cultural-biased features should be considered when developing interactive systems. Thus, taking into account these features during the whole system development process persist as a crucial challenge to achieve. Understanding how cultures vary and how to address this diversity within the design of the interface is becoming critical to ensure the quality of any final product, in particular EADs. However, few cultural-based guidelines or recommendations were founded related to the development of EADs.

To cope with the above problem this paper presents a set of cultural-based recommendations (guidelines) related to [18]. These guidelines can be used during the EDAs development processes in order to ensure EDAs quality related to culture. To illustrate de proposal, the development of a physical EDA prototype called "Emoti-Picture Frame" (EPF) for the particular cultural context of Latinoamerica is discussed. Future work includes the use of the proposed guidelines to conduct the development of the next EPF version with the inclusion of people comming from different cultural environments. More evidence is required to assure the impact of the proposed guidelines in EADs development. Work in this direction is being pursued.

Acknowledgments. This work was partially supported by Colombian Colciencias Projects No. 4128-14-18008 and No. 030-2005, Cicyt Projects TEN2004-08000-C03 and TIN2004-08000-C03-03, and Project SGR-00881 (Gen. Catalunya, Spain).

References

1. Altarriba, J., Basnight, D.M., Canary, T.M.: Emotion representation and perception across cultures. In: Lonner, W.J., Dinnel, D.L., Hayes, S.A., Sattler, D.N. (eds.) Center for Cross-Cultural Research, Western Washington University, USA (2003)
2. Bentley, R., et al.: Ethnographically-informed systems design for air-traffic control. In: Proc. of the Fourth ACM CSCW '92, pp. 123–129. ACM Press, New York (1992)
3. Brave, S., Dahley, A.: InTouch. In: Proc SIGCHI Conference, ACM Press, New York (1997)
4. Buck, R.: The communication of emotion. Guilford Press (1984)
5. De Souza, C.S., Preece, J.: A framework for analyzing and understanding online communities. In: Interacting with Computers, The Interdisciplinary Journal of HCI (2004)
6. Dourish, P., Adler, A., Bellotti, V., Henderson, A.: Your place or mine? In: Proc. of the ACM CSCW'96, ACM Press, New York (1996)
7. Fogg, B., Cutler, L.D., Arnold, P., Eisbach, C.: HandJive: a device for interper-sonal haptic entertainment. In: Proc. of ACM SIGCHI'98 Conference, ACM Press, New York (1998)
8. Geertz, C.: The Interpretation of Cultures. Basic Books ed. New York, USA (1975)
9. Greenberg, S., Fitchett, C.: Phidgets: Easy development of physical interfaces through physical widgets. In: Proc. of the ACM UIST'01 Conference, ACM Press, New York (2001)
10. Gelfand, M.: The Handbook of Negotiation and Culture. Stanford Univ. Press (2004)
11. Marcus, A., West Gould, E.: Crosscurrent. ACM Interactions, nro. 7 4, 32–46 (2000)
12. Parkinson, B.: Emotion. In: Colman, A.M. (ed.) Companion encyclopedia of psy-chology, vol. 2, Routledge Press, UK (1994)
13. Picard, R.W.: Affective Computing. MIT Press, Cambridge, MA (2000)
14. Primo, N.: Gender Issues in the Information Society. UNESCO WSIS Pub. Series (2003)
15. Saarni, C.: The Development of Emotional Competence. Guilford Press (1999)
16. Scheirer, J., Picard, R.: Affective Objects. In: MIT Media Lab Report N 524 (2000)
17. Schneiderman, B., Plainsant, C.: Designing the user interface: Strategies for effec-tive human-computer interaction. Addison-Wesley, Reading (2004)
18. Sturm, C.: TLCC Towards a framework for systematic and successful product internation-alization. In: Proc. of IWIPS'02. Product & Systems Internationalisation, Inc (2002)
19. Tollmar, K., Junestrand, S., Torgny, O.: Virtually living together. In: Proc. of the Conference on Designing Interactive Systems: Processes, Practices, Methods, and Techniques, pp. 83–91. ACM Press, New York (2000)
20. Weiten, W.: Psychology: Themes and Variations. Thomson Wadsworth 6th edn (2005)

User Interaction with User-Adaptive Information Filters

Henriette Cramer[1], Vanessa Evers[1], Maarten van Someren[1], Bob Wielinga[1],
Sam Besselink[1], Lloyd Rutledge[2], Natalia Stash[3], and Lora Aroyo[4]

[1] University of Amsterdam, Human Computer Studies Lab, Kruislaan 419, 1089 VA
Amsterdam, The Netherlands
hcramer@science.uva.nl
[2] Telematica Instituut, P.O. Box 589, Enschede, The Netherlands
[3] Vrije Universiteit Amsterdam, De Boelelaan 1083a, Amsterdam, The Netherlands
[4] Technische Universiteit Eindhoven, P.O. Box 513, Eindhoven, The Netherlands

Abstract. User-adaptive information filters can be a tool to achieve timely
delivery of the right information to the right person, a feat critical in crisis
management. This paper explores interaction issues that need to be taken into
account when designing a user-adaptive information filter. Two case studies are
used to illustrate which factors affect trust and acceptance in user-adaptive
filters as a starting point for further research. The first study deals with user
interaction with user-adaptive spam filters. The second study explores the user
experience of an art recommender system, focusing on transparency. It appears
that while participants appreciate filter functionality, they do not accept fully
automated filtering. Transparency appears to be a promising way to increase
trust and acceptance, but its successful implementation is challenging.
Additional observations indicate that careful design of training mechanisms and
the interface will be crucial in successful filter implementation.

Keywords: user-adaptive systems, information filtering, transparency, trust,
acceptance, recommenders.

1 Introduction

In crisis situations it is vital to have the right information at the right place at the right
time. Emergency management personnel, possibly from multiple organisations, need
to work together and need to make sense of often dynamic, chaotic and unexpected
situations. They have to deal with high-risk situations and both information over- and
underload. A diversity of actors needs to be provided with the information they need.
Especially in case of international crises, substantial personal and cultural differences
might have to be overcome. User-adaptive information filters have been suggested as
a possible tool to deliver crisis management actors with the information they need in a
personalised, effective and efficient manner (e.g. Meissner, 2006, Van Someren,
2004). However, user interaction with user-adaptive filters is not yet completely
understood. The dialogue between a user-adaptive information filter and the user is

N. Aykin (Ed.): Usability and Internationalization, Part II, HCII 2007, LNCS 4560, pp. 324–333, 2007.
© Springer-Verlag Berlin Heidelberg 2007

extremely important in achieving filtering adequate performance and acceptance in the user (Waern, 2004, Höök, 2000, Hanani, 2001). This dialogue needs to build an appropriate level of trust in the user. Users need to decide how well the system is suited for use in the task at hand and in what situations they can or cannot depend on the system. Over time, users need to assess how well the filter is adapting well to their feedback and is improving its filtering results and possibly becoming more suited to these tasks – or less suited when adaptation is less successful. A relationship needs to be built where the user trusts the system and feels it is useful to invest effort in training the filter, even though the filter might not yield high-quality results from the first moment on. The filter has to convince the user to keep using the filter and provide feedback on its filtering results so the system can improve its future results. This interaction needs to be satisfying to the user, while not detracting from the user's task. Additionally, usability concerns for adaptive systems might have to be addressed, such as limited predictability, controllability and obtrusiveness (Jameson, 2003). Such complexities of user interaction with adaptive systems will in all probability even be greater in crisis situations. Filters will have to adapt to very dynamic, complex situations and the stakes for users are high; achieving appropriate user trust will be crucial. Before user-adaptive information filters are deployed in high-risk situations to address the needs of a diverse set of users we need to understand what factors affect trust in and acceptance of such systems in general. The research discussed in this paper contributes to research in user diversity and usability by aiming to explore the factors that affect trust in automation and the effects of transparency across various types of user contexts. After a short discussion of trust and transparency, two studies are discussed as examples of such research

Parasuraman et al. (2000) propose a model of levels of reliance that could help deciding what level of automation is appropriate in a certain situation to ensure effective performance. They consider human performance areas (mental workload, situation awareness, complacency, skill degradation) and evaluative criteria such as automation reliability, risks and the ease of systems integration. However, even when an appropriate level of automation has been determined, there is no guarantee users will trust a system to the same appropriate degree and will actually decide to use it. Lee and See (2004) provide a comprehensive review of trust from various perspectives (including organisational, sociological, and interpersonal). They define trust as 'the attitude that an agent will help achieve an individual's goals in a situation characterized by uncertainty and vulnerability'. A similar definition is provided by Jøsang, (2004), who define trust as 'the extent to which one party is willing to depend on somebody or something, in a given situation with a feeling of relative security, even though negative consequences are possible'. An appropriate level of trust should match the reliability of the technology. Muir (1994) however shows that automation is distrusted by users, even if trust would be warranted. Trust is mostly determined by perceived competence of a system. Muir found that any signs of incompetence diminished trust, even when performance was not hindered. However, trust is not just determined by the perceived reliability of a tool. Factors such as perceived risks of using a system, previous experiences with the automation, user's workload, 'good manners' of the automation such as confirming to human etiquette, match of the user's personality and the system's are examples of factors that play a role as well (Parasuraman, 2004, Lee and See, 2004). Furthermore, the information items the system presents to the user need to be trustworthy as well, focus here is however on trust in the system itself. Lee and See conclude that trust does influence whether users are willing to rely on a system, but that it does not determine reliance completely. They state that trust only plays a role in uncertain and complex situations, where exhaustive evaluation whether to use a system is impractical. Assessing whether a system can be trusted in a complex situation can be made easier by making a system transparent. This entails offering the user insight in how a system works and increasing user understanding of the system's inner workings, for example by offering explanations for filtering results. In previous studies it is suggested that making an adaptive system more transparent to the user could lead to increased trust and acceptance, an increase in system performance and a more positive user attitude towards using a system (e.g. Herlocker, 2000; Pu 2006, Sinha, 2002; Höök, 2000; Waern, 2004; Cortellessa 2005). What types and levels of transparency are feasible and appropriate in which contexts and what type of effects they have on trust and acceptance is not yet fully understood. As Fogg (2003) states, the impact on credibility of any element depends on to what extent it is noticed (prominence) and what value users assign to the element (interpretation). Parasuraman (2004) notes that as automation gets more complex, users will be less wiling and able to learn about the mechanisms that produce the automation's behaviours. Besides the effort needed from the user to process transparency information, additional possible adverse affects have to be considered as well. Dzindolet (2003) for example found that explaining why errors might occur increased trust in automated tools, even when this was not appropriate. Even though transparency is thought to increase trust, there also might be a conceptual limit to the effect on usage behaviour. Trust is only thought to be an issue in situations that are too complex to understand for the user (Lee and See, 2004). If a system is fully transparent, and the user has the resources to do so, s/he can fully understand the system. It could be argued then that in such a situation, trust no longer plays a role.

2 Problem Statement

Understanding what factors affect how users provide feedback to a system and the mechanisms that lead to trust and acceptance of filters in general are important to be able to design user-adaptive information filters suitable for crisis situations. The relationship between risk, trust and transparency is not yet fully understood, especially not in the context of user interaction with user-adaptive systems. From the discussed literature we expect that transparency both influences perceived competence of a system through users' understanding of a system, and possibly also directly influences trust. The research project aims to further explore the factors influencing acceptance/trust in adaptive information filters. How do user perceptions of risk, system transparency and user control affect acceptance and trust? In what situations does transparency affect trust and acceptance? We aim to offer guidance on how a system can offer appropriate transparency and user control and benefit users, their task and context. While the characteristics of crisis situations include a diverse set of multiple users, high-risk and complex situations, we first aim to understand single user situations in less critical contexts and build on our findings in further research.

3   Case Studies

Below a selection of results from two studies are discussed. These studies have been carried out to investigate the relationship between training, transparency, trust and acceptance in interaction with user-adaptive information filters. Both studies address interaction with user-adaptive information filters that are dependent on explicit user feedback and base their filtering on content features of information items. First a study is discussed exploring user interaction with a trainable spam filter. This study investigates which factors affect user attitudes to information filter use in practice. The second study explores user interaction with a content-based user-adaptive art recommender system. This study focuses on the effects of transparency on trust and acceptance. Possible implications of the findings of both studies are discussed for designing an information filter for use in crisis situations. The studies are part of a larger research program investigating interaction with user-adaptive information filters.

3.1   Spam Filter Study

The first example study aimed to investigate what factors in practice influence use, trust and acceptance of adaptive systems that rely on direct user involvement. Interaction with user-adaptive spam filters was chosen as a case study. 48 participants were observed while interacting with their email client and spam filter in their regular work setting. Both participants with and without knowledge of AI-techniques were involved, 30 male, 18 female. Participants were relatively well-educated, ranging from some college-level education to PhD's. All participants were employees of either a university or a research organisation, ranging from researchers to administrative personnel. Use of two types of filters was observed: the built-in Bayesian trainable spam filter of the Mozilla email client, and an additional non-adaptive rule-based filter. After observation, interviewing addressed participants' understanding of their spam filter, and explored their attitude towards using and training their filters. The questionnaire addressed participants' trust and acceptance of their spamfilter, with questions adapted from Venkatesh, (2003) and Jian, (2000).

The study showed that the choice of users for a specific filter setting mainly depended on whether participants thought information overload spam was a problem for them and the way they wanted to manage the risk of losing email. 23 of the 44 participants (out of 48) with an active spam filter spam considered spam a problem, with 14 mentioning that spam wasn't a problem anymore because of their spam filter(s). However, even while the majority of these participants thought their spam filter was useful (average=5.3, st.dev=1.1, N=46, a=.869 on a Likert-scale from 0-6) and had a positive attitude towards the filter (mean = 5.7, st.dev 0.7, N=48), letting the filter actually delete messages was not acceptable to most of them. Only four participants let their filter automatically delete (a portion of) the spam they received. Participants based their level of trust mainly on observed filter errors. Some participants gave examples of 'critical errors' where the filter did not recognize obvious spam or filtered out email that was important to them. Participants reported they trusted their filter in the interview, but scored only slightly positive on trust-related items in the questionnaire (mean= 3.1, st.dev=1.3, N=46, a=.733). The way participants managed the risk of losing an email appeared decisive in the choice for a particular filter setting. The only participant who let the filter delete all alleged spam for example reasoned that missing an important email was a risk he could easily take, as senders of really important emails would contact him if he didn't answer them anyway. Other participants did not feel this was a viable option for them. Such differences thus occur even within one organisation. Diversity of users and their (social) context and the way these affect the way in which users rely on automation have to be taken into account when designing an information filter. Especially when designing for crisis management, where multiple organisations, a wide diversity of actors and changing task contexts will occur, this will be a major design challenge.

Participants were willing to train their filters and both correcting and more extensive training efforts such as importing old spam as training set were reported. Interestingly, participants appeared to report that training the filter by correcting its errors did appear to have increased trust, but they did not report less controlling behaviour. These user efforts thus mainly appear to have cost the users; they did not benefit from the filter's capabilities. This extra effort spent on a filter instead on the task at hand, without any benefits the user takes advantage of later on, might be fatal in more critical situations.

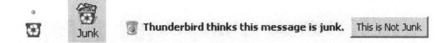

Fig. 1. a. Mozilla Junk icon b. Mozilla Junk button and c. Mozilla warning text and correction button

Careful interface design is very important in raising awareness of filter activity and avoiding user mistakes in training a filter. Even though the Mozilla client shows icons, buttons and warning labels (figure 1), participants did not always recognize the filter's activity. Such lack of awareness of filter activity might have grave conesquences in crisis situations. If filter errors occur, users might do not even realise a breakdown in communication has occurred, or are even possible, which might lead to uninformed actions and inappropriate reliance on automation. One participant in this study for example confused the filter's button to train the filter for a delete button, essentially training the filter to recognize any email similar to any email ever deleted by that participant as spam. This could potentially be very dangerous in more critical situation when a user decides to actively use the filter, without realising it has been wrongly trained. If even in a situation such as in this study, where participants user their email client everyday, they are not always able to report filter settings and sometimes confuse interface elements, this certainly has to be taken in account for crisis situations. Mistakes appear to be even more likely in less-familiar crisis situations in which users will not be able to spend time to fully examine a filtering interface. It appears that while users do appreciate the concept of adaptive filters, and are willing to invest effort to train them, filters are not used to their full extent mainly because of the perceived risks associated with their use and imperfections in interface design leading to lack of awareness and understanding of the filter.

3.2   Transparency, Trust and Acceptance of a User-Adaptive Recommender System

Transparency, giving the user insight in the inner workings of a system, could be a way to increase trust and acceptance of filters when filter usage will actually benefit task performance. The second study described in this paper is a pilot study, part of an ongoing study, exploring how transparency affects user trust in and acceptance of user-adaptive content-based information filters. An art recommender prototype, the CHIP system was used in this study as an example of a user-adaptive information filter. The CHIP system recommends artworks from the collection of the Rijksmuseum Amsterdam based on annotations of content features of artworks. Annotations used for recommendations include for example artist (for example Rembrandt), place & time (such as Amsterdam, 1700-1750), and topics (such as 'food and drink', or Buddhism).

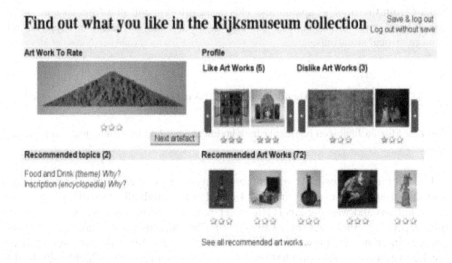

Fig. 2. Transparent version of the CHIP prototype

Using a between-subject experimental set-up the effects were investigated of offering a more transparent versus a less transparent recommender on trust and acceptance. Two groups of participants individually used either a transparent or a non-transparent version of the CHIP recommender system. The transparent CHIP version showed the topics in the user profile the system thinks the user finds interesting and on which its art recommendations are based (figure 2). The non-transparent version did not show these topics. Observation of participants' interaction with the system, interviews and a questionnaire were combined to gain insight in the effects of transparency on perceived understandability, perceived competence, trust and acceptance of the system and its recommendations. Questionnaire items were adapted from Jian (2000) for trust and Venkatesh (2003) for acceptance.

Fifteen participants took part in the study. Participants were 14-61 years old, 10 male, 5 female. Thirteen of the 15 participants had received some form of college level education. Participants were asked to prepare a presentation about their personal art interests. For this presentation they needed to choose 10 artworks as their favourites. These artworks could be any artwork they had seen using the CHIP system, either recommended or not. If participants chose more recommendations over other artworks they had seen in the system, this was taken as an indicator of acceptance of the system's recommendations. Afterwards, participants were presented with an 'acceptance task'. They were asked to find one additional interesting artwork within one minute and were offered the choice to either find this artwork from a fixed list, not based on their profile, or use the recommended artworks.

Trust, Acceptance and Transparency Effects. Participants generally thought the recommender was moderately useful, scoring a mean of 4.93 on a 7-point Likert scale (st.dev=1.43, N=15; questionnaire items=2, a=.7396). They liked system recommendations (mean=5.23, st.dev=1.18; items=2, a=.6998) and reported trusting the filter (mean=5.2, st.dev=.666, N=15; items:10, a=.869). However, 10 of the 15 participants still reported they would not let the system choose artworks for them. Transparency did not increase trust and acceptance in a significant way in this study. There were also no differences between the conditions in the levels of trust reported in the questionnaire. Participants in the transparent condition did not prefer the system's recommendations to their own selection more often than those in the non-transparent condition. Participants in the transparent condition were even significantly less convinced the system's recommendations were improving using their feedback than participants in the non-transparent condition (U=12.500, W=40.500, Z=-1.83, p(1-tailed)=.036, Ntrans=7, Nnon-trans=8).

A number of possible explanations are possible for the lack of effect of transparency on trust and acceptance, and its unexpected additional negative effects on the perceived benefits of training the system in this study. First of all, the number of participants in this exploratory study was small and the manipulation might not have been strong enough. There was no significant increase in perceived understanding of the system in the transparent condition in this study (U=26.00, W=62.00, Z=-.239, p(1-tailed)=.434). This could be explained by the potential unfamiliarity of the topics shown. If the user for example does not understand what a topic such as 'inscriptions' entails and why it would be interesting, showing this topic does not necessarily increased perceived understanding of the system's criteria. Additionally, not all features of the transparent version were noticed by participants. A 'why?' button was offered for every listed recommended topic, clicking this button opened a screen explaining what ratings this recommendation was based on. This feature was not used by any of the participants. Whether they didn't notice or did not have the need for this information is unclear. This illustrates that it is important to make sure that transparency features are actually helping the users understand the system better and not just require attention and mental effort from the user. Participants in the transparent condition did find learning how to use the system more difficult (U=13, Z=-1,93, p=0,05; mean transparent condition=6.00, mean non-transparent condition=6.75). For many participants, the transparency feature became an extra screen item that had to be processed instead of a helpful feature. This type of issue certainly has to be taken into account in designing information filters for crisis situations. A full understanding of the risks and benefits of using a filtering system might be crucial in deciding whether using the system would be appropriate in a crisis situation. In emergency management applications however users cannot be expected to notice unfamiliar screen features or spend the effort to get to know how a system works during a crisis. It appears that instruction of potential users on how a system works cannot be avoided, if it has to be made sure users can make informed decisions on whether the system is suitable for the tasks at hand. It also appears that there are limits to the effects of transparency even if it makes the system more understandable. Trust and acceptance in this study appeared more determined by the immediate evaluation of the recommendations by participants and not by the type of transparency offered here.

4 Discussion and Conclusion

Participants in the discussed example studies appear to value the concept of user-adaptive information filters. Participants in the first study thought their spam filter helped them deal with a spam problem. Participants in the second study reported to appreciate the recommendations made by the system. However, these studies also show that most users do not want to hand over complete control to an adaptive system. In case of the spam filter, letting the filter automatically delete messages was not accepted by the great majority of the participants. In case of the relatively low-risk situation of using the art recommender, most participants did not let the system choose artworks for them. In both studies, even if participants report trusting a filter, they might not actually want to rely on the system. This issue has to be taken into account in further study and system evaluations; reported trust does not necessarily mean actual usage behaviour will occur that would indicate this trust. Training of the system by the users by correcting it or rating how interesting certain information items are, does appear to increase trust. It does however not necessarily lead to less controlling behaviour. Participants in both the spam filter and recommender study thought training the filter improved it, but this didn't necessarily mean they handed over control to the filter after they observed it making fewer mistakes. The benefits of user-adaptivity, training the filter, and seeing it improve, appear less important to users in their final decision to accept system decisions, than overall potential risks and consequences of using of the filter.

This supports the findings of Cortellessa et al (2005), who argue that focus should be on developing an efficient mixed initiative approach, instead of completely autonomous systems, and users should be offered an appropriate level of transparency of an adaptive system's actions. Additionally, authors such as Kaber and Endsley (2004) describe the dangers associated with handing over control completely: full automation potentially hurts situation awareness, monitoring performance and failure detection and might not result in a decline in perceived workload. The challenge is how to balance benefits of a filter and the risks of its use, how to provide users with appropriate control and training a system to optimal performance, without taking too much time and effort away from the user's primary tasks.

Even though previous literature does state transparency increases trust and acceptance, the art recommender transparency study shows that just showing any transparency feature does not necessarily help trust and acceptance. This particular transparency feature did not appear to help the user understand the system, illustrating that designing a useful transparency feature is not an easy task (as is also discussed by Herlocker, 2000). In a crisis situation weighing the costs and benefits of a transparency feature will be challenging, but even more important. A relationship between the system and user has to be built before a crisis occurs. As training a filter during a crisis situation is not a very viable option, training should probably occur offline such as in simulated training sessions. This way, in case the filter fails no immediate consequences occur and the user has the chance to get to know the system in a less stressful situation. Raising awareness of filter activity and its adaptivity features in the user is not trivial. Interface choices matter, as illustrated by the participant in the spam filter study who confused a filter train button with a delete button, not realising she was (inaccurately) training a filter. Participants in the spam filter study also could not always accurately report filter settings. In the second study involving the art recommender, interface items such as the additional 'why?' button were not always noticed or used. Lack of awareness might not appear very serious in the case of using a spam filter or an art recommender. In crisis situations however, not knowing whether a filter is active or how to use it, could lead to uninformed choices, increased risk and difficulty in recovering in case of filter mistakes.

Introducing user-adaptive information filters in crisis management practice is challenging. Ways for the user to manage the risk associated with their use have to be devised before they will be accepted. A longer-term relationship has to be built in a setting where the user keeps control over the system but can still benefit from efficiency gains from using it. Perceived benefits of use of a filter have to outweigh the perceived efforts required from users to understand, train and correct them. Transparency has potential to help users make informed choices and develop appropriate trust and acceptance. Producing explanations for users that help them understand the complexities of a filtering system's decisions during a crisis, that also are concise and understandable will not be a trivial matter however. Until it is completely clear how to design a transparent system, careful instruction on such a filtering system, explaining the users on how a system works and how to use and correct could be crucial. The implementation of a user-adaptive information filtering system in emergency management will thus require a lot of user effort before it can actually be used. It appears that trust will remain playing an important role in usage as full system transparency appears difficult to achieve; crisis situations are by nature uncertain and complex, and spending extensive effort and time deciding whether to use a system is impractical. The studies discussed here are steps towards a fuller understanding of these issues, but also show that more research into the relations between acceptance, trust and transparency is necessary.

Acknowledgments. This research is funded by the Interactive Collaborative Information Systems (ICIS) project nr: BSIK03024, by the Dutch Ministry of Economical Affairs under contract to the Human-Computer Studies Laboratory of the University of Amsterdam. The CHIP system is developed by the CHIP (Cultural Heritage Information Personalization - www.chip-project.org) project, part of the CATCH (Continuous Access To Cultural Heritage) program funded by the NWO (Netherlands Organisation for Scientific Research).

References

1. Cortellessa, G., Giuliani, M.V., Scopelliti, M., Cesta, A.: Key Issues in Interactive Problem Solving: An Empirical Investigation on Users Attitude. In: Costabile, M.F., Paternó, F. (eds.) INTERACT 2005. LNCS, vol. 3585, pp. 657–670. Springer, Heidelberg (2005)
2. Dzindolet, M.: The role of trust in automation reliance. Int. J. of Human-Computer Studies 58(6), 697–718 (2003)
3. Fogg, B.J., Tseng, H.: The Elements of Computer Credibility. In: Proc. CHI 1999, pp. 80–87. ACM Press, New York (1999)
4. Fogg, B.J.: Prominence-Interpretation Theory: Explaining How People Assess Credibility Online. In: In Proc. CHI 2003, ACM Press, NewYork (2003)
5. Hanani, U., Shapira, B., Shoval, P.: Information Filtering: Overview of Issues. Research and Systems, User Modeling and User-Adapted Interaction 11(3), 203–259 (2001)
6. Herlocker, J.L., Konstan, J.A., Riedl, J.: Explaining collaborative filtering recommendations. In: Proc. CSCW 2000, pp. 241–250. ACM Press, New York (2000)
7. Höök, K.: Steps to Take Before Intelligent Interfaces Become Real. Interacting with computers 12(4), 409–426 (2000)
8. Jameson, A.: Adaptive Interfaces and Agents. In: Jacko, J.A., Sears, A. (eds.) Human-computer interaction handbook, pp. 305–330. Erlbaum, Mahwah, NJ (2003)
9. Jian, J.Y., Bisantz, A.M., Drury, C.G.: Foundations for an empirically determined scale of trust in automated systems. Int. J. of Cognitive Ergonomics 4(1), 53–71 (2000)
10. Jøsang, A., Lo Presti, S.: Analysing the Relationship between Risk and Trust. In: Proc. International Conference on Trust Management, pp. 135–145. Springer, Heidelberg (2004)
11. Kaber, D.B., Endsley, M.R.: The effects of level of automation and adaptive automation on human performance, situation awareness and workload in a dynamic control task. Theoretical issues in ergonomic science 5(2), 113–153 (2004)
12. Meissner, A., Wang, Z., Putz, W., Grimmer, J.: MIKoBOS - A Mobile Information and Communication System for Emergency Response. In: Proc. ISCRAM 2006 Van de Walle, B., Turoff, M. (eds.), Newark, NJ, USA (2006)
13. Muir, B.M., Moray, N.: Trust in automation. Part II. Experimental studies of trust and human intervention in a process control simulation. Ergonomics 39(3), 429–460 (1996)
14. Parasuraman, R., Miller, C.: Trust and etiquette in high-criticality automated systems. In: Proc. CHI 2004, pp. 51–55. ACM Press, NewYork (2004)
15. Pu, P., Chen, L.: Trust Building with Explanation Interfaces. In: Proc. IUI 2006, pp. 93–100. ACM Press, NewYork (2006)
16. Sinha, R., Swearingen, K.: The Role of Transparency in Recommender Systems. In: CHI'02 extended abstracts on Human factors in computing systems, pp. 830–831. ACM Press, New York (2002)
17. Venkatesh, V., Morris, M., Davis, G., Davis, F.: User Acceptance of Information Technology: Toward a Unified View. MIS Quarterly 27(3), 479–501 (2003)
18. Wærn, A.: User Involvement in Automatic Filtering: An Experimental Study. User Modeling and User-Adapted Interaction 14(2-3), 201–237 (2004)

A System for Adaptive Multimodal Interaction
in Crisis Environments

Dragoş Datcu, Zhenke Yang, and Léon Rothkrantz

Delft University of Technology
Faculty of Electrical Engineering, Mathematics and Computer Science
Mekelweg 4, 2628 CD Delft, The Netherlands
{D.Datcu,Z.Yang,L.J.M.Rothkrantz}@ewi.tudelft.nl

Abstract. In the recent years multimodal interfaces have acquired an important role in human computer interaction applications. Subsequently these interfaces become more and more human-oriented. Humans use multimodality to reduce ambiguity and incompleteness of information. Seemingly they are able to switch easily from one modality to the other and fuse the information from different multimodal sources. The goal of our research was to develop a crisis based human like multimodal system. In particular, we bring into focus the multimodal interaction between human users and the automatic crisis system and its correlation with the adaptability to the human behavior in crisis situations. Our system is capable of conceding for an optimal interaction process by taking into account the major informational human channels while gathering the user inputs and producing the system feedback. In this paper we describe the design of our system which is implemented as a running prototype. We have conducted a simulation of a crisis event to measure the degree of user satisfaction. At last we discuss the drawbacks as well as the premises of our solution in the context of the high level of performance achieved by our approach.

Keywords: Multimodal human computer interfaces, adaptive interfaces, crisis support systems, multimodal framework.

1 Introduction

Recently a special focus has been noticed on areas concerning the development of support systems for crisis situations. More and more attempts are engaged to automate processes to manage the communication and enhance the interaction of actors at different crisis sites. In addition, the current developments of hardware platforms and equipments allow for highly demanding processing and device interconnectivity. A specific requirement in such a context points to reliable multimodal interfaces to link different components and to sustain the information flows through characteristic layers of abstraction.

The main contribution of the research described in the current paper, is given by the diversity in multimodal human computer interaction. This comes as part of the solution for improving the usability of automatic systems for the management of

N. Aykin (Ed.): Usability and Internationalization, Part II, HCII 2007, LNCS 4560, pp. 334–343, 2007.
© Springer-Verlag Berlin Heidelberg 2007

crisis situations. During a crisis event, panic and confusion are two reasons that usually lead to an increase of the typical damaging effects. We aim at limiting these effects by developing system interfaces that are self-adaptive given the variety of users and situations. The interaction between the users and the automatic system is eased by the intelligent information aggregation and the continuous adaptation to the user needs and to each crisis situation. The behavioral differences between all the actors interacting through our multimodal system are efficiently managed by a common strategy on the plan to solve the crisis situation.

At the global scale, we have achieved a high degree of internationalization for the users interacting with the system by focusing on the selection of modalities to support language independent user communication.

The adaptive crisis multimodal framework being described in this paper is centered on the shared memory paradigm. Comparing with the traditional way implying direct connections between the system components each connection having its own data format, the new approach suggests a more human-modeled alternative to store, retrieve and process the data. The information is conferred an underlying structure that complies with eXtended Markup Language (XML). The shared memory in the current design of the multimodal framework takes the form of XML data spaces. The use of shared memory allows for loosely coupled asynchronous communication between multiple senders and receivers. The communication decoupling is realized both in time and location. The specification fully complies with the requirements of data manipulation in a multimodal environment where the availability of data is time-dependent and some connections might be temporarily interrupted.

Considering the study case of the automatic crisis application, wireless devices such as PDAs or mobile phones can communicate and exchange essential crisis multimodal information. One distinct remark concerning our multimodal system is the adaptability to various working conditions. The adaptation induces an in-built context-aware mechanism to intelligently interfere with the external world in a natural manner. In the case of crisis applications it assumes dynamic and transparent system auto-configuration to get optimal performance given any crisis specific environments, human actors and hardware devices. The system adapts the information extraction in terms of audio and visual channels. An example is the case when specific information regarding the emotion from the speech of one person cannot be computed due to noisy environment or lack of a special processing component. In such a case and if there is no occlusion of the person's face, equivalent information is generated by employing the proper component to perform facial expression recognition. The network data transfer is optimized so as to avoid data blockage and to generate a good flow of the information through the connected processing components. The system feedback is generated taken into account the informational channels and the human computer interfaces available. An example is that the system automatically decides to ask the user a question via a loud message in the speakers instead of a panel text message if the lighting conditions in the room are poor.

A throughout technical description of the multimodal framework that supports the adaptive interfaces detailed in the paper, is given in [2]. In the next section we present related work in the research field of multimodal interfaces in crisis management. In section 3 we describe the system architecture. Section 4 presents the results of the experiment we done for determining the performance of the system.

2 Related Work

Recent research advancements on the area of support applications in crisis situations have accentuated the need for new algorithms and methods to cope with the specific issues of adaptive work environments and adaptive data distribution. Novel techniques have come into play for connecting users over dynamic wireless networks and for providing the user with the most relevant information given specific crisis environments. The work of [7] describes a system for routing people outside a dangerous area using a personalized dynamic routing algorithm in case of emergency. The architecture is based on multi and mobile agents. Each human user is supervised by a specialized agent that learns the behavioural peculiarities of its human counterpart. The interface of the system uses a set of graphical iconic representations that allow the user to provide his input accordingly. The research in [8] presents the use of an icon language for describing crisis situations and its integration with blackboards in MANETs [1]. The work of [9] investigates the use of the emerging computing model of Dynamic Data-Driven Applications Systems as base for the support of emergency medical treatment decisions in response to a crisis. By linking real-time sensors, procedural and geographic data, the system manages to produce decision support at the site of the incident, at local centres and at the central point of coordination. [12] gives extensive discussions over the role of multimodal interfaces on the specific elements regarding the crisis management and tackles various issues in enriching human computer interfaces with dialog and speech-gesture capabilities. [10] tackles the issues that rise from the integration of an intelligent agent software robot into a crisis communication portal for sending news alerts on mobile devices. The work of [13] adopts novel techniques in mixed and virtual reality technologies to enhance systems aiming at the surveillance, security and emergency, prevention plans in crowded environments. The interactive control room processes video data from airborne and fixed cameras and along with GPS driven maps generates real-time augmented 3D videos with the crowd for risk and prevention planning. The data can be also visualized by on-field human agents. The human computer interface is enriched with an eye tracker based mechanism to allow for the control of camera functions and views by gaze. The research described in [15] proposes a distributed multi-agent architecture for crisis response management and discusses the solutions for providing the necessary support. The work presented in [14] provides a classification of artificial coordination strategies in terms of skill, rule and knowledge. The research is applied in a case study of medical personnel to casualty allocation in the crisis response domain. The conclusions reflect the trade-off between efficiency and flexibility indicating the strategies of knowledge-level coordination as the most effective, and skill-level as the most efficient. The change of operational requirements can be optimally handled through the knowledge-level strategies as opposed to the performance of skill-level strategies in such context. The work of [11] addresses the requirements of disaster relief operations and proposes a solution based on an extension of the existing Belief-Desire-Intention BDI model having the capability of situation awareness.

3   The Architecture of the Adaptive Multimodal System

The automatic crisis system aims at solving the problems occurring during the process of collecting the input from different human users located at different points in the crisis scene and at fusing these partial observations so as to provide pertinent information related to the evacuation, help and coordination of specific actions for attenuating the causes of the crisis. The usual scenario for this case consists of a set of human observers and qualified personnel equipped with personal mobile devices (Fig. 1) that communicate with the system through a powerful multimodal interface. They are entitled to dynamically make reports on their own experience with respect to the crisis scenario while making use of information as it is offered by the system. The interface keeps track of the individual user inputs and updates the user profile. The information is eventually used in the attempt to solve the ambiguity in the personal reports. When possible, all the interfaces are interconnected through XML data spaces that run over existing wireless networks. The special issues that are taken into account focus on the possibility of sudden breakdowns of the infrastructure, the interoperability and limited processing power of various user mobile devices and the possible occurrence of individual and global ambiguous user reports.

Fig. 1. Zaurus PDA (*left*) and the fireman user profile using the crisis multimodal adaptive system (*right*)

3.1   The User Interface

During a crisis event different people have access to the system through individual multimodal interfaces, running on personal mobile devices. The acquisition of data from the users follows an as natural as possible process allowing the user to use different modalities to produce the relevant input to the system. The interface is able to conveniently take the multimodal input from the user and to send it to the other devices in the crisis informational network. Seemingly in order to create an input the user can use the visual set of crisis icons, text messages, pen input, photos and direct speech. Depending on the hardware of the user mobile device, the interface should furnish with as many as possible of these input modalities. The interface adjusts the input and output according to the characteristics of the device. The standard view generated by the interface consists in a 2D image (Fig. 2) showing a map associated to the location of the user. If the hardware facilitates the 3D rendering of images, the user can switch to this visualization mode (Fig. 3).

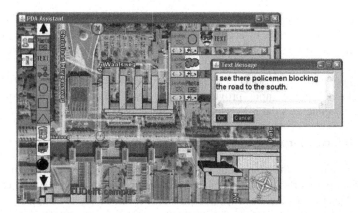

Fig. 2. The 2D user interface used by the external observer to report on the smoke crisis event

The use of GIS data in decision support systems for crisis management has been already adopted in systems as those presented in [3], [5] and [6]. By making use of GPS data, the interface introduces geographical based information into the process of interacting with the user. At this level the system can already create particular correlations among the user observations and the environmental area.

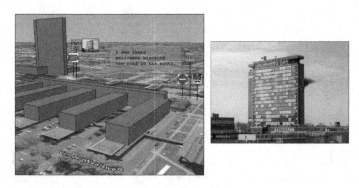

Fig. 3. The 3D user interface (*left*) used to report a crisis event and a photo of the view (*right*) taken by the user with his mobile device

In the case GPS data are not available the user has the option to simply mention the area where he is located. The interface will take the notice regarding the location as reference. Eventually, the location parameter is assigned with a slightly higher degree of uncertainty in all his further reports on the crisis event. The user can use both the 2D and 3D interfaces of the crisis application. To report about an event, the user can drag icons on special locations on the map or accentuate a special point of interest using geometrical symbols [4]. The icons are ordered in a hierarchical way. Firstly, the user has to select an appropriate context (accident, fire, terrorist attack, etc.). Given a certain context, a special set of icons is available to the user. The interface is also adapted to the role the user plays during the crisis event.

Laymen and professionals have different interfaces and different set of icons. For example a fireman is able to accurately report about the smell and color of a toxic cloud. That expertise can not be expected from a civilian and so the specific icons for such observations are not available. An automatic synchronization is realized on the information on each view so as to preserve the consistency of the crisis informational content. Based on the input provided by the user (Fig. 2), the system interface automatically generates the 3D crisis event scene (Fig. 3).

3.2 The Informational Disambiguation Model

The system manages the communication on the informational channels and supports the collaborative work for the specialized personnel working at the site of crisis. The specialized users hold functional precedence over the category of common users. This requirement is due to the fact that regular users are more exposed to failure in providing essential information over the crisis context when compared with personnel qualified in performing such activities.

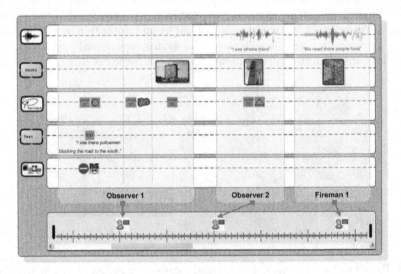

Fig. 4. The timeline with the integration of different contextual crisis multimodal information

All the previous user reports are taken into account when deciding for a certain operation to change the internal world knowledge of the system. All the observations coming from the field are stored and tracked while the system attempts to classify the crisis event as being one of the standard crisis scenarios from the system repository. At this level the solution for removing the ambiguity on different crisis scenarios is solved by employing the description and properties of each crisis context available in the repository as system knowledge. The classification represents a continuous process updating the event properties as soon as new evidence is made available by the system reasoning. According to the description of the current recognized crisis context, the system is able to generate feedback to the users in the form of support for distinct ongoing actions. All the user reports are collected and processed in an automatic manner. Human experts can also access the preliminary information of such automatic modules of the crisis system and can finally make adjustments on particular parameters of the results. This stands for the highest layer at which the ambiguity in partial, user observations can be decreased. Although is the most accurate among the all types of disambiguation, the manual procedure is time consuming and involves the presence of specialized people.

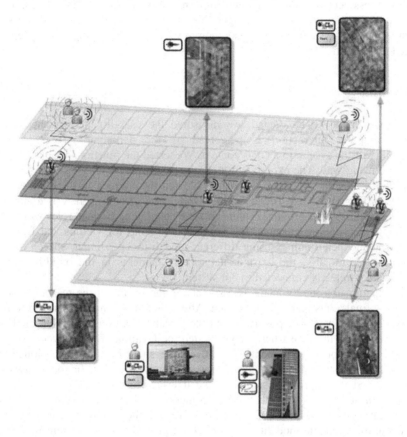

Fig. 5. The individual observations of the multimodal adaptive system. Multi-hop networks among mobile devices allow for data exchange in situations when the connection to the central system is seriously affected.

In fig. 4 the user-oriented multimodal information regarding an example of a crisis event is presented in a timeline manner. The system automatically synchronizes the user reports between different modalities. The meaning of a user observation is generated by extracting and correlating the atomic informational clues related to the crisis event from each user informational stream. The illustration shows an example of the original input of a user, split in separate multimodal information flows.

The disambiguation model incorporates the fusion and filtering of the user reports stored using a common representation format.

Fig. 5 illustrates an example for a schematic representation of the users of the adaptive crisis system on the map in the crisis context. Some of the regular as well as special users provided snapshots of the event taken from the locations in the crisis scene. The users are characterized through the types of inputs they use while working with the adaptive system interface for generating the desired observation reports. From the picture, it can be noticed that the users which work close to the fire site have direct wireless access to the communication infrastructure. As for the others, as it is the case of the one fireman on the right side of the picture, they can still access the resources of the system and to send their own reports by using adhoc networks created at the spot.

4 Results

In the experiment we conducted, we measured the usability performance for the human computer interaction as perceived by the participating users and the adaptability of the system to a crisis context. We tested the functionality of the system in the following way. The experiment took place during a training session of real fire brigade in the faculty building. Students followed the firemen in their exercise and acted according to the real fire scenarios. During the session there was a simulated fire in the building. We provided volunteer students playing firemen roles with PDAs' and they were supposed to enter the building searching for victims and fire. They reported about their findings using different modalities: pen input, speech and text messages. Additionally, the existent network of cameras in the building and the PDA's were wirelessly connected to our system.

The experts subjectively made assessments on the results of the reasoning system and set the final adjustments to these data. After this session the firemen had to fill in a questionnaire. They were positive about the possibilities to use different modalities as for example in the case where they reported the location of a fire event using pen with additional spoken comments. Following the analysis of the questionnaire, it resulted that the students were able to use the iconic interface. In some cases they could not find the appropriate icons on the interface to report about events/special locations. In those cases students used SMS messages. The preferred modalities were iconic messages and SMS text. During the interaction the system gave advices to the user about the available modalities. In the end it proved that our system was able to handle the information from different devices and different modalities.

The drawback of the system was the unstable wireless connection and the interface which was not properly designed for firemen undergoing specific fire brigade actions. Especially the lighting conditions, the background noise and the improper firemen outfit such as firemen gloves had a negative impact on the quality of the human friendly system interaction. Because of failing technology, on average only text, icons, pictures were available. The interface with styluses is not suitable for being used by firemen in action. Firemen use special gloves and are unable to use a stylus. The use of the speech interface was complicated. Students didn't use close to mouth microphones (unfortunately not available for the experiments). So, the speech signal was corrupted by background noise. In addition to this, the network communication problems and the restricted bandwidth restricted the use of the video streaming that could make possible the run of facial expression recognition on other computers. The communication between users was far from optimal due to the failing communication of the wireless ad hoc network. Many times users couldn't be reached or data got lost. It is expected that the next generation of PDAs will come with specific hardware solutions to these problems.

5 Conclusion

In the current research we have detailed the functionally and the constituent modules of a multimodal system aiming to support the human computer interaction and to provide proper information to help special categories of people in crisis situations.

The novelty of our system consists in the algorithms to provide the human support in different crisis situations. The interface of the system automatically adapts to the conditions in the working environments and to the user preferences and abilities. Subsequently we have conducted a research on the quality of the interaction between humans and the automatic system during an experimental setup. The context of the experiment focused on a simulated crisis situation that assumed the presence of a fire event and various people acting different roles ranging from common observers from outside the site to qualified fire brigade personnel trying to evacuate civilians and to stop the fire.

During the development of the system, a special attention was given to the graphical user interface more exactly to the tools the users can access in order to create certain reports of their own observations on the crisis. The graphical tools supported during the interaction process involved the use of pen input, icon sequences, text and direct snapshots taken with the user mobile device. Moreover, the interface has been enriched with speech recording capabilities to ease the collection of the user input. This modality was preferred in situations when poor illumination or low visibility caused by smoke altered the use of the graphical interface.

The conclusions related to the underlying multimodal framework emphasized the system tolerance to the coincidental communication breakdowns as a positive aspect though the user difficulty at perceiving the optimal solutions in acting in conditions of lack of updated information about the crisis.

The people that played the role of firemen during our simulation also experienced the difficulties induced by the wearing of the real fireman equipment. That was obviously not suitable for a regular activity of interacting with the Zaurus PDA device. Especially the gauntlet that is indispensable while working close to the fire place seemed to be the cause of the problem. Ultimately the experimentation of the automatic multimodal system for crisis situations underlined the superiority of such an automatic approach to help people produce and collect information in reference to the crisis events.

Acknowledgments. The research reported here is part of the Interactive Collaborative Information Systems (ICIS) project, supported by the Dutch Ministry of Economic Affairs, grant nr: BSIK03024.

References

1. Corson, S., Macker, J.: RFC2501: Mobile Ad hoc Networking (MANET): Routing Protocol Performance Issues and Evaluation Considerations (1999)
2. Datcu, D., Zhenke, Y., Rothkrantz, L.J.M.: Multimodal workbench for automatic surveillance applications, In: Multimodal Surveillance: Sensors, Algorithms and Systems Chapter 14 (2007)
3. Delhay, S., Idrissa, M., Lacroix, V.: PARADIS: GIS Tools for Humanitarian Demining. In: The 2nd International ISCRAM Conference, pp. 213–219 (2005)
4. Fitrianie, S., Datcu, D., Rothkrantz, L.J.M.: Constructing Knowledge of the World in Crisis Situations using Visual Language. In: IEEE International Conference on Systems, Man, and Cybernetics (2006)
5. Fuhrmann, S., MacEachren, A.M., Dou, J., Wang, K., Cox, A.: Gesture and Speech-Based Maps to Support Use of GIS for Crisis Management: A User Study. AutoCarto (2005)
6. Granica, K., Nagler, T., Eisl, M.M., Schardt, M., Rott, H.: Satellite Remote Sensing Data for an Alpine Related Disaster Management GIS. In: The 2nd International ISCRAM Conference, pp. 221–232 (2005)
7. Rothkrantz, L.J.M., Datcu, D., Fitrianie, S., Tatomir, B.: Personal Mobile Support for Crisis Management Using Ad-Hoc Networks. In: The 11th International Conference on Human-Computer Interaction, Lawrence Erlbaum Associates, Inc, Mahwah (2005)
8. Tatomir, B., Rothkrantz, L.J.M.: Crisis Management using Mobile ad-hoc Wireless Networks. In: The 2nd International ISCRAM Conference, pp. 147–149 (2005)
9. Gaynor, M., Seltzer, M., Moulton, S., Freedman, J.: A Dynamic, Data-Driven, Decision Support System for Emergency Medical Services, ICCS2005, pp. 703–711. Springer, Heidelberg (2005)
10. Goh, O.S., Ardil, C., Fung, C.C., Wong, K.W., Depickere, A.: A Crisis Communication Network Based on Embodied Conversational Agents System with Mobile Services. International Journal of Information Technology (3) 4, (2006) ISSN 1305-2403
11. Jakobson, G.N., Parameswaran, J., Burford, L., Lewis, P.: Ray: Situation-aware Multi-Agent System for Disaster Relief Operations Management. In: Proc. ISCRAM, pp. 313–324 (2006)
12. Sharma, R., Yeasin, M., Krahnstoever, N., Rauschert, I., Cai, G., Brewer, I., MacEachren, A.M., Sengupta, K.: Speech–Gesture Driven Multimodal Interfaces for Crisis Management. Proceedings of the IEEE 91(9), 1327–1354 (2003)
13. Thalmann, D., Salamin, P., Ott, R., Gutierrez, M., Vexo, F.: Advanced Mixed Reality Technologies for Surveillance and Risk Prevention Applications. In: Levi, A., Savaş, E., Yenigün, H., Balcısoy, S., Saygın, Y. (eds.) ISCIS 2006. LNCS, vol. 4263, pp. 13–23. Springer, Heidelberg (2006)
14. Veelen, J.B., van, Storms, P., van, Aart, C.J.: Effective and Efficient Coordination Strategies for Agile Crisis Response Organizations. In: Proc. ISCRAM 2006 pp. 202–213 (2006)
15. Weigand, H.: Agent Community Support for Crisis-ResponseOrganizations. In: On the Move to Meaningful Internet Systems 2006: OTM 2006 Workshops, vol. 4277, pp. 218–226. Springer, Berlin, Heidelberg (2006)

Integrating Emotions and Knowledge in Aesthetics Designs Using Cultural Profiles

Rosa Gil[2] and César A. Collazos[1]

[1] Department of Systems, FIET, Universidad del Cauca,
Sector Tulcán, Popayán-Colombia
ccollazo@unicauca.edu.co
[2] Departament d'Enginyeria i Informàtica, EPS, Universitat de LLeida,
25001 LLeida, Spain
{rgil,tonig}@diei.udl.es

Abstract. Emotions have been described as complex organized states and some Tangible User Interfaces (TUIs) have been developed based on them. TUIs using some kind of physical interfaces called Phidgets, have included a strong emphasis on touch and physicality as well as on exploiting the meaning and cultural usage associated with everyday physical objects. However, there is a gap between emotions and knowledge management. This paper presents a detailed analysis to show how this relationship is developed in several cultures, trying to find a common understanding to relate them. From a cognitive point of view, some image schemas have been established and extended using metaphors. As a result it is possible to relate schemas that come from perception to abstract schemas. For instance, several physical properties as position in a frame or curve shape properties used in aesthetics designs can be associated to some kind of emotions as '*joy for speed*'. Cultural profiles are the missing element to formalize it because emotion expression can be different in every culture; moreover scientific knowledge and emotions come together in the same representation in some cultures. As conclusion, a research line is exposed for integrating knowledge management in TUIs, and in this paper a previous prototype has been developed.

Keywords: emotions, interfaces, aesthetics designs, and cultural relations.

1 Introduction

In order to explain the model, section 1 introduces cognitive linguistics, this section illustrates how human beings conceptualize knowledge, following section 2 refers to mathematical properties, trying to establish connections to the way human beings conceptualize knowledge using them, section 3 introduces emotion and its connections to knowledge, some aspects relating to emotions as color or geometry are included. Section 5 and 6 explains the proposed approach: a knowledge model related to emotions, its prototypes and the previous knowledge management implementation from Semantic Web.

N. Aykin (Ed.): Usability and Internationalization, Part II, HCII 2007, LNCS 4560, pp. 344–353, 2007.
© Springer-Verlag Berlin Heidelberg 2007

2   Cognitive Approach

In order to relate abstract knowledge to physical, cognitive linguistics approach is going to be considered. The root of this research is based on the construction of the human beings knowledge from perceptions and afterwards they use it to express their feelings and emotions.

2.1   Cognitive Linguistics

Neural Theory of Language (NTL). This theory attempts to explain how many brain functions (including emotion and social cognition) work together to understand and learn language. The NTL assumption is people understand narratives in a sub-conscious manner imaging the situation being described. There is both linguistic evidence (from classifier languages) and imaging data supporting the idea the meaning of a noun depends on the uses of the underlying thing.

At the NTL core, cognitive linguistics is based on "Image Schemas", which are regularities in our perceptual, motor and cognitive systems. Image schemas are conceptual or perceptual and they represent a link between language and spatial perception. The brain's visual system is also active when a person dreams [1]. Moreover, congenitally blind people, most of whom have the visual system of the brain intact, can perform visual imagery experiments perfectly well, with basically the same results as sighted subjects, but a bit slower [2], [3]. Thus, it makes neurological sense that even the congenitally blind people can use structures in the visual system for conceptual purposes.

The visual system is linked to the motor system via the prefrontal cortex. Via this connection, Image-Schemas are related to body parts [4]. This explanation allows understanding the way human beings could conceptualize concepts.

Spatial Image Schemas. Two roles sharing a location, define these Image Schemas:

- A trajector (TR) which is an object being located
- A landmark Schema (LM) representing the reference to the object.

Topological schema arises from trajector and landmark. The simplest topological schema is the CONTAINER schema, where another concept exists: boundary. This schema is used to reason in language structure, for instance, IN and OUT are universal concepts in language, however each culture exploit them in a different sense.

A similar effect happens with reference frames. Usually, in mathematics, physics or even in graphic design an object has to be referenced. This fact is universal too; however in every culture different reference frame is used. For instance, Australian aborigine tribes do not have the concept of *left* or *right*, they understand the objects position in terms of *north, south, west* or *east*. It follows that world and the objects that are positioned on it are referenced in an absolute frame (*planet Earth*).

2.2   Emotional Approach from Cognitive Linguistics

The currently work in emotions is based on the following 10 proposals [5] taken from cognitive science:

1. Appraisals are constituents of, and therefore also necessary conditions for emotions.
2. Emotions are affective states with objects
3. There are two routes to emotional appraisal (reinstatement and computation)
4. These forms of appraisal parallel two kinds of categorization (prototype and theory based)
5. The two routes to emotional appraisals and the two kinds of categorization are governed by two forms of reasoning (associative and rule based).
6. The two routes to emotional appraisal or categorization may serve different behavioral functions (preparedness and flexibility).
7. The fact that some components of an emotion can be triggered before full awareness of its cause does not conflict with a cognitive view
8. Unconscious and conscious affect elicitation differs only in the episodic constraints on emotional meaning.
9. Automated, conditioned, imitated, and reinstated emotions are all manifestations of reinstated appraisals.
10. The experiential and motivational/behavioral manifestations of appraisals, while difficult to describe in language, can be communicated through connotative meaning.

3   Mathematical Properties

In a frame, the simplest concept to be conceptualized is the point, however it can describe more than a mathematical property. In the previous section, cognitive linguistics showed us how human beings conceptualize topological schemas and how they are related to language. However, if these concepts have to be represented in a 2D interface, some facts have to be explored if knowledge management has to be integrated: geometrical meaning in different cultures.

3.1   Point, Lines and Shapes in 2D

Point. In mathematics, coordinates represent points. For instance, in a space of dimension one, we need just one coordinate (a number), in a space of dimension two, two coordinates... A line needs two coordinates in a space of dimension one and so on. However, a point, or a line can represent universe in a different sense.

There is within the spiritual universe of Islam a dimension that may be called "Abrahamic Pythagoreanism", or a way of seeing numbers and figures as keys to the structure of the cosmos and as symbols of the archetypal world and also a world, which is viewed as the creation of God in the sense of the Abrahamic monotheisms.

The nature of origins of creation point of a subject is grounded in mystery. The nature of point –the simple, self-evident origin of geometry- is one such mystery: is it possible that a point "has no dimension", except that it be a metaphysical point, and how can it occupy "place" if space has not yet been created from its unfolding?

It has been suggested that this basic truth is reflected in both the openings words of the Book of Tao and in the fundamental formula of Islam (no divinity if not the sole divinity). This formula consists of two pairs of words, each word representing a degree of reality, as well as each pair denoting the negation and the affirmation respectively; the negation refers to the manifest domain and the affirmation to the supraformal and the Principle together.

For instance, we take a point which, having emerged, proceeds to describe a line (the line-path can be taken as representing the point "externalizing" itself); the line moves laterally or in a curve to describe a plane; the plane rotates or moves in a further direction to describe (or create) the solid dimension – the third dimension – to which all phenomena of the manifest corporeal world are subject.

4   Knowledge and Emotion Through Language

4.1   Emotions, Knowledge and Language

Several studies aiming at identifying the links between a product's shape characteristic and its emotional message have been carried out. *'Joy for speed'* can be translated in terms of emotion? CAD designers work everyday in these terms.

The FIORES project [6] establishes two level mapping

- The first level links geometric properties with styling terms
- The second level links styling terms with those expressing the emotional character

Our approach includes metaphors for building knowledge (see the next sections where metaphor is discussed and knowledge management, too)

4.2   Shapes and Emotions

This section goes further in the concept of geometry, mathematical properties have been explored. This section relates geometry with emotions.

Geometric shapes. The circle reflects the unity of the original point. The circle has always been regarded as a symbol of eternity. As a symbol within the limits of time, or rather subject to that condition of existence, it passes around just as the active compass point returns to its first position it necessarily passes over it and in principle establishes a helix – the expression in time of the circle. The circle expresses "threeness" in itself, i.e. centre, domain, periphery; and "fourness" in a manifest context, i.e. centre, domain included, boundary, domain excluded.   Emotions associated: PROTECTION, FEAR (Claustrophobia)

The position of the triangle is relevant to emotions. The triangles with a horizontal base enhance emotions as strength, personal stability or equilibrium. These concepts evoke physical mountain shape. The triangle positioned over the vertex has the opposite considerations.

Shapes properties: Curve properties to achieve emotions
Following the '*joy for speed*' example, it was necessary to express in a design this emotion. Some curve properties were tested to achieve it:

- Acceleration: deviation of the tangent to the curve
- Convexity/concavity
- Softness/Sharpness
- Tension
- Crown: blowing up the curve
- Lead-in: particular way to connect two edges/surfaces

Color properties
Emotion is balanced by color and its properties as Contrast, hue or saturation. Moreover, color can be a powerful tool in the realm of information design, where it is used to help the viewer organize data into various structures [7].

Psychologists have proved that we see the color of an object before its shapes and details.

Wilhelm Ostwald[1], a Nobel Prize winner in chemistry, studied color associations. His search for a law based on color order led him to the conclusion that people respond to colors emotionally.

Color in culture
Color and culture are two aspects very correlated. Briefly, some remarks [8]:

- Black – mourning and death in the industrialized west, whereas in China and India is white
- Red – stop (only in countries where automobiles are still rare)
- Green – in the 19th there is links to arsenic, associated with poison, for instance see cartoons, whereas today it is seen as the color of spring and environmental awareness.

Meanings of colors: Cheeriness (red, oranges), good wealth (yellows stimulate), Safety (blue), aggression (red), peace and depression (blue and violet)

4.3 Metaphor: Relating Emotions

Mappings
As a premise to formalize emotions as mental knowledge, the first will be considered as expressions based on physical knowledge, as has been explained previously (point 1). Metaphors will be used to understand how an emotion is internally understood and transmitted.

In order to build these metaphors, the concept of mapping is introduced. Mapping [9] is a correspondence between two sets that assigns to each element in the first a counterpart in the second.

Mappings between domains are at the heart of the unique human cognitive faculty of producing, transferring and processing meaning. Meaning construction is visualized as an iceberg where the visible part is used and known language.

---

[1] http://nobelprize.org/nobel_prizes/chemistry/laureates/1909/ostwald-bio.html

Cognitive science successfully takes into account *cultural and situational data as well as computational and biological data.*

Mappings construction

There are two main domains: source domain and target domain. In order to build a mapping, both are needed.

TIME as SPACE is a mapping that is widely used. Language is plenty of expressions where time is seen in terms of space. In fact, the conceptualization of reasoning is linked to our conceptualization of space and motion, for instance: 'try to think straight. This line of reasoning is taking you in the wrong direction'.

Mental spaces

Schema mappings operate to build and link *mental spaces*, which are structured by ICMs (Idealized Cognitive Models) [10]. They operate when a general schema, frame, or model is used to structure a situation in context.

Mental spaces are the domains that discourse builds up to provide a cognitive substrate for reasoning and for interfacing with the world. They set up in this manner and are internally structured by frames and cognitive models, and externally linked by connectors. In order to illustrate this concept a sentence where the verb is an emotion is analyzed: Maybe Romeo is IN LOVE with Juliet. The connectors are ROMEO and JULIET.

Further grammatical techniques and strategies for building spaces in Japanese and English have been compared [11] and also the psychological effects of using explicit space builders in discourse [12].

Sometimes blending and conceptual integration extends a mapping in a sense that a new identity is created. For instance, the concept of VIRUS illustrates this process. Initially, virus was only defined in a biological domain; when some programs were developed in a computer science domain, a mapping was created because these programs aimed to destroy/alter programs in the computer. This concept was so extended, those strange inferences about computer VIRUS where formulated: Can the computer virus infect human beings? Or can biological virus infect computers?

Emotional mapping example

Anger is one of the most primitive emotions in different cultures. A metaphor used in language (English and Spanish) for this emotion is to associate it to a *steaming pot*. The consequence is that the properties and behaviors are translated to anger emotion from the knowledge we have about a steaming pot.

Language allows us to collect physical knowledge and metaphors relate it to emotions. One main consequence is the communication of emotions to human beings. The idea is going beyond human beings language and to tend a bridge to computers language. The next section will show how it can be possible.

5 Emotional Design Including Knowledge Management

5.1 Emotions and Graphic Design

In an exercise in graphic design asks for relating emotions to geometrical positions in a square. [13] The exercise also takes into account the color and the contrast of color. For instance, some patterns appear:

Negative emotions as Fear or Envy are represented at the bottom of the square. Positive emotions as Courage are represented at the top of the square. In other words, when actions or in this case, emotions are perceived as positive or negative, automatically are represented in terms of spatial dimensions, i.e. verticality

5.2 Knowledge Management

Knowledge is perhaps one of the most complicated concepts to be defined. If the goal is to achieve knowledge management between human beings and computers, the task is already impossible to end. In order to reach it, some steps have been done, it means that some constrains have to be done, for instance, applications will be developed over the web as a first step. This is due to the fact that an effort has been made in knowledge management in the Semantic Web, where there are specific languages, which allow formalizing ontologies. These languages behind the interfaces have to accomplish several points:

- Be able to adapt to different cultural profiles instantaneously
- Provide a mechanism to learn and exchange new knowledge to human beings and machines.

In order to achieve it, RDF[2] and OWL[3], which are languages from Semantic Web, are proposed. Metaphors will allow us to pass from abstract concepts to physical and vice versa. To allow interoperability between concepts it was necessary to establish which are the common concepts among different cultures around the world (see point 2). In fact, this is a revolutionary point of view; nowadays the newest initiatives that come from Semantic Web as Semantic Web Portal project[4] or PiggiBank[5] do not achieve to relate metaphors. They are specialized in semantic annotation.Metaphors can be explicated using ontologies as well as the knowledge behind the web interface

As it has been seen in the previous sections emotions are related to physical properties. Every user has his/her own relations, usually conditioned by cultural aspects. Model flexibility allows incorporating cultural aspects as ontologies themselves, which can be connected. One of the key aspects was the fact that many times there is not agreement to connect emotions, for instance, for me blue color can represent happiness because it remembers me blue sky in a sunny day and not sadness or coldness. This kind of problems can be solved with patterns over cognitive aspects. It means that human beings associate <color> to <emotion>. This is the interesting relation as many others. **Fig. 1.** Shows these kind of relations. There are different clouds with different colors, which symbolized that they come from ontologies, in fact they can be instances. Every 'cloud' is influenced by culture and it can establish relations to other profiles.

---

[2] http://www.w3.org/RDF/
[3] http://www.w3.org/TR/owl-features/
[4] Semantic Web Portal: http://sw-portal.deri.at/
[5] AQUA Question Answering System.

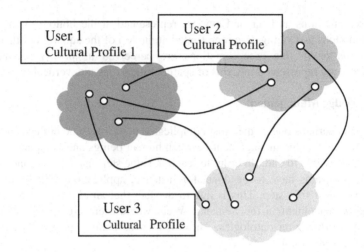

Fig. 1. Ontologies used in the cultural profiles design in the knowledge management

6 Implementation

Currently, knowledge management using Web Semantics has been implemented in a portal called Rhizomik[6] (see **Fig. 2.**). It is possible to visualize, edit and delete the data structure and also the instances of the ontology. The use of a Wiki[7] allows it. However, there is a gap because the goal is to design an emotional interface.

In order to solve this fact, an extension of the portal is being defined following the criteria of the paper (cognitive science, graphic design, CAD techniques, psychology, mathematics…). A prototype has been built (see **Fig. 3.**) to make an experiment about relations of music and emotions. Actually is in phase of improvement, OpenLaszlo[8] has been chosen to extend portal capabilities. OpenLaszlo is an open source platform for creating zero-install web applications with the user interface capabilities of desktop client software.

OpenLaszlo programs are written in XML and JavaScript and transparently compiled to Flash and soon DHTML (this is a very interesting characteristic). The OpenLaszlo APIs provide animation, layout, data binding, server communication, and declarative UI.

Rhizomik will be responsible of knowledge management. This kind of interfaces will interact to the user in the following way:

– The user will associate songs to emotions. There will be a special part to do it.
– It will be possible with a displacement toolbar change our mood and automatically, the interface will show us the music associated.
– It will be possible to modify metadata about songs/albums

---

[6] http://www.rhizomik.net
[7] http://en.wikipedia.org/wiki/Wiki
[8] http://www.openlaszlo.org/

- The design process will be developed following the User Centered Design
- Mash-up's[9] applications will be used.
- User can create new relations if he/she has the permission to do it.

Fig. 2. Rhizomik Semantic Web Portal

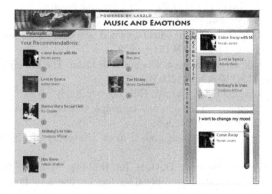

Fig. 3. Music and Emotions interface proto0074ype

7   Conclusions and Future Work

This work aims to make a new research line between to established disciplines: Web semantics and TUIs. The first needs to have powerful interfaces to show knowledge management advantages while the second has the inverse problem. TUIs are not restricted to web, so the following step is to migrate applications over the web to different kind of devices.

Our approach deals with the fact that we have some experience over knowledge management over the web, concretely Semantic Web, and a Semantic Web portal is presented and a prototype as well to illustrate a connection to emotions as an extension of the portal. Nowadays, it is not a TUI yet. Some aspects, which have been taken from several disciplines, have been considered to make this model. Cultural profiles fit perfectly in the knowledge model. The direction of our research goes to convert our portal in a new kind of TUI.

---

[9] http://en.wikipedia.org/wiki/Mashup_(web_application_hybrid)

Acknowledgments. This work was partially supported by Colombian Colciencias Projects No. 4128-14-18008 and No. 030-2005, Cicyt Projects TEN2004-08000-C03 and TIN2004-08000-C03-03.

References

1. Hobson, J.A.: The dreaming brain. Penguin Books, London (1988)
2. Marmor, G., Zaback, L.: Mental rotation by the blind: Does mental rotation depend on visual imagery? Journal of Experimental Psychology: Human Perception and Performance 2, 515–521 (1976)
3. Kerr, N.H.: The role of vision in visual imagery experiments: Evidence from the congenitally blind. Journal of Experimental Psychology: General, 112, 265–277 (1983)
4. Bailey, D., Feldman, J., Narayanan, S., Lakoff, G.: Modelling Embodied Lexical Development. In: Proceedings of the 19th Annual Conference of the Cognitive Science Society (1997)
5. Clone, G.L., Ortony, A.: Cognitive in Emotion: Always, Sometimes, or Never. In: Richard, D., Lane, Nadal, L. (eds.) Paper in Cognitive Neuroscience of Emotion, pp. 24–62. Oxford University Press, NewYork (2000)
6. Giannini, F., Monti, M.: Design intent-oriented modeling tools for aesthetic design. Journal of WSCG, vol. 11(1), ISSN 1213–6972
7. Dabner, D.: Graphic Design School. Thames & Hudson. The Principles and Practices of Graphic Design (2004) Reprinted (2005)
8. Heller, E.: Psicologia del color. Gustavo Gili (January 2005)
9. Fauconnier, G.: Mappings in thought and language. Cambridge University Press. (1997). Reprinted 1999, 2000, 2002, 2003, 2005
10. Lakoff, G.: Women, Fire and Dangerous Things. University of Chicago Press, Chicago (1987)
11. Fujii, S.: English and Japanese Devices for Building Mental Spaces. University of California, Berkeley. In: Paper presented at the International Pragmatics Conference, Kobe, Japan (1993)
12. Traxler, M., Sanford, A., Aked, J., Moxey, L.: Processing Causal and Diagnostic Statements in Discourse Human Communication Research Centre, University of Glasgow. Manuscript (1995)
13. Lewandowsky, P., Zeischegg, F.A.: practical guide to digital design. (2000) Reprinted 2002, 2003, 2004, 2005 (Spanish edition)

"Only Famous Companies I Would Ever Buy": Understanding How People Learn to Trust Web Sites

Emilie W. Gould

Manning School of Business, Acadia University, Wolfville, Nova Scotia, Canada
emilie.gould@acadiau.ca

Abstract. Many studies of e-commerce continue to be constrained by classic marketing concerns like product type. However, new aspects emerge when Fogg's (2003) Typology of Web Credibility is applied to the development of trust. Results from a set of focus groups with Malaysian students highlight interesting issues associated with process, cultural values, and global inequities in infrastructure. The pilot study reported here will be updated with information from additional focus groups at the HCI International 2007 Conference in Beijing.

Keywords: trust; credibility; e-commerce; advertising; cultural values.

1 Introduction

I am currently engaged in conducting a series of focus groups with students from three different countries to examine the way they have learned to use (or not use) the web for e-commerce. The results from a pilot study with Malaysian students are reported here; results from additional focus groups will be reported at the HCI International 2007 Conference in Beijing.

2 The Malaysian Focus Groups

A pilot study with male and female Malaysian students examined their use of the Internet. All of the students were studying in the United States, but none had lived there more than one year. The students discussed their use of the Internet in Malaysia and how it had changed once they moved to the United States. Trust was a recurrent theme and, for some of them, trust was specifically connected to type of site. The students also identified specific design elements that enhanced credibility in e-commerce sites. In general, their comments corroborated the findings of Fogg's (2003) Stanford Web Credibility Survey [3]; the ten elements that most enhanced credibility in the second Stanford survey were similar to their own concerns.

However, the students did not define e-commerce sites in a static way; almost all of them described the development of their trust in the Internet and specific web sites as a process that took place over time. Again, I found Fogg's work useful; his

N. Aykin (Ed.): Usability and Internationalization, Part II, HCII 2007, LNCS 4560, pp. 354–362, 2007.
© Springer-Verlag Berlin Heidelberg 2007

typology of web credibility appeared to describe the students' evolution from suspicion to enthusiasm for the web. They first learned to trust the web as a site for commerce and then to trust specific web sites on the basis of reputation, inspection, and interaction.

The focus groups surfaced one last theme. Another barrier to the development of commercial web sites in Malaysia was infrastructure. Limited bandwidth, lack of access to computers, and lack of access to credit all interacted with web credibility. Once these infrastructure constraints disappeared after their arrival in North America, the students began their process of investigation.

2.1 Initial Attitudes to e-Commerce

The ten students who participated in the focus groups first learned to use the Internet in Malaysia so that they could communicate with friends, play games, or listen to music. Their first applications were email and IRC. Very few had access to networked computers at home or school so they spent a lot of time in cybercafés.

Although the students said they often logged into chat rooms to talk with strangers (something that might be considered quite risky in the United States), they never used the Internet for e-commerce. That, they felt, was much too dangerous. Students in three of the four groups talked about Internet frauds and claimed to know friends and acquaintances who had lost hundreds of dollars on the Internet. For instance:

> S3: One of my friends, he tried to buy a Sony camera, J point, ... zero pixel. And he wait for like a month, and then checked back through the web site, and the web site doesn't exist any longer. So he just lost like three, three hundred something.

Auction sites such as eBay were particularly distrusted because they provided no real controls on sellers. Students were also concerned about the security of their credit card information:

> S3: You know what I was told when I first used eBay, very good, they say that you know that the Internet is not secure and like that. [S4: agrees] That's what prevented Malaysian people. S5: Maybe we hear more about cases of frauds and stuff. They are listening from the US. Cases of online fraud. So we prefer safer, face-to-face transactions.

Another student had rarely used the Internet; before coming to the United States, it didn't seem real:

> S10: Ah, actually, back then in Malaysia, I did not use it much. I don't know, how they... I don't believe (group laughs) Ah, because the Internet is like, you know is, like on the air, like. How do you say it? So, I just cannot believe everything I see through the net.

These risks and the insubstantiality of the web were not problems when chatting anonymously with others but they were major factors retarding e-commerce.

Moreover, e-commerce just didn't seem necessary in Malaysia. Two students told me why they thought there weren't many online shopping sites back home:

> **S2:** Probably because Malaysia is just a small country and everything is within reach. [**S1:** Yeah] I mean, you know where to get stuff. Here, I mean, you have to shop around. Even the mall here is quite [**S1:** expensive] far out. **S1:** If you want to get something cheap, you know you're supposed to go here (thumps table for emphasis), in Malaysia. And we get all the cheap stuff there. [**EWG:** Oh, really!] [**S2:** Yeah] You do. So there's really no need of online...
>
> **S1:** We get a lot of bargains. [**S2:** agreeing] You can get something for ten bucks and you can bargain. It will go as low as 5 bucks. [**S2:** Right.] That's the beauty of it. [**S2:** I can do that.] You don't need eBay.

Other students also talked about the convenience of shopping in Malaysia: knowing whom to buy from, feeling the merchandise, and bargaining until you got the best price. Two groups said that Malaysian web sites were intended to get people to come into stores, not to sell merchandise online. These "bricks and clicks" sites should be thought of as advertisements rather than e-commerce. In a 2000 comparison of Malaysian and United States web sites [4], my co-authors Norhayati Zakaria and Shafiz Mohd. Affendi Yusof noted the same issue.

2.2 Attributes of Trustworthy Sites

After the students came to the United States, their feelings changed. Most of them began to buy things online and were happy with their experiences. The young woman who had not believed in the Internet said she now surfed the net in her spare time to look for "cute" things. Her friend said it was much more convenient to buy products from web sites than go to American shopping malls.

Three explanations emerged from the focus groups. First, Malaysian students already in the United States told the newcomers that they could trust the general security of the Internet. Second, they saw everyone else at their university using the web. Third, the students evolved their own strategies for selecting or testing certain types of sites.

When the Malaysians began to initiate purchases on their own they tended to buy from a limited number of companies. Sometimes they picked sites that they had heard about from others:

> **S5:** People before us use them [sites] and they find trustworthy and they pass it on to us.

But a far more powerful strategy was to buy from "famous," well-established sites.

> **EWG:** And are there any characteristics that make you trust [Amazon, eBay, and Overstock] as opposed to some other online companies? **S10:** No, because it's famous. [Okay] Yeah, it's true. Because Amazon, I mean everybody knows it for its credibility and stuff like that, yeah. That's fine... Only famous companies I would ever buy. If I don't know that company then, I don't really trust them.

Another student emphasized that big companies were inherently more trustworthy.

> **S5:** Like for me, I start from big companies first because big companies usually have big stakes and usually they won't betray, they won't easily, they won't certainly commit fraud. And if they do, then I think they will be much more visible. Like, most of my purchases are in Amazon.com. If I purchase from somewhere else, usually it's when it's linked by that site or by any other major sites. I disagree with like searching Yahoo for like stuff and then, go to people's web site, no.

Linking from reputable sites increased confidence. But sometimes students had to buy from unknown sites. Certain products, such as phone cards to Malaysia, are not sold by well-established companies. So the students evolved the strategy of buying something small and evaluating the transaction. If the purchase was successful, they would go back again to that company.

> **S2:** I usually stick to one. Once I trust one company, that's it.

> **S8:** Or, if we don't know anything, like we just try to buy one, like one time, [**S6:** Yeah] and then we maybe the next time just try the same thing. **S6:** The trust develops, I think.

Certain aspects of site design increased student confidence. Students mentioned the importance of general appearance, security, contact numbers or email addresses, and information on management (rather than information for consumers).

Although well-known companies like Yahoo and Amazon were assumed to be more reputable because they had an incentive not to commit fraud, they must still deploy appropriate sites:

> **S1:** I think I trust Yahoo and the Amazon. One, because I know the company and two because of the web site. It looks more professional so I know they have enough, they can pay people enough money to make a really nice web site. Compared to eBay, it's yeah a growing company but I don't really trust it because the web site's kind of flimsy. And I can't, it's hard for me, it's not really user friendly.

This subtheme of "professional-looking" sites came up several times. Malaysian web sites were criticized for not being "developed" ("in its baby stage"), for not using Flash or interactive features, and for not updating themselves on a regular basis. Sometimes the students ascribed these problems to slower networks but they also gave me examples of "good" Malaysian web sites that were highly interactive and well designed. Good sites were attributed to the national Multimedia Super Corridor (MSC) initiative; this program was established in 1996 to make Malaysia a major global player in information technology.

Secure servers were another essential:

> **EWG:** ... I mean, how do you say to yourself, I'm going to spend some money on this web site, I'm not going to spend some money on another web site? **S3:** Usually there's a little "s" in the address. That makes me... **S5:** https. [**S3:** Yes] [Okay] **S3:** When there's a little "s" – https – that's secure... **S5:** They meant business when they purchased that.

Having some way to contact someone at the site was also very important to the Malaysian students. They were quite conscious of the presence (or absence) of webmasters. A contact address signified that the company was responsive to customer needs. The existence of a webmaster signified that the company had a real commitment to maintaining the site.

Finally, special types of information enhanced credibility. One student explained why she thought one bank web site was better than another.

> **S1:** But the bank I trust most is the bank, is Chase Manhattan Bank. Because they have both JP Morgan and Chase on the same web site. So, for businesses, they go to JP Morgan, for personal, they go to Chase and the Chase web site has also has the investor relations site. They tell me how much they have done for the past few years, who their board members are, so I know who's behind the scenes running the whole thing. So I trust them more.

I asked other students if they wanted that kind of information in a web site. One of them said it wasn't always necessary:

> **S5:** Maybe because it depends on how deep is our interaction with the company. If we just going to buy stuff online and that's it, then probably we don't need to know much about their corporate infrastructure.

These conversations suggest that some (but not all) of the students wanted to do research to increase their understanding of the organization and build their sense of confidence before they processed the product message for certain types of sites.

One aspect of site design not mentioned by the Malaysians was graphics (except for animation, which was linked to level of technical development). I asked why images of customers were not common on Malaysian sites. I was told:

> **S5:** Maybe it is not our style. In terms of television advertisements, we rarely see like people coming to the screen and talking, buy this product and stuff. Here is this. Its advantage. Rarely. Usually what we see is all those animations and the bottle comes springing out, something like that. Rarely people go, come out and speak. That's not, that's not the Malaysian style. And, yeah, usually when they do so, they look stupid. (all laugh) Maybe that's why they don't like to do it. There is always something unstylish about it.

Another student supported this.

> **S8:** Like in Malaysia, most of the people are quite shy. I don't know. To put yourself on a web site, maybe that's one of the reasons people don't.

This discomfort with personal images may also derive from prohibitions in Islam. Restrictions on portrayals of the human body are much more stringently observed in Arab countries but, according to Deng, Jivan, and Hassan (1994) [2], the Malaysian government also censors advertising images to protect public decency. Whatever the root cause, this lack of customer images may contribute to an apparent lack of focus on consumers in Malaysian web sites.

3   The Stanford Web Credibility Survey and Fogg's Typology of Computer Credibility

I was struck by the amount of research done by the Malaysians before they would buy anything through the Internet. But many people have told me they investigate online organizations this same way. The 1999 and 2002 results of the Stanford Web Credibility Surveys (Fogg, 2003) [3] show that people in Finland and the United States look for much the same data as the students in my focus groups.[1] Many of the items cited by the Malaysian students match the ten elements that most enhanced site credibility in the second Stanford survey:[2]

1. The site represents an organization you respect
2. The site lists the organization's physical address
3. The site provides a quick response to your customer service questions
4. The site gives a contact phone number
5. The site sends emails confirming the transactions you make
6. The site looks professionally designed
7. The site gives a contact email address
8. The site is arranged in a way that makes sense to you
9. The site links to outsides sources and material
10. The site has been updated since your last visit

On specific items, the differences between the Stanford surveys and the focus groups seem to be differences in degree rather than kind. Similarly, in my thesis research [5], Malaysian evaluators in Malaysia expressed stronger skepticism towards e-commerce (and greater initial suspicions) than United States students.

The focus groups support Fogg's (2003) typology of computer credibility which grew out of the Stanford studies. Fogg identifies 4 types of web credibility:

Presumed	General assumptions in the mind of the perceiver
Reputed	Third-party endorsements, reports, or referrals
Surface	Simple inspection or initial firsthand experience
Earned	Firsthand experience that extends over time

Some of the specific elements he associates with each type of credibility differ from those mentioned by the Malaysian students. However, as Fogg himself notes, his results could change with a more culturally diverse set of users. In the meantime, his typology describes the process used by the Malaysian students to select e-commerce sites in the United States surprisingly well.

In Malaysia, the Internet was not presumed trustworthy but, in the United States, the students found the opposite presumption. As they began to settle in, senior students told them that certain sites could be used. This reputed credibility gave the newcomers enough confidence to search for books and clothing online and to analyze new sites for themselves. Famous sites had a natural advantage. However, web sites

---

[1] A list of web design elements was elicited in research studies with 6000 participants and rated by 3000 more respondents.
[2] Elements associated with online newspapers from the original survey are not included.

that looked professional, used secure servers, and provided contact information or the address of a webmaster also met student standards for surface credibility. (Some students also looked for information about company management.) When students were able to purchase good quality items successfully, the sites earned more credibility. Trust also increased if new sites were linked to trusted sites.

4   Moderating Effects and the Role of Cultural Values

Fogg suggests that variations in the operator, information content, functionality, and design of a web site may all increase or decrease credibility. Similar moderating factors are known to influence preference for different types of ads. In this study, cultural values seemed to play a role.

Deng, Jivan, and Hassan (1994) [2] found that target audience (general audience or youth audience) and product type (used by women or by men and women) determined whether to localize Western ads for Malaysia. Han and Shavitt (1994) [6] found that the context of use (products to be purchased and used by individuals or with others) modified individualistic and collectivist appeals in ads targeted to consumers in Korea and the United States. Zhang and Neelankavil (1997) [9] found similar effects for China. When selling products for personal use, culturally-congruent appeals were not always necessary.

These findings support the notion that people can be both independent and interdependent (Markus and Kitayama [7]). As a result, individualistic appeals for personal use products often succeed with nominally collectivist people.

A year 2000 content analysis [4] I did with Norhayati Zakaria and Shafiz Mohd. Affendi Yusof found fundamental differences in online information in Malaysian and United States web sites. We hypothesized that Malaysians viewed their interactions with web sites in a relational perspective related to their cultural values. The necessity of establishing personal relationships seemed to be limiting the growth of e-commerce. By contrast, the focus groups show that Malaysian students in the United States are quite capable of coming to trust web sites. Yet the amounts of their online purchases remain small, mainly for books, music, and clothing. Except when discussing fraud, none of the students talked about using online banks or buying expensive electronics or computer products online. Perhaps type of site moderates the requirement for information about the organization. How might this happen?

Triandis (1995) [8] says that collectivists are more cautious about joining groups than individualists. Once committed, they remain loyal – even to the point of putting group interests ahead of their own. As a result, they try to gather a great deal of information before committing themselves. Individualists often join more groups than collectivists but rarely let these memberships impede their self-interest or freedom of action; if it suits them, they will leave one group and join another.

Buying a product for personal use is not like joining an organization. Most of the products cited by the Malaysian students are used alone. Even clothing, often viewed as public in the West, is hidden under traditional dress by many Malay women. But putting money in a bank or selecting a university is much more like joining a group. Each requires a longer term commitment and involves a much greater element of risk. Some of the people in the focus groups specifically cited the importance of identifying organizational information about bank web sites. This may be because Malaysians are more conscious that their investments have an impact on their extended families. Researching a university from its web site could be similar.

5 The Importance of Infrastructure

Finally, the focus groups surfaced the importance of infrastructure on the development of trust. When I asked students why commercial web sites had not taken hold in Malaysia, many cited infrastructure problems. Limited bandwidth, lack of access to computers, and lack of access to credit all made e-commerce more difficult in Malaysia than the United States. Bin, Chen, and Sun [1] reported similar problems in the People's Republic of China in 2003.

Until 2000, ISDN lines were relatively uncommon in Malaysia. Low-speed networks limited interactivity because sites took a long time to download and process information. Two students complained about the bandwidth problem:

> **S3:** I think that's the reason why most people won't create web sites that really use Flash or something is because it really takes time to load. You can't really, can't enjoy that. **EWG:** You can go out and drink a whole bottle of water. **S5:** Or we could have lunch.

Other students reminded me that parts of the country remain off the net. One student from East Malaysia mentioned villages near his hometown that lack electricity (let alone network connections). Another said that poor people have to use cybercafés. But cybercafés also cost money. Even though the government's Vision 2020 and MSC initiatives are building up Malaysia's technical infrastructure, the consensus was that e-commerce will remain limited until everyone has access to adequate service.

A third problem concerned Malaysia's economic infrastructure. Credit cards are hard to get. Two focus groups said lack of access to credit had slowed the development of e-commerce.

> **S4:** Big gap between US and Malaysia is the, the use of credit cards. Yeah. [**S3:** agrees] In Malaysia, we, we don't use credit cards that much compared to here, so I think that's the difference in, in, in the purpose of building a web site in Malaysia and the US.

> **S8:** I mean it's hard to get credit approval too. **EWG:** Oh, is it? **S8:** I think so. Yeah. (All laugh) **S7:** Like not at our age, right. We don't have,... **S6:** Yeah, we don't, like here, we can apply and we usually get one credit card but like in Malaysia I have to use my father's. (All laugh)

Banks do not approve young people for credit cards and even older people seem reluctant to use them to replace cash. One student mentioned that his father preferred to send personal checks for mail-order purchases rather than provide his credit card number.

A final problem was hinted at but not strongly stated. Censorship has existed in Malaysia and may reinforce distrust of the web. One student made the point that you don't always know the real source of information on the Internet. She was referring to a spoofing incident, but all the students reported that they were more engaged by the medium since coming to the United States because they were able to read uncensored material reflecting a variety of views. When I asked students for the best Malaysian web sites, each focus group told me to look at malaysiakini.com – an online newspaper that has battled censorship in the past.

6   Conclusion

Additional research is continuing with Chinese (PRC), Canadian, and Caribbean students to look at the determinants of trust for different groups of people. These results will be reported at the HCI International 2007 Conference.

Acknowledgments. My thanks to my Malaysian colleague Norhayati Zakaria who helped me start this research program.

References

1. Bin, Q., Chen, S.-J., Sun, S.Q.: Cultural differences in e-commerce: A comparison between the U.S. and China. Journal of Global Information Management 11(2), 48–55 (2003)
2. Deng, S., Jivan, S., Hassan, M.-L.: Advertising in Malaysia - A cultural perspective. International Journal of Advertising 13, 153–166 (1994)
3. Fogg, B.J.: Persuasive technology: Using computers to change what we think and do, Amsterdam. Morgan Kaufmann, San Francisco (2003)
4. Gould, E., Zakaria, N., Yusof, S.A.M.: Applying culture to website design: a comparison of Malaysian and US websites. In: Proceedings of 2000 Joint IEEE International and 18th Annual Conference on Computer Documentation (IPCC/SIGDOC 2000), pp. 161–171. IEEE Press, New York (2000)
5. Gould, E.W.: Applying cultural dimensions to website design: A case study from Malaysia and the United States (Doctoral dissertation, Rensselaer Polytechnic Institute, 2004). In: Dissertation Abstracts International (2005)
6. Han, S.-P., Shavitt, S.: Persuasion and culture: Advertising appeals in individualistic and collectivistic societies. Journal of Experimental Social Psychology 30, 326–350 (1994)
7. Markus, H.R., Kitayama, S.: Culture and the self: Implications for cognition, emotion, and motivation. Psychological Review 98, 224–253 (1991)
8. Triandis, H.C.: Individualism and collectivism. Boulder, CO: Westview Press (1995)
9. Zhang, Y., Neelankavil, J.P.: The influence of culture on advertising effectiveness in China and the United States: A cross-cultural study. European Journal of Marketing 31(2), 134–149 (1997)

A User Experience Study on C2C E-Commerce Localization in China

Dan Guo, Zhengjie Liu, Zhiwei Guo, and Kai Qian

Sino European Usability Center, Dalian Maritime University, 116026, Dalian, China
{guodan,nicolas,gzw}@newmail.dlmu.edu.cn, liuzhj@dlmu.edu.cn

Abstract. Chinese online commerce develops rapidly. How to give user the good shopping experience in C2C e-commerce website is discussed. In this research, we selected 22 college students, and let them try their first online shopping experience on two Chinese C2C e-commerce websites-Ebay(China) and Taobao which are designed under two different cultures, through the analysis of their experience process and satisfaction questionnaire, we found that in user's purchase decision process, the transfer and expression of function/ concept provided by website play a decisive role, shopping flow control have certain effect to the purchase implement process, and the main factor which impacts user total experience is whether the website provides the necessary function for shopping. Both websites have their own advantages in either interaction or interface, although they do not have effect to user's total shopping experience, but they do effect to the user's shopping feeling.

Keywords: E-commerce, localization, user experience, user testing, satisfaction questionnaire.

1 Introduction

With the rapid development of China's economy and information technology, many business activities are transferred to the internet. According to the report by iResearch Marketing, China's e-commerce transactions in 2005 have come to 740 billion yuan. It is expected that by the end of 2007 only B2B transaction will reach 210 billion dollars [1]. Chinese e-commerce potential is very huge, many world famous e-commerce company are coming to China: in 2004 Amazon acquired Joyo; in 2003 Ebay completed the acquisition of entire eachnet shares. But the final winners are rare: Dangdang and Joyo are still in the competition; Ebay(China) lost its dominant position in the competition with Taobao.

What brings to this? Is it because of the different strategy and function provided to meet users among websites? Or is it because of the different design styles under different cultural background? Or have other reasons?

We tried to do some studies in this area. We select two C2C e-commerce websites ebay.com.cn and taobao.com which are designed in different cultural backgrounds. In

N. Aykin (Ed.): Usability and Internationalization, Part II, HCII 2007, LNCS 4560, pp. 363–371, 2007.
© Springer-Verlag Berlin Heidelberg 2007

our study, user testing and satisfaction questionnaires are used to measure the user's initial online shopping experience. According to the analysis of the user's behaviors in the shopping process and their evaluation of satisfaction, we will find out the existing problems and the factors which affect the total experience of users' initial purchase on website, which can provide design ideas of localization and good experience for C2C e-commerce website.

The rest of this paper is organized as follows: Section 2 examines existing related work on the research of e-commerce website user experience and localization. In section 3 we discuss the research background, shopping process and our hypotheses. Furthermore, we will describe our experiment design and the data analysis in section 4, and we will end by drawing the results, conclusions and identifying opportunities for further work.

2 Related Work

2.1 E-Commerce Website User Experience Research

In the research of user experience on e-commerce website, many academicians make their contributions. Because the asymmetry of information in online market-places is the main cause of the potential risk to online traders [2], so trust is often discussed [6], [8], [10], [15], [16], [17], [18], [19]. Patricia Lanford's research shows that trust in online stores strongly affects consumers' purchase decisions[10], Troy's research about C2C e-commerce website trust also shows the importance of trust for the purchase decision, and he think the reputation of the seller and quality of previous dealings with the seller are the key factors[16], Florian N. Egger described the trust model from Graphic Design, Structure & Navigation Design and Content Design[15],.and the researchers from South Africa give a 'ABCD' trust model for e-commerce in South Africa[2]. Chinese researchers try to give the trust model [6], [17], [18], and some academicians even discuss the usefulness of credit [8]. The researchers also attempt to do some works on the e-commerce website usability evaluation, website comparing and design methodology [3], [11], [12], [14].

2.2 E-Commerce Website Localization Research

There are some researchers engage in cross-cultural studies on e-commerce. British researchers did a study on the interaction design of globalization and localization [9]. Through a comparative study between Amazon and Dangdang, Chinese researchers discuss the impact of cultural factors on the behavior of user's shopping [13]. Another paper is about Taobao and Ebay, the researchers compare the data of reputation scores of two websites [7].Now the C2C e-commerce localization user experience research is not much.

3 Hypotheses

3.1 Background

Nowadays, about two-thirds netizens who purchase products online select C2C e-commerce website in China [4]. Taobao and Ebay(China) are most famous C2C e-commerce websites in China, both of them have strengthen registration members, and the product number and transaction are both more than the other similar websites. Among the users who have visited e-commerce website, at lest 50% didn't buy anything, but if user had bought once on the website, then the possibility he becomes a regular user is close to 50% [4]. So users' initial shopping experience is very important for the C2C e-commerce websites. So we select Taobao and Ebay(China), and study the user's initial shopping experience.

3.2 Shopping Process Analysis

A total initial online shopping process contains four phases: attracted and enter, making a decision, implementing purchase and waiting. The process is shown in figure 1.Two key stages of user's initial experience is the stage of decision and the stage of implementation. In the stage of making a decision, users should do the following things: first of all, finding out the product they wanted, then compare a the product information and seller information, if they want to know some product detail information they should contact with seller. And in the stage of implementation, user should find the payment enter, register to become the website member, and after e-mail confirm and activation on another website, they should come back to the website and recover the product again, then study the secure online payment system, enter E-bank, and end this phase by writing the mail address .

3.3 Hypotheses

In the process of making a decision to purchase, users may contact with a lot of concepts and functions which are provided by websites in order to dispel user's worry or help purchase convenient, such as seller's credit feedback system, secure online payment system. Are these concepts and functions which is provided by websites is effectively for user's purchase? We give the hypotheses:

H1: The concepts and function the website provided have enough effect for users' purchase.

There are so many differences between internet shopping and real life shopping, especially in the initial shopping process. The difference in the stage of implementing purchase is much greater. For example, they are required to be find the payment enter, registered members, use the secure online payment system and E-banking…, the process is so Complex, so will the difference between online shopping process and real life shopping process affect the user's purchase experience on website?

H2: The difference between website and real shopping process affect the user experience.

In addition, will the different design style under different cultural backgrounds in the two websites affect the user's purchase behavior?

H3: The difference between interaction and interface has effect to user's initial shopping experience.

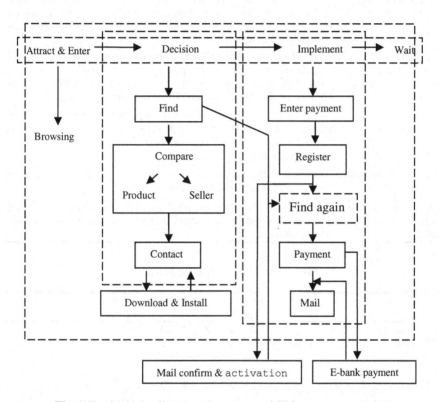

Fig. 1. Total initial online shopping process of C2C e-commerce website

4   Experiment Process

4.1   Method

We recruit 22 students without any online shopping experience from a university in Dalian as participants. They are divided into two groups for the evaluation of the two websites. The test is implemented in usability laboratory. The task scenarios are shown in table1. After the test, each user will fill in a satisfaction questionnaire, as shown in table 2.

Table 1. User task scenario

Task	Scenario description and explanation
Browsing	Let the users browsing on the website leisurely. This task inspects the initial impression and feelings the website brings to the user.
Product finding	Let the user find out a favorite MP3. This task inspects the way user used to find out the product.
Product comparing	Let the users take a comparing among the MP3 they have been searched, and choose one. This task inspects the gist of making decision and their understanding of the functions and concepts provided by the website.
Find the product visited before	Find out a product visited before This task inspects the compositor of merchandise and the function "product browse before".
Study the concept and function	Explain the functions and concepts they used, and dispel their concerns before their decisions, and transit to the implementation stage
Purchase-1(registration)	Complete the purchase-1. This task inspects the usage of search of payment enter , registration, and recover the product ever visited .(after registration, user have to recover the product again in both of the two website)
Purchase -2(payment)	Complete the purchase-2. This task inspects the understanding and usage of secure online payment system
Purchase -3(fill out mail address and contact)	Complete the last step of purchase-write the mail and contact address. This task inspects users' understanding and usage of mail address and contact.

Table 2. User satisfaction questionnaire

Question	Strongly Agree						Strongly Disagree	NA
1.The system is easy to use	O	O	O	O	O	O	O	O
2.The system provides the necessary function.	O	O	O	O	O	O	O	O
...								
16.I like the interface of the system	O	O	O	O	O	O	O	O
...								
20.Overall, I am satisfied with the system	O	O	O	O	O	O	O	O

4.2 Data Analysis

The analysis of user testing data. We describe the issues we founded from two ways: task and function. Meanwhile, classified the issues according to the issue number which user meet, the impact for the final completion of the task, and the effect on user's cognition of purchase process and website concept. For example, serious issues are the issues that most of the users meet or user's task is paused, or user's cognition of purchase process and website concept has a big mistake because of the issue.

The analysis of satisfaction questionnaire data. Except the overall satisfaction (the 20th question), we classify the nineteen questions into five factors: system usability factor, information quality factor, interface quality factor, emotional factor and the functions users expect. We consider user's overall satisfaction is decided by the five factors. We calculate the average of every questionnaire question of the two website and the average of every factor (for example the system usability factor). The item which is missed or NA is filling in with the average.

5 Result

Based on the analysis of user test results, we know the concept/function transfer and expression have very large effect during their purchase decision process. The flow control and the experience conflict are all work at the purchase implement process; the data of the satisfaction questionnaire show that both websites have its own advantage on either interaction or interface. The functions that the website provides will affect the user's evaluation to the whole website. Although system usability and interface don't affect the user's total experience directly, it works on the user's feeling to the whole system.

5.1 Transfer and Expression of Function/Concept

Trust and security are the key factors which let user make purchase decision. Both websites provide relevant function to solve these problems, for example, secure online payment system and credit feedback of the sellers. Especially Taobao provides IM for users to contact the sellers to understand the product information better, and for user's convenient shopping it provides the functions of "Product comparing" and "Finding the product visited before".

Many users didn't make a purchase decision after their task 2, 3, 4(the purchase decision phase). But after training, they express their concerns dispelled a lot and can accept the online shopping. They all express that they need these functions, but most of the time the functions are not "visual". Even the users find out these concepts, it can't "explain" and "express" by itself, that is to say, users can not simply judge its meaning simply, but also unable to estimate how much they will pay for understanding and using these concepts and functions. The result is the users abandon their purchase and leave the website before they dispel their worry.

5.2 Flow Control and Experience Conflict

Generally speaking, if the users make a decision to buy, they can stick to complete the entire shopping process. However, the initial shopping experience is not ideal, they have to suffer flow skip and experience conflict incessantly.

Not continuous shopping process. As it is shown in fig 1, we can see that user has to skip to another two websites in the phase of their implement purchase. One is member confirm and activation, the other is going to the e-banking to pay. According to he website's restrict, users have to recover the product they want to buy after they successfully registrant as a member. These seriously break the fluency of the shopping process, and if the product was expired during user's registration process, it may lead the user's reproved and dissatisfaction.

Additional and Complex operation and study process. In the process of payment, users do a lot of things that has no matter with shopping itself. In reality user can gain the product as long as he pay for it. But shopping on website are not so easy, users has to suffer registration, recover the product they visited, studying and understanding online payment system, entering e-banking, filling in the mail address and so on, which makes the purchase process too long.

5.3 Satisfaction Questionnaire Analysis

The average score the user give on the satisfaction questionnaire of the two websites is shown in figure 3. Ebay(China) has got a higher score than Taobao in many questions. So the result is Ebay(China) is better than Taobao on total experience.

The similar tendency. According to the user's evaluation to the two websites, the users all give the highest score on the 20th question 'Generally speaking, I am satisfied with the system.' Meanwhile, the users all give the lowest score to the 17th question 'The system is very attractive.' In addition, the 5th question 'I think using this system can improve productivity.' and the 7th question 'I can use this system to complete task efficiently.' also displayed the same trend. Our testing verified their argument exactly. After the initial purchase experience on website, the users say that there are indeed some tangible benefits shopping in the website, and they say that even if they don't buy anything in the website, they may still enjoy in searching the information of products and take the comparison of goods. But the complex initial purchase process made them tired, and they don't think the initial purchase have high effective.

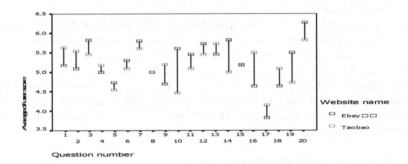

Fig. 3. The average of user score description of Taobao and Ebay(China) satisfaction questionnaires

The analysis of ANOVA. We carried out an independent-samples T test, the data analysis result shows that the score of the 10th question 'The system show the information clearly' (Ebay(China) gets the higher score) and the 16th question 'I like the interface of the system' (Taobao gets the higher score)are significant different. We speculate if it is because the colorful interface and rich pictures fit with the aesthetic needs of users in china. But it may also because of too many interface elements that bring on the uncertainty, which decentralized user's attention, and then lead to their dissatisfaction to the clear information present on the website.

Regression analysis of correlation factors. We carry a regression analysis on the five factors which may affect the total satisfaction, the five factors are system usability factor, information quality factor, interface quality factor, emotion factor and the functions that user expect. The result show that the functions the website provides will affect user's evaluation to the website most, though system usability and interface don't affect the total satisfaction directly, but they do have an impact on user's feelings to the system.

6 Conclusions

Based on our test and analysis, we summarize a concept model of good shopping experience for C2C e-commerce website. They should be satisfied from the function level, interaction level and impact level, as shown in figure 4. For the initial users, their needs are focused on the function level. They pay more attention to whether the website provides the functions that can dispel their worry and are convenient for their purchase. That is to say, the function's effective transfer and express is especially important to C2C e-commerce website to attract the initial users.

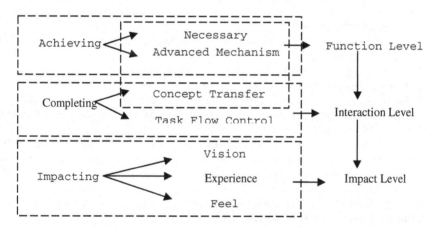

Fig. 4. Good online shopping experience concept model

Although the differences of two websites' interaction and interface do not affect the initial user's total experience to the website, the usability and interface quality do affect the initial user's feeling on shopping process. Then with the deep understanding of the function and concept, will the usability and interface quality affect the regular user's shopping experience? We know that usability affect user's shopping feeling then is user's emotion and cognition relative?

We select college students as subjects according with online shopping distribution, but can our subjects cover all the circs? In addition, the restriction of sample size may reduce the credibility of the result, and then it needs a further improvement.

References

1. iResearch marketing: B2B transaction China. (2006), http://info.it.hc360.com/2005/05/19134983069.shtml
2. Albert, M.R.: E-buyer Beware: Why Online Auction Fraud Should be Regulated. American Business Law Journal 39(4), 575–643 (2002)
3. Minocha, S., Petre, M.: Evaluating e-commerce environments: approaches to cross-disciplinary investigation. In: Human factors in computing systems CHI '06 (2006)
4. CNNIC: The research report of Chinese internet (2004), http://www.cnnic.net.cn/download/manual/2004111601.pdf
5. Nielsen, J.: Usability Engineering, pp. 105–131. Academic Press, San Diego (1993)
6. Yang, Y., Hu, Y., Chen, J.: A web trust-inducing model for e-commerce and empirical research. In: Proceedings of the 7th international conference on Electronic commerce ICEC '05 (2005)
7. Lin, Z., Li, J.: The online auction market in China: a comparative study between Taobao and eBay. In: Proceedings of the 7th international conference on Electronic commerce ICEC '05 (2005)
8. McKnight, D.H., Choudhury, V.: Distrust and trust in B2C e-commerce: do they differ? In: Proceedings of the 8th international conference on Electronic commerce (2006)
9. De Angeli, A., Kyriakoullis, L.: Globalisation vs. localisation in e-commerce: cultural-aware interaction design. In: Proceedings of the working conference on advanced visual interfaces AVI '06 (2006)
10. Lanford, P., Hübscher, R.: Trustworthiness in e-commerce. In: Proceedings of the 42nd annual southeast regional conference ACM-SE 42 (2004)
11. Tilson, R., Dong, J., Martin, S., Kieke, E.: A comparison of two current e-commerce sites. In: Proceedings of the 16th annual international conference (1998)
12. Callahan, E., Koenemann, J.: A comparative usability evaluation of user interfaces for online product catalog. In: Proceedings of the 2nd ACM conference on Electronic commerce EC '00 (2000)
13. Su, Q.-Y., Adams, C.: Will B2C e-commerce developed in one cultural environment be suitable for another culture: a cross-cultural study between amazon.co.uk (UK) and dangdang.com (China). In: Proceedings of the 7th international conference on Electronic commerce ICEC '05 (2005)
14. Fang, X., Salvendy, G.: Customer-centered rules for design of e-commerce Web sites. Communications of the ACM, 46(12) (2003)
15. Egger, F.N.: Trust me, I'm an online vendor: towards a model of trust for e-commerce system design. In: Human factors in computing systems CHI '00 (2000)
16. Strader, T.J., Ramaswami, S.N.: The value of seller trustworthiness in C2C online markets. Communications of the ACM, 45(12) (2002)
17. Peng, L., Chen, Z., Li, Q.: Model and method for evaluating creditability of C2C electronic trade. In: Proceedings of the 8th international conference on Electronic commerce (2006)
18. Zhang, X., Zhang, Q.: Online trust forming mechanism: approaches and an integrated model. In: Proceedings of the 7th international conference on Electronic commerce ICEC '05 (2005)
19. Barnard, L., Wesson, J.: A trust model for e-commerce in South Africa. In: Proceedings of the 2004 annual research conference of the South African institute of computer scientists and information technologists on IT research in developing countries SAICSIT '04 (2004)

Towards Cultural Adaptability in Driver Information and -Assistance Systems

Rüdiger Heimgärtner

Siemens AG, Im Gewerbepark C25, 93055 Regensburg, Germany
Ruediger.Heimgaertner@siemens.com

Abstract. This paper elucidates and discusses some aspects of cultural adaptability. It describes the concept, influence and Use Cases of cultural adaptability in driver information and assistance systems exemplified by driver navigation systems. Thereby, the reasons, advantages and problems of using adaptability regarding driving safety and driver preferences will be addressed. The results of two online studies concerning use cases of navigation systems revealed differences in interaction behavior, which depend on the cultural background of the users (e.g. attitude, preference, skill etc.). Furthermore, cultural adaptability can improve usability and share in universal access.

Keywords: cultural adaptability, cultural user interface design, adaptive HCI (Human Computer Interaction/Interface), adaptive HMI (Human Machine Interaction/Interface), driver navigation systems, driver information systems, driver assistance systems, tool, cross-cultural HCI analysis, cultural adaptability, cultural user interface design, intercultural usability.

1 Cultural Differences in User Interfaces

Culture influences the interaction of the user with a computer system or a machine because of the movement of the user in a cultural surrounding [13]. Cultural dimensions are models to describe the behavior of the members of different cultures. They allow to analyze and to compare the means of the characteristics of different groups quantitatively [6]. For HCI the cultural dimensions are interesting that are directly connected to communication, information, interaction and dialog design, e.g. those cultural dimensions concerning the culturally different concepts of space, time and communication [2]. Space and time are physical variables influencing the communicative behavior of human beings, which form the social processes of a group of humans and their culture: by learning of certain kinds of behavior, the human being matures according to his cultural surrounding. Basic patterns of such kinds of behavior are time handling, density of networks of information, communication speed and the time behavior of action chains. In this respect, it is also reasonable to assume that *variables connected to information science* like information speed (distribution speed and emergency frequency of information), information density (number and distance of information units) or information order (appearing sequence and arrangement of information) *correlate with cultural different basic patterns of kinds*

N. Aykin (Ed.): Usability and Internationalization, Part II, HCII 2007, LNCS 4560, pp. 372–381, 2007.
© Springer-Verlag Berlin Heidelberg 2007

of behavior. Therefore the differences that Hall [2] found in communication speed between cultures imply differences in information speed ("duration of information presentation"), information density ("number of parallel pieces of information during information presentation") and information frequency ("number of information presentations per time unit").

To be able to design user interfaces for the global market that can adapt to the cultural needs of the user automatically, the first step is to find out the differences in the cultural needs of the users and hence the cultural differences in HCI on all levels of HCI localization (surface, functionality, and interaction) concerning Look & Feel [3], [5]. In this context, topics such as presentation of information (e.g. colors, time and date format, icons, font size) and language (e.g. font, writing direction, naming) or dialog design (e.g. menu structure and complexity, dialog form, layout, widget positions) as well as interaction design (e.g. navigation concept, system structure, interaction path, interaction speed) are affected [13], [4].

One promising method to accomplish this task is to observe and analyze the interaction behavior of users, from different cultures, with the system by an appropriate automated analysis tool to determine different interaction patterns according to the cultural background of the users (if any).[1] From this, cross-cultural usability metrics can be derived, which can be used for cultural adaptability.

2 Adaptive Driver Information and -Assistance Systems

Today, driver information and assistance systems are very complex both in functionality and in usage, which tend to need strong mental power of the drivers. The mental workload of the driver has to be as low as possible for the sake of preventing accidents in traffic. Hence, especially when the driver is becoming mentally overloaded (e.g. in dangerous traffic situations) the characteristics of the interaction between the system and the driver must be adapted automatically to reduce mental workload or at least to prevent mental *overload*.

According to the Use Cases, there are several areas in driver information and assistance systems where adaptability is reasonable, e.g. maneuver generation, voice guidance (instructions and timing), guidance pictograms, map display, dynamic routing / traffic message data handling, multimedia / multimodal HMI in general, destination input, speech recognition, help concept controlled by speech, interaction management and dialog management. Therefore, cultural adaptability does not only concern the look and feel of the user interface, but also the interaction devices as well as the number and the kind of system functions that can dynamically change according to the driver preferences, the driver state and the driving situation.

Within the infotainment systems of a car, alongside other components – including radio, telephone, CD or DVD player and telematics unit – especially the car navigation system demands many interactive activities from the driver. Furthermore, it also provides many important and calculated pieces of information together with vehicle data to other devices (e.g. data about the driving situation). In this sense, the

---

[1] For information about such a tool in more detail, see [3], [4] and "A Tool for Cross-Cultural Human Computer Interaction Analysis" in this conference proceeding.

driver navigation system plays a prominent role of intersection within the round dance of driver information and assistance systems. Therefore, it will be used as an exemplary system in this paper to elucidate cultural adaptability.

Use Cases, which need massive interaction in navigation systems, are e.g. destination input, map interpretation and maneuver guidance [3]. To be able to take into account these complex information structures simultaneously and to let the driver's mental workload be as low as possible at the same time, it is necessary to employ adaptability additionally to pre-settings or profiles. Adaptability is an appropriate solution for this because the driver does not have the opportunity to adapt manually the setup of the information presentation according to the special requirements depending on the situation. Especially for stressful situations, the HMI of the driver information system has to be adaptive to reduce the mental workload of the driver [12], depending on the driver's cultural background [15].

According to the principle of cross-cultural adaptation of HMI [3], the culturally dependent behavior of the driver has to be measured and recorded over time in order to obtain information about the parameters necessary to be able to culturally adapt the HMI. Either the system suggests the adequate form of information presentation to the driver (Computer Supported Adaptation) or it adapts it automatically (Automatic Adaptation) whilst the driver is actually concentrating on driving [10]. E.g., difficult routes with high rate of accidents can be avoided most notably for beginners by analyzing the routes as well as the driving behavior and by adapting the route calculation and the information presentation according to the recognized facts.

3 Cultural Adaptive Driver Information and -Assistance Systems

If a driver information or -assistance system knows the culturally influenced preferences of the driver, it can adapt its behavior to the expectations of the driver to reduce mental workload, to prevent mental distress and to increase driving security [11]. The objective of cultural adaptive HMI in driver information and assistance systems is the situation-referential adaptation of cultural aspects of the Graphical User Interface and Speech User Interface. For cultural adaptive HMI user models are employed, which are averaged over all users of a cultural group (e.g. information dimming or multi-modal dialogs according to the different requirements in China and Germany respectively, according to the current situation and context) [5].

There are some target user groups of drivers which have their own characteristics of using driver information or -assistance systems in vehicles depending on their preferences (e.g. driving beginners vs. experienced drivers, old vs. young people, female vs. male users) that are influenced by their primary culture. In this sense, the meaning of the usual conception of *culture* as ethnical determined is extended to the *individual culture* of the driver (e.g. individualistic but culturally influenced style of using a device, interacting, driving, etc.). E.g. the individual driving behavior, including aspects such as fast, stressed, hectic, sporty, or unsteady driving, depends on the kind of cultural influences to the driver by the group he belongs to (beginners, intermediates, professionals, experts), or gender and on the cultural background (using bumpers for parking, buzzer frequency, interaction times, interaction frequencies, etc. cf.

e.g. [15]). [2] The data collected about driving contains important information about the preferences of the driver such as the preferred type of routes, average speed, default tours, short or long tours, along rivers or hills, etc. Moreover, the interaction styles can vary strongly (e.g. reasonable, rational, arbitrary, sequen-tially fast, well-considered, haptic, visual, auditory, linguistic, etc.). By associating these aspects with the cultural models, implications can be made to culturally adapt the HMI and the functionality of such systems.

To make driver information and assistance systems culturally adaptive, at least three steps are necessary, determine the differences in the HCI of the cultural different users (cultural preferences), design the system architecture according to the preferences (personalization) and enable the system to detect the driver behavior to adapt the HMI accordingly and automatically (adaptability).

4 The First Step to Cultural Adaptability: Determining Cultural Differences in HCI

The first step has been started doing two online studies to get the preferences of users according to their cultural background. The "Intercultural Interaction Analysis" tool (IIA tool) was developed to obtain automatically quantitative data regarding cultural differences in HMI by simulating use cases of navigation systems. [3] Using literature research and analytical reasoning, 118 potentially culturally sensitive parameters in HCI have been identified, implemented into the IIA tool and applied by measuring the interaction behavior of the test persons in relation to the culture. Some of the most impressing results will be presented and discussed here to demonstrate the difficulties, but also the importance to accomplish the first step for personalization and adaptability.

Employees of SiemensVDO all over the world were invited to do interaction tests by downloading the IIA tool from a central server. The differences in HCI in these studies have been analyzed according to the selected test languages by the participants (Chinese (C), German (G), and English (E)).

Some of the considered variables have shown significant differences that therefore can be called *cultural interaction indicators*. They represent significant differences in user interaction due to the different cultural background of the users. E.g., *Message distance* denotes the temporal distance of showing the maneuver advice messages in the maneuver guidance test task. (C) desired about 30% more pre-advices ("in x m turn right") than other users before turning right. This can be an indication for higher information speed and higher information density in China compared to Germany, for example. *POI* counts the number of points of interest shown in the navigation map display. Information density increases with the number of POI and is two times higher for (C) than for (G) or (E). *MaxOpenTasks* represents the maximum number of open

---

[2] Cf. "Towards Cultural Adaptability to Broaden Universal Access in Future Interfaces of Driver Information Systems" in this conference proceeding.

[3] For a detailed description of the test settings and the results please refer to [3], [4] or to "A Tool for Cross-Cultural Human Computer Interaction Analysis" in this conference proceeding.

tasks in the working environment (i.e. running applications and icons in the Windows ^{TM} task bar) during the test session. (C) tend to work on more tasks simultaneously than (G) or (E) (ratio (C,G,E) = 1.7:1:1) which can be possibly explained by the way of work planning (polychrome vs. monochrome timing, cf. [2]) or the kind of thinking (mono-causal (sequential) vs. multi-causal (parallel) logic, cf. [13]). *Infopresentation-duration* means the time the maneuver advice message is visible on the screen. (C) and (G) wanted the advices to be about 40% longer than (E) do. *Number of Chars* contains the number of characters entered by the user during the maneuver guidance and map display test tasks in answering open questions ((C) less than (E) or (G)). This is explained by the fact that the Chinese language needs considerably less characters to represent words than English or German.

Age had influence on the cultural interaction indicators, which should not correlate with the test language (Table 1).

Table 1. Similarity matrix between test language and control variables

Study	1	2
	Test language	Test language
Test language	1,000	1,000
Age	0,370**[4]	0,161**
Gender	-0,038	-0,017
Computer experience	0,174	-0,048

This high correlation came from the fact that the age of the test persons of the different countries was not distributed equally: there were no Chinese test persons above the age of 40 in the first study (n=102). This influence was lower using only test persons whose age is distributed equally in the user groups (separated by the test language) or by calculating partial correlations or univariate tests. This conclusion has been confirmed by the collected data of the second study: Pearson correlation and Kruskal-Wallis-test showed a lower correlation coefficient for the variable *Age* than in the first study because of n=916. In both cases, the statistical methods used justified the results of the studies as correct and representative for employees of SiemensVDO. None of the control variables influenced the cultural interaction indicators in a way that they cannot be called *cultural interaction indicators*. Nevertheless, the influence of the user age has to be observed and considered very carefully when looking for adequate samples and test groups in future data collections.

Even if computer experience is the most significant variable directly connected to interaction behavior (e.g. interaction speed and frequency) it did not interfere with the measuring process of the different cultural interaction behavior (of the users) employing the cultural interaction indicators. This results can be explained by the fact that computer experience was almost equally distributed in the test users at the worldwide locations of SiemensVDO because the link to the IIA tool has been sent per e-mail only to users who have Internet access and hence, who have some basic computer experience.

---

[4] The level of significance is referenced with asterisks in this paper (* p<.05, ** p<.01).

There are many combinations of cultural interaction indicators that contribute positively to a high discrimination rate in assigning users to their test language without knowing their nationality. Only the interaction patterns within use cases or applications are known. The resulting discriminating rate for classifying all test users to their selected test languages simultaneously and correctly is 60%.[5] Applying the same method classifying the cases into two groups (instead of three at the same time), the discriminating rate increases tremendously: between German and English test language the discriminating rate goes up over 70% and between Chinese and German test language the discriminating rate is even higher than 80%. This outcome in conjunction with the weak influence of disturbing variables supports the high reliability and criteria validity of the statistical results received in these two studies and the reliability of the IIA tool. This is also supported by the discriminating rates according to different group variables including or excluding the control variables in the set of input variables of the step-by-step discriminance analysis (Table 2).

Table 2. Classification rates according to different group variables excluding or including the remaining control variables

	Classification rate		
Group variable	Excluded	Included	Most discriminating cultural interaction indicators
Test language (df = 2)	60 %	65 %	Information speed value, uncertainty avoidance value, speed (MG), interaction exactness value, number of maneuver, ~ POI, ~ restaurants, ~ streets, ~ chars, ~ maximal open tasks
Age (df = 46)	10 %	10 %	Number of help, ~ error clicks, ~ exceptions, ~ mouse clicks, ~ chars, interaction exactness value
Gender (df = 1)	82 %	82 %	Speed (MG), message distance, number of help, ~ mouse clicks, ~ chars, ~ street names, ~ maximal open tasks
Computer exp. (df = 3)	53 %	54 %	Interaction speed, uncertainty avoidance value, number of mouse clicks, ~ open tasks before test
Nationality (df = 10)	42 %	69 %	Information speed value, interaction exactness value, total dialog time, speed (MG), number of help, ~ exceptions, ~ maneuver, ~ error clicks, ~ POI, ~ streets, ~ maximal open tasks

It seems that the combination of the most discriminating cultural interaction indicators points to the characteristics of the group variables. The users grouped by test language or nationality exhibit almost the same HCI characteristics mirrored by almost the same high discriminating cultural interaction indicators. In contrast, the users grouped by age, gender or computer experience are characterized by different cultural interaction indicators. For example, number of help and number of error clicks as well as interaction exactness value classify users of different age. Experienced users can be recognized by interaction speed, uncertainty avoidance value, the number of mouse clicks and the number of open tasks before doing the test. The classification of the user to his cultural background needs the combination of many more cultural interaction indicators than to classify the user in respect of age, gender or computer experience because those variables influence the culture of the user.

---

[5] For detailed statistical explanations and results, please refer to [4] or to "A Tool for Cross-Cultural Human Computer Interaction Analysis" in this conference proceeding.

There have been also implemented potential cultural interaction indicators that are statistically not discriminative. In the first study *ScrollBarChanges_norm* (F (2) = 0.954, p=.389) e.g. shows that the number of the scrolling events triggered when moving a scroll bar slider by the user is not significantly different between the groups. In the second study *TotalDialogTime* (F (2, 916) = 1.370, p=.255) e.g. shows that the time needed by the users to pass the dialogs of the test tasks is not significantly different between the groups. In both studies, *NumberOfHelp* counts the number of initiations of online help by the test persons. Usually this variable was zero, which shows that help was not needed. This fact can be exploited, e.g. to indicate that the test tasks were self-explaining and comprehensible for the users. Nevertheless there are differences between the groups in using the help function (χ^2 (2, 916) = 1.619, p=.445, ratio (C:G:E) = 5.6:1:1.4). This can possibly explained by the fact that the IIA test was developed by a German designer. Hence, the German imprinted design and explanation of the test shall be optimized for the Chinese users even more profoundly in future regarding the aspects for intercultural usability engineering [8].

Even if the cultural characterization of the users asked by the VSM94 questionnaire based on Hofstede [6] is very similar for all users [4], the *HCI between the Chinese, German and English speaking participants differs significantly*. A possible implication of that is grounded in subconscious cultural differences imprinted by primary culture and learning the mother tongue, which leads to different HCI independently of the conscious cultural propositional attitudes. However, this explanation has to be verified in future studies.

Nevertheless, *some results are expected to be valid for HCI design in general* because there are culturally sensitive variables that can be used to measure cultural differences in HCI only by counting certain interaction events without the necessity of knowing the semantic relations to the application. Such indicators are e.g. mouse moves, breaks in the mouse movements, speed of mouse movements, mouse clicks, interaction breaks and possibly the number of acknowledging or refusing system messages. Surely, all those indicators can also be connected semantically to the use cases or applications. Nevertheless, simply counting such events related to the session duration from users of one culture and comparing them to users of another culture is obviously sufficient to indicate differences in interaction behavior of culturally different users.

This preparatory work contributes to the first step to establish cultural adaptability, which is the basis to be able to tackle the next steps: personalization and adaptability.

5   Discussion: Problems, Benefit and Implications of Cultural Adaptability

It is problematic that an automatic adaptation (adaptability) depends on maximum data when observing new users: the system needs more data in order to be able to release information about the user as well as to be able to infer the characteristics of the user regarding information presentation, interaction and dialogs. Furthermore, the knowledge gathered about the user can be *misleading or* simply *false*. Hence, the reliability of assumptions can be a problem [10]. The user model has to match the system model to prevent unexpected situations for the user, which may confuse him.

Another problem is that legal restrictions also have to be taken into account. Because of legal restrictions, only the effects of driver actions in a driver model are allowed to be permanently stored, but not the log file of the personalized driving sessions themselves [1]. As long as no solution is available, which can achieve meaningful adoptions from minimum data automatically, it remains necessary to investigate standard parameters and their values very early in the design-phase, and long before runtime, in order to integrate them into the system. Therefore, it is necessary that the system already has corresponding user-knowledge (standard parameters) before the user's first contact with the system occurs. Before using the system for the first time, it must be adjusted e.g. to the nationality of the user (which indicates the main affiliation of the user to a cultural group) and the corresponding cultural parameters can be placed simultaneously as standard parameters for the desired country. Thus the adaptive system also obtains adequate characteristics of the user more quickly at runtime, because there is "more time" to collect the culture-specific data for the user, since a basic adaptation to the most important user preferences has already been performed before runtime (by putting the standard parameters into the system). Hence, designing an appropriate system according to the user in the design phase helps to avoid the problems rising from adaptability.

The benefit of cultural adaptability hopefully lies in the reduction of driver workload by recognizing and knowing the cultural expectances of the user by the system, which improves the usability of the system ([7], [9]) by adapted user and system models, shorter training times by fast adaptation to the driver as well as in less distraction from traffic and mental workload by automatically optimizing and adapting the HMI according to the current driving situation to increase driving safety ([5], [12]). Finally, the resulting effect of improved usability by cultural adaptability is that many more drivers are able to use the same systems in the car more easily and with contentment that contributes to universal access. [6]

However, many questions remain open and have to be addressed very carefully in future studies. How many dynamic changes are optimal for the driver? When does a "hidden" adaptation occur? How can this be prevented? How much does the driver trust the adaptive system? Adaptability must not surprise the driver but has to be in accordance with his mental model [4]. Additionally there are culture dependent questions [3], which have to be answered because cultural adaptability underlies more than the problems of adaptability. E.g., what cultural aspects *must* be adapted? Which of them can be adapted automatically? How is the acceptance of cultural adaptability?

Additionally, studies that are more detailed must show whether or not changing the metrics of potential cultural interaction indicators (or using them in other situations, use cases or circumstances) will improve their discriminating effect and yield appropriate values accordingly to show the *general validity* of some cultural interaction indicators. Moreover, cultural parameters regarding different user groups (elderly vs. younger drivers, experienced vs. beginning drivers, female vs. male drivers, drivers of different vehicles etc.) have to be found.

---

[6] Cf. "Towards Cultural Adaptability to Broaden Universal Access in Future Interfaces of Driver Information Systems" in this conference proceeding.

6 Conclusion

Cultural adaptability in driver information and assistance systems is necessary. The functional and informational complexity of infotainment systems today cannot longer be handled only by the driver alone without employing adaptability. Drivers do have individual preferences that are culturally influenced: the cultural background of the driver determines the behavior in certain (especially dangerous) driving situations. There are many different groups of drivers, which exhibit their own "culture" whether regarding groups at international level (e.g. countries) or within the national level (e.g. social, ethnic, or driver groups). A study with a tool for cross-cultural human computer interaction analysis revealed different interaction patterns according to the cultural background of the users regarding e.g. design (ample vs. simple), information density (high vs. low), menu structure (high breath vs. high depth), personalization (high vs. low), language (symbols vs. characters) and interaction devices [4]. These results are partly confirm by qualitative studies e.g. [14]. The cultural differences in HCI found using *special combinations of cultural interaction indicators* are *statistically discriminating enough* to enable computer systems to detect different cultural interaction patterns automatically and to relate users to a certain culture behavior, which in turn makes *cultural adaptability possible* in the first place. Many kinds of interaction patterns are only recognizable over time. Hence, enhanced algorithms are needed to enable the system to automatically and correctly adapt itself to the cultural imprinted needs of the user to bring the "mental model" of the system in accordance with the users' mental model. The reduction of the mental workload by recognizing and knowing the cultural expectances of the driver by the system supports system usability and driving security. To design cultural adaptive systems formation principles in the vehicle context have to be taken into account to hold the mental workload of the driver as low as possible and using methods of artificial intelligence can help to get cultural adaptability and to broaden universal access.[7] Further studies have to be done to yield more precise values and relevant cultural parameters regarding different user groups as well as the degree of acceptance of and the power to reduce the mental workload by cultural adaptability in driver information and assistance systems.

7 Outlook

The near-term objective is to apply enhanced techniques using statistical and data mining methods and semantic processing to extract the cultural variables and its values as well as guidelines for cross-cultural HMI design in a more automatic way. The mid-term objective is to analyze and evaluate the test data in more detail to generate several algorithms for adaptability based on neural networks as well as structured equal models to prove basic theoretical cultural interaction models. The best discriminating algorithms for adaptability will be transformed and implemented into driver information systems to be evaluated qualitatively using intercultural usability tests with users of different culture and under mental stress.

---

[7] Cf. "Towards Cultural Adaptability to Broaden Universal Access in Future Interfaces of Driver Information Systems" in this conference proceeding.

Acknowledgments. I like to thank all persons who supported my dissertation project.

References

1. De Bra, P., Aroyo, L., Chepegin, V.: The Next Big Thing: Adaptive Web-Based Systems. In: Journal of Digital Information, 5 (1)
2. Hall, E.T.: The Silent Language. Doubleday, New York (1959)
3. Heimgärtner, R.: Research in Progress: Towards Cross-Cultural Adaptive Human-Machine-Interaction in Automotive Navigation Systems. In: Day, D., del Galdo, E.M. (eds.) Proceedings of the Seventh International Workshop on Internationalization of Products and Systems. IWIPS 2005, The Netherlands, Grafisch Centrum, Amsterdam pp. 7–111 (2005)
4. Heimgärtner, R.: Measuring Cultural Differences in Human Computer Interaction as Preparatory Work for Cross-Cultural Adaptability in Navigation Systems. In: Useware 2006, VDI-Bericht Nr. 1946, VDI-Verlag, Düsseldorf pp. 301–314 (2006)
5. Heimgärtner, R., Holzinger, A.: Towards Cross-Cultural Adaptive Driver Navigation Systems. In: Workshops-Proc. HCI UE Usability Symposium Vienna 2005 pp. 53–68 (2005)
6. Hofstede, G.: Cultures and Organizations: Software of the Mind, London. McGraw-Hill, New York (1991)
7. Holzinger, A.: Usability Engineering for Software Developers. Communications of the ACM 48(1), 71–74 (2005) (ISSN: 0001-0782)
8. Honold, P.: Interkulturelles Usability Engineering. Eine Untersuchung zu kulturellen Einflüssen auf die Gestaltung und Nutzung technischer Produkte. VDI-Verlag, Düsseldorf (2000)
9. Jameson, A.: Adaptive Interfaces and Agents. In: Jacko, J., Sears, A. (eds.) Human Computer Interaction Handbook. Erlbaum, New Jersey, pp. 305–330 (2003)
10. Kobsa, A.: User modeling in dialog systems: potentials and hazards. AI & Society, 4 (3), 214–240
11. Piechulla, W., Mayser, C., Gehrke, H., Konig, W.: Reducing driver's mental workload by means of an adaptive man-machine interface. In: Transportation Research Part F: Traffic Psychology and Behaviour, 6 (4), 233–248
12. Recarte, M.A., Nunes, L.M.: Mental Workload While Driving: Effects on Visual Search, Discrimination, and Decision Making. In: Journal of Experimental Psychology: Applied, 9 (2), 119–137
13. Röse, K., Liu, L., Zühlke, D.: Design Issues in Mainland China: Demands for a Localized Human-Machine-Interaction Design. In: Johannsen, G. (ed.): 8th IFAC/IFIPS/IFORS/IEA Symposium on Analysis, Design, and Evaluation of Human-Machine Systems. Preprints, Kassel, 17–22 (2001)
14. Vöhringer-Kuhnt, T.: Asiatische vs. europäische HMI Lösungen von Fahrerinformationssystemen. In: Useware 2006, VDI-Bericht Nr. 1946, VDI-Verlag, Düsseldorf pp. 279–287 (2006)
15. Xie, C.-q., Parker, D.: A social psychological approach to driving violations in two Chinese cities. In: Transportation Research Part F: Traffic Psychology and Behaviour, 5 (4), 293–308

Sound Detection as an Aid to Increase Detectability of CCTV in Surveillance System

Yongjun Kim, Sang Won Lee, Daniel Hyundo Lee, Jaeyong Kim, and Myun W. Lee*

Human Factors Labs. Dept. of Industrial Engineering
Seoul National University, Seoul, 151-744 Korea
mwlee@snu.ac.kr

Abstract. An operator in CCTV surveillance system is required to detect abnormal events over long working hours, and the events are intermittent, unpredictable and infrequent. Therefore, Operators often show lower performance than desirable. This paper proposes an automated surveillance system that integrates vision and audition to increase detectability. Sound surveillance system using TDOA (Time Difference of Arrival) can locate a sound source accurately, turn the camera towards it, and it has more advantages in reliability and cost-effectiveness than the existing surveillance system. The system is verified by conducting experiments in various environments.

Keywords: Automated Surveillance System, Sound Localization.

1 A Need for Development of an Automated Surveillance System

Due to an increasing need for surveillance and security, size of the market for surveillance system is growing. Accordingly, application of CCTV is increasing. Since CCTV system usually requires operators to watch a number of monitors. Therefore, surveillance system is not reliable because of human factors of vigilance task. For these reasons, the need for an automated surveillance system is rising in order to reduce cost and increase effectiveness [1].

Due to an increasing need for surveillance and security, size of the market for surveillance system is growing. Accordingly, application of CCTV is increasing. A CCTV system usually requires an operator to watch a number of monitors. Therefore, a surveillance system is not reliable due both to performance degradation over time and to divided attention during vigilance task. For these reasons, a need for an automated surveillance system is increasing in order to reduce cost and increase effectiveness [1].

Related technologies have been evolving in recent years. Especially, due to recent improvements in digital image processing, automated surveillance system (AVS) is experiencing rapid innovation. An objective of such automated surveillance system is to process information gathered by sensors, understand current situation, and act accordingly in order to maximize efficiency of surveillance [2].

---

* Corresponding author.

N. Aykin (Ed.): Usability and Internationalization, Part II, HCII 2007, LNCS 4560, pp. 382–389, 2007.

Since CCTV system is already in use in many areas, a market potential of AVS is remarkably high. Although the market is growing, the growth rate is not high as previously anticipated. One reason for this limited growth rate is that AVS is not commercialized enough due to limited reliability, high cost, and high complicacy [1].

1.1 Evolution of Automated Surveillance System

Regazzoni categorized surveillance systems into three generation according to technological advances [3].

Technological innovation of video surveillance system started from analog CCTV system. These systems consist of a number of cameras located in a multiple remote location and a set of monitors usually placed in a single control room. The early version of analog CCTV systems had technical shortcomings, such as noises from analog transmission and massive volume of records. Moreover, due to the decrement of operator's attention and concentration, infrequent events often slipped away.

In 1980's, thanks to the technological progress of converting analog signal to digital signal, the second generation surveillance system which takes advantage of the digital format, were developed. This digital system, also called a semi-automatic system, achieved tremendous progress in transmitting and storing the data. Also, researches on automatic real-time detection, which, with its digital image processing technology, helps the users grasp the situation, came into mainstream.

Nowadays, with the rapid developments in digital and wireless technologies, researches on the third generation surveillance system are on their way. The third generation surveillance system is a robust system which uses a large network of cameras. It monitors a large area with increased flexibility and reliability.

1.2 Limitations of a Video Surveillance System

As we saw earlier, most of the researches on automated surveillance system are focused mainly on video signals and image processing, lacking study of the other sensors. Many researchers brought up following issues concerning video surveillance system [1].

1. Due to the limitations in FOV (Field of View), it is difficult to cover a large area.
2. Natural changes such as light, movement of camera, wind, or fog can affect reliability of the system.
3. Installation and setup of the system is too complicated.
4. It's difficult to commercialize due to the high cost.

2 Proposal of a Surveillance System Supported by Auditory Sensors

Although most of the surveillance systems gather information only via camera, auditory information can provide more meaningful clue than visual information [4]. Many ergonomics researches already showed the results that audition shortens the time required to locate a specific object. In the research of robotics, searching direction or identifying obstacle by sound information has been studied actively. Especially, based on the fact that human and other animals recognize their surroundings by identifying the location of sound source, applying sound localization to machines for tracing object is being studied robustly [5].

2.1 Characteristics of Sound Information

When human hears something through ears, eyes move towards the direction of sound source by using sound localization. This ability can be applied not only to human but also to machine which locates a specific object. As seen in the research of Huang (1999), vision and audition have the following characteristics [6].

Table 1. Audition verses vision

	Audition	Vision
Directivity	Omni directional	Directional
Time resolution	High	Low
Spatial resolution	Low	High
In darkness	Works	Not works
Occlusion	Not occurs	Occurs
Computation	Little	Much

Even though audition has less space resolution than vision, audition has an important characteristic – omni-directional. That is, when a sound comes from a specific location, the sound sensors can receive the signal from every direction. On the other hand, camera can recognize an object only within its field of view. This means that audition can cover wider angle than vision. Moreover, audition, unlike vision, is not affected by lighting or obstacle, and it can calculate the location of event faster than visual information.

In conclusion, automated surveillance system with auditory sensor can overcome the shortcomings of visual system and solve the problems of decreasing concentration and attention of the operator monitoring a large area.

2.2 Sound Localization

When wave comes from the origin of a sound, auditory sensor with microphone receives the signal. Determining the location (direction and distance) of the signal is called sound localization.

If multiple microphones are installed remotely from each other, the location of sound source can be calculated. The calculation is based on the time difference of an arrival from sound source to the sensors. This research used the calculation method of using TDOA (Time Difference of Arrival) received by 3 different microphones.

Fig. 1 shows a sound geometrically from a specific location arriving, with time difference, at 3 different microphones.

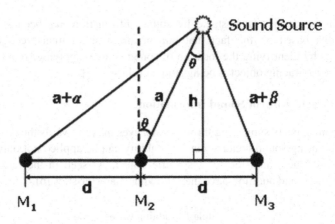

Fig. 1. Time difference of sound that arrives to the microphones

If we suppose a camera is at the location of the second microphone(M2), the location of the sound source can be defined by azimuth angle (θ) and distance (a). For the simplification, three cameras are located on the same line at regular intervals (d). Since speed of sound is a function of temperature, knowing the temperature of the environment, the distance between the sound source and each microphones (α, β) can be expressed as:

$$\alpha = (speed\ of\ sound \times time\ difference\ between\ microphon\ 1\ and\ 2) \quad (1)$$

$$\beta = (speed\ of\ sound \times time\ difference\ between\ microphon\ 2\ and\ 3) \quad (2)$$

By expressing cosine values of each angle in two triangles which share M2 using The Law of Cosines, the distance (a) between the camera and the sound source can be given by:

$$a = \frac{2d^2 - \alpha^2 - \beta^2}{2(\alpha + \beta)} \quad (3)$$

The azimuth angle (θ) is

$$\sin \theta = \frac{\alpha^2 + 2a\alpha - d^2}{2ad} \quad (4)$$

Solving this using arcsine, the inverse function of sin, it can be expressed as:

$$\theta = \arcsin(\frac{\alpha^2 + 2\alpha d - d^2}{2ad}) \quad (5)$$

3   The Architecture of Sound Surveillance System

As the location of a sound source is known by the method in the previous chapter, a surveillance system, which can obtain the information of the location, can be activated and moves the camera towards the location. Following Fig. 2 is the overall

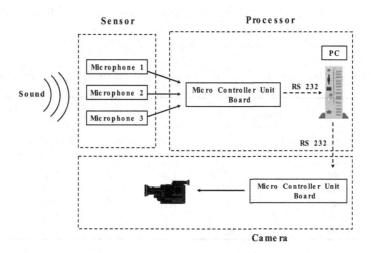

Fig. 2. Structure of an auditory surveillance system prototype

structure of an automated system that identifies the location of sound source and moves the camera angle to the sound source in order to record the visual information.

4   Test of Sound Surveillance System

To verify the sound surveillance system proposed in this research, two experiments were conducted.

4.1   Measuring Accuracy of Sound Detection

In order to measure the accuracy of a system that calculates the location of the sound source, sound sources were located every 15 degrees from 0 to 90 degree either side. Sounds of sufficient volume were created 20 times at each location. Distances were

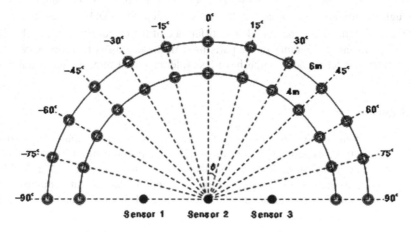

Fig. 3. The structure of accuracy measuring experiment

4m and 6m at each angle, and the room temperature was controlled at 20 degrees Celsius, so that the speed of sound was controlled at 343m/s.

The summary of the experiment is in Table 2 and Table 3.

Table 2. The measuring of azimuth angle of the sound surveillance system (4m)

Actual angle	Calculated angle			Difference between actual angle and calculated one			
	mean	minimum	maximum	mean	minimum	maximum	standard deviation
0°	0.65	0.5	0.9	0.64	0.53	0.97	0.11
15°	14.88	12.29	17.86	1.36	0.03	2.86	0.71
30°	29.94	28.91	31.86	0.73	0.20	1.86	0.49
45°	45.45	43.71	48.98	1.28	0.06	3.98	1.08
60°	58.96	57.94	62.56	1.4	0.05	2.56	0.7
75°	74.89	70.67	82.12	3.52	0	7.12	3.52

Table 3. The measuring of azimuth angle of the sound surveillance system (6m)

Actual angle	Calculated angle			Difference between actual angle and calculated one			
	mean	minimum	maximum	mean	minimum	maximum	standard deviation
0°	0.89	0.56	2.12	0.89	0.56	2.12	0.48
15°	13.62	12.76	16.91	1.75	0.1	2.23	0.61
30°	37.43	34.6	43.7	7.43	4.66	13.7	3.12
45°	43.68	43.34	44.08	1.31	0.91	1.65	0.25
60°	60.82	50.72	68.00	3.69	0.16	9.27	3.44
75°	72.13	70.56	74.98	2.86	0.01	4.43	1.78

As shown in the result, system usually has the error of about 5 degrees. Through experiments, we found out that the most important thing in order to increase the accuracy of the system is to minimize the errors from the three sound sensors. Although the sounds were created at the same location, the TDOA varies from 1 μ s to 100 μ s, and that difference yields the difference of the calculated angles. The main reason for this error is mainly in the parts used in these sensors had tolerance of 5% rate. Applying electric parts which have less tolerance will improve the accuracy of system.

4.2 Case Study

In order to confirm the operation of the system for various sounds in various environments, three experiments were conducted in environments different from the laboratory. The three different environments were street outside of a building, underground parking lot with reverberation, and indoor hallway in a building. We selected many kinds of sounds at each location. Selected types of sounds are stated in Table 4.

Table 4. Success rate of sound surveillance on the street

Type of sound	# of times	detection (rate)	etc
Driving sound	10	0 (0%)	Miss (100%)
Honking	10	6 (60%)	Malfunction (20%) Miscalculation (20%)
Opening & Closing door	10	8 (80%)	Malfunction (20%)
Breaking window	5	5 (100%)	
Yelling	10	4(40%)	Malfunction (40%) Miscalculation (20%)

Table 5. Success rate of sound surveillance in the underground parking lot

Type of sound	# of times	detection (rate)	Etc
Driving sound	10	0 (0%)	Miss (100%)
Honking	10	4 (40%)	Malfunction (30%) Miscalculation (30%)
Opening & Closing door	10	9 (90%)	Malfunction (10%)
Breaking window	5	5 (100%)	
Yelling	10	5 (50%)	Miss (30%) Malfunction (10%) Miscalculation (10%)

As seen in the result, system recognized sound, calculated the location for the sound of "breaking window" and "opening and closing door," turned the camera towards the sound source, and secured the image of the scene. However, the sensor received "yelling" and "honking" but was not able to calculate the location because those sounds were long-lasting so the time difference and the azimuth angle could not be calculated logically (malfunction). Sometimes, camera did not get the right image because the error in the calculation of azimuth angle was too big (miscalculation). One noticeable finding is that the sensor did not react to the driving sound which was more than 1m away. This is because the pitch of driving sound has low. It means that in the real life situation, the system considers driving sound as "noise", and distinguishes it from a meaningful signal like crash.

5 Conclusion

As verified in the experiment, the sound surveillance system developed in this study can locate a sound source accurately, operates cameras towards the calculated location of the sound source. This system has several advantages over existing ones.

First, traditional CCTV system had a shortcoming that human had to makes decision about those infrequent events or objects, thus error rate including miss and false alarm was high. On the other hand, this system offers secondary information of sound source so that the system can support human vigilance.

Second, since the camera moves according to the change in the environment, the system can cover larger area with fewer cameras. This, again, gives two advantages. One is that operator gets less information from less monitors so that he or she can continue attention easily. The other is that the amount of record is far less than the traditional surveillance system – it can reduce both initial cost in the installation and operating cost in storing data.

Last, shortcomings of new, intelligent visual surveillance system - environmental limitation, complicacy of system, and lack of reliability – can be overcome. Especially it costs less than those systems which requires advanced logic of image processing.

This system that is supported by sound detection could be a beginning to replace the existing CCTV products in the intelligent surveillance market. Moreover, while traditional visual analysis system can detect events only within the stationary camera angle, sound detection and sound localization technologies can commercialize a more intelligent surveillance system that can move around its cameras to look for meaningful information.

References

1. McLeod, A.: The impact and effectiveness of low-cost automated video surveillance systems. In: Security Technology. 30th Annual International Carnahan Conference, pp. 204–211 (1996)
2. Valera, M., Valestin, S.A.: Intelligent distributed surveillance system: a review. IEEE Proceedings of Image Signal Process 152, 192–204 (2005)
3. Regazzoni, C.S, Visvanathan, R., Foresti, G.L.: Scanning the Issue/Technology-Special issue on video processing, understanding and communications in Third Generation surveillance systems. Proceedings of the IEEE 89, 1419–14440 (2001)
4. Clavel, C.T., Ehrette, G.: Richard.: Events detection for audio-based surveillance system. In: IEEE International Confrerence on Multimedia and Expo pp. 1306–1309 (2005)
5. Aarabi, P., Zaky, S.: Robust sound localization using multi-source audiovisual information fusion. Information Fusion 2, 209–223 (2001)
6. Jie Huang, T., Supaongprapa, I., Terakura, et al.: A model-based sound localization system and its application to robot navigation. Robitocs and Autonomous System 27, 199–209 (1999)

Approaches to Create a Universal User Experience in Handheld Electronic Product

Joonhwan Kim, Wanje Park, Scott Song, Boeun Park, and Hyunkook Jang

Samsung Electronics Co., Ltd
416 Maetan3, Yeongtong, Suwon, Gyeonggi 443-742 Republic of Korea
{joonhwan.kim,wanje.park,sangkon.song,be.park,
hyunk.jang}@samusung.com

Abstract. A study with the purpose of providing user experience that is consistent with various devices was conducted at a global electronics company that manufactures a variety of digital electronic products. Products selected as study subjects were handheld devices that can receive DMB (Digital Media Broadcasting), play multimedia files, and create files such as photos. The study was conducted by a task force team with User Interface practitioners of managing divisions of each product. In this study, methods and processes that were attempted in order to establish consistency principles of user experiences, enhancing the various characteristics of each product, are described. The results and practical experiences obtained through the processes are introduced.

Keywords: User Experience, Design Process, Usability, Handheld Device, Multimedia Player.

1 Introduction

For companies that release various types of digital electronic devices targeting the global market, in addition to enhancing performance and providing useful features of their products, they reach a point in which they must also provide consistent user experience between products to consumers. This is related to efficiency and performance of development and management from the internal aspect of the company and further, it also has an influence on the company's brand identity. Besides, due to the digital convergence era, there are no significant differences between products, and increase in the level of complexity leads usability problems. Therefore, at this point in time, integration of elements of user experience including Information Architecture (IA), Graphical User Interface (GUI), and Physical User Interface (PUI) is needed. With handheld products as the subject of this study, the actual processes and approaches taken at the actual work site in order to accomplish common user experience and UI (User Interface) identity between each product are introduced. The contents introduced in this study are processes and results of cross-divisional co-work that was actually conducted by a company that manufactures various digital electronic devices including handheld products that can receive digital media broadcasting, play multimedia files, and create files such as pictures as subjects

N. Aykin (Ed.): Usability and Internationalization, Part II, HCII 2007, LNCS 4560, pp. 390–396, 2007.
© Springer-Verlag Berlin Heidelberg 2007

of study. Examples of such products include DMB (Digital Media Broadcasting) TV, Digital Still Camera, Digital Movie Camera, MP3 Player, and Convergence Multimedia Player.

1.1 Significance of Study

As the number of products being launched increased providing user interface and operation methods that are different for each product gradually became a problem. In addition, an environment in which various products can be connected was created through enhancement of connectivity which resulted in a higher level of complexity the actual user can utilize, and as a result of digital convergence, the gap between products decreased significantly. In such an environment, providing a consistent user experience for similar products serves as an extremely important factor for both manufacturers and users. Therefore, the necessity of establishing user interface design identity surfaced naturally.

1.2 Problems

Digital handheld devices used in this study had the following similarities and differences, and the task of this study was to reach the purpose taking such circumstances under consideration. That is, it needed to establish the unity of usage on the level of respecting the existing characteristics of each product, and the coordination between the individual identity of the products and the level of standardization was important.

Similarities of products used in the study are as follows.

- All are mobile handheld devices
- All have a display window that displays information and content, and have minimum input button users can control
- All are capable of playing multimedia files
- All have characteristics of convergence with many functions integrated
- Because they are released in different countries, the design cannot be confined to any particular country.

Differences of products used in the study are as follows.

- Although they are convergence product, each product possesses its unique key function, and the weight of each function is different. For example, when comparing a movie camera whose main function is to take motion pictures and an MP3 player that has a function for movie taking, although they both have the ability to take motion pictures, the level of importance of the function and the weight of the function are different.
- User interface environments are different. For example, system performance, hardware specification, display size, and resolution are different.

Under such an environment, the following approach was made in order to establish consistent user experience principles.

2 Methods and Activities

The main task of this study was to establish consistency between the many characteristics of the above various products. Realistic attempts based on traditional UCD (User-Centered Design) that emphasizes user's task and interactive design through substantial assessment of usability were made [1]. Description of the time line is as follows.

2.1 The Makeup of Study Staff and the Organization

A task force team was organized by UI related practitioners from managing divisions of each product. UI designers and graphic designers of each product, and UI researchers of research organizations were included. The task force team members have direct and indirect experience in the UI process and the development process through production experience in the organization to which they belong. They also possess human network for gathering data and verification through contact with their related divisions such as development, quality assurance, and customer service, in case of any rising problems. The members established plans that are needed for fulfilling the task such as responsibilities and schedules of each member.

2.2 Deciding the Direction of Study and the Scope of Outcome

The first step in performing the practical task was to define the products used for the purpose of study. Since products that cannot be easily classified due to convergence of products are already being released, mobility, size of screen, and other standards were used to define the products used. In addition, because new UI design based on the binding power of the outcome of this study can be difficult, flexibility in the part that maintains UI concept consistent with each product and other exceptions were allowed. In addition, through literature survey, information on stages and necessary contents of management of user interface design were referenced [2, 3].

2.3 Fundamental Studies Focusing on Major Products

Centered on products launched by each division, a comparison analysis of UI elements including features, information architecture, navigation rules, graphical design style, and OSD (On Screen Display) terminologies was conducted. Each product was compared under similar conditions, and similarities and differences were recorded. Moreover, a study on products with high market share was also conducted through a comparison analysis.

2.4 User Interface Design Stage 1: Defining the Basic Elements of Design

Through literature research, characteristics and elements of handheld devices were checked [4]. It was conducted by dividing the process into stage 1 and stage 2, and each stage was divided into cognitive elements and visual elements. In cognitive elements of stage 1, direction of IA and terminology were defined, and physical user interface such as buttons, navigation movement methods were also included. In the visual elements, direction of overall design, icon, color, and screen layout were addressed.

2.5   User Interface Design Stage 2: Defining Outcome Details

The second stage was also divided in to cognitive elements and visual elements and was based on those discussed in stage 2; each element was organized in a form that is closer to the outcome of the task. In cognitive elements, outcome guideline, physical input methods and their labels, menu structure, and detailed navigation were defined; and in visual elements, a library type design management method were planned.

2.6   Direction of Graphical and Physical Design

Through the outcome obtained in the second stage of UI Design, elements to be included in the UI design guideline were developed initially. Based on this, a graphic design was conducted, and a design style was defined and drafted. Physical design element related to usability such as input method and labeling were suggested.

2.7   Initial User Study

The initial user study was conducted with two purposes. First, areas that require data of high quantity such as location and name of buttons, preference of basic elements of IA and GUI, and name of functions were conducted using a web survey in Korea, the USA, and England. Second, in order to gather basic and thoughtful opinions pertaining to the direction of design of elements defined in 2.6, a FGI (Focus Group Interview) was conducted with professional groups residing in Korea. Specific opinions on the draft for graphic design and representative interaction methods were collected. The FGI also had the purpose of a pilot test of the international user studies that will be addressed in 2.9.

In the web survey, in Korea, 1,000 users who own at least two handheld portable devices participated with age range of 18 to 39. Gender ratio was 57.8% of males and 42.2% of females. The average use frequency was 42.5% of high and 57.5 of light, and knowledge level of the owned devices was 42% of expert level and 58% novice level. In USA and England, 300 users in total (150 in each country) participated with same condition with Korea. Gender ratio was 47.3% of males and 52.7% of females. The average use frequency was 67.1% of high and 32.9 of light, and knowledge level of the owned devices was 66.7% of expert level and 33.3% novice level. The results of the survey revealed that differences between Korea and other two countries in several points such as physical button labels of function list and going back to previous depth while similar patterns were found overall. This indicated that careful approaches were needed to localize the User Interface of the outcomes in this study. In FGI in Korea followed by the web survey, more insights were gathered about preferences of design, functionality, information hierarchy, and suggested interaction methods.

Table 1. Key results of web survey

Category	Korea	USA / England
Physical button	Left to LCD screen (49%)	Upper to LCD screen (38%)
Major functionalities	Photo taking, Music	Photo taking, Music
Button goes to top level	MENU (39%), HOME (43%)	MENU (65% USA, 71% England)
Button activates function list	MENU (37%)	FUNCTION (47% USA, 46% England)
Button selects and confirms item	OK (53%)	SELECT (38% USA, 45% England)
Button goes back to previous level	Left Arrow (50%), BACK (44%)	BACK (69% USA, 78% England)
Handheld device carrying	In the bag (41%), Designated carrier (30%)	Designated carrier (47% USA, 39% England)
Multitasking Frequency	Often (64%)	Often (32% USA, 39% England)
Buttons support multiple functionalities	Convenient (60%), Inconvenient (36%)	Inconvenient (37% USA, 43% England) Convenient (30% USA, 41% England)
Preference of Touch Screen	High (63%)	High (63% USA, 67% England)

2.8 Initial Redesign

Through data analysis of information gathered from the initial user evaluation, direction of the existing UI design was modified, and graphic style, icon, color, and other elements of visual design were supplemented.

2.9 Secondary User Study (International Usability Testing)

There was a need to evaluate usability and the level of preference with key countries in which products with results obtained in 2.8 will be released as the subjects of study. Korea, China, the US, and England were selected. Participants were gathered by their age bracket, gender, and product usage experience of each country. A total of 32 participants (8 in a group) performed the test with age range of 18 to 49 and average gender ratio was 52% (males) and 48% (females). A method of combining a FGI and a 1:1 task performance test was planned. In the FGI, thoughtful data on the direction of GUI and IA elements were studied, and in the 1:1 task performance test, user reaction and manipulation of representative action scenarios were measured through an interactive prototype. It was first conducted in Korea with the purpose of a pilot test and after making partial supplementation, the evaluations were then conducted simultaneously in the US, England, and China. For quality evaluation, the research center within the company and local usability firms located in each country cooperated.

As the results, it was found that the suggested graphical design was clean and easy to follow overall. In the physical button layout of HOME, MENU, and BACK, difference results were found between the countries (Table 2). 2.5D graphical icons were preferred in China and Korea, while pictogram style icons were slightly preferred in USA and England (Table 3). The suggested user customization features of GUI appeals to all age groups in USA and England, while that only appeals to younger groups in Korea and China. The navigation interaction was considered very usable (82% successfully complete in 1:1 task performance test in average). In all countries, participants tended to use both LEFT and BACK button to go back to the previous level, and both RIGHT and OK button to activate or select items.

Table 2. Physical button layout

	Left Side	Middle	Right Side
Korea	HOME (56%)	MENU (60%)	BACK (60%)
China	HOME (82%)	MENU (92%)	BACK (87%)
USA	HOME (62%)	MENU (66%)	BACK (60%)
England	BACK (56%)	MENU (60%)	BACK (56%)

Table 3. Graphic icon preference

	2.5D	Pictogram
Korea	56%	44%
China	66%	34%
USA	42%	58%
England	46%	54%

2.10 Secondary Redesign and Final Outcome

Through analysis of user data gathered in various countries, strength and weaknesses of products were verified and areas that need improvements were redesigned. In part, additional user evaluation was needed, and needed data were obtained through an informal tertiary user evaluated that was limited to domestic users. Through such processes, the final result within the scope of the initial study task was produced.

2.11 Finalization and Maintenance

The end outcomes of the study completed through 2.1 to 2.10 needs to be managed in a fashion in which members of each division that develop the actual product can access it for review. Therefore, such requirement was fulfilled by using a method of registering the end outcomes by using an electronic management system in the company, and also prepared the organizational basis that allows continuous supplementation and maintenance through Q&A.

3 Conclusion and Future Work

Finding User Interface design identity of products released by a company will require a greater amount of time and effort than presented in this study. It can be stated that fundamentals for establishing identity of mobile multimedia devices with various characteristics have been identified and a system which manages outcomes has been built through these processes. Through application of products, we expect this study to have positive effects such as increasing usability of products and development efficiency, providing common elements of user experience, and further, strengthening of company's brand image [2].

As the subject of future studies, there are tasks such as commercialization of the end product obtained through the processes of this study and expansion of user environment such as connection scenarios between products that can actually occur. In addition, additional assessment of whether the product that is released has elements that influence more than language due to cultural differences in regions of sales can be considered [4].

Acknowledgements. Expressions of gratitude is extended to the task force team members who participate and lead the study to satisfactory results, partnering companies, and the participants of the user studies in each country.

References

1. Barnum, C.M.: Usability Testing and Research. Longman. New York, NY, USA (2002)
2. Kuniavsky, M.: Observing the User Experience. Morgan Kaufmann, San Francisco (2003)
3. Lindhlom, C., Keinonen, T., Kiljander, H.: Mobile Usability. McGraw-Hill, New York, USA (2003)
4. Weiss, S.: Handheld Usability, Chichester, West Sussex, England. John Wiley & Sons, Ltd, NewYork (2002)

Statistical Modeling of Affective Responses from Visual and Auditory Attributes in the Movies

In Ki Kim[1], Kyung Jae Lee[2], Woojin Chang[1], and Myung Hwan Yun[1]

[1] Departement of Industrial Engineering, Seoul National University,
San56-1, Sillim-dong, Gwanak-gu, Seoul, 151-742, Repbulic of Korea
{lookat2,changw,mhy}@snu.ac.kr
[2] Graduate Program in Technology and Management, Seoul National University,
San56-1, Sillim-dong, Gwanak-gu, Seoul, 151-742, Repbulic of Korea
strutjet@tam.snu.ac.kr

Abstract. The affective responses of audience watching movie are selected and the visual and auditory attributes in movie, which have a significant effect on the affective responses of audience, are measured. The relationship between the movie attributes and affective responses are modeled using regression analysis. Fun of a movie is evaluated based on the audiences' affective responses and an affective response is explained using either movie attributes or other affective responses. These structures are visually summarized in the hierarchical diagram.

Keywords: movie, visual and auditory attribute, affective response.

1 Introduction

Movies consist of visual and auditory contents and have long historical background. When people watch a movie, they usually pay attention to screen and sound. For this reason, movie is a good research subject about affective responses from visual and auditory stimulus.

The research on the mutual interaction between movies and audiences studies the visual and auditory perception [3,10,12]. The previous researches on Hollywood movies maintained that characteristics of Hollywood style are the integration of all the elements related to the storytelling in the purely cognitive view and the management of the elements in the narrative structure [21]. This implies that Hollywood style focuses on the storytelling keeping the audiences from recognizing the operations of camera, lightning, setting, and film cutting in the movie. Recently, Zillmann [24] asserted that the researches on the Hollywood style were restricted to the analysis of cognitive narration in movies, so that they cannot fully explain the affective response of audience.

The psychological aspect of the interaction between movie and audience was analyzed by studying the movie attributes having causal relationship with affective responses of audiences. For example, there were attempts to theoretically explain the process that the movements of camera and editing style give rise to an empathy with movie characters and immersiveness [17] and the processes that the audiences have

N. Aykin (Ed.): Usability and Internationalization, Part II, HCII 2007, LNCS 4560, pp. 397–406, 2007.
© Springer-Verlag Berlin Heidelberg 2007

the psychological identification with movie characters [1,4,15,16], immersiveness [5,6,12]. However, these explanations were made qualitatively so that the related theories can be applied only in qualitative way and have a weakness that they are not confirmed by experimental results of the audiences' reactions.

To make a theory, which can be described in quantitative way, the quantification of various visual and auditory attributes in movie and the measurement of affective responses should be conducted. The first research on the measurement of affective response was to gauge galvanic skin response (GSR) of 7000 of people reading a movie script. But this research was not noticeable since GSR was not validated as an explanatory variable [2]. Eliashberg [7] modeled the audiences' reactions in the way that they press the "Like/Dislike" buttons of Lazarsfeld-Stanton Program Analyzer, which measure the affective response of audience, while watching movie. Zawilinski [20] designed the system to statistically analyze the measurement of the affective responses of audiences generated when they watch movie. These researches under-stood a movie as a whole subject rather than the combination of independent entities, so that there was a limitation to analyze each visual and auditory attribute of movie in detail.

There were researches that analyze the affective responses of audiences by focusing on each attribute of movie. Gregson [9] researched on the affective response of audience to the color tone of screen and the storytelling of movie based on the experimental results of 215 audiences. Roberts [19] measured the affective responses to the ethnic identification between audiences and movie characters by self-reports, facial expressions, and biomedical signals of 168 male and female subjects with various ethnic and cultural backgrounds. These researches focusing on the individual attributes of movie have difficulty in finding the integrated effects generated from the interactions between attributes and in including the levels of attribute, which is almost limitless, since relatively small number of movies need to be considered to control the experiments with test subjects of large size.

To make a research reliable and valid in the affective perspective, the integration of a movie and its audience is essential. In view of a movie, the research selecting the core attributes significant for the affective responses and the analysis of the relation-ship between these core attributes and the affective responses need to be conducted in order. To understand various causal relationships between attributes of a movie can provide the current movie production environment, which depends on intuition and experiences, with a structural evaluation basis built upon statistical model.

Visual and auditory attributes in movie can be considered design attributes in production design process. However, design attributes in movie vary dynamically as time goes on, and have a large number of degrees of freedom in accordance with genre and specific properties of each movie. For example, the color tone in a movie is quite various and a lot of combinations of colors are used in each image frame and varied through the changes of scene in general, while the color tone as a design attribute of a home electric appliance is relatively simple and can be restricted to the several patterns. However, when a dominating color tone exists throughout a movie, the color tone of the movie can be considered as an attribute of movie.

The first objective of this research is to recognize the visual and auditory attributes in movie, which have a significant effect on the affective responses of audience. The second objective of this research is to model the relationship between affective responses of audience and the attributes of movie. This attempt is valuable in that the knowledge on the causal relationships between affective responses and movie attributes can be applied to construct a design strategy to maximize the amusement of movie, and to estimate the fun level of a new movie for audience.

2 Model

In this section, we model how visual and auditory attributes of movie give rise to affective responses including fun. When considering a movie as the process of interaction with audiences, movie contents provide the audiences with affective responses and allow them to have fun as a result.

2.1 Selection of Affective Responses

The variables of affective responses are summarized in Table 1. These 21 variables are selected by the following criteria. First, the variables related to visual and auditory attributes of movie are preferred to variables related to story only. Second, the variables should be selected to cover all the areas of perception, memory, and information processing. Third, the variables should be conceptually clear enough to understand. Fourth, the value of variable should be easily decided by questionnaire with easy expression. Fifth, the variables have their own conceptual contents so that their meanings are not overlapped with each other. The 'Fun' variable, which reflects compound affects and is expected to have large variance was measured by 100-scale. The other variables were evaluated by 7-likert scale.

The questionnaire for the variables was designed in consideration of the following ideas: easy understanding, general expression, and consistency of questions. The outline of our questionnaire is as follows. Whether a subject (student) watched a movie or not is questioned to investigate how previous experience of watching movie affects the affective responses. The personality model with five dimensions was applied to the questionnaire to investigate how the personality of an audience affects the affective responses. Age and gender were asked to investigate how the affective responses are changed according to age and gender differences. The seat location of each audience was reported to investigate how viewing position affects the affective responses. The audience's preference in movie genres was asked to investigate how audience's preconception about genres affects the affective responses.

The 42 male and 8 female undergraduate students responded to the questionnaire after watching movie sample clips composed of the scenes, each of which is about 2 minutes long, from 9 Korean movies played between years 2005 and 2006. The scenes in a sample clip represent the genre of a movie well. To investigate the fact that audiences may have different affective responses according to the scene even from the same movie, the 50 subjects (students) were evenly separated into the two groups and their test results were compared and analyzed. Each group watched the 10 minutes long sequences of the different scenes from a movie and answered the questionnaire.

Table 1. Variables of affective responses

Variables	Description
Reality	Scene looks real.
Loose	Scene is loose.
Artificial	Scene seems to be artificially constructed.
Color	The overall color tone of scene is in harmony with the theme of movie
Edit	The connection between scenes is smooth.
Relief	Scene has strong image relief.
Intense	Scene is visually intensive.
Speed	Scene makes audiences feel speed.
Shock	Scene makes audiences feel shock.
OST	OST appeals to audiences.
Texture	The texture of a scene appeals to audiences.
Brightness	The brightness of a scene appeals to audiences.
Arousal	Scene arouses audiences
Dialogue	Dialogues well represent movie characters' personality.
Clear	The intention or the thoughts of characters are clearly revealed in characters' actions or conversations.
Familiar	Audiences are familiar with the scene.
Focus	Audiences focus on characters or objects in the scene.
Divided	Audiences watch the scene from bird's eye view.
Salient	Movie character or object is distinguished in the scene.
Immersiveness	Audiences identify themselves with movie characters.
Fun	Audiences are satisfied with a movie

2.2 Measurement of Visual and Auditory Attributes in the Movie

Gong et al.[8] suggested SDL (Scene Description Language), which is manually operated by a classifier, to simplify the video processing algorithms and to reduce the processing errors, and defined SDL elements such as Color, Object, Event, Position, Shape, Area, Motion, and Camera Operation etc. In this research, we selected 10 visual and auditory attributes of movie that have significant effects on affective responses based on biomedical signal analysis. These attributes are visual and auditory contrast, lightness, color, motion, scene change rate, object size, video signal peak frequency, amplitude of video signal peak frequency, sound power level, and sound to noise ratio, which are shown in this order in Table 2. In this paper, we measure the values of the continuous variables categorized in these 10 attributes in each of 9 movies used to make sample clips in section 2.1, and analyze the measured values.

Table 2. Measurement of 10 visual and auditory attributes of 9 movies

	Cont-rast	Light-ness	Color	Motion	Scene rate	Object size	Peak freq.	Peak amp.	Power	SN ratio
1	0.334	0.211	0.161	0.859	0.203	0.255	0.447	0.119	0.147	0.433
2	0.170	0.383	0.240	1.087	0.109	0.772	0.927	0.098	0.096	0.544
3	0.236	0.149	0.151	1.626	0.106	0.206	0.911	0.387	0.333	0.589
4	0.202	0.295	0.275	0.821	0.067	0.260	1.143	0.162	0.177	0.444
5	0.232	0.537	0.514	0.732	0.382	0.499	1.604	0.067	0.018	0.525
6	0.248	0.747	0.962	0.463	0.154	0.741	0.811	0.453	0.094	0.776
7	0.056	0.016	0.016	1.075	0.200	0.574	0.719	0.479	0.535	0.644
8	0.571	0.490	0.500	1.164	0.114	0.324	1.145	0.177	0.170	0.547
9	0.162	0.305	0.323	0.649	0.323	0.220	0.906	0.056	0.041	0.348

2.3 Modeling Procedure

If each movie has a specific pattern of design attributes and the means and standard deviations of these attributes are almost independent of each other, regression models, whose dependent variables are variables of affective responses shown in Table 1 and whose explanatory variables are the means and standard deviation of the attributes in Table 2 or the affective responses in Table 1, can be constructed. The overall statistical modeling procedure is as follows.

1. Construct a regression model using variables of affective response in Table 1. Use "Fun" as a dependent variable and other variables as explanatory variables. Call "Fun" the level 0 variable. Find the significant explanatory variables and call these level 1 variables.
2. Construct regression models between a level 1 variable and movie attributes in Table 2. Use a level 1 variable as a dependent variable and movie attributes as explanatory variables.
3. If a level 1 variable is not explained by movie attributes, then construct a regression model, whose dependent variable is the level 1 variable and whose explanatory are the variables of affective response belong neither to level 0 nor to level 1. Find the significant explanatory variables and call these level 2 variables.
4. Construct a hierarchical diagram (see Figure 1 in section 4) based on level 0, level 1, level 2, and movie attribute

3 Results

In this section, some findings about affective responses of movies and the results of statistical models based on affective responses and visual and auditory attributes in movies are provided.

3.1 Findings About Affective Responses of Movies

The following 6 hypothesis about affective responses and the corresponding test results are as follows.

Hypothesis 1: *Age and gender do not make any significant difference in fun valuation.*

We found the test result supportive of the hypothesis.

Hypothesis 2: *Distinct scenes in one movie do not make any significant difference in affective responses.*

To verify hypothesis 2, we conducted an experiment that two subject groups watch different scenes (each two minute long, respectively) of the movie, 'Family Crisis'. T-test result for the comparison of population mean showed significant differences on fun, artificiality, concentration, and speed between two subject groups (p-value<0.001). Hence, the hypothesis is rejected. This implies that the analysis of a short scene is insufficient for the overall movie evaluation. Subsequently, there arises a question on how long a scene should be shown to subjects. This question is roughly examined in hypothesis 3.

Hypothesis 3: *The length of a scene is nothing to do with affective responses.*

To verify hypothesis 3, we conducted questionnaire survey after showing two minutes movie clip to one subject group and ten minutes movie clip including the previous two minutes sequence as well to the other subject group (clips composed of the scenes from the movie 'Island'). T-test on means of collected data showed that there is statistically no significant difference between two groups, thus supporting hypothesis 3. However, we observed that the variance of answers to most of the questions decreases, as the length of movie clip increases. This tendency can be interpreted in the way that, as clip length increases, the each subject's affect become difficult to observe. The acceptance of hypothesis 3 allows us to limit all movie clips to be played for two minutes at most.

Hypothesis 4: *Watching a movie again makes no difference in affective responses.*

To verify hypothesis 4, each subject was instructed to report whether he or she had previously watched the movie. The subjects were separated into two groups: one with watching experiences and the other without. T-test on the difference of these groups verified that there exist significant differences in following variables of attribute responses: 'Familiar', 'Loose', 'Texture', and 'Fun' (p-value<0.01). Hypothesis 3 is rejected regarding these variables. The subjects with previous exposure tend to evaluate movie as "familiar in visual impressions", "with less distractedness", "satisfactory at screen quality", and "more funny". As subjects' previous exposure to a movie can make a difference in affective responses, we showed the movies that every subject or none of them had watched to our research subjects.

Hypothesis 5: *Personality makes no significant difference in affective responses.*

Analysis of personality in the perspectives of extroversion, openness, neurosis, affinity, and sincerity is widely accepted to be precise and comprehensive after the verifications of its validity and reliability by numerous actual studies [14]. Each subject was requested to evaluate himself or herself in accordance with those five perspectives mentioned above. The subjects were classified into 7 groups using the cluster analysis based on self personality evaluation results. ANOVA test showed that there is no significant difference in 'Fun' variable between the groups (F-statistic =0.376, p-value=0.894). Most of the variables of affective responses did not show any significant difference between the groups. However, in 'Relief', 'Brightness', and 'Arousal', there observed significant differences between some groups. Despite of this significance, the personality factors do not explain well these variables (R-square value is less than 0.1). Hence, the result was not supportive of hypothesis 5.

Hypothesis 6: *The favorite genre does not influence affective responses.*

To verify hypothesis 6, each subject was requested to choose his or her favorite genre among comedy, action, drama, fantasy, romance, SF, and thriller and allowed to have multiple choice. For most of the genre, the ratio between favorite and unfavorite groups was almost 1:1, while the four times larger unfavorite groups were observed in action, SF, and Fantasy genres. We checked if favorite genre could affect evaluation of fun, and there exists a significant difference in valuation of fun between those who prefer comedy, action, SF, fantasy and those who do not. Those who prefer comedy, action, SF, fantasy tend to be generous in scoring of fun. We also conducted t-tests to examine the difference between two subjects groups about other variables besides fun. T-test found significant difference only when the subject watches the movie of favorite genre. For example, when the subjects, who like comedy, watches 'Family Crisis', they showed significant differences in 'Reality', 'Edit', 'Intense', and 'Texture' variables from those who do not (p-value<0.01). In other words, the subjects whose favorite genre is comedy assessed 'Family Crisis' as "more realistic", "smooth scene change", "visually intensive", and "satisfactory screen quality". Likewise, those who prefer action/fantasy genre showed significant difference in 'Divided' variable from those who do not while watching 'Island' (p-value<0.01). In other words, those who prefer action movie tends to look out the movie in more perspective view than those who do not. However, except for comedy and action/fantasy, it turned out to be the favorite genres do not have any effect on affective responses. Thus, hypothesis 6 can be accepted in general except for a few cases.

3.2 Results of Statistical Model

Fun is evaluated individually on the personal utility basis. Thus, fun can be measured as a universal index to represent the personal satisfactory level for a movie. This is confirmed by the evaluation result of audiences for 35 movies with various genres such as drama, action, comedy, and horror on the website, 'http://movie.naver.com', from year 2000 and year 2006. In this result, 97.1% of people participating in the evaluation expressed their satisfaction with movies using "funny" and "not funny" even for horror movies. Based on the questionnaire results, we can construct the following regression equation for fun.

(Fun) = 0.13633 + 0.65560 × (Immersiveness) − 0.25687 × (Clear)
      − 0.60204 × (Divided) + 0.95167 × (Brightness)

According to this regression model, the higher 'immersiveness' and 'brightness' and the less 'clear' and 'divided' give rise to more fun. This can be interpreted as follows. The funny movies used to

1. let the audiences feel empathy with movie characters,
2. keep scenes bright in general,
3. hide the intention or the thoughts of characters throughout the storytelling,
4. make the audiences pay attention to a specific subject of each scene.

'Immersiveness' and 'Clear' among the variables affecting 'Fun' could be directly explained by some design attributes of movie shown in Table 2. 'Divided' and 'Brightness' which are the other factors affecting the fun were interpreted by other variables of affective responses such as 'Focus', 'Reality', 'Familiar', 'Dialogue', 'Relief'.The results of other regression models were described in Table 3.

Table 3. Results of regression models

Dependent variable	Explanatory variables	p-value	Goodness of fit
Fun	Immersiveness, Clear, Divided, lightness	0.0022	0.9457
Divided	Reality, Focus	0.0039	0.7893
Brightness	Familiar, Dialogue, Relief, Reality	0.0001	0.9913
Familiar	Edit, Intense	0.0070	0.7445
Immersiveness	Ave. of lightness, Std. of lightness,, Ave. of SN ratio	0.0179	0.7537
Clear	Ave. of lightness, Ave. of SN ratio, Ave. of object size	0.0044	0.8607
Reality	Std. of peak frequency	0.0941	0.2556
Visual Intense	Ave. of lightness, Std. of lightness,, Ave. of object size, Sdt. of SN ratio	0.0019	0.9496
Edit	Ave. of lightness, Ave. of object size, Std. of object size, Ave. of peak frequency	0.0020	0.9485
Dialogue	Ave. of lightness, Sdt. of SN ratio	0.0011	0.8603

We could see that most of the affective response variables except 'Familiar' were explained by the movie attributes in Table 2. For example, 'Intense' is affected by the average of the 'lightness', the standard deviation of the 'lightness', the average 'size of the object', and the average of 'the sound-to-noise ratio'. In the other hand the affective response variables, 'Edit' and 'Intense', have influences on the 'Familiar'. The regression results in Table 3 are visually summarized in Figure 1.

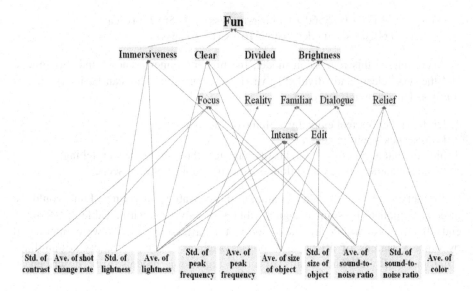

Fig. 1. Hierarchical diagram of the relationship between affective responses and movie attributes

4 Discussion

In this paper, we recognized the movie attributes that have a significant effect on the affective responses of audience and modeled the relationship between affective responses of audience and the visual and auditory attributes of movie. We found that the variables of affective responses, 'Immersiveness', 'Brightness', 'Clear' and 'Divided', have a significant effect on 'Fun', which is a universal index to represent the personal satisfactory level for a movie. These variables can be explained by the visual and auditory attributes of movie or other affective responses.

Our quantitative model is insufficient to fully describe the delicate causal relationships between affective responses and visual and auditory attributes of movie. However, our model provided an essential method to measure affective response of audiences using the values of the visual and auditory attributes. This model enabled us to score the 'Fun' level of movie. Further research considering a large number of movies and subjects is necessary to upgrade our current model to the extent that a design strategy to maximize 'Fun' of movie can be constructed.

Acknowledgments. This work was supported by Korean Film Council.

References

1. Affron, C.: Cinema and Sentiment. University of Chicago Press, Chicago (1982)
2. Austin, B.A.: Movie Genres: Towards a Conceptualized Model and Standardized Definitions. In: Current Research in Film: Audiences, Economics and Law, vol. 3, Alex Publishing Corporation, Norwood, NJ (1987)

3. Boring, E.G.: A factual textbook. Wiley, New York (1935)
4. Choi, M.J.: The Study of Fantasy Identification of Visual Text Audience. Korean Society for Journalism and Communication Studies 48(3), 222–247 (2004)
5. Deleuze, G.: Cinema: The Movement-Image. University of Minnesota Press, Minneapolis (1986)
6. Dick, B.F.: Anatomy of Film. St Martins (1990)
7. Eliashberg, J., Sawhney, Mohanbir, S.: Modeling Goes to Hollywood: Predicting Individual Differences in Movie Enjoyment. Management Science 40(9), 1151–1173 (1994)
8. Gong, Y., Chuan, C.H., Yongwei, Z., Sakauchi, M.: A generic video parsing system with a scene description language. Real-Time Imaging 2, 45–49 (1996)
9. Gregson, K.S.: Extreme media: Factors that Influence Enjoyment. Indiana: p. 210 (2003)
10. Hochberg, J., Fallon, P.: Perceptual Analysis of Moving Patterns. Science 194, 1081–1083 (1976)
11. Kim, W.B.: Between Immersion and Awakening: Fantasy and Drive Reversal in Electronic Media Art. Korean Association for History of Modern Art. 16(0), 71–100 (2004)
12. Koffka, K.: Principles of Gestalt Psychology. New York, Harcourt, Brace (1935)
13. Koster, R.: A Theory of Fun for Game Design, Paraglyph (2005)
14. Lim, J.W.: Consumer Behavior: Strategic Use for Comprehension and Marketing. Kyung Moon Publishers (2006)
15. Münsterberg, H.: Hugo Munsterberg on Film: The Photoplay: A Psychological Study and Other Writings. Routledge (2001)
16. Metz, C.: The Imaginary Signifier: Psychoanalysis and the Cinema, Indiana University Press (1986)
17. Mitry, J.: The Aesthetics and Psychology of the Cinema, Indiana University Press (1999)
18. Reisz, K., Millar, G.: The Technique of Film Editing. Hastings House, New York (1968)
19. Roberts, N.A.: Ethnic and Cultural Influences on Subjective, Behavioral, and Physiological Emotional Responses to Film Clips. University of California, Berkeley vol. 138 (2003)
20. Zawilinski, K.M.: Emotional Response Analyser System with Multimedia Display. U.S. (1997)
21. Zillmann, D.: Cinematic Creation of Emotion. Moving Image Theory. B. F. A. Anderson, J.D. Carbondale. Southern Illinois University Press: pp. 164–165 (2005)

User-Specific Service Generation: A Morphological Approach to Customized Blog Creation

Namjoong Kim[1], Hyojeong Lim[1], Sookyeong Seo[1],
Yoo Suk Hong[1,2,*], and Yongtae Park[2]

[1] Graduation Program in Technology and Management, Seoul National University, Korea
[2] Department of Industrial Engineering, Seoul National University, Korea
yhong@snu.ac.kr

Abstract. As the growth of service industry, new service creation has become as important as traditional view on new product development. It is particularly recognized that users want customized services for their intention. This study weighs blog-service characteristics (functions) based on user intentions and suggests a new service design method to combine functional levels among the existing blog service characteristics to meet each user intention. This research conducts online surveys to identify different user intentions, clusters them into five user intention groups, and then determines functional levels for a specific blogger group for an exemplified application. Morphology analysis is used to combine functional characteristics and the existing service levels at each function to generate a new blog concept for the target user group.

Keywords: new service generation, morphology, web service, blog.

1 Introduction

'Blogging' has exponentially increased as an online activity and has been fueled by reports from mainstream media of the massive power of blogs as an alternative news source since 1999, especially in the aftermath of 9/11 and the Iraq war. As web 2.0, which is the trend represented by information share and participation, has made blogs rapidly diffused, people use blogs to exchange their thoughts each other and participate in discussing social issues.

When blogs are firstly introduced into Korea, they did not intend to be used for participating in the social issues but for building social networks. Another trend occurred as the diffusion of Cyworld. It is the first successful online service as personal media and strongly focused on building social relationship. However, as nowadays portal sites such as naver.com, yahoo.com, daum.net are adopting blog services as a way of new services and blog-specified sites are becoming more popular, blogs settle down as a personal media just as in the western countries.

While blogs become one of the major online services, research in various fields has been conducted. In social engineering, some studies have been progressed to examine

---

* Corresponding author.

N. Aykin (Ed.): Usability and Internationalization, Part II, HCII 2007, LNCS 4560, pp. 407–416, 2007.
© Springer-Verlag Berlin Heidelberg 2007

why people use blogs and how bloggers behave. Moreover, a number of marketing managers have interests in so-called 'buzz effects' through blogs. On the other hand, computer science researchers and designers have tried to approach to blog concept generations based on functions and suggest more efficient interface designs. However, there has not been much research on the linkage between social engineering and computer engineering fields. Combined with user intentions in the area of social engineering, blogs have to support some important functions to customize for specific user needs, which are designed by engineers. Therefore, research to link between the user intentions and functions of blogs is required.

In this research, we explore which functional characteristics of blogs should be focused according to different user intentions and pursue an effective combination between functional characteristics and existing blog services in order to generate a new blog concept for an exemplified target user group.

2   Literature Review

2.1 Definition of Blogs

The term 'blog' is a combined word between 'web' for the Internet and 'log' for an official written account of what happens each day. The first generation of blogs starts in 1991 as a personal website of Tim Berners-Lee, who is the creator of World Wide Web services [1]. Blogs are defined as frequently updated web pages with a board in order that recently posted articles comes at top, distinguishing them from the traditional web pages that are not frequently updated and from board-type homepages [2]. Since blogs have rapidly evolved and still changed the patterns, the definitions and characteristics of blogs have not yet been clearly clarified. Meanwhile, blogs are defined with some basic characteristics as an unedited voice of a person, a diary-type board in order of recent updates to old articles, exposure of both titles and contents in the front page, frequently updated web pages by daily online posting, entry and post saved as HTML document with characteristics of publication, reflection and permalink, articles posted with mainly short content, categorized and networked by track back [3].

The wider definition is suggested by Blood that blogs are personal website for posting articles with users' own interests [4]. Blood classifies blog types into three types according to contents: log-style blog contains short memos of personal daily lives; filter-style blog includes news articles mainly focusing on social issues; and notebook-style blog is a mixed type between the other two, dealing with quite long articles about bloggers' own feelings and thoughts on their daily lives and social issues.

Blogs can also be classified into homepage, portal, and professional types [2, 5]. First, homepage type blog is used to maintain friendship among users in their 10s and 20s. Second, portal type blog is provided by portal web sites, which enables users to easily scrap any content from the portal sites into their own blog pages. Third, blog-specified sites have more advantages in terms of flexibilities to control menus than homepage type and portal type blog, as well as provide a good quality of content and information.

This paper suggests a new typology of blogs. In addition to previous three types of blogs, installation type blog is included as a new type of blog, which users are able to install programs for managing and operating their own blog environment such as skins and BGMs through modifiable source codes. Naver blog(blog.naver.com), Cyworld(www.cyworld.com), Egloos(www.egloos.com), and Tattertools (www. tattertools. com) are selected as representatives for portal, community, blog-specified, installation type of blog respectively.

2.2 User Intentions of Blogging

Various types of blogs meet different user needs with unique services, and the users seldom switch their blog services. This is what sociology researchers concerned about to which function people expect for blogs. The user intentions of blogging include social relationship/public sharing, self-satisfaction, social/business purposes and distinction of intergroup in extents of usage [6]. Moreover, existing user intentions of online communities with priority given to blogs are one of the online communities [7]. For example, user intentions are characterized by the following ten factors: representation of identification, memory sharing, studying tool, documen-tation, epidemic, habit, interaction, pride, voyeurism, and publication of image.

Thus, these 10 factors representing user intentions are tested in this research by online survey.

2.3 Functional Characteristics of Blogs

Blog functions are diversified. Even though design components of blogs change with variability, there are six essential functions of blogs [8]. They are 1) archives that make recent articles come first, 2) comment system with which visitors append reply, comment and remote comment on articles. Blogs support 3) categorization of articles, and provide 4) permalinks, through which one can move to the original article and blogs that locate in head or back link of posting. 5) Trackback function of blogs provides continuous public sharing of contents in similar interests and among people, which therefore contributes to make a powerful community in the same interest. Finally, a search tool in blogs is convenient not only to search for previous postings but also to give a guide to who drops in blogs through web searching.

2.4 Method of New Service Development

Sequential models for new product or service development have been investigated by several researchers [9, 10, 11]. These sequential models are made up of well-defined steps, as illustrated by the *stage-gate* model [10]. This research focuses on the service generation stage in the sequential process of service development.

The former research uses conjoint analysis and the theory of inventive problem solving (TRIZ) to generate new services, which are also traditional methods to develop new products [12]. However, since those models have limitations that there are fundamental differences between products and services, a new service development process has to be treated with more flexibilities and generalities than the new product development process [13].

This research suggests a morphology-based method for a service concept generation to increase flexibility and generality of service changes.

3 Research Hypothesis

Tried to observe from preceding research, the intentions of blogging are already revealed by differences of every each person in sociology field. It is possible to guess that users who have different intention of using can select blogs on their taste. Therefore our objectives are to clarify the important components according to user intentions and to suggest a new blog concept for a specified blogger group.

Hypothesis 1. User intentions of blogging are divided into several groups.
Hypothesis 2. Each user group emphasize on different functional characteristics of blogs.

After testing *Hypothesis 1*, one of the user intention groups is targeted to develop a new blog concept. Then once *Hypothesis 2* is tested, specific functional characteristics for the targeted bloggers are selected from the existing service options, focused on the weights of functional characteristics.

4 Methodology

4.1 Morphology Analysis

Morphology analysis is famous for its systematic approach to generate ideas traditionally for a product development. A morphological matrix is composed of the rows of key parameters at each product or service design level and the columns of available alternative components. Therefore, several combinations of selected alternatives at each key parameter can be new ideas [14, 15].

While the method is simple and reasonable, it has a serious limitation that the number of possible ideas is too large to consider all the alternatives. To solve this problem, a weighted morphology matrix is suggested in this research for an efficient parameter selection. A weighted morphology matrix is constructed according to the survey results on the functional characteristics of four different existing blog services, and then the service levels with the highest weight score at each functional characteristic are selected to efficiently make an alternative combination among the functional characteristics and existing blog services.

4.2 Variables and Measurement

Survey questionnaires are composed of five user intentions, 12 important functions and user satisfactions in each function for bloggers. The user intention consists of self-satisfaction, social/business purposes, friendship, storage of information, and representation of identification, which will be tested by confirmatory factor analysis. Respondents are asked with questionnaires for those user intentions and satisfactions on the blog functions, which are measured by 5-point scale (the same items used in the research for [6, 7]).

4.3 Data and Methodologies

Online survey is conducted to gather data on user intentions and importance of functional characteristics at each consistent user group. The survey is progressed by randomly selected bloggers. Out of total 298 answers received from the survey, 287 data except for 9 unreliable data are used for analysis[1]. Then the averages, frequencies, rates of variables are calculated and ANOVA is taken to see if there are statistically significant differences among blog types.

5 Results and Discussions

5.1 Results of Reliabilities Test and Factor Analysis

Before analyzing the survey results, a Cronbach's alpha test is conducted to check if there are internal consistencies among survey questionnaires explaining five factors of user intentions. Out of total 20 survey items asking bloggers of user intention, 16 items prove to have significant reliabilities with satisfactory Cronbach's alpha coefficients over 0.7 except for the other four items with values under 0.6, which are therefore excluded from the analyses. The results of factor analysis for user intentions confirm the five dimensions as designed for the survey questionnaires in Table 1: self-satisfaction (26.03%), social/business purposes (14.77%), relationship management (10.87%), information storage (10.39%), and expression of personality/identity (6.51%). The overall explanatory capability of these five factors is 68.57 %.

5.2 Hypothesis Testing

In order to test *Hypothesis 1*, ANOVA is conducted to examine if there are significant differences in user intentions among four different blog types.

With the assumption of homoskedasticity, ANOVA result with Levene statistics is statistically significant at a 0.05 level, which means the variances of five factors for user intentions do not follow the assumption of homoskedasticity among different blog types. Therefore, ANOVA without homoskedasticity is conducted, and then post-hoc Tamhane T2 and Dunnett T3 statistics are tested.

---

[1] 287 people (150 males, 137 females) participated in the survey (Under 20 years old: 71 people, 21~30: 182, 31~40: 30, Above 41: 4).

Table 1. Result of factor analysis on user intention of blogging

	Factors				
	1	2	3	4	5
Expression of own feelings and thoughts	**.848**	.030	.110	-.076	.075
Documentation of daily life	**.789**	.019	.200	.069	-.023
Self-reflection	**.714**	.307	.083	-.061	.141
Personal usage	**.692**	-.017	-.259	.059	.157
Getting to know social issues	.135	**.845**	.052	-.020	.115
Participation to discuss social issues	.019	**.755**	.215	.101	-.091
Helpful information for study/business	.075	**.745**	.094	.269	.063
Communication with others through blogs	.092	.120	**.823**	.037	.042
Exchange with information and ideas	.026	.382	**.742**	.115	.117
Importance of number of visitors and comments on the blog	-.097	-.112	**.668**	.154	.368
Helpful way to understand other people	.325	.329	**.538**	-.210	.043
Blog as a scrapped book	-.049	.036	-.094	**.862**	-.028
Scrap of good information or articles from other sources into my own blog	.012	.099	.136	**.839**	.125
Blog as a knowledge warehouse	.047	.445	.171	**.602**	.107
Importance of good-looking blogs	.079	.078	.189	.104	**.865**
Blog as the reflection of my characteristics	.205	.037	.103	.027	**.864**

Factor extraction method: PCA.
Rotation method: Verimax with Kaiser Normalization. a. Factor rotation converged after 6 iterations.

Table 2 shows descriptive statistics of means and standard deviations of the five factors according to four different blog types. While Egloos blogs intend to be used as a way of self-satisfaction (0.207), Cyworld mini homepages seem to use for personal uses with minus value (-0.650) for social/business purposes. Naver and Egloos blogs provide relationship management functions with mean value 0.07, Naver bloggers tend to have information storage purposes (0.452) rather than Egloos and Tattertools. Also, Naver bloggers highly intend to express their personality/ identity (0.221) through the blogs. However, those user-wise comparisons according to each blog type need to be clarified by ANOVA test and the post-hoc test.

Table 2. Descriptive statistics of user intention of blogging

	Cyworld(61)	Naver (71)	Egloos(112)	Tattertools(36)
Self-satisfaction	-.108(.936)	-.159(1.16)	**.207**(.813)	-.146(1.190)
Social/business purposes	**-.649**(.815)	.181(1.078)	.112(.942)	.393(.828)
Relationship management	-.196(.994)	**.070**(.993)	**.075**(.969)	-.040(1.107)
Information storage	.284(.909)	**.451**(1.056)	-.405(.800)	-.109(1.094)
Expression of personality/ identity	-.003(.985)	**.221**(1.040)	-.148(.928)	.031(1.112)

Number with blog's name means each blog users number from the survey.
Data are presented with a format 'mean(stan. dev.)'.

The result of ANOVA test in Table 3 shows significant differences in the mean values among four blog type of user groups in the factors of self-satisfaction, social/business purposes, and information storage within 5% significance level, while those in the factors of relationship management and expression of personality/identity are not significant. Therefore, *Hypothesis 1* that supposes different blogger groups have different user intentions is partially supported. Post-hoc Tamhane T2 and Dunnett T3 tests prove the multiple comparisons of each blog type. In the comparison of blog types for the social/business purposes, Cyworld users with lower intention to this are generally different from the other groups. As for use for information storage, there are significant differences that Naver bloggers have a higher intention while Egloos users have a lower intention.[2]

Table 3. Result of ANOVA test on the differences among blog user groups

	Differences	Sum of squares	Deg. of freedom	Mean square	F	p-value
Self-satisfaction	Between groups	8.13	3	2.71	2.76	**.042**
	Within groups	270.87	276	.98		
Social/business purposes	Between groups	35.06	3	11.68	13.22	**.000**
	Within groups	243.93	276	.88		
Relationship management	Between groups	3.40	3	1.13	1.13	.335
	Within groups	275.59	276	.99		
Information storage	Between groups	38.28	3	12.76	14.63	**.000**
	Within groups	240.71	276	.87		
Expression of personality/ identity	Between groups	5.98	3	1.99	2.01	.112
	Within groups	273.01	276	.98		

Hypothesis 2 is tested to see if the user groups by the four different blog services can be re-clustered by the importance of blog sub-functions from their usage. First, the correlation coefficients between the important levels of twelve blog sub-functions and five factors of user intentions are calculated. The correlation between information storage and scrap, as well as between expression of personality/identity and makeup of blogs are significant with coefficient over 0.4, while other sub-functions and factors of user intentions are not significantly correlated. Second, four regression analyses are conducted with each user intention as the dependent variable and all the blog sub-functions as independent variables. After the regression analyses, independent variables are finally selected by the backward selection method.

From the results of each regression analysis the followings are revealed: people using blogs for self-satisfaction need the functions of board/article posting and flexibility of menu control, whereas plug-ins and track back functions are more important to people using blogs for social/business purposes; the interactivity with friends and the RSS functions is significantly essential to bloggers who manage friendship through blogs, and bloggers who want to express their personality and identities emphasize on making-up their blogs. The conclusion through these results is that important sub-functions of blogs are varied according to user groups with different user intentions. Thus, *Hypothesis 2* is supported.

---

[2] While Naver users gave high scores (0.452) to information storage purpose, Egloos users gave low scores (-0.406) to this, which results in the group differences with the significant level near 0.

5.3 Application of a New Concept Development: Morphology-Based Case Study

As previously mentioned this research assumes that there is a specified user group with user intention and suggests a new blog concept.

The first step is to re-cluster the integrated users with variables of user intentions. This enables to select a specified target for a case study, therefore from which a new blog concept is generated. To re-cluster the sample, five factors of user intention are selected as variables for k-means clustering method. The value of k is determined as five by an ex-ante hierarchical clustering analysis and calculation of the distances among cluster centers. As the result of the cluster analysis is shown in Table 4, Clusters 1-5 are characterized as a group for information scrap, self-satisfaction, personal expression, social/business activities, and relationship management, respectively.

Table 4. Result of 5-means clustering

	No. of user clusters (no. of cases in each cluster)				
	1 (59)	2 (68)	3 (42)	4 (46)	5 (65)
Self-satisfaction	.349	**.600**	-1.480	-.265	.199
Social/business purposes	.063	.083	-.027	**1.106**	-.910
Relationship management	.055	-.963	-.376	.630	**.754**
Information storage	**1.279**	-.416	-.223	-.156	-.471
Expression of personality/ identity	.293	-.021	**.662**	-.722	-.160

In the investigation of each blog to see the distribution of clusters 1-5 in each blogger groups, it shows that each cluster is included in one user group with different ratios. This result shows that each blog has lured the bloggers with various user intentions by using distinctive service functions.

The next step is to target a specified user cluster and develop a new blog concept. In this research, the user cluster 2 (self-satisfaction) is selected for a morphology-based case study. In the morphology matrix, the score of alternative technologies is calculated by averaging the satisfaction score on the design parameters from whom are in the target user cluster 2. The important levels of each sub-function provided by the target user cluster 2 are shown as design parameter's weight in Table 5. Alternatives are evaluated and selected by one of the maximum weighted values.

The highlighted items in Table 5 are the results of this newly suggested approach with the maximum score among the alternatives. The combination of the resulted alternative items suggests a new blog service that intensifies the scrap of articles, interactivities with neighbors, and RSS functions for a target cluster 2. As for scrap function, Naver blog has been given more scores, which reflects the fact that Naver is a portal type blog so that it can be enable users to scrap contents from 'Naver news' or 'Jisik-iN[3]' services. Therefore, this function can be constrained unless the new concept of blogs includes various sources of contents. An easy way to approach to this is to enlarge the compatibilities with portals or other content websites. In terms of interaction with neighbors, services are provided by Egloos have the highest value to consider the design parameter. Since Egloos provides a simple neighboring

---

[3] An open knowledge-sharing house and dictionaries for Naver portal users, where Q&As actively occurs regarding any issues ranged from personal interest to professional areas.

management system with link to neighboring blogs and list of recent visitors, while Cyworld and Naver blogs provide more powerful operations. This result shows that a complicated neighboring system such as Cyworld is not important to target cluster 2. For operations of skin/accessories, installation type blogs such as Tattertools has significantly high score since the flexibilities in its source codes are higher than others.

Table 5. Morphology matrix for a new blog concept generation targeting user cluster 2

Design parameters (weight)	Cyworld			Naver			Egloos			Tattertools		
	Mean	N	σ	Mean	N	σ	Mean	N	σ	Mean	N	σ
Scrap (2.72)	3.44	9	0.73	3.73	11	1.10	3.11	18	1.08	2.63	8	1.19
Posting/editing of articles (4.72)	3.00	10	0.82	3.75	12	0.97	3.86	36	0.93	3.90	10	0.88
Selection of categories (4.41)	2.90	10	0.74	3.83	12	1.11	3.81	36	0.86	3.44	9	1.01
Control/storage of articles (4.41)	2.90	10	0.74	3.92	12	1.00	3.89	36	0.89	3.90	10	0.74
Structure of menus (4.20)	2.78	9	0.83	3.25	12	1.06	3.69	36	0.92	3.30	10	1.16
User interface (4.20)	2.63	8	0.92	3.50	12	0.80	3.64	36	0.87	3.70	10	0.82
Administration mode(4.20)	2.00	9	0.87	3.00	12	1.04	3.69	36	0.95	3.50	10	0.97
Statistics of visitors (3.40)	2.22	9	0.67	2.91	11	1.14	3.61	36	1.15	3.33	9	1.00
Link to neighboring blogs (3.40)	3.50	10	0.53	4.00	11	1.00	3.85	33	1.00	3.00	9	0.87
Relationship management (3.40)	3.11	9	0.60	3.09	11	1.38	3.24	33	1.03	2.67	9	0.87
Skin/accessories of blogs (3.35)	2.78	9	1.09	3.00	11	1.26	3.24	34	0.89	3.56	9	1.13
Plug-ins (3.14)	1.83	6	0.75	2.67	9	1.41	2.67	18	0.77	3.78	9	0.97
RSS (3.31)	3.00	6	0.89	3.22	9	1.48	3.43	23	0.95	3.56	9	0.88
Track back (3.45)	2.67	6	0.82	3.13	8	1.73	3.82	33	0.77	3.50	8	0.76
Modification of source (4.13)	2.80	10	1.48	3.08	12	1.38	3.46	35	1.12	3.70	10	0.95
Limits to data storage (4.09)	1.56	9	0.73	3.17	12	1.11	3.30	33	1.19	3.70	10	1.16
Level of content security (4.09)	3.30	10	1.25	3.58	12	1.24	3.69	36	1.09	4.30	10	0.67

6 Conclusions

This paper confirms that user intentions of blogging are characterized by five factors such as self-satisfaction, social/business purposes, relationship management, information storage and expression of personality/identities. In addition, this paper examines that four various types of bloggers have differences in the preference of blog sub-functions depending on the five factors of user intentions. Based on the survey data, users of four different blog types (Cyworld, Naver, Egloos and Tattertools) are regrouped into five distinct clusters classified by user intention factors. To develop a new blog concept for a specific user group, a morphology-based approach is proposed to generate alternatives with various levels of new blog sub-functions. In this research, one of the five clustered user groups is selected and a morphology-based concept generation is conducted to the clustered group 2 in which users tend to fulfill self-satisfaction through their blogs.

The new concept generation approach has a potential to be a good tool to examine the characteristics of bloggers according to the user intentions. However, since the morphology matrix that is calculated from the survey results has a small number of cases in each cell, the mean value of each cell is hardly reliable. Also, the verification of a new blog concept will be discussed further as the success of new blogs not only depends on the right targeting and right services for the targeted user groups but also the other management capabilities such as marketing, etc. Therefore, future research will include clarification of how the design parameters are combined with blog sub-functions in the existing blog services, and which features of blogs influence on the user satisfaction.

References

1. Winer, D.: The history of weblogs (2002), available at http://newhome.weblogs.com/historyOfWeblogs
2. Herring, S.C., Scheidt, L.A., Bonus, S., Wright, E.: Bridging the gap: A genre analysis of weblogs. In: Proceedings of the 37th Annual Hawaii International Conference on System Sciences pp. 101–111 (2004)
3. Kim, J.S.: Blogs' social and cultural advances and issues. Korea Telecommunications Policy Review 16(8), 18–36 (2004)
4. Blood, R.: The weblog handbook: Practical advice on creating and maintaining your blog. Perseus Publishing, Cambridge, MA (2002)
5. Miller, C.R., Shepherd, D.: Blogging as social action: A genre analysis of the weblog (2004), available at http://hochan.net/archives/2004/04/13@12:29am.html
6. Kim, Y.J.: A study on the blog as a media: Focused on media functions and the problems of the blog. Korean Journal of Journalism & Communication Studies 50(2), 59–90 (2006)
7. Choi, J.W., Lee, J.H., Kim, B.C.: Intention to use online community: Case of blog users. Korea Society of Management Information Systems, Spring Conference, pp. 575–581 (2005)
8. Lee, J.H.: Interface design in Blog (Web+Log) service. Journal of Korean Society of Basic Design & Art. 5(1), 87–95 (2004)
9. Stevens, E., Dimitriadis, S.: Managing the new service development process: towards a systemic model. European Journal of Marketing 39(1/2), 175–198 (2005)
10. Cooper, R.G.: Stage-gate systems: a new tool for managing new products. Business Horizons 33(3), 44–54 (1990)
11. Johnson, S.P, Menor, L.J., Chase, R.B, Roth, A.V.: A critical evaluation of the new services development process: integrating service innovation and service design. In: Fitzsimmons, J.A., Fitzsimmons, M.J. (eds.) New services development, creating, memorable experiences, Sage Publications, Thousand Oaks, CA (2000)
12. Chai, K.H., Zhang, J., Tan, K.C.: A TRIZ-based method for new service design. Journal of Service Research 8(1), 48–66 (2005)
13. Menor, L.J., Takikonda, M.V., Sampson, S.E.: New service development: area for exploitation and exploration. Journal of Operation Management 20, 135–157 (2002)
14. Ritchey, T.: General morphological analysis: A general method for non-quantified modeling.In: The 16th EURO Conference on Operational Analysis, Brussels, pp. 1–11 (1998)
15. Zwicky, F.: Discovery, invention, research: Through the morphological approach. The Macmillan Company, Toronto (1969)

Computer Task-Based Evaluation Technique for Measuring Everyday Risk-Taking Behavior

Kentaro Kotani, Chiho Tateda, and Ken Horii

Department of Systems Management Engineering, Kansai University,
3-3-35, Yamate-cho, Suita, Osaka 564-8680, Japan
{kotani,tateda67,khorii}@iecs.kansai-u.ac.jp

Abstract. Human risk-taking behavior is a major factor for accidents. Several techniques for quantifying human risk-taking tendency include questionnaire and observation methods. These techniques, however, have been questioned their validity and reliability. Our objective was to propose and evaluate a computer task-based evaluation technique for measuring everyday risk-taking tendency. In this technique, the users perform tracing a certain length of pathway, from start to goal, shown on the display by mouse. The system monitors the trajectory of the mouse cursor and detects the point of decision-making when users change their strategy from steering motion to ballistic motion as the mouse cursor approaches to the goal, yielding the level of risk-taking behavior represented by the Index of Difficulty (ID) at the location of strategy change. The results of experiment showed that IDs were highly correlated with probabilities of risk-taking behaviors obtained from 16 question items.

Keywords: Risk-taking behavior, Fitts task, Steering task, Decision making.

1 Introduction

Risk-taking behavior is one of the factors for accidents such as traffic, medical and industrial accidents. Risk-taking behaviors are defined as those include potential negative consequences even though the actors realize its potential risk [1]. Many studies investigate the risk-taking behaviors by using techniques such as self-report scales and observation methods. These studies try to quantify the level of personal risk-taking tendency. It was, however, criticized their reliability and validity since the results may be biased by respondents' unwillingness of uncovering truthful responses.

The objective of this study is to address a new computer-task based technique for evaluating the risk-taking behaviors by utilizing the changes in strategy of tracking motions, one of characteristics of human movement.

1.1 Changes in Strategy in Steering Task

The technique uses changes in strategy of tracking motions in a steering task. We provided the steering task completed with a custom-developed software program

N. Aykin (Ed.): Usability and Internationalization, Part II, HCII 2007, LNCS 4560, pp. 417–421, 2007.

developed in JAVA. The steering task requires users to move the cursor through eight virtual two-dimensional horizontal and vertical tunnels of varying widths displayed as two parallel lines without going outside of these lines. If users steer the cursor outside the lines, they have to redo the steer until successful, before the next tunnel is displayed. When each trial is performed, users change their strategy from steering task requiring feedback control, to the Fitts task requiring ballistic motions at the point where subjects judged as no longer feedback control is necessary for completing the trial. The index of difficulty for steering task can be calculated such that the value is the length remaining to complete the trial divided by the width of the tunnel [2].

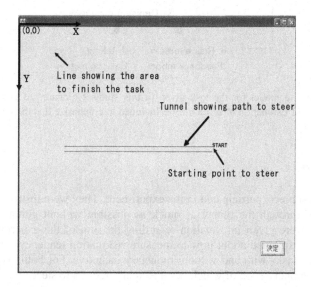

Fig. 1. Computer display of software program made for estimating tendency of risk-taking behavior. Users steer mouse cursor from the starting point (at the right of the tunnel showing "START") to the vertical line showing on the left. While steering the cursor, the software user changes his/her strategy from feedback motion to ballistic motion at the point they estimate that no longer feedback control is necessary. The program then detects the point by the change in speed of trajectory and calculates index of difficulty at the point of strategy changes.

1.2 Model of Risk-Taking Behavior in This Study

We proposed a risk-taking model for the steering task, shown in Figure 2, based on the general risk-taking model [3] and the model for risk-taking tendency at driving [4]. The initial process of the model is called hazard perception where hazard implies the objects or conditions that increase the possibility of misses. The utility in the model includes the motivation for haste and the feeling for thrill seeking. Even though the risk is accurately evaluated, the utility determines whether the person acts the risk-taking behavior, hence, the utility becomes the important factor for observing risk-taking behaviors.

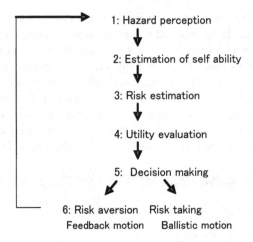

Fig. 2. Risk-taking model for the task given in this study. Compared to general risk-taking model, process #2 Estimation of self ability is included to emphasize that the model is based on user performance.

2 Methods

A total of 10 subjects participated in the experiment. They were instructed to steer the mouse cursor through the tunnel as quick as possible without going outside of the tunnel. They were given information regarding the aim of the experiment, however they were not explained about how to measure risk-taking tendency. There were two types of tasks: tasks with and without monetary incentive. For both tasks, there were four types of tunnels, each of which has different direction to steer.

Table 1. Question items (in part, translated)

Item Number	Questions
1	I Steal someone's belongings
2	I gamble very often
3	I ignore traffic lights when I walk crossing roads
4	I ignore traffic lights when I drive
5	It is OK to drive if I drink two glasses of beer one hour ago.
…	…

Note: They are originally written in Japanese.

Experimental procedures were as follows: (1) the practice session was given prior to the trials. The practice session consisted of 60 trials. (2) The subjects performed set of trials. Each trial was shown to the subjects in randomized order. (3) After all trials were completed, the subjects were asked to answer 50 question items regarding everyday risk-taking behaviors including driving safety, impulsivity, and thrill-seeking activity. The subjects answered their probability of risk-taking behavior for each item ranging from 0 to 100. Samples of question items are shown in Table 1.

Detection for strategy change from steering task to Fitts task was based on the velocity changes.

3 Results and Discussion

3.1 Detection of Risk-Taking Tendency

Figure 3 shows the trajectory of mouse cursor while a subject performed the trials. It is apparent to detect from the figure that IDs are distributed between five and 15 bits, where the trajectories of mouse cursor show changing trends of moving velocity.

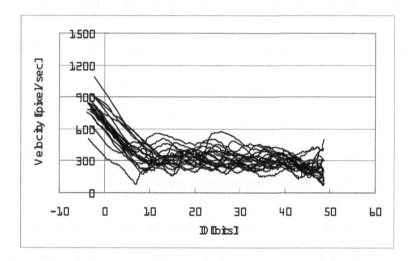

Fig. 3. Trajectory of steering trials with time converted to IDs. A total of 20 trials, performed by subject A, are overlapped. From right to left, the subjects steer the route path. The distance of the route, with the width of the path are converted to IDs in this figure.

Analysis of variances revealed that index of difficulties were different by subjects ($F(9, 1482) = 2608.5$, $p<.01$) and level of incentive($F(1, 1482) = 18.65$, $p<.01$). All in all, 95.0% of trials were able to detect the point to change the strategy by observation.

3.2 Relationship Between Index of Difficulty Obtained by the Task and Probabilities for Risk-Taking Behaviors

Analysis of variances for probability for risk-taking performance obtained by questionnaire revealed that the probability for risk-taking performance was significantly affected by subjects and by the question items. Correlation between indices of difficulty and probability for risk-taking performance showed that four out of 50 question items showed high positive correlations with individual indices of difficulty and 12 out of 50 question items showed high negative correlations with individual indices of difficulty. Among question items, seven items were associated with driving performance. Three of them were positively correlated with indices of difficulty, whereas four of them were negatively correlated.

4 Conclusion

In this paper, a computer task-based evaluation technique for measuring everyday risk-taking behavior was introduced and whether or not IDs determined by the strategy change from steering task to Fitts task was evaluated as a potential index for risk-taking behavior with a proposed risk-taking model. Frequency of the observed strategy change and the association with every-day risk-taking behaviors obtained from questionnaire suggested validity of the proposed technique. The next phase of this study includes the effect of *a priori* knowledge and detailed comparison with other techniques for measuring levels of risk-taking behaviors.

Acknowledgments. This work was supported by "Academic Frontier" Project for Private Universities: matching fund subsidy from Ministry of Education, Culture, Sports, Science and Technology, 2006-2011.

References

1. Haga, S., Akatsuka, H., Kusukami, K., Konno, S.: Factors of risk-taking behavior: A questionnaire survey. RTRI Report (In Japanese with English abstract) 8(12), 19–24 (1994)
2. Zhai, H., Woltjer, R.: Human action laws in electronic virtual worlds – An empirical study of path steering performance in VR. Teleoperators and Virtual Environments 13(2), 113–127 (2004)
3. Haga, S.: Factors behind unsafe acts. Technical Report of IEICE (In Japanese with English abstract) 99(238), 29–34 (1999)
4. Renge, K.: Psychological processes of risk-taking behavior in driving and new approach toward promoting risk-avoiding behavior. IATSS Review (In Japanese with English abstract) 26(1), 12–22 (2000)

Validating a Multilingual and Multimodal Affective Database

Juan Miguel López[1], Idoia Cearreta[1], Inmaculada Fajardo[2], and Nestor Garay[1]

[1] Laboratory of Human-Computer Interaction for Special Needs (LHCISN).
Computer Science Faculty. University of the Basque Country
Manuel Lardizabal 1; Donostia - San Sebastian
[2] Cognitive Ergonomics Group
Department of Experimental Psychology. University of Granada
Cartuja Campus; Granada
juanmi@si.ehu.es, icearreta001@ikasle.ehu.es, ifajardo@ugr.es,
nestor.garay@ehu.es

Abstract. This paper summarizes the process of validating RekEmozio, a multilingual (Spanish and Basque) and multimodal (audio and video) affective database. Fifty-seven participants validated a sample of 2,618 videos of facial expressions and 102 utterances in the database. The results replicated previous findings of no significant differences in recognition rates among emotions. This validation has allowed having the audio and video material in the database classified in terms of the emotional category expressed. This normative data has proven to be useful for both training affective recognizers and synthesizers and carrying out empirical studies on emotions by psychologists.

Keywords: Affective computing, affective resources, user validation, multilingual and multimodal resources, semantics.

1 Introduction

Human beings are eminently emotional, as their social interaction is based on the ability to communicate their emotions and perceive the emotional states of others [1]. Affective computing, a discipline that develops devices for detecting and responding to users' emotions, and affective mediation, computer-based technology which enables the communication between two or more people, displaying their emotional states [2, 3], are growing areas of research [4].

Affective mediation tries to minimize the filtering of affective information carried out by communication devices, due to the fact they are usually devoted to the transmission of verbal information and therefore, miss nonverbal information [5]. Applications of mediated communication can be textual telecommunication technologies such as affective electronic mail, affective chats, etc.

In the development of affective applications, affective resources, such as affective stimuli databases, provide a good opportunity for training such applications, either for affective synthesis or for affective recognizers based on classification via artificial neural networks, Hidden Markov Models, genetic algorithms, or similar techniques

N. Aykin (Ed.): Usability and Internationalization, Part II, HCII 2007, LNCS 4560, pp. 422–431, 2007.
© Springer-Verlag Berlin Heidelberg 2007

(e.g., [6, 7]). As seen in [8], there is a great amount of effort devoted to the development of affective databases. Affective databases usually record information by means of images, sounds, speech, psychophysiological values, etc. One of the main risks with affective databases is not having correctly labeled information. Therefore, they should be validated by human subjects in order to ensure that the stimuli adequately express the affects they are supposed to.

In this paper, the validation of the multilingual (Spanish and Basque) and multimodal (utterances and facial expressions videos) RekEmozio affective database is presented. In the following sections, affective models and related work are briefly revised. Next, RekEmozio database characteristics, validation process and main results are presented. Finally, a number of conclusions are outlined and future work is proposed.

2 Related Work

2.1 Models of Emotions

There are many possible ways where emotional parameters can be registered, codified or interpreted by computers. Models of emotions proposed by cognitive psychology could be a useful starting point. Generally speaking, models of emotions can be classified into two main groups: categorical and dimensional emotional models.

Categorical models of emotions have been more frequently used in affective computing (see [8] for a revision). In the research of emotions, different category groups related to emotions have been suggested. For example, authors such as [9] think that there are six basic emotions and that they are universal and shared by all humans, from which the rest of affective reactions are derived. These emotions, also called "Big-Six" emotions, are *anger, joy, sadness, disgust, fear* and *surprise.*

Dimensional approach to emotion has been advocated by a number of theorists, such as [10, 11]. Emotion dimensions are a simplified description of basic properties of emotional states [12]. The most frequent dimensions found in the literature are *Valence, Activation,* and *Control.* Therefore, a stimulus can be classified according to these 3 dimensions, for instance, it can be said that a concrete utterance has high valence, low activation and high control.

2.2 Affective Databases

Cowie and colleagues carried out a wide review of existing affective databases [8] which are described according to diverse features such as naturalness (e.g., emotion elicitation method) and scope (e.g., material: audio, video, mix; language).

Regarding material, there are databases of speech, sounds, text, faces or video scenes. With respect to speech, most references found in literature are related to English, while other languages have less resources developed, especially the ones with relatively a low number of speakers. This is the case of Basque. To our knowledge, the first affective database in Basque is the one presented by [13]. In Spanish, the work of [14] stands out.

Our understanding is that there is no validated database in Basque and Spanish which includes multimodal material (audio and video). Consequently, this type of database is essential for research in affective recognition and production, a database called RekEmozio, which includes these features, is described in the next section.

3   RekEmozio Database

3.1   Database Description

The RekEmozio database was created with the aim of serving as an information repository for performing research on user emotion. Members of different work groups involved in research projects related to RekEmozio performed several processes for extracting speech and video features such as frequency, volume, etc. This information is described in [15]. The characteristics of the RekEmozio database are described in Table 1 [16].

Table 1. Summary of RekEmozio database features

Scope			Naturalness					Context
Language	Description given of emotions	Number of actors/ actresses	Emotion elicitation methods	Semantically meaningful content	Material	Same text per emotion		Mode
Spanish	sadness, fear, joy, anger, surprise, disgust; neutral	10 (5/5)	Contextualized acting	Combined	2,618 audio stimuli and 102 video stimuli	Non-semantically meaningful texts		Audio-Visual
Basque		7 (4/3)						

As shown in Table 1, the RekEmozio database was created using recordings carried out by skilled bilingual actors and actresses. They received financial support for their cooperation. They were asked to read a set of words and sentences (both semantically and non-semantically relevant) trying to express emotional categories by means of voice intonation. The emotional categories considered are the classical "Big-Six" plus the neutral one, as shown in Table 1 ("Description given of emotion" column). In addition, they were asked to express facial expressions related to these emotional categories.

Regarding spoken material, the paragraphs and sentences used were constructed by using a group of words extracted from an affective dictionary in Spanish (1,987 words dictionary with nouns, adjectives, verbs and interjections). This emotional dictionary is built on top of words contained in the database of [17].

Semantically meaningful paragraphs and sentences were built from this group of words. Moreover, non-semantically meaningful words with the "neutral" label were used. For Basque sentence creation, sentences from Spanish were translated.

4   RekEmozio Database Validation

The procedure for performing the normative study to obtain affective values from the given audio-visual material is described next.

4.1 Method

4.1.1 Participants

Fifty-seven volunteers participated in the validation, 36 men (average age of 26.25, sd=9.7; age range=17-56) and 21 women (average age of 27.5; sd=10.7; age range=18-52). The mother tongue of 31 participants was Spanish and the mother tongue of the remaining 26 participants was Basque. They received financial support for their cooperation.

4.1.2 Material and Tools

A set of 2,720 stimuli were obtained from RekEmozio database, from which 2,618 were oral expressions (words, sentences and paragraphs) and 102 were videos with facial expressions. In order to ask subjects to validate affectively the stimuli, subjects were asked to select an emotional label for each stimulus (categorical test). Finally, in order to automate data recovery and facilitate the analysis of collected data, a tool called Eweb [18] was used.

4.1.2.1 Categorical Test. For the RekEmozio database validation, categorical measures were used, as the recordings within the database itself were performed by actors and actresses trying to express the above mentioned seven categorical emotions. Thus, when validating the database, human subjects were asked to indicate what emotion they thought the actors and actresses were attempting to express in each different database recording or stimulus.

4.1.2.2 Instruments. In order to automate data recovery and facilitate the analysis of collected data, Eweb [18, 19], a tool for designing and implementing controlled experiments in Human-Computer Interaction (HCI) environments, was used.

4.1.3 Design

A mixed multifactorial design was followed. The *Language* (Spanish, Basque) variable and *Actor* variable (10 or 7 levels, depending on the number of actors per language) were manipulated between-groups, while *Emotion* (joy, sadness, anger, disgust, surprise, fear, neutral) and *Media* (audio, video) were manipulated within-subject. In the case of audio material, according to RekEmozio database features, two more variables were manipulated: *Text Length* (word, sentence, paragraph) and *Semantics* (semantically meaningful, non-semantically meaningful). Each subject validated 160 stimuli (154 oral expressions and 6 videos) corresponding to one single actor.

4.1.4 Procedure

The participants used the interface provided by Eweb to perform their validation. First, participants received general and specific instructions for performing the experiment and they had to fulfil a demographic questionnaire. Afterwards, they began the session itself. Each participant performed the validation for one language, thus, they received the instruction about the language in which they had to perform.

The session was divided into two blocks (audio and video) and Eweb randomly presented each one to the participants. They had to perform several trial sessions for each block (three for oral and three for facial). They later performed the experimental session for the 154 stimuli in audio (where the audio block was selected) and 6 in video (otherwise). Participants had to complete a questionnaire for each stimulus, by selecting the emotional category. Each stimuli was heard/seen only once by the participants. They could only select one value for the category in the questionnaire. When participants finished with their first block, Eweb assigned them a second. The validation session finished after participants had completed both audio and video blocks. The procedure was the same for each language.

4.2 Results

4.2.1 Emotion Recognition in Vocal Expression

First of all, the data in the categorical test was analyzed. Recognition accuracy percentages for the different types of utterances (depending on the language) are presented in Table 2. Replicating previous data [20], Fear and Disgust obtained the lowest success percentages while Neutral, Joy, Sadness and Anger obtained the highest ones.

With the aim of contrasting whether the differences between emotions and languages were significant, a multifactorial ANOVA was performed with *Emotion*, *Text Length* and *Semantic* as within-subjects variables and *Language* as between-group variable. The percentage of recognition in the categorical test was introduced as dependent variable. The main effects of *Emotion*, $F(6,330)=34.11$; Mse=0.13; $p<0.000$ and *Text Length*, $F(2,110)=44.37$; Mse=0.05; $p<0.000$, were significant. In the case of the *Emotion* variable, the highest percentage of recognition was for Sadness (76%), followed by Anger (73%), Joy (73%), Surprise (63%), Fear (51%) and Disgust (51%). On the other hand, subjects obtained a higher percentage of emotion recognition with Sentences (M= 70%) and Texts (M= 71%) than with Words (M= 61%), $F(1,55)=67.6$; Mse= 0.07; $p<0.000$. Finally, the main effect of *Semantic* was also significant, $F(1,55)=175.32$; Mse= 0.1; $p<0.000$.

Table 2. Recognition Accuracy Percentages for Utterances in function of language and emotions

Language	Sadness	Fear	Joy	Anger	Surprise	Disgust	Neutral
Spanish	75%	51%	78%	71%	66%	52%	80%
Basque	77%	52%	68%	74%	59%	51%	77%

Semantically meaningful texts obtained higher scores than non-semantically meaningful ones (77% and 58% of recognition respectively). There was neither significant main effect of *Language* nor interaction of this variable with others. Recognition percentages in function of *Emotion*, *Language*, *Semantic* and *Text Length* can be seen in Table 3 and 4.

Table 3. Recognition Accuracy Percentages for Spanish Utterances depending on language, emotions, semantic and text length

Semantic	Text Length	Sadness	Fear	Joy	Anger	Surprise	Disgust	Neutral
Non-seman-tically Meaningful	Word	68%	38%	44%	58%	63%	39%	76%
	Sentence	72%	33%	74%	78%	49%	25%	74%
	Paragraph	79%	42%	78%	79%	40%	24%	71%
Seman-tically Meaningful	Word	80%	53%	63%	67%	63%	52%	77%
	Sentence	83%	75%	81%	90%	68%	93%	78%
	Paragraph	88%	78%	89%	92%	65%	81%	88%

Table 4. Recognition Accuracy Percentages for Basque Utterances depending on language, emotions, semantic and text length

Semantic	Text Length	Sadness	Fear	Joy	Anger	Surprise	Disgust	Neutral
Non-seman-tically Meaningful	Word	57%	41%	71%	53%	64%	38%	79%
	Sentence	76%	38%	72%	68%	62%	23%	70%
	Paragraph	75%	47%	79%	75%	42%	24%	86%
Seman-tically Meaningful	Word	75%	52%	75%	65%	71%	62%	76%
	Sentence	93%	68%	92%	91%	83%	89%	73%
	Paragraph	84%	66%	85%	87%	74%	79%	97%

The 2-way interaction between *Emotion* and *Semantic* was significant, F(6,330)=30.23; Mse=0.05; p<0.000. The percentages of recognition for Fear (40%) and Disgust (20%) were especially lower in the case of non-semantically meaningful.

4.2.2 Emotion Recognition in Facial Expression
In the categorical test, the general accuracy percentage for facial expressions was 90% (sd 18.62). Table 5 shows the recognition accuracy percentage for each emotional category.

Fear and Disgust (as in the case of utterances) and Sadness were the emotions with the lowest recognition rates whereas Joy, Anger and Surprise obtained the highest recognition rates. In order to contrast whether the differences between emotions were significant, an ANOVA of repeated measures was performed with the six levels of *Emotion*. The difference between Sadness, Fear and Disgust on the one hand and Joy, Anger and Surprise on the other hand, was significant, F(1, 56)=18.7; Mse=0.08; p<0.001. Neutral results are not mentioned as neutral face is used as a reference in this study.

Table 5. Recognition Accuracy Percentages and Standard Deviations of facial expressions videos for each emotional category

	Sadness	Fear	Joy	Anger	Surprise	Disgust
Mean	81%	81%	98%	96%	96%	89%
SD	40%	40%	13%	19%	19%	31%

4.3 Discussion

The main goal of this study was to validate the audiovisual and multilingual emotional database *RekEmozio*. The data of the categorical test allows us to conclude that both audio and visual stimuli are valid to express the intended emotion as the recognition accuracy percentage is over 50% (78% in the case of audio and 90% in the case of video).

In the case of utterances, the differences in recognition accuracy between emotions found by other authors (e.g., [20]) were replicated, that is, Joy, Sadness and Anger are the type of utterances with the highest percentages of recognition while Fear and Disgust obtained the lowest recognition percentages. These relatively stable differences are supporting the hypothesis of the role of specific vocal parameters in the communication of different emotions [21]. In addition, the fact that Anger has the highest recognition percentages in vocal expression seems to agree with the results of [22]. The authors suggest an evolutionary explanation for these results: emotions that express danger, such as Anger and Fear, must be perceived at long distances with the aim of being perceived accurately by members of the group or even by the enemies. In order to do so, voice would be the most effective way, while facial expressions would be more effective for emotions which must be transmitted in short distances. This would explain why Anger (danger related) in vocal expressions is better recognized than other emotions not related to danger such as Surprise or Disgust. It would also explain why Joy and Surprise (which are supposed to be transmitted in short distances) obtained higher recognition rates in the case of facial expressions (98% and 96% respectively) than in the case of vocal expressions (75% and 62% respectively). However, there are two results which are incoherent with the evolutionary hypothesis: 1) Fear (danger related) presents one of the lowest recognition rates of vocal expressions; 2) Anger recognition rates are also higher in the case of facial expressions than in the case of vocal expressions. It would suggest that actors simply interpreted facial expressions better than vocal ones.

Another important finding of this study was the significant effect of semantic in the case of utterances. The semantically meaningful texts where better recognized than the non-semantically meaningful ones. Nevertheless, non-semantically meaningful texts, obtained an accuracy percentage of 58%, which is closer to the values obtained in earlier work (e.g., [21]). This means that, although the semantic content is an important contributor, the vocal or prosodic cues contribute much more effectively to the decoding of certain emotions. However, the recognition percentage for Fear (40%) and Disgust (20%) were especially low in the case of non-semantically meaningful utterances. According to [21], the low rates could be due to the diversity of modalities involved in the expression of these emotions (e.g., in the case of Disgust: nasal, visual, oral, semantic, etc.).

Finally, another goal of this study was to compare emotion recognition patterns in different languages, in this case Spanish and Basque. No relevant differences were found between languages. This agrees with the findings of other authors such as [23, 24, 25], who found that there is little difference in emotion detection between subjects coming from different linguistic and cultural environments, but state that recognition success rate in users is far from perfect. Therefore, in spite of being very different languages regarding to their grammar and vocabulary, Spanish and Basque seem to express emotions with the same accuracy, not only in general terms, but they also showed similar recognition patterns. For example, Fear and Disgust were the worst recognized emotions in both Spanish and Basque. However, the fact that both languages were able to transmit emotions by means of vocal cues does not mean that such cues were identical. A matter of future work is to verify this by means of contrasting the utterance in function of the acoustic parameters.

5 Conclusions and Future Work

At the moment, the validated database is being used for training affective recognition applications applied to the cultural characteristics of the place where authors carried out their research. It is considered that training affective recognizers with subject validated databases will enhance the effectiveness of recognition applications. For example, the naturalness of the resources contained in the database is being analyzed taking voice parameters that have influence in the affective expression and recognition into account. Standard signal processing techniques have been used for extracting parameters involved in emotional speech. Several Machine Learning techniques have been applied to evaluate their utilities in the affective speech recognition [15]. The aim has been enhancing the results which are obtained with more traditional approaches

The aforementioned effectiveness must also take multimodal database features (images, linguistic parameters, vocabulary, etc.) into account. In the future, this database will be extended with combined recordings of audio and video.

Moreover, in future studies, social and contextual information will be added. All of this information will be described in an ontology with the aim of associating multimodal elements. Using this ontology in combination with software engineering, applications will assist in the development of affective systems [26], both for the scientific community and for industry.

Finally, another matter of future work is to contrast whether emotion transmission by vocal cues in Spanish and Basque are based on different or similar acoustic parameters.

Acknowledgements. The work carried out received financial support from the Department of Economy of the local government "Gipuzkoako Foru Aldundia" and from the University of the Basque Country (in the University-Industry projects area). The authors would like to express their gratitude to the people involved in the RekEmozio project in general and to the people that participated in the compilation and validation of the RekEmozio database in particular.

References

1. Casacuberta, D.: La mente humana: Diez Enigmas y 100 preguntas (The human mind: Ten Enigmas and 100 questions). Océano (ed.), Barcelona, Spain (2001)
2. Garay, N., Abascal, J., Gardeazabal, L.: Mediación emocional en sistemas de Comunicación Aumentativa y Alternativa (Emotional mediation in Augmentative and Alternative Communication systems). Revista Iberoamericana de Inteligencia Artificial (Iberoamerican journal of Artificial intelligence) 16, 65–70 (2002)

3. Picard, R.W.: Affective Computing. MIT Press, Cambridge, MA (1997)
4. Tao, J., Tan, T.: Affective computing: A review. In: Tao, J., Tan, T., Picard, R.W. (eds.) ACII 2005. LNCS, vol. 3784, pp. 981–995. Springer, Heidelberg (2005)
5. Garay, N., Cearreta, I., López, J.M., Fajardo, I.: Assistive technology and affective mediation. Human technology. Special Issue on Human Technologies for Special Needs 2(1), 55–83 (2006)
6. Fragopanagos, N.F., Taylor, J.G.: Emotion recognition in human-computer interaction. Neural Networks 18, 389–405 (2005)
7. Athanaselis, T., Bakamidis, S., Dologlou, I., Cowie, R., Douglas-Cowie, E., Cox, C.: ASR for emotional speech: clarifying the issues and enhancing performance. Neural Networks 18, 437–444 (2005)
8. Cowie, R., Douglas-Cowie, E., Cox, C.: Beyond emotion archetypes: Databases for emotion modelling using neural networks. Neural Networks 18, 371–388 (2005)
9. Ekman, P., Friesen, W.: Pictures of facial affect. Consulting Psychologist Press, Palo Alto, CA (1976)
10. Mehrabian, A., Russell, J.A.: An approach to environmental psychology. MIT Press, Cambridge, MA (1974)
11. Tellegen, A.: Structures of mood and personality and their relevance to assessing anxiety, with an emphasis on self-report. In: Tuma, A.H., Maser, J.D. (eds.) Anxiety and the anxiety disorders, pp. 681–706. Lawrence Erlbaum, Hillsdale, NJ (1985)
12. Schröder, M., Cowie, R., Douglas-Cowie, E., Westerdijk, M., Gielen, S.: Acoustic correlates of emotion dimensions in view of speech synthesis. In Proc. Eurospeech 1, 87–90 (2001)
13. Navas, E., Hernáez, I., Castelruiz, A., Luengo, I.: Obtaining and Evaluating an Emotional Database for Prosody Modelling in Standard Basque. Lecture Notes on Artificial Intelligence, vol. 3206, pp. 393–400. Springer, Berlin (2004)
14. Iriondo, I., Guaus, R., Rodríguez, A., Lázaro, P., Montoya, N., Blanco, J.M., Bernadas, D., Oliver, J.M., Tena, D., Longhi, L.: Validation of an acoustical modelling of emotional expression in Spanish using speech synthesis techniques. In: SpeechEmotion'00, pp. 161–166 (2000)
15. Álvarez, A., Cearreta, I., López, J.M., Arruti, A., Lazkano, E., Sierra, B., Garay, N.: Feature Subset Selection based on Evolutionary Algorithms for automatic emotion recognition in spoken Spanish and Standard Basque languages. In: Sojka, P., Kopecek, I., Pala, K. (eds.) TSD 2006. LNCS (LNAI), vol. 4188, pp. 565–572. Springer, Heidelberg (2006)
16. López, J.M., Cearreta, I., Garay, N., de López Ipiña, K., Beristain, A.: Creación de una base de datos emocional bilingüe y multimodal. In: Redondo, M.A., Bravo, C., Ortega, M. (eds.) Proceedings of the 7th Spanish Human Computer Interaction Conference, Interaccion'06, Puertollano, pp. 55–66 (2006)
17. Pérez, M.A., Alameda, J.R., Cuetos Vega, F.: Frecuencia, longitud y vecindad ortográfica de las palabras de 3 a 16 letras del diccionario de la lengua española (RAE, 1992). Revista Española de Metodología Aplicada 8(2), 1–20 (2003)
18. Arrue, M., Fajardo, I., López, J.M., Vigo, M.: Interdependence between technical web accessibility and usability its influence on web quality models. Int. J. Web Engineering and Technology 3(3), 307–328 (2007)
19. López, J.M.: Development of a tool for the Design and Analysis of Experiments in the Web. In: Lorés, J., Navarro, R. (eds.) Proceedings of The 5th Spanish Human Computer Interaction Conference, Interacción'04, Lleida pp. 434–437 (2004)

20. Scherer, K.R., Banse, R., Wallbott, H.G., Goldbeck, T.: Vocal cues in emotion encoding and decoding. Motivation and Emotion 15, 123–148 (1991)
21. Banse, R., Scherer, K.R.: Acoustic profiles in vocal emotion expression. Journal of Personality and Social Psychology 70(3), 614–636 (1996)
22. Johnstone, T., Scherer, K.R.: Vocal communication of emotion. In: Lewis, M., Haviland, J. (eds.) Handbook of Emotion, 2nd edn. pp. 220–235. Guilford Publications, New York (2000)
23. Abelin, A.: Cross-cultural multimodal interpretation of emotional expressions – an experimental study of spanish and swedish. In: Abelin, A. (ed.) SProSIG (2004)
24. Oudeyer, P.-.Y.: The production and recognition of emotions in speech: features and algorithms. International Journal of Human-Computer Studies 59(1-2), 157–183 (2003)
25. Tickle, A.: English and Japanese speaker's emotion vocalizations and recognition: a comparison highlighting vowel quality. In: ISCA Workshop on Speech and Emotion, Belfast (2000)
26. Obrenovic, Z., Garay, N., López, J.M., Fajardo, I., Cearreta, I.: An ontology for description of emotional cues. In: Tao, J., Tan, T., Picard, R.W. (eds.) ACII 2005. LNCS, vol. 3784, pp. 505–512. Springer, Heidelberg (2005)

Tools to Increase the Strategic Value of User Experience Design

James Nieters, David Grabel, and Vijay Agrawal

SJC-J4, 255 W Tasman Ave, San Jose, CA 95014
jnieters@cisco.com, dgrabel@cisco.com, vijagraw@cisco.com

Abstract. Case study describing tools and processes enabling accelerated adoption of Usability Standards, and increased efficiencies in development of accessible, internationalized, branded applications across large number of products in an enterprise. By building tools to support UE standards and best practices, the User Experience Team at Cisco not only achieved wide adoption of UE standards and best practices across Cisco applications, we also increased efficiencies in User Interface development and the ability to build internationalized, accessible software, thus increasing the strategic value of User Experience Design.

Keywords: User Experience, Branding, Tooling, Accessibility, Internationalization.

1 Introduction

Many experts in the field of HCI have talked about the value of human interface standards for graphical user interfaces (GUI's) [4] [3]. Such standards have been around since the early 1980's. Few, though, have discussed how User Experience Design (UXD) groups in a corporate culture can build tools to not only promote predictability and consistent brand experience, but to also drive a culture of usability, globalization and accessibility across application development teams.

The Cisco User Experience Design (UXD) Group built a set of application user interface standards in 2003. From the software development engineer's perspective, adhering to the standards required additional work- they had to read the specifications, interpret them, and spend time implementing hundreds of details [6]. While Cisco application development teams realized the value of consistent branding and design patterns, accessibility, and globalization, application features often received higher priority due to the high cost of compliance and time to market considerations [1].

In two case studies, application development teams only achieved full compliance with each of these requirements in the fifth release of the application. Doing so required three years of effort. Within Cisco, only three of over 100 teams developed entirely standards-conformant applications in the first year.

N. Aykin (Ed.): Usability and Internationalization, Part II, HCII 2007, LNCS 4560, pp. 432–440, 2007.

This resulted in:

- Inconsistent branding
- Minimal accessibility and globalization support
- Increased customer training
- Increased support costs

The Cisco UXD Group recognized an opportunity to help application development teams solve this problem [2]. We created standards-conformant GUI component libraries and tools. The goal was to make it faster and easier to create a standards-conformant application than to build an application that is not conformant. The Cisco UXD Group achieved much greater adoption after having built these component libraries and tools. As of this paper, more than 20 application development teams use the UXD Components and tools, with more adopting them every week. Experiences thus far show a reduction in time to full feature implementation by up to 67%.

This paper discusses the process, technology and tooling choices made to achieve these objectives.

2 Risks and Benefits of Common Tooling

The decision to implement tooling to support standards carries its own risks and benefits.

2.1 Implementation Risks

Cisco has over 100 software applications. The risks of implementing tooling targeted toward a large number of applications in an enterprise include:

- The solution may not address common ground across a sufficient number of teams
- The solution may not be ready for consumption by teams when they need it
- Providing solutions can reduce innovation

Building a Solution that Does not Address the Common Ground. For a tooling solution targeted to many application teams, it should meet the requirements of most teams planning to use the tool.

At Cisco, this risk was mitigated by carrying out a detailed requirements gathering and analysis process of the applications being built at Cisco, and building a set of tools that supported as many teams as possible.

Timing – Inability to Deliver the Tool in the Required Timeframe. The tools and feature enhancements should be made available to the teams at the appropriate time in their product development lifecycle.

This was achieved by anticipating needs of the teams and working with them from product conceptualization through the UI design phase to ensure the necessary tooling was available by the time teams were ready to consume it.

Innovation – Balancing Innovation and Standardization. Product marketing staff is tasked to understand customer requirements. Teams have been innovative in meeting these needs.

A balance was achieved when development teams understood that they could contribute to our standards and tooling.

2.2 Risks of Not Implementing

Within Cisco, we learned that not implementing tooling as a vehicle to promote standards leads to:

- Increased time to market
- Increased support costs
- Added time to address non-English speaking markets
- Engineering inefficiency
- Inability to leverage advances in UI technologies due to lack of centralized core competencies.
- Inconsistent branding where we 'touch' customers every day: software applications
- Non-adherence to Section 508 (U.S. government regulations regarding accessibility)

3 Getting the Executive Buy-In

At Cisco Systems, Inc., ensuring adoption of standards required innovative designs and designs that meet business requirements. Adoption has also required involving politically powerful organizations as co-owners and aligning with senior-level initiatives. Initially, the organization started small by supporting the most strategic initiative in the organization—working with a cross-technology business council, for sponsorship and initial governance. The Cisco UXD Group focused to deliver value to teams in this initiative—standards-conformant designs in a timely fashion. The UXD group produced examples of successful implementations, and worked with individual teams after this to sustain the momentum.

The biggest challenge was that while executives wanted to see teams adopt the standards, they would not require them to adopt the standards. Product teams can take on a "not invented here" attitude or view UE as a "speed bump". The UXD Group's response has been to approach this from two angles: Executive support and tooling that proved UE can speed time to market.

At this point, organizations that had not been on board are active supporters. In addition, we are closely aligned with Corporate Marketing, the Intranet standards team, and the Internet standards team. These collaborations give the UXD Group the added positional power it needs for the standards and tooling to be recognized by executives.

We continue to evolve the standards and tooling as the organization evolves. For example, we are defining a new icon language that reinforces the new Cisco brand, and will continue to evolve other assets as necessary.

4 Processes and Tooling

This section describes the processes and tooling that facilitated wide adoption of the tools and standards, and thereby, increased the strategic value of the UXD team.

4.1 Processes

The processes outlined below helped ensure we built the right set of tools:

- Early and continuous engagement with application teams
- A centralized standards and tooling team that works with Design Services to identify requirements
- Collaborative tools to help application teams provide insights and feedback to the tooling team. In our case, these included a wiki, jira, and email aliases.

4.2 Information Architecture Design

Applications can be geared to different types of users, whether they be the first-time, novice or advanced. Functionality can be presented linearly (often for the novice user), logically, or based on usage patterns.   Understanding the primary target audience has a direct effect on how functionality is presented. This is something that development teams seldom consider without UXD input.

On a more granular scale, due to the exposure to a broad range of applications, the UXD team has been able to identify design patterns; similar functionalities that can be presented in similar ways.

4.3 UI Prototyping Tools

Also known as interface builders, UI prototyping tools allow developers to rapidly design the UI for the application. Prototype Tooling has always been an evolving field.

[7] *Prototyping tools have enabled product developers to accelerate product cycles, to design products that have been better accepted, and to customize products . Unlike their counterparts in the manufacturing sector, software and Web designers have not always used prototyping tools. As a result, companies moving services to the Web have often failed to directly address real customer requirements.*

When defining and evolving the prototyping tools, the UXD Group established the following goals for delivering value to Cisco application teams:

- Adherence to Cisco's branded look and feel.
- Concept validation. Support communication of designs to all stakeholders.
- Illustrate the interactivity of the UI in the prototype.
- Enable teams to determine the viability of proposed designs.
- Support the ability to generate code.
- Facilitate project scoping.
- Allow comparison with other similar applications under design and development. Typical Cisco application UI is shown in Fig 1 below.

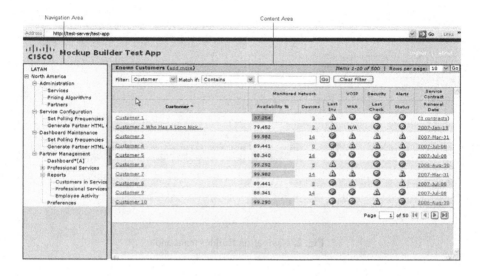

Fig. 1. Output of Navigation Builder

It consists of:

- Navigation area– drawers or tree based navigation pane
- Content area– The area containing UI components and content, such as tables, reports, and charts

We divided prototyping tools into two parts:

1. Navigation Builder
2. Content Builder

We will see that using some of today's tools, coupled with homegrown tooling, the UXD team achieved a robust prototyping platform.

The navigation builder enables designers to represent the navigation for applications via live prototypes. Designers use the following steps to use the navigation builder:

Step 1: Visual specification of navigation elements

The diagram in Fig. 2 shows how designers enter navigation data. The value on the right defines the content link for each navigation item. For example, a label "Device A" would refer to the page devicea.html. The content link can be a mockup built using an IDE, a visio file, an image, or any other web accessible resource. This gives the interface designers flexibility to wire all types of mockups into the navigation.

Step 2: Internally, the navigation builder tool saves the navigation definition in XML format.

Step 3: To render the resulting mockup, the tool processes the navigation definition XML using a stylesheet and the stylesheet processor available in the browser.

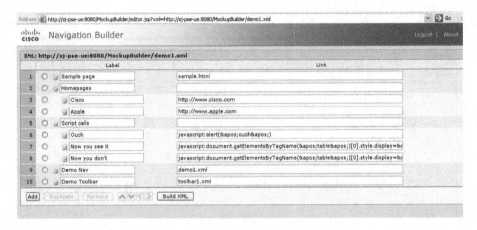

Fig. 2. Navigation Builder front end

The result is a standards-conformant application mockup with navigation and content areas presented to the designer.

An application prototype built in this manner is hosted on a shared server and can be accessed via a URL from anywhere. This supports easy collaboration among stakeholders of the prototype.

The Content Builder is a design tool enabling designers to build page content. Designers use tools such as Visio and Adobe Photoshop to build page content that is static. To prototype the interactivity of the next generation of UIs, a live mock-up tool based on Eclipse IDE is used. We built code templates, drag-and-drop wizard extensions to the Eclipse IDE to simplify mockup design:

- Code templates enable interface designers to start from a template. For example, a designer can choose to design a page containing panels of group boxes. This can be done by choosing the "Group Box Layout" template and specifying the number of group boxes when prompted. This results in the tool generating the necessary JSP tags using the SDK tag library and rendering them in the Design mode. An advanced designer may also choose the source mode and modify some of the html/jsp tag attributes to suit their needs.
- Wizards for complex widgets like table and scheduler enable designers to build the UI using easy-to-follow wizards, which reduces the need to understand or modify JSP tags.
- An added benefit is that the content builder generates code for the UI that can be used as a starting point by the application developer.

4.4 UI Development Tools

These tools serve as building blocks enabling application developers to rapidly build standards-conformant UIs.

The broad goals for these libraries are:

- Built-in standards compliance
- Branded look and feel
- Reduced engineering cost for development teams
- Incorporation of latest technology advances into the tools, such as Web 2.0, AJAX-enabled interactive components
- Globalization support
- Accessibility conformance

UI Component Libraries. There are over 100 software applications at Cisco. About half of them are desktop applications, and the rest are browser based.

UXD team decided to build JSP Tag library and Swing component libraries to meet the entire spectrum of applications.

JSP Tag libraries serve as the UI Components vehicle for browser-based applications. The team continually evolves these libraries to use the latest technologies such as AJAX, DHTML for rich, interactive look and feel. The standards define the visual behavior of the component and the tags implement them. This way, application teams automatically receive standards compliant, feature rich components

Swing components use a commercial component library and build a pluggable look and feel on top. This layer helps these components adhere to the Cisco UE Standards, thereby producing standards-conformant components ready for application teams to consume.

UI Components to Support Globalization. Supporting an interface for a global audience is more difficult than simply translating the text strings. It may include different number, date, and time formats, new input methods, redesigned layouts, different color schemes, and new icons [5]. Examples include:

- Text translations
- Orientation based on locale
- NumberFormat based on the client locale

Because internationalization issues do not readily emerge during development, teams do not notice them until close to the product shipment date. By this time, many such issues must remain unresolved due to release deadlines. The components in the UXD Group's library contain attributes to specify the locale and the key in the message bundle, thus supporting internationalization.

UI Components to Support Accessibility. Developing accessible UIs requires a sound understanding of accessibility requirements. The UXD Group worked with the Accessibility team at Cisco to help build UI components that comply with section 508 requirements. Examples include:

- Keyboard equivalents for all actions
- Appropriate color contrast and limits on animation
- Meaningful labels for tables and other objects
- Text Description for images

This enables application teams can build accessible UIs without having to spend effort on it.

Globalization Tools. A sustainable process to support globalization depends on many factors. These include leveraging translation memory and terminology databases, defining a taxonomy and globalization roles within the company, and establishing relationships with translation vendors in target countries. Although the Cisco UXD Group has helped promote this process, other teams own the non-tooling aspects of the Globalization program. The UXD Group has collaborated on the following elements:

Translation Memory. Many messages, such as error messages and tool tip text are repeated across multiple Cisco applications. For example, "Device x was successfully added." Without translation memory, the same message is often phrased differently, leading to a non-uniform experience for users. Clearly, this central message library (translation memory) ensures that translations for commonly used messages are reused to ensure uniformity of messages, enhancing the user experience.

Tools to Detect Globalization Issues. In the past, globalization issues were not discovered until late in the development life cycle, resulting in many internationalization challenges not being solved in time for product release.

The UXD team worked with the Globalization team to offer testing tools that as part of the development toolkit helped detect and remedy internationalization issues,. Doing so helped promote a culture of testing for internationalization issues as part of the day-to-day development process. The result is applications with robust globalization support.

Splash and Login Screen Generators. Splash and Login Screen Generators help generate images that application teams need for login screen, about, help and other places. A standard tool helps application teams quickly generate such images rapidly.

Icon Libraries. Icon Libraries are arguably the single most reused piece of software across Cisco applications. The UXD team offers a centralized repository of icons that helps application teams to readily integrate icons for various artifacts into their applications. It also ensures uniform look and feel. For example, an icon for wireless device looks same in all Cisco applications, facilitating predictability for an improved user experience.

Help System. A uniform Help System design has helped application teams to quickly build Help pages and plug into their application using a common framework.

5 Summary

Developing tooling to help application development teams rapidly build globalized, accessible, and standards-conformant applications, has placed the Cisco UXD Group in a position of greater strategic relevance. Rather than functioning as auditors of usability and standards, the team functions as solution providers.

As of this paper, 20 application development teams use the UXD Components, with more adopting them every week. Experiences thus far show a reduction in time to full feature implementation by up to 67%. As teams adopt these component libraries, they are helping to build a culture of usability, internationalization and accessibility across the development community.

References

[1] Bachman, Bill, Aliaga, Frederick– Four strategies for promoting common UI guidelines within Adobe - © ACM 1-58113-728-1 03/0006 5.00 (2003)
[2] Bazelmans, Rudy– Productivity – The role of the Tools group - ACM Sigsoft Software Engineering Notes vol 10(3) (July 1985)
[3] Grudin, Jonathan – Consistency, Standards, and formal approaches to interface Development and Evaluation – @ (1992) ACM 0734-2047/92/0100-0103
[4] Myers.: Challenges of HCI Design and Implementation – Interactions – (January 1994)
[5] Russo, Patricia, Boor, Stephen – How Fluent is Your Interface? Designing for International Users – InterCHI (April 1993)
[6] Thoutrup, Henrik, Nielsen, Jakob – Assessing the usability of a User Interface Standard - ACM 0-89791 -383 -3/91 /0004/033 (1991)
[7] Hakim, J., Spitzer, T.: - Effective Prototyping for Usability - 0-7803-6431-7/00/$10.00 © 2000 IEEE (2000)

Incorporation of User Preferences into Mobile Web Service Conversations

Jonghun Park[1], Wan Lee[1], Jae-Yoon Jung[1], and Kangchan Lee[2]

[1] Seoul National University, Seoul, Korea
[2] Electronics & Telecommunication Research Institute, Daejeon, Korea
jonghun@snu.ac.kr, {wanlee80,jjyjung}@gmail.com, chan@etri.re.kr

Abstract. WS-CDL (Web Services Choreography Description Language), a Candidate Recommendation from World Wide Web Consortium, facilitates the specification of rules to govern the ordering of message exchanges between web service participants. This paper considers a computing environment where a mobile client interoperates with a web service provider according to a WS-CDL specification that defines peer-to-peer interactions, and proposes a framework through which the client can specify its preference on how conversation should take place. The presented framework allows mobile clients to effectively cope with user and device mobility through providing a flexible means to reduce the number of exchanged messages without violating choreography requirement.

Keywords: Ubiquitous services, Mobile web services, Web service choreography, Conversation preference, WS-CDL.

1 Introduction

While web service is currently emerging as a dominant technology for supporting e-Business automation and integration, it is also increasingly considered as a promising platform for inter-connecting devices in mobile and ubiquitous computing environment. By embedding the web services into virtually any computing devices, it becomes possible for a device to discover and interoperate with other devices and remote services, establishing pervasive network of computers of all form factors and wireless devices.

Several recent efforts recognize the need for embedding web service capability into devices to enhance interoperability among them as well as with external services. Microsoft's invisible computing project [6] attempts to make small devices part of the seamless computing world by developing a platform to build custom smart devices and consumer electronics that implement web services on a chip. Researchers at Microsoft, Intel, Canon and BEA have published WS-Discovery that uses web services to make it easier for devices to find one another on a network [1]. For example, it will enable a personal digital assistant to locate available services such as printing or file sharing on a wireless network. In addition, Microsoft, Intel, Lexmark and Ricoh have co-authored a specification called the Devices Profile for Web

N. Aykin (Ed.): Usability and Internationalization, Part II, HCII 2007, LNCS 4560, pp. 441–450, 2007.

Services to provide guidance for how software makers and hardware manufacturers can inter-connect devices using WS-Discovery and web services [2].

In the meantime, OMA's mobile web services working group focuses on a framework that can support consistent and federated access to service enablers that exist within or connected to the wireless network and devices. It has published OMA Web Service Enabler (OWSER) specifications to define necessary infrastructure for offering and consuming web services and for providing network identity related capabilities [8]. Indeed, considering that the interoperability problem is the crux for realizing the vision of ubiquitous computing and the web services are meant to be consumed directly by programs not humans, we envision that making every device an autonomous web service appears to be a vital approach. In particular, when a mobile device is web service enabled and engages in a conversation with a service provider, it becomes necessary to define an interaction logic required for them. For this purpose, one can use a choreography language to specify the rules of engagement between the mobile client and the web service provider.

In such a mobile service environment, however, connection may be lost and the mobile device may move into out-of-service area any time during a conversation, and the user may not be attentive all the time. These may prevent the conversation from successful completion particularly when the conversation is long-running or involves several user interactions. Accordingly, performing mere step by step execution of a choreography specification defined for the mobile client may yield unsatisfactory results.

To address these problems, in this paper we propose a flexible framework, named Web Services Conversation Preference Profile (WS-CPP), through which mobile web service clients can express their preferences on how conversation should take place while being able to satisfy a choreography specification. The presented framework allows some of the activities defined in a choreography representation to be selectively skipped, providing an effective means to flexibly reduce the number of messages exchanged between the mobile client and the web service provider.

This paper is organized as follows. Section 2 provides a brief overview of the web service choreography language considered in this paper and then presents the proposed preference model and framework architecture. The detailed structure as well as the modeling entities defined for WS-CPP are described in Section 3. In Section 4, an example is presented to show usage of a WS-CPP specification. Finally, Section 5 concludes the paper.

2 Preferences on a WS-CDL Specification

Web service choreography aims at the coordination of interactions between distributed parties, which define web services to expose their externally accessible operations. The coordination of interactions becomes necessary in almost any autonomous web services conversations, including the areas ranging from simple printing request to complex multi-step device configuration.

Several new breed of specifications have been proposed to provide notations for describing interaction flows in web service based collaborations [7]. In particular, motivated by the need for an effective mechanism to coordinate the interactions among web services and their user agents, W3C formed the web services choreography working group that has been tasked with the development of such a mechanism in an interoperable way. As a result, the working group has published the Web Services Choreography Description Language (WS-CDL), aiming to provide the capability of composing interoperable collaborations between any type of party regardless of the supporting platform or programming model.

WS-CDL is an XML-based language that describes peer-to-peer collaborations of web services participants through defining, from a global viewpoint, their common and complementary observable behavior, where ordered message exchanges result in accomplishing a common goal [4]. A WS-CDL document can be used at design time by a participant to verify that its internal processes will enable it to participate appropriately in the choreography. It can also be used to develop a web services-based composite process that can be said to implement the required external observable behavior for the process. At run time, the choreography definition can be used to verify that everything is processed according to the predefined conversation protocol [4].

In this paper, we attempt to specify the client-side preferences on how a client should interact with a web service provider, and therefore we consider a masterslave style choreography in which the service provider manages conversations with clients and the clients interact only with the provider and not between themselves. The proposed preference specification model, WS-CPP, bases the WS-CDL as a choreography language, and focuses on the specific preference requirements that can arise during the multi-step interactions with a web service provider. It enables web service clients to express their interaction preferences in a standard format that can be delivered to and interpreted by service providers.

Given a WS-CDL description that represents a set of valid interaction sequences, WS-CPP allows conversation preferences to be associated with some of the interactions defined in the WS-CDL document so that they are not required during actual conversations. Specifically, from the WS-CDL entities, we identify a set of activities that can be associated with preferences as follows.

An activity notation in WS-CDL is the lowest level component of a choreography, and it is used to define an activity as either an ordering structure, a work unit, or a basic activity. An ordering structure consists of `sequence`, `parallel`, and `choice`, and it combines activities with other ordering structures in a nested way to specify the ordering rules of activities.

All activities enclosed within the `sequence` need to be executed sequentially in the same order that they are defined, and are not allowed to be skipped. In contrast, the `parallel` structure contains one or more activity notations that are enabled concurrently, and a preference can be introduced to specify the execution priorities among the activity notations within the `parallel` structure. Similarly, when two or more activity notations are specified within a `choice` element, requiring only one of them to be performed, a preference on which activity notation is to be selected can be defined for the `choice` element.

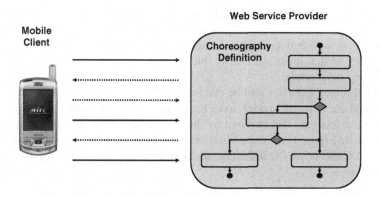

Fig. 1. Conversation behavior under WS-CPP

A workunit is used to describe a guard condition as well as a repetition condition on an activity notation. The guard condition expresses the interest on one or more variable information to be available under certain constraints. The workunit completes successfully when its repetition condition evaluates to be false. Since the number of iterations executed for a workunit can be controlled by the messages sent from a client in some cases, we define a preference notation that allows a client to specify a set of values that are pre-assigned to the variables of interest for the purpose of minimizing the number of interactions resulting from a loop execution.

As for the basic activity which contains interaction, perform, assign, silent action, no action, and finalize activities, we identify two activities that can be associated with preferences. The interaction activity is used to exchange information between collaborating parties, and in particular the message exchange is specified in an exchange element within the interaction. Therefore, a preference indicating whether a specific message exchange should take place or not can be defined for the exchange element.

On the other hand, with the assign activity that creates or changes the value of one or more variables in a WS-CDL document, we associate a preference that allows the value of a variable to be assigned beforehand in order to make some of the interactions defined in the choreography unnecessary at runtime.

Now that we have discussed the conversation preferences defined in WS-CPP, we proceed to describe a required runtime behavior when a WS-CPP specification is to be used. First, we assume that a WS-CDL document is publicly available from a web service provider so that it can be referred to by a client application's developer. The developer then needs to write a client application of which the interaction behavior conforms to the requirements specified in the service provider's WS-CDL document.

The client program must also be WS-CPP aware. That is, it must be able to interpret a WS-CPP specification and adjust its behavior according to the specification. Later, a WS-CPP document that reflects the client application's preferred conversation behavior is defined by a user agent, and then it is transmitted to a service provider when an actual conversation starts.

In the meantime, after the service provider has received the WS-CPP profile, it should be able to refer to the preference definitions in the profile throughout the conversation. In other words, while the service provider engages in a conversation following the prescribed choreography, it needs to look up the preference definition from the WS-CPP document for each activity notation that is associated with a preference so that it can seamlessly interact with the client without raising exceptions or waiting indefinitely.

The resulting behavior will be that the number of messages exchanged between the client and the service provider under the proposed WS-CPP framework will be always equal to or less than that required by the original WS-CDL definition as illustrated in Figure 1. In Figure 1, the dotted lines represent that some of the interactions that were required in the WS-CDL definition are skipped at run-time according to the WS-CPP specification.

3 Preferences on a WS-CDL Specification

The proposed WS-CPP document consists of a series of preference definitions. We have adopted XPath [3] to express conditions as well as to locate the elements in the WS-CDL and WS-CPP documents. The top level element of WS-CPP is preferences that has namespace definitions and a reference to the target WS-CDL document. A preferences may contain zero or more of the following entities: variableDefinitions, interactionSkip, workunitSkip, choicePriority, and orderPriority.

The variableDefinitions construct allows defining one or more variables to be used within a WS-CPP document. A variable defined in a WS-CPP document points to a data structure within an informationType of WS-CDL by using an XPath expression so that its value can be referred to for instantiating the corresponding variable in a WS-CDL document. The syntax of the variableDefinitions is:

```
<variableDefinitions>
    <variable name="NCName" type="QName"
       query="XPath expression" />+
</variableDefinitions>
```

The interactionSkip represents a preference on the exchange element within an interaction activity of WS-CDL. The target exchange element in the WS-CDL document is referred to by use of an XPath expression. This preference element indicates that a message expected to be delivered to a receiver will not be actually sent. Instead, the receiver should presume as if the message were received. This is accomplished by providing all the data required from the message with preAssignment element that pre-assigns a value to a variable defined in a WS-CDL document, making the actual interaction become unnecessary at runtime. In order to distinguish the client-initiated exchange from the service provider-initiated exchange, we use an attribute named type. The syntax of the interactionSkip construct is defined as follows:

```
<interactionSkip name="NCName"
    guard="xsd:boolean XPath expression"?
```

```
    target="XPath expression to an exchange tag"
    type="ignore|filter">
    <preAssignment name="NCName">
        <copy source="XPath expression" target="QName" />+
    </preAssignment>?
</interactionSkip>
```

The above preference definition employs a guard to express a condition that must be satisfied in order for the preference to be activated. The type with the value ignore indicates that the interaction to be skipped is a client-initiated exchange, and the type with the value filter represents the other case.

Continuing with our description of the preference constructs, the workunitSkip is used when a client wants to avoid iterative interactions required by a workunit activity notation. Through the use of workunitSkip, a client may pre-assign multiple values to a variable of a WS-CDL document for the purpose of avoiding sending messages repetitively to exit the loop. In case that the loop is not exited even after trying a list of possible values, the interactions in the workunitSkip may proceed as defined in the WS-CDL document or the entire conversation may be stopped, depending on the value of causeStop, an attribute of workunitSkip. The syntax of workunitSkip is shown below:

```
<workunitSkip name="NCName"
    guard="xsd:boolean XPath expression"?
    target="XPath expression to an exchange tag in workunit"
    causeStop="true|false">
    <multiPreAssignment name="NCName">
        <copy source="list of XPath expressions" target="QName" />+
    </multiPreAssignment>
</workunitSkip>
```

The choicePriority lets the selection be pre-specified when a client is required to make a decision among the available choices defined in the WS-CDL specification. A priority can be defined in terms of a string that refers to the position of an activity element within a choice structure. The syntax of choicePriority element is:

```
<choicePriority name="NCName"
    guard="xsd:boolean XPath expression"?
    target="XPath expression to a choice tag">
        <selection position="xsd:string" />
</choicePriority>
```

Finally, the orderPriority corresponding to the parallel structure specifies the client's execution ordering priority among the activities that can be enabled in parallel. The priorities among the activities are specified using a set of partial order expressions that must hold for the activity pairs [5]. The syntax is defined as:

```
<orderPriority name="NCName"
    guard="xsd:boolean XPath expression"?
    target="XPath expression to a parallel tag">
    <priority expression="Prioritization expression" />
</orderPriority>
```

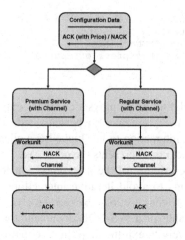

Fig. 2. A schematic diagram showing the conversation logic of the example scenario

4 Example

We consider the following simple scenario to demonstrate a usage of the proposed WS-CPP: A user with a web service enabled mobile device routinely visits an area where two types of on-demand multimedia streaming services, namely a regular service and a premium service, are provided to mobile devices within the range of wireless LAN.

In order to start the service, the device first needs to invoke the service by sending context data such as the authentication information, screen size, and media handling capability of the device to the service provider. For the sake of simplicity, we assume that only the screen size information is required.

When the service provider receives the context data, it immediately checks if the configuration of the device is valid. In case that the configuration is not supported, the service provider notifies the device with a negative ACK (NACK), and the choreography completes. Otherwise, it replies back to the device with an ACK message. Subsequently, the user is asked to choose a service type and a channel of interest. Occasionally the selected channel may not be available due to the problem of a content provider. If this happens, the user is expected to select another channel until the selected channel is found to be available. The whole conversation completes after the service provider sends an ACK message.

The conversation logic of this example scenario is shown in Figure 2. The choreography for the considered example is implemented by use of Pi4SOA package [9]. The Pi4SOA package is then used to export its internal choreography definition to a WS-CDL document. Because the entire specification generated from Pi4SOA is quite lengthy, we only show its abbreviated version in Figure 3. As this abbreviated code indicates, WS-CDL lets the developer define a choreography by composing various activity notations. We also remark that workunit is used in the code to define a loop.

```
<choreography name="multimediaService" root="true">
   <sequence>
      <interaction name="Provider accepts configuration"
         operation="configuration" channelVariable="D2PCh" initiate="true">
         <exchange name="acceptConfig"
            informationType="configDataType" action="request">
         <exchange name="supportedConfig"
            informationType="configAckType" action="respond">
         <exchange name="unsupportedConfig"
            informationType="configNackType" action="respond"
            faultName=" unsupportedConfigException">
      </interaction>
      <choice>
         <sequence>
            <interaction name=Client requests the premium service"
               operation="premiumService" channelVariable="D2PCh">
               <exchange name="acceptPremium"
                  informationType="premiumType" action="request">
            </interaction>
            <workunit name="Repeat until an available premium channel is found"
               repeat="channelFound = true">
               <interaction name="Handle unavailable premium channel"
                  operation="unavailablePremiumChannel" channelVariable="D2PCh">
               <exchange name="sendPremiumChannelNack"
                  informationType="premiumChannelNackType" action="respond">
               <exchange name="acceptAnotherPremium"
                  informationType="premiumType" action="request">
               </interaction>
            </workunit>
            <interaction name="Provider responds premium with ACK"
               operation="sendPremiumAck" channelVariable="D2PCh">
               <exchange name=" sendPremiumAck"
                  informationType="premiumAckType" action="respond">
            </interaction>
         </sequence>
         <sequence>
         <!-- Choreography definition for the case of the regular service here -->
            ...
         </sequence>
      </choice>
   </sequence>
</choreography>
```

Fig. 3. A WS-CDL code for the example scenario

In order to show a usage example of WS-CPP, we now make the following assumptions on the user's conversation preferences.

- P1: The user prefers not to receive an ACK message for the configuration data transmission.
- P2: The user prefers the premium service to the regular service if the price for the premium service is less than $5.
- P3: The user's preferred channels are "CH1", "CH2", and "CH3" in the order of his or her preference. If none of them are available, the user wants to be provided with the original channel selection menu.
- P4: The user does not want to receive a NACK message when a selected channel is not available.

```
<preferences name="multimediaServicePref" root="true" ...
  choreographyDefinition="cns:/package/choreography[1]">
  <variableDefinitions>
     <variable name="screenSize" type="cns:configDataType" query="/screen"/>
     <variable name="premiumPrice" type="cns:configAckType" query="/price"/>
     <variable name="channelNum" type="cns:premiumType" query="/channel"/>
  </variableDefinitions>
  <!- Preference 1 ->
  <interactionSkip name="Filter Configuration Ack"
     target="sequence[1]/interaction[1]/exchange[2]" type="filter"/>
  <!- Preference 2 ->
  <choicePriority name="Select Premium Service"
     guard="tns:premiumPrice &lt; 5" target="sequence[1]/choice[1]">
     <selection position="1"/>
  </choicePriority>
  <!- Preference 3 ->
  <interactionSkip name="Skip Channel Selection"
     target="sequence[1]/choice[1]/sequence[1]/interaction[1]/exchange[1]"
     type="ignore">
     <preAssignment name="mostPreferredChannel">
        <copy source="CH1" target="tns:channelNum"/>
     </preAssignment>
  </interactionSkip>
  <workunitSkip name="Avoid Interaction For Alternative Channel Selection"
     target="sequence[1]/choice[1]/sequence[1]/workunit[1]/interaction[1]/exch
     ange[2]" causeStop="false">
     <multiPreAssignment name="alternativeChannels">
        <copy source="CH2 CH3" target="tns:channelNum"/>
     </multiPreAssignment>
  </workunitSkip>
  <!- Preference 4 ->
  <interactionSkip
     name="Fliter Channel Unavailability Message"
     target="sequence[1]/choice[1]/sequence[1]/workunit[1]/interaction[1]/exch
     ange[1]" type="filter"/>
</preferences>
```

Fig. 4. A WS-CPP specification for the considered preferences

The resulting WS-CPP specification is shown as an abbreviated form in Figure 4 where tns and cns respectively indicate the namespaces defined for the WS-CPP and WS-CDL documents. In Figure 4, each preference requirement is represented by the corresponding preference modeling element available in WS-CPP. The interactions whose preferences are not specified in WS-CPP will proceed normally as defined in the WS-CDL document.

In the WS-CPP specification presented in Figure 4, the preference P1 is represented by interactionSkip where the target WS-CDL interaction that needs to be filtered is pointed to in terms of an XPath expression. Note that the type filter is used for this case as the message is supposed to be sent by the service provider. We also define choicePriority with a guard to reflect the preference P2. The preference P3 is taken care of through defining two preference elements. We use interactionSkip with a pre-defined value to skip sending the preferred channel number, and workunitSkip to avoid sending alternative channel information. Finally, as in the case of P1, the preference P4 is expressed by using interactionSkip. The completed

WS-CPP specification is sent to the service provider at the time the client invokes the service. Therefore, the interactions the user wants to avoid will not be necessary at runtime.

5 Conclusion

In this paper, we presented an overlay preferencing mechanism that can alleviate additional real time messaging requirements during web service based interactions. Specifically, we proposed a conversation preference specification framework, called WS-CPP, in an attempt to enhance the flexibility of mobile peer-to-peer web service applications that must adhere to the conversation rules defined in terms of WS-CDL.

WS-CPP allows some of the interactions defined in a WS-CDL document to be skipped selectively while satisfying the rules of conversation required by a service provider. In addition, it provides a means for the mobile clients to pre-specify their preferences on the choices, concurrencies, and loops that can arise during a conversation. We plan to test the proposed framework in a real mobile environment, and also effectively extend it for the multi-party choreography cases.

Acknowledgments. This work was supported directly by ETRI, and in part by Engineering Research Institute at Seoul National University.

References

1. Beatty, J., et al.: Web services dynamic discovery (WS-Discovery). Microsoft (2005), http://msdn.microsoft.com/library/en-us/dnglobspec/html/WS-Discovery.pdf
2. Chan, S., et al.: Devices profile for web services. Microsoft (2005), http://specs.xmlsoap.org/ws/2005/05/devprof/devicesprofile.pdf
3. Clark, J., DeRose, S.: XML Path Language (XPath) Version 1.0. W3C Recommendation (1999), http://www.w3.org/TR/xpath
4. Kavantzas, N., et al.: Web services choreography description language version 1.0. W3C Candidate Recommendation (2005), http://www.w3.org/TR/2005/CR-ws-cdl-10-20051109/
5. Kießling, W., Hafenrichter, B., Fischer, S., Holland, S.: Preference XPATH: A query language for e-Commerce. In: Proc. 5th Int. Conf. für Wirtschaftsin-formatik pp. 425–440 (2001)
6. Microsoft: The Microsoft invisible computing project web site. http://research.microsoft.com/invisible/
7. Muehlen, M., Nickerson, J.V., Swenson, K.D.: Developing web services choreography standards - The case of REST vs. SOAP. Decision Support Systems 40(1), 9–29 (2005)
8. OMA: OMA Web Services Enabler (OWSER): Overview (2006), http://www.openmobilealliance.org/release program/owser_v1_1.html
9. Pi4SOA: The Pi4SOA (Pi Calculus for SOA) web site. http://www.pi4soa.org

Dealing with Computer Literacy and Age Differences in the Design of a Ubicomp System to Cope with Cognitive Decline in Lonely Elders

Marcela D. Rodríguez[1], Alejandro Aguirre[1], Alberto L. Morán[2],
and Oscar Mayora-Ibarra[3]

[1] Ingeniería en Computación, Facultad de Ingeniería, UABC, Mexicali, B.C., México
[2] Ciencias Computacionales, Facultad de Ciencias, UABC, Ensenada, B.C., México
[3] Create-Net, Trento, Italy
{marcerod,alexaguirre,alberto_moran}@uabc.mx,
oscar.mayora@create-net.it

Abstract. The aging of the population is a phenomenon faced by many nations. In Mexico, it is estimated that in 2005, 7.5% of the Mexican population was 60 years or older and that by 2030 will be reaching 17.5%. Growing old is often accompanied by the loss of close companionship that can aggravate the elders memory loss. It has been identified that for coping with cognitive decline, older adults need to have diverse relationships by communicating with others across a wide array of ages and cultures, and extend their social networks. In this paper we present a case study that enable us to get an initial understanding concerning the relationships of older adults with their relatives and the barriers they have faced to integrate themselves to the current technologically-supported family networks formed by the younger. Based on the findings of our case study, we propose to reduce the generational gap through a pervasive collaborative game that enables elders and their relatives to select the most appropriate interaction interface according to their age, preferences and technical skills.

1 Problem Context

The aging of the population is a phenomenon faced by many nations [1]. In Mexico, as an illustrative case of the reality experienced in many other Latin-American countries, this phenomenon acquires particular significance since Mexico is a developing country in which there exists an enormous social disparity [2]. It is estimated that in 2005, 7.5% of the Mexican population was 60 years or older, and that by 2030 this figure will be more than double, reaching 17.5% [2].

Growing old is often accompanied by the loss of close companionship that can cause older adults to face feelings of loneliness and depression, that often may lead to a decrease of quality of life and other health problems. Additionally, as a consequence of growing old, it is common that older citizens suffer from gradual memory loss that may be aggravated by loneliness [3]. It is estimated that in 5.36% of Mexican homes, older citizens are living completely alone with no other relatives close to them; and 23.28% of Mexican homes are composed of at least 1 older adult who may stay alone at home during the day since other family members have to be away for their daily

N. Aykin (Ed.): Usability and Internationalization, Part II, HCII 2007, LNCS 4560, pp. 451–459, 2007.

activities [2]. The relationships of senior citizens with their family is affected in different ways, for instance: Children, who become the care-givers of their parents, worry due to the fact that they can not take care of them appropriately; children who live far away from their parents do not maintain frequent contact with them, and grandchildren miss the opportunity to get to know their grandparents. These situations do not help promote frequent face-to-face interaction between older adults and their relatives. It has been identified that for coping with cognitive decline, older adults need to have diverse relationships by communicating with others across a wide array of ages and cultures, and extend their social networks [3].

2   Understanding the Context of Lonely Elderly People in Their Homes

To gain an initial understanding concerning the relationships of older adults with their relatives, and how they have evolved and changed over the years, we conducted semi-structured interviews with six elders between 65 and 75 years old and their children. Our results show that:

- *Parent-children relationships change over the years.* When children were younger, one of the objects of communication was frequently and mainly about arguments dealing with the children's necessities, as one of the older citizens stated: *"...when the children were kids, they talked to me when they had a problem, i.e. they needed something for their school... Now that they are married, they call me just to know if I am fine".* One child stated that when he was younger, he could not share some important things with their working parents. However, we realized that in all the interviewed families that when the children became independent or formed their own family, the face to face interactions with their parents were limited up to one visit a week if they do not live in the same city or town.

- *Older parents become the focal point for family gatherings and news distribution:* i) Children receive recent family news through their parents who tend to become the "networkers" [4] who collect and distribute family news; As an evidence of this finding one of the children said: *"my mother is the one who tell us how the rest of the family is";* ii) visiting parents are the motivation for arranging family; with regard to this, an elder mentioned: *"The family meets every Sunday in my house..."*.

- *The intensity of the relation between parents and their children differs according to the child gender.* Female children tend to have a closer relationship with their old parents and can be more intense when parents become sick. Three children and two parents provided us comments supporting this finding. For instance, one of the female children stated: "When my mother is sick, I call her more frequently, or I take her to my home...", and an elder said *"it is my daughter who calls me two or three times a week to ask me if I am fine, and she always visits me on weekends"*

- *The social networks of the elders are formed by a diversity of members.* The social networks of the elders are mainly formed by relatives. But we also found, that in some cases their networks include friends and former co workers, as mentioned by two of the interviewed elders: *"I attend knitting classes for old people,...."*, *"I met with a group of retirees once a week at least to bowl"*.

- *Children encourage their parents to carry out different activities to cope with their loneliness.* Children encourage their parents to perform activities in which they can interact with other senior citizens, such as knitting classes. However, the activities that elders perform vary according to their personality and social position, as one of the participants stated: *"my mother only likes to interact with the family, she always has been a person dedicated to caring for us"*

- *Children do not consider the current cognitive decline of their parents as a problem.* All children subjects are aware of the type of things that their parents forget, but consider that this does not represent a risk. Similarly, all the parents stated that they forgot some things, but they considered that this was normal. However, three of the children mentioned that they are aware that their parents may present a cognitive decline problem in the future, as stated by one of the participants: *"I think that in the future I will be the driver of my father. I worry about the way he drives. I have realized that he forgets the names of the streets and that he sometimes does not see the stop signs"*.

- *The adoption of new communication technologies has positively affected the parent-children relationships.* The interviewed families considered that the parent-children relationships are different, since now they use technology, such as cell phones and the Internet, to stay in touch more frequently. One child said: *"We can communicate at any moment by using cell phones, and now the younger family members use the Internet"*. Another child commented: *"Technology keeps the family close during critical moments; for example, we can communicate faster when my parents are sick"*. We found that technology, such as appliances, had been adopted by the elders since they were considered as easy to use. In some cases, the elders' family has encouraged them to use some of these devices. One of the older adults said *"I started to use the microwave oven when my daughter in law gave me one and taught me how to use it"*; other older adult stated: *"I started to use a cell phone because my children suggested me having one in order to stay communicated with them"*

The above findings provide evidence that i) as the children grow, move away, and get further responsibilities, the nature and intensity of their relations with their parents change; ii) the use of newer communication technologies creates a generational gap between members of different ages, as these are easily adopted by younger members of the family, but not by the older ones; and iii) to reduce this generational gap, younger members of elders' family play an important role, since they encourage and teach older members to start using the technology, which will enable elderly can discover the affordances of these new means of communication. Thus, in order for elders adopt a new communication technology, it has to be easy to use and helps them to be added to the current technologically-supported networks of their younger relatives. If technology enables elders to "increase their social networks and closer intergenerational ties, they will have a sense of well-being and will reduce their social isolation" [10].

Our findings point out to a need for newer mechanisms that encourage older adults who may not have any computer skills, to communicate and spend time with family members who have different ages, computer skills, technology preferences, and that live in different places, which will enable them to reduce their feelings of loneliness while coping with cognitive impairment.

3   Coping with the Diversity of the Elders' Family Network Members

Proposing a new technology that is addressed to a diversity of users may be challenging. There exists a concern that elders are not receptive toward technology which is due to the challenging experience of learning and using it [5,6]. Studies about using mobile phones by elders, suggest that these devices are used for very limited purposes, and that they avoid using some functions due to the complexity of the interaction interface of these devices [7]. In order for new technology to be accepted by older users, it needs to offer facilities for making the interaction easier, or even possible. On the other hand, teenagers and kids are more prone to accept using new technology. For instance, teenagers tend to enjoy the use of mobile phone since it enables them to stay in touch with friends, and use a current technology to be part of this fashion trend. [8].

To address the inter-generational gap among younger and older members of a social network, several research projects propose technological solutions with different approaches. The Message Center is a system that aims to support cross-generational communication between elders and younger family. It enables elders to handwrite or typewrite to compose a message and then send it to an email, cell phone (SMS), PDA, or fax machine. The system can also receive messages from those devices in printed form [6]. The 'Keep in Touch' audio messaging system (or KiT) is an inter-generational communication appliance. The system aims to facilitate communication among the very young and very old people, the technically illiterate and the simply pre-literate. The KiT system involves a small-form-factor PC and a touch screen. In order to send a message using KiT, the user touches a portrait and the system starts recording a message [5]. Finally, the Age Invaders game was proposed with the aim to facilitate family entertainment [11]. It is an interactive social-physical game that allows the elderly to play together with children in physical space while parents can participate in the game play in real time through the internet. The game offers adaptable game parameters to automatically compensate for potential elderly disadvantages, for example slower reaction time and slow movement. This system promotes the intergenerational interaction through a game.

Our proposal aims to cope with the diversity of family members by enabling them to interact anytime and from anywhere through a pervasive system as explained in the following sections.

4   System Design

We identify the desirable features of our pervasive system in order to address the findings presented in section 2. These features have to deal with: the need of communicating family members that are geographically distributed, have different ages, computer literacy, and technology preferences.

4.1 Desirable Features of the System

For dealing with the distributed location of the elders' family members we propose that our system:

- provides mechanisms for creating and maintaining a distributed social network through collaborative activities. We propose to deal with this feature by providing a collaborative game that encourages older adults to incorporate themselves to their family network while coping with their cognitive decline.
- enables a synchronous interaction and communication among the family members playing the game who are geographically distributed.
- To deal with the diversity of the family members who may be very young or very old, technically illiterate or simply pre-literate, and have different technology preferences, we propose the system have the following features:
- As older adults tend to be left out of the social networks supported by communication technology due their lack of computer skills, they need mechanisms integrated to their home environment that enable them to be aware when their relatives are interacting through the system. To do this, we propose that the system provides context-aware notification mechanisms that let elders to know when their family members are playing.
- To facilitate the interaction with the system, it needs to provide appropriate interfaces that can be accessed from different devices. This will let users to select the interaction device that they consider more appropriate according to their ages, preferences and computer skills.
- Finally, it is desirable that the system can be easily extended to enable the integration of other pervasive devices. To do this we need to design a system flexible enough to allow its extension.

4.2 Scenario of Use

Our proposal is based in a previous work, the Electronic Family Newspaper, presented in [9], which was conceived with the aim to strength the relationships among elders and their relatives living abroad. In this paper we present an extension of this system in order to enable users to interact through the Memory Game provided by this system. To illustrate how we propose family members can interact through this game, (see Fig. 1), we present the following scenario of use:

Jose, a 10 year-old boy, lives in Tijuana, Mexico. This afternoon, he has accessed the Entertainment section of the Electronic Family Newspaper to play the Memory Game through his video game console. Mr. Juan is Jose's grandfather, who lives in Colima, Mexico and while Mr. Juan is watching the T.V., a message is displayed on it notifying him that his grandson Jose is playing the Memory Game. Mr Juan decides to join the game by using the remote control of his T.V. When his wife realizes that they are playing, she also decides to join the game, but she prefers using the tangible interface to interact with the system. The Memory Game is personalized according to the users' preferences by setting the game features.

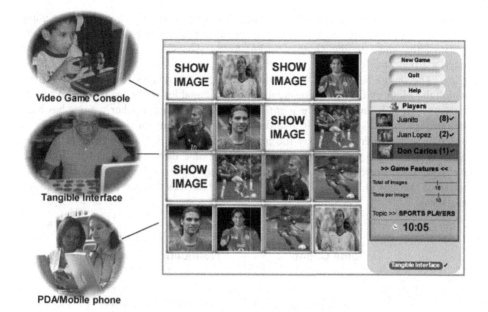

Fig. 1. Grandfather, daughter and grandson playing with the Memory Game

4.3 System Architecture

To facilitate the evolution of the Electronic Family Newspaper, it was conceived as a Multi-agent system. Following with this implementation paradigm, we also propose that the main components of the game system be autonomous agents that decide when and how to act. As presented in Figure 2, some of the agents will act as assistant agents that facilitate the users interaction with the system (such as, the Game Display Agent), other agents will hide a complex functionality of the system (such as the Game Control Agent), and finally, other agents will act as a proxy to system resources (such as the Image Repository (IR) proxy-agent).

The system architecture consists of three nodes. The *Agent Broker* that handles communication between agents which represent users, services and devices. Information is communicated through XML messages [12]. The implementation of this service is based on the Jabber open-source instant messaging which stores the state of people and agents and notifies their changes to other agents subscribed to them.

The *Game Server* contains the agents that will create and manage the game. The *Game Client* facilitates the interaction with the system of the diversity of users that may want to play the game through different interaction devices. The Game Client can be any device used of interacting with the system, for instance a Tablet PC or a PDA. Finally, the Notification Client enables elders to receive messages inviting him to join the game. We are considered that elders can receive notifications on his T.V, in this case the Notification Client will be a set-top box. Thus, the following are the autonomous agents of the system that are distributed among these nodes:

The *Game Control Agent* creates and manages the game by controlling the game sessions, control floor and replicating the game to all users by sending the current view of the game to the *Game Display Agent*. The Game Display Agent has an interface that enables designers to add devices that can be used to interact with the game. The *Image Repository Agent-proxy* manages the Images Repository (IR) from which the Memory Game will be created. Thus, it enables the Game Control Agent to recover images from the IR. The *Notification Agent* is aware of when a game has been initiated and who is playing. It also detects the availability of the elders' devices in order to select where to display the message in order to invite the elder to join the game by sending a notification message to his home device, such as the T.V. This message is received by the *Notification Display Agent*. This component has an interface that has to be specialized in order to add devices that can receive notification messages.

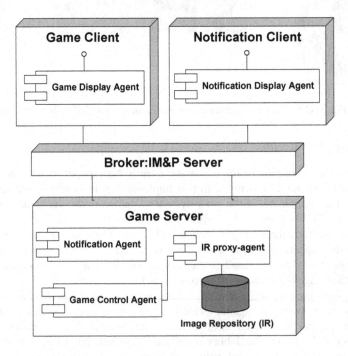

Fig. 2. System's components

5   Application Scenario

To explain the functionality of the proposed system, we present in Fig. 3 how the systems' components interact in order to support the scenario presented in section 4.2:

When Jose, a 10 years-old boy, accesses the Memory Game through his video game console, the Game Display Agent sends its presence to the agents subscribed to it. This indicates to the Game Control Agent that a new game session has started. Then it requests to the IR Proxy-agent to recover the images of the preferred character of Jose in order to create the Memory Game which is sent to the Game Display Agent to be displayed for Jose. The Game Display Agent notifies its presence and new state (playing) in order the other system' agents and users can be aware that Jose is playing. This presence is received by the Notification Agent, which checks which users are online or which devices are available. It detects that the T.V. of Jose's grandfather is turned on. Then the Notification Agent invites Jose's grandfather to start playing with Jose by sending a notification message to the Notification Display Agent to be displayed on the T.V. Finally, Jose's grandfather decides to join the game by using the T.V. remote control or any other interaction device of his preference, such as a tangible interface.

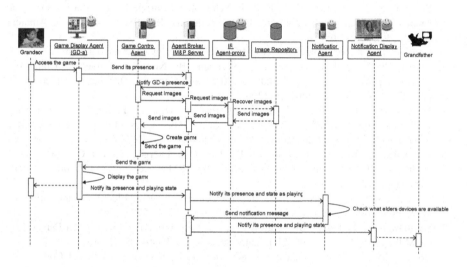

Fig. 3. Interaction of the system's agents

6   Conclusions and Future Work

In this paper we have presented evidence of the importance of providing technological support to reduce the generational gap between family members of different ages and technical skills. We consider that in order for older adults adopt a new communication technology, it has to be easy to use and helps them to be added to the current technologically-supported networks of their younger relatives. Thus, our technological solution aims to facilitate elders can be integrated to the current family networks supported by communication technology. This will help elders to reduce their social isolation which have a negative impact on their cognitive decline.

Our solution consists in a system that provides collaborative activities that encourage family members to spend time together by using the pervasive interaction devices appropriate for their age and computer skills. To explore this solution we have presented the design of a collaborative Memory Game that provides mechanisms to enable elders to be easily integrated to the family social network. Before implementing our system, we plan to conduct a usability evaluation with older persons using different interaction interfaces, such as Tablet PC, a tangible interface, and an interactive T.V. Based on the evaluation results, we will modify the current game interface by adding some of the interaction interfaces that resulted more appropriate for elders.

Acknowledgments. This work was supported by CONACYT. We would also like to thank the families that participated in the case study.

References

1. Steg, H., Strese, H., Loroff, C., Hull, J., Schmidt, S.: Europe Is Facing a Demographic Challenge:Ambient Assisted Living Offers Solutions. IST Project Report on Ambient Assisted Living (March 2006)
2. Consejo Nacional de Población (CONAPO) (2005), http://www.conapo.gob.mx/
3. Morris, M., Lundell, J., Dishman, E., Needham, B.: New Perspectives on Ubiquitous Computing from Ethnographic Study of Elders with Cognitive Decline. In: Ubicomp'03, pp. 227–242. Springer, Heidelberg (2003)
4. Isaacs, E.A., Tang, J.C., Morris, T.: Piazza: A Desktop Environment Supporting Impromptu and Planned Interactions. In: ACM Proceedings of Computer Supported Cooperative Work '96, Cambridge MA, USA, pp. 315–324 (1996)
5. Langdale, G., Kay, J., Kummerfeld, B.: Using an Intergenerational Communications System as a 'Light-weight' Technology Probe. In: ACM Proceedings of CHI'06, Montreal, Canada, pp. 1001–1006 (April 2006)
6. Wiley, J., Sung, J., Abowd, G.: The Message Center: Enhancing Elder Communication. In: ACM Proceedings of CHI'06, Montreal, Canada, pp. 1523-1528 (April 2006)
7. Kurniawan, S., Mahmud, M.: A Study of the Use of Mobile Phones by Older Persons. In: ACM Proceedings of CHI'06, Montreal, Canada, pp. 989–994 (April 2006)
8. Ito, M.: Mobile Phones, Japanese Youth, and the Re-Placement of Social Contact. In: Proceedings of Annual Meeting for the Society for the Social Studies of Science, Cambridge, MA (2001)
9. Gonzalez, V.M., Rodriguez, M.D., Santana, P.C., Favela, J., Castro, L.A.: Supporting Relationships Maintenance for Elders and Family Living Abroad. IEEE Pervasive Computing, Mobile and Ubiquitous Systems. Special Issue on Emerging Economies 5(2), 47 (2006)
10. Magnusson, L., Hanson, E., Borg, M.: A literature review study of information and communication technology as a support for frail older people living at home and their family carers. Technology and Disability 16, 223–235 (2004)
11. Khoo, E.T., Lee, S.P., Cheok, A.D., Kodagoda, S., Zhou, Y., Toh, G.S.: Age Invaders: Social and Physical Inter-Generational Family Entertainment. In: ACM Proceedings of CHI'06, Montreal, Canada, pp. 243–246 (April 2006)
12. Rodriguez, M.D., Favela, J., Preciado, A., Vizcaino, A.: Agent-based ambient intelligence for healthcare. In: AI Communications vol. 18(3), pp. 201–216. IOS Press, Amsterdam (2005) ISSN: 0921-7126

Sharing Stories: Learning with Stories

Nina Sabnani

Faculty, National Institute of Design
Ahmedabad, India

Abstract. The *e-kaavad* is inspired by the thousand year old *Kaavad* storytelling tradition in Rajasthan, India. The *Kaavad* is a travelling temple that came to the village with the storyteller, as not everyone had access to a temple. The *Kaavad* is a story box that has several doors that open up to reveal painted stories from the 'Great' epics and the 'Little' traditions. As the story evolves, the teller opens one door at a time and reveals the next part of the story. The last door opens to reveal the presiding deities, which ends the story session. The inspiration is its form as well as what it stood for; to take the school to the children if they don't have access to the school themselves. This paper presents the process by which the *e-kaavad* has been developed in form and content and how it has been received so far.

Keywords: Inclusive, Storytelling, traditional *Kaavad*, elementary education, self-learning, harnessing technology.

1 Introduction

Fig. 1.

Once upon a time in India, when there was no television, no cinema or even radio, there were stories. When there were no e-learning sites, no universities or even schools, there were teachers. These teachers were none other than the storytellers. These tellers travelled from place to place; mesmerizing audiences, triggering their imagination and curiosity and leaving them to draw the essence themselves from the stories told and to find their place in their own lives. These stories could be verbal and non-verbal. Painting, music and dancing were often integral to the telling and may have also included chanting and playing of instruments. These traditions may well have been the precursor to cinema and animation as several countries share similar forms of oral narratives such as story scrolls, puppets, dance drama amongst others. In India, telling and listening to stories was traditionally considered

N. Aykin (Ed.): Usability and Internationalization, Part II, HCII 2007, LNCS 4560, pp. 460–468, 2007.
© Springer-Verlag Berlin Heidelberg 2007

very sacred. Even today, amongst believers, it is very auspicious and sacred to hear and tell stories from the great epics. Such is the power of story that it often dissolves borders between the real and the virtual. One such tradition of storytelling is still alive in Rajasthan, India. This tradition know as the *Kaavad* recitation is on the edge of oblivion and can only survive if all stakeholders give it a new lease of life. (Fig. 1)

1.1 The *Kaavad* Tradition

Kaavad the term: The word *Kaavad* comes from the word *'Kivad'* meaning door (Bharucha) and the shrine does consist of several panels that open up like many doors. It consists of several wooden panels hinged together that are painted with images from the epics and other stories. There are also images of donors and local/folk heroes and heroines (Bhanawat). Interestingly, there are three kinds of persons from different times (mythical, historical, present) depicted on the same space (panel). The persons depicted are the Gods, the saints and normal mortals from all castes, all sharing the same space which in real life was denied to persons of different castes. The representations merge time and space here as a single vertical column in space divides different times. There is a sense of travelling inside a real temple as the panels open and close simulating the various thresholds in a temple, starting with the *dwarpals* (doorkeepers) and seated lions. The storytellers use painting, narration and gesture to tell stories from the Hindu epics of the *Mahabharata* and the *Ramayana* as well as about local heroes. The storytellers collaborate with a visual artist to create images onto the story boxes to assist the telling. Traditionally, the storyteller known as the *Kaavadiya Bhat* performed the role of record keepers, priest, entertainer, informer and teacher all in one. The painted images on the *Kaavad* serve as mnemonics for events from the epics and endorse the storyteller's claims to the occurrence of the events. The storyteller uses a peacock feather as a pointing device to validate his claim and uses the same image to tell different stories each time. The whole experience is multi-sensory as it begins with the lighting of an incense stick, followed by singing and narration and the storyteller pointing at the images and opening the door like panels to reveal the gods in the sanctum sanctorum. Finally the narration ends with the patron providing blessed food *(prasadam)* to all gathered. All gathered include persons from all castes and social standing. Like the 'Lota', the *Kaavad* could not have been made by one person, (Eames) but by several individuals over a long period of time to arrive at its magical form.

1.2 The Situation Today

Today, the *Kaavads* are being made for the tourism industry as well as the export market. The traditional *Kaavad* makers of Bassi and other middlemen who have entered the arena are busy making *Kaavads* to order, including those on various other subjects like the life of Jesus Christ, Meerabai, Prithviraj Chauhan, Mahavir etc. They rarely make them for the traditional client, the storyteller *Kaavadiya,* and the link between the maker and teller has weakened to a degree that some makers don't even know where the storytellers may be found. The storytelling device, the *Kaavad,* has been rendered mute and the storyteller has decided to hide his identity although it has been said that they do perform for their patrons, far away from their own homes

(Bharucha). However, there is an emergence of new tellers who have seen its potential to communicate.

1.3 *Kaavad* Inspired Work

The *Kaavad* form has inspired Vikalp Design, an NGO from Rajasthan to introduce young adults to sex education. The two parts or doors of the panels represent man and woman. Each side then provides its own private space to understand the inner workings of the body, while considering it all sacred. A design student has translated the *Kaavad* form onto a folding book, which allows it to be opened in different ways. The content of the book is again, sex education for young adults in Rajasthan. The folk museum, *Lok Kala Mandal* in Udaipur has encouraged the use of *Kaavads* for adult education, health awareness for pregnant women by initiating the making of *Kaavads* with these themes and also training potential storytellers. It was observed that information brought to the people in their traditional form was accepted more easily and enhanced credibility. This then formed the basis for exploring the *Kaavad* as a self-learning device.

1.4 e-*Kaavad*

The idea of a mobile temple has thus inspired the use of the *Kaavad* as an interactive learning experience for elementary education. Just the way, the temple came to the devotees; the *e-kaavad* comes to the student. The e-*kaavad* uses the current technologies and new media to bring quality education to all, without distinction, without any barriers of language, religion or economic status. The *e-kaavad* is a self-learning interactive haptic device. It provides an environment for learning through story-telling. The *e-kaavad* is a compact 53cm x 51cm x 15.5cm wooden box. It houses a monitor, keyboard and the necessary circuitry to enable it to be connected to a computer CPU. The box is made up of collapsible wooden frames. Each frame has a number of touch sensors attached to it. These touch sensors are connected to the keyboard such that when activated they simulate a

Fig. 2.

keyboard input to the CPU. In the front of the sensors are thin cardboard panels consisting of colourful pictures. When any of these pictures are pressed the associated story begins to play on the monitor of the *e-kaavad*. Various animated stories are created and stored in the CPU. The picture panels have the possibility of being changed and replaced by other images (fig.2). The design of the *e-kaavad* is such that it is easily portable and has the potential to be used in various indoor or outdoor locations. This indigenous design provides children as well as adults with a wonderful interface to learn interactively. It is a tool highly suitable for use in the rural India for education, health etc. One of the most powerful features of the *e-kaavad* is that it also gives the user an opportunity to create their own stories on the associated panels to make the whole experience more participatory.

It may be suitable at this point to briefly discuss the elementary education environment that continues to provide the brief and directions for future research and development. And in this case of the *e-kaavad* it was obvious that the brief for content and interaction could only emerge with the involvement of all the stakeholders which included the students, the teachers, parents, school principals, policy makers and NGOs who offer alternate education.

2 Elementary Education and Digital Technology

The New Media technologies are being used as a new means of communication, which are growing rapidly. Some of the issues that this global media is bringing into full focus are the role of education to empower and inform; the role of design towards making the reach more accessible for a people-centric technology. The New Media promise a rich, truly democratic future. A future where there will be quality education for all, regardless of distance or time. Designers can bring in their expertise to map the quality education onto the digital platform so that it is available to many. For that to happen, there needs to be a hiatus between the educators and designers that will allow them to collaborate successfully.

2.1 Research

A six-month research project was thus carried out by the National Institute of Design, Ahmedabad to assess the use of digital technology in schools. The primary research tools included interviews, learning hand-outs and focus group discussions. One hundred and fifty respondents were contacted in the cities of Ahmedabad and Delhi as one provided the local situation and the other an understanding from the centre where most decision making bodies are located. The attempt was also to comprehend the needs and requirements in the area of digital technology from the point of view of the children themselves. It also took into consideration any difference in opinion based on the city, urban and peri-urban areas, across gender, age, language and socio-economic category. In the assessment study, girls and boys, children from upper, middle and lower class schools, those from Hindi, English and Gujarati medium schools were included. Their individual opinions regarding fun, games, teaching, storytelling and the use of digital technology for elementary education were considered to arrive at the final conclusion. The first prototype of *e-kaavad* was tested in the urban and rural environment.

2.2 Research Findings

The objective of this research was to first have an understanding of the current scenario of elementary education in the country and how the stakeholders felt about the use of digital technologies. A study like this could help designers meaningfully participate in contributing towards fulfilling the constitutional right of every child to be educated. The salient findings of this study were as follows:

- While most children are aware of mobile phones, digital cameras, DVDs and the wider implications of digital technology, most understand it best in the context of computers. The same holds true for most teachers, parents and policymakers. It will take another couple of years for people to understand it in all its ramifications.
- The opportunity of moving away from standard delivery mechanisms has led to the fast adoption of digital technology at the elementary school level. Children are more technology savvy today and this is evident from the ease with which they handle even other gadgets that they confront for the first time.
- In almost all schools, computers are taught at the elementary level only as a supplement to the main curriculum and not as a subject. The computer curriculum does not include any level of programming but only usage of readymade software to create visual imagery around contexts and lessons being taught.
- Customised software is used to familiarise children with development of logical thought, following directions and motor coordination. Children from standard first to fifth are taught to use different programmes like Paint Brush, Crayolla, Kid Pics, Learner Rabbit, Logo different Levels, Linux, Opening-Shutting files, Level One of MS Word, Power Point, making Folders, MS Excel, Introduction to Basic language, Simple Programming, Emailing, accessing information from Internet and Websites, Drag and Drop software and Multimedia Presentations.
- Self-learning is encouraged to help the child overcome initial inhibitions and then develop confidence in working with the computer towards pre-set goals. Hands on experience with "a world of information at their finger tips" the child feels empowered. Guided usage of computers is encouraged at all levels to simplify the process of sifting and sourcing information through the Internet.
- The importance of using innovative techniques was stressed by all respondents, parents, teachers as also school principals across categories. Even the Government position was to make education joyful to attract more children, reduce the dropout rate and increase retention. The rationale for innovation was to maintain curiosity levels in children; a child's right to grow and learn in an environment that is friendly and fun, to keep a child's interests alive and to encourage "free flight of thoughts".

Some innovative techniques stressed by all were:

Activity based teaching that promotes self-learning, Holistic learning, integrated learning, Storytelling method, Demonstration method, Visualisation method, Project method, Multi-sensory approach, Multi-modal approach, Learning associated with real-life situation, Theme learning, Participatory learning, Interactive learning and Learning by doing.

Besides this there was also focus on social responsibility, making children aware of their duties and not just their rights. The stress was on achieving a balance between pursuit of the material needs and inculcation of values and respect and concern for the environment in which they lived. Spreading environment consciousness and generating awareness on alternate energy sources and to build a more responsible attitude towards the ecological system was another recurring concern. Most schools have structured programmes that attempt to reach the disadvantaged section of the society. Well funded schools use their infrastructure to reach out directly to underprivileged children from their immediate neighbourhood or associating with NGOs for the same.

2.3 Use of Storytelling in Elementary Education

The research also involved a focused study of the use of storytelling in schools and the response to the *e-kaavad* and the findings were as follows:

- Stories are being used as teaching aids in an attempt to make classroom teaching more enjoyable. Children are encouraged to read out stories in class and these sessions serve to build children's imagination, sharpen creative skills, structured thinking, language skills, pronunciation, writing skills, value system, strengthen basic concepts and being an interactive process help children overcome their inhibitions, stage fright and build confidence.
- Stories on current affairs are commonly made with a view to provide general knowledge and to create awareness about what is happening in the world around and often to help the child handle difficult situations like family problems, social and political problems like communal riots and natural calamities like an earthquake.
- Innovative learning through stories must be complemented by games to ensure holistic personality development. Games have the advantage of active rather than passive learning and foster interpersonal trust and also assist in nurturing team spirit.
- Children were naturally excited by the *e-kaavad*. The colours, illustrations, sound, as well as the concept appealed to them. They could follow the storyboard easily. And found it easy to handle. As a medium *e-kaavad* is full of possibilities and must be explored further.
- Computers have established themselves as an indispensable teaching and self-learning aid essentially because of their ease of operation and interactive nature. They are now being used extensively in schools and at home for information gathering, knowledge enhancement and entertainment.
- Many felt the need for Indianised CDs to help children understand and relate to software better. Especially for the underprivileged children the medium has to be related to their environment.

2.4 A Model for the *e-Kaavad*

Based on the above findings a model thus began to take shape (Fig 3). With the child as the centre of the universe and learning as the prime intention it became apparent that one of the ways to reach learners was to offer a learning experience that was imbued with traditional knowledge and modern values, that was local using global technologies which then made it possible to scale up the reach through a carefully designed Interface that allowed users to access it at their own pace and even allowed them to customize it to their needs.

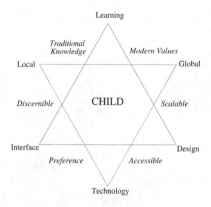

Fig. 3.

3   The Developing and Testing of the e-Kaavad

The *e-kaavad* evolved over several iterations and continues its journey beyond the initial user group of children to also reach out to rural crafts persons. At each stage the endeavour was to use the inclusive approach of story, its innate interactivity, and use of technology for a wider reach.

3.1 The First Prototype

The first prototype was made with ordinary thermocol with touch sensors wired on the inside and covered with painted images of animals on the outside. The *e-kaavad* was then attached to the CPU which was hidden from the user. Children were invited to touch the animals and as soon as they did that, the animal made a sound. The surprise pleased the children and they touched the entire animal images one after the other. Once the excitement of hearing all the animals was over, the students lost interest. When asked what more would they want it do they all said they would like to see them animated. This response was the same from the rural and urban children. For the initial test the *e-kaavad* was taken to the 'Floating School', a school set up for the children of salt miners near a village Dhrangadhra

Fig. 4.

near Ahmedabad. The response of the children there was similar to the one from children in an English medium school in Ahmedabad. They all wanted the images to be animated (Fig 4 and 5). The sensors were too delicate and the material too fragile. What was needed was a hardier material that could cope with the children's enthusiasm to touch and open doors and press all buttons.

Fig. 5.

3.2 The Second Prototype

The next prototype consisted of a wooden box not unlike the original *Kaavad* although it did not have as many panels. Based on the findings content was developed around the animals and each animal told something about itself when it was touched. An LCD monitor was placed inside so the animation could be viewed on this (Fig 6). This was tested in an exhibition India 2020 held at NID (National Institute of Design) and found a larger acceptance. Consequently several meetings were held with elementary school teachers from around Ahmedabad and Gandhi-nagar from the municipal schools under the District Primary Education Programme and the *Sarva Shiksha Abhiyaan.* It became clearer with every meeting that for the *e-kaavad* to find a useful long life it had to be adopted by its prime users, the students and the teachers. While the students seemed ready the teachers eyed it with interest but also a faint distrust. They could not at first understand

Fig. 6.

how designers could make learning material for students of elementary education, a user-group that the teachers understood better. It was only after they were convinced that they were to be active partners in the development of content that a vibrant collaboration began to emerge and make way for a wider platform where the role of the designer was that of creating systems not products.

3.3 The *e-Kaavad* for Rural Crafts Persons

The potential of the *e-kaavad* to be connected online presented a possibility to be also used for networking between crafts persons based in the rural areas with their clients in the urban settings. The *e-kaavad* could provide a user-friendly interface that could allow them to communicate, send images and movies to clarify briefs and communicate from their own power bases.

4 Conclusion

The journey from the shrine to a haptic device is not as long as the one from the first one door shrine to its many panelled one as that evolved with cultural changes over time. However, the journey of the *e-kaavad,* from its first prototype to its current form is far from over. The content builders need to work closely with technologists and designers and other stakeholders. The spirit of the *Kaavad* then lives on as that too evolved with close collaborations between the makers, the tellers and the patrons.

References

1. Bhanawat, M.: Kaavad. Lok Kala Mandal. Udaipur (1975)
2. Bharucha, R.R.: An Oral History. Penguins India (2003)
3. Das, U.: Qualitative Assessment of the use of Digital Technology in Primary Education, A Report. National Institute of Design. Ahmedabad, India (2004)
4. Eames, C.: The India Report. Government of India (1958)

The Digital Packaging of Electronic Money

Supriya Singh

Smart Internet Technology Cooperative Research Centre/RMIT University
Supriya.singh@rmit.edu.au

Abstract. In this paper I examine how money is digitally packaged (or not packaged) and its influence on the meaning of the gift and remittance. Remittances received by developing nations in 2005 were an estimated $US167 billion. These, together with gifts for ceremonial occasions demonstrate the importance of money as a medium of personal relationships. Gifts in particular have been wrapped in distinctive ways to express their ritual meanings. This wrapping of gifts has not easily translated to digital media. In this paper I draw on personal experience and participant observation in India, Malaysia and Australia. This is supplemented by literature, and content analysis of websites dealing with gifts and remittances.

Keywords: electronic money, digital wrapping, gifts, remittances.

1 Introduction: Money as a Gift

The ritual of gifting money is one of the most visible differences across cultures. In Anglo-Celtic society in Australia, the United Kingdom and the United States, there is a deep opposition between cash and gifts. Cash is seen as impersonal and tied to the market and therefore an unsuitable medium for the expression of personal, spontaneous feelings. In Anglo-Celtic society gifts of cash have traditionally been accepted from grandparents and sometimes from parents [11]. With the rising costs of education and housing, there has been an increase in parents gifting money to children

In Australia, there is a growing acceptance of cash as a gift, but in most cases, cash is only acceptable if it is transformed into gift certificates, tokens that sometimes come in their own boxes, or more recently generalized gift cards which work as electronic wallets. The use of the wedding registry or wish list is making the cash value of gifts more transparent.

At the same time, increasing de facto (oohabiting) relationships and re-marriage are making gift giving more fraught. Traditional wedding gifts to help set up the home are no longer suitable. Twelve per cent of Australian couples in 2001 were in de facto relationships [4]. The more telling statistic is that nearly three-fourths (72%) of people who got married had lived in a de facto relationship in 2001 [7]. Divorce and remarriage have also increased. In 1997, one third (33%) of all marriages involved a person who had previously been married, compared to 14 per cent in 1967 [3]. In the early 21st century in Australia, a person is most likely to go into a de facto relationship of about two years, get married though not necessarily to the same partner, have

N. Aykin (Ed.): Usability and Internationalization, Part II, HCII 2007, LNCS 4560, pp. 469–475, 2007.

children, may get divorced after 12 years, become single again, go into a de facto relationship again, re-marry and be part of a step or blended family [13].

Glenis Henderson, a friend of mine in Melbourne, has seen these changes take place in her life. Glenis is Anglo-Celtic, middle income and married for 40 years to the same partner. She and her husband have three daughters. The first two had traditional marriages, in that both husband and wife were marrying for the first time, without a prior de facto relationship. The third daughter, Elizabeth, recently married Steve who had been married before. Elizabeth used to have her own place. Steve had a house of his own. The last thing they wanted was another set of china. So Glenis who had never given money as a gift before, composed and sent the following doggerel in November 2005 to family and friends with the wedding invitation.

> Whatever shall we give them?
> It's a question asked a lot
> When a couple like our Liz and Steve
> Are about to tie the knot.
> They've lived in separate houses
> And collected many a thing.
> So we have formed a plan to help you
> Know just what you can bring.
>
> We hope you think our idea great
> And decide that you'll participate
> By placing in an envelope
> An amount you'll feel is best
> To help this happy couple
> Feather their own little nest.
>
> At Ashton Manor, we'll provide
> A little wishing well.
> Just place your wedding gift inside
> And enjoy the day with our groom and bride....

After some shocked reactions from Glenis' network, 95 per cent gave cash in plain envelopes in the wishing well. She says the cash amount was less than what the guests would probably have spent on gifts[1]. In due time, I received a thank you note from the couple, saying that the cash I had gifted went towards the construction of their new car port. This wedding did not set a trend of receiving cash as gifts. Glenis has only had one other similar request. It was her nephew's wedding and he and his partner had been in a de facto partnership. They requested that people contribute to their honeymoon flight by directing their money to a designated travel agency.

Though Glenis was making up the rules responding to changes in relationships, in other societies, cash is the mandatory gift at marriages, births and deaths. In India, at a recent family wedding, there was a special occasion just before lunch where the guests were photographed as they gave their gifts of money (*shagun*) or sometimes

---

[1] Personal communication, Glenis Henderson, 14 November 2006.

other gifts. The shagun from family members came before the wedding and would be expected to be more substantial than from non-family guests. It is not only the bride and the groom who receive the shagun but also their parents, most often the mother. Every family has a different arrangement as to whether the shagun will be used to defray wedding expenses or will be gifted to the couple.

The amount of money is carefully thought out. The minimum condition is that it reflect reciprocity, and be in tune with gifts previously received. The closeness of the relationship and the financial condition of the household is also a factor. In North India, the preference used to be for ritual odd numbers, such as Rs 21, Rs 51, Rs 101, Rs 501. But with the one rupee having no substantial monetary value, and sometimes difficult to find, the gift is more likely to be in even numbers. The ritual significance of number is also found with the Chinese ang-pow given at Chinese New Year, weddings and births. The ang-pow should ideally end with an eight, for it sounds like fortune or a nine, as it sounds like longevity [6].

2 Wrapping Gift Money

The wrapping of gifts is in many Western cultures and in Japan, an important part of gift giving. Similarly, in cultures where money is a preferred gift, ceremonially wrapping cash is part of the ritual of gift giving. The wrapping of cash transforms money from a unit of value and a medium of exchange to a medium of relationship. As Poster [10] says there is an important distinction between "communicational efficiency" and the "configuration of communication exchange". He says "Changes in the configuration or wrapping of language alters the way the subject processes signs into meanings" (p. 11).

In New Delhi, it is possible to buy colorful and patterned gift envelopes for the *shagun* – the ritual presentation for weddings and births. They used to come with a one rupee coin stuck on the outside. Automated Teller Machines (ATMs) are popular sources of cash for they dispense clean, crisp notes. In Japan too, some ATMs deodorise and clean the notes before delivering them [1]. Parents, grandparents and relatives traditionally give children "otoshidama" - presents of money in colourful packets for the New Year [2]. In Pakistan, garlands of currency as wedding gifts are openly sold.

Amongst the Simunul Bajaus of Sabah, Malaysia, cash is the most appropriate gift from most of the guests at weddings or funerals. Gifts of cash are taken into account when planning the expenditure. In order for the receiver to keep a record, this cash is often presented in envelopes with the giver's name on the outside. Sometimes, the cash is elaborately transformed, as with the payment of bride-price (the money that is paid by the groom). At one particularly ostentatious wedding in the late 1970s, the MR 3,000 was arranged in the shape of the National Mosque. At another wedding, the money was arranged in floral designs with the red of ten ringgit notes and the green of the fifty ringgit notes being carefully matched[12].

2.1 The Ang-Pow

My children in the Malaysia of the 1970s and 1980s used to look forward to Chinese New Year. This was not only for the sticky cakes made for the Kitchen God, but also because they would collect the red ang-pow packets given to all children. Even though we were not Chinese, we too had to take many ang-pows to distribute at the Chinese New Year functions. The packet would most often contain only MR5, but the notes were always new and crisp. Banks not only had a separate counter to distribute the traditional red envelopes for the ang-pow but also ensured they had a supply of crisp new notes during Chinese New Year.

The ang-pow is also a traditional gift for parents at the birth of a child, and for the bride and groom at their wedding. Ang-pows are also used to pay for services, such as from feng shui experts, moving the service beyond a purely contractual relationship.

The ang-pow is always red in colour, as the Chinese see red "as a protective colour, representing auspiciousness, prosperity, and with the power to exorcise evil spirits" [6]. The packet is illustrated with symbols of prosperity and longevity portraying, for example, the God of Wealth and the God of Longevity. Newer symbols include three or nine carps swimming among flowering lotuses, the dragon and the phoenix, peonies in full bloom, the three Immortals, golden pineapples or Chinese zodiac animals [6].

According to Cheah (2006), the ang-pow has crossed ethnic boundaries in Malaysia. Malays/Muslims give money to young children during Syawal (the month of Ramadan, ending with Hari Raya) in green packets decorated with Islamic motifs. Even Deepavali cash gifts come in ang-pow sized packets, but with distinctive Indian motifs.

3 Remittances: Sending Money Home

Remittances sent by family members overseas are an increasingly important way to express continuing membership of the natal or nuclear family. The World Bank estimates international remittances received by developing countries were $US167 billion in 2005 [14]. The top two countries in 2004 receiving remittances were India ($US21.7 billion) and China ($US21.3 billion) [14]. The formal figure for remittances may underestimate remittances by as much as 20 to 80 per cent, because many of these are sent through informal channels [5].

Remittances have been part of family support by family members who have moved out, either within the country, or increasingly, overseas. The quantum has risen with the increase in migration and the economic prosperity of migrants, particularly in the United States.

Remittances can come via the bank, or by money transfer that can be collected at the post office. New technologies are increasingly used, such as ATMs, direct transfer through the bank branch or via mobile phone. However, it is important not to under-estimate cash remittances via couriers, money transfer agents, or informal transfer.

3.1 Sending Money Home Via the Mobile Phone

The Philippines leads the world in the use of mobile phone to transmit remittances. Smart Communications, the largest mobile phone company in the Philippines together with other remittance partners, began its Smart remittance via a text message in 2004. Globe Telecom is also expected to enter the market [9, 14].

Smart Communications' partners include McDonald's, SM malls, SeaOil gas stations, Travelex Money Transfer, Forex International Hong Kong, Dollar America Exchange in California, CBN Grupo in Greece, Ireland, Japan, Spain, and the United Kingdom, New York Bay Remittance, and Banco de Oro Bank in Hong Kong, China. This network allows migrant workers to cheaply transmit their remittances. In Hong Kong, China, the fee is about $2. In the Philippines, the transaction costs one per cent plus the fee for the text message. The transaction is also secured by the need for a different PIN for the mobile phone and the Smart account. Moreover an ID is required when collecting cash. [14]

The Smart remittance works as follows [14]:

> A Filipino in Hong Kong, China, deposits money to be remitted with one of Smart's remittance partners, which then sends a text message to the beneficiary in the Philippines, informing him or her of the transfer. The remittance is credited into a Smart Money "electronic wallet" account by any Smart mobile customer. The money can be withdrawn from an ATM using the Smart Money cash card, which can also be used as a debit card for purchases (p. 150).

4   Designing for the Digital Wrapping of Gifts and Remittances

Though there is a greater use of digital channels for sending remittances, digital money is not ritually wrapped. There is no equivalent to the electronic greeting card. Even cash received via the post office, courier or the bank is not ritually wrapped.. It is an obvious area where social and cultural centered design can highlight the emotional and ritual element in the gifting and remitting of digital money. The following scenario illustrates how digital money can be transformed into a digital gift.

4.1   A Digital Ang-Pow

Eng Lin, 23, from Kuala Lumpur in Malaysia is studying at a university in Melbourne. She is supported by her parents and gets a monthly remittance for her living expenses. This year, she is feeling particularly homesick as she is unable to go home for Chinese New Year. She is going to miss the New Year Eve dinner with her extended family, with her grandmother saying "Man, man cher" – eat slowly. She will miss the dragon dances and the sound of fireworks. And she won't get the red ang-pows.

Eng Lin knows her family is thinking of her. On her mobile phone, she receives a text message from the bank wishing her *Kong Hee Fatt Choy*, that is, wishing her a prosperous New Year. With the message are three red ang-pows. Her parents had sent her an ang-pow; her Uncle No. 1 had sent her another ang-pow and her grandmother had also remembered her. Her eyes misted.

The next day she goes to her bank branch to the Gift Money counter. The teller wishes her a Happy Chinese New Year and hands her three ang-pows, each with a message. She does not open the ang-pows. For the moment, it is enough to hold them, and think of her family.

Later, in her room, she opens the ang-pows and sees her parents and Uncle No 1 have each sent her $A100. Her grandmother has sent her $50. She puts the money back in the ang-pow packets. She wants to keep the money separate for it is special ang-pow money. She does not want this money to get mixed up with her living expenses. Later, she will decide how to spend her ang-pow money in a way which will remind her of Chinese New Year in Melbourne.

Eng Lin called her parents and Uncle No. 1 and her grandmother wishing them *Kong Hee Fatt Choy*. She told them, "I have never had a bank teller wish me Happy Chinese New Year. And when I looked inside, the notes were crisp and new, just like at home."

Eng Lin began to plan sending an ang-pow through the bank to her nephew on his birthday next month.

5 Conclusion

There is a richness in the wrapping of gift money in the physical world that is not duplicated in the digital world. Reasons for the lack of ritual meaning in digital money still need to be explored. It could be because many designers of digital media themselves may not have received ritually wrapped gift money. As a result, digital money is efficient, but seldom as meaningful as the physical gifting of money between kin. Another reason may be that adding ritual meaning may distinguish the product in the first instance, but not significantly enough to influence market share.

The lack of meaningful digital money gifts also means that anthropologists have not been able to demonstrate the relevance of their insights to the designers (See [8]). There is a need for social scientists and designers to work more closely together, particularly in the early stages of design, so that digital money can have more symbolic meaning and act more effectively as a medium of relationship.

Bringing cultural meaning to the centre of digital money may also have a significant policy outcome. Ritually meaningful digital money may help increase the transparent and formal transmission of gifts and remittances. Globally, this is a desirable policy outcome for it would help combat money laundering and increase the economic transparency of remittances for the sending and receiving countries.

References

1. NSF/Tokyo Report: Control and Robotics Related Research Activities (1997)
2. Otoshidama (2006)
3. Australian Bureau of Statistics. 4102.0 - Australian Social Trends, 1999: Family Formation: Remarriage trends of divorced people, Australian Bureau of Statistics, Canberra (1999)
4. Australian Bureau of Statistics. Marriages, Australia, 2004, Australian Bureau of Statistics, Canberra, 2006, Marriages in Australia, including ethnic breakdown (2006)
5. Buencamino, L., Gorbunov, S.: Informal Money Transfer Systems: Opportunities and Challenges for Development Finance, United Nations, 2002, DESA Discussion Paper No. 26 (2002)
6. Cheah, A.: A packet of good tidings, The Penang Tourism Action Council (2006)

7. de Vaus, D.: Diversity and change in Australian families: Statistical Profiles. australian Institute of Family Studies, Melbourne (2004)
8. Dillon, A.: Why ethnography needs to show its relevance: Cultural Analysis and What Designers Need to Know -A Case of Sometimes Too Much, Sometimes Too Little, and Always Too Late. Journal of Computer Documentation 22(1), 13–17 (1998)
9. Opiniano, J.M.: Using text message to send cash: New technology transfers money cheaply and easily, Mercury News (2006)
10. Poster, M.: The Mode of Information: Postructuralism and Social Context. The University of Chicago Press, Chicago (1990)
11. Singh, S.: Marriage money: the social shaping of money in marriage and banking. Allen, Unwin, St. Leonards, NSW (1997)
12. Singh, S.: On the Sulu Sea. Angsana Publications, Kuala Lumpur (1984)
13. Singh, S., Cabraal, A.: Women, money and the bank. Financial Literacy, Banking and Identity Melbourne (2006)
14. World Bank Global Economic Prospects 2006: Economic Implications of Remittances and Migration. World Bank, Washington DC (2006)

Security Design Based on Social and Cultural Practice: Sharing of Passwords

Supriya Singh[1], Anuja Cabraal[1], Catherine Demosthenous[2], Gunela Astbrink[3], and Michele Furlong[4]

[1] Smart Internet Technology Cooperative Research Centre/RMIT University, GPO Box 2476V, Melbourne 3001, Australia
{Supriya.singh,anuja.cabraal}@rmit.edu.au
[2] Smart Internet Technology Cooperative Research Centre
[3] Smart Internet Technology Cooperative Research Centre/GSA Information Consultants, GSA Information Consultants
PO Box 1141, Toowong, QLD, 4066, Australia
g.astbrink@gsa.com.au
[4] Smart Internet Technology Cooperative Research Centre/GSA Information Consultants, GSA Information Consultants, PO Box 1141,Toowong, QLD, 4066, Australia
mfurlong@iinet.net.au

Abstract. We draw on a qualitative study of 108 people to examine the routine sharing of passwords for online banking among married and de facto couples, Aboriginal users and people with disability in Australia. The sharing of passwords goes against current banking authentication systems and consumer protection laws that require customers not to reveal their access codes to anybody, including family members. The everyday violation of these security requirements results from the lack of fit between security design and social and cultural practice, rather than a lack of security awareness. We argue for the need to go beyond individualistic user-centered design, so that social and cross-cultural practices are at the centre of the design of technologies. The need for a social and culturally centered approach to design is even more important when dealing with different notions of privacy across cultures and a culture of shared use in public and private spaces.

Keywords: Banking; security; Australia; sharing passwords, social and cultural centered design, privacy across cultures.

1 Introduction

Banking security design assumes an individual keeps his or her access codes confidential while conducting Internet transactions using a personal computer. In this paper we argue that these assumptions are against common social and cultural practices. There are multiple situations where the individual shares access codes particularly with members of the family. Internet transactions are also not always conducted on a personal computer, whether at home or in the work place. Hence we

N. Aykin (Ed.): Usability and Internationalization, Part II, HCII 2007, LNCS 4560, pp. 476–485, 2007.

are arguing that for the "effective use" of technologies, design and policy should be built on social and cultural practice.

Banks use what you know – usernames, Personal Identification Numbers (PINs) and passwords - as the first order of authentication. At times, this first order of security can be complemented by what you have (such as tokens) and who you are (biometrics). Australian banks like Westpac Banking Corporation tell consumers on their web sites not to disclose their access codes to "any third party including family, friends and institutions" [39]. If the access codes are disclosed, the consumer is not protected under the Electronic Funds Transfer Code of Conduct (2002) [5]. The Code states that the account holder is liable for losses where "the user voluntarily discloses one or more of the codes to anyone, including a family member or friend" (paragraph 5.6(a), p.14). Breaches of this confidentiality are primarily dealt with through consumer education leading to increased security awareness [3].

There is an equally strong presumption that Internet transactions will not be conducted in cyber cafes or on other publicly shared computers. Westpac drawing on material from the Australian Bankers' Association actively discourages consumers from using publicly accessed computers. Westpac says "It is important to use only a trusted and secure computer to access your Internet banking account. Using publicly shared computers, such as those at Internet cafes, is strongly discouraged"[39]. The State Bank of India has a similar warning on its site, despite the fact that for most Indians, Internet is accessed primarily via publicly shared computers. The State Bank of India while welcoming users to use Internet banking warns "However, as a matter of precaution and safety, he should avoid using PCs with public access"[35].

In Section 2 we draw on a qualitative study of 108 people in Australia to show that passwords are routinely shared in some situations by different user groups. In section 3 we draw attention to public and shared access to the Internet in India and different cultural notions of privacy. In the concluding section we build on perspectives of user centered security to propose a social and culturally centered approach to design so that security design is based on social and cultural practice.

2   The Study

We[1] conducted a qualitative study of how people deal with money and banking in the context of their relationships. This research is part of a wider project focusing on Security, Trust, Identity and Privacy in the Smart Internet Technology Cooperative Research Centre. Our qualitative study conducted between April 2005 and July 2006, covered 108 people in Melbourne, rural Victoria and Brisbane in Australia. We attempted to cover the diversity of the Australian population to understand the issues rather than to generalize. We conducted 84 open-ended interviews, two 'yarning' circles (these are more like group interviews) with six Indigenous people in Brisbane and three focus groups with 18 people with disabilities. The interviews, focus groups and yarning circles were transcribed. We used the N6 computer program for qualitative research to analyze the data and identify negative cases to ensure rigor. This meant we first broadly coded the data, then organized the data into matrices to check emerging themes in a

---

[1] We are grateful to Jan Browne, Jenine Beekhuyzen, Gabriele Hermansson, Margaret Jackson, Lesa Beel and Doug Lorman who also helped conduct the qualitative study.

transparent manner. It was a 'grounded' study in that there was a fit between data and emerging theory, rather than a testing of hypotheses [15].

2.1 Sample

The participants were accessed through personal and professional networks. The aim was to understand the issues across the major socio-economic groups in Australia, rather than to generalize. Our sample had:

- 45 men and 63 women. The high number of women was partially explained because more women were managing money particularly in the lower income households;
- Four participants were aged between 18-24; 24 aged 25-34; 28 aged 35-44; 21 aged 45-54; 18 aged 55-64; and 13 aged 65 or over. The 18-24 age group was under-represented as few of them were yet in de facto or marital relationships;
- We had a range of annual household income levels: 25 had an income below $25,000 (all dollar values are in Australian dollars); 25 between $25,000-49,999; 20 between $50,000-$74,999; ten between $75,000-$100,000; and 21 had over $100,000 a year. Seven participants did not want to disclose their household income.
- 37 participants had a Certificate or lower educational qualification, 64 had a BA or higher degree, four had other qualifications and three did not say. Of those who had a BA or higher degree, at least 11 were in IT.
- We had 70 Australians with an Anglo-Celtic background, 17 with other European heritage; 11 indigenous people (eight Australians of Aboriginal background, and three Australians from the Torres Strait Islands); six associated with Asia; and four associated with Africa and the Middle East.

2.2 Sharing Passwords

In our study, three groups of people shared banking passwords, in different social contexts. Married and de facto (cohabiting) couples who shared passwords to their individual accounts, saw it as a matter of trust and convenience. Indigenous people in remote areas shared passwords and cards to access EFTPOS and withdraw money from ATMs, because of a lack of banking services. People with disabilities had to share passwords because they needed help in order to complete a banking transaction.

Our qualitative study shows that when one person in a couple relationship manages the money, that is pays the bills, and monitors Internet banking, it is not unusual for that person to manage the joint accounts as well as all the individual accounts, including the accounts of the partner. The form of the account, whether it be joint or individual, remains important in terms of meaning. This is because different kinds of accounts earmark and separate money according to ownership and source of the funds [32, 43]. In the case of Internet banking where passwords are shared however, the form of the account no longer defines the boundaries of access to money, or information about money.

In our study we had eight couples with joint accounts where both partners also had individual accounts. In four of these cases, one partner managed all the accounts, including their partner's individual account. With the other four couples each person managed his or her own individual account.

Where the couple's joint and individual money was managed by one of the partners (4 of 8), this was possible because the spouse had given him/her the password. As Erin (all names are pseudonyms), an administration assistant, 25-34, with an annual household income between $75,000 and $100,000, said,

> As far as the bank is concerned they say that no-one else should have your password and that sort of thing but (my husband) trusts me as his wife to have that information and do the transactions that need to be done. We could be breaching security as far (as) the banks are concerned but as a married couple it's a trust thing. But I wouldn't go giving it to anyone else.

The sparse literature on Indigenous banking in remote areas shows that key cards and access codes are often shared [7, 26, 31]. In our study, Sanna, a Torres Strait Islander now living in Brisbane, 45-54, with a BA and earning more than $50,000 a year, talked of banking on her island. She described how the bank was only on one of the 17 inhabited islands. A plane trip and a one night stay were required to get to that island. She said "When one person goes into Thursday Island they [do] everybody's business and shopping". This means they take others' keycards with the PINs. "You have to" said Sanna, "It's a matter of survival".

Telephone and Internet banking have increased the independence of many people with disabilities. However, the lack of accessible banking services necessitates the sharing of passwords and PINs with partners or family members. This sharing also happens at times with carers/support workers or shop assistants in order for transactions to be completed.

Fiona who has a physical disability, aged 35-44, with a Masters' degree and a household income of $50,000-$74,000, said she withdraws money via EFTPOS, so that the cashier can help with the swiping of the card. She said, "When I go to do EFTPOS I tell the shop assistant my PIN... Some shop assistants say they can't do that and I say they have to because I can't do it."

Sharing of passwords, where studied, is equally common in other populations. Dhamija and Perrig [10] interviewed 30 people (most likely in the United States) to test the comparative usability of recognition-based and recall-based authentication. They found that:

> ...people viewed the ability to share passwords with others as a feature. Almost all participants shared their bank PIN with family or friends and several users shared account passwords with others because this was a convenient way to collaborate, share information or transfer files (no page numbers).

In this section we have presented qualitative data that reveals that the sharing of passwords for banking is found among couples, in remote Indigenous communities and with people with disabilities. There is evidence from other literature where people see the possibility of sharing passwords as a useful feature of design.

3 Public Access to the Internet

In this section we examine the second underlying assumption of banking security design and policy—that every household will have its own Personal Computer or other personal access device. The Australian pattern follows that of Internet access in developed countries. Sixty-seven per cent of Australian households in 2004-05 accessed the Internet from home [4]. In the same period however, seven percent of the Australian population aged over 18 years accessed the Internet from the public library, and 12 per cent from other sites (excluding home, work, educational institution, neighbours, and friends).

In countries like India, as Sadagopan reminds us "While PC stands for Personal Computer elsewhere, in India it represents a Public computer" [27]. This public access can be provided by commercial Internet access points where customers pay a fee for service (at times called cybercafés), or the free Internet access points for development, in libraries or other institutional places targeting a specific audience. There are also rural kiosks that are run by commercial entities such as ITC's e-chaupal, government initiatives such as e-Seva, and entrepreneurial projects run by NGOs such as those by the M. S Swaminathan Foundation. Others are run by individuals.

Concentrating only on the urban commercial cybercafés [16], Haseloff said, "...as much as one-third of the middle class is dependent on cybercafes as their only access point " (no page number). Estimates of the number of cyber cafés and Internet kiosks in urban and rural areas range from 105,000 to 200,000 cyber cafés in India in 2005 (accounting for 60% of net users) [19, 25].

3.1 Internet Banking and E-Commerce at Indian Cybercafés

Internet cafes and kiosks are important in India, not only for incidental communication and searching, but for Internet banking and the estimated $US 498 million e-commerce industry in 2006-2007 [19]. This is one of the main findings of surveys by industry associations Internet and Mobile Association of India and Internet & Online Association [20].

The Internet and Online Association's urban online survey of 3,099 Internet users in April 2005 [20] showed that more than a quarter (28 %) of these respondents accessed the Internet from the cyber café. This was not the dominant mode of access for e-commerce, as 65 per cent accessed e-commerce sites from the office, and 52 per cent from the home.

The Internet and Mobile Association of India (IAMAI) also conducted an online survey of 882 persons who regularly visited e-commerce sites from cyber cafés. Of these, 47 per cent (417 persons) had shopped online more than once. Of these 417 persons, 58 per cent did online banking. This sub-sample as with the IAOI survey had an over representation of males (87%), 18-35 years of age (84%) and those with graduate and postgraduate degrees (80%).

The survey findings are in conflict with bank advice that customers avoid banking using public computers. The need is to ensure that publicly accessed computers are secure and seen as secure by customers. As Sadagopan [27] notes, security "is indeed a serious problem & cannot be taken lightly".

The level of fraud in Internet banking in India is unclear. It is also unclear what protections the Indian consumer has in case he or she loses money from his or her Internet banking account accessed from a cyber café. However, the bank's warning against the use of Internet cafes for Internet banking reflects the greater potential for such fraud from public kiosks.

3.2 Shared Use of Mobile Phones in Developing Countries

Mobile phones are emerging as an important way of accessing the Internet. As the Internet and Online Association's urban online survey [20] shows, seven percent of their sample in India access the Internet from the mobile phone. Toyama et al. [36] noted it is possible

> ...that the most compelling scenarios will be hybrid experiences, where a shared-access kiosk provides a full Internet experience occasionally, and pre-paid mobile phones provide a shallow experience continuously. Neither mobile providers nor computing firms have emerged with such a solution thus far (p. 9).

The security problems posed by mobile phone access to the Internet are those of mobile applications everywhere. But unlike Japan, the United States, Europe and Australia, in India and other developing countries, individually owned mobile phones are often shared [6, 12, 24, 37, 38]. As noted in the Information Economy Report (2005) [37]

> ...in developing countries a single mobile phone is frequently shared by several people, particularly in poor, rural communities, and people at all income levels are able to access mobile services either through owning a phone or using someone else's (p. 12).

The leasing of mobile phones in the villages of Bangladesh by Grameen Bank is based on shared use [6]. A 2004 study of rural municipalities in the Philippines found that 15 per cent of the cell phones were family owned but 62 per cent allowed others in the household to receive and respond to messages [24].

The sharing of mobile phones is common in Africa [38]. In Rwanda as Donner notes [12]:

> ...in Africa, as elsewhere in the developing world, handsets often pull double-duty, used by multiple family members, shared among friends (perhaps by swapping SIM cards in and out), or perhaps by a whole set of users in a village or neighborhood. Across the region, many people make their living by selling individual calls on handsets. These micro-entrepreneurs play an important function in extending connectivity to people who can not afford their own handset, or who might only require an occasional call (p. 2).

3.3 Cross-Cultural Attitudes to Privacy

With an increasing global flow of money and information, it has become critical to study privacy attitudes and behaviours for different activities, social contexts and technologies, in a cross cultural framework. In our approach to privacy, we draw on user centered studies that have emphasized that privacy rests in the control of the sharing of personal information and presenting our version of ourselves [2, 8, 23, 34]. Cross cultural research is also important because the right to be left alone is seen as less important than connectedness to family and community in some activity contexts, in some countries. This argument draws on broader theories of the cultural differences between countries [18]. The move towards indigenous psychologies also emphasizes the relatedness of individuals over individual autonomy [17].

Some cross cultural research is happening in the context of the use of media. As Livingstone [22] says, in a global world, it is difficult not to do cross cultural research. Much of the comparative research, particularly with mobile phones and other new media, is happening within the Western developed countries, or across diverse groups within the same country. There is also the beginning of cross cultural research in the use of media in developing countries. Research on privacy laws across borders is also becoming more important. However, the cross cultural research on privacy, where it exists, still has to be more clearly linked to design and policy.

The sharing of mobile phones and the comfort with public telephones and cybercafés in India is part of broader boundaries of the privacy of personal information. Some of the most distinctive cultural differences related to privacy lie in the boundaries of domestic money [25]. Among middle income Anglo-Celtic married couples, money and information about money is often shared by the couple, but not always between the parents and children. Money also flows in one direction, between parents and children, and at times between grandparents and children. However in many other cultures, money and information about money also flows from children to parents. Using money as a medium of family relationships has been central to the $US167 billion in migrant remittances flowing back to developed countries in 2005 [41].

Even within Western countries, there are cultural differences about the privacy of money. In Australia, among Aboriginal groups, money is shared within an extended family, kinship group or household cluster. [28, 31]. Similar differences are also found for Islander and Maori families in New Zealand [14].

Greater research on the privacy of money needs to be done in developing countries. In what contexts is it appropriate to ask about money earned, money spent? What are the culturally appropriate ways of not answering these questions?

Personal information too is shared in different ways across cultures. Genevieve Bell, Director of the User Experience Group, Intel, in her keynote address at OZCHI 06 noted it was not unusual for Indian families to have a single email address. It is a common practice in India and Korea for educational institutions to post students' full names and grades on public notice boards or newspapers [21, 40].

There has been little discussion of the impact of these cross cultural differences in the privacy of personal information, particularly money, on design and policy. Kumaraguru (2005) drawing on a sample of 407 persons in companies and universities found that people in the high-tech workforce may not be "sufficiently aware of privacy issues in general, and more specifically, privacy issues related to technologies".

4 Conclusion: Social and Cultural Centered Design

Our study of banking in Australia showed that banking access codes were shared in some contexts by married and de facto couples, Indigenous people in remote communities and people with disabilities. The literature on public access and shared devices in India and other developing countries revealed that public access and shared devices are one of the main ways of accessing the Internet.

The security implications of these social and cultural practices have yet to be considered by designers, bankers and policy makers. The usual industry and policy reaction to access codes not remaining confidential is to propose further education of customers, or more stringent laws. Our study showed that people with a high education were also sharing access codes. The sharing was in response to a customer need, whether it be trust in the couple relationship, lack of banking services or accessibility.

We argue that social and cultural practices need to be placed at the center of design. To do this we need to extend the perspectives of user centered design (UCD) in three directions. The UCD approach places the user at the centre of security design, aligning usability and security [1, 9, 11, 13, 29, 30, 33, 42]. First, we need to expand from the individual alone or the individual in an organisation to the domestic context of individual and shared activities in the household. Second, these activities and values need to be studied in the field. Third, the cultural meanings of online financial transactions have to be taken into account. This is particularly important as money is used, managed and owned in different ways in various cultures [32].

These approaches will help link design, policy and practice. They will also bridge the household experience with national and international approaches. It is only with such connections, that the Internet can deliver its potential for individual and community empowerment across cultures.

References

1. Ackerman, M.S.: The intellectual challenge of CSCW: The gap between social requirements and technical feasibility. In: Carroll, J.M. (ed.) Human-Computer Interaction in the New Millennium, pp. 303–324. ACM Press, New York (2002)
2. Agre, P.: Introduction. In: Agre, P., Rotenberg, M. (eds.) Technology and Privacy: The New Landscape, pp. 1–28. The MIT Press, Cambridge, Mass (1998)
3. Australian Bankers' Association Inc. Stay safe online: ABA supports the e-security awareness week, Australian Bankers' Association Inc. (2006)
4. Australian Bureau of Statistics. Household Use of Information Technology, Australia, 2004-05, Australian Bureau of Statistics, Canberra (2005) Cat No. 8146.8140
5. Australian Securities and Investment Commission. Electronic Funds Transfer Code of Conduct: As revised by the Australian Securities & Investments Commission's EFT Working Group, Australian Securities and Investment Commission, Sydney (2002)
6. Bayes, A., Braun, J.v., Akhter, R.: Village Pay Phones and Poverty Reduction: Insights from a Grameen Bank Initiative in Bangladesh, ZEF Bonn, Zentrum für Entwicklungsforschung, Center for Development Research, Universität Bonn, Bonn (1999)

7. Birdsall, C.: All in the family. In: Keen, I. (ed.) Being Black: Aboriginal cultures in 'settled' Australia, Aboriginal Studies Press for the Australian Institute of Aboriginal Studies, Canberra, 137–158 (1994)
8. Castro, M., Singh, S.: Rigour at a trotting pace: A story from the user-centred design of smart internet technologies. In: QualIT, Brisbane (2004)
9. Cranor, L.F., Garfinkel, S.: Preface. In: Cranor, L.F., Garfinkel, S. (eds.) Security and Usability: Designing Secure Systems that People Can Use, O'Reilly, Sebastopol, CA, ix-xviii (2005)
10. Dhamija, R., Perrig, A., Déjà, V.: A User Study Using Images for Authentication. In: Proceedings of the 9th USENIX Security Symposium Denver, Colorado, USA, 2000, The USENIX Association, No page numbers (2000)
11. D'Hertefelt, S.: Trust and the perception of security (2000)
12. Donner, J.: User-led innovations in mobile use in sub-Saharan Africa Receiver Newsletter#14 (2005)
13. Erickson, T., Kellogg, W.A.: Social translucence: Designing systems that support social processes. In: Carroll, J.M. (ed.) Human-Computer Interaction in the New Millennium, pp. 325–345. ACM Press, New York (2002)
14. Fleming, R., Taiapa, J., Pasikale, A., Easting, S.K.: The Common Purse. Auckland University Press, Auckland (1997)
15. Glaser, B.G., Strauss, A.L.: The discovery of grounded theory: Strategies for qualitative research. Aldine, Chicago (1967)
16. Haseloff, A.M.: Cybercafes and their Potential as Community Development Tools in India, The Journal of Community Informatics (2005)
17. Ho, D.Y.F.: Indigenous Psychologies: Asian Perspectives. Journal of Cross-Cultural Psychology 29, 88–103 (1998)
18. Hofstede, G.: Cultures and Organizations: Software of the Mind. McGraw-Hill, New York (1997)
19. Internet and Mobile Association of India. Cybercafé Users Ecommerce Activities, Internet and Mobile Association of India (2005)
20. Internet and Online Association. IOAI Survey: Ecommerce Security 2005, Internet and Online Association (2005)
21. Kumaraguru, P.: Internet Privacy in India Hot Topics, Carleton University (2005)
22. Livingstone, S.: On the Challenges of Cross-National Comparative Media Research. European Journal of Communication 18(4), 477–500 (2003)
23. Palen, L., Dourish, P.: Unpacking privacy for a networked world. In: Proceedings of the conference on Human factors in computing systems, Ft. Lauderdale, Florida, USA, pp. 129–136. ACM Press, New York (2003)
24. Pertierra, R.: Mobile Phones, Identity and Discursive Intimacy. Human Technology 1(1), 23–44 (2005)
25. Ranjan, A.: Milestones in India's Internet Journey (2005)
26. Renouf, G.: Bookup - some consumer problems. A report for ASIC (2002)
27. Sadagopan, S.: Why I feel e-commerce will fly in India?, IIITB, Bangalore, n.d.
28. Sansom, B.: A grammar of exchange. In: Being Black: Aboriginal cultures in 'settled' Australia, Aboriginal Studies Press for the Australian Institute of Aboriginal Studies, Canberra, pp. 159–177 (1988)
29. Sasse, M.A., Flechais, I.: Usable security: Why do we need it? How do we get it? In: Cranor, L.F., Garfinkel, S. (eds.) Security and Usability: Designing Secure Systems that People Can Use, O'Reilly, Sebastopol, CA, pp. 13–30 (2005)

30. Schneier, B.: Secrets and lies: Digital security in a networked world. John Wiley & Sons, New York (2000)
31. Senior, K., Perkins, D., Bern, J.: Variation in material wellbeing in a welfare based economy. In: South East Arnhem Land Collaborative Research Project, University of Wollongong, Wollongong (2002)
32. Singh, S.: Marriage money: the social shaping of money in marriage and banking. Allen & Unwin, St. Leonards, NSW (1997)
33. Singh, S., Cabraal, A., Demosthenous, C., Astbrink, G., Furlong, M.: Password Sharing: Implications for Security Design Based on Social Practice. In: Computer Human Interaction, San Jose, ACM, San Jose, New York (2007)
34. Singh, S., Zic, J., Satchell, C., Bartolo, K.C., Snare, J., Fabre, J.: A Reflection on Translation Issues in User-Centred Design. In: 7th International Conference on Work with Computing Systems, WWCS 2004 (Kuala Lumpur, 2004) (2004)
35. State Bank of India. Internet Banking: Welcome Aboard, State Bank of India (2006)
36. Toyama, K., Kiri, K., Ratan, M.L., Nileshwar, A., Vedashree, R., MacGregor, R.F.: Rural Kiosks in India, Microsoft Corporation (2004)
37. United Nations Conference on Trade and Development. Information Economy Report 1005, United Nations, New York and Geneva (2005)
38. Vodafone. Africa: The Impact of Mobile Phones The Vodafone Policy Paper Series (2005)
39. Westpac Banking Corporation. Internet Banking Terms and Conditions, Sydney (2006)
40. Woo, J.: Invasion or giving up of Internet privacy? A personal divide emerges. In: Pacific Telecommunications Conference (Honolulu, 2001) (2001)
41. World Bank Global Economic Prospects 2006: Economic Implications of Remittances and Migration. World Bank, Washington DC (2006)
42. Yee, K.-P.: Aligning Security and Usability. IEEE Security and Privacy 02(5), 48–55 (2004)
43. Zelizer, V.: The social meaning of money. Basic Books, New York (1994)

Mobile Personalization at Large Sports Events
User Experience and Mobile Device Personalization

Xu Sun and Andrew May

Ergonomics and Safety Research Institute, Holywell Building, Holywell Park, Loughborogh University,
LEICS, LE11 3UZ, UK
{x.sun3,A.J.May}@lboro.ac.uk

Abstract. Mobile personalization is frequently discussed, and has been shown in relation to a number of usage scenarios. However, this research has focused mainly on technology development. There have been few studies of mobile user experience, and personalization in sports. This paper is devoted to the new field of studying the user experience related to mobile personalization at large sports events (LSE). In order to support and enrich the user experience at LSE with mobile personalization, this study investigates the current audience experience at stadiums and derives the usage patterns that device personalization could usefully support in this context.

Keywords: User experience, mobile personalization, usage pattern.

1 Introduction

The large sports event (LSE) is a large environment with a lot of excitement and information, during which spectators are often overloaded with information from a variety of sources [1]. Mobile devices offer potential benefits within this distributed information environment; however, it is not clear how individuals can best benefit from the capabilities they offer. A possible solution is personalization, making the mobile device adapt to the user - ensuring that only relevant information is retrieved, and is presented in a way that is suitable. Research has been conducted on enriching the user experience of media in different ways [2] [3] [4] [5]. However, there have been few studies of the mobile user experience in sports. The research of the mobile user experience at a LSE is a relatively new research domain. The user experience at LSE in this study incorporates the viewing of the sports event, the engagement of the individual in the LSE, and the subjective experiences with mobile personalization in a stadium environment.

This research explores the role of mobile personalization at LSE. Mobile personalization in paper means mobile adjusts itself to provide content based on an understanding of the user; the understating includes the user's interests, preferences, behavior and context; it helps the user to achieve certain goals. It contributes to existing research by exploring how mobile personalization can enhance the user

N. Aykin (Ed.): Usability and Internationalization, Part II, HCII 2007, LNCS 4560, pp. 486–495, 2007.

experience at LSE. This research also explicitly takes the Chinese culture into consideration – this provides some methodological guidance for research and design for Chinese users.

1.1 Research Problem

Nowadays LSE are a prime social, economic and media phenomena [6]. It implies large groups of spectators gathering within a large spatial distribution to co-experience a lively atmosphere and exciting sporting moments. As an LSE is a large environment with lots of stimuli, visitors can be overloaded by the amount and diversity of information they are exposed to, and can lose track of that which is relevant to them [1]. In order to avoid the overwhelming experience of a large and complex real/virtual information environment, and to satisfy individual difference, personalization is recommended for the mobile device design to enhance the user experience at LSE. In order to enhance the user experience at LSEs it is necessary to identify (1) the nature of the current user experience, and (2) the role that personalization of a mobile application can play. To address these questions, user studies were carried with target Chinese mobile users, investigating their current experiences in the context of LSEs.

2 Field Study

A field study was used for gathering data on the audience experience within a LSE. In this study, the *user experience* refers to the subjective experience that a visitor gets when interacting with a mobile device within the stadium environment. It includes both experiences with the mobile device as well as the experiences within the context of the LSE. The context of the LSE makes the mobile user experience unique in this study. This study stresses the importance of these experiences in the LSE context of social interaction, in which people interpret the LSE and create interactions involving other individuals, events occurring, and the mobile device.

This study is grounded in the collaborative aspects of the user experience from the literature [7,8,9,10,11,12,13]. This has the following aspects: user (expectations, needs, motivation, mood); the characteristics of the designed mobile device (e.g. usability, functionality); the context of LSE (e.g. physical context and social context); social interactions occurring within LSE context (e.g. interactions); the culture (e.g. values, beliefs) These five levels of components cover the aspects defined within the literature; however the lists of attributes for each component in brackets are still incomplete. This study therefore examines user experience at LSE from personal, social, functional and cultural perspectives.

2.1 Methods

The field study is a method used in a number of design contexts, inspired by ethnography [14]. It encompasses participant observation, interviews, literature analysis and information gathering. It can be summarized as, 'the study of people in naturally occurring settings, involving the researcher participating directly in the setting, in order to collect data, without meaning being imposed externally' [15]. It combines observation, contextual interview and questionnaires.

Observation was a suitable method for gathering user experience data emanating from non-verbal expressions. It can capture information relating to their user experience which the user may not be aware of, or is unable to express verbally. Also, this method was compatible with the ethos of ethnography, where the researcher is immersed in the user's naturally occurring environment in order to collect data without meaning being imposed externally.

Contextual interviews were selected as a means of investigating a user's anticipation and expectation, which have been identified as central elements of user experience [16]. This kind of data cannot be observed directly. In addition, it provided an opportunity to make the user study flexible.

A questionnaire was used to collect a user's opinions toward their experience in the stadium. It answers question relating to 'what', such as what they felt about watching the events, and what problems occur. It was used at the end of the field study with the aim of gathering user experience of mobile personalization in context.

2.2 Field Study

Preparation. The field studies took place at four sports events, namely two swimming galas and two football matches. Those events were held at sports stadium in shanghai. Eighteen Chinese participants, who are mobile users and have prior experience of watching sports events, were involved in the study which lasted for 16 hours over four days.

Fig. 1. The field studies undertaken at sports stadiums

Procedure. Users were firstly informed of the research purpose and the concept of mobile personalization. This was done before the sports events. During the events, the observer sat behind them observing and recording their user experience in a relatively unobtrusive way. Each participant involved in the evaluation had a mobile phone that prompted them by SMS to fill in the 'wish list' during the breaks – this reminded them to write down on paper their wish for improving the audience experience. The lists were collected and recorded for later analysis. This method is referred to as a 'beeper study' [17]. It tends to be relatively intrusive and may encourage participants to be more expressive than when being simply interviewed.

Follow-up context interviews were carried out immediately after the events to investigate user's levels of anticipation and their expectations. It was conducted while the participants' memory of the event was still fresh in order to promote recall of relevant detail. During the interview, users acted as informants as well as co-designers. The interviews covered questions regarding their audience experience and user requirements at LSE. Summative user experience at the LSE was measured at the end of the interview using a five-point Likert scale ('very negative', 'negative', 'just so so', 'positive', 'very positive'). Note that 'just so so' is an appropriate translation of the Chinese word representing an 'OK' or 'neutral' response.

Observers were placed among the users to record observable aspects of the user experiences from the user, social, contextual and cultural perspectives. The data relating to user experience factors is summarized in Table 1. This was done to provide an overview of what the current audience experience was, what kinds of information resources were predominantly used, and the relevance to mobile personalization. It was also a means of capturing what the type of information that the users were interested in, or were unable to access.

2.3 Analysis

After the field studies were conducted, the affinity diagram technique [18] was used for data analysis. Affinity diagrams are good for sifting through large volumes of data and encouraging new patterns of thinking. Furthermore, they allow grouping of ideas based on their natural relationships before sorting through them and analyzing which kinds of requirements the data represented.

2.4 Results

The current user experience at the LSE was not positive. Based on a simple five point scale 43.75% of users rated their experience as 'just so so' on the questionnaire; the other 56.25% users described a 'negative experience' (refer to Figure 2).

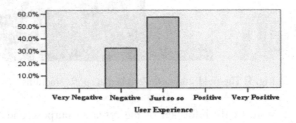

Fig. 2. Current user experience rating at sport stadiums

Analysis further revealed the negative user experiences relating to the LSE context, social interaction, user, and user culture.

Table 1. User experience captured during studies Interviews (I), observation (O) and user questionnaire (Q)

Factors	I	O	Q	Analysis
User				
Behavior		Y		watch, navigate, talk, taking pictures, cheering
Emotions	Y	Y		excited (peak movement), distracted, bored
Expectations	Y			understanding the competition, enjoy the live atmosphere
Motivation	Y			sports, social interaction
Experience			Y	43.75% 'just so so', 56.25% 'negative'
Culture				
Characteristics	Y	Y		emphasis on group image, interactions within groups;
Social interaction				
With events	Y	Y		cheering, creating multimedia records
With friends	Y	Y		talking to friends nearby, taking photos
With stranger	Y	Y		glancing at each other
LSE Context				
Stadium layout		Y		round stadium, stage was centered for competition, seats were closely related to each other; audience could not easily move around.
Physical Objects		Y		two outdoor 15x17-foot video stadium displays, hanging on the front and back side of stadium
Audio Information		Y		at the beginning/end of each competitions, audio presentation of information on who was competing, and who scored afterwards
Visual Information		Y		public screen display of information on scores, time, and replay of scoring moments, (not visible from a distance)
Paper based Information		Y		program list was available from the internet or prepared in advance (few users had it and looked at it)
Mobile Device				
Use of mobile media		Y		peak moments: taking photos, video recording breaks: sending message, taking photos
Interaction with device		Y		moving around trying to get a good view when creating multimedia records, one hand used to send message, put in pocket after using

2.4.1 LSE Context

The LSE was conceptualized as a large group of individuals within a particular spatial distribution who co-experience a lively atmosphere and the momentary excitement of sports. The field studies discovered that the LSE context influenced the user experiences in relation to the flow of information and the stadium environment that they were part of.

It was important to realize that the predominant experiences for users at the LSE related to the competitions in the field; the general event information became of secondary interest. There was an overloading of competition information published/ distributed in several ways, including audio, visual and paper 'channels' at stadiums.

It was not easy for the audience to search or assimilate the large amount of information while experiencing the events. The spectators were therefore cognitively overloaded and often failed to notice information which was potentially relevant.

Detailed information can be lost at a LSE. Unlike watching TV, spectating at a LSE meant missing the detailed ongoing information such as that usually provided on television. The information broadcast in the stadium (via the stadium loudspeaker system and large screens) was used to inform the audience of the competitions. This information was located at the hot spots of the events where many spectators were located. However, many spectators were not at the critical locations and therefore they missed event information. The event was watched by spectators, but the significance of the events within the wider competition was often not known until later. Within the overall LSE atmosphere, the detailed competition information can be lost.

The characteristics of the published information at the LSE were not under the user's control and only partly relevant. The audiences interest in information varied. At particular moments, some spectators were interested in athlete information while others were interested in information relating to the competitions taking place. Currently, the diversity of the audiences' interests was not satisfied by the information provided. The host published/broadcast the information, while the audience had no influence on what, when or how information was received during the ongoing events.

The stadium environment also influenced the user experience. Due to a large number of spectators and limited stadium space, the use of a mobile device and related personal activities were constrained in the stadium environment. Examples included buying food or going to the toilet, which occurred during the break or before or after the competition.

The mobile device was inconvenient to use. In the stadium environment, it was not possible to perform complicated mobile tasks except by simply clicking. Other personal activities were somehow constrained in the stadium environment: it was not easy to locate seats among the audience, specially when arriving late; it usually took two and a half or more hours to watch a competition, during which was inconvenient to obtain refreshments because of the crowds in stadium; after the events, crowds caused difficulties in meeting friends in the stadium.

2.4.2 Social Interaction

One of the characteristics of being a LSE spectator was that their experience of the event was socially constructed by seeing people go there to enjoy the company of others. However, there were limited social interactions formed in-situ. Spectators were seldom involved in other activities besides quietly watching the competition; they seldom directed attention to social interaction. The social interaction happened infrequently – and included asking questions, and discussion among friends. It took place in a less explicit way with passers-by through the exchanging of glances. The experience itself was often dominated by long periods of watching, with the social interactions only comprising a small portion of the time spent watching the event. This led to spells of considerable boredom amongst the audience. The lack of social interaction could promote audience experience at a shared level of attention – this becomes part of a social interpretation process that can influence what the experience means to individuals and others.

2.4.3 User

Users staged their experiences mainly by watching, and moving around the stadium to optimize their viewing angles. Other activities were undertaken occasionally such as creating multimedia records, and interacting with each other. Being in a sport stadium, users expected to experience the events in a more dynamic fashion. The dynamic experience would consist of a better understanding of the competition, more active social interaction, and engagement in their local environment (i.e. the stadium). This was not supported in the current sporting event which were studied.

2.4.4 Culture

An interesting finding was that most social interactions arose within specific groups. For example, the Chinese audience demonstrated their distinctive group image by wearing specific uniforms or using particular accessories when cheering. Interactions happened by taking picture, talking to group members, or chanting group slogans during the peak moments of the events. Interviewing the users highlighted their anticipation of a greater level of interaction within their group, such as discussing what they had just seen, and sharing their experiences at the LSE. This finding highlights the collective orientation of Chinese culture [19], which emphasizes extended group relationships.

3 Usage Pattern of Mobile Personalization

The field studies charted a new design space for mobile personalization that renders user experience more active and engaging in a socially and culturally relevant way. Mobile personalization could contribute value by supporting a user's control over the information, facilitating their actions within a stadium environment, and enhancing social interactions of audiences in a LSE context. Those Implications for how mobile personalization could supplement the user experience are summarized in the following.

Support information flow. To address current problems of overload due to general and only partially relevant information, audiences should be provided with information in a personalized way - letting them decide what information is desired, and applying a user's requests as an information filter. It is also important to allow users to decide when the information should be sent. Information should by no means constrain the viewing of the LSE, as the primary interest of user in this context is the competition taking place. Users' control over information should be supported by allowing them specifying their requests, including interests, preferences and relevant context.

Reduce environmental constraints. The environment is a major influence on the user experience, especially in terms of the usability of the mobile device [16]. Means of facilitating users in the stadium environment are proposed with the aim of mobile personalization: *Simply interaction.* A clear finding from the field studies was that interaction with the mobile device needs to be simple: interaction should be personalized for the stadium environment to allow impromptu interaction with the device with low commitment from the user.

Support of other personal services. To avoid the embarrassment involved in locating seats, ordering food and trying to meet up with friends, a mobile device should provide users with personal guidance. Users could get personalized guidance to their stadium seat according to their location, with seat identification integrated into an e-ticket function. Food and refreshments could be ordered based on individual and group preferences; meeting points can be arranged on request according to users' locations.

Enhance Social interaction. Social interactions are key to a fulfilling user experience at a LSE, as demonstrated by the enjoyment derived from being a member of a group of people who support the same team. A personalized mobile device can help to create and maintain a relationship in a virtual social network - this supports the group's co-experiencing of the event and caters to the Chinese culture of underpinning group relationships [19, 20]. For example, mobile personalization can help generate virtual groups with people sharing common interests and profiles. By doing so, interaction opportunities can be proposed based on users' interests, and greater social interaction can be promoted.

Design for Chinese users who showed a high preference for group relationships during the field studies. Mobile personalization, besides being able to assign each individual to a virtual group to promote a sense of group belonging, can help to emphasis group image by presenting personalized group information and creating personalized features, such as group grants and anthems.

The usage patterns derived from the field studies demonstrate that mobile personalization can contribute value by enriching the user experience. It can provide timely, relevant information, create supportive environment and enhance social interaction. Figure 3 illustrates these themes.

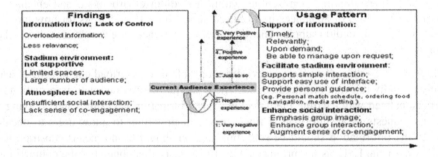

Fig. 3. The role of mobile personalization at LSE

4   Conclusion

This research reported that for the participants studied within this research there was a negative audience experience in large sports stadiums. This emanated from multiple perspectives relating to the LSE context, social interaction, the mobile device, user centered issues and the wider culture of this particular group of users. In summary, the audience were limited in their ability to select from a variety of different information sources, assimilate the content and control their interaction with information in the LSE context. The social interaction between spectators only played a small role during events, which lead to considerable boredom amongst the spectators; mobile devices were not convenient to use due to the LSE context. For Chinese users (as were studied in this research), sporting events were important not just in themselves but also as a means for social interaction amongst groups. Users expressed a high expectation of greater group interaction within the stadium: the user experience should be enhanced since spectating is a rich, social experience.

This research serves as a starting point to employ mobile personalization concepts to enrich the user experience at a LSE. Usage patterns are proposed in support of human-information interaction, the stadium environment, user culture and social interaction within the LSE context. While personalization is considered important, users may fail to personalize effectively or be unwilling to invest the time and effort needed to complete this. Thus, research will continue to generate visualizations of these personalization concepts on a mobile user interface. This will then be evaluated with target users as part of an iterative design process to better understand if/how mobile personalization could improve the user experience at large sporting events.

References

1. Marx, M., Schmandt, C.: 'CLUES: Dynamic Personalized Message Filtering'. In: proceedings of Computer Supported Cooperative Work (1996)
2. Bluetooth Module WML-C10 Class 2. Mitsumi Electric Co., Ltd (2004), http://www.mitsumi.com
3. Boll, S., Westermann, U.: Mediether: an event space for context-aware multimedia experiences. In: Proceedings of the 2003 ACM SIGMM workshop on Experiential telepresence, pp. 21–30. ACM Press, New York (2003)
4. De Bra, P., Brusilovsky, P., Conejo, R.: Tv scout: Lowering the barrier to personalized tv program recommendation. In: Proceedings of the 2nd International Conference on Adaptive Hypermedia and Adaptive Web Based Systems (2002)
5. Olsson, D., Nilsson, A.: Mep: a media event platform. Mobile Networks and Applications, pp. 235–244 (2002)
6. Jacucci, G., Oulasvirta, A., Salovaara.: A Multimedia experience: a field study with implications for ubiquitous applications. Personal and Ubiquitous Computing, Special issue on Memory and sharing of experiences (2006)
7. Shedroff, N.: Experience Design. New Riders (2001)
8. Sanders, E.B.-N.: Virtuosos in the Experience Domain. In: Proceedings of the 2001, IDSA Education Conference (2001)
9. Norman, D.A.: The Invisible Computer. MIT Press, Cambridge (1998)
10. Kankainen, A.: UCPCD - User-Centred Product Concept Design. In: Proceedings of DUX03, ACM, San Francisco (2003)
11. Koskinen, I., Battarbee, K., Mattelmäki, T. (eds.): Empathic design. Forthcoming. IT press, Helsinki (2003)
12. Dewey, J.: Art as Experience, New York: Perigee (reprint) (1998)
13. Oinas-Kukkonen, H.: Mobile Electronic Commerce through the Web. In: Proceedings of the Second International Conference on Telecommunications and Electronic Commerce, Nashville, TN, USA, pp. 69–74 (1999)

14. Wolcott, H.F.: Ethnography: A Way of Seeing. AltaMira Press, Walnut Creek, CA (1999)
15. Brewer, J.: Ethnography. Open University Press, Buckingham (2000)
16. Kuniavsky, M.: Observing the User Experience – A Practitioner's Guide to User Research. Morgan Kaufman, Elsevier, USA (2003)
17. Dey, A.K.: Evaluation of Ubiquitous Computing Systems: Evaluating the Predictability of Systems. In: UBICOMP 2001 Workshop on Evaluation Methods for Ubiquitous Computing (September 30, 2001)
18. Hackos, J., Redish, J.: User and task analysis for interface design. John Wiley & Sons, New York (1998)
19. Hofstede, G.: Culture and Organizations: Software of the Mind, Intercultural Cooperation and its Importance for Survival. McGraw Hill, New York (1997)
20. Marcus, A.: Fast Forward, User-Interface Design and China: A Great Leap Forward, Interactions, January +February issue (2003)

How Should You Frame Questions to Measure User Attitudes Accurately? An Experimental Design Study

Seema Swamy

10828 Alderbrook Lane, Cupertino, CA-95014
seemavasanth@yahoo.com

Abstract. Attitudes are most frequently measured through responses to questionnaires. The validity of the results is strongly dependent on the quality of the instrument. Questionnaires employed to evaluate users' attitudes toward issues, products, or services frequently tend to have several biases yielding inflated responses. A 2 x 2 experimental design study established that rating attitudinal items on a Likert scale in a questionnaire with all statements framed in positive valence tend to produce higher attitudinal scores than when statements are balanced with both positive and negative valence.

Keywords: Attitude measurement, validity, reliability, survey, experimental design, questionnaire, and Likert scale.

1 Introduction

Attitude measurement is the basis of consumer and market research and is central to the field of social sciences [3, 8]. As Gordon Allport stated in the *Handbook of Social Psychology,* "An attitude is a mental and neural state of readiness, organized through experience, exerting a directive or dynamic influence upon the individual's response to all objects and situations with which it is related [1]."

Attitudes clearly exist, but can rarely be observed and measured directly. They are often considered precursors of conscious behaviors. The measurement of attitudes within individuals is extremely important as they determine product loyalty and brand perceptions, affecting actions such as purchasing products or services, and the quality of future interactions.

Users' perceptions and attitudes are most often measured through self-reports obtained through questionnaires. Questionnaires tend to have closed-ended items in which respondents are instructed to select their responses based on a list of options provided [4]. Closed-ended questionnaires are generally cheaper, more reliable, and faster to code and analyze the data collected.

2 Literature Review

Questionnaires should be designed not only to ensure that the constructs measured are reliable, but also to maximize the accuracy of the measured attitudes. Frequently, in market research and consumer service surveys, participants are asked to state their

N. Aykin (Ed.): Usability and Internationalization, Part II, HCII 2007, LNCS 4560, pp. 496–505, 2007.
© Springer-Verlag Berlin Heidelberg 2007

agreement to a set of statements on a number of issues. One of the most common biases evident in these questionnaires is that the statements are frequently framed with only positive affect without balancing it with statements framed in negative affect, thereby introducing an acquiescence bias.

Meaningless acquiescence to attitude items by the sample of respondents is not generalizable to the population [7]. Concerns over the acquiescent response set bias first became prominent in the measurement of attitudes in the California F scale research [5]. In addition to acquiescence bias, respondents are also less likely to read the statements carefully when all the statements are framed positively. When the questionnaire is balanced with both positive and negative valence items, participants are compelled to read each of the statements more carefully to rate them consistently.

Most research that has tested best practices in research methods has employed college students as participants. This has frequently been cited as a limitation in the generalization of findings about optimal questionnaire construction to other populations.

Therefore, for this study, the target sample consisted of users of a customer-to-customer e-commerce site where sellers and buyers interact with each other to transact products and services. When the users of this e-commerce site encounter any problem or issue, they contact customer support. The most frequent form of communication is through email. To assess the existence of acquiescence bias, attitudes in three main areas were measured - the artifact itself, that is, the email response provided by the customer support representative (CSR), the responder of the email, that is, the customer support representative, and how valued the recipient of the email felt based on the reply of the CSR.

> *Hypothesis 1: When a questionnaire is designed with statements framed in the affirmative or with only positive valence, the responses will be significantly more positive than when the statements are balanced with both positive and negative valence.*
>
> > *Sub-hypothesis 1a: The positive bias of affirmative questionnaire would lead to more positive evaluation of artifacts such as emails compared to evaluations obtained through balanced questionnaire.*
> >
> > *Sub-hypothesis 1b: The positive bias of affirmative questionnaire would lead to more positive evaluation of the responder of the emailed question compared to evaluation obtained through balanced questionnaire.*
> >
> > *Sub-hypothesis 1c: Evaluation of how valued the recipient of the email response felt would be significantly more positive when it is measured with the affirmative questionnaire than when it is measured with a balanced questionnaire.*

Two types of emails were employed to ensure that the effects of questionnaire design were not due to the type of email issue and response. The two types of emails were – one pertained to a policy of the customer-to-customer e-commerce site and the second pertained to the transgression of a partner transacting on the site. Generally, individuals tend to have stronger affect toward another individual due to social presence [6] compared to a more diffuse entity such as a company policy of relatively less consequence. Thus, negative experiences with another transacting user would likely engender a relatively more negative perception compared to an issue with a company policy.

> *Hypothesis 2a: Individuals will rate an email more positively when the issue pertains to a clarification of a company policy than when the issue pertains to a transgression by a transacting partner.*

> *Hypothesis 2b: Individuals will rate the responder of an email more positively when the issue pertains to a clarification of a company policy than when the issue pertains to a transgression by a transacting partner.*

> *Hypothesis 2c: Individuals will rate how valued they felt significantly more when the issue pertains to a clarification of a company policy than when the issue pertains to a transgression by a transacting partner.*

3 Method

3.1 Participants

1133 participants participated in the between-subjects experimental design study. Participants were users of a customer-to-customer e-commerce site.

3.2 Procedure

In the 2 x 2 between-subjects experimental design study (type of questionnaire vs. type of email issue), participants were asked to assume that they had written a question to the CSR and had received a response. The study was run online. Participants were provided with an online copy of a question written to customer support and a response to the question written by a customer support representative.

Following this, they were asked to complete a questionnaire online. The questionnaire consisted of statements about perceptions of the email, perceptions of the CSR, and how valued the user of the customer-to-customer e-commerce site felt after reading the response. Participants were asked to indicate the extent to which they agreed or disagreed with the statements.

There were two types of questionnaires – one with affirmative statements and other with balanced statements. In the affirmative questionnaire, participants received a questionnaire with all items constructed in positive valence. In the balanced questionnaire, the items contained both positive and negative valence statements. Participants were randomly assigned to provide their evaluations on one type of questionnaire.

There were two types of emails employed in the study – one related to the billing policy and the second related to the behavior of a transacting partner on the customer-to-customer e-commerce site. The billing policy issue pertained to a general support question about fees charged by the e-commerce site. A customer-to-customer e-commerce site seller wrote an email inquiring about a $1.65 charge to his account and was mistaken that this amount was a monthly charge. The CSR clarified that the charges were related to two items he had listed on the site and that it was not a recurring charge as there was no monthly fee. The second email pertained to a seller's negative experience with a buyer on the site. Specifically, the issue pertained to a complaint from a seller about a bidder who backed out of a winning bid. The CSR responded that appropriate action was taken on the transgressing partner and offered credit to the complainant for listing the item on the site. Participants were randomly assigned to receive one type of emailed question and response.

The online questionnaire consisted of attitudinal measures. Participants were asked to rate their degree of agreement to a set of statements on a 5-point Likert scale ranging from Strongly Disagree to Strongly Agree. The statements appeared in a random order to control for order effects [2]. Participants' perceptions of the email and the customer support representative who wrote the email response were measured. In addition, participants were asked to evaluate how valued they felt by the response.

Various constructs such as the effectiveness of the response in resolving the consumer's problem, structure of the emails, quality of the emails, perception of CSR supportiveness, friendliness and respectfulness of the CSR, and perception of how valued the consumer felt, were measured by multiple items through factor analysis. *Effectiveness of the email response* was made up of the following items - the email summarized consumer's problem well, the email addressed consumer's concern, the email included relevant web links that consumer could click on for more information, the email provided the consumer with all the information needed, and the consumer found the email informative. The *structure of email* was composed of items including - the email was well structured, the format of the email made it easy to read, and extraneous information was not presented. The *quality of the email* was composed of items including - the email was well written, consistent, directed, straightforward, transparent, and had appropriate length.

The factor measuring *supportiveness of CSR* was composed of items including - CSR responded to the consumer's concern adequately, understood the consumer's concern, provided the consumer with concrete steps to take, addressed the consumer's questions, was familiar with the consumer's situation, took steps to help resolve the consumer's situation, and was effective in responding to the consumer's question. The factor measuring perception of *friendliness and respectfulness of the CSR* included the items – the CSR was friendly, helpful, supportive, knowledgeable, and treated the consumer with respect. The factor measuring perceived *empathy of CSR* included the items – CSR was empathetic, firm, even-keeled, and no-nonsense.

The factor measuring how *valued consumers* felt by the email response was composed of the following items – the consumer felt valued, was treated fairly in this interaction, was addressed personally, felt good about being a consumer, felt that the company cared about the consumer's situation, and found the company's policies to be fair.

The factors were computed through principal components analysis. In the balanced questionnaire, the items that were framed with negative valence were reverse coded. The factors were highly reliable with Cronbach's alpha scores ranging from 0.77 to 0.93.

4 Results

The data were analyzed employing multivariate analysis of variance. There were no significant interaction effects. As predicted, participants gave significantly higher responses on perceptions of the CSR, the email, and how valued they felt during the interaction in the affirmative statements condition compared to responses obtained through the balanced questionnaire.

4.1 Questionnaire Type

Participants rated the email as having solved the consumer's issue significantly more positively in the affirmative questionnaire compared to the balanced questionnaire $F(1, 885) = 198.15$, $p < 0.0001$, $\eta^2 = 0.86$, $M = 3.79$ & 3.13, $SD = 0.92$ & 0.41 respectively. The effect size was high.

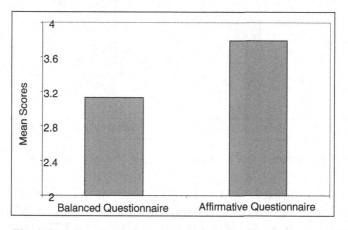

Fig. 1. Participants' rating of the effectiveness of the email response

Participants rated the structure of the email as being significantly better in the affirmative questionnaire compared to the balanced questionnaire $F(1, 885) = 304.86$, $p < 0.0001$, $\eta^2 = 1.03$, $M = 3.92$ & 3.12, $SD = 0.89$ & 0.39 respectively. The effect size was extremely high.

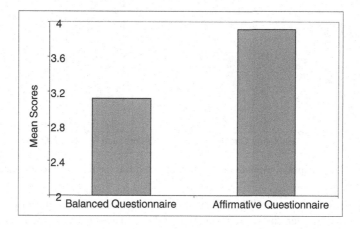

Fig. 2. Participants' evaluation of the structure of the email response

Participants rated the quality of the email as being significantly better in the affirmative questionnaire compared to the balanced questionnaire $F(1, 885) = 31.99$, $p < 0.0001$, $\eta^2 = 0.38$, $M = 3.80$ & 3.54, $SD = 0.81$ & 0.52 respectively. The effect size was relatively low.

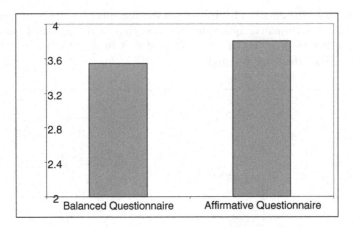

Fig. 3. Participants' evaluation of the quality of the email response

In particular, participants rated the email responder (in this case the CSR) as being significantly more supportive in the affirmative questionnaire than in the balanced questionnaire $F(1, 885) = 347.88$, $p < 0.0001$, $\eta^2 = 1.06$, $M = 3.77$ & 2.93, $SD = 0.93$ & 0.29 respectively. The effect size was extremely high.

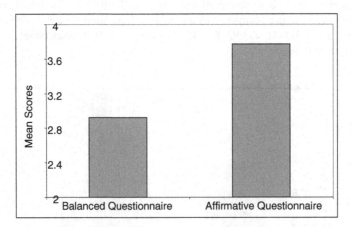

Fig. 4. Participants' evaluation of how supportive was the responder of the email

Participants rated the CSR responding to the consumer's question as being significantly friendlier and more respectful in the affirmative questionnaire compared

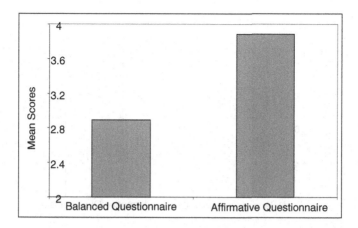

Fig. 5. Participants' evaluation of how respectful and friendly was the responder of the email

to the balanced questionnaire $F(1, 885) = 511.76$, $p < 0.0001$, $\eta^2 = 1.23$, $M = 3.89$ & 2.89, $SD = 0.88$ & 0.33 respectively. The effect size was extremely high.

Participants rated the CSR as being significantly more empathetic in the affirmative questionnaire compared to the balanced questionnaire $F(1, 885) = 39.22$, $p < 0.0001$, $\eta^2 = 0.41$, $M = 3.76$ & 3.45, $SD = 0.84$ & 0.62 respectively. The effect size was moderate.

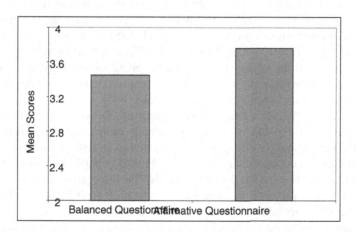

Fig. 6. Participants' evaluation of how empathetic was the responder of the email

Participants reported feeling significantly more valued by the CSR when they responded to the affirmative questionnaire compared to the balanced questionnaire $F(1, 885) = 72.03$, $p < 0.0001$, $\eta^2 = 0.54$, $M = 3.68$ & 3.25, $SD = 1$ & 0.40 respectively. The effect size was moderate.

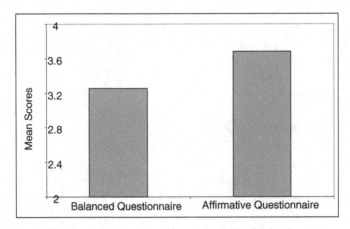

Fig. 7. Participants' evaluation of how valued they felt by the response

4.2 Email Type

Participants rated the email as having resolved the consumer's issue significantly more when the issue pertained to the company's billing policy compared to an issue with another user in the customer-to-customer e-commerce site $F(1, 885) = 14.44, p < 0.0001, \eta^2 = 0.23, M = 3.53$ & $3.35, SD = 0.77$ & 0.77 respectively. The effect size was low.

Participants rated the structure of the email as being significantly better when the issue pertained to the company's billing policy compared to an issue with another user in the customer-to-customer e-commerce site $F(1, 885) = 4.6, p < 0.0001, \eta^2 = 0.14, M = 3.55$ & $3.44, SD = 0.77$ & 0.79 respectively. The effect size was low.

Participants rated the quality of the email as being significantly better when the issue pertained to the company's billing policy compared to an issue with another user in the customer-to-customer e-commerce site $F(1, 885) = 18.61, p < 0.0001, \eta^2 = 0.28, M = 3.76$ & $3.57, SD = 0.66$ & 0.69 respectively. The effect size was low.

Participants rated the CSR as being significantly more supportive when the issue pertained to the company's billing policy compared to an issue with another member in the customer-to-customer e-commerce site $F(1, 885) = 8.05, p < 0.0001, \eta^2 = 0.16, M = 3.39$ & $3.26, SD = 0.83$ & 0.76 respectively. The effect size was low.

There was no difference in participants' rating of the CSR's friendliness and respectfulness in responding to the consumer's question when the issue pertained to the company's billing policy or when the issue pertained to a transaction problem with another user in the customer-to-customer e-commerce site $F(1, 885) = 2.85, p = 0.09, M = 3.41$ & $3.32, SD = 0.88$ & 0.76 respectively.

There was no difference in participants' rating of the CSR's empathy in responding to the consumer's question when the issue pertained to the company's billing policy or when the issue pertained to a transaction problem with another user in the customer-to-customer e-commerce site $F(1, 885) = 3.67, p = 0.06, M = 3.65$ & $3.54, SD = 0.75$ & 0.74 respectively.

Participants reported feeling significantly more valued by the CSR when they received a response to the company's billing policy related issue compared to the response received for an issue with another user in the customer-to-customer e-commerce site $F(1, 885) = 12.94$, $p < 0.0001$, $\eta^2 = 0.33$, $M = 3.55$ & 3.36, $SD = 0.74$ & 0.80 respectively. The effect size was low.

5 Discussion

When participants confirmed research hypotheses for the type of issue in the email, the effect sizes were low. Possibly, the statistical significance was the result of high power as a consequence of high cell-sizes.

Participants confirmed research hypotheses for the type of questionnaire employed to measure attitudes. In the case of framing statements in questionnaire design, when all the statements are framed positively, participants may assume that a positive response is sought by the researchers. Thus, they may try to be helpful by confirming what they believe to be the research hypotheses. Thus, respondents are likely to provide more positive responses in affirmative questionnaires. Clearly, responses to the affirmative questionnaire with only positive valence statements are affected by acquiescence bias.

In general, the effect sizes for the difference in attitudes between the balanced questionnaire and affirmative questionnaire were high both for the responder of the email and the artifact - email. The effect size for perception of self was somewhat lower. The smaller standard deviation for the balanced questionnaire compared to the questionnaire with items framed in only positive valence suggests that the respondents likely paid more attention to the individual items in the balanced questionnaire. Thus, the responses were probably more accurate reflections of their perceptions and attitudes, resulting in significantly less variability. Possibly, participants did not read the items as carefully in the questionnaire consisting of only positive valence items, thereby resulting in response set bias and greater variability. The reliability of the responses in both the questionnaires - balanced and affirmative, may be high. However, the validity of the outcome based on balanced questionnaire may be higher. Hence, assessments about the larger population based on the results obtained through balanced questionnaires would likely be more accurate. Consequently, user findings obtained with a balanced questionnaire administered to a random sample would have greater external validity, compared to findings derived from data collected though a questionnaire with items framed in only one direction.

6 Conclusion

Accurate measurement of attitudes is of paramount importance particularly in market and consumer research as inflated assessments of users' satisfaction or propensity to use products could have deleterious consequences in terms of investment in resources. Controlling for biases in the measurement of attitudes would provide stakeholders with a more accurate assessment, allowing them to take appropriate measures to improve user satisfaction, trust, and loyalty.

References

1. Allport, G.W.: Attitudes. In: Murchison, C. (ed.) Handbook of Social Psychology, pp. 798–884. Clark University Press, Worcester, MA (1935)
2. Brace, I.: Questionnaire Design: How to plan, structure and write survey material for effective market research. Kogan Page, London (2004)
3. Fishbein, M., Ajzen, I.: Belief, attitude, intention, and behavior: An introduction to theory and research. Addison-Wesley, Reading, MA (1975)
4. Krosnick, J.A.: Response strategies for coping with the cognitive demands of attitude measures in surveys. Applied Cognitive Psychology 5, 213–236 (1991)
5. Ray, J.J.: Reviving the problem of acquiescent response bias. The. Journal of Social Psychology 121, 81–96 (1983)
6. Reeves, B., Nass, C.: The Media Equation: How People Treat Computers, Television, and New Media Like Real People and Places. Cambridge University Press, Cambridge (1996)
7. Rorer, L.G.: The great response style myth. Psychological Bulletin 63, 129–156 (1965)
8. Tesser, A., Whitaker, D., Martin, L., Ward, D.: Attitude heritability, attitude change and physiological responsivity. Personality and Individual Differences 24, 89–96 (1998)

Measuring the Emotional Drivers of Visual Preference in China

Hsun Tang, JiaMing Lang, JinYu Lou, and Kenneth Farmer

eBay Inc.
2145 Hamilton Ave. San Jose CA 95125, United States
itsdesire@gmail.com, {jlang,jlou,kfarmer}@ebay.com

Abstract. The purpose of this research is to understand the visual preference of Chinese internet users and to create a visual language system that elicits key emotional experiences. Designers carefully selected a rich variety of visual stimuli that spanned different products / environments as well as abstract forms. A laddering interview methodology was used to elicit the emotions evoked by the different visual design cues. The results of the research were used to modify web page design.

Keywords: Emotion, Laddering Interview, Visual Design, Chinese.

1 Background

Over the past few years, the term "localization" has become increasingly popular among international companies in China. This often means that a company adapts local language and content to fit in a particular market. But what does that really mean to users? Can we just translate a product and discard the fact that each market has its own specific needs? Consumers in China often say that "our product is not Chinese enough" or "we have to do something to make it a better fit for this market." What does "not Chinese enough" really mean? How do we measure it? We decided to learn more about this topic from the perspective of visual design and conducted research to determine the visual elements, trends and styles that will meet user's needs.

The goal of this research is to find out how to connect with our user at the emotional and visual level in order to further improve the desirability of our product. One of the challenges of this type of research is to elicit personal feelings and emotions from people in an impersonal interview setting. Since the 1960's, market research has used an interviewing technique commonly referred to as "laddering" to identify the linkages among product features, personal benefits and emotions. Reynolds and Guttman (1988) formalized this approach in a paper entitled "Laddering theory, method, analysis and interpretation."[1] We used a modified laddering interview method to elicit personal thoughts and feelings in our research.

2 Laddering

Laddering traditionally utilizes a series of questions to probe on the reasons why successively more abstract concepts are important to people. For example, if we were

N. Aykin (Ed.): Usability and Internationalization, Part II, HCII 2007, LNCS 4560, pp. 506–509, 2007.
© Springer-Verlag Berlin Heidelberg 2007

to ask a participant why he likes his favorite writing pen, the participant might say "I like the way it looks, it feels comfortable in my hand, I bought it for a good price and I like the way it writes." Once we have elicited these attributes of the pen, we then focus on each attribute in turn and ask why each is personally important to the participant. For example, if we ask the participant why it is important that the pen "feel comfortable", the participant might reply "so that my hand will not get tired." That is, the benefit of the pen to the participant is that his hand will not tire. Continuing this line of questioning, we then ask the participant why it is important that his hand not get tired. The participant might reply, "Because I can be more productive." Finally we ask the participant why it is important to be productive, and the participant reply "so that I can be successful in my job." In this case we have taken the participant up the ladder from attributes of the pen all the way to success.

Laddering is a very effective tool to get respondents to discuss emotions and feelings in a short period of time during an interview. In order to further create a comfortable setting in which to discuss emotions, we decided to interview friends together in this research.

3 Methodology

3.1 Narrow Down Objectives

This research project was designed to understand the characteristics and emotions of visual preference among general Chinese internet users, and to apply these findings to design of our website. There are 3 key phases to this project. This paper focuses on Phase I of the research

Phase I: Collection of broad and general information from users in seven Tier 1 and Tier 2 cities in China using a combined laddering interview and card sort methodology. Our goal was to get a deep understanding of visual preferences and to identify any similarities and differences in preferences among different regions in China.

Phase II: Design exploration using the visual preferences that we uncovered in Phase I. We selected a few key flow page designs as a template for designers to explore different types of design styles. The content and layout of the pages were exactly the same, and only the visual styles and elements differed. This ensured that our respondents did not get distracted by page content when we gathered feedback.

Phase III: Based on Phase II findings, we had a clear understanding of user preference. We verified the findings through application to our website design.

3.2 Laddering Interview

We employed a variation of the traditional laddering interview method, as outlined below. There are five steps to this modified laddering interview process:

- Step 1: Respondents sorted different types of products, images and other stimuli displayed on cards into 3 to 5 groups based on aspects of visual appearance such as shape, texture, color, material, complexity, simplicity, etc. We asked respondents not to focus on things such as price, whether they personally would buy the object, etc. We encouraged them to take their time and to think creatively about how they sort the objects and to have fun with the task. The interviewer kept a list of which objects were sorted into what groups.

- Step 2: Respondents were asked to describe the features that each group had in common and how the groups differed. These object features or "attributes" formed the bottom of the ladders.
- Step 3: The interviewer asked respondents why each attribute was personally important to them. For example the interviewer might say to a respondent "You mentioned that some objects have rounded edges. Do you like objects that have rounded edges? Why or why not?" The interviewer then probed for the personal reasons why the attribute Rounded Edges is liked or disliked. The respondent might reply "I like objects with rounded edges because they are easy to hold." The interviewer then recorded that Rounded Edges connects with Easy to Hold. The interviewer repeated this for each attribute. In this example, Easy to Hold is a benefit. The interviewer repeated this process for all attributes elicited in Step 2.
- Step 4: The interviewer asked each respondent why each benefit was important to them. For example, "You mentioned that Easy to Hold is important to you. Why is it important that an object be Easy to Hold?" The interviewer probed for personal reasons why Easy to Hold is important. For example, the respondent might say "when an object is Easy to hold my hand does not get tired." The interviewer recorded that Easy to hold connects with Hand Does Not Get Tired." In this example, Hand Does Not Get Tired is a higher-order benefit. The interviewer repeated this process for all benefits elicited in Step 3.
- Step 5: Finally, the interviewer asked why each high-order benefit was important to respondents. For example, the respondent might say that "Hand Does Not Get Tired" is important because "I Feel Good That I Can be More Productive and Successful at My Job." This type of emotion or feeling marked the end of the laddering sequence of questions.

3.3 Card Sorting

The cards presented to users included 4 groups of stimuli:

1. 5 sets of pictures of different types of cars;
2. 6 sets of pictures of different models of mobile phones;
3. 6 sets of pictures of different scenes of shopping environments;
4. 63 pictures of abstract stimuli, varying in content, color, shape or arrangement.

Method for selection of stimuli. All the stimuli were selected purposely and carefully by visual designers. The designers worked to ensure that stimuli in each group had design characteristics unique to each group, but between the four groups, the design characteristics were thematically connected and consistent.

For example, our target was to narrow down the final set to include 5 or 6 different models of mobile phones. The designers first collected pictures of over 50 different mobile phones. Then the designers started to remove similar models from the collections, based upon shape, color, size, function etc. It was relatively easy to reduce the total number of mobile phones to 10-15.

At the final stage, the designers compared and selected the mobile phones very carefully so that each model was distinguishable from the others. It must have design characteristics that the other phones do not have, and the final 5 to 6 models must cover all design characteristics of interest. This selection method was applied for each of the four groups of stimuli.

Respondent card sorting task. During the interview, the respondents first were asked to select their favorite car, mobile phone and shopping environment from the card groups. The laddering interview elicited the emotional reasons (or "emotion keywords") behind this preference.

The emotional keywords helped our designers understand what kinds of visual design characteristics were popular among our target users, and what kinds of emotions these attributes triggered. The moderator chose about 5 most frequently mentioned emotion keywords, and then asked the respondents to sort the cards in group 4 (the abstract stimuli) into 5 piles according to how well the stimuli seemed to be associated with each emotion. This sorting exercise provided designers with additional detailed information about how different design characteristics drive different emotions.

4 Application

The research provided a type of dictionary of visual cues and associated emotions across many different regions of China. These findings were used to modify the visual design of our site so as to better align it with the desired emotional experience of our users.

References

1. Reynolds, Thomas, J., Gutman, J.: Laddering Theory, Method, Analysis, and Interpretation, Journal of Advertising Research, pp. 11–31 (February/March 1988)

Developing Adaptive Mobile Support for Crisis Response in Synthetic Task Environments

Guido te Brake and Nanja Smets

TNO Defence, Safety and Security
PO Box 23, 3769 ZG Soesterberg
The Netherlands
{guido.tebrake,nanja.smets}@tno.nl

Abstract. This paper presents an experimental platform for the development and evaluation of mobile decision support for crisis response operations. Using a game-engine, synthetic task environments can be created in which coordination support and the usability of adaptive user interfaces for first responders can be examined in a highly controlled manner. Results of the first experiment in which the platform was used to examine the influences of map size and spatial ability on task performance and situational awareness are presented, and ongoing work is described.

Keywords: crisis response operations, synthetic task environments, adaptive support systems.

1 Introduction

Information technology is developed to support first responders with communication, information sharing, and situational awareness, to enable more effective crisis response operations. Because of the variability and dynamics of their work environment and task sets, first responders may benefit from support tools with adaptive user interfaces. Adaptive interfaces can change the content, presentation, or dialogue, to match user demands real-time without the explicit control of the user and have the potential to improve human–machine performance. However, when not properly designed adaptivity can degrade performance as well. Besides variation in environmental factors, great diversity in user preferences can be expected as well. To be effective, the adaptive system needs a good understanding of the user's capacities and preferences, his or her current tasks, and the location and characteristics of the surroundings of the user.

Due to the complexity of designing adaptive interfaces, frequent testing of intermediate prototypes by future users is important. However, evaluations of crisis response applications in real-world settings are expensive, potentially dangerous, and may sometimes even be impossible to execute [1]. Evaluation in a synthetic task environment (STE) can provide an appropriate alternative for real-world testing.

This paper describes a game-based experimental platform for the development of mobile support systems for crisis operations. Modern game engines can create

N. Aykin (Ed.): Usability and Internationalization, Part II, HCII 2007, LNCS 4560, pp. 510–519, 2007.

realistic yet low cost STEs that are suited for multiparty testing. We think that using STEs for development and testing is a powerful approach, both for exploration of new support concepts as for evaluation of final implementations of user interfaces for specific tasks. The platform consists of two parts: a 3D synthetic task environment and a support tool on which new support concepts can be implemented for evaluation.

In Section 2, a brief introduction is given to other work on games and STEs for crisis management. Next, the platform is described and the results of the first experiment studying the effects of map size and spatial ability on task performance and situational awareness are presented. Finally, we show the versatility of the platform by describing ongoing work.

2 Related Work

The term serious gaming is often used to describe the use of games in science, education, training, health, and public policy [2,3]. Although the term is relatively new, the concept to exploit computer games for purposes other than entertainment is not. The National Research Council envisioned prospects for the usage of game engines as early as 1997 because game engines come at low costs yet provide effective and efficient graphics, replication mechanisms, and modeling options [4]. This led to the wide application of games in the field of training and education, as the topics of the majority of articles in the journal Simulation & Gaming show. For example, the United States Army uses Rogue Spear [5] to teach strategy and tactics and to train troops to fight in urban terrain. Other domains in which games have been used are artificial intelligence research [6,7], human robot interaction and robotic behavior in urban search and rescue [8], recruitment (America's Army [9]), and experimentation. Recent publications describe the possibilities of using COTS systems for military experimentation [10], and some of the pros and cons of using STEs for psychological experimentation [11].

Game technology has been used in the crisis management domain. Unreal Triage [12] is an analysis and training tool for emergency responders using a synthetic task environment, created by the Unreal Tournament game engine. The player's objective is to perform primary triage. Players must locate and classify the casualties into one of four treatment categories. The player interviews each casualty to determine cognitive health and then examines the casualty for the status of the airway, breathing and circulation. Victims are then tagged as red (immediate), yellow (urgent), green (delayed), or black (fatally wounded). Hazmat: Hotzone is a networked, multiplayer simulation, created at Carnegie Mellon University in cooperation with the New York Fire Department, which uses game technology to train first responders for chemical and hazardous materials emergencies. FiRSTE is a first responder training environment that focuses on training first responders with a high level of immersion and physical interfacing [13].

Other more technical work has been committed on developing architectures for simulation of crises that can be used for training of emergency response [14,15].

3 Experimental Platform

The Unreal Tournament 2004 game engine is very popular in the academic community. Besides the quality of the engine, attractiveness lies in the modification called Gamebots [6], which allows external software to communicate with the game engine. Gamebots was developed at the University of Southern California for artificial intelligence research and provides two application programming interfaces (APIs). The first API allows controlling virtual characters in the game, the second pipes information out of the game.

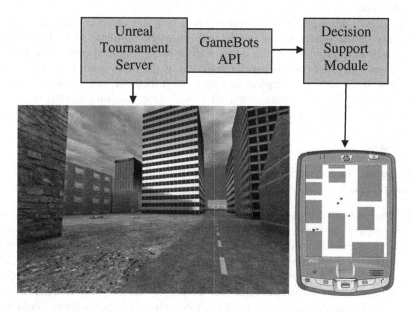

Fig. 1. Generic platform architecture, showing an urban STE and a support tools with a map presenting the locations of the player (a first responder) and several civilian victims

Fig. 1 shows the architecture of our experimental environment [16]. The main component of the architecture is the Unreal Tournament 2004 server that hosts the game. Each player, representing a first responder, has the synthetic world at its disposal via the replication mechanism of Unreal Tournament 2004. All types of scenes can be created varying from simple block worlds to very realistic urban areas using the Unreal Level Editor UnrealEd 3.0 that comes with Unreal Tournament 2004. The Gamebots script was slightly changed and recompiled using the Unreal Tournament 2004 compiler to enable transfer from additional information from the game to the support tool, such as the location of the team members. The basic support tool is created using Microsoft's Visual Studio's C# language and communicates with the Unreal Tournament server using a TCP/IP channel.

Logging data for analysis is one of the main advantages of experimenting in simulated environments. The platform logs trajectories, actions, and communication. Performance parameters can easily be measured based on the logged data.

4 Experiment

The platform has been tested in an experiment with naive participants in June 2006. Goal of the experiment was twofold: to test the platform, and to do a baseline experiment to which results of future experiments using advanced adaptive concepts can be compared. The experiment, the results and some lessons learned are described in this section.

The participant's task was to be a first responder and to search and rescue victims of a chemical cloud as quickly as possible. In the meantime he or she had to build an understanding of the situation to be able to answer questions from the commander about the area.

The focus of the experiment was the effect of map size and user's spatial ability on the quality of the situational awareness and rescue performance of first responders. Participants were provided with a small map showing a limited part of the environment in one condition (in this paper referred to as the PDA condition), and a larger map showing almost the complete environment (called the tablet condition) in the other condition. The maps were displayed on a desktop monitor. A better rescue performance and situation awareness was expected for the condition with the large map.

4.1 Method

Participants. Twenty university students participated in the experiment as paid volunteers, nine male and eleven female. Average age of the participants was 22.

Task. The task of the participant was to search and rescue 30 victims that were distributed over the synthetic environment and whose locations were shown on the map of the support tool. Victims in the game were rescued by walking up to them, after which they disappeared from the simulated environment and from the map. They were not rendered realistically, because this did not seem required for our purposes. A second task was to remember important landmarks and events (like a burning car), because a commander could ask for this information. The participants could move forward, backward, sideways, and turn using a game controller. In a pilot study, we noticed that some participants hardly looked at the STE, but navigated though the area solely by looking at their support map. In real life, it is not possible to walk around and pay attention to your support tool at the same time (with the exception of head-up support tools). We solved this problem by turning the support screen black when the participant walked.

Design. The experiment had a within subjects design. The map size was the independent variable with two levels: a big map (tablet condition) and a small map (PDA condition). To exclude learning effects, we balanced the map size condition with two different urban synthetic environments using a Latin square design.

A map of the area was available on the support screen, showing buildings (pink), office buildings (grey), streets (yellow/white) and parks, grass and trees (green). The colors of the map were taken from the colors of maps on www.routenet.nl, to create a familiar look and feel. Victims on the map were indicated by a green circle and a unique number, the location of the participant was shown as a red circle with a bar indicating viewing direction. An impression of the 3D STE is given in Fig 2.

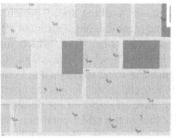

Fig. 2. Left: screenshot from one of the used STEs. Right: the large and small size support map, of which one was provided to the users.

Dependent variables measured for the search and rescue task were:

- Performance data. This includes the distance participants walked in the environment and the number of victims rescued in the game.
- Situation awareness (SA). SA was measured using the SAGAT method [17,18], a questionnaire, and performance measures. The SAGAT method focuses on global SA and has the advantage that it avoids retrospective recall like the questionnaire. The questionnaire, however, is less intrusive because it does not interrupt the scenario played by the participants.
- Subjective data gathered in questionnaires

Procedure. At the start of the experiment participants were given a general, written instruction about the experiment, and were asked to fill in a general questionnaire containing questions about computer and game experience. Subsequently a spatial test was conducted. After instruction participants navigated a testing trail in an environment similar to the test environments to assess the game controller handling skills of the participant. Next, they were given instruction of the task. The main part of the experiment consisted of two blocks of 30 minutes, with a ten minute break, in which the participant performed the search and rescue task in both conditions. Afterwards they navigated through the testing trail (in reverse direction) for the second time, and filled in a questionnaire about the experiment. The whole experiment took approximately three hours.

Material. Each participant used two computers, both with a 17 inch computer screen. The support screen displayed either the small or the large support map; the environment screen displayed the STE, as was shown in Fig. 2. The two screens were placed in front of the participant, next to each other. A Logitech game controller was used to navigate in the virtual environment.

4.2 Results and Discussion

Goal of this study was to examine the effect of map size on situation awareness and route planning efficiency. Participants in the tablet condition had a better overview of the amount of victims they rescued than participants in the PDA condition, but no other significant effects on performance were found. These findings may (partly) be a result of the chosen walking speed, which was so high that running around was as efficient as route planning. No significant effects were found for SA either. The SA of the participants was rather poor, which may be due to the main task of rescuing victims for which not much SA was required.

A non-significant trend suggests that in the tablet condition participants with a high spatial ability rescued more victims than participants with a low spatial ability. Spatial ability did not have an effect on the number of victims rescued in the PDA condition. This suggests that in the tablet condition participants with a high spatial ability were able to plan efficient routes. These results were also supported by the subjective data. Participants were asked whether they navigated mainly using the STE, the support map, or both. The outcome shows that participants in the PDA condition looked mainly at the STE or the map and the STE combined, whereas in the tablet condition participants looked mainly at the map or at the map and the STE combined.

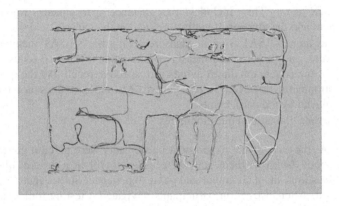

Fig. 3. Routes of five participants in the tablet condition

During the experiment and analysis some known advantages of synthetic environments became apparent. The software makes it possible to log events in a scenario that would be difficult to log in a real-life environment. For instance the route walked by the participants, pauses, and the time they used the support tool. Logging in Unreal Tournament 2004 can be done extensively, because every interaction with the environment is captured. It is easy to extract the data from the game environment and then process it into useful visualizations to interpret the results (Fig. 3).

Navigating performance of participants improved during the experiments, as was shown by the smaller time required by the participants to walk the testing trail after the experiments. Sufficient practice before the experiments may eliminate this effect. An alternative is to correct the measurements based on the difference in speed before and after the experiment. It was also found that difference between participants were considerable, mainly correlated with gaming experience and age, which should be taken into account when designing experiments [11]. Use of the platform was enjoyed by the participants, and did not cause serious usability problems. This can be explained by the fact that most were computer-savvy university students. However, even for participants without gaming experience use of the virtual environment and the game controller proved to be easy.

One problem sometimes encountered when using dynamic synthetic environments is simulation sickness [11]. No problems were encountered during this experiment, although in pilot runs when the turning speed was higher and people were seated closer to the screens, one participant had to stop because she did not feel well. Hence, simulator sickness is an issue that should be paid attention to when designing this type of experiments.

5 Current Work

The platform is currently being used in other projects to develop and evaluate intelligent support for fielded virtual teams. All projects make use of the same platform and technology, and require only the design or alteration of a synthetic environment to match the research requirements. Because of this, follow-up experiments can be designed very rapidly and results can be compared with previous findings because all other factors can be kept constant.

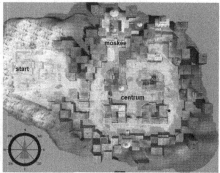

Fig. 4. STE and support tool to examine the effect of a decision aid on situational awareness

Fig. 4 shows the STE and the supporting map that were used in a project that examined the effect of supporting maps on situational awareness. Task of the participants was to follow a person on the move whose location is reported once in a while and presented on the map. An existing Unreal Tournament modification generating an urban Middle Eastern environment, Strike Force 2004 (www. strikeforce2004.com), was adopted and slightly modified. The experiment was recently done with military personnel, who stated that this type of environment is very suited for evaluation of support tools. The data of the experiment is currently being analyzed.

Another project, committed in cooperation with the Nijmegen Institute of Cognition and Information, focuses on heading-up and north-up maps. For some tasks, heading-up maps have shown to be superior, but it is expected that the development of a proper cognitive representation of the area may be influenced negatively. Fig. 5 shows the STE and the support map that were designed for this experiment. Participants survey the maze area supported by either a north-up or a heading-up map, and afterwards their cognitive representation is examined. Participants are shown an image of a particular place in the maze and are asked in which direction and at which distance a particular item can be found. The experiment is currently ready to be committed.

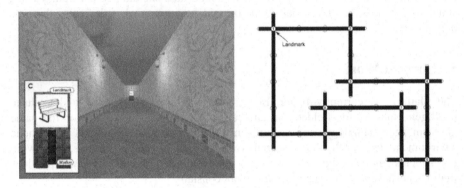

Fig. 5. STE and support tool for research on the effect of rotation of maps on the development of a cognitive representation of the area

In a related project, an adaptive interface concept will be developed that can help the user to choose between heading-up versus north-up visualization. It is known that some users prefer north-up and others heading-up. In this study it will be examined whether task performance of the user using his or her preferred visualization can be improved if the 'appropriate' visualization is selected automatically depending on the task at hand. Personalization of the interface according to user preferences will be an important topic. This experiment is currently being designed.

The projects described above focus on support of single users, but the platform is also very suited to examine virtual teams. Game engines generally allow up to 16 or 32 players, creating ample opportunities for research on multiparty cooperation. One of the main problems with virtual teams is their sensitivity to a breakdown of wireless communication channels. One project will examine whether showing uncertainty about the positions of team members of which no recent location updates are available improves SA and team performance. This experiment is currently being designed.

6 Discussion and Conclusions

The platform was used in two experiments and has shown the advantages of experimenting in simulated task environments. Especially the high level of control over events and the ease of logging have proven very powerful. The reusability of STEs and the generic architecture of the platform enable fast design of materials for new and follow-up experiments. Follow-up experiments with a focus on virtual teams and adaptive user interfaces are currently being designed and executed.

A number of issues has come up during experimentation. One is the relation between the level of immersion and the development of situational awareness in virtual environments. Little is known on how realistic STEs must be to get situational awareness that is similar to situational awareness build in real-world experiments. A relevant question is whether the relatively poor level of SA of the participants can (partly) be attributed to the low level of immersion reached at desktop virtual environments.

Another issue that must be taken into account when designing experiments is the diversity in user virtual navigation skills. Although both the university students that participated in the experiment described in Section 3 as well as the military personnel that participated in the first experiment described in Section 4 found the platform easy to use, differences in navigation skills could influence measurements. This issue, which has also been addressed by others [11], warrants further research.

The evidence that mobile use of maps and support effectiveness is related to user spatial ability suggests that different users may benefit from different types of navigation support. The experiments mentioned in the previous section that look at heading-up versus north-up displays will address this issue. Task and cultural differences between the various parties in crisis management are other important factors to address. Adaptivity and user diversity are key concepts for applications that aim at supporting emergency operations in real-time and dynamic environments.

Acknowledgments. The research reported here is part of the Interactive Collaborative Information Systems (ICIS) project, supported by the Dutch Ministry of Economic Affairs, grant nr: BSIK03024. The ICIS project is hosted by the DECIS Lab (http://www.decis.nl), the open research partnership of Thales Nederland, the Delft University of Technology, the University of Amsterdam and the Dutch Foundation of Applied Scientific research (TNO).

We thank Oliver Lindemann of Nijmegen Institute of Cognition and Information and Robert de Bruin of TNO for permission to show their implementations in Fig. 4 and Fig. 5.

References

1. Jenvald, J., Morin, M.: Simulation-supported live training for emergency response in hazardous environments. Simulation & Gaming 35(3), 363–377 (2004)
2. Serious Games: Serious Games Initiative. Retrieved April 10, 2006 (2006), from www.seriousgames.org
3. Lewis, M., Jacobson, J.: Game Engines in Scientific Research. Communications of the ACM 45(1), 27–31 (2002)
4. National Research Council: Modeling and Simulation: Linking Entertainment & Defense. National Academy Press, Washington (1997)
5. Rogue Spear: Tom Claney's Rainbow Six Rogue Spear. Retrieved January 26, 2006 (2006), from www.roguespear.com
6. Kaminka, G.A., Veloso, M.M., Schaffer, S., Sollito, C., Adobbati, R., Marshall, A.N., Scholer, A., Tejada, S.: GameBots: a flexible test bed for multiagent team research. Communications of the ACM 45(1), 43–45 (2002)

7. Laird, J.E., van Lent, M.: Human-level AI's Killer Application: Interactive Computer Games. In: AAAI Fall Symposium Technical Report. North Falmouth, Massachusetts, pp. 80–97 (2000)
8. Wang, J., Lewis, M., Hughes, S., Koes, M., Carpin, S.: Validating USARsim for use in HRI research. In: Proceedings of the 49th Annual Meeting of the Human Factors and Ergonomics Society pp. 457–461 (2005)
9. Armerica's Army: Developed by the U.S. Army. Washington, DC: U.S. Army Office of Public Affairs (2002)
10. Fong, G.: Adapting COTS games for military experimentation. Simulation & Gaming 37(4), 452–465 (2006)
11. Frey, A., Hartig, J., Ketzel, A., Zinkernagel, A., Moosbrugger, H.: The use of virtual environments based on a modification of the computer game Quake III Arena ® in psychological experimenting. Computers in Human Behavior 23, 2026–2039 (2007)
12. McGrath, D., McGrath, S.P.: Simulation and Network-Centric Emergency Response. In: Interservice/Industry Training, Simulation, and Education Conference (I/ITSEC) (2005)
13. Leu, M., Hilgers, M., Agarwal, S., Hall, R., Lambert, T., Albright, R., Nebel, K.: Training in Virtual Environment for First Responders. In: Proceedings of Midwest Section ASEE meeting, Rolla, MO (2003)
14. Jain, S., McLean, C.R.: Integrated simulation and gaming architecture for incident management training. In: Winter Simulation Conference, pp. 904–913 (2005)
15. Mehrotra, S., Butts, B., Kalashnikov, D., Venkatasubramanian, N., Rao, R., Chockalingam, G., Eguchi, R., Adams, B., Huyck, C.: Project Rescue: challenges in responding to the unexpected. SPIE 5304, 179–192 (2004)
16. Te Brake, G., de Greef, T., Lindenberg, J., Rypkema, J., Smets, N.: Developing Adaptive User Interfaces Using a Game-based Simulation Environment. In: Proceedings of the 3rd International ISCRAM Conference. Newark, NJ (2006)
17. Endsley, M.R., Garland, D.J.: Situation Awareness Analysis and Measurement, pp. 147–173. Lawrence Erlbaum Associates, Mahwah, USA (2000)
18. Endsley, M.R., Bolté, B., Jones, D.G. (eds.): Designing for situation awareness. Taylor & Francis (2003)

Structural User Preferences of Interfaces and Time Orientation

Nancy Thiels, Theresa Maxeiner, and Kerstin Röse

Center for Human-Machine-Interaction
University of Kaiserslautern
P.O. Box 3049, 67653 Kaiserslautern
Germany
{thiels,roese}@mv.uni-kl.de, maxeiner@rhrk.uni-kl.de

Abstract. Today the user orientation within the development process of user interfaces in production environment is concentrated on tasks. This is realized by focusing on user groups. To enhance the usability of user interfaces, the development process is expanded by the personalization of user interfaces. Thus user preferences and their attributes e.g. individual differences concerning the structure of interfaces have to be examined for being able to develop appropriate interfaces for specific users. Different test methods to gain these preferences and attributes are described within this paper. The found structural preferences can be connected to the concept of time orientation: it classifies people in two different categories: polychrons and monochrons. The test results confirm that these characteristic are rather individual differences than intercultural variables.

Keywords: Cross-cultural, Usability Engineering, Time orientation, User interface development.

1 Introduction

The personalisation of user interfaces has entered many fields - particularly the consumer product industry. The advantages of personalisation concepts become clear when using such systems: offered information is adjusted to the needs or previous use habits of users. In contrast to the consumer product industry, the personalisation of user interfaces and the orientation on users' needs are still rare in the production environment. Developers have a certain understanding of user needs and interests related to user interfaces. This understanding – no matter, how far or whether at all it is applicable – is realised in the development of user interfaces. The actual needs of users remain unconsidered [17]. One approach overcoming this lack are user groups. Studies in the field of user-group-specific prototypes showed that distinctive advantages result from these user interfaces; higher efficiency and a faster learnability could be obtained by specific structuring and design of prototypes for diverse user groups for example [15]. Personalisation which goes beyond role aspects in the vocational surrounding field and includes the design of user-specific interfaces was

N. Aykin (Ed.): Usability and Internationalization, Part II, HCII 2007, LNCS 4560, pp. 520–526, 2007.

examined in a study for colour design [10]. Extroverted and introverted users performed different tasks with user interfaces, especially designed for their needs in comparison to a neutral interface. The use of specially implemented user interface could not be proved significantly favourable. However users showed clear reactions to different designs: Those – mainly extroverted people – who preferred the extroverted interface considered the introverted one as boring and vice versa.

For developing user interfaces, the structure of task and functions is the basis for the further user interfaces design process and consequently for the usability of the user interface itself. Therefore it is important to know the structural preferences of those users working with the interface. The structural preferences of users can be connected to different time orientation concepts of users, as Zhang and Goonetilleke [16] found that user having different concepts of time orientation, referred to as monochrons and polychrons, solving tasks, e.g. by working with user interfaces, differently. Monochrons can just do one thing at a time, whereas polychrons do many things at once. Thus Zhang and Goonetilleke [16] concluded the concept of time orientation could be an individual difference within a culture, rather than an intercultural difference.

In this paper user characteristic and structuring preferences within the production environment will be tested. On basis of the test results it will be attempted to corroborate that the concept of time orientation are individual variables rather than intercultural variables.

2   User Interface Development

Most user interfaces in the production environment are the results of a systematic development process, consisting of the phases analysis, structuring, design and realisation. An evaluation accompanies all these phases (see Fig. 1).

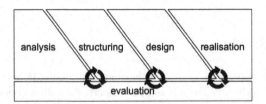

Fig. 1. Useware Engineering Process [2]

Within the analysis user tasks and their needs, as a result of these tasks, are worked out. The analysis phase is divided into the phases preparation, questioning and evaluation. During the preparation users who are to be questioned are selected. Furthermore questioning methods and materials are specified and completed. Then users are asked in order to reveal their tasks and needs, which have not been considered so far and as well as how the system is used. Finally the collected data of all users is aggregated and combined to a task model. Within the structuring phase the task model of the analysis is extended by functionalities of the system for which the user interface is developed. From these data a platform-independent use model [12] is created, which results in elementary use objects that describe inseparable and elementary user tasks. Through the selection of a hardware platform the usage structure for the future user interface derives from the former use model. In the design phase navigation and interaction concepts are specified on the basis of the usage structure. Furthermore the fundamental layout of the user interface is developed. The evaluation phase takes place accompanying all previously mentioned phases. On this respective results and/or partial results of the phases are evaluated in each case with the users. The aim is the integration of the evaluation outcomes into the specific phase of the user interface development process.

Apart form the evaluation phase direct user integration takes place in the analysis [14]. A user friendly system cannot be archived by the mere involvement of the user at the end of the development process. Quality and user orientation cannot derive from a usability test at the end of the process, but a continuous check must take place comparable to quality management concepts [13].

3 Personalisation of User Interfaces

Today, the personalisation of user interfaces within the production environment is mostly limited to user groups. User groups can be distinguished by different tasks what means that users of one group share the same tasks. Particularly in this environment, personalised user interfaces that consider specific individual charac-teristics and possible needs are not common. Even the adjustment to user groups is usually limited to the definition of the rights of access for certain areas of user interfaces or to the choice of different functions on a direct access within the user interface.

This kind of personalisation is technically accomplishable for today's operations, because only limited access to information and interactions is available for users. Due to ever changing technology, the development of individual user interfaces for every usage situation would not be efficient. However, a further personalisation of user interface design in production environment shall be permitted in order to cope with the variety of information and interaction. Accounting for requirements of a future, in which the complexibility and amount of information will steadily rise, user interfaces have to be personalised in order to present interaction and information possibilities user-adequately. Personalisation concepts differ by their technical implementation. The concepts can be divided into variable and fixed systems. Variable systems adapt to user's inputs. They can be divided into adaptive systems on the one hand and adaptable systems on the other hand [11]. The former are systems which adapt dynamically to user inputs. The latter are systems adapted by the user [8] by speci-fying his preferences before actually using the interface. Fixed systems do not respond to different user inputs. Different aspects of personalisation are considered during their development. At the end of the development process, different personalised interfaces result for different users.

In the production environment users have to habituate to one user interface and feel comfortable with it in order to be able to react fast and intuitively when using the interface. Therefore personalised user interfaces cannot change their structure and design with every login. Fixed personalised user interfaces with regard to the user attributes are the most promising concept. To consider and specify these attributes in personalized user interfaces, user test have to be performed in order to reveal required factors.

4 The Time Orientation Concept

The concept of time orientation by Hall [4; 5; 6] divides people in two extremes: monochrons and polychrons. Monochrons do one thing at a time and polychrons do many things at once. Originally Hall developed the time orientation concept to describe different cultures and their behavior concerning time. He also adds other attributes to this concept [7]: For example monochrons are low-context, need information and committed to the job. Polychrons are high-context, already have information and are committed to people and human relationships (see Table 1).

Table 1. Characteristic of monochronic and polychronic people [7]

Monochronistic	Polychronistic
Do one thing at a time	Do many things at once
Concentrated on the job	Are highly distractible and subject to interruptions
View time commitments as critical	View time commitments as objectives
Are low-context and need information	Are high-context and already have information
Are committed to the job	Are committed to people and human relationships
Adhere strictly to the job	Change plans often and easily
Emphasize promptness	Base promptness on the importance of and significance of the relationships
Are accustomed to short-term relationships	Have a strong tendency to build lifetime relationships

Through this concept it is possible to order user who differ by geographic parts to one of the two extremes: For example northern Europeans are said to be monochronic and Latin America polychronic. But it is important to note that these cultures have not to be exclusively one concept of time orientation: The Japanese, for example, are polychrons in dealing with other people and monochrons by working for official business [9]. Other research in this field showed that polychrons are able to perform multiple tasks better than monochrons [3]. Zhang and Goonetilleke [16] performed tests once to find out the ability of monochrons and polychrons to control of two parallel processes and second to evaluate further attributes concerning monchrons and polychrons. The first test showed a better performance of the polychrons, as was expected because of the former research in this field.

5 Test Methods

5.1 Psychological Scales

Apart from demographic data, the usage of and the knowledge about technical equipment and devices was prompted. Furthermore, a questionnaire was included in order to examine the belief of control of users within the handling of technical devices [2]. Additionally parts of an intelligence test were integrated to appraise the technical ability and linguistic skills. Finally questions aiming at different traits of character such as an extroverted or introverted personality were used, as it was verified in a study by Karsvall [10] that those aspects have a significant influence on the design of user interfaces. These variables were collected within pre-tests. Therefore they perform as independent variables for the further test to collect the structuring preferences.

5.2 System Tests

To reveal preferences regarding the structure of user interfaces, the user had to perform different tasks with different kind of information systems belonging to a specific machine. While the content of the systems remained the same, the structure differed. Four different systems were tested: two hierarchical systems in one case embellished within a side map, in another case within a tree map; a network structure embellished with hyper links and as a reference system the original system which contained a tree map and hyper links. All systems were equipped with a search function.

5.3 Interviews

Afterwards users were interviewed about their impressions of the systems during the test. Thereby users were asked about their previous knowledge of the content as well as of the machine type belonging to the information system. Furthermore they were asked to estimate their own performance regarding errors and time to solve the tasks. Finally users were to state the preferred system without consideration of their performance and why. They were asked to rate all tested systems in a hierarchical order, beginning with the most preferred one and ending with the system they disliked most.

6 Results

In this study 38 German users (30 male, 8 female; with an average age of 28 years, varying between 18 and 56 years) from the production automation field were tested in three different groups: students, engineers and technicians.

The statistical evaluation of the system tests and the questionnaires about user attributes showed that there was a significant correlation between the hierarchical order of the preferred systems of users and their technical ability. Users who preferred working with the hierarchical system in tree-map-style, showed a higher technical ability than users which preferred working with the network system. Another significant result regarding tested users was the clear preference of only one of the five different systems: users judging a hierarchical system as the preferred one disliked the network-structure and vice versa. In general this meant that the hierarchical systems were located at one end and the network structured system at the other end of the ranking scale. But the most surprising results were that preferences for network structured system correlated significantly positive with the performance on the verbal skills – one part within the intelligence test. And it could also be shown that the preference for hierarchical systems correlated positively with the performance of a part of the intelligence test which tested the ability of users to recognize the essential. These two last results confirm the finding of Zhang and Goonetilleke [16] that structural preferences really are individual attributes and not cultural dependent.

7 Conclusion

Tests results have shown that there are different structural preferences within the tested persons. This shows as well as Zhang and Goonetilleke [16] (see Fig. 2) have found that the concept of time orientation and the characteristic of persons as monochron and polychron are individual culture-independent variables.

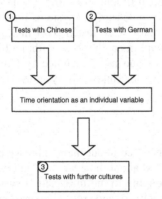

Fig. 2. Previous test to proof the time orientation concept as an individual variable

Next steps will be further tests (see Fig. 2) on the relation between structural preferences, time orientation and individual differences performed within other cultures in order to verify the structural preferences and the concept of time orientation as individual differences within a culture rather than intercultural differences. Therefore first of all tests with other European cultures are intended.

References

1. Beier, G.: Kontrollüberzeugungen im Umgang mit Technik; Ein Persönlichkeits-merkmal mit der Relevanz für die Gestaltung technischer Systeme Verlag im Internet GmbH, Berlin (2004)
2. Boedcher, A., Ehrmann, M.: Usability-Test versus Useware-Engineering. In: atp – Automatisierungstechnische Praxis, vol. 10 (Oldenbourg Industrieverlag, Muenchen) (2005)

3. Frei, R.L., Racicot, B., Travagline, A.: The impact of monochronic and Type A Behavior patterns on research productivity and stress. Journal of Managerial Psychology 14(5), 374–387 (1999)
4. Hall, E.T.: The silent language. Fawcett Publications, New York (1959)
5. Hall, E.T.: The dance of life: the other dimension of time. Anchor Press, New York (1989)
6. Hall, E.T.: The Hidden Dimension. Anchor Press, New York (1990)
7. Hall, E.T.: Understanding cultures differences: Germans, French and Americans, Yarmouth: Intercultural Press (1990)
8. Hinz, M., Fiala, Z., Wehner, F.: Personalization-Based Optimization of Web Interfaces for Mobile Devices. In. Mobile HCI, Lecture Notes in Computer Science 3160, 204–215 (2004)
9. Hoft, N.J.: Developing a cultural model. In: del Galdo, E., Nielsen, J. (eds.) International user interfaces, pp. 41–73. John Wiley & Sons, New York (1996)
10. Karsvall, A.: Personality Preferences in Graphical Interface Design; NordiCHI Conference, Aarhus, Denmark, October 19-23, pp. 19–23. ACM Press, New York (2002)
11. Mertens, P., Stoeßlein, M., Zeller, T.: Personalisierung und Benutzermodellierung in der betrieblichen Informationsverarbeitung. Arbeitspapier Nr.2, Wirtschaftsinformatik I, Universität, Erlangen-Nürnberg, (05/12/2006) (2004), http://www.wi1.unierlangen.de/veroeffentlichungen/suche.php
12. Mukasa, K., Zühlke, D., Bödcher, A., Reuther, A.: useML: A Human-Machine Interface Description Language. In: Proceedings of the Workshop on Developing User Interfaces with XML: Advances on User Interface Description Languages, May, Gallipoli, Italy (2004)
13. Roese, K., Ziegeler, D.: Mehrwert und Qualität durch prozessbegleitende Evaluation. In: atp – Automatisierungstechnische Praxis, 03/2006. Oldenbourg Industrieverlag, München (2006)
14. Thiels, N., Ehrmann, M., Zuehlke, D.: Model-based development of user-centred control systems in ambient intelligent production environments. In: The 9th IFAC Symposium on Automated Systems Based on Human Skill and Knowledge.Nancy, France (2006)
15. Wittenberg, C.: Requirements analysis and UI concept development for personalized mobile devices. In: 9th IFAC/IFIPS/IFORS/IEA Symposium on Analysis, Design, and Evaluation of Human-Machine Systems, Preprints (Atlanta) (September 2004)
16. Zhang, Y., Goonetilleke, R.: Time orientation and multitasking. In: IFAC Symposium on Analysis, Design and Evaluation of Human-Machine-Systems, Atlanta, Georgia, September 7-9, pp. 7–9. ACM Press, New York (2004)
17. Zuehlke, D.: Useware-Engineering für technische Systeme. Springer, Berlin (2004)

Overcoming the Language Barrier:
The Potential of the Visual Language LoCoS in
International Human-Computer Communication

Marleen Vanhauer, Karina Oertel, and Jörg Voskamp

Fraunhofer Institute for Computer Graphics, Department for Human-Centered Interaction
Technologies, Joachim-Jungius-Str. 11, 18059 Rostock, Germany
marleen@vanhauer.de, {Karina.Oertel,
Joerg.Voskamp}@igd-r.fraunhofer.de

Abstract. The present paper investigates whether the artificial language LoCoS is suited for application in international Human-Computer Communication, in comparison to natural and extended-natural foreign language. In the present study, LoCoS was examined with regard to criteria of effectiveness, encoding, efficiency, acceptance, learnability and functionality in contrast to English or English in combination with emoticons. The random sample yielded 47 persons from 19 different countries totally. A tentative acceptance of LoCoS as a symbolic language was observed, although the effort required to learn it was rated notably lower than that required to learn a foreign language. Communication occurred more efficiently because fewer LoCoS symbols than words were used. A general trend towards the use of extended natural languages could be detected, indicating that symbols are not exclusively accepted (yet), but are increasingly used in combination with a natural language.

Keywords: International Human-Computer Communication, Visual Communication, Internationalization, Artificial Languages, Visual Languages, Iconic Languages, Semiotics.

1 Introduction

The development of written and spoken language over several thousand years to its present diversity represents one of the most important aspects of human evolution. The creation of a universal writing system, enabling communication regardless of native language and cultural background, would be a major achievement for science and society. In the future, people would not have to study for months to pick up a new language [1]. Multilingual communities are already using machine translation to overcome the language barriers which are arising with growing frequency. However, inevitable semantic translation errors still occur which make precise interpretation difficult [2]. English is often declared language of the World Wide Web [3], but how optimal and effective do we communicate using English [4]? Internationally unambiguous visual languages, such as LoCoS, could help overcome cultural and linguistic barriers [4], and thus facilitate international human-computer communication.

N. Aykin (Ed.): Usability and Internationalization, Part II, HCII 2007, LNCS 4560, pp. 527–536, 2007.

Moreover, recognition of symbols may be more intuitive, as fewer people suffer from dyslexia in cultures with symbolic written language such as that used in China [5]. The increasing use of acronyms and emoticons, which, except for Japanese emojis, generally have conserved meaning world-wide, indicates a trend for internationally universal expression. However, attempts to artificially create and popularise international auxiliary languages in the past, such as *Leibniz' Universal Language, Solresol, Volapük, Lingua Franca, Esperanto* and *Interlingua* have failed largely due to either their initial effort required to learn them [6] or due to their origins in Indo-European languages [7]. Whereas *Blissymbolics* by Charles K. Bliss, based on rather abstract than iconic symbols [8], found its use in special education, Otto Neurath's *Isotype* had a big influence on graphical user interface design. Still, computer-based visual languages intentionally designed for research purposes in the past decade, such as the *Elephant's Memory, VIL, CAILS* and *Musli*, did not experience a break-through in use. This failure may be because contrary to the sophisticated English language no official grammars were published, and except for a basic prototype no cutting-edge GUI-applications were developed and projects were abandoned [9]. The international visual language LoCoS is based on 19 major iconic symbols and can be learned in 1-2 days, which makes it perfectly suitable for use in international Human-Computer Communication or Human-Computer Interaction [10]. The LoCoS-for-Mobile-Devices Prototype by AM+A (Fig.1) provides a method of utilization of LoCoS in mobile devices [8]. The present study links to it in that way, that it aims to examine LoCoS to be used by people of different linguistic and cultural backgrounds in an Human-Computer Communication environment.

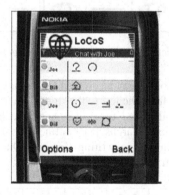

Fig. 1. LoCoS-for-Mobile-Devices Prototype [8]

2   LoCoS

2.1   Concept and Development

LoCoS is an artificially created, universal iconic language originally developed by the Japanese Graphic Designer Yukio Ota in 1964. *LoCoS* stands for *Lovers' Communications System* [11, 12]. It aims at facilitating international communication among people regardless of their linguistic and/or cultural background. Among artificially created languages, in addition to being associated with pictographic symbol languages, it also classified as an international auxiliary language. Since its first publication, over the years the system has been widely expanded, so that today more than 1,000 distinct symbols exist. The majority of literature has been published in Japanese, with hardly any translations into English or other languages. Moreover, LoCoS has its own pronunciation system [10] which will not be included in the current analysis.

2.2 Morphology and Syntax

Single words in LoCoS are represented by pictographs. By combining 19 major symbols (Fig. 2) with each other, new terms can be formed. A circle (*sun* or *day*) with a dot (*point existence*) in the center can stand for *day* or *today*, for example. Past and future tense are expressed by a line (*to do*) proceeded or followed by a dot. *To see* (Fig. 3) results from combination of the symbols for *to do* and *eye* [10].

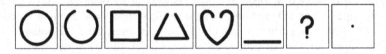

Fig. 2. Selection of some of the 19 major LoCoS symbols (*day, man, thing, thought, feeling, place, question, point existence*) [10]

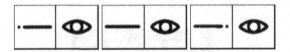

Fig. 3. Past (*saw*), present (*see*) and future tense (*will see*) of the verb *to see* [10]

Complete sentences in LoCoS can be created by arranging symbols in a triple-lined grid. The symbols are read from the left to the right. The main content is placed in the middle row. Adverbs are allocated to the top and adjectives the bottom row [10]. However, due to save space, Marcus [8] confined his LoCoS-for-Mobile-Devices prototype application to single-line writing (Fig. 4). Due to this and technological limitations, in this study, a triple-line grid was not used.

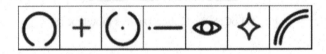

Fig. 4. Example for a complete declarative sentence in LoCoS: *You and I saw a beautiful rainbow* [10]

3 Experiment

To define Human-Computer Communication, i.e. the quality criteria and correspond-ding measurements (dependent variables), 3 different models were considered. The first model included the requirements of an artificially created international language as defined by the International Auxiliary Language Association (IALA): *learnability, correlation to native language, functionality, consistency* and *neutrality*.

The second model consisted of the 3 core aspects for usability evaluation as defined by the International Organization for Standardization (ISO) in the ISO guideline 9241-11: *acceptance, effectiveness* and *efficiency*.

The third model employed the quality criteria (primary capability principles) used by Leemans [13] to evaluate the applicability of his created visual language VIL in human-computer communication. To receive specific measurements, he assigned his criteria to Shneiderman's measurable human factors (in brackets) [14]: *learnability* (time to learn, retention over time), *extensibility, encoding* (speed of performance, error rate) and *decoding* (speed of performance, error rate).

Emerging from the 3 models mentioned above and taking into consideration practical restrictions on time, technical possibilities and the limitations of a remote test, the present study focused on the 6 quality criteria *acceptance, learnability, functionality, effectiveness, encoding and efficiency*. The corresponding objective and subjective variables of error rate, satisfaction and effort to learn were extended by including more specific items such as number of words or LoCoS symbols, preference and utilization (Table 1).

Table 1. Analyzed criteria with corresponding subjective and objective measurements

Criteria	Subj. Measurement	Obj. Measurement
Acceptance	Preference	
	Satisfaction	
Learnability	Effort to Learn	
Functionality	Utilization	
Effectiveness		Error Rate
Encoding		Error Rate
Efficiency		Number of Words/Symbols

3.1 Hypotheses

The following hypotheses were posited:

H1 (Acceptance). LoCoS facilitates communication among people of different linguistic and cultural backgrounds.

H2 (Learnability). Learning a symbolic language like LoCoS requires less learning effort than learning a natural foreign language, because symbol recognition happens more intuitively.

H3 (Functionality). LoCoS is suitable for modern forms of communication, i.e. chatting and sending short text messages (SMS).

H4 (Effectiveness, Encoding). Fewer errors occur while encoding messages from English into LoCoS compared to encoding messages into a natural or an extended natural foreign language like English.

H5 (Efficiency). Communication using LoCoS is more efficient and requires fewer symbols than words used to express the same thought.

3.2 My LoCoS Community – Test Application

As we wished to gather data from a culturally diverse sample, the study required participants to be recruited from as many countries as possible. The most efficient way to achieve this was to use a remote test conducted online via the world wide web. Therefore, an online forum was set up as the test application. Based on the open source SMF software, *My LoCoS Community* was implemented. It simulated an imaginary application environment for testers, accessible from anywhere in the world with unrestricted internet access. Through integration of a WYSIWYG-editor (Fig. 5) into the software, graphic LoCoS symbols were incorporated into the application, so that the participant could select them via a simple mouse-click from a pop-up-menu. The LoCoS pop-up menu included more than 280 different LoCoS symbols arranged thematically into several categories.

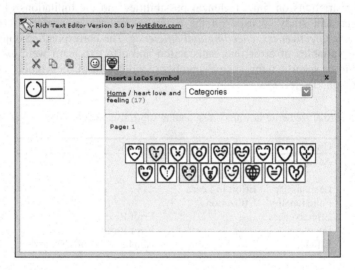

Fig. 5. WYSIWYG-editor with LoCoS pop-up menu

3.3 Method and Material

Communication within the *My LoCoS Community* was divided into 3 conditions: firstly, via a natural language, secondly via an extended natural language and thirdly via an international symbolic language. This resulted in participants being allocated to one of 3 groups: the control group using English (Group C), the first experimental group using English with Emoticons (Group E_1) and the second experimental group LoCoS (Group E_2).

The first part of the test, in which objective variables were measured, consisted of an assignment to verbalize (Group C and E_1) or encode (Group E_2) 10 standard sentences – 6 declarative, 2 interrogative and 2 imperative. The second part of the test was a survey to collect subjective data, such as demographical, behavioral and attitudinal information. The test application, the online-forum *My LoCoS Community*, was activated for a period of 4 weeks between February and March 2006. Test persons were recruited through an e-mail invitation letter which was posted to several mailing lists and newsgroups shortly before and during the testing period. The average time to participate was estimated at 30-45 minutes. After registering and logging-in, test subjects had access to different pdf files, containing extended test instructions and an introduction to LoCoS (LoCoS Manual), according to the group to which they were assigned. The only prerequisite for participation to be a non-native English-speaker, to equalize linguistic background as far as possible among subjects. An exception existed for Group E_2 (LoCoS), as the tasks were completed using LoCoS and not English. Other differences among participants were controlled by randomly allocating them to either Group C, Group E_1 or Group E_2 [15].

Overall, 47 people (N=47) participated in the study. Of these, 20 participants were in Group C, 18 participants were in Group E_1 and 9 participants were in Group E_2. The apparently uneven allocation of the groups was due to the fact that although 130 people registered to participate, only 15.4% of Group C, 13.8% of Group E_1 and 6.9% of Group E_2 entirely submitted their results. Differences between groups in regard to gender, native language, country of residence, age, English proficiency, online-forum experience and habit of emoticon use were not significant (p>0,05). The random sample yielded participants from 19 different countries including Germany, South Korea, United States, Italy, Pakistan, Slovenia, Bulgaria, China, Finland, Ireland, Israel, Canada, Mexico, Poland, Sweden, Slovakia, Spain, Hungary and United Kingdom. Nearly two-thirds of participants (30) stated either German, French, Russian or Spanish as their (first) native language. The ratio between male and female test-takers was 1.3:1. The average age was between 18 and 35 years.

Table 2. Means and standard deviation of selected variables between groups

Group	English	English w/ Emoticons	LoCoS	Sig.
Gender (Male/Female)	12/8	10/5	3/6	$\chi2(2)=2.699$, p=0.259
Native Language				$\chi2(10)=14.411$, p=0.155
Country of Residence				$\chi2(36)=33.607$, p=0.538
Age (Categories 1-7)	2.60±0.503	2.50±0.522	3.11±1.264	p=0.174
English Proficiency (1-5)	3.50±0.761	3.80±0.414	3.56±0.726	p=0.398
Online-Forum Exp. (1-4)	2.17±1.150	2.38±1.088	2.33±1.118	p=0.853
Emoticon Use (1-4)	2.75±1.020	2.38±0.719	2.44±0.882	P=0.428

4   Results

4.1   Subjective Data

Acceptance (H1). Hypothesis H1 was analyzed by questioning the preferred communication method – if no common language between conversational partners was shared – and also the extent of participant's subjective satisfaction. 3 respondents reported a preference for communicating in English, whereas 5 respondents would favour using English in combination with emoticons. Only 1 person stated a preference for LoCoS from the 3 tested communication methods. An interesting finding was that 7 out of the 8 people who preferred English with or without emoticons were non-native-English speakers. Subjective satisfaction on a scale between 1 (very easy) and 7 (very hard) was rated on average 3.2 in Group E_2, 1.8 in Group E_1 and 2.5 in Group C. Summarily, a tentative acceptance of LoCoS as a symbolic language was observed, but hypothesis H1 could not be verified in this study.

Learnability (H2). Contrary to H1, a majority 7 out of 9 participants from Group E_2 agreed that learning a visual symbolic language like LoCoS requires less time and effort than learning a natural foreign language. They also shared the opinion that this is because symbol recognition takes place more intuitively, though this could not be objectively verified.

Functionality (H3). The statement that LoCoS is as suitable for use in Human-Computer Communication (SMS, instant messaging) as natural languages since communication of complex information is possible, was both confirmed by 4 participants and disconfirmed by 4, while 1 interviewee neither provided no response. Furthermore, 8 of 9 participants could imagine the use of LoCoS for communication among hearing-impaired people. 7 of 9 interviewees could imagine LoCoS to be useful in scientific or formal communication. 6 respondents shared the opinion that LoCoS is ideal for teenage communication, while another 6 felt it would be useful for any age groups. The fewest number of endorsements were given to the uses of LoCoS as machining operating language (2 votes) and for poetry (1 vote).

4.2 Objective Data

Effectiveness/Encoding (H4). For examination of hypothesis H4, the mean semantic, tense, spelling and word-order errors for all of the 10 sentences were calculated for each group. The system of error measurement derives from natural languages, since to our best knowledge there is no specific metric for visual languages. A One-Way ANOVA showed that there was no significant difference in average error rate between groups (C, E_1 and E_2) ($p=0.779$). A post hoc LSD test also did not reveal any significant differences between individual pairs of groups. Therefore, the hypothesis could not sufficiently be supported with these data.

Efficiency (H5). For evaluation of efficiency and validation of hypothesis H5 the mean numbers of words or LoCoS symbols used for all 10 sentences in each group were calculated. In this study efficiency reflects the effort needed for typing and keying in letters or LoCoS symbols. It does not attempt to serve as a measure of cognitive processing. Assuming the standard length of an English word to be 5 letters, the total numbers of letters for every 10 sentences in Group C and E_1 were divided by 5 to calculate the average number of words to be compared with LoCoS symbols used in Group E_2 (1 LoCoS symbol = 1 word). Each emoticon used in Group E_1 counted as five letters (1 word). A One-Way ANOVA revealed a significant difference between groups ($p=0.022$). A post hoc LSD test showed that this significance was due to a significant difference between Groups C and E_2 (p=0.008), as well as between Groups E_1 and E_2 (0.017) (Fig. 5). Overall, communication occurred more efficiently because fewer symbols than words were used to express the same thought.

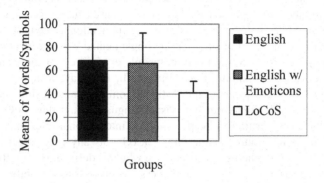

Fig. 6. Means of words/LoCoS symbols used and standard deviation

5 Discussion

A general trend towards the use of extended natural languages could be detected, indicating that while symbols are not exclusively accepted (yet), they are increasingly used in combination with a natural language in Human-Computer Communication. The reason for the tentative acceptance of an artificially created iconic language like LoCoS may be that while learnability is an important theoretical evaluation of a language, it does not predict practical success [16]. Publications in several major spoken languages are essential for an increasing awareness and natural distribution of LoCoS. The creation of symbols representing technical functions could facilitate application of LoCoS in the context of Human-Computer Interaction. However, LoCoS' advantage in comparison to other artificially created visual languages is that it does not claim to be a replacement for natural languages [11].

In previous studies there have been many approaches for creating different visual languages. Future experiments should employ a professionally developed mature iconic language like LoCoS to focus research findings in relation with Human-Computer Communication or Interaction, and ensure results are comparable across studies. In addition, LoCoS itself could be examined for the usefulness of multimedia attributes such as color [8], animation, audio or tool-tip help.

To optimize the assessment procedure, there is a need for a non-ambiguous system of measurement developed specifically for evaluation of visual languages, to compliment the current criteria. It is critical to determine whether the number of words used by subjects indicate the powerfulness of a language or simply the restricted vocabulary of a novice. To include people who may not have access or exposure to computers, a future test could be conducted by collaborating lab sites worldwide. Moreover, offering the test in participants' native languages would provide a better comparison of their task performance. Through an individually implemented test application and a test design which allows for tracking of cognitive effort and physiological data (eye fixation duration, saccade rate etc.), assessment measurements could be determined objectively. Imaginative, partly incomplete dialogues as part of the test task would provide a more natural communicative situation to subjects, as opposed to the sentences used here. We suggest use of a common communication device prototype as test application as the best possibility.

In addition, we imagine LoCoS could be implemented within educational learning software for speech- or learning-impaired people or children, or integrated in e-mail or instant messaging communication software. In this way, it could aide intuitive language acquisition and promote international communication using state-of-the-art technology. Horn [17] points out that visual languages, and thus LoCoS, could be applied in distance learning or help managing international telephone conferences between multi-ethnic groups. In the end, LoCoS – as any other artificially created language – relies on psychological acceptance which is defined by initially motivating as many people as possible [18], a process which assesses viability rather than theoretical criteria.

Acknowledgements. Deep thanks and appreciation to Aaron Marcus as a source of inspiration and for providing rare, original LoCoS material. Many thanks also to Yukio Ota as inventor and designer of LoCoS.

References

1. Katz, J.E.: Magic in the Air: Mobile Communication and the Transformation of Social Life. Transaction Publishers, p. 158 (2006)
2. Yamashita, N., Ishida, T.: Automatic prediction of misconceptions in multilingual computer-mediated communication. In: Proceedings of the 11th International Conference on Intelligent User Interfaces. IUI '06, pp. 62–69. ACM Press, New York, NY (2006)
3. ORF: Auf der Suche nach international gültigen Schriftzeichen - Symbolsprachen. Broadcasting Series Matrix, recorded July 17th, 2005. ORF, Wien (2005)
4. Fan, M., Ko, K.: Managing Icon Abundance on eBay. In: CHI '04 Extended Abstracts on Human Factors in Computing Systems. CHI '04, pp. 1555–1555. ACM Press, New York, NY (2004)
5. Spaeth, A.: Minds at Risk. TIME Asia Magazine, vol. September 8, 2003. TIME Inc. Hong Kong (2003)
6. Mealing, S., Yazdani, M.: A computer-based iconic language. Department of Computer Science. University of Exeter, England (1990)
7. Crystal, D.: The Cambridge Encyclopedia of the English Language, 2nd edn. Cambridge University Press, Cambridge (2003)
8. Marcus, A.: LoCoS for Mobile Devices: A Case Study. Aaron Marcus and Associates (AM+A), Inc. Berkeley, California (2005)
9. Maurer, H., et al.: Foundations of MIRACLE: Multimedia Information Repository. A Computer-supported Language Effort. Journal of Universal Computer Science 9(4), 309–348 (2003)
10. Marcus, A.: All About LoCoS. Aaron Marcus and Associates (AM+A) Inc. Berkeley, California (2006)

11. Ota, Y.: LoCoS - Experimente mit der Bildersprache. In: Bild der Wissenschaft. vol. February. DVA, Stuttgart, pp. 152–159 (1973)
12. Ota, Y.: Pictogram Design. Popular edn. Kashiwashobo Publishers, Ltd, Japan (1993)
13. Leemans, N.E.M.: VIL: A Visual Inter Lingua. Worcester Polytechnic Institute, USA (2001)
14. Shneiderman, B.: Designing the User Interface: Strategies for Effective Human-Computer Interaction, 3rd edn. Addison Wesley, Reading (MA) (1998)
15. Bortz, J., Döring, N.: Forschungsmethoden und Evaluation für Human- und Sozialwissenschaftler, 3rd edn. Springer, Berlin, Heidelberg, New York (2002)
16. Bußmann, H.: Lexikon der Sprachwissenschaft. Kroener Alfred GmbH + Co., Stuttgart (1990)
17. Horn, R.E.: Global Communication for the 21st Century. MacroVU, Inc. Bainbridge Island, Washington (1998)
18. Richards, I.A.: Basic English and Its Uses. W.W. Norton & Company Inc, New York (1943)

A Remote Study on East-West Cultural Differences in Mobile User Experience

Qifeng Yan[1,2] and Guanyi Gu[1]

[1] Nokia Corporation, Itämerenkatu 11 – 13, 00180, Helsinki, Finland
[2] Media Lab, University of Art and Design Helsinki
Hämeentie 135 C, 00560, Helsinki, Finland
{qifeng.yan,guanyi.gu}@nokia.com

Abstract. Most of current user interfaces and interaction systems are based on psychological and social models drawn from the European and American research traditions. However, recently, the applicability of these models is reconsidered after many products and services were proved to be failed in eastern cultures. This paper proposes that different user experiences should be designed for different cultures. In this research, East-West cultural differences are found in 3 user experience areas: 1, correlation of subjective and objective results; 2, Personal mobile networks; 3, Device interaction learning style. Some problems found during this research and some possible future improvements are also discussed.

Keywords: Cultural Differences, User Experience, Mobile experience, Cross-cultural design.

1 Introduction

Many scholars have begun reconsidering the applicability of western models in user experience design for eastern people. Eastern countries, with most of the world's population, a quickly growing economy, should not be ignored.

Is it really meaningful to deep explore cultural differences in user experience? This is maybe politically wrong according to cultural equality notion. However, it has been proved to be economically right by sales records of cross-cultural product makers and service providers.

In order to clarify the concept within the context here we can apply the following definition of "culture" as proposed by A.J.Marsella (1994):"Culture is shared learned behavior which is transmitted from one generation to another. For purposes of promoting individual and social survival, adaptation, and growth and development. Culture has both external (e.g., artifacts, roles, institutions) and internal represent-tations (e.g., values, attitudes, beliefs, cognitive/affective/sensory styles, conscious-ness patterns, and epistemologies.)". Internal representations are invisible and often overlooked but they are highly related to user experience design. Thus our research focuses on that.

N. Aykin (Ed.): Usability and Internationalization, Part II, HCII 2007, LNCS 4560, pp. 537–545, 2007.
© Springer-Verlag Berlin Heidelberg 2007

Cultural difference research has been an old story. Many relevant theories and models have been presented by sociologists, soci-psychologists, and intercultural communication educators since 1960s'. Dutch cultural anthropologist Geert Hofstede (1997) formulated his theory that world cultures vary along 5 consistent, fundamental dimensions: 1, Power distance; 2, Individualism vs. collectivism; 3, Femininity vs. masculinity; 4, Uncertainty avoidance; 5, Short vs. long-term orientation. "Understanding Cultural Differences", ([7] Hall and Hall 1990) explain several culture-dependent variables: 1. Fast and Slow Messages: Finding the Appropriate Speed; 2. High And Low Context: How Much Information Is Enough? (The level of detail people desire when presented with information) 3. Time As Communication: Monochronic and Polychronic Time (Whether or not people like to perform tasks in parallel, attitudes towards personal space); 4. Past- and Future-oriented; 5. Tempo, Rhythm, and Synchrony. These 2 scholars' theories mentioned above are the most systematic and influencing ones. However, the goal of their research is to facilitate man-man intercultural communication, while the user experience-related cultural differences we discuss in this paper mainly concern man-machine communication and user experience.

Therefore, above cultural difference dimensions can not be used directly for our research purposes. But they are good references for us to come up some hypotheses for research topic definition.

2   Research Methods

A new user research tool, Smartphone360 application for NOKIA S60 devices, the 1st implemented mobile user interaction tracking tool in the world is used in this research. Since S60 is an open software platform, so phones powered by S60 from other phone makers are also applicable.

To some extend Smartphone360 can be regarded as a spy ware tracking all mobile phone usage data in real life but not users' privacy. It can automatically encrypt and upload the collected data to our server through GPRS connection periodically without any security warning on the phone screen. The uploading timing is adjustable according to the phone memory size. Some of the settings can be changed remotely to meet the new requirements of our research. So all data collection and transportation happens automatically in the background and users can use the phone as usual without disturbing. We promised the participants that no communication contents are tracked and the collected data are for research purpose only and are never linked to any phone number or individuals.

We have done a series of such remote studies on more than 5 thousands users in US, Europe and China. In the most recent research, we tested 2 new features of this new user research tool: 1.Key Press observer: It automatically monitors precise time of all key down and key up events, only excluding number keys for privacy protection reasons. 2. Mobile Questionnaire: Triggered by certain operations, or scheduled beforehand, some context sensitive mini questions can pop-up to ask users' opinion about usability, pleasure or other subjective feelings and the context of the use of certain features. For example, after users take a photo using phone camera, a question can pop up to ask the user how satisfied are they with the last photo taking experience, or what they just took a photo for, for people, animals, landscape or something else. In this way we can analyze the collected data to understand how the users use the phone features in different contexts in real life. The length and frequency of questionnaire are well controlled to avoid abusing of lengthy question-naires, which always tire the testees and affect their answers. In the concluding survey, we found that participants think the pace of the questionnaires (4 questions per week) was acceptable and the feedbacks are quite positive. Many participants even think the mini questionnaire did make them feel funny instead of disturbed during the testing.

The collected data are analyzed combining quantitative and qualitative methods. In order to find out some significant differences behind the huge amount of data, SPSS statistic software is used in quantitative analysis. The most challenging part of the research is to writing suitable program scripts to process the huge data.

Previously, sociologists and soci-psychologists mainly conducted cultural differ-ence research by interview and observation in certain contexts. However, the resear-cher is also responsible for establishing a context for the "correct" interpretation of the research objects. Actually that is also part of doing research. Thus researchers always tend to establish contexts more research-friendly for the expected results, which normally make the research too subjective.

However, traditional academic attempts in relevant areas are still valuable for this research. We try to use some existing cultural models and user experience models in data analysis to interpret the cultural difference phenomenon and conclude the research.

For quantitative research, the number of samples is important. To find common rules from empirical results of user studies, we mainly use quantitative methods in this research.

Because Smartphone360 tool provides a means to reach large and diverse samples all over the world, it seems ideally suited for cross-cultural research. We compare the results of remote experiments and those of laboratory experiments to see whether the remote research results agree with those of face-to-face research. Actually, we can also track the place where the phone users are located in precisely to get some context information about the usage of the phone. To keep the promise of privacy protection to the participants, we disable this function. Lots of context information is missing in the research, but hopefully this can be compensated with large amount of usage data.

In traditional usability testing, psychological pressure on testees caused by many facilitators and observers has been proved to be a problem, which does not exist in this study anymore.

In the most recent research, 110 volunteers with 12 different nationalities including Chinese, Danish, Finnish, French, German, Hungarian, Indian, Irish, Romanian, Russian, UK, and USA participated in this research. They were told to use the phone as usual. According to users' feedbacks, they did not feel that Smartphone360 application running in the background slows down the responsiveness of the phone user interface. So this research tool is perceived as having very little effects on phone user interface performance.

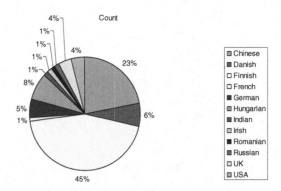

Fig. 1. Cultural Nationality Diversity of the samples

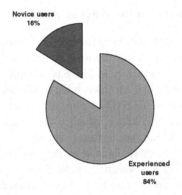

Fig. 2. S60 experiences of the samples

About the skillfulness of the testees, 16.2% of them have less than 1 month S60 experience, and are categorized as novice users. 51.5% of all the testees have used the phone for more than 6 months and are categorized as experienced users.

The age distribution in this study is also broad: 27.9% are 16-24 years old; 46% are 25-35 years old;18.4% are 35-45 years old; and 7.4% are older than 45.

In average each user generated 27.5 days' usage data. And millions of key presses were recorded.

There are also some risks in our research sample composition. 84% participants are male because most technical fans are male and they are dominant in smart phone users.

In this research, we focus on Finnish-Chinese culture comparison because Finnish and Chinese are dominant among the participants. Furthermore, Nordic culture and Chinese culture are usually described as 2 extremes in many cultural dimensions proposed by Hofstede and Hall. For example, Long (China) vs. short (Finland) power distance; Individualism (Finland) vs. collectivism (China); Femininity (Finland) vs. masculinity (China); High (China) vs. Low (Finland) uncertainty avoidance; Short-term (Finland) vs. long-term (China) orientation; High (China) and low (Finland) context in conversation.

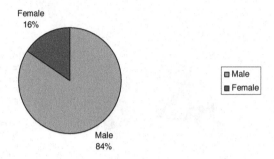

Fig. 3. Gender Proportion of the samples

3   Data Analysis

3.1   Differences in Face Issues or the Ways of Thinking?

In the paper "Towards Effective Usability Evaluation in Asia: Cross-Cultural Differences" by Linda Herman, it was reported that research results of objective and subjective evaluation correlated poorly in Far East samples because it is considered culturally unacceptable in the Far East to criticize too openly or directly, as this may cause designers hurt or loss of face ([1] Craig, 1993). Is it because of losing face issues? In this research, we also check whether this situation exists in our remote anonymous questionnaire without face to face contacting.

In some research topics, objective data shows that the differences between Chinese and Finnish are within 2%. The subjective evaluations in those topics from Chinese and Finnish users are compared to find the cultural differences in subjective evaluations. For example, objective data analysis results of number of key presses and time spent to finish a task in average, and subjective easiness and phone responsiveness evaluations of relevant applications collected with the mobile questionnaire tool. To standardize the questionnaire, we use opposite adjective pairs for example Easy/Hard, Fast/Slow and some adverbs to form a standard 5 level scale options to measure subjective feedbacks.

As shown in the graph below, 11% more Chinese users selected "neutral" than Finnish users. And 5% more Finnish users selected "Very positive" than Chinese users. 7% of Finnish users selected "Very Negative" but no Chinese users selected it. From the data we can easily reach a conclusion that Chinese users are more neutral and more careful about giving extreme evaluations especially extremely negative evaluations to avoid criticism.

In this research, we promise the participants that privacy is strictly protected without linking users' answers and key presses to their personal information. So theoretically most of the participants make selection according to their own opinions without thinking about any face issues. However, the same problem exists in anonymous remote survey. It seems that it is not only a matter of face, but also the ways of thinking.

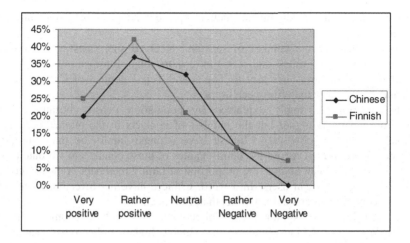

Fig. 4. Subjective evaluations on the same interaction performance from Chinese and Finnish users

Table 1. Percentage of the answers

	Chinese	Finnish
Very positive	20%	25%
Rather positive	37%	42%
Neutral	32%	21%
Rather Negative	11%	11%
Very Negative	0%	7%

"The doctrine of the mean" is emphasized in classic Confucian literatures and has become one of the core ways of thinking in Confucian cultures. It is quite different from "equality" which is one of core values in western cultures. Confucius said "Over is like not enough". The meaning is a bit similar to the English proverb "the last drop makes the cup run over". Confucian culture tends to avoid extreme especially negative extreme to keep space for further flexible actions. So "keeping your opinion neutral" is a very popular Chinese wisdom, and has deep influence on educated people in other Eastern Asian countries. Comparing to face issues which also exist in western cultures, this "The doctrine of the mean" inside people's mind can better explain this problem.

3.2 Differences in Personal Mobile Networks

In the previous smartphone360 studies on 429 Chinese users and 444 European users (including Finland, Germany and UK), the average number of contacts in the phones of Chinese users is 6.4% less than European users. We analyze the receivers' diversity of voice call and short messages, and find that short messages are mainly sent to familiars who are frequently contacted and listed inn the phone book in the phone, but voice calls are to everybody including strangers and service numbers. So short message sending and receiving can better represent people's behaviors in mobile social networking.

However, the average number of sent and received short messages per day of Chinese users is 3.5 times and 2.9 times more than European users. And the percentage of short messages sent to Top 5 and Top 1 contact of Chinese users is 6.9% and 13.9% more than European users.

This can not be simply explained by population density because Chinese population density is higher but the number of contacts in the phones is less than European. However, obviously Chinese have stronger family tie than Europeans. Even though we did not record the family names of those contacts to validate this for privacy reasons, we can assume the proportion of family members in the top contacts are higher than European users. In a word, Chinese have narrower but more active and more convergent personal networks than European.

This can be also explained by Collectivism VS Individualism theory ([6] G,Hofstede, 1993). Chinese culture has much higher collectivism value than European culture. So the communication among a group of people is more intensive and more convergent.

Another reason for the huge volume of short messages among Chinese users is that in China, a land of amenity, local style communication is a typical high context communication ([7] Hall and hall, 1990), and much more extra context information is needed in daily oral communication than low context communication cultures in Europe, especially in Nordic countries. For example, simply answering "yes" or "no" or directly asking for help in oral communication is impolite in China. Much more unrelated information is needed and communication efficiency is low. However, SMS (Short Message Service) provides a good reason and excuse for short and effective communication in China since Chinese character input is not easy for everybody.

In addition, life tempo in China is faster than in Europe ([7] Hall and hall, 1990), Modern Chinese people prefer concise communication but they can not ignore traditional high-context oral communication in personal networking. As a new technology not belonging to traditional culture, SMS provides a good platform for short and efficient communication.

All in all, new technology is providing good excuses for not using Chinese traditional complicated and lengthy ways of communication.

3.3 Differences in Interaction Problem Solving and Learning Style

Usability is not everything for a good user experience. "Learnability" is also important since the growing number of phone features is making user interface inevitably more and more complicated.

Through online concluding questionnaire, we asked the users which way they prefer when facing difficulties in phone operation and feature understanding in previous large scale studies. It is interesting that most of US users tend to find the problem solving information from the internet, and most of European users prefer to find the answers in the printed manuals, while most Chinese users prefer to ask other users for answers. We do not clarify the answer options that they prefer to ask other users in real life or in internet forums. Anyway, there are lots of Chinese online forums full of discussion of usage tips of mobile phones. The forum masters and advanced forum members always try to answer every simple and even stupid question from beginners. This kind of situations can be rarely found in English mobile phone forums. Why the users prefer to ask other users to solve their problems? The precondition is that other users are very willing to answer those questions.

In Confucian cultures, teacher is a highly respected profession. Chinese people are so eager to act as teachers. As Mencius, a Confucian master said "A common trouble with Chinese people is that they are too eager to assume the role of teacher." Such examples can be easily found in real life. Family elders in China take much more education responsibilities than in Europe. The elder colleagues are often called "teacher" by junior colleagues, because most Chinese enjoy the feeling of teaching others and being called "teacher", so do the web forum masters in virtual world. In this "Teaching" culture, everybody is teaching others and taught by others and enjoys the experiences, so it is natural that Chinese people tend to be taught by others and give nice feelings to the teachers when facing phone interaction problems. More important is that this is the most efficient way of problem solving.

4 Conclusion

User experience is not culture independent, so does user experience research. Not only manufacturing, but also usability testing is moving to China, India and other developing countries, because it is easier to access large number of samples and it is much more cost efficient to do user research there. But cultural differences in user experience should be well understood before conducting cross-cultural user studies and using data collected from other cultures as references to the targeted culture. Because Smartphone360 tool provides a means to reach large and diverse samples all over the world remotely, it seems ideally suited for cross-cultural user experience research. Comparing to counting key presses manually, this tool can record all key presses more precise and make data analysis easier. With S60 system emulator, we can reproduce user interface and key presses on the PC screen with recorded data for detailed observation. All in all, it is a very powerful and cost saving solution for user experience research.

From this research, it was found that the reason why research results of objective and subjective evaluation correlated poorly in China is not only "Face" issue. More important is that the "Doctrine of Mean" way of thinking is so popular in Confucian cultures, since the same kind of problem is also found in this remote anonymous research.

Cultural differences in mobile personal networks are also found in this research. Comparing to Chinese mobile personal networks, European personal mobile networks are a bit broader and top contacts are more diverse.

Nowadays, learnability has been attached more and more importance to in user experience design. However, different cultures tend to learn mobile interaction in different ways. US users prefer searching in the internet, European like to check from printed manual, while Chinese tend to ask other users due to their "enjoying teaching" culture. This result provides a reference for designing good experiences for mobile interaction problem solving and new phone feature promotion.

Context is still important in user experience research. For example in this research, we do not know some strange key presses happening in users' pockets accidentally or not. We are planning to develop a more context sensitive questionnaire tool with use observation functions to support this kind of research, or cooperate with mobile phone operators to get more context information of phone usage in the future. So not only key press observer, but also context observer will be implemented in 360 tools in the future.

Acknowledgments. We thank all Smartphone360 user experience research volunteer participants, all supporting colleagues, and the reviewers, who wrote and provided helpful comments on previous versions of this document. Some of the references cited in this paper are included for illustrative purposes only.

References

1. Craig, J.M.: Culture Shock! Singapore, Times Books International (1993)
2. S60 Software platform Application blog http://blogs.s60.com/tommi/2006/01/some_results_from_our_smartpho_1.html
3. McLoughlin, C.: Culturally responsive technology use: developing an online community of learners. British Journal of Educational Technology (1999)
4. Dray, S., Mrazek, D.: A Day in the Life: Studying context across Cultures. In: del Galdo, E.M., Nielsen, J. (eds.) International User Interfaces, John Wiley and Sons, New York (1996)
5. Fernandes, T.: Global User Interface Design, http://www.acm.org/sigchi/chi95/proceedings/tutors/tf_bdy.htm
6. Geert, H.: Cultures and Organizations: Software of the Mind. In: Intercultural Cooperation and its Importance for Survival, McGraw-Hill, New York (1997)
7. Hall, E.T., Hall, M.R.: Understanding Cultural Differences. Intercultural Press, Yarmouth, Maine (1990)
8. Honold, P.: Culture and Context: An empirical Study for the Development of a Framework for the Elicitation of Cultural Influence in Product Usage. The International Journal of Human-Computer Interaction, 12 (2000)
9. Ito, M., Nakakoji, K.: Impact of culture on user interface design. In: del Galdo, E.M., Nielsen, J. (eds.) International User Interfaces, John Wiley & Sons, New York (1996)
10. Noiwan, J., Norcio, A.F.: Designing for Effective Information Presentation: The Effects of Cultural Differences on Speed, Accuracy, and Perceptions on Usability and Aesthetics. In: Proceedings of the HCI International 2001 Conference, vol 1 (2001)
11. Marcus, A.: Cultural Dimensions and Global Web User-interface Design: What? So What? Now What? In: the Proceeding of the 6th Conference on Human Factors and the Web in Austin, Texas (June 19, 2000)
12. Marcus, A.: Globalization, Localization, and Cross-Cultural Communication in User-Interface Design. In: Jacko, J., Spears, A. (eds.) Handbook of Human-Computer Interaction, Lawrence Erlbaum Publishers, New York (2002)
13. Matsumoto, D.: Culture and Emotion. In: Adler, L.L., Gielen, U.P. (eds.) Cross-Cultural Topics in Psychology, Praeger (1994)

Cultural and Social Aspects of Security and Privacy - The Critical Elements of Trusted Online Service

Yinan Yang[1], Ed Lewis[2], and Lawrie Brown[2]

[1] IEEE Society on Social Implicatins of Technology, Australia
dr_yyang@ieee.org
[2] School of IT&EE, UNSW@ADFA, Canberra, Australia
ed.lewis@adfa.edu.au, lawrie.brown@adfa.edu.au

Abstract. The lack of trust is identified as the key concern for consumers in the eCommerce environment. Service providers attempt to address this concern by implementing Public Key Infrastructure (PKI) systems for online security and privacy and to enhance user confidence. Much research has focused on the technical implementation of online security and privacy systems. This paper discusses social and cultural influence as critical elements of a trusted online service environment. It suggests a mechanism for enhancing trust in e-commerce that takes account of these influences.

Keywords: Trust, social factors, PKI.

1 Introduction

The growth of eCommerce is being hampered by a lack of trust between providers and consumers of Web-based services. Both online service providers and consumers have been reluctant to establish new business relationships via open electronic networks like the Web. This lack of Web trust has a direct effect on user confidence in online services and is increasingly affecting the rate of growth of eCommerce [1].

Many researchers have tried to address multi-disciplinary trust issues [2, 3]. Electronic (Digital) security technology does play an important role in establishing trust in an eCommerce environment [4]. It also provides a tangible perception of trust for online consumers. Public Key Infrastructure (PKI) technology [5] uses digital certificates and a combination of public and private encryption keys for authenticating the legitimate parties before transactions. Public-key cryptography has been used for anti-spoofing, authentication, authorisation, non-repudiation, and secure data communications. Despite some technical issues with X509-compliant PKI [6], the use of PKI in the eCommerce environment is still rising.

However, with the increasing use of PKI technology for cross-border eCommerce transactions and delivery of services by various governments, there are challenging social, cultural and legal issues that require further research [7]. Shneiderman et al identified two principles and associated guidelines to enhance cooperative behaviours and win user/customer loyalty [8]. Several trust factors were identified such as

N. Aykin (Ed.): Usability and Internationalization, Part II, HCII 2007, LNCS 4560, pp. 546–553, 2007.
© Springer-Verlag Berlin Heidelberg 2007

assurances, references, certifications from third parties, and guarantees of privacy and security. These identified trust factors are also referenced and more or less agreed among researchers of empirical trust studies and surveys [9, 10].

The proposed W3 trust-profiling framework [11] identifies a range of trust factors including professional association, reputation, policies and legal status in its trust categories [12]. This generic trust-profiling framework attempts to assist consumers to assess the trustworthiness of webcontent of service provider. Based on this trust profile [13], online consumers can make better-informed decisions and User Confidence is improved.

There is a need for enhancing user confidence through improving the organisational culture and consequently improve the reputation of the service provider [14]. Online service providers (or organisations) need to know how to increase cooperative behaviours and win customer trust by understanding the social and cultural elements that are embedded in online security and privacy systems.

2   Identified Gaps Between PKI Technology and Social and Culture Elements

Many researchers have identified the *Reputation* of a service provider as an important factor of trust [8, 9, 10]. To build online trust, service providers need to be able to demonstrate their reputation and credibility to online consumers. In other words, the reputation and credibility of an online service provider needs to be assessed and measured in a meaningful way [12].

For example, normally, a professional association logo is displayed on a service provider's website to symbolize its trustworthiness by showing its professional affiliation. However, a logo provides little tangible meaning of the Reputation of the service provider to online consumers. A GIF file can be easily copied, downloaded and created. For customers to be able to trust an organization, they must be able to establish that it has a trustworthy reputation, supported by sound governance of its use of PKI technologies.

To focus this discussion, the following is a simple way to describe implementation of an online security and privacy solution:

- *Governance with Embedded Social Values* represents the principles and standards that provide a sound basis for online security and privacy. This includes legal requirements, social factors, policy and architecture, such as the Gatekeeper PKI Framework in the Australian Government.
- *Development Approaches and W3TF Adoption* [14] represents the technologies and approaches that implement business solutions to create a trusted environment for online services.
- *Monitoring and Feedback Mechanism* to measure the outcomes of the above aspects and provides factual and measurable information that permits improvements and fine-tuning of the above two aspects.

To further complicate matters, social and cultural differences can play key roles with online security and privacy when dealing with each aspect above.

3 Challenges in Social and Cultural Aspects of PKI Implementation

PKI technologies have been developed and utilised by various groups and communities for a secure communication on the Internet to provide various trust models [13]. Many research works focus on the improvement of technical deficiencies of PKI. However, to achieve a trusted and credible online service environment, service providers should also examine their organisational culture that is influenced by its inhabited social environment. This self-assessment and self-regulation of Governance framework presents more challenges than technical improvement.

The following social and cultural aspects illustrate some challenges that face organisations as online service providers.

3.1 The Healthier the Organisational Culture, the Better the Reputation

Nowadays, most organisations have codes of conduct to regulate employees' behaviour. The company's reputation relies upon its employees for they are also the trust agents of organisation and carry the implementation of PKI.

Organisations that operate a trusted online service often ensure that staff associated with the trusted systems are required to have regular vigorous and intrusive security checks based on the level of information protection required by the organisation. Staff who pass background and character checks are considered to be trusted staff and have privileges to view and access the information that they are cleared to see. However, organisations sometimes find that major security and privacy breaches were carried out by these trusted staff, e.g. possible inside trading [15], and unauthorised access to personal information [16]. This indicates there can be a gap between an organizational culture and individual values.

These diverse individual values are often based on the varied cultural inheritances of individuals and groups. The cultural bases of privacy values are very difficult to regulate through a simple mechanism, such as the code of conduct of the organisation. Indeed, legal prosecution can be utilised for those serious cases of security and privacy breaches, but by that stage great damage may have been done to the organisation's reputation.

There are differences between individuals in their value systems, which can lead to tensions in decision-making. There are differences between organisations in their cultures – the sum of the value systems. These differences can lead to loss of collaboration and delays in action. These losses can, in turn, lead to loss of reputation. In which case, displaying a reputable logo on its website adds no value.

There are a number of possible ways to encourage and consolidate the positive organisational culture and sharing of common values.

- Building up various leadership groups at all levels of the organisation. Each group (or a business unit) acts as a trust agent to translate the organisational value into daily interactions and dealings among themselves and other stakeholders.
- Some organisations provide an induction session for new staff and ongoing training for existing staff. These induction sessions inculcate common values and state clearly the organisational values and expectations for individual of the company.

- Some organisations adopt an organisation maturity model [17] as a tool for attracting, developing, motivating, organising and retaining an outstanding workforce as well as bench-marking of the current state of the organisation with a desirable organizational culture and value ahead.
- Providing coaching to some senior executives to be a role model to lead the organisational change requirements.

Although common sense is probably the most important ingredient, persistence, resilience and commitment are required from the top executives to the lower ranking staff. With sufficient time, a desirable organisational culture may prevail, which will see organisational Reputation enhanced. The question now is, how does this repute-tion translate into increased trust? How can the user of the organisation's e-commerce come to know if it has a trustworthy reputation?

3.2 Taking Social and Culture Elements into PKI Implementation

PKI technologies have been developed and utilised by various groups and communities for online security and privacy protection. Different PKI offers different trust models [18]. PKI technology is continuing to improve from its deficiencies because of many researchers and security communities' contributions. However, there is little research on how different cultural and social factors may influence implementation of PKI and various levels of trust.

According to Australian Standard 8015: 2005 *Corporate Governance of information and communication technology,* ICT governance is

> The system by which the current and future use of ICT is directed and controlled. It involves evaluating and directing the plans for the use of ICT to support the organization and monitoring this use to achieve plans. It includes the strategy and policies for using ICT within an organization.

The principles of ICT governance given in the Standard include Principle 5 (Ensure that ICT conforms with all external regulations and complies with all internal policies and practices) and Principle 6 (Ensure that ICT meets the current and evolving needs of all the 'people in the process'). That is, governance must incorporate social and cultural values in such as way as to show clearly that its use of ICT is acceptable to all stakeholders.

Gatekeeper PKI Framework (Gatekeeper) is the Australian Government's strategy for the use of Public Key Infrastructure (PKI) to enable the delivery of online government services. Gatekeeper Strategy governs the use of PKI in government for the authentication of external clients (organisations, individuals and other entities). Gatekeeper ensures a whole-of-government framework that delivers integrity, interoperability, authenticity and trust for Agencies and their clients [19]. The Gatekeeper PKI framework covers a range of areas, including policy documentation requirements, online authentication requirements, privacy impact assessments and risks and threats assessments and Gatekeeper accreditation requirements.

Gatekeeper has been in action since May 1999 and was developed through a comprehensive consultation process involving all Gatekeeper accredited service providers, Federal, State and Territory governments. The Australian Government led consultation process aimed to balance various stakeholder requirements including legal requirements, all levels of government responsibilities, and Australian public expectations. Through this consultation process, the Australian government sought to demonstrate its commitment [20] to the Australian public that culture and social values are reflected in its governance strategy.

Different countries may embed different social and cultural values in their Governance models. To illustrate variations in regulatory environments in countries, ASIA Public Key Infrastructure (PKI) Forum [7] reported:

> Laws and regulations in Australia have had federal privacy legislation since 1988 that applies to government conduct. In 2000, Australian federal law was extended to private sector (in an attempt to come into line with European Union law). Most Australian has passed mirror legislation. The 2000 Australian Law is broadly based on the OECD principles. It was intended to harmonise Australian Private Sector regulations with those of the European Unit. However, most commentators agree here that the Australian federal privacy law is not as stringent as Europe's. Some states have adopted somewhat tougher health privacy law (page 8).

ASIA PKI Forum [7] found some differences in laws and regulations among the participant countries. These differences may cause some technical difficulties such as interoperability as well as the legal status of digital signatures across various countries. Given that the 2000 Australian Law is broadly based on OECD countries, the Gatekeeper-compliant PKI in Australia may offer acceptable levels of trust to OECD countries when they deal with Australian government service providers.

The Gatekeeper PKI framework is the governance model for PKI implementations adopted by Australian government agencies for their online services. The development of this governance model continues, based on extensive consultation with other Gatekeeper-compliant PKI stakeholders, including State and Territory governments and industries. This ongoing redevelopment of the governance framework often requires regular updating to meet new business and consumers expectations and demands. These changes in Governance can result in technical implementation changes. At the same time, technical advances can also force Governance to catch-up. Therefore, an ability to develop a strategy and sufficient resources around PKI implementation become critical for an organisation.

The Gatekeeper PKI framework is developed based on Australia's culture and social values, which are also deeply embedded in Australian organisations' culture and practice. This broader social context dictates individual's thinking and interprettation of government policies (i.e. Gatekeeper PKI Framework), legal requirements (e.g. Privacy Act) and how to implement the online security and privacy solutions to meet Australian consumers' expectations.

3.3 Development Approaches and W3TF Adoption

Although Australia's use of PKI does meet the governance principles, how is this made known to the users of its certificates so they can trust this use? PKI technologies have been developed and adopted world wide on various platforms and devices by individuals, small and medium service providers to large government organisations.

However, there are different approaches to implementing it, which may offer different levels of trust to consumers.

Some organisations require implementing PKI with a well-developed governance strategy, while others just simply install the technology. The Australian government requires federal government agencies to comply with the Gatekeeper PKI Framework when implementing PKI technology. This requirement increases User Confidence through alignment of the PKI technological component with the Gatekeeper policy and strategy framework.

In contrast, some companies could easily ignore their obligations to their customers by implementing a system without adequate security and privacy protection. So it can be difficult for consumers to differentiate the reputable ones from disreputable ones. To address this issue, a conceptual W3 trust-profiling framework (W3TF) was developed by Web trust researchers [14]. W3TF has proposed a trust metadata mechanism for online service providers to implement and to improve trustworthiness as described in its trust categories.

W3TF provides a means of establishing Web trust and indicates where to start to assess the trustworthiness of online service information before committing to business dealings on the Web. W3TF is also capable of providing a generic framework to integrate different trust requirements and factors into a coherent but flexible framework to allow it to grow. As shown, W3TF is based on various trust principles and incorporates important trustworthiness factors and trust requirements from various empirical studies. In addition, the simplicity and practicability of W3TF offers a sensible and a logical way to perform trust assessments on both standalone and hyperlinked webcontents.

In a heterogeneous Web environment, transitivity of trust can be achieved through a combination of various trustworthiness assessments using the proposed trust categories of the W3TF. This mechanism brings hidden information into its trust categories that communicate with the end-user and enable consumers to find out more about the potential service providers. Consumers can make the right choice about using a service, after checking what might be artificial or spoofed certification. The system based on the trusted information provided by W3TF [16] shall assist consumers to determine the acceptable level of trust.

3.4 Monitoring and Feedback Mechanism

Ongoing monitoring is important to maintain the trusted online service environment. Any glitch will hinder user confidence in the system and the organisation that operates the system. PKI offers online authentication and privacy protection to online consumers.

Often, the cost of the ongoing monitoring of the PKI system is very high including resources, disaster contingency plan, updated equipment, software components, knowledge and skills. It can be difficult to convince management to budget for ongoing monitoring of the trusted systems to prevent undesirable events. Many organisations do not see the importance of a sufficient budget for ongoing monitoring activities. In some cases, there could be a tension between a technical team and a non-technical team as to whom is responsible when things go wrong.

Continuing monitoring can improve PKI environment over time. The proposed W3TF mechanism provides factual and measurable operational information that indicates the health status of the existing PKI operational environment.

As well, the organisation should use monitoring within the guidelines established in AS 8015 to enable it to improve and fine-tune its strategy and development approaches. Monitoring also can be a timely sensing of any deficiencies in the environment before disaster occurs and causes political embarrassment. Any disaster in business services will certainly damage the reputation of the organisation as well as consumers' confidence.

To address this issue, organisations should follow the AS8015 principles to build a trustworthy reputation that is obvious to its customers. In order to do so, it should encourage an organisational culture of collaboration, cooperation and coordination.

4 Summary

This paper identifies social and cultural influences as critical elements for a trusted online service environment. The ability to incorporate diverse cultural and social values into online service implementation should enhance user confidence through the demonstrable reputation of the service providers. Some issues in Governance include roles and responsibilities, the maturity of security architectures and implementation of standards.

This paper also identifies a number of issues and potential options to improve online trust, including the adoption of W3TF and the use of sound governance principles. Through collaboration between the research and practitioner communities, the identified issues can be narrowed and more user-centric online security and privacy systems can be achieved.

References

1. Princeton Survey Research Associates: A Matter of Trust: What Users Want From Web sites (January 2002), http://www.consumerwebwatch.org/news/report1.pdf
2. Belanger, F., Sridhar, V., Slyke, C.V.: Comparing the Influence of Perceived Innovation Characteristics and Trustworthiness Across Countries. In: Proceeding of the International Conference on Electronic Commerce Research (ICECR-5) (November 2002)
3. Hoffman, D.L, Noyak, T.P., Peralta, M.: Building Consumer Trust Online. Communications of ACM 42(4), 80–85 (1999) ISSN: 0001-0782
4. Yang, Y., Brown, L., Newmarch, J.: Tokens of Trust: Different Certificates for Different Trust Models. In: Proceedings the UniForum New Zealand Conference (April 1999)
5. ITU-T Recommendation X.509, Information Technology - Open Systems Interconnection - the Directory: Authentication Framework, International Telecommunication Union, (June 1997)
6. Gutmann, P.: PKI: It's Not Dead, Just Resting. Computer 35(8), 41–49 (2002) ISSN: 0018-9162
7. Legal Infrastructure Working Group, Asia PKI Forum. Legal Issues on New Security Technologies and CA's Risk Management (July 2006)

8. Shneiderman, B.: Designing trust into Online Experiences. Communications of the ACM 43(12), 57–59 (2000) ISSN: 0001-0782
9. Cheskin & Studio Archetype/Sapient, San Francisco, eCommerce Trust Study (January 1999), www.cheskin.com/think/studies/ecomtrust.html
10. Grandison, T., Sloman, M.: A Survey of Trust in Internet Applications, IEEE Communications Surveys, 4th quarter, IEEE (2000)
11. Yang, Y., Brown, L., Newmarch, J., Lewis, E.: IWSM 2000. LNCS, vol. 3841. Springer, Heidelberg (2006)
12. Yang, Y., Brown, L., Lewis, E., Newmarch, J.: W3 Trust Model: a Way to Evaluate Trust and Transitivity of Trust of Online Services. In: Proceedings Internet Computing Conference, Las Vegas, USA (June 2002)
13. Yang, Y., Brown, L., Newmarch, J., Lewis, E.: A Trusted W3 Model: Transitivity of Trust in a Heterogeneous Web Environment. In: Proceedings of the Fifth Australian World Wide Web Conference, Queensland, pp. 59–73 (April 1999)
14. Yang, Y.: W3 Trust-Profiling Framework (W3TF) to assess Trust and Transitivity of trust of Web-based services in a heterogeneous Web environment, PhD Thesis, School of Information Technology and Electrical Engineering, University of New South Wales, ADFA, Canberra, Australia (August 2004)
15. 06-025 NAB Forex trader pleads guilty to ASIC charges, (February 7, 2006) URL at http://www.asic.gov.au
16. Shanahan, D., Karvelas, P.: Welfare Spies Sacked, Australian (February 5, 2007)
17. Curtis, B.: Capability Maturity Model, (2001), at http://www.gartner.com/measurement
18. Yang, Y., Brown, L., Newmarch, J., Lewis, E.: Trust Metadata: Enabling Trust and a Counterweight to Risks of E-Commerce. In: Proceedings Asia Pacific World Wide Web Conference, pp. 197–203 (1999)
19. Australian Government Information Management Office. Gatekeeper Public Key Infrastructure (PKI) Framework, (September 2006), URL at http://www.agimo.gov.au/infrastructure/gatekeeper
20. Office of the Federal Privacy Commissioner. Office of the Federal Privacy commissioner Consultation paper. (accessed on December 2006), URL at http://www.privacy.gov.au/publications/dpki.html

Dynamic Scripting in Crisis Environments

Zhenke Yang and Leon J.M. Rothkrantz

Man-Machine-Interaction Group,
Faculty of Electrical Engineering, Mathematics and Computer science,
Delft University of Technology
Mekelweg 4 2628CD Delft, The Netherlands
Z.Yang@tudelft.nl,
L.J.M.Rothkrantz@tudelft.nl

Abstract. This paper presents a system that focuses on improving event reporting in crisis situation management. The idea is to provide reporters with software with an intelligent adaptive interface based on dynamic scripting to ensure report consistency and minimize composing time. The dynamic scripting approach is modeled after human reasoning with specific knowledge. Our approach differs from other approaches to adaptive interfaces in that, instead of trying to fit the users' interpretation of observations into sensible reports, we use possible crisis scenario as the starting point of the reports.

Keywords: Dynamic scripting, Adaptive interfaces, Expert system, specific knowledge, Jess.

1 Introduction

In the movie industry scripts and storyboards are used frequently to help actors to memorize their lines and to aid directors to keep the overall view of the movie. Storyboards illustrate key moments in a scenario and thus can function as a memory aid. In experiments we conducted with semi-professional actors, it seemed that during key moments in the acting process, resemblance to the storyboard triggers parts of the movie scripts in the minds of the actors [1]. Shank et. al. [2] explain this by suggesting that the sequence of events that constitute such situations are stored in human memory as scripts. It seems that humans are very capable of recognizing and participating in situations that they have experienced before. The recognition of these scripts is triggered by the key events being perceived by the human. Interestingly, humans are quite capable of recognizing the scripts without having perceived all the events that constitutes the script. Furthermore, the recognition process seems to be very efficient (requiring very little processing power) and effective. Recognition errors can easily be corrected if more features become available.

In crisis situations, reports from eye witnesses and crisis responders are invaluable in creating a good assessment of the size and nature of the crisis. This is true provided that the reports are speedy, un-ambiguous and consistent. In a previous project, we developed a language independent icon interface for crisis reporting [3]. This

N. Aykin (Ed.): Usability and Internationalization, Part II, HCII 2007, LNCS 4560, pp. 554–563, 2007.

interface had a disadvantage in that all icons, even the ones irrelevant to the crisis situation, are shown. This made it sometimes very hard for users to find the desired icons, especially if the number of icons is large. The main contribution of this paper is an adaptive interface with increased usability by using dynamic scripting to select the icons to be shown.

In our model of the crisis situation, all reporters are equipped with a handheld device, containing a graphical interface to make reports. The interface presents the reporter with a number of icons using which he has to describe the situation he wants to report about. As the number of possible situations that can be reported is very large, the interface has to make a selection of icons to show. This selection of icons is determined by a rule based selection algorithm powered by competing scripts, hence the term dynamic scripting. Each script represents the chain of events that identify a possible scenario; each script also has a set of icons associated with it (each icon represents a key event in the script). At the onset of the crisis, when few events have been observed, there are many competing scripts. The reporter is presented with a number of icons representing the key concepts most common to the competing scripts. As the reporter selects icons, more key concepts in the crisis environment become clear. As a result, certain scripts become impossible and are removed from competition. The interface is then populated with icons provided by the remaining competing script. This process continues until, there is only one script left. Apart from selecting new icons, error handling mechanisms are also built in to the interface. The reporter can remove an icon anywhere in the list of selected icons or undo a previous selection. In both cases all the possible scripts are re-evaluated. In this way scripts that have been removed from competition previously can become competitive again.

Although the system has not been completed we have prototyped and tested parts of it in several simulated crisis scenarios. These parts will be described in the current paper. The remainder of the paper is structured as follows. First we give an overview of the background and the related work in the area, then we describe how we gathered information about crisis situations, next we give an overview of the system. After that we present the experiments and their results. Finally we conclude with some discussions and give directions for further research.

2 Background and Related Work

2.1 Dynamic Scripting

Dynamic scripting is inspired by the Conceptual Dependency theory developed by Schank and Abelson [2]. The dynamic scripting approach assumes that knowledge about crisis and crisis events is represented in the human mind as scripts. These scripts are triggered by the observation of special features or events occurring in the environment. In the beginning, when a small number of features are observed, many competing scripts may be in our mind. But by reasoning and the additional information from further observations, we arrive at a final hypothesis.

We can illustrate scripting in humans with a very simple example. Image yourself as a witness of a traffic accident in which some people got injured. After observing the accident, you would be triggered to call the alarm line and you expect the ambulance and police to arrive shortly after. In the described scenario, it is clear that this behavior and the corresponding expectancy will be triggered only if we have experienced the situation before. We call this knowledge about events that we have experienced many times before specific knowledge [4, 5]. The example also shows that a scenario with an event sequence consisting of many events may be recognizable or even identifiable from just the first few of those events. Humans take advantage of this property of specific knowledge all the time, giving them the ability to rapidly interpret, recognize and participate in situations that resemble scenarios stored in their memory as specific knowledge. The flow from recognition to actions is also efficient since humans don't spent time reasoning about irrelevant matters or asking irrelevant questions. Thus, specific detailed knowledge about a situation allows humans to perform intelligent actions and do less processing and wondering about frequently experienced events [2].

The sequence of events that represents a specific scenario we call a script (in this sense a script is comparable with scripts used in the movie industry). Furthermore, we can view the human specific knowledge as a database containing many scripts (one for each scenario). As we perceive events occurring in our environment, certain scripts become more plausible then others. As more events are perceived, the evidence in favor of the correct scenario increases. This in turn increases the plausibility of the corresponding script. On the other hand, evidence might contradict a scenario. In this case another script becomes more plausible.

2.2 The Crisis Situation

Since the bombings in London and Madrid in 2005 the challenge of robust, reliable and effective crisis management has become an increased area of interest. Apart from the problems involving organizational and management issues [6], these events are also reminders of the problems in crisis management technology. Good supporting technology to help people of different backgrounds, roles and professions to collaborate with each other is a necessity when facing crises. The potential benefits of extensive information sharing and wider cooperation have historically been mitigated by the unavailability of robust communications or transportation systems to support them. Increasingly, however, this barrier is being eliminated. More complex and potentially superior disaster response strategies become feasible as advances in these technologies empower fast, widespread information and resource sharing within the disaster zone and between that zone and neighboring areas [7]. Extensive information sharing can aid in resource assessment and contribute valuable information to plan the response effort more effectively, especially in the first few hours after the onset of the crisis.

Recent catastrophes however, have shown that the technology was unable to cope with the non deterministic environment, information explosion and operational chaos [8] that ensues in crises of large proportions. Immediately after the beginning of the crisis, an explosion of eye witness reports of incidents will begin flowing from observers and responders into the crisis centre. These reports will be of varying significance and accuracy. They will also be highly subjective, geographically dispersed, erroneous, partial or contradicting. They might even be describing different phenomena possibly unrelated to the current crisis. The need of a standard representation of reports to reduce the ambiguity and multitude of semantic interpretation of human observers is obvious. Moreover, it is necessary to provide reporters with an interface to compose these reports rapidly and effectively.

In crisis situations, reporters (observers, responders) may be forced to communicate with their mobile device (e.g. PDA) on a Mobile Ad-Hoc Network due to potentially overloaded or destroyed communication infrastructure [9]. Because of the hardware constraints of these devices (e.g. small screen, small or no keyboards), these devices do not lend themselves well for traditional user interfaces for crisis event reporting. Many attempts have been made to adapt user interfaces to cope with these constraints. (E.g. [10] propose a multimodal approach, [11] propose speech recognition and [3, 12] propose a natural interaction style based on an iconic interface.) In this paper, we choose the iconic interface as the main user interaction. The advantages of this interface for crisis reporting are discussed in [3]. By making this interface intelligent and adaptable we can increase the speed, clarity and objectiveness of the reports while decreasing the number of errors and contradictions.

3   Constructing Scenarios and Knowledge of the World

To manage the size of the project, we have limited our scope to crisis situations caused by gas and fire incidents. In the period of august 2005 to April 2006, we carried out interviews with experts from the Southern Rotterdam Fire Department and the crisis center of the Rijnmond environmental agency (DCMR). With the information from interviews with firemen and chemical experts we created a list of possible crisis scenarios, we also created a list of named concepts (and their relationships) that play an important part in the crisis situation [13]. Next we used these named concepts to formulate the crisis scenarios. We tested if the scenarios thus formulated where discriminative enough so that each scenario was identifiable by a unique set of concepts. Finally, a selection of the scenarios we further developed into scripts to test the system.

The icon selection scheme we devised (Fig. 1) works as follows. At the onset of the crisis, when few features have been observed, there are many competing scripts.

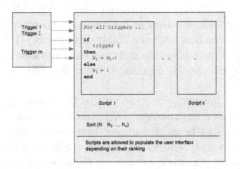

Fig. 1. Icon selection scheme

The reporter is presented with a number of generic icons representing the key concepts most common to the competing scripts. As the reporter selects icons, more and more key concepts in the crisis environment become clear. As a result, certain scripts become impossible and are removed from competition. The interface is populated by icons provided by the remaining competing scripts. This process continues until finally, there is only one script left.

4   System Overview

The system consists of three parts: a user interface to present the reporter with icons, an icon selection module that populates the user interface with icons from the competing scripts and a message generation module that fills in the missing icons once a conclusion has been made. The message generation module is also responsible for generating the appropriate message to send to the crisis centre.

4.1   User Interface

Due to the limitations of mobile devices (small screen, small or no keyboard) we have chosen to use an iconic interface as the main user interaction method in our reporting system (see Fig. 2). Direct manipulation of the icons on a GUI with a pointing device allows for fast interaction as pictorial signs can be recognized more quickly then written words [14], [15]. Furthermore, [3] has shown that with NLP it is possible to generate consistent messages from a collection of icons.

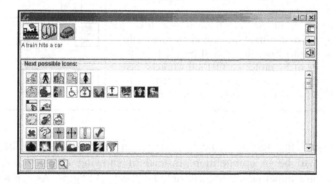

Fig. 2. Iconic interface for composing crisis reports

4.2   Icon Selection Module

The icon selection module is responsible for selecting the icons to show on the screen based on the remaining competing scripts. We used the same icons as in [3]. Each competing script is allowed to propose icons to be shown. The icon selection module is also responsible for limiting the number of proposals so that the interface does not become too crowded. On the other hand, the module has to make sure that the interface does not become too limited in expressiveness as a result of a lack of icons.

In our system, a script is made of two parts: a list of icons and a description of the scenario. The icons are the graphical representations of the events in the script. The description can be viewed as a knowledge base containing a priori information about the scenario at hand. It is essentially a set of rules.

Specifying a Script. A script can be specified by writing the sequence of events as rules. An expert system's inference engine [16] controls the application of these rules. Jess [17] was used as the expert system shell as it provides the capabilities needed to develop the inference engine that is used for the icon selection task. To get an idea of the icon selection process, let us consider the three simplified scenarios depicted in Table 1.

Table 1. Three example scenarios with their associated icons. The arrows in the icon representation are added to show the order of the events in the scenario.

nr	Scenario description	Icon representation
1	A building is on fire and there are injured people. After a while an ambulance comes to take care of the injured and the fire department arrives to distinguish the fire.	
2	A building is on fire but there is also toxic gas coming out of the fire. In this case, people in the neighborhood have to be evacuated. The fire department arrives (properly equipped) to distinguish the fire.	
3	A building is on fire but there is also toxic gas coming out of the fire. Furthermore there are injured people. In this case, the injured people have to be taken care of by protected first aid workers, people in the neighborhood have to be evacuated. Properly equipped firemen have to distinguish the fire.	

Let us assume that these are the only scripts in the system. In the beginning, all three scripts will be in competition. Instead of showing all six icons, the icons proposed by the competing scripts will only be "fire" and "gas". As can be seen from the table, all three scenarios include the fire event, so if the fire icon is selected from the user interface, all scripts still stay in contention, but the "injured people" icon is added and the "fire" icon is removed. However, if the gas icon is selected, script 1 drops out of contention and the "evacuation" icon will be shown.

In order to work in the Jess, the rules of a script have to comply with the Jess rule syntax. Each Jess rule contains a condition and consequence separated by a "=>" token. The condition is a logical statement and the consequence specifies the hypothesis if the condition is true. The example below shows a listing of the Jess rules for the second script in our example.

```
(defrule script2-init "this is the initial rule for script 2,
it proposes the possible icons to start this script"
=>
  (assert (propose fire))
  (assert (propose gas))
)

(defrule script2-r1-1 "this rule proposes the gas icon if fire
has been detected"
  (percept fire)
  =>
  (assert (propose gas))
)

(defrule script2-r1-2 "this rule proposes the fire icon if gas
has been detected"
    (percept gas)
=>
    (assert (propose fire))
)

(defrule script2-r2 "this rule proposes evacuation icon if gas
and fire have been detected"
    (or (percept fire) (percept gas))
=>
    (assert (propose evacuate))
)

(defrule script2-r3 "this rule proposes firemen icon if people
have been evacuated"
    (or (percept fire) (percept gas))
    (percept evacuate)
=>
    (assert (propose firemen))
)
```

Rule Based Icon Selection. As many competing scripts propose icons to be displayed, a selection process determines which icons will actually end up in the GUI. The selection process depends on the conflict resolution strategy of the Jess inference engine. In rule based systems, when the conditions of multiple rules are satisfied (these rules are called activated), a conflict resolution strategy is applied to determine the order in which the rules have to be fired. When a rule fires, the consequence of that rule is executed. The default conflict resolution strategy in Jess is known as depth. Here, the most recent activated rules are placed above the older ones. This tends to cause the system to pursue a single line of reasoning until it is done. The complexity of the condition of the rule also determines the priority of a rule. With all other things being equal, a rule with a more complex condition (one that is more difficult to satisfy) has precedence over a rule with a less complex condition. In general, the conditions of the rules in a script become more complex further on in the script; therefore, this strategy allows the order of the events in the script to influence the icon selection process.

In our system, the selection process continues until the maximum number of icons to display is reached or until all competing scripts have given their proposals (whichever comes first). This behavior is achieved by letting the inference engine fire the activated rules in the order determined by the conflict resolution, until there are no activated rules left. This works because (1) rules that have fired do not activate again. This prevents a rule from firing continuously, (2) the rules are written such that the firing of a rule does not add or remove other scripts from competition since the consequence of a rule only proposes new icons to be displayed. This ensures that only icons of currently competing scripts are proposed, (3) the rules with the most common icons will be ordered first by the conflict resolution. This ensures that the most common icons of the competing scripts are displayed first, (4) When a rule proposes an icon that is already perceived or selected for display it is ignored. This ensures that there are no duplicate icons shown.

5 Experiments

Unfortunately, the system can't be tested in a real crisis, because (1) the message generation module has not been implemented yet (2) it is difficult to create a controlled experiment of a disaster just to test the interface. Therefore, some preliminary experiments had to be done in simulated crises situations.

In one experiment, we deployed a prototype of our interface in the MACSIM [18] crisis simulator. This simulator contains models of physical phenomena and is able to simulate such phenomena and show them on a minute by minute basis. We have tested the first prototype in several crisis simulation scenarios with students being the reporters. These students take the role of eye witnesses and report back to the crisis center. In another experiment, we tested the interface using a scenario presented to respondents in the form of photographs. A disadvantage of photographs is that it is very hard to determine ones position just by looking at them. To compensate for this, all respondents were provided with a map of the environment with explicitly information on what direction they are looking at. During the experiments, the respondents were asked to think aloud, telling what they are thinking and what they are trying to accomplish. This allows us to determine if specific tasks need to be made more intuitive, or need more functionality.

In the experiments we only focused on the usefulness of the interface. Preliminary results show that the total amount of icons shown decreased significantly. However we have not done comparisons with a non adaptive icon interface under the same conditions, as some issues emerge during experiments that need to be resolved first. The issues can be classified in two categories.

1. Not all objects or events were identified for the correct script to be concluded. The combination of the unrealistic experiment setup (simulation and photographs) and the respondents not being experienced reporters may have caused them to miss important events.
2. Users wanted to report about events but miss the appropriate icon. In these cases the reporters wanted to report about events that the system deemed irrelevant. Further analysis of the results have to show is the reporters were correct or if the events where really irrelevant.

6 Discussion and Conclusion

In crisis situations, reports from eye witnesses and crisis responders are invaluable in creating a good assessment of the size and nature of the crisis. This is true provided that the reports are speedy, un-ambiguous and consistent. In this paper we presented a language independent, adaptable interface for crisis reporting. Language independence is required to bridge the gap between differences in crisis management as a result of user diversity. By using an adaptable interface for crisis reporting based on possible crisis scenarios, we can increase the ease and speed with which reports are composed and the consistency of the resulting reports. Our approach differs from other approaches to adaptive interfaces in that, instead of trying to fit the users' interpretation of observations into sensible reports, we use possible crisis scenarios as the starting point of the reports. In this sense, it is the user who has to fit its interpretation of observations into a possible scenario.

During a crisis simulation experiment, the basic crisis events occur according to a predefined script. However, the order and timing in which the reports about the events enter the crisis centre cannot be determined beforehand. The situation in the crisis centre may soon become chaotic and unmanageable. Because our adaptive interface only generates messages based on scripts, this becomes somewhat easier to manage. Furthermore, the rule based nature of the interface, make decisions and inferences easier to verify afterwards. Another advantage is that, even though the scripts may be executed in a different order, the scripts themselves may be designed and specified sequentially in order of the basic physical events of a crisis scenario.

As a drawback, all scripts have to be designed and specified in advance. This means that for the interface to be fully expressive, all possible scenarios have to be converted into scripts since reports about scenarios that have not been specified are not possible.

A topic for further research could be a mechanism to generate new scripts for scenarios that have not been encountered before i.e. learning. The Conceptual Dependency theory sheds light on this issue by assuming that humans reason about new situations by applying general knowledge or common sense to the problem. This would suggest that we also have to apply domain specific common sense knowledge about concepts and their relationships to situations never encountered before. We could combine this knowledge with observations of new situations to generate new scripts such that the new script is (1) expressive and (2) discriminative.

Finally the possible relationships between events are very limited e.g. the possibility to specify that the occurrence of one event excludes another event or that one event highly increases the probability of another are lacking. More research should be done to increase the expressiveness and flexibility of the scripts.

References

1. Wang, X.: Storyboard-based world modeling, Master of Science thesis TU Delft, The Netherlands (2006)
2. Schank, R., Abelson, R.: Scripts, Plans, Goals and Understanding. Erlbaum, Hillsdale, NJ (1977)
3. Fitrianie, S., Rothkrantz, L.J.M.: Communication in Crisis Situation using Icon language. In: Proc. of IEEE ICME 05 (2005)
4. Reategui, E.B., Campbell, J.A.: Leão, B.F.: A Case-Based Model that Integrates Specific and General Knowledge in Reasoning, Journal of Applied Intelligence, vol 6(1) (1997)
5. Aamodt, A., Plaza, E.: Case-Based Reasoning: Foundational Issues, Methodological Variations, and System Approaches. AI Communications 7(1), 39–59 (1994)

 6. Oomes, A.: Organization Awareness in Crisis Management: dynamic organigrams for more effective disaster response. In: Proc of the First International Workshop on Information Systems for Crisis Response and Management, Brussels, pp. 63–68 (2004)
 7. Scott, P.D., Rogova, G.L.: Crisis Management in a Data Fusion Synthetic Task Environment. In: Proc. of the 7th International Conference on Information Fusion (2004)
 8. Dymon, U.J.: An Analysis of Emergency Map Symbology. Int. Journal of Emergency Management 1(3), 227–237 (2003)
 9. Tatomir, B., Rothkrantz, L.J.M.: Crisis Management using Mobile Ad-hoc Wireless Networks. In: Proc. of ISCRAM05 (2005)
10. Wahlster, W., Rethinger, N., Blocher, A.: SmartKom: Multimodal Communication with a Life-Like Character. In: Proc. of EUROSPEECH'01, Denmark (2001)
11. Comerford, L., Frank, D., Gopalakrishnan, P., Gopnanth, R., Sedivy, J.: The IBM Personal Speech Assistant. In: Proc. of the ICASSP 2001, USA (2001)
12. Kjeldskov, J., Kolbe, N.: Interaction Design for handheld Computers. In: Proc. of APCHI02, Science Press, China (2002)
13. Benjamins, T.: MACSIM,: Multi-Agent Crisis Simulator, Interpreter and Monitor Master of Science thesis TU Delft, The Netherlands (2006)
14. Frutiger, A.: Signs and Symbols, their Design and Meaning. Van Nostrand Reinholt: New York (1989)
15. Littlejohn, S.W.: Theories of human Communication, 5th edn. Wadsworth (1996)
16. Giarrantano, J., Riley, G.: Expert Systems: Principles and Programming. PWS-KENT Publishing Company. Boston (1989)
17. Friedman-Hill, E.: Jess in Action. Manning Publications Co (2003)
18. Benjamins, T., Rothkrantz, L.J.M., MACSIM: Serious Gaming in Crisis Management via Script-based Simulation. In: proc of 9th International Conference on Computer Games: AI, Animation, Mobile, Educational & Serious Games (2006)

How to Quantify User Experience:
Fuzzy Comprehensive Evaluation Model Based on
Summative Usability Testing

Ronggang Zhou

Department of Industrial Engineering, Tsinghua University,
Beijing 100084, China
zhourg@tsinghua.edu.cn

Abstract. The concept of usability is complicated and fuzziness. Fuzzy theory
is developed to provide comprehensive evaluation capabilities in the presence
of imprecise and uncertain information. Starting with the ISO 9241 dimensions
(effectiveness, efficiency and satisfaction), a fuzzy comprehensive model based
on fuzzy theory for evaluating usability is proposed instead of conventional
methods. The model has ability to assess user experience comprehensively with
defuzzied score. Combined with data of summative usability, it can be applied
to benchmark product usability, and a case study indicated the approach can
quantify user experience directly and comprehensively.

Keywords: user experience, usability, usability testing, fuzzy comprehensive
evaluation, analytic hierarchy process (AHP).

1 Introduction

As technology advance, usability has become an important criterion for decision
making for end-users and consumers to chose, and users are less willing to put up
with uncomfortable product when there are many competitive alternatives. So product
usability captures more devotion from product designers and developers for their
competitive purpose in the market. Nowadays, usability has become a special field
consisted of multi-disciplines, called usability engineering. And many useful methods
are available to evaluate the usability. However, less effective tools or approaches are
efficient to evaluate comprehensively product's usability integrating objective and
objective measure, since usability is a concept of fuzzy and its definition is dependent.
The purpose of this study is to propose a comprehensive evaluation model based on
fuzzy evaluation approach. The model can be used to measure the level of products
usability in usability engineering processes, such as for designers and developers to
know the best one in the corresponding stage of develop.

1.1 Definitions of Usability

As a core term in human-computer interaction, usability has been defined by many
researchers in many ways [1] [2] [3] [4] [5] [6]. By focusing on the perception of the

N. Aykin (Ed.): Usability and Internationalization, Part II, HCII 2007, LNCS 4560, pp. 564–573, 2007.

product, Shackel proposed an operational definition of usability, and provided a set of usability criteria [1]. They were effectiveness, learnability, flexibility, and attitude or satisfaction. The definition has been generally accepted in usability community [7]. Another well-accepted definition of usability which received more attention from HCI was offered by Nielsen, he described five operational usability dimensions: learnability, memorability, efficiency, satisfaction and errors [2]. Based on the effort of whole usability community, the international Standards Organization (ISO) attempted to establish standards definition on usability, and defined usability as "the extent to which a product can be used by specified users to achieve specified goals with effective, efficiency and satisfaction in a specified context of use" [5]. However the dimensions of usability have been described by ISO/IEC 9126-1 as understandability, learnability, operability, and attractiveness [6]. From the overview of the usability definition, usability could be a combination of different dimensions, such as effectiveness, usefulness, learnability, flexibility, attitude/likeable, memorability, efficiency, satisfaction, errors, understandability, operability and attractiveness. So in some degree "the concept usability is ill defined in research and practice alike. Usability can mean different things to different people, even when it is defined, it still remains intuitive, circular, or elusive." [8], and the meaning of usability is context dependent and still ambiguous [1] [9] [10].

1.2 Attempts to Evaluate Usability Comprehensively

The definition of usability is related with usability measurement, "what we mean by the term usability is to a large extent determined by how we measure it" [4]. Many different metrics can be used for measuring one dimension of usability. For example, with binary task completion, accuracy, error rate, recall and/or completeness, we can measure the effective [10]. In a summative usability evaluation, several metrics are available to the analyst for benchmarking the usability of a product for comparing with its previous versions or competitor's systems. But generally it is difficult to make a comparison between different evaluations, since metrics, test tasks and numbers of task are used differently. If analyst could draw a comprehensive evaluation for overall usability, the comparison would become possible. From the literatures, we have seen some attempts to derive a single measure based on data of usability evaluation.

Only based on objective data of user performance time, key stroke time and error rate, Babiker et al derived a metric for measuring overall usability of hypertext system [11]. The metric was based on three individual important attribute: access and navigation, orientation, and user interaction. They found their metric correlated to subjective assessment measures, but it could not be generalized to other systems since proper weights need to be determined. With the method of Principle Components Analysis, Sauro et al also tried to derive a way to represent system or task usability in a single, standardized and summated metric, and they claimed that the metric do include all usability aspects, such as effectiveness, efficiency and satisfaction[12]. But the evaluated aspects were weighted equally.

Focusing on user's personal interactive experience with a product, several well-known subjective usability questionnaires were developed such as Software Usability Measurement Inventory (SUMI) [13], the Questionnaire for User Interaction (QUIS)

[14] [15], and Post-Study system Usability Questionnaire (PSSUQ) [16] [17]. The authors of these questionnaires do not necessarily intend for the questionnaires to act as a single measure of usability [12]. Based on human information processing theory and eight human factors considerations which are relevant to software usability, Purdue Usability Testing Questionnaire (PUTQ) was developed as a checklist for comparing the relative usability of different software systems [7]. Also in development of usability questionnaires for electronic mobile (MPUQ), Ryu tried to use decision making methods based on the Analytic Hierarchy Process (AHP) and linear regression analysis to make comprehensive usability evaluation of mobile [18]. These questionnaires can provide a subjective assessment for recently completed tasks and there were claimed to derive a reliable and low-cost standardized measure of the overall usability or quality of use of a system, but they are only suitable to subjective assessment and are not appropriate for integrating objective data.

These methods are not enough dynamic to apply to the practice for evaluating overall usability of product. Since the complication and fuzziness of the usability, the selection of evaluation approach is very important. Fuzzy theory is developed to provide decision-making capabilities in the presence of imprecise and uncertain information. Starting with the ISO 9241 dimensions (effectiveness, efficiency and satisfaction), this paper aims to propose a comprehensive evaluation model with the approach of fuzzy comprehensive evaluation integrating the AHP, and apply it to present a single usability score based on summative usability testing.

2   A Proposed Usability Comprehensive Evaluation Model

In this section, first we provided general description for fuzzy comprehensive evaluation and how to use the AHP to weight the evaluated factors. Then we proposed a comprehensive evaluation model for usability.

2.1   General Description of Fuzzy Comprehensive Evaluation

Fuzzy analytic hierarchy evaluation is the process of evaluating an objective utilizing the fuzzy set theory. When evaluating an objective, multiple related factors must be considered comprehensively in order to give an appropriate, non-contradicting and logically consistent judgment. The general steps of fuzzy evaluation may be simplified as the following [19]:

Step 1: Determining a set of evaluation factors. With these factors we can get a structural index system for evaluation. Assuming that the objective being evaluated contains n factors, then the index set can be represented as $U = \{u_1, u_2, ..., u_n\}$.

Step 2: Determining a set of appraisal grades. The appraisal set can be represented as $V = \{v_1, v_2, ..., v_m\}$, for instance $\{excellent, good, medium, poor, very\ poor\}$ could be used as appraisal comment for specific objective.

Step 3: Setting fuzzy matrix for general evaluation. In this case, we'll get the mapping from U to V. For a specific factor, the appraisal is $R_i = \{r_{i1}, v_{i2}, ..., v_{im}\}$. The overall fuzzy appraisal matrix of all n factors can be mapped a fuzzy relationship:

$$R = \begin{bmatrix} r_{11} & r_{12} & \cdots & r_{1m} \\ r_{21} & r_{22} & \cdots & r_{2m} \\ \vdots & \vdots & & \vdots \\ r_{n2} & r_{n2} & \cdots & r_{nm} \end{bmatrix}. \tag{1}$$

Step 4: Determining the weight of evaluation factors. In making a comprehensive evaluation, the importance of each factor should be quantified. The weight vector can be represented by A $(a_1, a_2, ..., a_n)$, which can be formulated by the AHP.

Step 5: Getting the appraisal result. The overall appraisal result set of comprehensive evaluation is B, presented as follows.

$$B = (b_1, b_2, b_3, ..., b_m) = A \circ R. \tag{2}$$

Where, b_j could be operated by many operation models, such as M ($\wedge$, $\vee$), M ($\cdot$, $\vee$) and M ($\cdot$, $\oplus$) [20]. In this study, every single factor should be considered. So the M ($\cdot$, $\oplus$) was used for calculated b_j, where "$\oplus$" defined as $\alpha + \beta = \min(1, \alpha + \beta)$, then the model is

$$b_j = \sum_{i=1}^{n} a_i r_{ij} = \min\left\{1, \sum_{i=1}^{n} a_i r_{ij}\right\}. \tag{3}$$

2.2 How to Determine the Weight Vector by the AHP

In this paper, we used the AHP to obtain the weight vector A. The procedures may be simplified as follows [21][22]:

Step 1: Based on pair-comparison of n factors shown in Table 1, the weight comparison could be represented in $n \times n$ matrix as follows:

$$A = \begin{bmatrix} a_{11} & a_{12} & \cdots & a_{1n} \\ a_{21} & a_{22} & \cdots & a_{2n} \\ \cdot & \cdot & \cdots & \cdot \\ \cdot & \cdot & \cdots & \cdot \\ a_{n1} & a_{n2} & \cdots & a_{nn} \end{bmatrix}. \tag{4}$$

Each a_{ij} of the matrix represents the importance intensity of factor A_i over factor A_j. The a_{ij} value is supposed to be an approximation of the relative importance of A_i to A_j, i.e., $a_{ij} = (W_i/W_j)$. Each of a_{ij} $(i,j=1,2,...,n)$ follows $a_{ji}=1/a_{ij}$, for $a_{ij}\neq 0$.

Table 1. lineal scale of preferences in the pair-wise comparison process

Numerical rating	Judgments of preferences between factor i and factor j.
1	factor i is equally important to factor j
3	factor i is slightly more important than factor j
5	factor i is clearly more important than j
7	factor i is strongly more important than factor j
9	factor i is extremely more important than factor j
2, 4, 6, 8	Intermediate values

Step 2: Calculating the weight vector *A*. We can use the method of ANC (average of normalized columns) to estimate the vectors of weights function, ANC can be presented as:

$$w_i = \frac{1}{n}\sum_{j=1}^{n}\frac{a_{ij}}{\sum_{i=1}^{n}a_{ij}}.$$ (5)

Step 3: Computing consistence ratio of the judgments matrix. Accordingly, Saaty defined the consistency ratio as:

$$CR = CI / RI.$$ (6)

The CR is a measure of how a given matrix compares to a purely random matrix in terms of their consistency indices. A value of CR≤0.1 is considered acceptable. RI is the average random index, which is a statistical value. For a 3 ×3 matrix, the value of RI is 0.58. And where consistency index (CI) was defined as:

$$CI = (\lambda_{max} - n)/(n-1),$$ (7)

where n is the number of factors, and λ_{max} represents the maximum eigenvalue of the pairwise comparison matrix, the closer the λ_{max} is to n the more consistent, and the λ_{max} can be formulated by:

$$\lambda_{max} = \sum_{i=1}^{n}\frac{(A\bar{w})_i}{nw_i}.$$ (8)

2.3   A Weighted Hierarchical Index Proposed for Evaluating Usability

Usability cannot be directly measured, but we can construct it into attributes that can be measured. The choice of such attributes not only fleshes out what usability means, it also raises the question if that which is measured is a valid indicator of usability [10]. The framework of usability provided by ISO is pervasive [5], and was selected as a basis for structure of usability evaluation index in this paper like previous studies [12] [18] [23], i.e. effectiveness, efficiency and satisfaction structured as three attributes of usability. Since the two measures are product-independent and used most frequently, in order to structure a universal usability evaluation index for different systems, *task success* and *task completion time* were selected as a single metric for measuring effectiveness and efficiency respectively. The PSSUQ was developed exclusively for measurement of satisfaction for user testing, and had the highest percentages of redundancy with the other sets of questionnaire items [18], and so was chosen for measuring user's satisfaction after a test in this study.

Since single metric was employed to measure effectiveness, efficiency and satisfaction, we only need to determine the weight vector of the three attributes for overall usability. We had a six-expert panel to perform pair-wise comparison according to Table 1. They discussed together and gave agreeable pair-wise comparison with respect to the three attributes of usability, and they would repeat the process if the CR>0.1. Table 2 presented the matrix of pair-wise comparisons, and according to section 2.2, and the weight vector *A* could be given as (0.443, 0.169, 0.387).

Table 2. Pairwise comparison with respect to user satisfaction

	Effective	Efficiency	Satisfaction	Weight
Effective	1	3	1	0.443
Efficiency	1/3	1	1/2	0.170
Satisfaction	1	2	1	0.387

Note: λmax=3.018, CI=0.009, CR=0.016.

So the fuzzy evaluation model can be constructed as shown in Fig. 1.

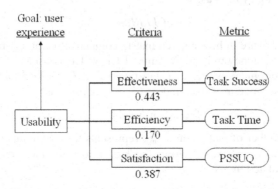

Fig. 1. Fuzzy comprehensive usability evaluation model

2.4 Determining the Fuzzy Member Function for Appraisal Matrix *R*

In this study, the metric of task success was valued by 0~1, "0" indicates one participant can not finish a test task, "1" means he complete the test task very well, intermediate value means corresponding degree of success. Satisfaction was scaled by PSSUQ, which is 7-point scale. Task time was recorded from the beginning to the end of task. How to value or record the success and time was described operationally. When determining the membership function for factors, corresponding score of each task on each metric would be ranked as "*excellent, good, medium, poor* or *very poor*". Table 3 presented the membership mapping, which was determined based on expert's experience.

Table 3. The membership mapping for metric score ranking

Ranking	*very poor*	*poor*	*medium*	*good*	*excellent*
Success	$0 \leq x < 0.3$	$0.3 \leq x < 0.6$	$0.6 \leq x < 0.8$	$0.8 \leq x < 0.95$	$0.95 \leq x \leq 1$
Time	$x < 0.3$	$0.3 \leq x' < 0.6$	$0.6 \leq x' < 0.8$	$0.8 \leq x' < 0.95$	$0.95 \leq x'$
Satisfac.	$1 \leq x < 2$	$2 \leq x < 3.5$	$3.5 \leq x < 5.5$	$5.5 \leq x < 6.5$	$6.5 \leq x \leq 7$

In Table 3 x is the mean performance. Before test, the shortest complete time was given as a expect value for each task, so x' was transformed by x according to the following formula:

$$x' = 1 - \frac{x-E}{E} = 2 - \frac{x}{E}, \qquad (9)$$

where "E" means expectable shortest task time, when $x'=1$, the performance on task time is the best. Then the factors in fuzzy relation matrix could be calculated as following formula [24]:

$$R_{ij} = \text{(Num. of corresponding average rank)} / \text{(Num. of the participants)} \qquad (10)$$

3 Case Study

In order to illustrate fuzzy comprehensive evaluation model could be applied to benchmark usability of product, one summative usability testing process was used as an example in this section. Based on integrated user-centered design approach [25], a software product was developed. Before releasing, a standard summative usability testing was conducted in a standard usability testing lab to benchmark the usability of the product [2] [25]. There were 16 typical users participated the testing. And the testing was processed by one experienced facilitator, and two usability engineers collected the data respectively as observers in the watching room.

3.1 Determining the Fuzzy Appraisal Matrix

According to section 2.1 and 2.4, the average performance of all tasks on each metric is calculated. Then each of mean value is ranked as "excellent, good, medium, poor or very poor", which is presented judgment set in the paper. According to Eq. (10), the fuzzy appraisal matrix for these three factors was obtained. The process could be illustrated from Table 4, which indicated the membership for task success.

Table 4. The membership mapping for task success value ranking

	$M_{success}$	Excellent	Good	Medium	Poor	Very Poor
P1	0.945		×			
P2	0.963	×				
P3	0.981	×				
P4	0.985	×				
P5	0.955	×				
P6	0.966	×				
P7	0.949		×			
P8	0.963	×				
P9	0.946		×			
P10	0.935		×			
P11	0.956	×				
P12	0.952	×				
P13	0.955	×				
P14	0.964	×				
P15	0.937		×			
P16	0.989	×				
Total		11	5	0	0	0
R_j		0.6875	0.3125	0	0	0

Similar way, we can get membership mapping for task time and satisfaction. So the fuzzy appraisal matrix could be presented as following.

$$R = \begin{bmatrix} 0.6875 & 0.3125 & 0 & 0 & 0 \\ 0.25 & 0.3125 & 0.0625 & 0.25 & 0.125 \\ 0.125 & 0.625 & 0.25 & 0 & 0 \end{bmatrix}. \tag{11}$$

3.2 Getting the Appraisal Result

In this paper, we consider very single factor overall, so B was calculated based on Eq. (2).

$$B = A \circ R = (0.4434, \ 0.1692, \ 0.3874) \circ \begin{bmatrix} 0.6875 & 0.3125 & 0 & 0 & 0 \\ 0.25 & 0.3125 & 0.0625 & 0.25 & 0.125 \\ 0.125 & 0.625 & 0.25 & 0 & 0 \end{bmatrix}. \tag{12}$$

$$= (0.3956, \ 0.3711, \ 0.1758, \ 0.0156, \ 0.0313)$$

This was the final appraisal vector, and it can be defuzzified to a comprehensive score [25]. In this paper, we defined excellent, good, medium, poor, very poor in appraisal grading as 95, 82, 67, 50, 31, respectively, so the appraisal vector B can be defuzzified according to the following formula:

$$a = \left. \sum_{i-1}^{m} b_i^2 a_i \middle/ \sum_{i-1}^{m} b_i^2 \right., \tag{13}$$

where a is the defuzzified score, $a_1=95$, $a_2=82$, $a_3=67$, $a_4=50$, $a_5=31$, b_i is appraisal vector. Base on the appraisal vector, the defuzzified score was 86.63, which can present the comprehensive usability of the software.

4 Discussion and Conclusion

Based on the fuzzy evaluation theory, a model for evaluating usability of a system was proposed instead of conventional methods. Fuzzy comprehensive evaluation theory is an effective approach for quantifying and qualifying the uncertain, and is appropriate to evaluate usability comprehensively. Based on the fuzzy evaluation model, the defuzzified score can provide a synthetic judgment for user experience of product using. Integrated with data of summative usability testing (e.g. performance measurements), the model can be used to measure the level of products usability in corresponding developed processes, such as for designers and developers to know the best one in the stage of the competitive analysis process or to validate the success of their own new product before releasing, since it can provide one continuous variable that can be used for hypothesis testing statistically. In addition, the approach can also be applied to structure other usability evaluation data systematically.

References

1. Shackel, B.: Usability - context, framework, design and evaluation. In: Shackel, B., Richardson, S. (eds.) Human factors for informatics usability. Cambridge, pp. 21–38 (1991)
2. Nielsen, J.: Usability Engineering. Academic Press, San Diego (1993)
3. Rubin, J.: Handbook of Usability Testing: How to plan, design and conduct effective tests. John Wiley & Sons, New York (1994)
4. Barnum, C.M.: Usability Testing and Research. Longman Publications, New York (2002)
5. ISO 9241-11: Ergonomic requirements for office work with visual display terminals (VDTs) – part 11: Guidance on usability. International Organization for Standardization (1998)
6. ISO/IEO 9126 -1: Software engineering- product quality – part 1: Quality model. International Organization for Standardization (2001)
7. Lin, H.X., Choong, Y.-Y., Salvendy, G.: A Proposed Index of Usability: A Method for Comparing the Relative Usability of Different Software Systems. Behaviour & Information Technology 16, 267–278 (1997)
8. Kim, K.: A model of digital library information seeking process (DLISP model) as a frame for classifying usability problems. Doctoral dissertation, The State University of New Jersey. New Brunswick, New Jersey (2002)
9. Newman, W., Taylor, A.: Towards a methodology employing critical parameters to deliver performance improvements in interactive systems. In: Proceedings of IFIP TC.13 International Conference on Human-Computer Interaction, pp. 605–612. IOS Press, Amsterdam (1999)
10. Hornbæk, K.: Current practice in measuring usability: Challenges to usability studies and research. International Journal of Human-Computer Studies 64, 79–102 (2006)
11. Babiker, E.M., Fujihara, H., Boyle, C.D.B.: A metric for hypertext usability. In: Proc. 11th Annual International Conference on Systems documentation, pp. 95–104. ACM Press, New York (1991)
12. Sauro, J., Kindlund, E.: A Method to Standardize Usability Metrics Into a Single Score. In: CHI 2005, Portland, OR, pp. 401–409. ACM Press, New York (2005)
13. Kirakowski, J.: The Software Usability Measurement Inventory: Background and usage. In: Jordan, P., Thomas, B., Weerdmeester, B. (eds.) Usability Evaluation in Industry, pp. 169–178. Taylor and Francis, London (1996)
14. Chin, J.P., Diehl, V.A., Norman, K.L.: Development of an instrument measuring user satisfaction of the human-computer interface. In: Proceedings of SIGCHI '88. ACM/SIGCHI, New York pp. 213–218 (1988)
15. Harper, B.D., Norman, K.L.: Improving User Satisfaction: The Questionnaire for User Interaction Satisfaction Version 5.5. In: Proceedings of the 1st Annual Mid-Atlantic Human Factors Conference. Virginia Beach, VA, pp. 224–228 (1993)
16. Lewis, J.R.: IBM computer usability satisfaction questionnaires: Psychometric evaluation and instructions for use. International Journal of Human–Computer Interaction 7, 57–78 (1995)
17. Lewis, J.R.: Psychometric evaluation of the PSSUQ using data from five years of usability studies. International Journal of Human-Computer Interaction 14, 463–488 (2002)
18. Ryu, Y.S.: Development of Usability Questionnaires for Electronic Mobile Products and Decision Making Methods. Doctoral dissertation, Virginia Polytechnic Institute and State University. Blacksburg, Virginia (2005)

19. Liang, Z., Yang, K., Sun, Y., Yuan, J., Zhang, H., Zhang, Z.: Decision support for choice optimal power generation projects: Fuzzy comprehensive evaluation model based on the electricity market. Energy Policy 34, 3359–3364 (2006)
20. Lan, H., Ding, Y., Hong, J.: Decision support system for rapid prototyping process selection through integration of fuzzy synthetic evaluation and an expert system. International Journal of Production Research 43, 169–194 (2005)
21. Saaty, T.L.: The analytic hierarchy process. McGraw Hill, New York (1980)
22. Hsiao, S-W., Chou, J-R.: A Gestalt-like perceptual measure for home page design using a fuzzy entropy approach. International Journal of Human-Computer Studies 64, 137–156 (2006)
23. Park, K.S., Lim, C.H.: A structured methodology for comparative evaluation of user interface designs using usability criteria and measures. International Journal of Industrial Ergonomics 23, 379–389 (1999)
24. Vredenburg, K., Isensee, S., Righi, C.: User-Centered Design: An Integrated Approach. Prentice Hall, New Jersey (2001)
25. Kuo, Y.-F., Chen, L.-S.: Using the fuzzy synthetic decision approach to assess the performance of university teachers in Taiwan. International journal of management 19, 593–604 (2002)

Author Index

Lecture Notes in Computer Science

For information about Vols. 1–4478

please contact your bookseller or Springer

Vol. 4523: Y.-H. Lee, H.-N. Kim, J. Kim, Y. Park, L.T. Yang, S.W. Kim (Eds.), Embedded Software and Systems. XIX, 829 pages. 2007.

Vol. 4522: B.K. Ersbøll, K.S. Pedersen (Eds.), Image Analysis. XVIII, 989 pages. 2007.

Vol. 4521: J. Katz, M. Yung (Eds.), Applied Cryptography and Network Security. XIII, 498 pages. 2007.

Vol. 4519: E. Franconi, M. Kifer, W. May (Eds.), The Semantic Web: Research and Applications. XVIII, 830 pages. 2007.

Vol. 4517: F. Boavida, E. Monteiro, S. Mascolo, Y. Koucheryavy (Eds.), Wired/Wireless Internet Communications. XIV, 382 pages. 2007.

Vol. 4516: L. Mason, T. Drwiega, J. Yan (Eds.), Managing Traffic Performance in Converged Networks. XXIII, 1191 pages. 2007.

Vol. 4515: M. Naor (Ed.), Advances in Cryptology - EUROCRYPT 2007. XIII, 591 pages. 2007.

Vol. 4514: S.N. Artemov, A. Nerode (Eds.), Logical Foundations of Computer Science. XI, 513 pages. 2007.

Vol. 4513: M. Fischetti, D.P. Williamson (Eds.), Integer Programming and Combinatorial Optimization. IX, 500 pages. 2007.

Vol. 4511: C. Conati, K. McCoy, G. Paliouras (Eds.), User Modeling 2007. XVI, 487 pages. 2007. (Sublibrary LNAI).

Vol. 4510: P. Van Hentenryck, L. Wolsey (Eds.), Integration of AI and OR Techniques in Constraint Programming for Combinatorial Optimization Problems. X, 391 pages. 2007.

Vol. 4509: Z. Kobti, D. Wu (Eds.), Advances in Artificial Intelligence. XII, 552 pages. 2007. (Sublibrary LNAI).

Vol. 4508: M.-Y. Kao, X.-Y. Li (Eds.), Algorithmic Aspects in Information and Management. VIII, 428 pages. 2007.

Vol. 4507: F. Sandoval, A. Prieto, J. Cabestany, M. Graña (Eds.), Computational and Ambient Intelligence. XXVI, 1167 pages. 2007.

Vol. 4506: D. Zeng, I. Gotham, K. Komatsu, C. Lynch, M. Thurmond, D. Madigan, B. Lober, J. Kvach, H. Chen (Eds.), Intelligence and Security Informatics: Biosurveillance. XI, 234 pages. 2007.

Vol. 4505: G. Dong, X. Lin, W. Wang, Y. Yang, J.X. Yu (Eds.), Advances in Data and Web Management. XXII, 896 pages. 2007.

Vol. 4504: J. Huang, R. Kowalczyk, Z. Maamar, D. Martin, I. Müller, S. Stoutenburg, K.P. Sycara (Eds.), Service-Oriented Computing: Agents, Semantics, and Engineering. X, 175 pages. 2007.

Vol. 4501: J. Marques-Silva, K.A. Sakallah (Eds.), Theory and Applications of Satisfiability Testing – SAT 2007. XI, 384 pages. 2007.

Vol. 4500: N. Streitz, A. Kameas, I. Mavrommati (Eds.), The Disappearing Computer. XVIII, 304 pages. 2007.

Vol. 4499: Y.Q. Shi (Ed.), Transactions on Data Hiding and Multimedia Security II. IX, 117 pages. 2007.

Vol. 4498: N. Abdennahder, F. Kordon (Eds.), Reliable Software Technologies – Ada Europe 2007. XII, 247 pages. 2007.

Vol. 4497: S.B. Cooper, B. Löwe, A. Sorbi (Eds.), Computation and Logic in the Real World. XVIII, 826 pages. 2007.

Vol. 4496: N.T. Nguyen, A. Grzech, R.J. Howlett, L.C. Jain (Eds.), Agent and Multi-Agent Systems: Technologies and Applications. XXI, 1046 pages. 2007. (Sublibrary LNAI).

Vol. 4495: J. Krogstie, A. Opdahl, G. Sindre (Eds.), Advanced Information Systems Engineering. XVI, 606 pages. 2007.

Vol. 4494: H. Jin, O.F. Rana, Y. Pan, V.K. Prasanna (Eds.), Algorithms and Architectures for Parallel Processing. XIV, 508 pages. 2007.

Vol. 4493: D. Liu, S. Fei, Z. Hou, H. Zhang, C. Sun (Eds.), Advances in Neural Networks – ISNN 2007, Part III. XXVI, 1215 pages. 2007.

Vol. 4492: D. Liu, S. Fei, Z. Hou, H. Zhang, C. Sun (Eds.), Advances in Neural Networks – ISNN 2007, Part II. XXVII, 1321 pages. 2007.

Vol. 4491: D. Liu, S. Fei, Z.-G. Hou, H. Zhang, C. Sun (Eds.), Advances in Neural Networks – ISNN 2007, Part I. LIV, 1365 pages. 2007.

Vol. 4490: Y. Shi, G.D. van Albada, J. Dongarra, P.M.A. Sloot (Eds.), Computational Science – ICCS 2007, Part IV. XXXVII, 1211 pages. 2007.

Vol. 4489: Y. Shi, G.D. van Albada, J. Dongarra, P.M.A. Sloot (Eds.), Computational Science – ICCS 2007, Part III. XXXVII, 1257 pages. 2007.

Vol. 4488: Y. Shi, G.D. van Albada, J. Dongarra, P.M.A. Sloot (Eds.), Computational Science – ICCS 2007, Part II. XXXV, 1251 pages. 2007.

Vol. 4487: Y. Shi, G.D. van Albada, J. Dongarra, P.M.A. Sloot (Eds.), Computational Science – ICCS 2007, Part I. LXXXI, 1275 pages. 2007.

Vol. 4486: M. Bernardo, J. Hillston (Eds.), Formal Methods for Performance Evaluation. VII, 469 pages. 2007.

Vol. 4485: F. Sgallari, A. Murli, N. Paragios (Eds.), Scale Space and Variational Methods in Computer Vision. XV, 931 pages. 2007.

Vol. 4484: J.-Y. Cai, S.B. Cooper, H. Zhu (Eds.), Theory and Applications of Models of Computation. XIII, 772 pages. 2007.

Vol. 4483: C. Baral, G. Brewka, J. Schlipf (Eds.), Logic Programming and Nonmonotonic Reasoning. IX, 327 pages. 2007. (Sublibrary LNAI).

Vol. 4482: A. An, J. Stefanowski, S. Ramanna, C.J. Butz, W. Pedrycz, G. Wang (Eds.), Rough Sets, Fuzzy Sets, Data Mining and Granular Computing. XIV, 585 pages. 2007. (Sublibrary LNAI).

Vol. 4481: J. Yao, P. Lingras, W.-Z. Wu, M. Szczuka, N.J. Cercone, D. Ślęzak (Eds.), Rough Sets and Knowledge Technology. XIV, 576 pages. 2007. (Sublibrary LNAI).

Vol. 4480: A. LaMarca, M. Langheinrich, K.N. Truong (Eds.), Pervasive Computing. XIII, 369 pages. 2007.

Vol. 4479: I.F. Akyildiz, R. Sivakumar, E. Ekici, J.C.d. Oliveira, J. McNair (Eds.), NETWORKING 2007. Ad Hoc and Sensor Networks, Wireless Networks, Next Generation Internet. XXVII, 1252 pages. 2007.